Child Psychology and Psychiatry

# Child Psychology and Psychiatry

Frameworks for Clinical Training and Practice

*Edited by*
*David Skuse*
*University College London*
*UK*

*Helen Bruce*
*East London NHS Foundation Trust*
*UK*

*Linda Dowdney*
*UK*

Third Edition

*Edition History*
Wiley-Blackwell (2e, 2011)

*Registered Office(s)*
John Wiley & Sons, Inc., 111 River Street, Hoboken, NJ 07030, USA
John Wiley & Sons Ltd, The Atrium, Southern Gate, Chichester, West Sussex, PO19 8SQ, UK

*Editorial Office*
The Atrium, Southern Gate, Chichester, West Sussex, PO19 8SQ, UK

For details of our global editorial offices, customer services, and more information about Wiley products visit us at www.wiley.com.

Wiley also publishes its books in a variety of electronic formats and by print-on-demand. Some content that appears in standard print versions of this book may not be available in other formats.

*Library of Congress Cataloging-in-Publication Data*

Names: Skuse, D. (David), editor. | Bruce, Helen (Consultant psychiatrist),
    editor. | Dowdney, Linda, editor.
Title: Child psychology and psychiatry : frameworks for clinical training and
    practice / edited by David Skuse, Helen Bruce, Linda Dowdney.
Description: Third edition. | Hoboken, NJ : John Wiley & Sons, Inc., 2017. |
    Includes index. |
Identifiers: LCCN 2016059981 (print) | LCCN 2017016743 (ebook) | ISBN
    9781119170228 (Adobe PDF) | ISBN 9781119170204 (ePub) | ISBN 9781119170181
    (cloth) | ISBN 9781119170198 (pbk.)
Subjects: LCSH: Child psychology. | Child psychiatry.
Classification: LCC BF721 (ebook) | LCC BF721 .C5157 2017 (print) | DDC
    155.4—dc23
LC record available at https://lccn.loc.gov/2016059981

Cover Image: The Children's Game, c.1955 (oil on hardboard), Everts, Anneliese (1908–1967) / Private Collection / Bridgeman Images
Cover Design: Wiley

Set in 10/12, WarnockPro by SPi Global, Chennai, India

Printed in Singapore by C.O.S. Printers Pte Ltd

10 9 8 7 6 5 4 3 2 1

# Contents

# Notes on Contributors

**Gillian Baird** is Professor of Paediatric Neurodisability at King's College London and Consultant Paediatrician in Neurodisability at Guy's and St Thomas' Evelina Children's Hospital. Her research interests have been in speech, language and communication disorders, autism and cerebral palsy.

**Dickon Bevington** is a child and adolescent psychiatrist in Cambridgeshire and Peterborough NHS Foundation Trust, specializing in youth with substance use problems and multiple co-morbidities. He is Medical Director of the Anna Freud National Centre for Children and Families and a developer of mentalization-based treatments (MBT-Families, co-lead of AMBIT). Previous publications include co-authorship of the second edition of *What Works For Whom: A Critical Review of Treatments for Children and Adolescents* (Guilford, 2015).

**Sarah-Jayne Blakemore** is Professor of Cognitive Neuroscience at UCL. She is Deputy Director of the UCL Institute of Cognitive Neuroscience and leader of the Developmental Cognitive Neuroscience Group. Her group's research focuses on the development of social cognition and decision-making in the typically developing adolescent brain.

**Ruma Bose** was Consultant in Child and Adolescent Psychiatry at the East London NHS Foundation Trust, Tower Hamlets, London, for several years. Prior to her appointment in the UK, she had worked as a psychiatrist in India. She has researched, published and taught on the subject of cross-cultural psychiatry and medical anthropology, particularly in relation to child and adolescent mental health.

**Helen Bruce** is a Consultant Child and Adolescent Psychiatrist in Tower Hamlets for East London NHS Foundation Trust and Honorary Senior Clinical Lecturer at Barts and the London School of Medicine and Dentistry. She is also an Associate Dean at the Royal College of Psychiatrists and Senior Teaching Fellow at University College, London. Her particular interests are medical education and transition to adult care.

**Alan Carr** is Professor of Clinical Psychology and Head of the School of Psychology at University College Dublin in Ireland. He also has a family therapy practice at the Clanwilliam Institute in Dublin. He has published over 20 books and 200 papers in the fields of clinical psychology and family therapy.

**Elaine Chung** is a Consultant Child and Adolescent Psychiatrist at the Royal Free Hospital working in paediatric liaison, neurodevelopmental psychiatry and general CAMHS. She is Vice Chair of the London and South East Branch Committee of the Association of Child and Adolescent Mental Health (ACAMH.)

**Gina Conti-Ramsden** is Professor of Child Language and Learning at the University of Manchester, UK. She is a Fellow of the Royal College of Speech and Language Therapists, a Fellow of the British Psychological Society and an Academician of the Social Sciences. Gina is interested in raising public awareness of language disorders in childhood, adolescence and adulthood. She is a founder member of the RALLI campaign to raise awareness of language learning impairments (www.youtube.com/RALLIcampaign).

**Anna Coughtrey** is a Clinical Psychologist working in the Psychological Medicine Research Team at UCL Great Ormond Street Institute of Child Health. Her research focuses on the integration of mental healthcare for children and young people with long-term physical illness with co-occurring common mental health difficulties, including anxiety, depression and behavioural problems.

**Cathy Creswell** is a Professor in Developmental Clinical Psychology and a National Institute of Health Research (NIHR) Research Professor at the University of Reading. Her work focuses on the development and treatment of common mental health problems in childhood, particularly anxiety disorders, with the overarching aims of improving both treatment accessibility and outcomes.

**David Dossetor** is a Child Psychiatrist with a special interest in intellectual disability and autism, Director of Mental Health at Sydney Children's Hospital Network and Associate Professor at Sydney Medical School. He is head of the Developmental Psychiatry Team that has developed emotions-based social skills training for autism spectrum disorder and also the free electronic *Journal for the Mental Health of Children and Adolescents with Intellectual and Developmental Disabilities* (www.schoollink.chw.edu.au).

**Linda Dowdney** is a Consultant Child Clinical Psychologist who has worked extensively in child and adolescent mental health services. She has a particular interest in the impact of bereavement upon children's well-being. She was Head of the Doctoral Clinical Psychology course at the University of Surrey, and an honorary Senior Lecturer at University College London.

**Kevin Durkin** is Professor of Psychology at the University of Strathclyde, Glasgow. His research interests span areas of developmental and social psychology, including the development of language and communication in typical and atypical children, media use by young people, problem behaviour in adolescence, and social adjustment in young adults with language impairment.

**Pasco Fearon** is both a developmental and a clinical psychologist. He is joint Director of the Doctoral Clinical Psychology training programme at University College London. His research focuses on understanding how children's social and emotional development, and mental health difficulties are influenced by parent–child interactions, attachment relationships and biological and genetic factors. He contributes to a range of clinical studies focusing on the development of mental health interventions for parents, infants and young children.

**Peter Fonagy** is Head of the Research Department of Clinical, Educational and Health Psychology, University College London; Chief Executive of the Anna Freud National Centre for Children and Families; and National Clinical Lead of NHS England's CYP IAPT programme. His clinical and research interests centre on the development and dissemination of evidence-based psychotherapeutic treatments for children, young people and adults, as well as issues of early attachment relationships, social cognition, borderline personality disorder and violence.

**Paolo Fusar-Poli** is a Consultant Adult Psychiatrist at the South London and Maudsley NHS Foundation Trust and leads the largest European clinical service for those at clinical high risk for psychosis. He is a Clinical Senior Lecturer at the Department of Psychosis Studies, Institute of Psychiatry, Psychology and Neuroscience, King's College, London. His research focuses on the assessment and treatment of individuals at risk for psychosis and on youth mental health. Paolo has been recognized as one of the most influential scientific minds in the 2015/2016 Thomson Reuters Highly Cited Researchers.

**Elena Garralda** is Emeritus Professor of Child and Adolescent Psychiatry at Imperial College London and Honorary Consultant Child and Adolescent Psychiatrist with the CNWL Foundation Trust, London, UK. Her clinical and research interests include the interface between physical and mental health in children and young people. She is involved in the 11th revision of mental disorders in the *International Classification of Diseases* (ICD).

**Jane Gilmour** completed her PhD and DClinPsy at University College London, where she has senior teaching fellow and clinical lecturer roles. Her publications reflect her research interests, including growth disorders, appetite dysregulation, neuropsychology and neurodevelopmental disorders. She also works as a clinical psychologist developing interventions for children and families who have neurodevelopmental conditions, particularly autistic spectrum disorders, obsessive compulsive disorder and Tourette's syndrome.

**Danya Glaser**, previously a developmental paediatrician, is Honorary Consultant Child & Adolescent Psychiatrist at Great Ormond Street Hospital for Children, and Visiting Professor at University College London. Within the field of child maltreatment she is a clinician, researcher and teacher, and has written widely. She is a past president of the International Society for the Prevention of Child Abuse and Neglect (ISPCAN).

**Julia Gledhill** is a Consultant Child and Adolescent Psychiatrist in Harrow CAMHS and Honorary Clinical Senior Lecturer at Imperial College. Her research has focused on the outcome and management of adolescent depressive disorders in primary care, with her MD thesis investigating the outcome of depressive disorder and subsyndromal mood symptoms in adolescents consulting their GP. Her other research interests have focused on psychiatric outcome for children and parents following acute life-threatening illnesses and paediatric intensive care unit admission.

**Isobel Heyman** is a consultant Child and Adolescent Psychiatrist who leads the Psychological Medicine Team at Great Ormond Street Hospital for Children. She is Honorary Professor at the Institute of Child Health, University College London. She is nationally/internationally known for her clinical and research work on obsessive compulsive disorder and neuropsychiatry. She has a commitment to the integration of physical and mental health care. In 2015 she was awarded Psychiatrist of the Year.

**Peter Hindley** is a retired Consultant Child and Adolescent Psychiatrist and Chair of the Faculty of Child and Adolescent Psychiatry at the Royal College of Psychiatrists. Before retiring, he was a Consultant in Paediatric Liaison at St Thomas Hospital and Director of Training in Child and Adolescent Psychiatry for south London. He currently works as a medical member of the Mental Health Tribunal Service.

**Matthew Hodes** is a Consultant Child and Adolescent Psychiatrist in Central and North West London NHS Foundation Trust and an Honorary Senior Lecturer in Child and Adolescent Psychiatry at Imperial College London. His interests include the interface of physical and mental health, migration and refugees' mental health, and evidence-based practice in child and adolescent psychiatry.

**Bettina Hohnen** is a Child Clinical Psychologist specialising in Paediatric Neuropsychology as well as general Child and Adolescent Mental Health. She lectures at University College London where she holds a post as a Senior Clinical Teaching Fellow. She is a regular speaker at conferences and writes, lectures and speaks on topics including neuroscience and education, adolescent brain development, neurodevelopmental differences in children and parenting.

**Sajid Humayun** is a Senior Lecturer in Psychology at the Department for Psychology, Social Work and Counselling at the University of Greenwich. He conducts research on callous-unemotional traits in children and adolescents, ran the first UK RCT of Functional Family Therapy and has written a number of reviews of interventions for antisocial behaviour in children and adolescents. He is a member of the Early Intervention Foundation evidence panel for gangs and youth violence.

**Anthony James** is an Honorary Senior Lecturer University of Oxford. He is a Consultant Child and Adolescent Psychiatrist at the Highfield Unit, Oxford. He has research interests in early-onset psychosis, bipolar disorder, obsessive compulsive disorder and dialectic behavioural therapy. He has undertaken MRI studies including longitudinal studies and magnetoencephalography in a number of adolescent-onset disorders. His recent research interest is in stem cell work in adolescents with psychosis.

**Eilis Kennedy** is a Consultant Child and Adolescent Psychiatrist and Director of Research at the Tavistock Clinic and an Honorary Reader in the Research Department of Clinical, Educational and Health Psychology at University College London. She is currently Joint Editor in Chief of the Journal Clinical Child Psychology and Psychiatry. Her research interests focus on the evaluation and development of interventions in Child and Adolescent Mental Health Services.

**Anup Kharod** is an Assistant Psychologist within the Psychological Medicine Team at Great Ormond Street Hospital. She has previously worked in child and adolescent mental health services and with children with acquired brain injury. Anup has a particular interest in child mental health in the context of neurodevelopmental disorders and the role of cognitive assessments in informing the delivery of evidence-based treatments.

**Thomas Klee** is Professor and Head of the Division of Speech and Hearing Sciences at the University of Hong Kong. He trained as a speech-language pathologist and taught at universities in the USA, UK and New Zealand before moving to Hong Kong. His current research focuses on improving the way in which children with development language disorders are identified.

**Graeme Lamb** has been working in psychiatry in East London for over 20 years. He is a Consultant in Child and Adolescent Psychiatry in East London NHS Foundation Trust (ELFT). Graeme is Clinical Director for Children's Services at ELFT with clinical responsibility for child and adolescent mental health and community child health services across the Trust.

**Cindy H. Liu** is the Director of Multicultural Research at the Commonwealth Research Center at Beth Israel Deaconess Medical Center, an Instructor in the Department of Psychiatry at Harvard Medical School and an Assistant Research Professor at University of Massachusetts Boston. Her research focuses on community-based and translational research related to the measurement of stress in diverse mothers and infants and its role on mental health in the family.

**Sonia Livingstone,** OBE, is a professor in the Department of Media and Communications at LSE. Sonia researches the opportunities and risks for children and young people afforded by digital and online technologies. Author of 20 books, her latest is The Class: Living and Learning in the Digital Age. She leads the projects Global Kids Online, Preparing for a Digital Future and EU Kids Online (see www.sonialivingstone.net).

**William Mandy** is a Clinical Psychologist and academic who works at University College London. His research is aimed at better understanding the lives of autistic people, and finding new ways to help them address some of the challenges they face. This involves developing new assessment methods and interventions for clinical and educational settings. He has a particular interest in autism as a condition that is characterized by strengths as well as difficulties; and in improving understanding of the female autism phenotype.

**Laura Markham** is a clinical psychologist who works in a Pupil Referral Unit in Sutton and consults to various schools in the area. She previously worked at the Department of Child and Adolescent Mental Health, Great Ormond Street Hospital. Her clinical work has involved the assessment and treatment of children with medically unexplained symptoms, mental health difficulties, neurodevelopmental difficulties and physical health problems.

**Barbara Maughan** is Professor of Developmental Epidemiology at the Institute of Psychiatry, Psychology and Neuroscience, King's College London. Her research focuses on psychosocial risks for disorder in childhood, and the long-term impact of disorder and early risk exposures for well-being across the life course. She has undertaken a number of long-term longitudinal studies and has extensive collaborations with national and international investigators in life course epidemiology.

**Eve McAllister** is a Clinical Psychologist within the Psychological Medicine Intervention Service, Department of Child and Adolescent Mental Health, Great Ormond Street Hospital. Her clinical work involves the assessment and treatment of children with a combination of functional symptoms/medically unexplained symptoms, mental health difficulties, neurodevelopmental difficulties and physical health problems.

**Eamon McCrory** is a Professor of Developmental Neuroscience and Psychopathology at UCL and a Consultant Clinical Psychologist. He is a Co-Director of the Developmental Risk and Resilience Unit. His research focuses on early adversity and the impact of maltreatment, the neurocognitive mechanisms associated with resilience and the emergence of mental health problems.

**Philip Messent** is a Consultant Family Therapist who has worked in East London CAMHS since 1986. He has a particular interest, born out of his experience in working in such a culturally diverse and socially disadvantaged area, in how we can best connect with others across differences in culture, class and socioeconomic status. This interest has extended in recent years to making connections across countries, making contributions to the development of international health links in Uganda and Bangladesh. He is a member of the teaching staff at the Institute of Family Therapy, London.

**K.A.H. Mirza** has over 30 years' experience in the assessment and treatment of children, young people and adults with psychiatric disorders and substance misuse. He has worked in general adult psychiatry and addiction sciences for a decade before specializing in child and adolescent psychiatry at the Maudsley Hospital, London and University of Cambridge. He has held senior academic and clinical positions in major universities across the world, including University of Cambridge, Dalhousie University Canada, and Institute of Psychiatry, King's College.

**Sudeshni Mirza** is a graduate of Trivandrum Medical College, University of Kerala, from where she also obtained her MD in Forensic Medicine in 1987. She was co-founder and consultant in a specialist drug and alcohol service in India. Currently Sudeshni works as Professor of Forensic Medicine in DM Wayanad Institute of Medical Sciences, Kerala. Sudeshni has co-authored many publications and co-edited several textbooks on both psychiatry and forensic medicine.

**Antonio Muñoz-Solomando** works as a Child and Adolescent Psychiatrist with Cwm Taf University Health Board and holds a managerial role within the service. He is actively involved in research, training and development of the local child and mental health services in South Wales. His clinical and research interests include neurodevelopmental disorders, mental health strategy, specifically the development of care pathways and service transition.

**Valerie Muter** is an honorary research associate at the Institute of Child Health, University College London. Before that, she was a Consultant Clinical Neuropsychologist at Great Ormond Street Children's Hospital for 15 years. Her clinical and research interests are in the fields of literacy development and disorders, and cognitive sequelae following neurological injury.

**Dasha Nicholls** is a Consultant Child and Adolescent Psychiatrist in the Feeding and Eating Disorders service at Great Ormond Street Hospital and Honorary Senior Lecturer at UCL Institute of Child Health. She chairs the Eating Disorders Faculty of the Royal College of Psychiatrists, is Past President of the Academy for Eating Disorders, chaired the Junior MARSIPAN group, is a member of the Eating Disorders NICE Guideline Committee and Expert Reference Group, and co-founded the Child and Adolescent Psychiatric Surveillance System (CAPSS).

**Thomas G. O'Connor** is a Professor in the Department of Psychiatry and the Director of the Wynne Center for Family Research at the University of Rochester. His clinical research focuses on the role that early (including prenatal) exposures and experiences play in shaping psychological, physiological and immunological processes underlying behavioural and somatic health.

**Anne O'Herlihy** currently works within the Children and Young People's Mental Health Programme (Medical Directorate, NHS England), supporting the CYP IAPT service transformation programme. She is project lead for the CYP eating disorder programme, curricula development, and related mental health work within NHS England. Prior to this post she managed CAMHS health service research projects (NICAPS, 2001; CIRS, 2007; COSI-CAPS, 2007) and quality improvement and accreditation programmes at the Royal College of Psychiatrists Centre for Quality Improvement (CCQI).

**Tony O'Sullivan** is a retired Consultant Paediatrician who until March 2016 was based at Kaleidoscope, Lewisham Centre for Children & Young People, Lewisham & Greenwich NHS Trust, London, UK.

**Christine Puckering** is a Clinical, Forensic and Neuropsychologist with a longstanding interest in parent–child interaction in the early years. She is Programme Director of Mellow Parenting, a charity aiming to help parents and young children make good relationships, particularly in families with complex needs. She was awarded a Winston Churchill Travelling Fellowship in 2015 to explore how other countries prioritize infant mental health.

**Vanessa B. Puetz** is a Postdoctoral Research Associate at the Developmental Risk and Resilience Unit at UCL. Her research focuses on the impact of childhood maltreatment on brain development and employs both neuroimaging (s/fMRI) and behavioural approaches with the longer-term aim of informing more effective ways to support and intervene with children exposed to early adversity.

**Kathryn Pugh** leads the Children and Young People's Mental Health Programme which contributes to NHS England's implementation of Future in Mind and the Five Year Forward View for Mental Health. She has extensive experience in developing and commissioning NHS clinical services for children and young people, and was previously Head of Policy at Young Minds.

**Paramala Santosh** is Head and Consultant Child & Adolescent Psychiatrist at the Centre for Interventional Paediatric Psychopharmacology and Rare Diseases (CIPPRD), Maudsley Hospital, London, and Honorary Reader in Developmental Neuropsychiatry & Psychopharmacology at the Department of Child and Adolescent Psychiatry, Institute of Psychiatry, Psychology and Neuroscience, King's College London, London. He is internationally recognized as an expert in paediatric psychopharmacology, web-based health monitoring, developmental neuropsychiatry, and rare diseases.

**Sanjida Sattar** has worked as an NHS Consultant Psychiatrist for 8 years and is currently based in Mid Cornwall CAMHS. She has expertise in assessment and management of complex neurodevelopmental disorders and learning disabilities. She has special interests in paediatric psychopharmacology and the effect of culture on child development and mental illness in children and young people.

**Stephen Scott** is Professor of Child Health and Behaviour at the Institute of Psychiatry, Psychology and Neuroscience at King's College London and a consultant psychiatrist with the National Conduct Problems Clinic at the Maudsley Hospital, London. He has carried out several randomized controlled trials of interventions for antisocial children and has researched their attachment security. He chaired the 2013 NICE guidelines on conduct disorders.

**Ajay Sharma** is a Consultant Neurodevelopmental Paediatrician in London, UK. He has extensive clinical and teaching experience of child development and developmental disorders. He has written articles and book chapters, and has co-authored and edited books on child development.

**David Skuse** is Head of Behavioural and Brain Sciences at the Institute of Child Health, University College London and an Honorary Consultant in Developmental Neuropsychiatry to Great Ormond Street Hospital for Children. He is an academic and Clinical Child Psychiatrist, whose approach to research is quintessentially interdisciplinary and translational. He has fostered a range of current national and international research collaborations, ranging from basic science through epidemiology to clinical applications.

**Virginia Slaughter** is Professor of Psychology at the University of Queensland, Australia, where she founded the Early Cognitive Development Centre. Her research focuses on social and cognitive development in infants and young children, with particular emphasis on social behaviour in infancy, theory-of-mind development and the acquisition of peer interaction skills. She is a Fellow of the Academy of the Social Sciences in Australia and serves as an Associate Editor for Child Development.

**Peter K. Smith** is Emeritus Professor of Psychology at Goldsmiths, University of London. He has researched extensively on school bullying and cyberbullying and chaired a COST Action on Cyberbullying (2008–2012), co-editing a book *Cyberbullying through the New Media* (Psychology Press, 2013). He is co-author of *Understanding Children's Development* (6th edn, Wiley, 2015) and author of *Understanding School Bullying: Its Nature and Prevention Strategies* (Sage, 2014) and *Adolescence: A Very Short Introduction* (OUP, 2016).

**Margaret J. Snowling** is President of St John's College at the University of Oxford and professionally qualified as a clinical psychologist. Appointed CBE for services to science and understanding of dyslexia in 2016, she is Fellow of the British Academy, Fellow of the Academy of Medical Sciences and Fellow of the Academy of Social Sciences. Her research is at the interface of language and reading development.

**Giulia Spada** is a Child Neuropsychiatrist, clinician and researcher, PhD student in Biomedical Sciences at the University of Pavia, Italy. She is a Consultant Child Neuropsychiatrist for the National Neurological Institute C. Mondino in Pavia where she set up and leads a prodromal service for children and adolescents at risk for psychosis. She has participated in international research collaboration with the Department of Psychosis Studies of King's College of London.

**Ramya Srinivasan** is a specialist registrar and NIHR academic clinical fellow (ACF) in Child and Adolescent Psychiatry working in East London, and with Prof. David Skuse at the UCL GOS Institute of Child Health. Ramya is particularly interested in adolescent mental health and neurodevelopmental disorders and their relationship to adult psychopathology.

**Paul Stallard** is Head of Psychological Therapies for Oxford Health NHS Foundation Trust and Professor of Child and Family Mental Health at the University of Bath. He has worked with children and young people for over 30 years since qualifying as a clinical psychologist. Clinically, he works within a specialist child mental health team where he leads a cognitive behaviour therapy (CBT) clinic for children and young people with emotional disorders. He is an active researcher and has led national multi-site randomized controlled trials evaluating the effectiveness of school-based CBT programmes and is currently evaluating the use of technology to support mental health interventions.

**Howard Steele** is Professor and Chair of the Clinical Group in the Psychology Department at the New School for Social Research. He is Co-Director of the Centre for Attachment Research at The New School and is founding and senior editor of the academic journal, *Attachment & Human Development*. He is also the Founding and Past President of the Society for Emotion and Attachment Studies.

**Stephanie F. Stokes** is a Speech Pathologist and a Professor in the Division of Speech and Hearing Sciences at the University of Hong Kong. She has held academic positions in Australia, New Zealand and the UK. Her research interests include the interface of lexical and phonological learning in children, and early identification of speech and language disorders in children.

**Roshin M. Sudesh** qualified in medicine from King's College London in 2013, and completed a master's in public health from the London School of Hygiene and Tropical Medicine and an honours degree in homeopathy from London Homeopathic Institute concurrently. Currently she is a specialist trainee in accident and emergency at Medway Maritime Hospital, Gillingham, Kent. She has had clinical and research experience in working with young people with substance misuse and offending behaviour.

**Rakendu Suren** is a Consultant Child and Adolescent Psychiatrist at Windsor, Ascot and Maidenhead CAMHS (Berkshire Health Foundation NHS Trust). He completed his specialist training in child and adolescent psychiatry in the Great Ormond Street Hospital-Royal London Hospital training scheme. He has a special interest in neurodevelopmental disorders and paediatric psychopharmacology.

**Anita Thapar** is head of the academic Child & Adolescent Psychiatry section at the Division of Psychological Medicine and Clinical Neurosciences, Cardiff University

School of Medicine. Her research focuses on the origins, development and complications of neurodevelopmental disorders. She runs a tertiary service for children with complex neurodevelopmental problems and, more recently, a transition clinic for 15- to 25-year-olds with attention deficit hyperactivity disorder.

**David Trickey** is a Consultant Clinical Psychologist who has specialized in working at the Anna Freud National Centre for Children and Families since 2000. He also trains and supervises other clinicians working with traumatized children and young people, and has published research in this area.

**Ed Tronick** is Director of the Child Development Unit in the Developmental Brain Sciences Program at the University of Massachusetts Boston and a Research Associate at Harvard Medical School. He is a developmental neuroscientist and clinical psychologist. His research interests include neurobehavioural assessment of infants, social-emotional development and the effects of stress on psychobiological systems in children and parents. His model of the infant–caretaker dyadic system as a common transducing or buffering pathway of the effects of resource-depleting factors unites micro-temporal and epidemiological conceptualizations of the development of well-being.

**Aaron Vallance** is a Consultant in Child & Adolescent Psychiatry in Surrey CAMHS (Surrey and Borders Partnership NHS Foundation Trust) and an Honorary Clinical Senior Lecturer in the Faculty of Medicine (Faculty of Education), Imperial College London. He has an MA (Oxon) in psychology, philosophy and physiology and a Masters in Education. His specialist interests include medical education, and he has written on various aspects of child and adolescent psychiatry.

**Angela Veale** is a lecturer in Applied Psychology, University College Cork. She is an academic and also a child and adolescent psychoanalytic psychotherapist and former Fulbright Scholar. Her academic work involves collaborative research with academics and non-governmental organization partners on community-based participatory action research and creative methodologies with children and communities in post-conflict, migration and refugee contexts.

**Essi Viding** is a Professor of Developmental Psychopathology at UCL. She is a Co-Director of the Developmental Risk and Resilience Unit. Her research focuses on different developmental pathways to antisocial behaviour and she uses multiple different methods, including neuroimaging and twin studies, in her research.

**Eileen Vizard,** CBE, is a Child and Adolescent Psychiatrist, Honorary Senior Lecturer at the Institute of Child Health, Honorary Consultant Child and Adolescent Psychiatrist in Great Ormond Street Hospital and Visiting Professor at New York University, London. She has published, researched and lectured extensively in relation to child maltreatment and emerging personality disorder traits in childhood. She was awarded the CBE in 2011 for services to children and young people.

**Cecilia Wainryb** is a Professor of Psychology at the University of Utah. Her research, spanning moral, social and emotional development, examines how young people construct meaning from moral transgressions and conflicts, and how such meanings contribute to the development of moral agency. She has studied these processes in community samples and samples of war-exposed youths. Her studies combine interview data, narrative methods, conversation analyses and psychophysiological measures.

**Justin Wakefield** is a Consultant Child and Adolescent Psychiatrist in Tower Hamlets CAMHS. He has research experience and clinical interest in working with LGBTQ young people. He has spoken at national conferences and contributed material on sexuality and gender to the MindEd project.

# Section 1

# Developing Competencies

1a: Contextual Influences Upon Social and Emotional Development

# 1

# Family and Systemic Influences

*Barbara Maughan*

Ecological theories of child development outline how numerous contexts interweave to support both normative and less adaptive socio-emotional development (for a review, see Dunn *et al.* [1]). Family networks are central to early child development. As their social worlds widen, children encounter childcare and school settings, and their expanding social systems encompass relationships with friends and peers. Children's growing competencies are influenced by each of these systems and by interactions among them. These systems, in turn, are influenced by broader social and cultural influences, and by variations in access to social and material resources (see Figure 1.1 for an illustrative model).

## Family Relationships and Parenting

Family relationships are complex: each dyadic relationship is affected by other relationships in the family system, and children influence, as well as being influenced by, those around them [2]. Even very young infants affect interactions with their caregivers, and variations in children's temperamental styles continue to evoke differing responses from carers at older ages. In part, variations of this kind reflect children's inherited characteristics; indeed, many aspects of family relationships and functioning once thought to be purely 'environmental' in origin are now known to reflect elements of 'nature' as well as 'nurture'. Children play an active part in shaping the environments they experience; their genetic make-up also affects individual differences in sensitivity to environmental influences, contributing to both resilience and vulnerability to stress [3].

Families are biologically and culturally evolved to promote children's development [4]. Some of the earliest steps in those processes – pre- and postnatal influences on neurobiological regulation, and early attachment relationships – are discussed in other chapters. But family relationships and parenting show ongoing links with the development of children's behavioural control and with the regulation of their attentional, arousal and emotional systems throughout childhood. In addition, parents contribute to children's cognitive development, socialize them into culturally appropriate patterns of behaviour and promote their understanding of moral values and the development of their talents. Parents also select and secure children's access to key resources beyond the family system.

*Child Psychology and Psychiatry: Frameworks for Clinical Training and Practice,* Third Edition.
Edited by David Skuse, Helen Bruce and Linda Dowdney.
© 2017 John Wiley & Sons, Ltd. Published 2017 by John Wiley & Sons, Ltd.

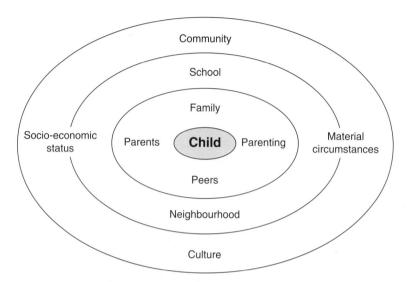

**Figure 1.1** Ecological model of influences on development.

Successful parenting involves numerous skills and capacities, varying with the age of the child, with culture and with social context. Underlying this diversity, most models of parenting highlight two central dimensions, one related to parental involvement and responsiveness (encompassing warmth, availability, positive engagement and support), the second centring on 'demandingness' or behavioural control, and incorporating monitoring, expectations and behaviour management. Combinations of these dimensions have been used to characterize four general styles of parenting [5].

- **Indulgent** (responsive but not demanding) – parents are non-traditional and lenient, allow considerable self-regulation, and avoid confrontation.
- **Authoritarian** (demanding but not responsive) – parents are obedience- and status-oriented, and expect orders to be obeyed without explanation.
- **Authoritative** (both demanding and responsive) – parents are assertive, but not intrusive or restrictive. Disciplinary methods are supportive rather than punitive. Children are expected to be assertive as well as socially responsible, self-regulated as well as cooperative.
- **Uninvolved** (both unresponsive and undemanding) – most parenting of this type falls within the normal range, but in extreme cases it might encompass both rejecting–neglecting and neglectful parenting.

Comparisons across these styles consistently highlight *authoritative* parenting as associated with more positive child outcomes in a range of domains: self-discipline, emotional self-control, positive peer relationships and school performance.

When children are under stress, family life can provide compensatory experiences. Cohesion and warmth within the family, the presence of a good relationship with one parent, close sibling relationships and effective parental monitoring are all known to represent protective influences of this kind. Finally, when parenting is compromised, risks of emotional and behavioural difficulties increase. Problems in four broad aspects of family relationships and parenting seem most important here:

- Discordant/dysfunctional relationships between parents, or in the family system as a whole
- Hostile or rejecting parent-child relationships, or those markedly lacking in warmth
- Harsh or inconsistent discipline
- Ineffective monitoring and supervision

Many family-based interventions and parenting programmes are designed to target difficulties of these kinds.

### Parent and Family Characteristics

Some parent and family characteristics show systematic links with children's risk of emotional and behavioural problems. Parents' own mental health is among the most important of these. In part, such associations reflect heritable influences; in part, they are also likely to index the effects of parents' mental health on family relationships and parenting. Mothers who are depressed, for example, are known to be less sensitive and responsive to their infants, and attend less, and respond more negatively, to older children [6]. Alcohol and drug abuse and major mental disorders in parents may impair parenting in more wide-ranging ways. When parents are antisocial, effects may also be mediated through the endorsement of antisocial attitudes and social learning.

### Sibling Relationships

Sibling relationships form a further key part of the family system for many children. The dynamics of sibling relationships show transactional links with relationships in other family subsystems and with aspects of parenting. Harsh and authoritarian parenting, for example, is associated with more conflictual relationships among siblings, while sibling conflict can constitute a major stressor for parents [7].

Bonds between siblings are intimate and often emotionally intense. Consequently, their potential for influencing children's trajectories is strong. Warm sibling relationships facilitate the development of social understanding [8] and are protective when families are under stress. Sibling conflict, by contrast, can compromise both emotional and behavioural development [9]. Evidence now suggests that up to 40% of children are bullied by their siblings, and that this intra-familial aggression can increase risks of being bullied outside the family [10]. In adolescence, siblings often show similar levels of problem behaviours such as delinquency and substance use. In part, these similarities are likely to reflect broader family-based processes; in part, they appear to reflect direct facilitation and 'deviancy training' by siblings. For all of these reasons, a focus on siblings is increasingly recommended as one element in therapeutic work with children and families.

## Changing Family Patterns

Recent decades have seen major changes in patterns of family formation, stability and complexity in many western societies [11,12]. Families are formed later, and are smaller, than in the past. Fewer parents now marry and there is more divorce, meaning that many children face transitions in their family lives. Parental separation can be followed by periods in single-parent households, and later by the establishment of new step-families. In addition, increasing numbers of children are now conceived following the use of new reproductive technologies, and more are growing up with same-sex parents – factors that have been examined for their potential to influence children's development. On average, children in single-parent and step-families show somewhat higher levels of emotional and behavioural difficulties than those in stable two-parent homes. [13,14]. Typically, however, these differences are modest and there is much variation within as well as between family types. Importantly, associations between the quality of mother–child relationships and children's adjustment are similar across family settings. Additionally, single-parent and reconstituted families often face economic and other stresses and may lack social and family supports. Taking these variations into account, research indicates that family type *per se* shows few consistent links with children's adjustment. Similar conclusions emerge from studies of 'non-traditional' family forms: children's adjustment typically reflects the quality of family relationships and the well-being of family members to a much greater degree than variations in family structure [15,16].

### Parental Separation and Divorce

When parents separate, most children show some short-term behavioural or emotional difficulties. In general, these are not severe [17]. School progress and motivation can be affected, and longer-term influences on young people's own patterns of relationship formation and stability later in life are found. Research suggests that these responses are not simply 'one-off' effects of parental separation: many children experience parental discord before their parents separate, and divorce itself is often followed by a cascade of other changes. Parents themselves are likely to be distressed, and many families face marked declines in economic circumstances. Some children can subsequently encounter house moves, school changes and disruptions to their social networks. Children's outcomes may be impacted by any element of this complex network of change.

## Childcare and Schooling

In most western societies at least half of mothers now return to work before their youngest child reaches the age of 3 years [18], resulting in a major interest in the impact of non-maternal care on children's development. Research suggests that multiple features of early childcare should be considered when assessing its effects. Higher-*quality* childcare (including, for example, variations in sensitive and responsive caregiving, and cognitive and language stimulation) has developmental benefits. For example, it is associated with gains in cognitive and language domains, academic skills [19] and prosocial behaviours, and fewer adjustment difficulties. Especially in the first year of life, a higher *quantity* of childcare (i.e. hours/week in any kind of non-maternal care) is associated with an increased risk of behaviour problems and disobedience [20]. As in family settings, however, individual children's sensitivity to non-maternal care will vary. For example, out-of-home care has been shown to have positive effects on the development of at-risk young children.

School life provides further opportunities, demands and challenges. Starting and changing schools are significant events in children's lives. Most adapt well, but a significant minority show some difficulties when starting school, and many young adolescents show short-term declines in academic performance and self-esteem on transfer from primary to secondary school. Tests are high up on children's lists of fears, and major examinations are often associated with increased psychological distress. Bullying can be frequent and is a key risk factor for children's mental health. Surveys suggest that many children experience occasional bullying at school, and smaller groups are persistently victimized. Although some may have been anxious and insecure prior to starting school, recent evidence demonstrates that bullying has independent effects on risks of later adjustment problems [21].

Variations in the social and organizational 'climates' of schools have modest independent effects on children's academic progress and behaviour [22]. In part, such variations reflect differences in the background characteristics of pupils, although differences in organizational characteristics and the tenor of day-to-day school life are important. Schools with more positive child outcomes have purposeful leadership, an appropriate academic emphasis, constructive classroom management and consistent, though not over-severe, discipline. The composition of pupil groupings also appears important – for instance, young children are more likely to become aggressive in classes with other very aggressive children. Both school- and classroom-based interventions can provide highly effective in behaviour management. For some severely disadvantaged children, schooling can provide significant positive experiences and support. Importantly, experimental studies of preschool programmes show long-term reduced risks of participant delinquency and unemployment many years after school leaving.

## Wider Social and Environmental Influences

### Poverty and Social Disadvantage

Poverty and social disadvantage are consistently associated with variations in children's health, cognitive skills and academic achievements, and – somewhat more modestly – with their social and emotional development [23]. Disruptive behaviours, in particular, show links with persistent family poverty, although effects are more marked for boys than for girls and are stronger in childhood than in adolescence. Research suggests that these associations reflect elements of both social selection and causal influences. Especially in families of young children, effects are likely to be indirect, operating through processes whereby poverty imposes stresses on parents that, in turn, have an impact on family relationships and parenting. In more affluent societies, relative deprivation – the perception of disadvantage by comparison with others – may also contribute to parental stress.

## Neighbourhood and Community Contexts

Rates of behavioural difficulties (and other markers of child health status) also vary with neighbourhood context [24]. Problem levels may be especially high in chronically disadvantaged inner-city areas, and the task of parenting may be more challenging when neighbourhood supports are poor. Again, many of these effects seem likely to be indirect in early childhood, operating via increased stress on families. But in severely disadvantaged settings, even quite young children may be directly exposed to community violence and, later in development, neighbourhood influences may be mediated through associations with delinquent peers.

## Multiple Stressors

For many children, exposure to these and other adversities will covary: children in stressed families often live in poor neighbourhoods, attend poorly resourced schools, and are exposed to deviant peers. Research suggests that risks at the child, parenting, sibling, peer and sociocultural levels each add uniquely to the prediction of emotional and behavioural problems. The total number of risks explains further variance in outcomes, and evidence is beginning to accumulate that differing *configurations* of risk are associated with specific emotional and behavioural difficulties [25]. Exposure to poverty, for example, may differ in its impact depending on parental characteristics and the quality of family relationships. Comprehensive assessments of family and systemic influences require that each of these levels of influence, and the interplay between them, be taken into account.

# References

1 Dunn EC, Masyn KE, Yudon M et al. (2014) Translating multilevel theory into multilevel research: Challenges and opportunities for understanding the social determinants of psychiatric disorders. Social Psychiatry and Psychiatric Epidemiology, 49, 859–872.
2 Leclère C, Viaux S, Avril M et al. (2014) Why synchrony matters during mother child interactions: a systematic review. PLoS ONE 9(12): e113571.
3 Pluess M (2015) Individual differences in environmental sensitivity. Child Development Perspectives, 9, 138–143.
4 Masten AS, Shaffer A (2006) How families matter in child development: reflections from research on risk and resilience. In: Clarke-Stewart A, Dunn J (eds) Families Count. Cambridge: Cambridge University Press, pp. 5–25.
5 Maccoby, EE, Martin, JA (1983) Socialization in the context of the family: Parent–child interaction. In: Mussen P, Hetherington EM (eds) Handbook of Child Psychology, volume IV, 4th edn. Socialization, personality, and social development. Wiley, New York, pp. 1–101.
6 Beardslee WR, Gladstone TRG, O'Connor EE (2011) Transmission and prevention of mood disorders among children of affectively ill parents: a review. Journal of the American Academy of Child and Adolescent Psychiatry. 50, 1098–1109.
7 Feinberg ME, Solmeyer AR, McHale SM (2012) The third rail of family systems: sibling relationships, mental and behavioral health, and preventive intervention in childhood and adolescence. Clinical Child and Family Psychology Review, 15, 43–57.

8  Dunn JF (2006) Siblings. In: Grusec JE, Hastings D (eds) Handbook of Socialisation: Theory and Research. New York: Guilford Publications, pp. 309–27.

9  Buist KL, Dekovic M, Prinzie P (2013) Sibling relationship quality and psychopathology of children and adolescents: A meta-analysis. Clinical Psychology Review, 33, 97–106.

10  Wolke D, Tippett N., Dantchev S (2015) Bullying in the family: sibling bullying. Lancet Psychiatry, 2, 917–929.

11  Furstenberg FF (2014) Fifty years of family change: from consensus to complexity. Annals of the American Academy of Political and Social Science, 654, 12–30

12  Thomson E (2014) Family complexity in Europe. Annals of the American Academy of Political and Social Science, 654, 245–258.

13  Dunn J, Deater-Deckard K, Pickering K et al. (1998) Children's adjustment and prosocial behaviour in step–, single-parent, and non-stepfamily settings: findings from a community study. Journal of Child Psychology and Psychiatry, 39, 1083–95.

14  Thomson E, McLanahan SS (2012) Reflections on "Family Structure and Child Well-Being: Economic Resources vs. Parental Socialization". Social Forces, 91, 45–53.

15  Illioi EC, Golombok S (2015) Psychological adjustment in adolescents conceived by assisted reproduction techniques: a systematic review. Human Reproduction Update, 21, 84–96.

16  Lamb ME (2012) Mothers, fathers, families, and circumstances: factors affecting children's adjustment. Applied Developmental Science 16, 98–111.

17  Lansford JE (2009) Parental divorce and children's adjustment. Perspectives on Psychological Science, 4, 140–152.

18  OECD (2105) http://www.oecd.org/els/family/LMF_1_2_Maternal_Employment.pdf. Accessed: January 2017.

19  Laurin JC, Geoffroy MC, Boivin M et al. (2015) Child care services, socioeconomic inequalities, and academic performance. Pediatrics, 136, 1112–1124.

20  Huston AC, Bobbitt KC, Bentley A (2015) Time spent in child care: how and why does it affect social development? Developmental Psychology, 51, 621–634.

21  Arseneault L, Bowes L, Shakoor S (2010) Bullying victimization in youths and mental health problems: 'Much ado about nothing'? Psychological Medicine 40, 717–729.

22  Rutter M, Maughan B (2002) School effectiveness findings 1979–2002. Journal of School Psychology 40 451–475.

23  Bradley R, Corwyn R (2002) Socioeconomic status and child development. Annual Review of Psychology, 53, 371–399.

24  Sampson RJ (2003) The neighborhood context of well-being. Perspectives in Biology and Medicine 46, 853–864.

25  Evans GW, Li D, Whipple SS (2013) Cumulative risk and child development. Psychological Bulletin, 139, 1342–1396.

## 2

# Child Development and Cultural Considerations in Clinical Practice

*Ruma Bose and Sanjida Sattar*

## Introduction

With increasing contact between cultural and ethnic groups, the concept of childhood has evoked renewed interest. Anthropologists, historians and cultural child psychologists have attempted to study children's lives and conceptions about childhood in different cultural contexts. There are wide differences across cultures [1,2]. For professionals working in multicultural contexts, an important question is: how are ethnic differences accounted for in prevailing concepts regarding parenting and childhood behaviours, both 'normal' and 'variant'? Ethnic variations in parenting may express adaptations to different conditions for child development necessitated by divergent ecological, socio-political and cultural priorities, rather than inherent 'ethnic differences'.

## Developmental Niche and Eco-Cultural Pathways

The concept of the developmental niche was developed as a framework for studying the production of children's health and development through the interaction between the physical and social settings of the child's everyday life, culturally determined customs of child care and parental theories about children [2], which inform the larger strategy for child care and the daily routines for children in a culture. The everyday routines embody the core cultural goals and fashion developmental pathways for children in the specific eco-cultural context or niche [3]. LeVine *et al.* [4] demonstrates how in parts of the world where child survival is precarious, close physical proximity to the baby is maintained by carrying, co-sleeping, breast-feeding, immediate response to crying, and substitute care by siblings when the mother is working. The pursuit of learning is postponed until survival is assured. The increased physical contact and stimulation promote growth, as well as development of attentional processes and early neuromuscular competency [5]. By contrast, in technologically advanced North America, where child survival is of less concern, but preparation for competency in future occupational roles is graded by mastery of literacy-based skills, mothers emphasize the attainment of language skills and mastery of the object world through communicative interaction and naming of objects from an early age, rather than close physical proximity. Parents respond to new eco-cultural contexts, after migration, for example, by changing parenting strategies.

*Child Psychology and Psychiatry: Frameworks for Clinical Training and Practice*, Third Edition.
Edited by David Skuse, Helen Bruce and Linda Dowdney.
© 2017 John Wiley & Sons, Ltd. Published 2017 by John Wiley & Sons, Ltd.

## Childhood and Parenting Across Cultures

As most accounts of children's development and needs are framed within writings from North America and Europe, the normative description of childhood is often based on children growing up within the northern cultures, and even within this are subsumed differences in class and socio-economic status. Culture is often consigned to the role of an 'add-on' variable to assumed normative standards applied universally. Recent cultural studies have questioned assumptions about 'cultural universals' and highlighted the centrality of culture in shaping human behaviours, crucially here of parents and children.

How integral is culture to concepts regarding childhood, child development and the goals that frame parental strategies for bringing up children? Although children achieve developmental maturity along broadly similar species-specific lines, and the goal of parenting is similar across cultures, i.e. seeing children become competent adults in one's own cultural, moral and economic world, there are wide differences in what constitutes the desired competencies and the means for achieving them. Shweder *et al.* [6] make the point that any aspect of human nature that we endeavour to understand must have a central essence, but that this essence consists of a heterogeneous collection of structures and inclinations substantiated by the historical experiences of different cultural communities, resulting in 'one mind, many mentalities: universalism without uniformity'. This is different from culture being perceived as variations from a normative standard. James *et al.*'s [7] question, 'One childhood or many?', is explored below via examples from the findings of cultural research across the globe.

## Infancy

### Developmental Stages

The very notion of stages of childhood is culturally constructed. Developmental psychologists mark the end of infancy with the beginning of 'toddlerhood', normatively defined at 2 years and marked by language and motor competency. However, this is not a biological fact, but a cultural convention based on the assumption that life stages should be delineated by absolute points in time. It is different from norms in cultures where the crucial reference point is the acquisition of moral sense [8]. Puritans of New England began strict discipline at 1 year of age, when they believed infancy ended and the Devil began to exert control. The ethnographic record shows that in most parts of the world, active teaching begins at least after 5 years, as it is believed that before this children are too immature or lacking in 'sense' to be taught important lessons [1]. The Baganda people of Uganda typically train their infants to sit independently as early as 4 months, as sitting up and smiling is an asset amongst this group who value face-to-face contact highly [8].

### Attachment

Cross-cultural research on attachment behaviour has thrown up challenging questions regarding how deviation from supposed universal norms is to be understood at a population level. The Bowlby–Ainsworth model of attachment describes a universal model of attachment behaviour predicated on the primary carer's sensitivity to the infant's signals. Ainsworth's work in different parts of the world testifies to the universality of attachment behaviour in infants, with group B attachment behaviour (secure attachment) being modal in most cultures [9]. However, the model does not allow for variations other than as suboptimal or pathological.

A review of the literature on attachment, taking into account population variations, raises the question of whether there is a multiplicity of optimum patterns for humans [10] reflecting different meanings attributed to optimal patterns of attachment behaviour in different sociocultural groups [9]. For example, a study of attachment in Bielefeld (Germany) [11], showed that 49% of the infants had anxious-avoidant attachment behaviour, which was related to a highly valued cultural emphasis on obedience and self-reliance, the training for which began in infancy. It was an accepted practice to leave infants in bed alone for short periods, and mothers compared the extent to which their babies could play alone as an indication of their developing self-reliance. Given the absence of evidence for a higher prevalence of personality disorder in Bielefeld, it could be argued that the drive for self-sufficiency engendered behaviours that, at that time, counted as virtuous in some German communities, and highlights a different pathway towards normal emotional development. Historically, the prevention of infant dependency was also highly valued amongst British and American middle classes until the end of World War II.

The variety in infant caretaking patterns is highlighted by the hunter-gathering Efe people (Zaire), where multiple caretakers alongside the mother provide both lactating and non-lactating care, resulting in Efe infants being more diffusely attached to many caregivers rather than intensely attached to one. Tronick *et al.* [12] propose that this model of caretaking is moulded by specific ecological demands and cultural values that emphasize group identification.

### Parental Involvement in Play and Learning

Parental facilitation of the child's academic preparedness through proto-conversations with babies, active teaching through toys and make-believe is considered critical by middle-class Euro-American parents, as it promotes skills required for future school and occupational success. Although the parent as teacher is often enshrined as an ideal in manuals for parents, it is essentially a cultural model that promotes important developmental skills required in complex urban societies. It is not an ideal in agrarian pastoral societies where processes are less demanding and where everyone one is a potential teacher or role model. Instead, qualities such as initiative, attention to detail, sharing, obedience and respect for elders attract greater value.

## Middle Childhood

With the introduction of compulsory education in most parts of the world, middle childhood has received relatively less attention in cultural work. However, a closer examination reveals startling differences in how children's lives are structured at this stage. Ethnographic description of the Girima people in Kenya demonstrates some differences from the North American normative expectations of children at this stage, but also seen in many other cultural groups in the developing world [13]. Girima people attach importance to providing children with duties that teach responsibility and mutuality necessary for future adult cooperative roles. Children aged 2–3 years take pride in running errands, and from 8 years onwards a girl may be expected to pound maize and a boy to herd. Work constitutes opportunities for acquiring skills in future gender-specific roles, as well as opportunities to participate in cooperative activities with other children. These activities are often combined with attending school. Assistance within the home is different from wage labour, which, however, remains a reality for children from very socio-economically deprived families in many parts of the world, and which also keep the world price of commodities down [14].

**Adolescence**

Adolescence as a stage between childhood and adulthood where the participants behave and are regarded differently appears to exist worldwide. This stage may therefore not be a product of culture, although many of its descriptions are [15]. In many cultures in which socialization into adult occupational roles begins early, it is less, as understood in the west, a stage where identity questions about future roles begin, but rather a stage for preparation for future reproductive roles, within which individuation is subsumed. The stress on individuation and identity formation at this stage, which is adaptive for industrial and mobile capitalist economies, is not shared across cultures where the social-relational self is emphasized.

## Culture and Disability

The definition of disability is complex, as reflected in the current World Health Organization definition, which encompasses impairments, activity limitations and participation restrictions, and reflects the interaction between features of a person's body and features of society [16]. Ingstad and Reynolds Whyte [17] highlighted important cross-cultural questions for conceptualizing disability, such as the family's ability in any society to care for an infirm person, particularly in the context of labour migration and the changing the structure of large families previously able to share care. Furthermore, it is easier for disabled people to contribute where the family is the basic unit of production. Impairment interacts with gender, age and economic standing in ways specific to a society, e.g. not being able to arrange marriage for a child has a great impact on a family in an economically deprived area of India.

Antonovsky [18] suggests that maintaining a sense of coherence makes a key difference to staying psychologically healthy in an apparently disordered world. Alongside biomedical explanatory models, parents may have spiritual explanations such as recognition by God of their ability to parent a disabled child, or retribution from a higher power, curse or magical force such as witchcraft [19]. Importantly, these explanatory models are often used inconsistently, are malleable and are shaped by individual circumstances [17].

## Ethnicity and Mental Health

In clinical practice, when a cultural explanation is offered to explain differences between ethnic groups regarding mental health, methodological considerations need to be taken into account, such as comparisons in terms of socio-economic variables, population versus clinic rates, and cross-cultural validation of research instruments. Cross-cultural epidemiological studies remain too varied for firm conclusions to be drawn about worldwide rates and patterns. For example, in Polanczyk *et al.*'s [20] meta-regression analysis of attention deficit-hyperactivity disorder (ADHD) studies, two-thirds of the 135 studies were from North America and Europe, and the variations in methodology were wide and accounted for the variability in the ADHD prevalence estimates.

Goodman *et al.*'s [21] systematic review of the mental health of children of the main ethnic groups in England underscored the need to research the interplay between risk and protective factors in different communities. There have been a number of studies illustrating this, including Goodman *et al.*'s [22] subsequent study, which found that British Indian children have a large advantage in a lowered risk for behavioural and hyperactivity problems. This advantage is partly mediated by family type and academic abilities. Reese [23] found that migrant parents who perceive higher risk to young people in the new environment exercise greater boundary control over adolescents than would be exercised in the country of origin, resulting in greater inter-generational conflict in the family. This may lead, in turn, to adolescents experiencing emotional difficulties and exhibiting behaviours communicating distress.

There is little evidence for culture-specific syndromes, but dissociative disorders such as trance and possession in adolescence related to rapid social change in parts of the world where possession beliefs exist have been reported [24].

## Conclusion

As culture and ethnicities are dynamic entities, a foreclosure of the discussion is never possible. A more useful approach is to develop a framework for understanding the centrality of culture in child development, based on the extensive evidence from cross-cultural research. However, as familiarity with one's own cultural norm is often the starting point for studying difference, there is always the risk of subsuming the issue of 'cultural difference' under that of 'different cultural moralities'. For mental health professions, culture is a potent tool for promoting reflexivity and widening our horizons by including knowledge about the everyday lives of children from parts of the world where the majority of children live.

## References

1  Lancy DF (2008) The Anthropology of Childhood: Cherubs, Chattel, Changelings. Cambridge University Press.

2  Harkness S, Super CM (1994) The developmental niche: a theoretical framework for analyzing the household production of health. Social Science and Medicine, 38, 217–226.

3  Weisner TS (2002) Ecocultural understanding of children's developmental pathways. Human Development, 45, 275–281.

4  LeVine RA, Dixon S, Levine S et al. (1996) Child Care and Culture: Lessons from Africa. Cambridge University Press.

5  Harkness S, Super CM (2002) Culture structures the environment for development. Human Development, 45, 270–274.

6 Shweder RA, Goodnow J, Hatano G et al. (1998) The cultural psychology of development: one mind, many mentalities. In: Damon D, Lerner RM (eds) Handbook of Child Psychology, Vol 1. Theoretical Models Of Human Development. New York: Wiley.

7 James A, Jenks C, Prout A (1998) Theorizing Childhood. Cambridge: Polity Press.

8 Gottlieb A (2000) Where have all the babies gone? Toward an anthropology of infants (and their caretakers). Anthropological Quarterly, 73. Youth and the Social Imagination in Africa, Part 1, pp. 121–132.

9 Harwood RL, Miller JG, Irizarry NL (1995) Culture And Attachment. New York: Guildford Press.

10 LeVine RA, Norman K (2008) Attachment in anthropological perspective. In: LeVine RA, New RS (eds) Anthropology and Child Development: A Cross-Cultural Reader. Blackwell Publishing, pp. 127–142.

11 Grossmann K, Grossmann KE (1981) Parent infant attachment relationships in bielefeld: a research note. In: Immelman G, Barlow G, Petrovich L, Main M (eds) Behavioural Development: The Bielefeld Interdisciplinary Project. New York: Cambridge University Press, pp. 694–699.

12 Tronick EZ, Morelli GA, Winn S (2008) Multiple caregiving in the Ituri Forest. In: LeVine RA, New RS (eds) Anthropology and Child Development: A Cross-Cultural Reader. Blackwell Publishing Limited, pp. 289–306.

13 Wenger M (2008) Children's work, play, and relationships among the Girima of Kenya. In: LeVine RA, New RS (eds) Anthropology and Child Development: A Cross-Cultural Reader. Blackwell Publishing, pp. 289–306.

14 Nieuwenhuys O (2005) The wealth of children: reconsidering the child labour debate. In: Qvortrup J (ed.) Studies in Modern Childhood: Society, Agency, Culture. Palgrave Macmillian, pp. 167–183.

15 Schegel A (1995) A cross-cultural approach to adolescence. Ethos, 23, 15–32.

16 World Health Organization (2011) World Report of Disability, 7. WHO.

17 Ingstad B, Reynolds Whyte S (1995) Disability and Culture. University of California Press, pp. 7–24.

18 Antonovsky A (1987) Unravelling the Mystery of Health: How People Manage Stress and Stay Well. San Francisco: Jossey-Bass.

19 Anthony J (2011) Conceptualising disability in Ghana: implications for EFA and inclusive education. International Journal of Inclusive Education, 15, 1073–1086.

20 Polanczyk GV, Willcutt EG, Salum GA et al. (2014) ADHD prevalence estimates across three decades: an updated systematic review and meta-regression analysis. International Journal of Epidemiology, 43, 434–442.

21 Goodman A, Patel V, Leon DA (2008) Child mental health differences amongst ethnic groups in Britain: a systematic review. BMC Public Health, 8, 1.

22 Goodman A, Patel V, Leon DA (2010) Why do British Indian children have an apparent mental health advantage?. Journal of Child Psychology and Psychiatry, 51, 1171–1183.

23 Reese L (2002) Parental strategies in contrasting cultural settings: families in Mexico and 'El Norte'. Anthropology & Education Quarterly, 33, 30–59.

24 Fabrega H, Miller BD (1995) Towards a more comprehensive medical anthropology: the case of adolescent psychopathology. Medical Anthropology Quarterly, 9, 431–461.

# 3

# Neurobehavioural Development in Infancy: The Buffering and Transducing Role of the Mother/Caretaker–Infant Dyad

*Cindy H. Liu and Ed Tronick*

## Introduction

Infant neurobehaviour and its development are behaviours generated by neurophysiological and psychological processes, which mediate infants' internal processes and engagement with the world. Ideally, neurobehaviour becomes adaptive as infants confront daily environmental challenges. We introduce theory-driven and empirically supported influences on neurobehavioural development, emphasizing mechanisms exemplifying the interaction of neurobiological and social domains of development. Neurobehaviour is not self-contained, nor is it preset or a simple unfolding controlled by genetic maturational processes, but rather it is embedded in regulatory processes between infants and caregivers, operating in a continuous, bidirectional and dynamic manner. These regulatory processes are affected by multiple factors, ranging from health status to toxic exposures. Furthermore, they are sculpted by culture, in addition to biological and physiological processes – the processes that make up human experience.

## Infant Neurobehavioural Capacities

Previously, newborns were seen as reflexive beings. Infant neurobehaviour was modelled on spinal frog behaviour where responses to stimuli were thought to be fixed, under stimulus control and automatic. This model is wrong [1]. It did not recognize that the quality of neurobehaviour and its intensity and robustness of expression, such as infant reflexes of knee jerking and sucking, are mediated by the infant's current state [2], i.e. the organization of neurophysiological (heart rate, respiration, EEG) and behavioural systems (tone, movements) at any given moment. Six states are now used to understand infant neurobehaviour: two *sleep* states (state 1, quiet sleep; and state 2, REM sleep), an *awake* but not alert state with eyes opening and with movement (state 3), two *awake or alert* states (state 4, quiet alert; and state 5, active alert) and a *distress* state (state 6) [3,4].

There are four domains of complex neurobehaviour [5]:

1. *attention* – visual and auditory abilities to process information such as discriminating faces;

*Child Psychology and Psychiatry: Frameworks for Clinical Training and Practice*, Third Edition.
Edited by David Skuse, Helen Bruce and Linda Dowdney.
© 2017 John Wiley & Sons, Ltd. Published 2017 by John Wiley & Sons, Ltd.

2. *arousal* – the expression and intensity of states from sleep to alert to distress and their self-modulation;
3. *action* – fine and gross motor skills for acting on the world of things and people such as reaching for an object;
4. *affective social processes* – communicative emotional displays.

The quality of these domains and the infants' repertoire of complex motor and attentional processes are affected by infant state [2,6], which determines various infant response modalities. For example, facial brightening and alerting to visual stimuli only occur during the alert states; startles occur in states 1, 4, 5 and 6, but seldom in state 2; movements are smooth in state 4 but jerky and uncoordinated in state 6, and largely absent in state 2 [4]. Furthermore, infants collect information and modulate their behaviour differently in different states. Head turning to sound and cuddling occur primarily in states 4 and 5 but not in state 2, and habituation can occur in states 1, 2 and 4, but is difficult to achieve in state 5. Repeated exposure to a stimulus often leads to a transition to state 6.

Infant neurobehaviour can be evaluated. The NICU (neonatal intensive care unit) Network Neurobehavioural Scale (NNNS) is the most refined and established measure [7]. A standardized assessment tool for infants [8,9], it assesses normally developing and at-risk infants from the newborn period to the postnatal period. Using different stimuli (e.g. bell, human face and voice) and handling techniques (e.g. cuddling,), the NNNS evaluates the four domains of infant neurobehavior. Critically, the NNNS considers infant state for each neurobehaviour and tracks the range of states and their lability.

The NNNS is sensitive to risk factors affecting infant neurobehaviour, such as gestational age, birthweight, *in utero* exposure to recreational drugs and maternal stress and depression [7]. Impressively, NNNS profiles of infants' neurobehavioural organization ('well organized' to 'poorly organized') have predicted long-term outcomes related to school readiness and IQ at 4.5 years of age [7] as well as cerebral palsy even when lesions are taken into account [7]. These findings indicate the significance of infants' self-organized neurobehavioural capacities for their long-term psychosocial development.

Epigenetic mechanisms are affected by environmental experience and, in turn, affect genetic functioning. In an exciting development, the NNNS has been found to be related to stress-related epigenetic changes (methylation). Methylation of the placenta gene (*HSD11B2*) that inactivates maternal cortisol, which is toxic to the foetus, is related to stress and the extent of its methylation was associated with poorer scores for the quality of infant movement [10]. Ongoing research promises to provide information on the mechanisms for neurobehavioural phenotypic neurobehavioural characteristics [11,12].

## Culture

Neurobehavior is a socially regulated process and not simply a physiological process. As a social process, the brain and physiological processes controlling neurobehaviour are enculturated in caretaking from the moment of birth, if not before [13]. Culture determines both caregivers' implicit and explicit views of infant capacities and caregiver behaviour. Depending on the culture, infant cries may reflect infant fragility and dependence or, conversely, infant robustness. Caregiving responses depend on these views. Social neuroscience research [14] indicates that prenatal and postnatal culturated experiences sculpt neurodevelopmental functional and structural characteristics [15].

Neonatal intensive care unit caretaking practices represent a set of 'cultural' practices that may relate to differing neurobehaviour in very preterm infants [16]. Infants from NICUs with high scores on infant-centred care (e.g. swaddling, parental involvement) showed higher attention and regulation, less excitability and hypotonicity, and lower stress/abstinence NNNS scores than infants from low-care units.

Unique caretaking practices by the Peruvian Quechua people appear to influence the biological and behavioural processes underlying infant neurobehavioural development. Quechua dwelling at high altitude (4250 m) use a culturally created caretaking technology, the manta pouch, to 'house' their infants – a layered set of cloths and blankets that tightly wrap around and fully enclose the infant. The practice buffers infants from the extremes of the environment (i.e. freezing temperatures, reduced oxygen, lack of humidity) [17]. Within the manta pouch, the temperature is stabilized and high, the air is humidified, and infant movement is limited. Paradoxically, the $O_2$ levels are lower and $CO_2$ levels are higher in the pouch compared to hypoxic conditions at high altitude. While these hypoxic conditions would be considered dangerous in other environments, the increase of $CO_2$ may actually be a microstressor that induces adaptive functional and structural changes. In combination with other features of the manta microclimate, high $CO_2$ levels increase the duration of infant sleep, which conserves energy; this in turn leads to faster physical growth and resistance to temperature loss. Raised $CO_2$ levels are partly responsible for inducing the left shift of the Quechua's $CO_2$ sensor, allowing them to tolerate otherwise debilitating high levels of $CO_2$. This is a developmentally sculpted phenomenon directly related to the length of time an individual lives at high altitude prior to puberty. Thus, truly fundamental physiological processes such as tolerance for $CO_2$, sleep quantity and motor development, which may appear to be 'built in', are affected by Quechua caretaking practices. Certainly no practices in the west mimic these practices, but one can wonder if there are biological optima for $CO_2$ sensitivity or sleep patterns.

While not denying that there are pathologies of functioning and development, cultural comparisons indicate that there are no fixed and universal norms, but that such norms are set by cultural practices. As an example, western practitioners, for safety reasons, currently urge caregivers to place their infants on their backs for sleep. After noticing motor delays (e.g. crawling) due to this change in sleep position, many practitioners consider it essential for caregivers to practice 'tummy time' with their infant – 30 minutes of daily exercise where the infant strengthens neck muscles in preparation for sitting up and crawling [18]. Caregivers are recommended to socially engage their infant during this time [19]. By modifying infant neurobehaviour, motor and social development is once again viewed as 'normal'. However, 'tummy time' may not be readily adopted by caregivers from certain cultures. For instance, Asians have always placed their infants on their back to sleep and never considered infant motor milestones delayed. In another example, African infants who were carried in a sling from birth had *accelerated* motor development compared with western infants [20]. Yet, we would probably never regard western infants as having a motor delay.

## Mutual Regulation and Buffer–Transducer Models

Although infants are competent beings with an impressive ability to self-regulate and to act upon the world, their capacities are limited and immature. The quality of neurobehaviour dissipates unless infants receive external support to scaffold their organization. Infants are capable of processing stimuli in a self-organized alert state. However, that state is energetically costly and often short-lived, but, with postural support and soothing from their caregivers, can become more sustained and robust [15]. Infants and caregivers are thus involved in a dyadic process that we refer to as the mutual regulation model (MRM) [21,22]. The MRM proposes that neurobehavioural processes are jointly regulated by infants using internal self-organized capacities in coordination with regulatory input from caregivers and their success or failure depends on both infant and caretaker capacities [23,24].

The MRM operates on the micro-temporal process of exchanging regulatory information. We now propose the buffer–transducer model (BTM). It extends the MRM model to include biological and cultural factors as well as the mechanisms that underlie and influence neurobehavioural development (see Figure 3.1). It conceptualizes the caretaker–infant mutual regulation as a final common pathway, either buffering or transducing the effects of different factors that affect neurobehavioural development to the infant.

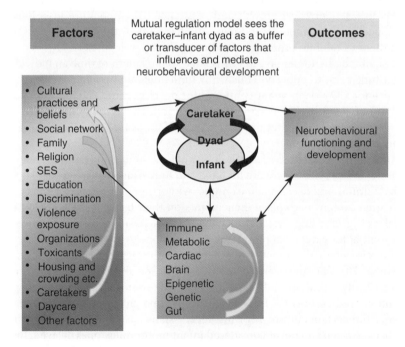

**Figure 3.1** Mutual regulation model sees the caretaker–infant dyad as a buffer or transducer of factors that influence and mediate neurobehavioural development.

There are four components to the BTM:

1. Infant outcome is reflected in the form of neurobehavior and development.
2. Risk factors are conceptualized as resource depletion or resource enhancement factors that affect resources available over time. These resources are physiological, psychological and relational or regulatory. They determine the quality of the child's outcome. For instance, low maternal education (e.g. less than high school) and associated factors deplete resources because such mothers are likely to have poorer self-regulatory and infant regulatory capacities, whereas high maternal education and its associated factors typically enhance regulatory resources [23].
3. Underlying mechanisms such as epigenetics or the immune system may deplete or enhance functioning depending on how they are affected by the interplay of the other components of the model, such as noise levels or community coherence.
4. The central component is the mother/caretaker–infant dyad, which can either buffer the infant from resource-depleting exposures or transduce the effects of resource-depleting or -enhancing factors to the infant. For example, neighbourhood violence typically does not directly affect the infant, but it does affect the caregiver. If the caretaker can self-regulate the dysregulating effects of violence on herself, he or she is more likely to be able to buffer the infant from its effects. By contrast, a caretaker dysregulated by the exposure to violence will be less able to regulate the infant and, in effect, transduces its dysregulating effects to the infant.

Within the BTM model, the dyad operates in a culturated manner – i.e. how caretakers buffer or transduce effects has a cultural form. For example, the Quechua initially buffer their infants from the depleting conditions of high altitude, but over the course of the first year they increasingly expose the infant to those conditions. This process leads to the enhancement of infants' physiological resources.

Space precludes discussion of many features of the BTM – e.g. the amplifying effects of the interplay of its components that affect neurobehavioural development or transduce their effects to the infant. What is most important to see is that what unites these different components into a dynamic regulatory system is the interplay of different components over time and the central role of the infant–caretaker dyad.

## Conclusion

The consideration of only biological factors is insufficient for understanding neurobehavioural development. A broader view of neurobehavioural development is necessary to capture the complexity of the processes that unfold over time. Infant state is needed to conceptualize the overall organization of an infant's physiological and behavioural systems as it receives external inputs from others. Through the MRM perspective, the caregiver and infant jointly make efforts to maintain infant neurobehavioural coherence and organization and the BTM model integrates the MRM by focusing on the central role of the mother/caretaker–infant dyad. Over the long run, the interplay of self-organized neurobehavioural processes, caregiver practices and resulting interpersonal states – however they differ across cultures – organizes infants in a coherent and culturally appropriate manner. Infants who are unable to engage socially in an appropriate way within their culture will not develop normally. Fortunately, good parenting naturally flows when caregivers function well in their environments, which in turn helps infants to develop into culturally appropriate beings.

## References

1 Sherrington CS (1906) The Integrative Action of the Nervous System. New Haven, CT: Yale University Press.

2 Prechtl HFR (1981) The study of neural development as a perspective of clinical problems. In: Connolly KJ, Prechtl HR (eds) Maturation and Development: Biological and Psychological Perspectives. Philadelphia, PA: JP Lippincott, pp. 198–215.

3 Prechtl HFR, Beintema D (1964) The Neurological Examination of the Newborn Infant. London, UK: Lavenham Press.

4 Lester, BM, Tronick, EZ (2004) History and description of the Neonatal Intensive Care Unit Network Neurobehavioral Scale. Pediatrics, 113, 634–640.

5 Lester BM, Tronick EZ (1994) The effects of prenatal cocaine exposure and child outcome. Infant Mental Health Journal, 15, 107–20.

6 Brazelton T (1973) Neonatal Behavioral Assessment Scale. London (England): Spastic International Medical Publications.

7 Tronick E, Lester B (2013) Grandchild of the NBAS: The NICU Network Neurobehavioral Scale (NNNS): A review of the research using the NNNS. Journal of Child and Adolescent Psychiatric Nursing, 26, 1073–6077.

8 Lester BM, Tronick EZ (2004) The Neonatal Intensive Care Unit Network Neurobehavior Scale (NNNS). Pediatrics, 113, 631–99.

9 Fink N, Tronick EZ, Olson K, Lester BM. Clinically healthy infants' neurobehavioral performance: Norms and percentiles from the Neonatal Intensive Care Unit Network Neurobehavioral Scale (NNNS). Pediatrics. Under review.

10 Marsit C, Padbury J, Lester B (2012) Placental 11-beta hydroxysteroid dehydrogenase methylation is associated with newborn growth and neurobehavioral outcomes. PLoS ONE,7(3).

11 Marsit C, Lambertini L, Maccani M et al. (2011) Placenta-imprinted gene expression association of infant neurobehavior. Journal of Pediatrics, 160, 854–860.

12 Lester B, Marsit C, Conradt E (2014) Are epigenetic changes in the intrauterine environment related to newborn neurobehavior? Epigenomics, 6, 175–178.

13 Tronick EZ, Morelli G (1991) Foreword: The role of culture in brain organization, child development, and parenting. In: Nugent JK, Lester BM, Brazelton TB (eds) The Cultural Context of Infancy: Multicultural and Interdisciplinary Approaches to Parent-Infant Relations, 2nd edn. Ablex Publishing.

14 Nelson CA, Thomas KM, de Haan M (2006) Neuroscience of Cognitive Development: The Role of Experience and the Developing Brain. Hoboken, NJ: John Wiley.

15 Tronick E (2007) The Neurobehavioral and Social-Emotional Development of Infants and Children. New York, NY: WW Norton, Co.

16 Montirosso R, Del Prete A, Cavallini A, Cozzi P, Gruppo di Studio NEO-ACQUA (2009) Neurobehavioral profile in a group of healthy preterm infants. Utilization of the NICU Network Neurobehavioral Scale (NNNS). Child Development, Disabilities – Saggi, 3, 96–116.

17 Tronick EZ, Thomas RB, Daltabuit M (1994) The Quechua manta pouch: A caretaking practice for buffering the Peruvian infant against the multiple stressors of high altitude. Child Development, 65, 1005–1013.

18 Persing J, James H, Swanson J (2003) Prevention and management of positional skull deformities in infants. Pediatrics, 112, 199–202.

19 Ma D. Babies should sleep on backs, play on stomachs (2009) American Academy of Pediatrics News, 30, 30.

20 Super CM (1976) Environmental effects on motor development: The case of African infant precocity. Developmental Medicine, Child Neurology, 18, 561–567.

21 Blumberg NL (1980) Effects of neonatal risk, maternal attitude, and cognitive style on early postpartum adjustment. Journal of Abnormal Psychology, 89, 139–50.

22 Tronick EZ, Beeghly M (2011) Infants' meaning-making and the development of mental health problems. American Psychology, 66, 107–119.

23 DiCorcia JA, Tronick EZ (2011) Quotidian resilience: exploring mechanisms that drive resilience from a perspective of everyday stress and coping. Neuroscience of Biobehavioral Reviews, 35, 1593–1602.

24 Beeghly M, Tronick E (2011) Early resilience in the context of parent-infant relationships: a social developmental perspective. Infant mental health: relationship issues, social-emotional development and pediatric practice. Special Issue of Current Problems in Pediatric and Adolescent Health Care, 41, 197–201.

# 4

# Genetic and Biological Influences

*David Skuse*

## Introduction

The Human Genome Project was completed in 2003 [1], and the first draft sequence of DNA in a human cell was then available for everyone to scrutinize. What have we learned since, and have those insights benefited patients with psychiatric disorders?

Until relatively recently, what little was known about genes that contribute to neurodevelopmental conditions came from the study of single gene mutations, in which the normal activity of an individual gene is disrupted. Disorders attributable to errors in a single gene are exceptionally rare (typically with an incidence of no more than 1 per 10 000). Remarkable advances are being made in the development of novel treatments, based on gene modification, for conditions that are due either to mutated genes, such as Rett syndrome [2] and fragile X syndrome [3], as well as coding problems that allow genes to be switched on that are faulty, such as Angelman syndrome [4].

Unlike single gene disorders, most psychiatric conditions are highly complex in terms of their underlying genetic predisposition. Whilst twin and adoption studies indicate an important role for heredity, in general, the risk of developing a major psychiatric disorder is attributable to the sum of individual differences in hundreds or even thousands of genes. We are beginning to identify many of the more important individual differences, but there is a continuing debate about how they aggregate to increase the chance of disorder, because each one has a tiny impact on the variation in individual risk [5]. In order to take advantage of our developing knowledge of DNA sequences, we need to bridge the gap between identifying those individual differences and their manifestations as phenotypes. Increasing evidence indicates that similar genetic risk factors (and potentially the associated developmental pathways that are malfunctioning) underlie a wide range of common psychiatric disorders, such as schizophrenia and autism [6]. Consequently, there has been a recent move to foster a new way of thinking about classification. The Research Domain Criteria Project originated at the National Institute of Mental Health (USA) and aims to develop a framework for conducting research in terms of 'fundamental circuit-based behavioural dimensions' that reflect findings in neuroscience and fundamental biology. This research framework may influence clinical classifications in due course; meanwhile, we will have to live with the convenience of our current diagnostic systems [7].

*Child Psychology and Psychiatry: Frameworks for Clinical Training and Practice,* Third Edition.
Edited by David Skuse, Helen Bruce and Linda Dowdney.
© 2017 John Wiley & Sons, Ltd. Published 2017 by John Wiley & Sons, Ltd.

## How Many Genes Are There?

Humans have around 19,000 protein coding genes, far fewer than the approximately 120,000 predicted 10 years ago [8]. We possess about the same number of genes as a mouse, and rather fewer than rice plants.

The information content of human DNA is built from a sequence of four basic building blocks: the nucleotides arginine, guanine, thymine and cytosine, which are usually depicted by the letters A, G, T and C. The nucleotides in a DNA strand are arranged in pairs, and our genome is made up of around three billion nucleotide pairs per haploid set of chromosomes. We normally have 23 pairs of chromosomes, and each member of the pair is identical in females. In males, one of the sex chromosomes is a Y rather than an X, but the total is just the same (46, the full diploid set). To fit such an enormous amount of information into a cell nucleus, the DNA double helix is incredibly tightly coiled. Recent research has focused on how that coiling occurs, by what rules, and how the machinery that wants to read the DNA sequence, to make proteins and regulate cellular activity, gets access to it [9]. (For a glossary of basic terms, see Box 4.1.)

---

**Box 4.1  Glossary of basic terms[a]**

**Allele** – one of two or more versions of a genetic sequence at a particular location in the genome.

**Base pair (bp)** – two nitrogenous bases paired together in double-stranded DNA by weak bonds; specific pairing of these bases (adenine with thymine and guanine with cytosine) facilitates accurate DNA replication; when quantified (e.g. 8 bp), bp refers to the physical length of a sequence of nucleotides.

**Complex condition** – a condition caused by the interaction of multiple genes and environmental factors. Examples of complex conditions, which are also called multifactorial diseases, are cancer and heart disease.

**Copy-number variation** – variation from one person to the next in the number of copies of a particular gene or DNA sequence. The full extent to which copy-number variation contributes to human disease is not yet known.

**Deletion mutation** – a mutation that involves the loss of genetic material. It can be small, involving a single missing DNA base pair, or large, involving a piece of a chromosome.

**Diploid number** – refers to the number of chromosomes in a human somatic cell. Such a cell normally contains 46 chromosomes, comprising two complete haploid sets (see *Haploid number*), which together make up the 23 homologous chromosome pairs.

**DNA** – deoxyribonucleic acid, the molecules inside cells that carry genetic information and pass it from one generation to the next.

**Epigenetic change** – a change in the regulation of the expression of gene activity without alteration of genetic structure.

**Gene** – the fundamental physical and functional unit of heredity. A gene is an ordered sequence of nucleotides located in a particular position on a particular chromosome that encodes a specific functional product (i.e. a protein or an RNA molecule).

**Gene chip** – a solid substrate, usually silicon, onto which a microscopic matrix of nucleotides is attached. Gene chips, which can take a wide variety of forms, are frequently used to measure variations in the amount or sequence of nucleic acids in a sample.

---

**Genome** – the entire set of genetic instructions found in a cell. In humans, the genome consists of 23 pairs of chromosomes, found in the nucleus, as well as a small chromosome found in the cells' mitochondria.

**Genome-wide association study** – an approach used in genetics research to look for associations between many (typically hundreds of thousands) specific genetic variations (most commonly single nucleotide polymorphisms) and particular diseases.

**Genome-wide scan** – an assay that measures hundreds of thousands to millions of points of genetic variation across a person's genome simultaneously, either for research or for clinical application.

**Genotype** – a person's complete collection of genes. The term can also refer to the two alleles inherited for a particular gene.

**Haploid number** –the number of chromosomes in a gamete, i.e. in an ovum or a sperm (in the human this is 23). A somatic cell (anywhere else in the body apart from the germ cells) has twice that many chromosomes (46 – see *Diploid number*).

**Human Genome Project** – an international project completed in 2003 that mapped and sequenced the entire human genome.

**Insertion mutation** – a type of mutation involving the addition of genetic material. An insertion mutation can be small, involving a single extra DNA base pair, or large, involving a piece of a chromosome.

**Methylation** – the attachment of methyl groups to DNA at cytosine bases. Methylation is correlated with reduced transcription of the gene and is thought to be the principal mechanism in X-chromosome inactivation and imprinting.

**Microarray** – a technology used to study many genes at once. Thousands of gene sequences are placed in known locations on a glass slide. A sample containing DNA or RNA is deposited on the slide, now referred to as a gene chip. The binding of complementary base pairs from the sample and the gene sequences on the chip can be measured with the use of fluorescence to detect the presence and determine the amount of specific sequences in the sample.

**Mutation** – a change in a DNA sequence. Germ-line mutations occur in the eggs and sperm and can be passed on to offspring, whereas somatic mutations occur in body cells and are not passed on.

**Nucleotide** – the basic building block of nucleic acids. RNA and DNA are polymers made of long chains of nucleotides. A nucleotide consists of a sugar molecule (either ribose in RNA or deoxyribose in DNA) attached to a phosphate group and a nitrogen-containing base. The bases used in DNA are adenine (A), cytosine (C), guanine (G) and thymine (T). In RNA, the base uracil (U) takes the place of thymine.

**Pharmacogenomics** – a branch of pharmacology concerned with using DNA sequence variation to inform drug development and testing. An important application of pharmacogenomics is the correlation of individual genetic variations with drug responses.

**Phenotype** – the observable traits of an individual person, such as height, eye colour and blood type. Some traits are largely determined by genotype, whereas others are largely determined by environmental factors.

**Rearrangement** – a structural alteration in a chromosome, usually involving breakage and reattachment of a segment of chromosomal material, resulting in an abnormal configuration; examples include inversion and translocation.

*(continued)*

---

**Box 4.1 (Continued)**

---

**Ribosome** – a cellular particle made of RNA and protein that serves as the site for protein synthesis in the cell. The ribosome reads the sequence of the mRNA and, using the genetic code, translates the sequence of RNA bases into a sequence of amino acids.

**RNA** – ribonucleic acid, a chemical similar to DNA. The several classes of RNA molecules play important roles in protein synthesis and other cell activities.

**Single nucleotide polymorphism (SNP)** – a single-nucleotide variation in a genetic sequence; a common form of variation in the human genome.

**Small (or short) inferring RNA (siRNA)** – short, double-stranded regulatory RNA molecule that binds to and induces the degradation of target RNA molecules.

**Systems biology** – research that takes a holistic rather than a reductionist approach to understanding organism functions.

**Translation** – during protein synthesis, the process through which the sequence of bases in a molecule of messenger RNA is read in order to create a sequence of amino acids.

[a] Glossary adapted from: Feero WG, Guttmacher AE, Collins FS (2010) Genomic medicine – an updated primer. New England Journal of Medicine, 362, 2001–2011.

---

Reading the complete sequence of our DNA for the first time was a mammoth achievement. Let us imagine each nucleotide has the dimensions of an American 1 cent piece (equivalent to a 1 penny piece in UK), which both have a diameter of about 2 cm. This is, of course, blowing up the size of each nucleotide enormously from their actual dimensions. If laid down side-by-side, three billion pennies would stretch about 35 000 miles, which is more than the circumference of the earth at the equator (25 000 miles).

## Sources of Genomic Variation

Nucleotides are read by the cell's genetic machinery in triplets, by convention from left to right in any illustration (e.g. AAA, CCC, TTA, ATG). Each triplet codes for an amino acid, or a signal of some sort (e.g. start, stop), or it has no meaning at all that we currently recognize.

Until relatively recently, we thought that the main reason individuals (of the same gender) differed from one another was due to small differences in the typical nucleotide sequence of their DNA. These changes are known as single nucleotide polymorphisms (SNPs) if they are known to have been identified in a population at a reasonable frequency. As we start to develop knowledge of the complete genomic nucleotide sequences (whole-genome sequence, WGS) of larger and larger samples of individuals (using the technique known as next-generation sequencing) we are identifying exceptionally rare variants that appear that may be inherited. The term single nucleotide variant is also used to refer to a nucleotide substitution.

On average, our DNA sequence of nucleotides is very similar from one person to another, with only about 0.4% of our genome differing due to these SNPs. Nucleotide substitutions occur on average once in every 800 base (nucleotide) pairs. If the change in our nucleotide sequence (e.g. . . .TCTGATTG. . . becoming . . . ACTGATTG. . .) occurs in a genetic coding, or a regulatory, region there may be an impact on gene expression or in the shape of the protein ultimately formed from the gene in question. Alternatively, the substitution may be 'silent' in its consequences.

We call such differences in gene sequence *polymorphisms,* if they are fairly common. Polymorphisms occur by definition in more than 1% of the population. The prevalence of polymorphisms is strongly influenced by the genetic background of the population being studied. This means that their distribution could be very different, for example, in Americans of African and of European origins. By convention, polymorphisms are benign markers of a population of origin.

There are other sources of genetic variation too. These include insertions and deletions of relatively small numbers of nucleotides (so-called indels) as well as grosser structural rearrangements within or between chromosomes (the latter can often be detected by microscopy). Where these indels are relatively large (larger than 1000 base pairs) and cause an increase or decrease in the number of copies of a single gene or a series of genes, these are known as copy-number variations (CNVs). Either increasing or decreasing the number of copies of particular genes may alter susceptibility to a variety of disorders. Several large-scale studies of autism and schizophrenia have shown that particular CNVs are much more common in both conditions than in control populations, and may also affect cognitive functioning in controls too [10].

Copy-number variations comprise both deletions and duplications of small segments of DNA. They are more likely to be pathogenic if they are deletions rather than duplications of DNA sequences, and there are some 'hotspots', such as a region on the short arm of chromosome 16 (16p11.2), where both events occur relatively frequently [11]. Determining the specific developmental processes that are disrupted, leading to psychiatric risk, is difficult because by definition they tend to disrupt large sequences of DNA, and several genes are either deleted or duplicated.

## Mechanisms of Genomic Regulation

Advances in technology are giving us new insights into the consequences of individual differences in DNA sequences. There is a lot of DNA in every human cell, but rather fewer genes than we expected. Most of the DNA is identical in all humans, but as we have seen, the variability that does exist can have significant consequences for the prediction prevention, diagnosis and treatment of disease.

Surprisingly, perhaps, we are faced with a number of unexpected and rapidly increasing problems concerning exactly how we define genes and how they are regulated. We used to think that a gene was a segment of DNA, in the cell nucleus, that coded for a protein and that the production of that protein was mediated by the action of RNA that read the genetic material and transported the code to protein-building machinery on the ribosome, elsewhere in the cell. In recent years we have found that there are many more classes of RNA than we ever suspected and that there is tremendously complex regulatory machinery.

Understanding how susceptibility to psychiatric disorder, measured at the level of a small change in a DNA sequence, leads to phenotypic differences at the level of observed behaviour and mental activity will be captured by integrating information from a host of different levels of analysis – from cellular activity to synaptic control, from the efficiency of neural transmission to cognitive processing.

## Mechanisms Influencing Neurodevelopmental Integrity

We now know that our conventional classification of psychiatric disorders reflects a set of historical precedents, but it is just a heuristic to enable clinical communication to be effective. There is no biological reality to the distinction we make between 'autism' and 'attention deficit hyperactivity disorder' (ADHD), for instance, and these conditions share many characteristics at the trait level. Furthermore, we know that certain CNVs increase the risk of a range of such disorders, presumably because they share neurodevelopmental regulatory pathways in common [10]. There is no genomic system that codes for one or other neurodevelopmental disorder (no genes, or set of genes, for autism as conventionally defined), but nevertheless research is beginning to identify variants and structural anomalies that are more strongly associated with what we recognize clinically as one distinct condition than with another. We also now know that many risk genes [12] are important for fundamental processes of brain function, including neuronal proliferation and migration, synapse formation and remodelling, and the configuration and connectivity of neural networks [13]. It is perhaps not surprising that synaptic plasticity has come to be seen as a crucial component of efficient neural functions, and that if it is compromised, a range of phenotypic variants can ensue. Whether there is a fundamental 'system' that, if disrupted, leads to a variety of possible psychiatric outcomes within the range of neurodevelopmental disorders (depending on the genetic background) is not known. At this point in time, we might put our money on glutamatergic synapses [14], which are crucial components of the systems that process sensory and cognitive information. If there are functionally damaging mutations in the genes that affect the function of the glutamate receptor, or the presynaptic release of glutamate, the outcome is often intellectual disability. Intellectual disability is on the spectrum of neurodevelopmental disorders affected by common genetic mechanisms [6].

## Measuring Genetic Susceptibility to Psychiatric Disorders

### Gene–Environment Interactions

It is self-evident that our genes do not wholly determine our development. Even identical twins, who share 100% of their genetic make-up, are not exactly the same in their personality or propensity to develop psychiatric disorders. But how do our family circumstances, the unpredictable events that happen in our lives, and our genetic make-up interact? Can we meaningfully predict that some people with a particular genetic predisposition will be vulnerable – but *only* if exposed to a certain sort of risky environments? For instance, is it true that children who had maltreatment experiences and who have a particular variant of the serotonin transporter gene (5-HTTLPR) area at greater risk of depression [15]? Should we warn young people who have a particular variant of the COMT gene that they should not smoke cannabis because of a disproportionate increase in their risk of psychosis [16]? The interpretation of the model, whereby a gene variant that has no independent impact upon the risk of a disease nevertheless confers an enhanced risk if that individual has been subject to a particular sort of adverse environment, has subsequently been subject to enormous independent scrutiny. We call this a candidate gene × environment (G × E) interaction.

The argument about whether the claim made by Caspi and colleagues [15,16] is true, or artefactual, hangs on whether one believes it is possible or improbable that a significant G × E effect could be observed in the absence of a main effect of the genetic risk (although there is a main effect of environmental risk) [17]. In other words, is it credible that a single gene variant could disproportionately increase the risk of a deleterious outcome only in the presence of a particular environment? Strange as it may seem, after 10 years and literally thousands of papers since the original publications, there is still no resolution to this debate [18]. There have been many attempts at replication of the original findings; when these have been successful, those who support the concept of G × E interactions argue that the replication studies were credible. On the other hand, when further studies (and meta-analyses) did not support the original findings, adherents claim the studies were flawed. The debate has been termed an 'epistemological or evidential divide' [19].

## Genome-Wide Association Studies (GWAS)

In recent years, psychiatrists have been keen to use our newly found knowledge of the sequence of the human genome, and of the genes contained within it (about 1% of the total) to evaluate associations between genetic variation (usually at the level of SNPs) and risk of disease. In principle, this is simple, and the number of genetic variants that are associated with complex disorders such as ADHD, schizophrenia or bipolar disorder is growing rapidly. The basic idea is to test whether a particular genotype is more commonly associated with the disorder than we would expect by chance, given the prevalence of the polymorphism in the general population. There are many pitfalls in the interpretation of such findings, not least the risk of false-positive results that do not replicate [20]. Now, independent replication is mandated for studies that aim to be published in leading journals.

Genome-wide association studies are generally far larger than candidate gene studies, because of the very large number of markers of possible risk (SNPs) that are measured in the population under investigation. It is possible to measure over one million gene variants on a single gene chip [21]. The aim is to identify, among these mass of possible susceptibility loci, a relatively small number that are of particular importance in conferring risk. With that information, it might be possible to infer neurodevelopmental pathways that are disrupted, and hence to facilitate drug development aimed at improving outcomes. The underlying rationale of GWAS is that common variants are likely to be responsible for common diseases (including autism, bipolar disorder and schizophrenia). However, most common variants of relevance to the disease confer only a relatively small increment in risk of disease, whether considered individually or in combination [22]. There is 'missing heritability', in the sense that we cannot explain from shared variants in those members of a population with the disease the majority of risk that is attributable to inherited factors, as estimated from twin or family studies. There is general agreement nowadays that enormous samples are required to conduct a statistically valid GWAS study (up to tens of thousands of patients), and this usually requires international collaborations. Inevitably, it also requires a loosening of criteria for 'diagnosis'. Recent work has suggested that much of the missing heritability may not be missing after all [23].

### Epigenetic Variation

Our chance of developing a psychiatric disorder may also be influenced by changes in the complex regulatory structure that enables genes to be read efficiently, as a consequence of exposure to certain environmental circumstances. Changes in the myriad mechanisms by which genetic activity is regulated but which do not alter the fundamental DNA sequence, are termed 'epigenetic'.

Epigenetic influences on gene expression are almost certainly not heritable in humans. Once acquired, epigenetic marks can nevertheless allegedly change gene expression for life. There are several mechanisms by which this could happen. The most intensively studied of these entails the attachment of methyl groups to specific nucleotides in a regulatory region of the gene, thereby silencing it. DNA methylation is a dynamic process and has been shown to be responsive to external stimuli.

There have been replicated studies showing that, in specific brain regions of people who committed suicide, especially in the prefrontal cortex, there is hypermethylation of promoters of gene function, resulting in decreased expression of those genes [24]. The changes are apparently not directly reflective of psychopathology, but were thought to increase vulnerability to commit suicide. The mechanism of risk could involve cognitive systems, with some support from animal studies in which knocking out the genes that were hypermethylated in humans had adverse consequences for behavioural regulation. Although most studies showing epigenetic markers that appear to be abnormal have been done on brain tissue, there is evidence that child maltreatment could influence DNA methylation in peripheral blood cells in patients with post-traumatic stress disorder [25].

There is increasing interest in the idea that a study of epigenetics could help us to identify some of the 'missing heritability' in studies of psychiatric risk [26]. The field is expanding rapidly and is becoming bewilderingly complex. The key unifying concept is that biochemical changes can regulate gene function without altering the fundamental DNA sequence, and that those changes can persist – potentially for a lifetime. Recently, some evidence is emerging that suggests there could be reversibility, indicating possibilities for therapeutic interventions. Whilst the field is still growing (exponentially) it is of enormous potential significance because it suggests there could be transmission of acquired changes to the genome's functional capacity across generations. This could occur indirectly, for instance by altering the behaviour of a parent in such a way that the same epigenetic change is engendered in the offspring. Alternatively, it is possibility that experience-dependent heritable changes do occasionally occur, in response to exceptional environmental events [27].

## Future of Psychiatric Genetics: Precision Medicine

In January 2015, President Barack Obama stated, in his State of the Union address, that he was launching a new Precision Medicine Initiative [28]. This concept has the potential to revolutionize the treatment of a wide range of human diseases, because it emphasizes the importance of taking individual variability into account. We have already seen that the foundations of psychiatric classification have been undermined by genetic research that has shown a paucity of evidence to support conventional diagnostic criteria at the level of biology. We also have seen emerging evidence that the role of environmental risk may be to alter gene function and the neural functions that enable us to maintain good mental health. The corollary of this finding is that the biological predisposition to psychiatric disorders is likely not only to be very complex, but that we also need to understand more about individual susceptibility in order to tailor appropriate treatment to the individual. Currently, the focus of precision medicine is on somatic diseases such as cancer. But increasingly, we will be using the findings from genetic research to discover more effective ways of managing child mental health disorders. In this regard, the nascent field of neuroepigenetics could turn out to be of particular importance. For decades, psychologists and psychiatrists have pointed to the experiences of early childhood as having a lifelong impact upon adjustment. There has been an assumption that the consequences of adverse experiences could be ameliorated by therapy – could it be that deleterious epigenetic changes can be reversed by 'talking therapy'?

Another focus of the Precision Medicine Initiative is to find appropriate therapeutics for individuals, based on their biological susceptibility. This is the field of psychiatric pharmacogenomics, pioneered at the Mayo Clinic [29]. We are aware as clinicians that not all children will respond to medical interventions in the same way, but we rarely understand why some are effectively treated whilst others do not improve or develop unacceptable side-effects. A simple screening test to characterize genetic variation in a subset of genes involved in that medication's metabolism could have enormous benefits in terms of efficiency and efficacy of drug treatment.

Finally, the cost of genomic screening with next-generation sequencing is reducing dramatically. We are already beyond the point at which we could secure a '$1000 genome' (envisaged by the pioneers who produced the first human genomic sequence at the cost of over $1 billion). There are going to be WGSs obtained from huge numbers of the general population, such as the United Kingdom's recently launched 100,000 genome project, which aims to obtain WGSs on people with cancers or rare diseases. Whilst the focus of such large-scale projects is initially diabetes, cancer and other common causes of physical morbidity, in future we may hope that they will address the fact that there is 'no health without mental health'.

## Conclusions

We are increasingly able to measure human genetic variation reliably. The cost of mapping someone's personal genome is dropping rapidly. When that information is available, it will mark the end of an era where the focus has been on genetic sequencing, and the beginning of a new age in which the functional activity of that genome is front of stage. Inevitably, the world of '-omics', exemplified by genomics, transcriptomics, proteomics, epigenomics and so on, will come to impinge on every aspect of medical science. Ultimately, it will influence the assessment and treatment of all conditions discussed in this volume: forewarned is forearmed.

## References

1 Collins FS, Morgan M, Patrinos A (2003) The Human Genome Project: lessons from large-scale biology. Science 300, 286–290.

2 Castro J, Garcia RI, Kwok S et al. (2014) Functional recovery with recombinant human IGF1 treatment in a mouse model of Rett Syndrome. Proceedings of the National Academy of Sciences, 111, 9941–9946.

3 Schaefer TL, Davenport MH, Erickson CA (2015) Emerging pharmacologic treatment options for fragile X syndrome. The Application of Clinical Genetics, 8, 75.

4 Meng L, War, AJ, Bennett CF, Beaudet A et al. (2016) Towards a therapy for Angelman syndrome by targeting a long noncoding RNA to active UBE3A. Cancer Research, 76 (6 Supplement), IA28–IA28.

5 Marjoram P, Thomas DC (2014) Next-generation sequencing studies: optimal design and analysis, missing heritability and rare variants. Current Epidemiology Reports 1, 213–219.

6 Adam D (2013) On the spectrum. Nature, 496, 416–418.

7 Cuthbert BN (2014) The RDoC framework: facilitating transition from ICD/DSM to dimensional approaches that integrate neuroscience and psychopathology. World Psychiatry 13, 28–35.

8 Ezkurdia I, Juan D, Rodriguez JM et al. (2014) Multiple evidence strands suggest that there may be as few as 19 000 human protein-coding genes. Human Molecular Genetics 23, 5866–5878.

9 Taudt A, Colomé-Tatché M, Johannes F (2016) Genetic sources of population epigenomic variation. Nature Reviews Genetics 17, 319–32.

10 Stefansson H, Meyer-Lindenberg A, Steinberg S et al. (2014) CNVs conferring risk of autism or schizophrenia affect cognition in controls. Nature 505, 361–366.

11 D'Angelo D, Lebon S, Chen Q et al. (2016) Defining the effect of the 16p11. 2 duplication on cognition, behavior, and medical comorbidities. JAMA Psychiatry 73, 20–30.

12 Geschwind DH, State MW (2015) Gene hunting in autism spectrum disorder: on the path to precision medicine. The Lancet Neurology 14, 1109–1120.

13 Lesch KP (2016) Maturing insights into the genetic architecture of neurodevelopmental disorders–from common and rare variant interplay to precision psychiatry. Journal of Child Psychology and Psychiatry, 57, 659–661.

14 Volk L, Chiu SL, Sharma K, Huganir RL (2015) Glutamate synapses in human cognitive disorders. Annual Review of Neuroscience, 38, 127–149.

15 Caspi A, Sugden K, Moffitt TE et al. (2003) Influence of life stress on depression: moderation by a polymorphism in the 5-HTT gene. Science 301, 386–389.

16 Caspi A, Moffitt TE, Cannon M et al. (2005) Moderation of the effect of adolescent-onset cannabis use on adult psychosis by a functional polymorphism in the catechol-O-methyltransferase gene: longitudinal evidence of a gene X environment interaction. Biological Psychiatry 57, 1117–1127.

17 Bakermans-Kranenburg MJ, Van IJzendoorn MH (2015) The hidden efficacy of interventions: Gene X environment experiments from a differential susceptibility perspective. Annual Review of Psychology 66, 381–409.

18 Tabery J (2015) Debating interaction: the history, and an explanation. International Journal of Epidemiology, dyv053 (epub).

**19** Munafò MR (2015) Understanding the candidate gene X environment interaction debate: epistemological or evidential divide? International Journal of Epidemiology 44, 1130–1132.

**20** Munafò MR, Flint J (2010) How reliable are scientific studies? British Journal of Psychiatry 197, 257–258.

**21** Ha NT, Freytag S, Bickeboeller H (2014) Coverage and efficiency in current SNP chips. European Journal of Human Genetics 22, 1124–1130.

**22** Manolio TA, Collins FS, Cox N J et al. (2009) Finding the missing heritability of complex diseases. Nature 461, 747–753.

**23** Zuk O, Schaffner SF, Samocha K et al. (2014) Searching for missing heritability: designing rare variant association studies. Proceedings of the National Academy of Sciences 111, E455–E464.

**24** Labonté B, Suderman M, Maussion G et al. (2013) Genome-wide methylation changes in the brains of suicide completers. American Journal of Psychiatry, 170, 511–20.

**25** Mehta D, Klengel T, Conneely KN et al. (2013) Childhood maltreatment is associated with distinct genomic and epigenetic profiles in posttraumatic stress disorder. Proceedings of the National Academy of Sciences 110, 8302–8307.

**26** Sweatt JD (2013) The emerging field of neuroepigenetics. Neuron, 80, 624–632.

**27** Bohacek J, Gapp K, Saab BJ et al. (2013) Transgenerational epigenetic effects on brain functions. Biological Psychiatry 73, 313–320.

**28** Collins FS, Varmus H (2015) A new initiative on precision medicine. New England Journal of Medicine 372, 793–795.

**29** Mrazek DA (2010) Psychiatric Pharmacogenomics. New York: Oxford University Press.

# Section 1

# Developing Competencies

1b: General Patterns of Development

## 5

# Clinical Evaluation of Development from Birth to 5 Years

*Ajay Sharma, Tony O'Sullivan and Gillian Baird*

The clinical evaluation of children with behavioural concerns includes a comprehensive consideration of physical, developmental, emotional, behavioural, social and environmental aspects, including possible organic and neurodevelopmental disorders. To identify neurodevelopmental disorders, the clinician's toolkit must include a working knowledge of typical developmental milestones and *'red flag alerts'* – developmental delays and differences that are significant. The competencies needed include the ability to elicit parental concerns, to take a relevant developmental history, to assess a child's development, to undertake relevant physical examination, to plan investigations and further assessment and to access local services as required.

## Child Development and Neurodevelopmental Disorders

Child development is a dynamic process shaped by a complex interplay between genetic factors and environmental factors, such as maternal health antenatally (including fetal exposure to toxins), *in utero* conditions, prematurity, low birthweight for gestational age, the birth process, nutrition, the economic and social conditions facing the family, and family interpersonal behaviour. The sequences of development are similar in most children, but there is enormous variation in both the rate and pattern of normal development. The developmental milestones are convenient markers to look at the rate of development.

Neurodevelopmental disorders are relatively common. Prevalence is higher in children with multiple risk factors (Box 5.1). Global developmental delay affects 1–3% of children in the general population. At least 1% of children have an autism spectrum disorder. Mild learning disability occurs in 1–2% and severe learning disability in 0.3–0.5% of the general population.

Most neurodevelopmental disorders are identified when parents raise concerns about the child's development or behaviour. Formal screening for developmental disorders is not currently recommended in the UK because of poor sensitivity and specificity of the available screening instruments and the difficulties in defining the 'caseness'. However, early identification is achieved by ongoing monitoring and surveillance of development, e.g. the Healthy Child Programme (HCP) in the UK (Box 5.2). Some parental checklists, e.g. Paediatric Evaluation of Developmental Status (PEDS) and Ages and Stages Questionnaire (ASQ), have also been found to be useful for early identification. Children

*Child Psychology and Psychiatry: Frameworks for Clinical Training and Practice,* Third Edition.
Edited by David Skuse, Helen Bruce and Linda Dowdney.
© 2017 John Wiley & Sons, Ltd. Published 2017 by John Wiley & Sons, Ltd.

---

**Box 5.1  Risk factors**

Risk factors increase the probability of negative psychological (cognitive and emotional) and social outcomes. There is a dynamic interaction between the child's vulnerabilities and risks, and multiple factors have a cumulative and exponentially adverse impact on outcomes.

| Child-related vulnerabilities | Parent-related risk factors | Environmental risk factors |
|---|---|---|
| • Prenatal exposure to drugs, alcohol, infections | • Poor parenting – negative control, rejecting/neglecting and harsh/abusive parenting | • Exposure to toxins, e.g. lead |
| • Prematurity, low birthweight | | • Overcrowding at home |
| • Neurological, sensory deficit. | | • Lack of developmentally appropriate opportunities or space |
| • Poor nourishment, iron deficiency | • Parental poor mental health/ learning difficulties | |
| • Difficult temperament | | • Lack of support for the family |
| • Poor self-regulation | • Low maternal education | • Lack of peer group/isolation |
| • Delayed development in itself | • Parental/family conflict, domestic violence | • Disadvantaged neighbourhood |
| | | • Exposure to violence |

Protective factors mitigate the detrimental effects of risks:

- some child-related characteristics, e.g. good problem-solving skills and positive temperament;
- some environmental features, e.g. a supportive and resourceful family, good relationship with an alternative carer and a stable and loving relationship.

---

**Box 5.2  The Healthy Child Programme (HCP)**

Every family is offered this programme of screening tests, immunizations, developmental reviews, and information and guidance. These services enable children and families to make healthy choices and achieve optimum health and well-being.

This includes neonatal examination, new baby review, 6- to 8-week examination, the 1-year and the 2-year review. Recently, a parent-reported screening test – the Ages and Stages Questionnaire (ASQ 3) – has become part of the 2-year review to gather information about children's developmental progress and help early identification.

Other screening tests currently include:

- Newborn Hearing Screening Programme.
- Newborn Bloodspot Screening programme (screens for nine conditions: sickle cell disease (SCD), cystic fibrosis (CF), congenital hypothyroidism (CHT), inherited metabolic diseases (IMDs) – phenylketonuria (PKU), medium-chain acyl-CoA dehydrogenase deficiency (MCADD), maple syrup urine disease (MSUD), isovaleric acidaemia (IVA), glutaric aciduria type 1 (GA1) and homocystinuria (HCU).
- Vision screening at 4–5 years to identify amblyopia, refractive errors and squints.

https://www.gov.uk/government/uploads/system/uploads/attachment_data/file/167998/Health_Child_Programme.pdf; www.screening.nhs.uk

presenting with some atypical qualitative and quantitative features of development (see Box 5.3) should always be referred for further evaluation.

## History-Taking

Obtaining a good history is the most useful aspect of developmental assessment in terms of establishing diagnosis, causative and associated conditions. This should cover the family history, social and family environment, and the pre-, peri- and postnatal history, paying attention to the risk factors associated with neurodevelopmental disorders (Box 5.4).

Start the clinical session with enquiry into parental or other caregiver's concerns. Elicit concerns proactively, beginning with the broad areas of function. Gather information from others who know the child, e.g. teachers and healthcare staff.

The most reliable history is elicited by asking open-ended questions and requesting supporting examples. All parents are very good at remembering whether or not they had concerns and, if so, what those concerns were. They are particularly good at describing current developmental abilities if the right questions are asked. Parents' *interpretation* of what their child does may be incorrect (e.g. 'He understands everything I say') but their observations are usually accurate (e.g. 'He will fetch his shoes only if he can see them').

---

**Box 5.3  Alerts for atypical development**

- *Delayed rate of development* beyond accepted normal range of variation in one or more developmental domains [e.g. mouthing objects beyond the second year; echolalia – repetitive imitation ('echoing') of speech heard – still present by 3 years]
- *Absolute failure to develop skills* (e.g. no canonical babble – multi-syllable babble with intonation – by 10 months)
- *Disordered developmental sequence* (e.g. hyperlexia – advanced reading – coexisting with delayed language)
- *Motor asymmetry* in hand use or walking
- *Developmental regression* – loss or plateauing of skills
- *Developmental difference*, e.g. unusual movements, repetitive spinning of objects

---

**Box 5.4  Limit ages/red flags for language, communication and social development**

- No multi-syllable babble by 12 months
- Pointing or other gesture by 12 months
- No joint attention by 18 months
- Absence of simple pretence play by 24 months (e.g. feeding doll)
- No single words by 18 months
- Lack of social interest in other children, e.g. preference for solitary play from 18 months
- No word combinations (non-echoed) by 30 months
- Cannot follow two-step command (e.g. 'Give ball to Daddy') by 30 months
- Echolalia still present at 3 years
- Speech largely unintelligible by 4 years
- No conversational interchange by 4 years

Establish the reason for obstetric intervention (e.g. fetal distress), the condition of the baby at birth (e.g. Apgar score < 5 at 5 or 10 minutes), and any history suggestive of neonatal encephalopathy (e.g. neonatal seizures). Ask about the child's general health (a history of serious illness may be relevant to understanding current behaviour or learning), sleeping, eating, elimination and self-help skills, e.g. dressing. Gestational age should be considered when seeing a child under the age of 24 months, and correction should be made when assessing age-appropriate attainments, especially in the first postnatal year.

## Observation and Interactive Assessment

The most meaningful and valid ascertainment of a child's abilities is obtained by combining history and observations made in a free-play and interactive session. Observe the child's social awareness, interests, flexibility, attention, anxiety, their initiating and responding to interactions and any repetitive movements, play or other behaviours. Any change in function and behaviour with increasing task complexity – such as coping with transition from non-verbal to language-based activity – and changes in performance as assessment time lengthens should be noted. If the child is unable to organize play materials and generate ideas on their own, this is a significant finding and may not be noticed if the adult is too helpful.

Look not only at *what* the child does, but also *how* s/he does it. The *quality* of response should therefore be monitored as well as the actual achievement.

Have a suitable selection of toys available before meeting the family and interacting with the child. These should be appropriate for the age of the child and for the domains of development to be assessed. A range of standardized assessments are available to gather detailed normative information for diagnostic or monitoring purposes e.g. Griffith's Mental Developmental scales and Bayley's Scales of infant Development. All such developmental assessment schemes have drawbacks as well as strengths.

## Developmental Domains

Developmental assessment involves establishing the child's progress in the sequence of development, the style of learning, behaviours that interfere with learning, e.g. avoidance, any sensory sensitivity or impairments and a qualitative description of the child's competences. Clinical interpretation requires that this information is combined with the findings of physical examination.

Developmental milestones are a way of describing developmental progress. Delays in some developmental sequences may indicate an underlying neurological, visual or hearing problem that requires an early referral for further assessment. These are indicated below as 'red flag' ages. Children with moderate or severe developmental delay, plateauing or regression of development require further assessment and investigations.

### Gross Motor

Delay in achievement of the gross motor milestones (Table 5.1) may be an indicator of neurological abnormalities. It is also sometimes associated with a global developmental delay. Although the correlation between gross motor skills and global developmental level is

**Table 5.1** Gross motor milestones

| Developmental milestones | Mean ages (months) | Limit ages – 'red flags' (months) |
|---|---|---|
| Hands open most of the time (not fisted) | 3 | 4 |
| Good head control when sitting and no head control on pull to sit | 4 | 6 |
| Sits independently | 7–8 | 10 |
| Walks alone | 11–13 | 18 |

weak, significant motor delay, particularly when associated with low muscle tone or other neurological concerns is often a marker for later cognitive difficulties. There may also be an impact on skills that depend on an intact motor system for their expression.

**Visual Behaviour, Eye–Hand Coordination and Problem-Solving**

These can be observed through creating a range of test situations, such as manipulation and use of pellet, rings, bell, cubes, crayon/pencil, form boards or puzzles. The use of a variety of such interesting and non-threatening test situations also helps to tease out the relative contributions of experience, emotional factors, motor and cognitive abilities. Children's achievements in this domain represent the precursor to later non-verbal problem-solving abilities, and correlate well with overall intellectual ability. *Always refer any concern about a child's visual interest or function for visual assessment.*

**Early Visual Behaviour**

The earliest developmental sequence starts with fixing gaze on the mother's face, then following a face with eyes only, and then being able to coordinate eye–head movements to turn the head to follow visually (Table 5.2). By six weeks a socially responsive smile accompanies this. Any abnormality of early visual behaviour should prompt an early referral for ophthalmological assessment.

**Eye–Hand Co-Ordination**

In this developmental sequence the infant shows visual awareness of hands and becomes increasingly refined in combining vision with hand movements for reaching, grasping, exploring and releasing objects (Table 5.3).

**Table 5.2** Early visual behaviour

| Early visual behaviour milestones | Limit age (months) | 'Red flag' (months) |
|---|---|---|
| Visually alert, orient to face | 1 | Any delay |
| Visually follows face | 2 | Any delay |
| Coordinates eye movements with head turning | 3 | Any delay |

**Table 5.3** Eye–hand coordination milestones

| Developmental milestone | Mean age (months) |
|---|---|
| Holds objects briefly when placed in hands without visual regard | 3 |
| Visually examines own hand | 4 |
| Reaches out with a two-handed scoop | 5 |
| Reaches out and grasps objects on table surface with a raking grasp | 6 |
| Transfers from hand to hand | 6 |
| Explores with index finger | 6 |
| Picks up a pellet/raisin between thumb and finger | 9 |
| Picks up a string between thumb/finger | 10 |
| Can release in a container | 10 |
| Has mature grasp | 12 |
| Has precise release – without pressing on surface | 13 |
| Builds towers of two cubes | 13 |
| Builds towers to three cubes | 16 |
| Turns pages of book one page at a time | 24 |

### Object Concepts and Relationships

This developmental sequence reflects infants' growing understanding of the nature of objects, their relatedness to each other and in space (visuo-spatial) combined with a refined grasp and release ability (Table 5.4).

### Imitating and Copying Cube Models

This sequence shows children's desire and ability to copy from models (combining the processes of encoding, decoding and executing) – moving on from vertical alignment to horizontal alignment to making two- and three-dimensional models (Table 5.5).

**Table 5.4** Object concepts and relationships milestones

| Developmental milestone | Mean age (months) |
|---|---|
| Permanence of object: looks for hidden object attention | 8 |
| Cause and effect: presses or pushes to activate a toy | 9 |
| Means-end relationship: pulls toy placed out of reach with a string | 9 |
| Relating two objects together | 10 |
| Relating objects: enjoys putting things in and out of container | 10 |
| Simple posting games: round shapes | 12 |
| Matches simple shapes | 16–18 |
| Matches three shapes with good 'scanning' | 24 |

**Table 5.5** Cube model copying milestones

| Developmental milestone | Mean age (months) |
| --- | --- |
| Builds tower of six cubes | 22 |
| Horizontal alignment of bricks | 24 |
| Three-cube bridge | 33 |
| Four-cube train with a chimney | 39 |
| Three steps with six cubes | 48–54 months |
| Four steps with 10 cubes | 60 months |

Imitating the adult's demonstration (e.g. of a circle) is a developmentally easier task than copying a circle (e.g. imitating at 33–36 months; copying at 39–42 months).

### Drawing

Children initially start jabbing pencil on paper just as they relate any other two objects together. This is followed by their interest in imitating others and first making a mark on the paper and going on to make vigorous uncontrolled scribble. By the end of the second year they can do controlled circular scribble and soon imitate others' hand movements to draw a line and later a circular shape before they are able to copy a pre-drawn circle and other shapes. Children gradually refine their grasp – 50% of children by the age of 3 years and 80% by 4 years have a good tripod grasp of a pencil (Table 5.6).

**Table 5.6** Drawing milestones

| Developmental milestone | Mean age (month) |
| --- | --- |
| *Shape copying* | |
| Makes a mark on paper | 15 |
| Scribble | 18 |
| Copies lines | 24 |
| Copies a circle | 36(90% by 42 months) |
| Copies a cross | 42(90% by 48 months) |
| Copies a square | 48 |
| Copies a triangle | 60 |
| Copies a diamond | 66–72 |
| | |
| *Drawing a person* | |
| Figure with head, other parts, no body | 36(80% by 45 months) |
| Figure with head, body, limbs | 54 |

**Language and Communication**

Identification of language impairment needs to combine information from parents and observations/assessment. Parents' reporting of expressive language is improved by making lists of spoken words or phrases. As children have good understanding of daily family routines, their language comprehension is often overestimated by parents and professionals!

Infants show a preference for the mother's voice within the first few days of birth, make responsive 'cooing' sounds within the first few months and play 'lap games' by 6 months. At around 9 months the infant begins to combine vocalizations and gestures to convey wishes, feelings, purpose and experience to others. At this stage, some infants may imitate the sounds of certain often-repeated family words. This is followed by the development of speech and language understanding and expression, with a considerable variation between children (Table 5.7). *Refer to the audiology clinic for any concern about a child's hearing.*

**Play and Social Behaviour**

Observation of play offers a unique opportunity to look at a number of developmental sequences as they come together, including initiation of and response to social interaction and communication (using both verbal and non-verbal skills), imagination and the ability to generate varied ideas in play and sustain these for period of time while remaining alert to the social environment (Figure 5.1).

Limit ages/red flags (see Box 5.4) indicate the need for a referral for further assessment.

**Development of Attention**

Attention and development of cognition are interdependent. A variety of conditions are associated with attention problems in pre-schoolers, including epilepsy, low birthweight, hearing loss, and prenatal exposure to teratogens (e.g. foetal alcohol syndrome, now common) or hypothyroidism (now rare)). Difficulties of behaviour, language, learning, social understanding and coordination often coexist with deficits of attention. Poor attention in a child with global delay may be in keeping with their general developmental levels.

Attention difficulties may contribute to poor performance at developmental tasks and/or to poor or disinhibited interactions or may indicate global developmental delay. Observations are made of the child's abilities to focus and sustain attention on tasks, to listen to instructions, and to shift attention between verbal and non-verbal tasks. Impulsiveness, distractibility, fidgetiness and activity level are noted, and any shift in attention with time or with change of activity. Knowing the stages of development of attention (see Box 5.5) is useful for working with children and identifying likely difficulties.

**Cognitive Development**

Development of cognition includes progression from cause and effect and object permanence to increasingly conceptual and complex thinking. This is observed non-verbally in the purposeful matching of shapes, patterns and pictures (not trial and error). Verbally and socially, this is seen in the development of conceptual vocabulary, e.g. which toys

**Table 5.7** Language and communication milestones

| Developmental milestones | Mean age (months) | Range(month) |
|---|---|---|
| *Comprehension/receptive language* | | |
| Understands 'no'/'bye' | 7 | 6–9 |
| Recognizes own name | 8 | 6–10 |
| Understands familiar names | 12 | 10–15 |
| Definition by use: using objects | | by 15 |
| Giving objects on request | | by 15 |
| Points to body parts on self/cares | 15 | 12–18 |
| Points to body parts on doll | 18 | 15–21 |
| Indentifying objects on naming | | by 24 |
| Follows a 2-step command | 24 | 18–27 |
| Functional understanding | 30 | 21–33 |
| Understands prepositions (in/on) | 24 | 18–33 |
| Understands prepositions (under) | 30 | 24–39 |
| Understands action words (e.g. eating, sleeping) | | by 36 |
| Understands simple negatives | 36 | 30–42 |
| Understands comparatives | 42 | 36–48 |
| Follows 2 instructions (4 ideas) | 42 | 36–48 |
| Understands complex negatives | 48 | 42–60 |
| Follows 3 instructions (6 ideas) | 54 | 48–66 |
| *Expressive language and non-verbal communication* | | |
| jargon | 12 | 10–15 |
| Syllabic and tuneful babble | 8 | 6–9 |
| Pointing to demand | 9 | |
| Pointing to share interest | 10 | 9–14 |
| One word | 12 | 10–18 |
| 2–6 words | 15 | 12–21 |
| 7–20 words | 21 | 18–24 |
| 50+ words | 24 | 18–27 |
| 2 words joining | 24 | 18–30 |
| 200+ words | 30 | 24–36 |
| 3–4 words joining | 30 | 25–36 |
| Speech usually understandable | 30 | 30–42 |
| Question words | 36 | 30–42 |
| Pronouns | 42 | 36–48 |
| Uses conjunctions(and, but) | 48 | 36–54 |
| Sentences of 5+ words | 48 | 36–54 |
| Complex explanations and sequences | 54 | 48–66 |

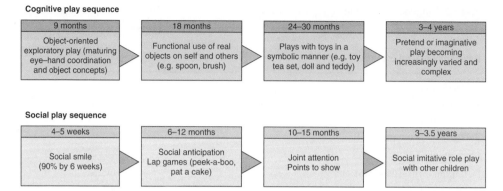

**Figure 5.1** Developmental sequences involved in play and social skills.

---

**Box 5.5  Development of attention**

- **Birth to 18 months.** Infants sustain attention in exploring toys by 5 months and, by 9–12 months, show sustained purposeful activities, correcting errors in looking for hidden objects. However, they are easily distracted towards dominant stimuli.
- **18 months to 3 years.** Children improve in their ability to undertake planned sequential activities – such as matching of shapes/forms of increasing complexity. They remain somewhat resistant to interference and have relative difficulty following directions while they are engaged in an activity (single channelled attention). The adult needs to first gain their attention, then talk and show the new activity in separate stages.
- **3 to 4 years.** Attention now becomes more flexible – easily shifting between tasks; selective – able to ignore irrelevant stimuli, and sustained, e.g. sorting cards by colour (36 months). As more integrated attention develops, children can listen to the adult and then shift their focus back on their play activity.
- **4 to 5 years.** Children now voluntarily ignore stimuli which are irrelevant to the task, controlling their focus of attention. They sustain attention to sort objects on two dimensions, e.g. colour and shape. By 5 years of age children integrate information from different sources, e.g. listening to directions without losing focus on the task.

---

go together for a particular attribute, and in the number of ideas shown in play. Many children with significant global developmental delay or with severe delay or abnormality in one particular domain have long-term cognitive and functional impairments.

## Clinical Decision-Making and Severity of Developmental Delay

When should the clinician take further action? Severe delay in any developmental domain (where development is equivalent to 50% or less of the expected milestones at that chronological age) is always significant and requires further investigations.

The full social, family, medical history and physical examination give context when deciding whether to watch and wait or to promptly investigate. If there is also delay in cognitive, non-verbal or motor skills or if there are any abnormal physical findings such as micro- or macrocephaly or neurology examination, or significant concern about social impairment, then further investigation would be warranted without further delay.

## Physical Examination

Physical examination (left until the end of the developmental assessment) contributes to clinical evaluation as outlined in Box 5.6; the key points to consider are outlined in Box 5.7.

---

**Box 5.6  How does physical examination contribute to clinical evaluation?**

- Providing clues for the cause of developmental impairment, e.g. dysmorphic features prompting a genetic test, small head circumference in foetal alcohol syndrome and, somewhat rarely, abnormal skin markings as an indicator for tuberous sclerosis.
- Identifying any associated neurological impairment, e.g. abnormal eye movements, large head, coarse features, liver enlargement or motor impairment in metabolic disorders; hypotonia in cerebellar problems and inability to run or get up quickly in Duchenne muscular dystrophy.
- Identifying a reversible physical explanation for a change of behaviour in children who are unable to communicate verbally, e.g. constipation, painful joint or tooth abscess.
- Physical signs of injury requiring explanation, e.g. while self-inflicted injuries (biting fingers, pulling out hair, poking eye) may be observed in some children with developmental impairment, signs suggestive of non-accidental injury (related to neglect or physical abuse) have a very different clinical significance and should trigger the local child protection procedures.

---

**Box 5.7  Key points to consider in physical examination**

- *Motor function* – determine whether the child has a motor disorder or if any delay is part of global learning difficulty. Observe movement patterns and posture during the appointment and developmental examination, when the child is walking, speaking and handling material. Formal examination of tone, reflexes and power is largely confirmatory.
- *Symmetry* – compare the two sides of the body and determine the child's hand preference. The motor skill, tone, reflexes or limb size may be significantly asymmetrical, suggesting hemisphere dysfunction or other pathology.
- *Malformation* – look for dysmorphic features and congenital malformations. They may suggest a particular syndrome or aetiology (e.g. foetal alcohol syndrome).
- *Skin* – carefully examine the skin for pigmented and hypopigmented spots.
- *Growth* – measure the head circumference, height and weight and plot on a centile growth chart.
- *Sight* – take seriously any concern about visual function. Arrange further examination via the ophthalmologist or paediatrician.
- *Hearing* – this will have been tested in the neonatal period, but some sensorineural losses may be progressive and some children will have persistent middle ear problems. Consider a referral to audiology for any concern about hearing, poor speech and delayed language.

## Planning Medical Investigations and Making Diagnosis

Investigations are done to ascertain any medical cause for the disorder and to identify any associated or exacerbating conditions, such as hypothyroidism, commonly found in Down syndrome, or hearing loss coexisting with autism. Table 5.8 offers an outline of

**Table 5.8** Investigation planning for developmental disorders

| Context | Recommended investigations | Comments |
|---|---|---|
| *First-line tests*<br><br>Children with severe developmental delay or moderate delay which is global or is associated with other significant findings in history and examination | Creatine kinase in boys<br><br>Thyroid function tests irrespective of neonatal screening<br><br>Array CGH (comparative genomic hybridization – if available)<br><br>Chromosomes for karyotype and fragile X if aCGH not available<br><br>MRI scan or CT scan in more severe mental retardation<br><br>Toxoplasma, rubella assay and CMV urine culture in children under 2 years | Some consensus guidelines also recommend serum lead, urate, U&E, ferritin and biotinidase<br><br>More recent genetic investigations provide a higher yield of positive and more informative results than previously.<br><br>For example, aCGH. Plasma calcium and alkaline phosphatase may help with diagnosis and management of DiGeorge syndrome, Williams syndrome and pseudohypoparathyroidism, and where motor delay is due to vitamin D deficiency. |
| *Second-line tests*<br><br>Associated abnormal head size (micro- *or* macrocephaly), seizures,<br><br>focal neurological features including severe oromotor impairment and speech abnormality | The above first-line investigations<br><br>*plus*<br><br>MRI<br><br>Where aCGH is not available, karyotype and specific molecular genetic tests, e.g. looking for 22q deletion in oromotor and speech dysfunction | |
| Specific history or examination findings suggestive of neurometabolic disorders | Metabolic investigations: serum amino acids, ammonia, VLCFA, carnitine, homocysteine, disialotransferrin<br><br>Urine: organic acids, orotate, GAGs, oligosaccharides | Key pointers for metabolic disorders in the clinical history include consanguinity, failure to thrive and episodic neurodevelopmental decompensations (often during minor illnesses). Examination findings may include coarse facial features or hepatosplenomegaly. |
| Specific history or examination findings suggestive of epilepsy or specific behavioural phenotypes, e.g. Angelman syndrome | EEG | In Angelman syndrome, characteristic EEG changes may precede seizures. Diagnosis is confirmed by deletion or uniparental disomy on chromosome 15<br><br>Specific EEG changes may also help in rare presentations such as regression in language and differentiation of seizure-like episodes such as in Rett syndrome |

| Context | Recommended investigations | Comments |
|---------|---------------------------|----------|
| Regression with or without associated features | Referral to a paediatric neurologist/consultation for planning further appropriate investigations. | In many countries human immunodeficiency virus (HIV) infections are becoming an important cause of regression, with neurological and neuropsychiatric manifestations usually presenting in the first 3 years of life |

U&E, urea and electrolytes; MRI, magnetic resonance imaging; GAGs, glycosaminoglycans ; VLCFA, very long-chain fatty acid; EEG, electroencephalogram.

the current evidence-based guidance for investigations. When planning further referrals and investigations, consider:

- What is the likelihood of the condition under investigation being present? What are the consequences of missing the diagnosis, however unlikely?
- Are there benefits from an early diagnosis: would it alter management, e.g. by informing genetic advice, and what 'bad outcomes' would be prevented?
- Would the target diagnosis give information of value to parents in their planning and coping?

## Further Reading

Bee H, Boyd D (2013) The Developing Child. Boston, MA: Pearson.
Sharma A, Cockerill H (2014) From Birth to Five Years – Practical Developmental Examination. London: Routledge.

# 6

# Emotional Development in the First Year of Life

*Howard Steele*

## Introduction

The range of emotions that young children feel and express stem from the meaning social interactions impart [1]. Trevarthen suggests that the human neonate begins life neurobiologically prepared for social and emotional interaction. Perhaps more provocatively, he asserts that when calm and alert, the neonate contributes 'to a precisely timed imitative exchange of expressions and pauses with another person, a dialog of movements that evolves as an emotional event lasting a few seconds' [2, p. 8].

Recent neurobiological studies using ultrasound techniques illustrate the apparent development of 'preparedness' for infant affective communication via the progressive development of fetal facial expressions. Between 26 and 36 weeks' gestation, these spontaneously become increasingly differentiated, simulating smiling and distress faces [3,4]. The authors suggest that this is an adaptive process likely to benefit the infant postnatally.

However, while evidence for neurobiological preparedness exists, there is less agreement on whether certain discrete emotions are present in the neonate as innate, universally, biologically determined phenomena [5,6]. Emotional development is a complex childhood process involving interaction not only between the infant's developing neurobiological and physiological systems, but also with those of cognition and emotion as well as the child's social and environmental world.

## Infant Emotional Expression

What emotions do infants feel in their first year of life? When, why and with what consequences? Two primary theoretical perspectives predominate in the study of emotional development – the structuralist and the functionalist [5]. Structuralists have focused on underlying physiological processes that constitute emotion, and also on developing a comprehensive taxonomy that identifies the age at which emotions appear, and their subsequent development. A functionalist theory of emotion assumes that emotions evolved as adaptive, survival-promoting processes with intrapersonal and interpersonal regulatory functions [7]. For example, fear of the dark and fear of being alone are adaptive because there is an obvious link between these events and potential danger [8]. From this perspective, emotions are organizers of personal and interpersonal life,

*Child Psychology and Psychiatry: Frameworks for Clinical Training and Practice,* Third Edition.
Edited by David Skuse, Helen Bruce and Linda Dowdney.
© 2017 John Wiley & Sons, Ltd. Published 2017 by John Wiley & Sons, Ltd.

enhancing or restricting development and mental health (for a recent review of these perspectives, see Wolan Sullivan [6]).

Infants develop emotional expressions and perceptions within social interactions, initially with their major caregivers. These influence the patterns of expectations and appraisals vis-à-vis the self and others. Emotional experiences can, therefore, result from or cause social interactions. For example, stranger anxiety (which typically appears at 8–9 months of age) may lead an infant to cling to the mother and only feel settled when she holds her/him close, so indicating 'I am here for you – you can get back to play or exploration, if you feel ready'. Regular interactions such as these lead infants to have a sense of trust in caregivers, and a hopeful attitude in the face of distress. Early caregiver–infant patterns of social interaction matter greatly because they become established and consolidated over the first year of life into relationship or attachment patterns [9]. These will be influenced by both caregiver and infant characteristics [9], vital because attachment patterns tend to persist with potentially long-lasting influences upon personality and mental health [10], see Chapter 12).

The infant's social and emotional development is also influenced by a wide range of biological, familial, social, cultural and environmental factors (see Chapter 1). Recently, ante-natal experiential influences upon the neurobiology of the developing foetus have been considered. For instance, high levels of antenatal maternal anxiety and depression have been linked to subsequent infant cognitive and social-emotional development – an effect that may persist into later childhood [11] (see Chapter 13).

Familiarity with the normative sequence of emotional development in the first year of life may aid the professional and parent alike in knowing how and when to respond to infants' emotional signalling. Six primary infant emotions appear over this time. Disgust (protruding tongue and scrunched together face), discontent (indicated by crying) or contentment (absence of crying) appear in the neonatal period or soon after, followed by smiling and laughter by 3–4 months, with sadness, surprise, anger and fear appearing in consolidated and consistent ways only in the second half of the first year. Normal age-related shifts in these emotions are discussed, although individual differences linked to deficits in neurobiological make-up or social experience can occur. Nonetheless, all children regardless of individual differences will thrive if their social and emotional needs are noticed and responded to sensitively, neither overwhelming them nor leading to feelings of neglect.

## The Development of Infant Emotional Expressions

### Crying

Infant crying is one way in which the infant signals its emotional state. As noted earlier, simulated facial expressions of distress evolve during fetal development [4]. Post-birth, three types of infant crying – hunger, fatigue and pain – have been reliably identified. The pain cry is a short, sharp, elongated piercing sound followed by apnoea. The hunger cry is one that builds steadily, while the fatigue cry is more of a whimper. While there is wide normal variation, newborn babies typically cry for about 30–60 minutes in a 24-hour period. This is about 10–20% of their waking time, as they sleep for approximately 16 hours, or two-thirds of the day. Some 10% of infants cry for more than 3 hours/day, showing distress for as much as half of their waking time. This causes great concern to caregivers and may be causally linked to postnatal depression, stress in the parental relationship and shaken baby syndrome. Fussiness appears to peak at 6 weeks [12], but fortunately, even very cranky newborns usually become much more settled by 3 months of age. Close caregiver proximity helps with the identification of the sources of infant distress. Babies whose cries are responded to promptly, sensitively and efficiently in their first 3 months, in the context of high satisfaction in the parental relationship, cry significantly less at 9 months [13].

### Smiling or Joy

It had previously been thought that newborns do not smile, though they can appear to do so as a result of sensory comfort or discomfort, such as feeding or wind. As previously noted, simulated smiling appears during fetal development [3] suggesting that full-term, healthy infants arrive 'hard-wired' for some facial expressions. Recent experimental research suggests that when newborns are stimulated by physical touch, they show different types of smiles according to whether they are awake or asleep [14]. This leads the authors to hypothesize that their awake smiles may have a social meaning. However, it is more generally agreed that only by 8–10 weeks do infants show fully elaborated social smiles – as, for example, when responding to familiar animate or inanimate objects such as the mother's face or a crib mobile. A full social chuckle appears between 12 and 16 weeks, and laughter by 4 months. Positive joyful expressions take on an increasingly differentiated range, dependent on the interaction partner.

### Surprise, Anger and Sadness

Surprise, anger and sadness represent a chain of emotions that result from a functioning memory and set of expectations regarding a hoped-for experience or interaction. Surprise is indicated by a vertical oval open mouth and raised eyebrows.

It can be either positive – as when the infant responds to peek-a-boo or jack-in-the-box games – or negative. The latter is the natural result when things don't appear as they should, or things don't go our way. Then, if restoration of the hoped-for event or interaction does not follow, surprise can quickly turn to protest or anger, with a characteristic furrowed brow and gritting of teeth [15]. Finally, should this not lead to a successful restoration of the hoped-for outcome, resignation and sadness, even depression, may follow [10].

A rather sophisticated cognitive appraisal process underpins these emotional expressions, and it is only in the latter half of the first year that we see the definite appearance of these facial expressions.

### Fear

Interestingly, the appearance of an organized expression of fear is directly linked to the onset of locomotion around 8–10 months, and the cognitive-motoric achievement of object permanence [16]. With organized knowledge that a valued object can be out of sight, but remains in mind, and can be recovered, infants show stranger anxiety [8]. Fearful protest may bring the caregiver back.

Fear is an adaptive response and one that typically leads to social referencing (looking at the trusted caregiver for cues as to how to behave). Caregiver positive and encouraging responses in fear situations – as, for example, in the classical visual cliff experiment – have been shown to encourage infants to overcome their fear – in this example, overcoming fear of an apparently imminent fall, and crawling safely towards their mothers. More recent research further indicates that infant social referencing also increases with the onset of infant locomotion [17]. Further, mothers report an increase in negative affect in infants after the onset of crawling. This occurs across a range of social and caregiving situations, including responsive distress to limitations being placed on activities resulting from increased exploratory mobility [17].

## Infant Detection of the Emotional Expressions of Others

Social interaction demands not only that the infant effectively signals its affective state, but also that she/he can detect and respond to the affective signals of others. Facial expressions play an important role in emotional communication, and by 2 months, infants can discriminate between distinct human expressions [5].

Recent work has focused on infant neural responses to a variety of emotional stimuli, illustrating that 7-month-old infants can reliably distinguish between facial expressions of happy, fearful and angry. Also, by 10 months, neural measures of attention show that they discriminate between angry and pain faces [18]. In other words, what infants show on their faces, they can perceive in others, and what they perceive, they can show.

Infant expectations regarding others' affective displays have developed well enough by 9 months for their caregivers to play with these expectations in peek-a-boo games [5]. Infants also appear sensitive to the emotional displays of others, showing goal-directed behaviour [19]. When responding to computer-generated geometric figures succeeding or failing to achieve simple goals, 10-month-old infants gazed significantly longer at displays of *incongruent negative* emotion after *successful* goal attainment than when congruent positive emotion was displayed. The authors hypothesize that these infants have developed expectations about future actions and likely emotional reactions.

However, the ability to discriminate between facial affective expressions is not the same as understanding or recognizing the meaning of emotions [5], the development of which begins to occur in the second year of life [20]. Neither do studies of attention or gaze relate directly to infant emotions and behaviour in meaningful social exchanges.

Discriminating between emotional signals is an important precursor of empathy. During their first year, infants show 'empathic distress', i.e. between the ages of 1 and 9 months of age, the majority of infants exposed to recorded infant cries will show rudimentary self-focused empathic arousal, such as crying or facial distress [21]. Empathic distress is distinguished from 'empathic concern', where the child expresses emotional concern via facial expressions, vocalizations, gestures and efforts to help or provide comfort. The latter has primarily been thought to develop in the child's second year, though Roth-Hanania *et al.*'s [21] research now suggests that infants as young as 8 or 10 months are able to show modest levels of empathic concern towards simulated maternal distress. This capacity increased gradually from 8 months to the beginning of the second year and was related to later displays of prosocial behaviour, leading the authors to infer a stable disposition in empathic concern.

**The Interactive Context**

Identifiable facial and vocal expressions of the primary emotions – joy, sadness, surprise, anger and fear – are recognizable across all cultures [15,22]. Nonetheless, emotional self-regulation and the clarity, organization and labelling of infant emotions have been linked to sensitive and responsive care over the first year of life [5,13,23]. Deficits in labelling emotional faces have been noted during middle childhood for those whose early emotional experiences included neglect and abuse, with recent neural research suggesting that even at 12 months of age, abused infants respond differently to facial affect than non-abused children [20]. Within the context of responsive parenting, infants also learn the rewards of feeling a range of positive and negative emotions, blended emotions, sequential and mixed emotions, coming to see the natural function and value of emotional experience.

Future directions in the study of infant emotions would usefully include further exploration of how infant genetic and temperamental variations influence parent–infant, inter-parent and familial interactions. Both infants and their parents contribute to the emotional tone of their dyadic interactions and, over time, their emotional availability to each other [24,25].

# References

1 Trevarthen C (2011) What is it like to be a person who knows nothing? Defining the active intersubjective mind of a newborn human being. Infant and Child Development, 20, 119–135.

2 Delafield-Butt JT, Trevarthen C (2015) The ontogenesis of narrative: from moving to meaning. Frontiers in Psychology, 6, 1157.

3 Reissland N, Francis B, Mason FB et al. (2011) Do facial expressions develop before birth? PLoS ONE, 6, e24081.

4 Reissland N, Francis B, Mason J (2013) Can healthy foetuses show facial expression of "pain" or "distress"? PLoS ONE, 8, e65530.

5 Rosenblum KL, Dayton CJ (2009) Infant social and emotional development. In: Charles H, Zeanah Jr (ed.) Handbook of Infant Mental Health, 3rd edn. New York: Guilford Press.

6 Wolan Sullivan M (2014) Infant expressions in an approach/withdrawal framework. Journal of Genetic Psychology, 175, 472–493.

7 Bretherton I, Fritz J, Zahn-Waxler C, Ridgeway D (1985) Learning to talk about emotions: A functionalist perspective. Child Development, 57, 529–548.

8 Bowlby J (1973) Attachment and Loss: Vol. 2, Separation, Anxiety and Anger. London: The Hogarth Press.

9 Beebe B, Jaffe J, Markese S et al. (2010) The origins of 12-month attachment: a microanalysis of 4-month mother-infant interaction. Attachment & Human Development, 12, 3–141.

10 Bowlby J (1960) Grief and mourning in early childhood. Psychoanalytic Study of the Child, 15, 9–52.

11 O'Donnell KJ, Glover V, Di Vito C et al. (2014) The persisting effect of maternal mood in pregnancy on childhood psychopathology. Development and Psychopathology, 26, 393–403.

**12** Barr RG, Konner M, Bakeman R, Adamson L (2008) Crying in !Kung san infants: A test of the cultural specificity hypothesis. Developmental Medicine and Child Neurology, 33, 601–610.

**13** Belsky J, Fish M, Isabella R (1991) Continuity and discontinuity in infant negative and positive emotionality: Family antecedents and attachment consequences. Developmental Psychology, 27, 421–431.

**14** Cecchini M, Baroni E, Di Vito C, Lai C (2011) Smiling in newborns during communicative wake and active sleep. Infant Behavior & Development, 34, 417– 423.

**15** Ekman P (2003) Emotions Revealed. New York: Henry Holt & Co.

**16** Piaget J (1954) The Construction of Reality in the Child. London: Routledge and Kegan Paul.

**17** Whitney PG, Green JA (2011) Changes in infants' affect related to the onset of independent locomotion. Infant Behavior & Development, 34, 459–466.

**18** Missana M, Grigutsch M, Grossmann T (2014) Developmental and individual differences in the neural processing of dynamic expressions of pain and anger. PLoS ONE, 9, e93728.

**19** Skerrya AE, Spelkea ES (2014) Preverbal infants identify emotional reactions that are incongruent with goal outcomes. Cognition, 130, 204–216.

**20** Curtis WJ, Cicchetti D (2013) Affective facial expression processing in 15 month-old infants who have experienced maltreatment: an event-related potential study. Child Maltreatreatment, 18, 140–154.

**21** Roth-Hanania, R, Davidovb M, Zahn-Waxler C (2011) Empathy development from 8 to 16 months: Early signs of concern for others. Infant Behavior & Development 34, 447–458.

**22** Sauter DA, Eisner F, Ekman P, Scott SK (2010) Cross-cultural recognition of basic emotions through nonverbal emotional vocalizations. Proceedings of the National Academy of Sciences, 107, 2408–2412.

**23** Steele H, Steele M (2008) Early attachment predicts emotion recognition at 6 and 11 years. Attachment and Human Development, 10, 379–393.

**24** Parade SH, McGeary J, Seifer R, Knopik RS (2012) Infant development in family context: call for a genetically informed approach. Frontiers in Genetics, 3, 1–7.

**25** Bornstein MH, Suwalsky JTD, Breakstone DA (2012) Emotional relationships between mothers and infants: knowns, unknowns, and unknown unknowns. Developmental Psychopathology, 24, 113–123.

# 7

# Young People with Learning Disabilities

*David Dossetor*

## Introduction

Learning disability is the accepted term in the UK for intellectual disability (ID) and is defined by the *International Classification of Mental and Behavioural Disorders*, 10th revision (ICD-10) as significant limitations in intellectual functioning and adaptive behaviour for everyday skills that onset before 18 years of age.

Around 2–3% of the population have ID (IQ < 70), of whom 1% have moderate, severe or profound ID. Generally, the rates are higher in boys than in girls and it is more likely to be identified at school age. Psychiatric disorder is found in 30–50% of children with ID. This constitutes 14% of all childhood psychiatric disorders, rising to 25% if autism spectrum disorders (ASDs) are included. Most young people with mild ID are seen in mainstream psychiatry services. This chapter focuses on the mental health challenges of those with moderate, severe and profound ID [1].

While caring for a child with ID is usually a greater challenge than caring for a neurotypical child [1], the presence of emotional or behavioural problems has a greater effect on the family than does the ID. Families who break down as a result of the challenge of caring for a child with ID generally fail to resolve four main adaptive tasks [2]:

- the need to adjust to a child with developmental differences;
- managing the burden of increased care persisting into adolescence and adulthood;
- understanding the child's emotional and behavioural disturbance and seeking appropriate help;
- dealing with the cumulative effects of the preceding factors on family wellbeing and relationships.

Comprehensive child and family services are needed to resolve all of these challenges [3] and can do much to mitigate the additional cost to families and communities of the associated emotional and behavioural disturbance.

## The Changing Context

### Human Rights, Equity of Access to Services and Social Inclusion

There is increasing awareness of the human rights of people with an ID to have equity of access to mainstream and specialist mental health service provision, and to be socially

*Child Psychology and Psychiatry: Frameworks for Clinical Training and Practice*, Third Edition.
Edited by David Skuse, Helen Bruce and Linda Dowdney.
© 2017 John Wiley & Sons, Ltd. Published 2017 by John Wiley & Sons, Ltd.

included in their communities. The long-term use of inappropriate inpatient care for those with mental health difficulties and/or challenging behaviours must be replaced with appropriate mental health care in the community [4,5].

The needs of young people with ID for specialist mental health provision are high due to the frequency and severity of their emotional and behavioural disturbance combined with their intellectual impairment. Mental health clinicians working with this population face a range of problems of greater complexity and differing in type from those generally presenting in child and adolescent mental health services, e.g. extreme repetitive self-injurious behaviour, extraordinary levels of anxiety and hyperactivity and insightless rage and violence sometimes driven by stereotypic preoccupation. Mainstream therapeutic interventions for such problems are less likely to be effective [6]. There is a paucity of research into these severe disturbances which, particularly in the context of behavioural phenotypes, could generate new understanding on the biodevelopmental–psycho-social–cultural mechanisms underlying these problems, and on alternative approaches to intervention.

This emotional and behavioural profile indicates a need for considerably greater access to services than that required by a neurotypical population. In fact, a lack of professional training, failure to understand the needs of those with disabilities, or just plain fear of not being able to provide appropriate help means that those with disabilities get *less* rather than equal access to appropriate expertise. Yet, the evidence shows that the provision of better mental health services enables families not just to adapt, but also to find advantages to having a family member with an ID [1]. Evidence suggests that with better services over time, more families with a child with ID experience an improved quality of life.

The quality of services for this population also affects both mortality rates and parameters of social inclusion, such as employment and sustained family care [1,4,5]. Yet the evidence shows that while the survival rates of people with an ID have increased, they still have a life expectancy of 15–20 years less than the mainstream population. In terms of social equity, while communities have become more affluent, the gap between the social inclusion and achievement of people with an ID and the mainstream population is seen to be widening [7]. Thus the mental health of this minority group has to be considered in a health, social and political context.

## Assessment and Intervention

### Quality of Life, Developmental and Mental Health Factors

The quality of life (QoL) of young people with long-term physical and mental health difficulties is now recognized as an important outcome criterion [8]. While satisfactory standardized QoL measures have yet be developed for this population [8], understanding what contributes to the QoL of young people with ID and their families is a prerequisite for working in this area (see Box 7.1) [1,9,10]. The aim of appropriate intervention is to enable any child with an ID to have a 'good enough' quality of life. Clinical assessment of this outcome will need to take into account both the family and young person's perspective, wherever possible.

Assessment of children and adolescents with disabilities requires a developmental perspective that considers the sequential acquisition of skills in the physical, intellectual, social and emotional domains of development (Box 7.2). Such a multidimensional

---

**Box 7.1 Quality of life assessments**

Quality of life assessments ask young people and their families, 'How satisfied are you with your life as a whole?' Assessment focuses on the primary domains underlying the concepts of inclusion and participation, i.e.:

- An adequate standard of living
- Feeling safe
- Reasonable health
- Connected to valued relationships
- Linked to a community
- Contributing a worthwhile role
- A sense of purpose, productivity and hope for the future

---

**Box 7.2 The main domains of development**

- **Motor and sensory development and integration** – e.g. coordination, sitting still, a capacity for calmness and concentration
- **Independence skills** – such as dressing, eating, hygiene and toileting skills. These provide a reasonable indication of general intelligence in the early years prior to school entry
- **Communication and language** – receptive and expressive verbal skills; non-verbal (including object and picture communication) skills
- **Emotional, social and play skills** – these are among the most complex developmental skills (fuller discussion of this area of development can be found in Chapter 10)
- **Quality of imagination** – stereotypic rigidity or imaginary preoccupation at the expense of social interaction versus the ability to build reciprocal ideas
- **Educational and adolescent community integration skills** – keeping safe, accessing services, managing money (schools are the primary setting in which these skills are developed and tested)

---

developmental approach provides a normative framework against which to consider disturbed behaviour, particularly in the context of extreme or challenging behaviours [10].

It is also important to assess the developmental mental competencies that are essential for initiating and sustaining satisfactory social interactions with others (see Box 7.3).

The assessment of psychiatric disorders in young people with ID is complicated by their behavioural presentation and their difficulties in reporting on, and evaluating, their mental states (see Box 7.4). It can also be difficult to differentiate between features of ID phenotypes and those of some psychiatric conditions, e.g. the difficulties in social anxiety that form part of the autism spectrum phenotype [11]. Diagnostic difficulties are exacerbated by the overlap between 'challenging behaviour' and 'psychiatric disorder' [12]. Thus, mental health assessments need to be undertaken by professionals with training in ID. Research in mild ID shows there is diagnostic reliability but differences in validity [13]. For example, while attention deficit hyperactivity disorder (ADHD) has diagnostic reliability, it differs from ADHD in a mainstream population. It has a

---

**Box 7.3 Development of the mind and mental competencies**

- Identification of self and non-self
- Motor regulation and coordination, sensory modulation
- Selective attention and attention switching
- Communication skills and theory of mind
- Emotion recognition, regulation and empathy
- Self-concept and self-esteem
- Reciprocal social interaction and relationship-building
- Reality-testing, perspective-taking and other executive function skills

These are best evidenced by the capacity to make new good quality peer attachments. The most important skills are:

- Development of attention and concentration, a prerequisite for learning
- Development of theory of mind to comprehend relationships

---

**Box 7.4 Difficulties in mental state assessment**

- Subjective mental phenomena cannot be reliably elicited < 7 years or IQ < 45 – cannot rely on for diagnosis of depression or psychosis.
- Difficulty articulating abstract or global concepts, e.g. describing mood
- Answers given to please the interviewer.
- Intellectual distortion: not understanding the implication of 'do you hear voices?'
- Diagnostic overshadowing – attributing psychiatric symptoms to the underlying intellectual disability.
- Baseline exaggeration or intensification, e.g. increase in self-injurious behaviour at a time of stress – an extreme response may be due to an anniversary of a loss or a change of a teacher/staff/classroom/accommodation/family visits that carers may not identify.
- Stress on coping with a lack of cognitive reserve leads to disintegration, disorganization or psychotic behaviour – distinguishing behaviour disorder from adjustment disorders and psychosis.
- Delusions and hallucinations are frequently difficult to distinguish from a range of normal developmental phenomena, e.g. concrete thinking, pretend friends, stereotypic thinking and imagination, especially in autism spectrum disorder.
- Irritability and explosive anger may be common problem of challenging behaviour but is associated with depression and mania.

---

prevalence of 30%, is as common in girls, and has stronger associations with family functioning, depression and social impairment. Standard treatment with stimulants is not as effective and is associated with more side-effects.

Problems of ASD, ADHD, anxiety disorders including, post-traumatic stress disorder and obsessive compulsive disorder, repetitive self-injury and disruptive behaviour disorder are more frequent in young people with ID than in the general population [10,11,14]. Substance abuse and conduct disorder are less frequent. Combinations of disorders are the norm [14]. There is almost no research on the reliability and validity of psychiatric diagnosis in young people with severe ID. The separation of disability services and behaviour support skills from mental health services leads to a lack of collaboration between disciplines on helping young people with ID. The contribution of developmental psychiatry has been held back by the lack of diagnostic research [14]. However, the specialist in ID psychiatry has to consider the explanatory value of different approaches, e.g. that of psychiatric diagnosis versus that of challenging behaviour with its inherent behavioural approach, and look at the implications for intervention and improvement. However, the best questionnaires on emotional and behavioural disturbance, such as the Developmental Behaviour Checklist, provide a useful checklist of symptoms but do not convert to psychiatric diagnosis [15].

**Child and Family Factors**

Interactions between a range of child and family factors influence child outcomes (Box 7.5). Child genetic differences elicit differences in parenting responses, and some children are more genetically sensitive to certain environmental factors, such as abuse/neglect [1]. Longitudinal studies show that biological qualities have a greater part to play in the persistence of child emotional and behavioural disturbance, with family factors making a smaller contribution (8%) to variances in outcome [15]. In general, therefore, young people with ID are more likely to contribute to problems of family functioning than the other way around, particularly those with challenging disorders such as ASD. Nonetheless, the ability of families to adapt to the demands of parenting a child with ID is important, and family relationships can be significant contributors to complex mental health presentations in young people. For example, parental mental health difficulties can impact upon parenting skills. The prevalence of chronic burn-out, stress, anxiety and depression in parents of young people with ID is high (approximately 25% in clinic studies) [16]. Accordingly, careful family assessment, on a number of family relationship dimensions is needed. These include, for example, problem-solving, communication, roles, affective responses, affective involvement and behaviour control [17].

**Educational and Service Influences**

In young people with mild to borderline ID, community and family factors are primary causal influences on child outcome [7], with school (and preschool) also exerting a major influence. Partnership between parents and teachers is important in meeting special developmental and well-being needs. In children with ID, engagement with, and the quality of management of other child services make important contributions. These include respite care services, and the other paediatric and health professionals who work with this population. These partners' professionalism, communication, and

---

**Box 7.5  Contributors to the ease or difficulty of child-rearing**

- Health problems, especially neurological, including sensory deficits
- Intellectual ability, including learning problems and neuropsychiatric deficits
- Temperament, with genetic and environmental contributors
- Environmental milieu – emotional warmth, stimulation, predictability and consistency
- Earlier experiences, positive or traumatic
- Attachment style and strength

collaboration are often key determinants of outcome. Complex cases necessarily involve many carers and professionals.

## Types of Intervention

Interventions for young people with ID and emotional and behavioural problems range from training in parenting skills to the use of fringe interventions such as chelating agents and oxygen therapy (see Figure 7.1). As can be seen, there is good evidence that

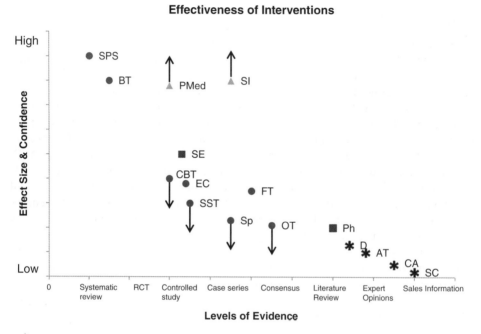

Figure 7.1 Effectiveness of modalities of intervention for emotional and behaviour disturbance. The *x*-axis is the confidence or effect size of a type of intervention, and the colour designates speed of intervention effect, which influences intervention in the context of acute presentation and family crisis. Triangles, rapid effect – days to weeks; circles, intermediate effect – weeks to months; squares, slow long-term effects – months to years. The arrow designates the change in importance in more severe disturbance. The graph also highlights the place of fringe and alternative approaches that naive, desperate families are often drawn to in the 'free market of economy of health'. Abbreviations are as follows: SPS, specialized parenting skills [21]; BT, behaviour therapy, including carer/staff training [19 ]; PMed, psychotropic medication; SI, safety intervention, including self-protective skills, room modification; CBT, cognitive behaviour therapy; SE, special education: skills to match needs; EC, emotion-based social skills training/emotional coaching; Sp, speech therapy and augmentative and alternative communication; SST, social skills training; FT, family and systems therapy; OT, occupational therapy/sensory integration; Ph, physiotherapy; D*, diet; AT*, alternative therapy; CA*, chelating agents, oxygen therapy; SC*, stem cell therapy; *, not approved by author.

parent training, behavioural intervention (including applied behavioural analysis) and psychotropic medication are effective, although there is less information on the persistence over time of intervention effects [18,19]. Evidence for effectiveness is based upon a combination of cohort studies and clinical consensus, as funding for randomized control trials has been limited.

## The Development of Services

There is a lack of international consensus on models of service provision, and limited evidence on service outcomes [4,20]. The components of various service models are outlined in Box 7.6. As an illustration, our own tertiary ID team consults to young people and their families, to mental health, disability and special educational services, and to non-government agencies. A wider range of disciplines and skills is required than is generally provided in mainstream child mental health services (see Box 7.7).

While consumers are clear that the failure to meet their disability mental health needs will continue without specialized mental health expertise [23], the support for professional specialization and funding of community-based services has been slow since the deinstitutionalization of the 1980s, and varies between countries. For example, in the UK, the 2004 National Service Framework [5] recommends a community-based ID service that includes input from psychiatrists and psychologists alongside other health professionals, such as speech therapists and occupational therapists. In contrast, across

---

**Box 7.6 Proposed service models**

- Assessment, including observation, clinical, behavioural and environmental assessment, and diagnosis
- Specialized individual therapies
- Pharmacological therapy
- Parent skill building, including stress management, problem-solving, coping strategies and building social support [1,21]
- Family and systems assessment and therapy
- An interdisciplinary team approach
- Individualized and structured group approaches
- Acute and 24-hour emergency services
- Consultation in-reach and community outreach programmes
- Short-term intensive in-patient/residential programmes
- Partnerships within/across clinical teams and community-based services, including education, respite, welfare, non-government disability organizations and employment services
- Wraparound approaches with relevant community-based services
- Highly specialized services for gaps in service provision such as forensic and youth offending
- Capacity-building of specialist skills across a range of disciplines
- Transfer of knowledge and relationship-building between developing specialist programmes and generic services

---

**Box 7.7  Range of skills within a tertiary young person's learning disabilities partnership clinic**

- Paediatrician and child psychiatrist for assessment of health, mental health, multidimensional formulation and medication
- Multidisciplinary allied health skills, including:
  - clinical psychology, occupational therapy, speech therapy, special education, pharmacy, case management
  - skill-building approaches: support specialist skills of treating teams [10]
  - specialized therapies, e.g. emotional/social learning, modified and trauma-focused cognitive behavioural therapy, play therapy.
- Family and system skills and cultural expertise
  - including specialized parent training, e.g. Stepping Stones Parent Training [21], parent–child interaction therapy [22]
  - the system issues (also separate special systems evaluation service)
  - the need to match environment to developmental/psychiatric need.
- Legal assessment of child protection, abuse and neglect
  - interface with welfare and intensive support services, e.g. for young people in out-of-home care
  - legal: human rights/child protection, e.g. when service systems are failing.
- High level of interagency collaboration and service agreement
  - to influence each other's service systems for the needs of the child and family
  - match service provision with clinical need versus business funding formulas.

---

Australia there is a dawning of recognition of the need for specialized ID services to be embedded in mental health service frameworks. Service provision is at different stages of development in individual states (see, e.g., NSW Ministry of Health [24]). Service requirements include a focus on reasonable adjustments, support, inclusion and participation. They also require early intervention for mental health needs facilitated by access to, and partnership between, paediatrics and general and specialist mental health services [25].

## Conclusion

Between 30% and 50% of children with ID will evidence a psychiatric disorder. Their complex presentation results in a high need for mental health services. Assessment and intervention need to address both child and family factors. The separation of disability services from mental health services is unhelpful. Over the last 25 years, the need for sub-specialist multidisciplinary learning disability mental health services has come to be appreciated, but the development of such services and sub-speciality skills has been slow. The rights of young people with learning disability of access to community-based mental health services, alongside the growth of neuroscience and psychiatric intervention research, make this an exciting and growing area of multidisciplinary multiagency clinical endeavour and collaboration.

# References

1  Families Special Interest Research Group of IASSID (2014) Families supporting a child with intellectual or developmental disabilities: the current state of knowledge. Journal of Applied Research in Intellectual Disabilities, 27, 420–430.

2  Nankervis K, Rosewarne A, Vassos M (2011) Why do families relinquish care? An investigation of the factors that lead to relinquishment into out-of-home respite care. Journal of Intellectual Disability Research, 55, 422–433.

3  Einfeld S, Ellis L, Doran C et al. (2010) Behavior problems increase costs of care of children with intellectual disabilities. Journal of Mental Health Research in Intellectual Disabilities 3, 202–209.

4  Transforming Care and Commissioning Steering Group (2014) Winterbourne View – Time for Change. Transforming the commissioning of services for people with learning disabilities and/ or autism. London: ACEVO. [The Bubb Report]. http://www.england. nhs.uk/wp-c ontent/uploads/2014/11/transforming-commissioning-services.pdf

5  NHS England (2015) Transforming Care for People with Learning Disabilities – Next Steps. London: NHS England. http://www.england.nhs.uk/wp-content/ uploads/2015/01/transform-care-nxt-stps.pdf

6  Emerson E, Hatton C (2014) Health Inequalities and People with Intellectual Disabilities. Cambridge: Cambridge University Press.

7  Llewellyn G, Emerson E, Honey A, Kariuki M (2011) Left behind: Monitoring the social inclusion of young Australians with self-reported long term health conditions, impairments or disabilities 2001–2009. Online: http://sydney.edu.au/health-sciences/ afdsrc/docs/left_behind_080811.pdf. Accessed: January 2017

8  Ravens-Sieberer U, Karow A, Barthel, D et al. (2014) How to assess quality of life in child and adolescent psychiatry. Dialogues in Clinical Neuroscience, 16, 147–158.

9  Cummins RA (2005) Instruments assessing quality of life. In: Hogg J, Langa A (eds) Approaches to the assessment of adults with intellectual disability: A service provider's guide. London: Blackwell Publishing, pp. 118–137.

10  Dossetor D, White D, Whatson L (eds) (2011) Mental Health for Children and Adolescents with Intellectual Disability: a framework for professional practice. Melbourne: IP Communications. www.IPCommunications.com.au.

11  Salazar F, Baird G, Chandler S et al. (2015) Co-occurring psychiatric disorders in preschool and elementary school-aged children with autism spectrum disorder. Journal of Autism and Developmental Disorders, 4, 11.

12  Emerson E, Einfeld S (2011) Challenging Behaviour, 3rd edn. Cambridge University Press.

13  Antshel K, Phillips M, Gordon M et al. (2006) Is ADHD a valid disorder in children with intellectual delays. Clinical Psychology Review 26, 555–572.

14  Dossetor D (2014) Diagnosis, Psychotropic medication and outcome in an audit of 150 child and adolescent neuropsychiatric patients. Journal of Mental Health for Children and Adolescents with Intellectual and Developmental Disabilities, 5, 4–9.

15  Tonge B, Einfeld S (2003) Psychopathology and intellectual disability: the Australian Child to Adult Longitudinal Study. In: Glidden LM (ed) International Review of Research in Mental Retardation, 26, pp. 61–91. Academic Press, San Diego USA.

**16** Hastings R, Beck A (2004) Practitioner review: stress intervention for parents of children with intellectual disabilities. Journal of Child Psychology and Psychiatry, 45, 1338–1349.

**17** Miller I, Ryan E, Keitner G et al. (2000) The McMaster Approach to Families: theory, assessment, treatment and research. Journal of Family Therapy, 22, 168–189.

**18** Furlong M, McGilloway S, Bywater T et al. (2012) Editorial Group: Behavioural and cognitive-behavioural group-based parenting programmes for early-onset conduct problems in children aged 3 to 12 years. Cochrane Database of Systematic Reviews, Issue 2.

**19** Ali A, Hall I, Blickwedel J, Hassiotis A (2015) Behavioural and cognitive-behavioural interventions for outwardly-directed aggressive behaviour in people with intellectual disabilities. Cochrane Database of Systematic Reviews 2015, Issue 4.

**20** Centre of Disability Studies (2014) Evaluation report on the Developmental Psychiatry Clinic and Partnership, The Children's Hospital at Westmead. Online: www.schoollink .chw.edu.au/. Accessed: January 2017

**21** Roberts C, Mazzucchelli T, Studman L, Sanders M (2006) Behavioural family intervention for children with developmental and behavioural problems. Journal of Clinical Child and Adolescent Psychology, 35, 180–193.

**22** Bagner D, Eyberg S (2007) Parent-child interaction therapy for disruptive behavior in children with mental retardation: A randomized controlled trial. Journal of Clinical Child and Adolescent Psychology, 36, 418–429.

**23** Dossetor D (2013) National Roundtable on the mental health of people with an intellectual disability: a summary. CHW School-Link Newsletter 4, 20–22. www .schoollink.chw.edu.au/newsletter/

**24** The NSW Health Service Framework for People with Intellectual Disability and Their Carers, NSW Ministry of Health 2012 http://www.health.nsw.gov.au/disability /Publications/health-care-of-people-with-ID.pdf

**25** Dossetor D (2015) What will the NDIS do for subspecialty expertise and the multidisciplinary services for complex mental health problems of young people with intellectual disability? Implications from the Centre for Disability Study's review of the Developmental Psychiatry Clinic. Journal of Mental Health for Children and Adolescents with Intellectual and Developmental Disabilities, 6, 1–11.

## Internet Resources

Chi-Mat: http://www.chimat.org.uk/ldcamhs – *some key resources on a range of topics relating to learning disabilities and child and adolescent mental health services*

Fletcher R, Barnhill J, Cooper S (eds) (2016) Diagnostic Manual – Intellectual Disability (DM-ID-2). A textbook of diagnosis of mental disorders in persons with intellectual disability. National Association for the Dually Diagnosed (NADD), United States. www.dmid.org/

Journal of Mental Health for Children and Adolescents with Intellectual and Developmental Disabilities: www.schoollink.chw.edu.au – *an Educational Resource & CHW School-link Newsletter; a free electronic interdisciplinary journal with review articles and reports on innovative treatment approaches*

Learning Disabilities: http://www.rcpsych.ac.uk/healthadvice/problemsdisorders /learningdisabilities.aspx – *the Royal College of Psychiatrists' page of readable and well-researched information for the public*

The Royal College of Psychiatrists Psychiatry of Learning Disability Reading List: http:// www.rcpsych.ac.uk/pdf/23%2009%202011%20LD%20PSYCH%20READING %20LIST.pdf

Young Minds: http://www.youngminds.org.uk/training_services/training_and_consultancy /resources/schools/1775_children_young_people_with_learning_disabilities – *an information pack including a chapter on mental health difficulties in children with learning disabilities*

## 8

## Language Development

*Thomas Klee and Stephanie F. Stokes*

The ability to communicate using language is one of the most basic human traits. It involves learning to understand and produce an abstract and complex linguistic code, providing the foundation for social interaction, personal relationships, reading, writing, problem-solving, formal learning and personal well-being. When children enter school at the age of 4 or 5 years, most have achieved near adult-like mastery of the sounds and grammar of their native language(s) and can easily and effectively communicate with others. We present some of the main developmental milestones of, and influences on, the language development of typically developing pre-school children.

## Processes and Components of Language Development

Figure 8.1 is adapted from a causal model of developmental disorders [1] and illustrates the relationship between language development and some of the factors known to affect it. The interaction between the child's genetic endowment and his or her environment is depicted. In the case of language development, the model proposes that the human genotype enabled a species-specific endowment for linguistic processing. While the nature and origin of infants' capacity for language acquisition remains to be fully elucidated, recent evidence supports this proposal (e.g. neonates listen preferentially to speech [2]). The key role played by environmental factors, in the form of both human (social) interaction and language input are also illustrated. The junction of these can be seen in the use of child-directed speech – developmentally sensitive speech and language adjustments made by parents and others when talking to children. Both genetic and environmental factors affect the developing brain and its neurobiological mechanisms [3,4]. These in turn underpin cognitive mechanisms, such as psycholinguistic processing and verbal memory [5], which affect language development. The child's language ability is also affected by development in the cognitive, psycho-social and motor domains.

Various components and modalities involved in understanding and producing language are also shown. Language comprehension (sometimes referred to clinically as *receptive language*) refers to the process of decoding speech – the chain of events in which sound waves produced by the human vocal tract are received, processed and given meaning by a human listener. Language production (also referred to as *expressive language*) refers to the process of encoding – the chain of events by which a message

*Child Psychology and Psychiatry: Frameworks for Clinical Training and Practice*, Third Edition.
Edited by David Skuse, Helen Bruce and Linda Dowdney.
© 2017 John Wiley & Sons, Ltd. Published 2017 by John Wiley & Sons, Ltd.

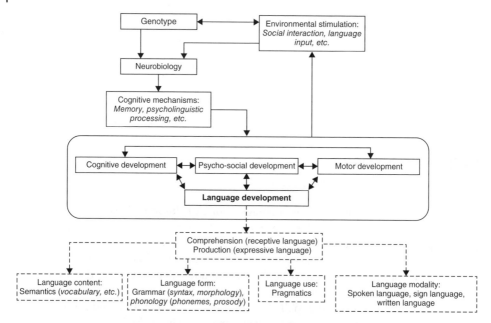

**Figure 8.1** Processes, components and modalities of language development.

generated by the brain is neurolocally relayed to muscles that move the structures of the vocal tract.

Figure 8.1 divides language into three components: content, form and use. Language content (semantics) refers to how meaning is conveyed by linguistic elements such as words, idioms and sentences. Language form encompasses grammar and phonology. One aspect of grammar involves the rules governing how words are combined to form phrases and sentences (syntax). For example, English grammar requires that the subject precedes the verb (e.g. *I should go.*) in declarative sentences while in questions, the verb precedes the subject (e.g. *Should I go?*). Morphology refers to the structure of words. For example, in English the past tense form of regular verbs is created by adding the *-ed* inflection to the verb stem (e.g. *climbed*). Language form also involves the language's sound system (phonology): both its contrastive sound segments (e.g. phonemes such as /p/, /t/ and /k/) and prosodic features such as stress and intonation. Language use refers to the interpersonal, communicative functions of language during social interaction (pragmatics), such as a speaker's communicative intentions. The model also illustrates various modalities of language, such as its spoken, signed or written forms.

This model is implicitly reflected in current theories of language development, such as usage-based accounts [6], in which general learning processes and cognitive mechanisms underpinning language development are mediated by environmental factors. Cognitive mechanisms include such things as pattern recognition and intention reading. Pattern recognition occurs when a child associates new information with something already known, recognizing similarities, such as when the child, knowing that the utterance *eat apple* describes that event, says *eat bread* to describe a similar event. Intention reading includes joint attention, such as when the adult and child share a focus on objects, events or interactions, or using pointing and gesturing to indicate objects and events.

There is little differentiation between the lexicon and syntax in early language development; rather, the child is learning to express relations in the world, such as *doggie eat* to describe a dog eating, rather than grammatical relations such as subject + verb. Language development is defined as form-function mappings or construction building.

## Milestones of Speech and Language Development

It is beyond the scope of this chapter to present detailed charts outlining children's speech and language development. These can be found on the websites listed at the end of the chapter. While the sequence of developmental milestones is broadly similar across children (e.g. babbling > first words > word combinations), there is wide variation in their attainment [3]. Thus when referring to developmental charts, it is important to remember that developmental milestones indicate the *average* age of attainment. Both genetic and environmental factors contribute to variation across children. For example, the development of infant phonetic discrimination is influenced by the quality of mother–infant interaction [4]. Socioeconomic status effects upon language development are apparent by 18 months [7]. Genetic factors contribute to both typical and atypical speech and language development [3]. Differences in definitions and research methods also influence reported developmental sequences. For example, proposed sequences of speech sound development may be affected by whether studies were based on children's spontaneous conversations with adults or picture-naming tasks, where words are elicited singly. Methods of data analysis can also be influential – for example, whether children's speech forms are analysed on their own (phonetic inventory) or in relation to adult forms (phonemic inventory). Moreover, national varieties (e.g. British, Australian or New Zealand English) or dialects (e.g. African American English) of the spoken language also affect acquisition. We now summarize general patterns of development in typically developing children.

## Developmental Phases

After 6–7 months of gestation, the foetus responds to sound, including the human voice, and neonates prefer to listen to sounds heard before birth, such as the mother's heartbeat and her voice. In its first 6 months after birth, the infant is highly responsive to adult interaction, intently watching human faces and turning in the direction of sounds. Turn-taking emerges and infants imitate adult tongue protrusion or raspberry blowing and laugh in response to the human voice. By 2 months of age, infants can discriminate between speech sounds [8] and produce a wide range of speech-like sounds, including those not present in their own language(s).

Between 6 and 12 months, infants' motor and cognitive development advance rapidly. Sitting and crawling allow exploration of the environment, increasing opportunities for object manipulation and learning about object function, shape and taste. Infants also begin appreciating the role of others as agents of change, seen in the use of simple communicative gestures and sometimes accompanied by vocalizations, to indicate and request objects (e.g. pointing) and action (e.g. raising arms to be lifted). At 6–7 months babbling emerges (e.g. *bababa*), becoming more diversified over the next few months.

At around 9 months conventional social gestures emerge (e.g. waving goodbye, shaking head to indicate rejection). At around 11 months infants start losing the ability to discriminate among all phonemes, beginning to better discriminate the speech sounds of their own language environment and fine-tuning their perception to be language-specific [9]. At 10 months the average receptive vocabulary size is about 50 words [10].

By 12–18 months, infants begin to understand the intentions of others, engage in joint attention (sharing attention and focus with an adult) and attend to books for brief periods. Walking contributes to a greater awareness of self-in-space, facilitating the developing comprehension of locative words, such as *in* and *on* and simple questions like *where's your teddy?* Parents often report that their child understands most of what is said to them, an impression fostered by the child's use of *comprehension strategies,* which capitalize on context in the absence of understanding exactly what is said (e.g. the parent says *Get the ball* as they point to one). Basic representational play emerges during this phase (e.g. 'drinking' from a toy cup), along with some single words. By now most children can identify some body parts (*Where's your nose?*) and pictures of family members. By 12 months, children's average receptive vocabulary size is 85 words, increasing to 250 words by 18 months [10].

By 24 months, representational play includes greater symbolism (e.g. using a block for a car). There is an understanding of *what* or *where* questions (e.g. *What's x doing?*) and some children begin to use the pronouns *me* and *you* and grammatical markers such as the *-ing* verb inflection, plurals (*cats*) and past tense *-ed.* While the average American toddler has an expressive vocabulary size of around 300 words by 24 months of age, large individual differences exist (seven to 668 words) [10]. Similar findings have been reported in 12 other languages [11]. It becomes difficult to estimate children's vocabulary size beyond the age of 2. Psycholinguistic processing mechanisms can be measured in 2-year-olds, with most children being able to imitate one-, two- and three-syllable nonsense words (e.g. *doe-per-lut*) [12]. By 20 months, 75% of children are reported by their parents to be combining words [10].

By 3 years of age, many children engage in cooperative play. Phonological awareness and other aspects of metalinguistic ability emerge, as seen in word play (e.g. *moo goo boo*). Print awareness emerges and the child can point to familiar words in books. Children understand the locative *under* and begin developing an awareness of causality, accompanied by an increase in asking *why* questions and producing complex sentences (e.g. *He's crying 'coz he fell down*), but sometimes with word order errors.

By 4 years, there is greater print and metalinguistic awareness, demonstrated by an appreciation of nursery rhymes. *Who* and *where* questions begin to be asked. Play becomes rule-based (e.g. role-taking) and children use language to organize and talk about their world (e.g. *you be the mummy*). Sentences contain embedded clauses and are almost adult-like (e.g. *Don't touch that 'coz you'll break it and I haven't finished yet*). They can now describe basic events, such as their birthday party.

By 5 years, the child understands purpose, function and consequence questions (e.g. *How can we open that jar? What will happen if he loses his keys?*). With knowledge of objects' locations comes an understanding of more locatives (*in front of, behind, next to, through*). The child can hold a conversation and, with an increase in schema (pattern) knowledge, can describe more abstract events, such as what happens at birthday parties in general.

## Atypical Language Development

Some children experience delays or problems in acquiring the sounds, meanings and grammatical structures of their language. Others experience difficulty using language socially. Such delays may or may not be transient and are often the first signs of a problem related to hearing, cognition or other areas of development. They may also be indicative of a developmental language disorder (see Chapter 35) or a social communication disorder (see Chapter 23). Pertinent to this chapter is a group of children with late onset of language, often referred to as *late talkers*: 2-year-olds with few words or no word combinations [13]. Epidemiological studies have identified factors associated with late onset of language, including male gender, family history of late talking or speech and language difficulties, early neurobiological growth, non-native language background, low maternal education and number of siblings [14,15]. Small-scale studies indicate that poor receptive vocabulary and limited gesture use may predict more persistent language problems [16], as has parent concern [17]. The American Speech-Language-Hearing Association suggests referring children to a speech and language therapist whenever a parent expresses concern (see http://www.asha.org/public/speech/disorders/LateBlooming.htm).

## Future Directions

Our understanding of language development is being advanced by progress in high-resolution, non-invasive neural studies. For example, it is suggested that there is increasing specialization of the developing cortical circuitry for speech between 1 and 4 months of age [18] and that the auditory and motor brain areas are involved in the developmental transition in infants' speech perception between 7 and 11 months of age [19]. Future advances in our understanding of language development will require further innovation and collaboration between disciplines, including those of neurobiology [20], speech-language sciences, cognitive science, linguistics and computer science.

## References

1 Bishop DVM, Snowling MJ (2004) Developmental dyslexia and specific language impairment: same or different? Psychological Bulletin, 130, 858–886.
2 Vouloumanos A, Werker JF (2007) Listening to language at birth: evidence for a bias for speech in neonates. Developmental Science, 10, 159–164.
3 Grigorenko EL (2009) Speaking genes or genes for speaking? Deciphering the genetics of speech and language. Journal of Child Psychology and Psychiatry, 50, 116–125.
4 Elsabbagh M, Hohenberger A, Campos R et al. (2013) Narrowing perceptual sensitivity to the native language in infancy: exogenous influences on developmental timing. Behavioural Sciences, 3, 120–132.
5 Parra M, Hoff E, Core C (2011) Relations among language exposure, phonological memory, and language development in Spanish-English bilingually-developing two-year-olds. Journal of Experimental Child Psychology, 108, 113–125.

6  Ibbotson P (2013) The scope of usage-based theory. Frontiers in Psychology, 4, 1–15.

7  Fernald A, Marchman VA, Weisleder A (2013) SES differences in language processing skill and vocabulary are evident at 18 months. Developmental Science, 16, 234–248.

8  Kuhl PK (2010) Brain mechanisms in early language acquisition. Neuron, 67, 713–727.

9  Kuhl PK, Conboy BT, Coffey-Corina S et al. (2008) Phonetic learning as a pathway to language: new data and native language magnet theory expanded (NLM-e). Philosophical Transactions of the Royal Society B, 363, 979–1000.

10  Fenson L, Marchman VA, Thal DJ et al. (2007) MacArthur-Bates Communicative Development Inventories: User's Guide and Technical Manual, 2nd edn. Baltimore: Brookes.

11  Bleses D, Vach W, Slott M et al. (2008) Early vocabulary development in Danish and other languages: a CDI-based comparison. Journal of Child Language, 35, 619–650.

12  Stokes SF, Klee T (2009) The diagnostic accuracy of a new test of early nonword repetition for differentiating late talking and typically developing children. Journal of Speech, Language, and Hearing Research, 52, 872–882.

13  Rescorla LA, Dale PS (eds) (2013) Late Talkers: Language Development, Interventions, and Outcomes. Baltimore: Brookes.

14  Zubrick SR, Taylor CL, Rice ML et al. (2007) Late language emergence at 24 months: an epidemiological study of prevalence, predictors, and covariates. Journal of Speech, Language, and Hearing Research, 50, 1562–1592.

15  Reilly S, Wake M, Bavin EL et al. (2007) Predicting language at 2 years of age: a prospective community study. Pediatrics, 120, e1141–1449.

16  Thal DJ, Marchman VA, Tomblin JB (2013) Late-talking toddlers: characterisation and prediction of continued delay. In: Rescorla LA, Dale PS (eds) Late Talkers: Language Development, Interventions, and Outcomes. Baltimore: Brookes, pp.169–201.

17  Klee T, Newbury J, Stokes, SF et al. (2015) Associations between parent concerns and clinical outcomes in children with and without early language delay at two points in development. Paper presented at the Symposium on Research in Child Language Disorders, University of Wisconsin-Madison.

18  Shultz S, Vouloumanos A, Bennett RH et al. (2014) Neural specialisation for speech in the first months of life. Developmental Science, 17, 766–774.

19  Kuhl PK, Ramirez RR, Bosseler A et al. (2014) Infants' brain responses to speech suggest Analysis by Synthesis. Proceedings of the National Academy of Sciences, 111, 11238–11245.

20  Hickok G, Small SL (eds) (2016) Neurobiology of Language. London: Academic Press.

## Internet Resources

American Speech-Language-Hearing Association: http://www.asha.org/public/speech/development/; http://www.asha.org/public/speech/development/chart.htm

Child Development Institute: http://childdevelopmentinfo.com/child-development/language_development/

National Institute on Deafness and Other Communication Disorders: http://www.nidcd.nih.gov/health/voice/pages/speechandlanguage.aspx

# 9

# Development of Social Cognition

*Virginia Slaughter*

Social cognition in humans is uniquely complex. Unlike other mammals, which respond primarily to each other's outward behavioural signals, we look deeper, into each other's minds, in order to understand one another. For instance, if we witness a stranger breaking into loud song on a crowded street, we might notice that outwardly she is smiling and acting exuberantly, but our primary reaction would be to interpret her unusual actions by considering what's going on inside her mind. She may want to communicate a message. Perhaps she thinks this is a good way to get a recording contract. Maybe she just feels great. This process of reasoning about what other people feel, want and know is referred to as mentalizing, mindreading or using our theory of mind. It is a fundamental skill that helps us to understand and get along with the other people in our world.

## Early Social Cognition

Until recently, most psychologists thought that the capacity for mentalizing only emerged in the pre-school period, because that is when typically developing children begin to pass tests assessing their ability to accurately report what is likely to be in someone else's mind in differing circumstances. Whether or not infants and toddlers also have a theory of mind has been debated for years. Recent experimental procedures, cleverly modelled on everyday situations, now confirm that some basic mentalizing is evident in infants' non-verbal communication and helping behaviours.

For instance, in one experimental procedure, 12- to 18-month-old infants watched an adult write on a piece of paper with a marker. Then the marker dropped off the table, unseen by the adult, who began to search around for it. Already on the floor were some other items, but the infants consistently pointed at or retrieved the marker, rather than the distractor items [1,2]. This showed that 1-year-olds could work out the specific item that the adult *wanted*. In another experiment, 18-month-old infants were invited to interact with two adults, who were playing with two different toys. After a while, the toys were put on a shelf and one of the adults left the room. The remaining adult then brought out a new toy, played with it and then put it on the shelf as well. When the first adult returned and pointed toward the three toys on the shelf saying, 'Oh look! Give it to me please!' the infants immediately retrieved the new toy – the one that this particular adult had not yet played with. This indicates that the infants interpreted the adult's pointing in terms of what the adult *thought* was new and interesting [3].

*Child Psychology and Psychiatry: Frameworks for Clinical Training and Practice,* Third Edition.
Edited by David Skuse, Helen Bruce and Linda Dowdney.
© 2017 John Wiley & Sons, Ltd. Published 2017 by John Wiley & Sons, Ltd.

Besides reading the mental states behind each other's actions, we also tend to antici-pate each other's states of mind and the behaviour they produce. For instance, if you know your friend likes sugar in his coffee, then, as he pours himself a cup, you are likely to shift your eyes to the sugar bowl, anticipating his desire as well as his next move. Recent eye-tracking research shows that 25-month-olds anticipate in this way and, furthermore, they can anticipate another person's next move even if that person is actually mistaken. In the eye-tracking study, toddlers watched a video in which an actor repeatedly reached to get his toy out of a box. When the actor wasn't looking, the toy was moved to a different box. Upon the actor's return, the toddlers anticipated his next move and looked to the first box, where the actor still *thought* his toy was located, rather than to where it really was [4]. This experiment shows unmistakable mentalizing because the toddlers focused on the inner experience of the actor, rather than on the actual location of the toy. Using a similar setup, this same pattern of eye gaze responses was observed in toddlers from rural, non-industrialized traditional societies in China, Ecuador and Fiji [5]. This cross-cultural pattern indicates that mentalizing is a universal skill that emerges in healthy children regardless of their particular language, socializa-tion or educational experiences.

Strikingly, another study showed that 6- to 8-year-old children with an autism spec-trum disorder (ASD), when presented with the same scenario, consistently failed to look to the box where the actor thought the toy would be [6]. This shows that automatic, non-verbal mindreading is disrupted in children with ASD, in addition to the more explicit social-cognitive and communicative problems characteristic of the disorder.

## Social Cognition in Preschool and Beyond

The research described above shows that in typical development, accurate mentaliz-ing is present, in some instances, within the second year of life. A direction for future research is to evaluate whether and how these early non-verbal theory of mind skills are linked to the more sophisticated social cognition that develops later in childhood. Although more research is needed, the results of one such study suggest a positive asso-ciation [7] between 12-month-olds' ability to convey new information to an ignorant actor (as in the pointing tasks described above) and their performance on measures of social cognition at 4 years of age.

Soon after children begin to use language, they also begin to talk about what they and others feel, want and think. This facile ability to communicate about what is in our own and others' minds has allowed researchers to expand the range of verbal tests used to assess young children's social-cognitive reasoning. The standard procedure is for children to listen to a description of a social scenario, sometimes accompanied by cartoons or acted out with puppets. Once the scenario is in place, they are then asked questions about what the protagonists feel, want or know, or what they will do next. While there are potentially as many different versions of these tests as there are unique social scenarios, a subset of them has recently been made into a highly reliable developmental scale, illustrated in Table 9.1. The theory of mind scale reveals that 3- to 10-year-old children gradually master different elements of social cognition in a pre-dictable sequence [8]. Children with clinical diagnoses that are characterized by delays or deficits in social cognition, such as deafness or autism, pass the tasks in essentially

**Table 9.1** Six tests that make up the theory of mind scale. Research shows that the majority of children acquire these concepts in order from diverse desires to sarcasm

| Test | Social-cognitive concept assessed | Approximate proportion of 3- to 6-year-old children who pass |
|---|---|---|
| Diverse desires | Different people may like and want different things | 95% |
| Diverse beliefs | Different people can hold different beliefs about the same thing | 88% |
| Knowledge access | People who see something also know about it; if they don't see then they don't know | 79% |
| False belief | People do things based on what they think, even if they are mistaken | 49% |
| Hidden emotion | People can deliberately conceal emotions by facial expression management | 27% |
| Sarcasm | In order to be humorous, people sometimes say the opposite of what they really mean | 20% |

the same order but at a later age. The one exception to scale conformity is that children with autism pass the hidden emotion task before they pass false belief [8]. This subtle difference reinforces the conclusion, following from years of research, that the mentalistic concept of false belief can be particularly difficult for people with autism to grasp.

## Individual Differences in Social Cognition – Implications for Children's Social Lives

Alongside the consistent developmental sequence for theory of mind concepts outlined in Table 9.1, there are measurable individual differences amongst children in their rates of social-cognitive development. These individual differences have been linked to some specific consequences for children's everyday social life. Although the effects are typically small to medium-sized, meaning that other factors play a role, children who perform well on theory of mind tests also tend to have relatively sophisticated social skills, as well as effective interpersonal relationships.

For instance, studies have shown that mentalizing is related to social competence in 3- to 10-year-old children. That is, those children who are good at working out what others feel, want and think are also likely to behave prosocially by helping, sharing, comforting and cooperating with others [9]. In light of this, it is understandable that children of this age who excel at mentalizing are also identified as popular by their teachers and peers [9,10]. It is important to note that much of this research is correlational, so we do not know for sure if skilful mentalizing causes children to be socially adept and popular, or if those qualities put them in the best position to develop their social-cognitive skills. Although more research is required, one recent study that tested children repeatedly at 5, 6 and 7 years of age suggested that a sound theory of mind in the earlier years is the foundation for positive peer behaviours that contribute to peer popularity.

Other studies indicate that 3- to 8-year-old children who perform well on theory of mind tests are also particularly good at keeping secrets, at distinguishing right from wrong in complicated social situations, and at deceiving and lying convincingly [11]. This last point highlights that mentalizing enables children to take part successfully in a wide range of social interactions, including potentially negative ones. For example, a recent study demonstrated that 3-year-olds who received training to facilitate their ability to predict others' mental states simultaneously improved their ability to deceive an experimenter in a guessing game [12]. These findings point out that acquiring a theory of mind does not necessarily make for a well-adjusted child; indeed, some research suggests that playground bullies, who are often somewhat popular as well as being feared for their manipulative and aggressive interpersonal tactics, possess good or even superior mentalizing skills [13]. Acquiring a theory of mind helps children to understand and navigate their social world, but how individual children choose to use their theory of mind – either prosocially or antisocially – is not yet well understood and is therefore an important direction for future research.

## Individual Differences in Social Cognition – Where Do They Come From?

Although it is in our nature to look past external behaviour and into each other's minds, analyses of genetic versus environmental influences on social-cognitive development suggest that nurture is more important in determining individual differences among children. In the largest such study to date, researchers compared mentalizing abilities of 1116 monozygotic and dizygotic 5-year-old British twin pairs. These analyses revealed that the majority of individual variation in the children's mentalizing (based on the kinds of tests listed in Table 9.1) was attributed to environmental influences rather than to genes [14]. Thus it appears that children's theory of mind is shaped primarily by their personal experiences.

One environmental variable that is crucial for theory of mind development is access to language and conversation about people's feelings, desires and thoughts. Mentalizing is consistently correlated with language ability, and there is also a specific link between children's ability to pass tasks such as those described in Table 9.1 and their comprehension and production of mentalistic vocabulary. The importance of language to mentalizing is perhaps most evident in the deaf; those deaf children who do not have access to fluent signing partners for daily conversation show social-cognitive delays similar to those observed in children with autism [15,16]. By contrast, deaf children who have regular access to signed conversation are comparable to typical hearing children in their social-cognitive development [16].

The role of language in social-cognitive development is further demonstrated by the fact that children's theory of mind is consistently associated with their participation in meaningful conversations about emotions, desires and thoughts with parents, siblings and friends [17]. The influence of parents' mentalistic conversation is especially well documented; in a nutshell, the more parents discuss and explain what they and others feel, want and think, the better their children understand those concepts. This principle has been documented in many conversational contexts from everyday disciplinary encounters ('It was really unkind of you to take her dolly; just imagine how it made her feel') to mutual reminiscences ('Remember when the bird stole the baby's fruit bun right out of her hand? She was so surprised and angry!') to book-reading ('Look at that boy's face in the picture; why does he feel so sad?'). It is important to note that the link between children's theory of mind and parents' mentalistic conversation extends to children with autism [18] and deafness [19]. While not yet translated into formal interventions, training studies have shown that exposure to mentalistic conversation boosts social-cognitive skill in typically developing children [20]. Therefore, parents should be encouraged to take the time to discuss feelings and thoughts with their young children. Not only will it make for engaging conversation, but, in conjunction with encouragement to behave prosocially, it may also benefit their children's social lives.

# References

1 Warneken F, Tomasello M (2007) Helping and cooperation at 14 months of age. Infancy, 11, 271–294.

2 Liszkowski U, Carpenter M, Striano T, Tomasello M (2006) Twelve- and 18-month-olds point to provide information for others. Journal of Cognition and Development, 7, 173–187.

3 Moll H, Tomasello M (2007) How 14- and 18- month-olds know what others have experienced. Developmental Psychology, 43, 309–317.

4 Southgate V, Senju A, Csibra, G (2007) Action anticipation through attribution of false belief in two-year-olds. Psychological Science, 18, 587–592.

5 Barrett HC, Broesch T, Scott RM et al. (2013) Early false-belief understanding in traditional non-Western societies. Proceedings of the Royal Society B-Biological Sciences, 280, 2012–2654.

6 Senju, A, Southgate, V, Miura et al. (2010) Absence of spontaneous action anticipation by false belief attribution in children with autism spectrum disorder. Development and Psychopathology, 22, 353–360.

7 Sodian B, Kristen-Antonow S (2015) Declarative joint attention as a foundation of theory of mind. Developmental Psychology, 51, 1190–1200.

8 Peterson C, Wellman H, Slaughter V (2012) The mind behind the message: Advancing theory of mind scales for typically developing children, and those with deafness, autism, or Asperger Syndrome. Child Development, 83, 469–485.

9 Caputi M, Lecce S, Pagnin A, Banerjee R (2012) Longitudinal effects of theory of mind on later peer relations: The role of prosocial behavior. Developmental Psychology, 48, 257–270.

10 Slaughter V, Imuta K, Peterson C, Henry J (2015) Meta-analysis of theory of mind and peer popularity in the preschool and early school years. Child Development, 86, 1159–1174.

11 Wellman HM (2014) Making Minds: How Theory of Mind Develops. New York: Oxford University Press.

12 Ding XP, Wellman HM, Wang Y et al. (2015) Theory of mind training causes honest young children to lie. Psychological Science, doi: 10.1177/0956797615604628.

13 Gasser L, Keller M (2009) Are the competent the morally good? Perspective taking and moral motivation of children involved in bullying. Social Development, 18, 798–816.

**14** Hughes C, Jaffee S, Happé F et al. (2005) Origins of individual differences in theory of mind: From nature to nurture? Child Development, 76, 356–370.

**15** Meristo M, Morgan G, Geraci A et al. (2012) Belief attribution in deaf and hearing infants. Developmental Science, 15, 633–640.

**16** Wellman HM, Peterson CC (2013) Theory of mind, development, and deafness. In Baron-Cohen S, Tager-Flusberg H, Lombardo MV (eds) Understanding other Minds: Perspectives from Developmental Social Neuroscience. Oxford: Oxford University Press, pp. 51–71.

**17** Hughes C (2011) Social Understanding and Social Lives: From Toddlerhood Through to the Transition to School. Hove, East Sussex: Psychology Press.

**18** Slaughter V, Peterson C, Mackintosh E (2007) Mind what mother says: Narrative input and theory of mind in typical children and those on the autism spectrum. Child Development, 78, 839–858.

**19** Moeller M, Schjick B (2006) Relations between maternal input and ToM understanding in deaf children. Child Development, 77, 751–766.

**20** Ornaghi V, Brockmeier J, Grazzani Gavazzi I (2011) The role of language games in children's understanding of mental states: A training study. Journal of Cognition and Development, 12, 239–259.

# 10

# Social and Emotional Development in Middle Childhood

*Alan Carr*

## Introduction

Social and emotional development (SED) involves the acquisition of skills for expressing emotions, regulating emotions and managing social relationships within the family, school and peer group [1,2]. Some of the milestones associated with these aspects of development are given in Table 10.1. Middle childhood, the period between 6 and 12 years, occupies a pivotal position between the preschool years and adolescence with respect to SED. During the preschool years, rudimentary skills are acquired, while in adolescence, sophisticated skills are refined. However, it is during middle childhood that particularly important developments occur within the emotional and social domains.

## The Preschool Years

During the first year of life there is a gradual increase in non-verbal emotional expression in response to all classes of stimuli, including those under the infant's control and those under the control of others. At birth, infants can express interest as indicated by sustained attention, and disgust in response to foul tastes and odours. Smiling, reflecting a sense of pleasure, in response to the human voice appears at 4 weeks. Sadness and anger in response to removing a teething toy are first evident at 4 months. Facial expressions reflecting fear following separation become apparent at 9 months. Infants also show an increasingly sophisticated capacity to discriminate positive and negative emotions expressed by others over the course of their first year of life. During the first year of life infants develop rudimentary self-soothing skills for regulating their emotions, such as rocking and feeding. They also develop skills for regulating their attention to allow themselves and their caretakers to coordinate their actions to soothe them in distressing situations. They rely on their caretakers to provide emotional support to help them manage stress. The capacity for turn-taking in games such as peek-a-boo develops once children have the appropriate cognitive skills for understanding object constancy. Social referencing also occurs towards the end of the first year when children learn the appropriate emotions to express in particular situations by attending to the emotional expressions of their caretakers.

During their second year, infants show increased verbal expression of emotional states, and increased expression of emotions involving self-consciousness and

*Child Psychology and Psychiatry: Frameworks for Clinical Training and Practice*, Third Edition.
Edited by David Skuse, Helen Bruce and Linda Dowdney.
© 2017 John Wiley & Sons, Ltd. Published 2017 by John Wiley & Sons, Ltd.

**Table 10.1** Social and emotional development

| Age | Expression of emotions | Regulation of emotions | Managing emotions in relationships |
|---|---|---|---|
| **Infancy (0–1 years)** | • Increased non-verbal emotional expression in response to stimuli under own control and control of others | • Self-soothing<br>• Regulation of attention to allow coordinated action<br>• Reliance on 'scaffolding' from caregivers during stress | • Increased discrimination of emotions expressed by others<br>• Turn taking (peek-a-boo)<br>• Social referencing |
| **Toddlerhood (1–2 years)** | • Increased verbal expression of emotional states<br>• Increased expression of emotions involving self-consciousness and self-evaluation such as shame, pride or coyness | • Increased awareness of own emotional responses<br>• Irritability when parents place limits on expression of need for autonomy | • Anticipation of feelings towards others<br>• Rudimentary empathy<br>• Altruistic behaviour |
| **Preschool (2–5 years)** | • Increased pretending to express emotions in play and teasing | • Language (self-talk and communication with others) used for regulating emotions | • Increased insight into others' emotions<br>• Awareness that false expression of emotions can mislead others about one's emotional state |
| **Middle childhood (6–12 years)** | • Increased use of emotional expression to regulate relationships<br>• Distinction made between genuine emotional expression with close friends and managed display with others | • Increased autonomy from caregivers in regulating emotions<br>• Increased efficiency in identifying and using multiple strategies for autonomously regulating emotions and managing stress<br>• Regulation of self-conscious emotions, e.g. embarrassment<br>• Distancing strategies used to manage emotions if child has little control over situation | • Increased understanding of emotional scripts and social roles in these scripts<br>• Increased use of social skills to deal with emotions of self and others<br>• Awareness of feeling multiple emotions about the same person<br>• Use of information about emotions of self and others in multiple contexts as aids to making and maintaining friendships |
| **Adolescence (13+ years)** | • Self-presentation strategies are used for impression management | • Increased awareness of emotional cycles (feeling guilty about feeling angry)<br>• Increased use of complex strategies to autonomously regulate emotions<br>• Self-regulation strategies are increasingly informed by moral principles | • Awareness of importance of mutual and reciprocal emotional self-disclosure in making and maintaining friendships |

self-evaluation, such as shame, pride or coyness. This occurs because their cognitive skills allow them to begin to think about themselves from the perspective of others. During the second year of life, toddlers show increased awareness of their own emotional responses. They show irritability – often referred to as the 'terrible twos' – when parents place limits on the expression of their needs for autonomy and exploration. In relationships they can increasingly anticipate feelings they will have towards others in particular situations. They also show rudimentary empathy and altruistic behaviour.

Between the ages of 2 and 5 years children increasingly pretend to express emotions in play and when teasing or being teased by other children. They use language in the form of both internal speech and conversations with others to modulate their affective experience. There is increased insight into the emotions being experienced by others and an increased awareness that we can mislead others about what we are feeling by falsely expressing emotions. More sophisticated empathic and altruistic behaviour also begins to develop within the family and peer group during the preschool years.

## Middle Childhood

During middle childhood (6–12 years), with the transition to primary school and increased participation in peer group activities, children's SED undergoes a profound change. Rather than regularly looking to parents or caregivers to help them manage their feelings and relationships, school-aged children prefer to autonomously regulate their emotional states and depend more on their own resources in dealing with their peers. As they develop through the middle childhood years, they show increased efficiency in identifying and using multiple strategies for autonomously regulating their emotions and managing stress. During this process they learn to regulate self-conscious emotions such as embarrassment and to use distancing and distraction strategies to manage intense feelings when they have little control over emotionally challenging situations. There is increased use of emotional expression to regulate closeness and distance within peer relationships. Within this context, children make clear distinctions between genuine emotional expression with close friends and managed emotional displays with others.

During middle childhood, children develop an understanding of consensually agreed emotional scripts and their roles in such scripts. There is also an increased use of social skills to deal with their own emotions and those of others. Children become aware that they can feel multiple conflicting emotions about the same person – for example, that they can be angry with someone they like. They use information and memories about their own emotions and those of others in multiple contexts as aids to making and maintaining friendships. As adolescence approaches they develop an increasingly sophisticated understanding of the place of emotional scripts and social roles in making and maintaining friendships.

Cooperative play premised on an empathic understanding of other children's viewpoints becomes fully established in middle childhood. Competitive rivalry (often involving physical or verbal aggression or joking) is an important part of peer interactions, particularly among boys. This allows youngsters to establish their position of dominance within the peer group hierarchy. Peer friendships in middle childhood are important because they constitute a source of social support and a context within which to learn about the management of networks of relationships. Children who are unable to make and maintain friendships, particularly during middle childhood, are at risk for the development of psychological difficulties.

## Adolescence

During adolescence, from 13 to 20 years, there is an increased awareness of complex emotional cycles, e.g. feeling guilty about feeling angry or feeling ashamed for feeling frightened. In adolescence, youngsters increasingly use complex strategies, such as reframing, to autonomously regulate emotions. These self-regulation strategies are increasingly informed by moral principles. However, alongside this concern with morality, self-presentation strategies are increasingly used for impression management. Adolescents gradually become aware of the importance of mutual and reciprocal emotional self-disclosure in making and maintaining friendships.

## Factors Contributing to SED

Available research indicates that SED in middle childhood is influenced by complex interactions among multiple personal and contextual factors. Personal factors include genetic endowment [3], pre- and perinatal factors [4], temperament [5], cognitive abilities [6], illness and disability [7] self-esteem [8], social cognition [9] and moral development [10]. Contextual factors include attachment [11], parenting style and child maltreatment [12], family structure and functioning [13], parental mental and physical health [14], school environment [15], peer group relationships [16], and the wider social, cultural and spiritual or religious environment [17–19]. From a clinical perspective, in any given case, we may expect more successful SED where there are more positive than negative personal and contextual factors. In contrast, where there are more negative than positive personal and contextual factors, problems with SED may occur.

## Positive SED

With regard to personal factors, young people are more likely to develop the skills for emotional expression and regulation and for making and maintaining relationships if they have favourable genetic endowments, a lack of pre- and perinatal adversity, easy temperaments, adequate cognitive abilities to understand their feelings and the emotional demands of their important relationships, good health, adequate self-esteem, the capacity to understand social situations accurately and a well-developed conscience. With regard to contextual factors, positive SED is more likely where children have developed secure attachments; where their parents have adopted an authoritative parenting style characterized by warmth and a moderate level of control; where their parents have no major mental or physical health problems; and where the family, school, peer group and wider social environments have been supportive. For example, in a UK study Bowes *et al.* [20] found that children from supportive families showed resilience when bullied in primary school.

## Problematic SED

Problematic SED may occur where there are difficulties with genetic endowment, the pre- and perinatal environment, temperament, cognitive abilities, health, self-esteem, social cognition and moral development. Problematic SED is associated with pre- and perinatal adversity and unfavourable genetic endowments indexed by family histories of psychopathology. A childhood history of difficult temperament is also associated with problematic emotional development. With regard to cognitive abilities, children with intellectual disabilities tend to acquire skills for expressing and regulating emotions and managing relationships at a slower rate than children without such disabilities. Disproportionately more children with intellectual disabilities than without show challenging behaviour associated with emotional regulation problems. Children with low self-esteem, who evaluate themselves negatively, have difficulty regulating negative mood states and managing relationships. Children who have problematic social cognition, notably those who have developed a hostile attributional bias where they inaccurately attribute negative intentions to others, have difficulties regulating anger and maintaining positive peer group relationships. Children who have not internalized social rules and norms and developed a conscience, particularly those with callous unemotional traits, have difficulties empathizing with others and making and maintaining social relationships. The foregoing are some of the ways in which personal vulnerabilities can compromise SED in middle childhood.

Social and emotional development during this period may also be compromised by environmental adversity characterized by difficulties with attachment, parenting style, parental health, family structure and functioning, the school environment, peer group relationships, and the wider social and cultural environment. Problematic SED is more common where children have developed insecure attachments to their parents or caregivers. Non-optimal family environments can also impair SED. Such family environments may be characterized by parenting problems, child abuse or neglect; parental mental or physical health problems or criminality; and interparental conflict or domestic violence. Where there is poor match between children's educational needs and educational placement, this can have an adverse effect on their SED. For example, problems with SED may be exacerbated where a child with a specific learning disability, intellectual disability or psychological disorder is placed in a mainstream class without adequate special educational resources. Schools with inadequate policies and procedures for managing bullying and victimization of pupils by peers or teachers can also have a negative effect on SED. Problematic SED may be exacerbated where children are rejected by their peers or where they spend a significant amount of time with antisocial peers. Within the wider social and cultural environment, a range of factors can have a detrimental impact on SED. These include a high level of extrafamilial stress and a low level of extrafamilial perceived social support and exposure to media (TV, films, computer games) that model and reinforce the inappropriate expression of aggression, anxiety, depression, elation and other emotions.

## Consequences of SED Problems in Middle Childhood

Emotional dysregulation is a risk factor for psychopathology [21], and many types of psychopathology and behaviour problems are associated with problematic SED. Anxiety and mood disorders and internalizing behaviour problems are associated with difficulties regulating fear and sadness. Disruptive behaviour disorders and externalizing behaviour problems are associated with difficulties regulating anger and aggression. Attention deficit hyperactivity disorder is associated with problematic impulse control. All of these types of disorders and behaviour problems are associated with problems in making and maintaining relationships, as are other conditions such as autism spectrum disorders and psychoses. There is significant continuity in social emotional development from middle childhood to adolescence. Those who are well adjusted in middle childhood tend to become well-adjusted adolescents [2], while problems tend to persist into the teenage years in children who showed social and emotional difficulties in primary school [22].

## Addressing SED Problems

Prevention and treatment programmes have been developed to address SED problems. Successful prevention programmes begin during the preschool years. They involve screening at-risk children on the basis of their status of personal and contextual risk factors, and offering complex interventions such as family support, parent training and child stimulation that target multiple risk factors [23,24]. With regard to treating children with SED problems, it is best to base interventions in any particular case on a formulation of factors relevant to that specific case and the current evidence base for effective interventions for such difficulties, because problems with SED are typically caused and maintained by the complex interaction of multiple personal and contextual factors [25].

## References

1 Lamb M, Lerner R (eds) (2015) Handbook of Child Psychology and Developmental Science, Vol. 3: Socioemotional Processes, 7th edn. Hoboken, NJ: Wiley.
2 Saarni C, Campos J, Cameras L et al. (2008) Emotional development: action communication understanding. In: Eisenberg N (ed.) Handbook of Child Psychology. Volume 3. Social, Emotional and Personality Development, 6th edn. New York: Wiley, pp. 226–300.
3 State M, Thapar A (2015) Genetics. In: Thapar A, Pine D, Leckman J et al. (eds) Rutter's Child and Adolescent Psychiatry, 6th edn. Chichester: Wiley-Blackwell, pp. 303–329.
4 Coall D, Callan A, Dickins T et al. (2015) Evolution and prenatal development: An evolutionary perspective In: Lamb M, Lerner R (eds) Handbook of Child Psychology and Developmental Science, Vol. 3: Socioemotional Processes, 7th edn. Hoboken, NJ: Wiley, pp. 57–105.
5 Chen X, Schmidt L (2015) Temperament and personality. In: Lamb M, Lerner R (eds) Handbook of Child Psychology and Developmental Science, Vol. 3: Socioemotional Processes, 7th edn. Hoboken, NJ: Wiley, pp. 152–200.
6 Burack J, Hodapp R, Iarocci G et al. (2012) Oxford Handbook in Intellectual Disability and Development. Oxford: Oxford University Press.

7  Crnic K, Neece C (2015) Socioemotional consequences of illness and disability. In: Lamb M, Lerner R (eds) Handbook of Child Psychology and Developmental Science, Vol. 3: Socioemotional Processes, 7th edn. Hoboken, NJ: Wiley, pp. 287–323.

8  Beale Spencer M, Phillips Swanson D, Harpalani V (2015) Development of the self. In: Lamb M, Lerner R (eds) Handbook of Child Psychology and Developmental Science, Vol. 3: Socioemotional Processes, 7th edn. Hoboken, NJ: Wiley, pp. 750–793.

9  Sharp C, Fonagy P, Goodyer I (2008) Social Cognition and Developmental Psychopathology. Oxford University Press: Oxford.

10  Killen M, Smetana J (2015) Origins and development of morality. In: Lamb M, Lerner R (eds) Handbook of Child Psychology and Developmental Science, Vol. 3: Socioemotional Processes, 7th edn. Hoboken, NJ: Wiley, pp. 701–749.

11  Music G (2011) Nurturing Natures: Attachment and Children's Emotional, Sociocultural and Brain Development. Hove: Psychology Press.

12  Cicchetti D, Toth S (2015) Child maltreatment. In: Lamb M, Lerner R (eds) Handbook of Child Psychology and Developmental Science, Vol. 3: Socioemotional Processes, 7th edn. Hoboken, NJ: Wiley, pp. 4513–4563.

13  Golombok S, Tasker F (2015) Socioemotional development in changing families. In: Lamb M, Lerner R (eds) Handbook of Child Psychology and Developmental Science, Vol. 3: Socioemotional Processes, 7th edn. Hoboken, NJ: Wiley, pp. 419–463.

14  Stein A, Harold G (2015) Impact of parental psychiatric disorder and physical illness. In: Thapar A, Pine D, Leckman J et al. (eds) Rutter's Child and Adolescent Psychiatry, 6th edn. Chichester: Wiley-Blackwell, pp. 352–363.

15  Wigfield A, Eccles J, Fredricks J et al. (2015) Development of achievement motivation and engagement. In: Lamb M, Lerner R (eds) Handbook of Child Psychology and Developmental Science, Vol. 3: Socioemotional Processes, 7th edn. Hoboken, NJ: Wiley, pp. 657–700.

16  Furman W, Tose A (2015) Friendships, romantic relationships, peer relationships. In: Lamb M, Lerner R (eds) Handbook of Child Psychology and Developmental Science, Vol. 3: Socioemotional Processes, 7th edn. Hoboken, NJ: Wiley, pp. 932–974.

17  Jenkins J, Madigan S, Arseneault L (2015) Psychosocial adversity. In: Thapar A, Pine D, Leckman J et al. (eds) Rutter's Child and Adolescent Psychiatry, 6th edn. Chichester: Wiley-Blackwell, pp. 330–340.

18  Luthar S, Crossman E, Small P (2015) resilience and adversity. In: Lamb M, Lerner R (eds) Handbook of Child Psychology and Developmental Science, Vol. 3: Socioemotional Processes, 7th edn. Hoboken, NJ: Wiley, pp. 247–286.

19  Ebstyne P, Boyatzis C (2015) Religious and spiritual development. In: Lamb M, Lerner R (eds) Handbook of Child Psychology and Developmental Science, Vol. 3: Socioemotional Processes, 7th edn. Hoboken, NJ: Wiley, pp. 975–1022.

20  Bowes L, Maughan B, Caspi A et al. (2010) Families promote emotional and behavioural resilience to bullying: Evidence of an environmental effect. Journal of Child Psychology and Psychiatry, 51, 809–817.

21  Keenan K (2006) Emotion dysregulation as a risk factor for child psychopathology. Clinical Psychology: Science and Practice, 7, 418–434.

22  Sterba S, Copeland W, Egger H et al. (2010) Longitudinal dimensionality of adolescent psychopathology: testing the differentiation hypothesis. Journal of Child Psychology and Psychiatry, 51, 871–884.

23 Manning M, Homel R, Smith C (2010) A meta-analysis of the effects of early developmental prevention programs in at-risk populations on non-health outcomes in adolescence. Children and Youth Services Review, 32, 506–519.

24 Sandler I, Wolchik S, Cruden G et al. (2014) Overview of meta-analyses of the prevention of mental health, substance use, and conduct problems. Annual Review of Clinical Psychology, 10, 243–273.

25 Carr A (2009) What Works with Children Adolescents and Adults. A Review of Research on the Effectiveness of Psychotherapy. London: Routledge.

# 11

# Social-Cognitive Development During Adolescence

*Sarah-Jayne Blakemore*

## Humans Are Exquisitely Social

Humans are an exquisitely social species. We are constantly reading each others' actions, gestures and faces in terms of underlying mental states and emotions, in an attempt to figure out what other people are thinking and feeling, and what they are about to do next. This is known as theory of mind, or mentalizing. Developmental psychology research on theory of mind has demonstrated that the ability to understand others' mental states develops over the first 4 or 5 years of life. While certain aspects of theory of mind are present in infancy [1], it is not until around the age of 4 years that children begin explicitly to understand that someone else can hold a belief that differs from one's own, and which can be false [2]. An understanding of others' mental states plays a critical role in social interaction because it enables us to work out what other people want and what they are about to do next, and to modify our own behaviour accordingly.

## The Social Brain

Over the past 20 years, a large number of independent studies have shown remarkable consistency in identifying the brain regions that are involved in theory of mind, or mentalizing. These studies have employed a wide range of stimuli, including stories, sentences, words, cartoons and animations, each designed to elicit the attribution of mental states (for a review, see Amodio & Frith [3]). In each case, the mentalizing task resulted in the activation of a network of regions including the posterior superior temporal sulcus (pSTS), the temporo-parietal junction (TPJ), the temporal poles and the dorsal medial prefrontal cortex (mPFC; see Burnett & Blakemore [4]). The agreement between neuroimaging studies in this area is remarkable and the consistent localization of activity within a network of regions, including the pSTS/TPJ and mPFC, as well as the temporal poles, suggests that these regions are key to the process of mentalizing.

## Development of Mentalizing During Adolescence

There is a rich literature on the development of social cognition in infancy and childhood, pointing to stepwise changes in social cognitive abilities during the first 5 years of life. However, there has been surprisingly little empirical research on social cognitive

*Child Psychology and Psychiatry: Frameworks for Clinical Training and Practice,* Third Edition.
Edited by David Skuse, Helen Bruce and Linda Dowdney.
© 2017 John Wiley & Sons, Ltd. Published 2017 by John Wiley & Sons, Ltd.

development beyond childhood. Only recently have studies focused on development of the social brain beyond early childhood, and these support evidence from social psychology that adolescence represents a period of significant social development. Most researchers in the field use the onset of puberty as the starting point for adolescence. The end of adolescence is harder to define and there are significant cultural variations. However, the end of the teenage years represents a working consensus in western countries. Adolescence is characterized by psychological changes in terms of identity, self-consciousness and relationships with others. Compared with children, adolescents are more sociable, form more complex and hierarchical peer relationships and are more sensitive to acceptance and rejection by peers [5]. Although the underlying factors of these social changes are most likely to be multifaceted, one possible cause is development of the social brain.

Recently, a number of functional magnetic resonance imaging (fMRI) studies have investigated the development during adolescence of the functional brain correlates of mentalizing. These studies have used a wide variety of mentalizing tasks – involving the spontaneous attribution of mental states to animated shapes, reflecting on one's intentions to carry out certain actions, thinking about the preferences and dispositions of oneself or a fictitious story character, and judging the sincerity or sarcasm of another person's communicative intentions. Despite the variety of mentalizing tasks used, these studies of mental state attribution have consistently shown that mPFC activity during mentalizing tasks *decreases* between adolescence and adulthood (Figure 11.1). Each of these studies compared brain activity in young adolescents and adults while they were performing a task that involved thinking about mental states (see Figure 11.1 for details of studies). In each of these studies, mPFC activity was greater in the adolescent group than in the adult group during the mentalizing task compared with the control task. In

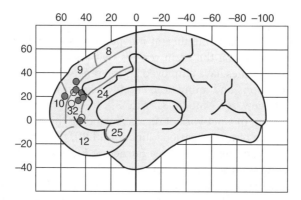

**Figure 11.1** A section of the dorsal medial prefrontal cortex (mPFC) that is activated in studies of mentalizing: Montreal Neurological Institute (MNI) *y*-coordinates range from 30 to 60, and *z*-coordinates range from 0 to 40. Dots indicate voxels of decreased activity during six mentalizing tasks between late childhood and adulthood (see Blakemore [10] for references). The mentalizing tasks ranged from understanding irony, which requires separating the literal from the intended meaning of a comment, thinking about one's own intentions, thinking about whether character traits describe oneself or another familiar other, watching animations in which characters appear to have intentions and emotions, and thinking about social emotions such as guilt and embarrassment. *Source:* Adapted from Burnett *et al.* [6] and Blakemore [7].

addition, there is evidence for differential functional connectivity between mPFC and other parts of the mentalizing network across age [6].

To summarize, a number of developmental neuroimaging studies of social cognition have been carried out by different laboratories around the world, and there is striking consistency with respect to the direction of change in mPFC activity. It is not yet understood why mPFC activity decreases between adolescence and adulthood during mentalizing tasks, but two non-mutually exclusive explanations have been put forward (see Blakemore [7] for details). One possibility is that the cognitive strategy for mentalizing changes between adolescence and adulthood. A second possibility is that the functional change with age is due to neuroanatomical changes that occur during this period.

Areas within the mentalizing network continue to develop in grey matter volume, cortical thickness and surface area across adolescence before relatively stabilizing in the early 20s [8]. In a study using a large sample of individuals with at least two brain scans between the ages of 7 and 30 years, we examined the structural developmental trajectories of the mentalizing brain network. Grey matter volume and cortical thickness in medial Brodmann area 10 (a proxy for dorsal mPFC), TPJ and pSTS decreased from childhood into the early 20s, whereas the anterior temporal cortex increased in grey matter volume until adolescence and in cortical thickness until early adulthood. The surface area for each region followed a cubic trajectory, reaching a peak in late childhood or early adolescence before decreasing into the early 20s [8]. This protracted development demonstrates that areas of the brain involved in deciphering the mental states of others are still maturing in terms of grey matter volume from late childhood into early adulthood.

Decreases in activity are frequently interpreted as being due to developmental reductions in grey matter volume, presumably related to synaptic pruning. However, there is currently no direct way to test the relationship between number of synapses, synaptic activity and neural activity as measured by fMRI in humans (for a discussion, see Blakemore [7]). If the neural substrates for social cognition change during adolescence, what are the consequences for social cognitive behaviour?

## Online Mentalizing Usage is Still Developing in Mid-Adolescence

Most developmental studies of social cognition focus on early childhood, possibly because children perform adequately in even quite complex mentalizing tasks at around 4 years of age. This can be attributed to a lack of suitable paradigms: generally, in order to create a mentalizing task that does not elicit ceiling performance in children aged 5 years and older, the linguistic and executive demands of the task must be increased. This renders any age-associated improvement in performance difficult to attribute solely to improved mentalizing ability. However, the protracted structural and functional development in adolescence and early adulthood of the brain regions involved in theory of mind might be expected to affect mental state understanding. In addition, evidence from social psychology studies shows substantial changes in social competence and social behaviour during adolescence, and this is hypothesized to rely on a more sophisticated manner of thinking about and relating to other people – including understanding their mental states.

Recently, we adapted a task that requires the online use of theory of mind information when making decisions in a communication game, and that produces large numbers of errors even in adults [9]. In our computerized version of the task, participants view a set of shelves containing objects, which they are instructed to move by a 'director', who can see some but not all of the objects [10] (Figure 11.2). Correct interpretation of critical instructions requires participants to use the director's perspective and only move objects that the director can see (the director condition). We tested participants aged between 7 and 27 years and found that, while performance in the director and a control condition followed the same trajectory (improved accuracy) from mid-childhood until mid-adolescence, the mid-adolescent group made more errors than the adults in the director condition only. These results suggest that the ability to take another person's perspective to direct appropriate behaviour is still undergoing development at this relatively late stage.

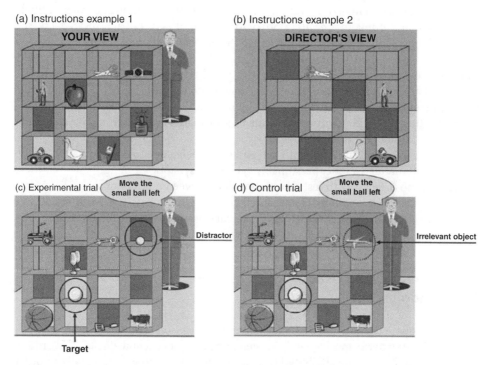

**Figure 11.2** (a, b) Images used to explain the 'director' condition: participants were shown an example of their view (a) and the corresponding director's view (b) for a typical stimulus with four objects in occluded slots that the director cannot see (e.g. the apple). (c, d) Examples of an experimental (c) and a control trial (d) in the 'director' condition. The participant hears the verbal instruction, 'Move the small ball left', from the director. In the experimental trial (c), if the participant ignored the director's perspective, she would choose to move the distractor ball (golf ball), which is the smallest ball in the shelves but which cannot be seen by the director, instead of the larger ball (tennis ball) shared by both the participant's and the instructor's perspective (target). In the control trial (d), an irrelevant object (plane) replaces the distractor item. *Source:* Adapted from Dumontheil *et al.* [10]. Reproduced with permission of John Wiley & Sons.

Many questions remain to be investigated in this new and rapidly expanding field. The study of neural development during adolescence is likely to have important implications for society in relation to education and the legal treatment of teenagers, as well as a variety of mental illnesses that often have their onset in adolescence

---

**Box 11.1 Key points**

---

- The social brain is involved in understanding others' minds.
- The social brain develops structurally and functionally in adolescence.
- Activity in medial prefrontal cortex decreases between adolescence and adulthood during social cognition tasks.
- Performance on an online theory of mind usage task improves during adolescence.

---

## References

1 Baillargeon R, Rose M, Scott RM, Hea Z (2010) False-belief understanding in infants. Trends in Cognitive Science, 14, 110–118.

2 Barresi J, Moore C (1996) Intentional relations and social understanding. Behavioral and Brain Sciences, 19, 107–154.

3 Amodio DM and Frith CD (2006) Meeting of minds: the medial frontal cortex and social cognition. Nature Reviews Neuroscience, 7, 268–277.

4 Burnett S, Blakemore SJ (2009) Functional connectivity during a social emotion task in adolescents and in adults. European Journal Neuroscience, 29, 1294–1301.

5 Steinberg L, Morris AS (2001) Adolescent development. Annual Review in Psychology, 52, 83–110.

6 Burnett S, Bird G, Moll J et al. (2009) Development during adolescence of the neural processing of social emotion. Journal of Cognitive Neuroscience, 21, 1736–1750.

7 Blakemore SJ (2008) The social brain in adolescence. Nature Reviews Neuroscience, 9, 267–277.

8 Mills KL, Lalonde F, Clasen LS, Giedd JN, Blakemore S-J (2014) Developmental changes in the structure of the social brain in late childhood and adolescence. Social Cognitive and Affective Neuroscience, 9, 123–131.

9 Keysar B, Lin S, Barr DJ (2003) Limits on theory of mind use in adults. Cognition, 89, 25–41.

10 Dumontheil I, Apperly IA, Blakemore S-J (2010) Online usage of theory of mind continues to develop in late adolescence. Developmental Science, 13, 331–338.

Section 2

Promoting Well-being

# 12

# Attachment in the Early Years: Theory, Research and Clinical Implications

*Pasco Fearon*

## What is Attachment?

Attachment broadly speaking refers to the tendency of infants and young children to rely on parent or carer figures for comfort and support when frightened, stressed or ill. It is thought to be a form of bio-behavioural adaptation, shaped by the forces of natural selection to maximize infants' and young children's chances of survival [1].

It is important to distinguish between attachment *behaviour* and an attachment *bond*. Attachment behaviours are defined on the basis of their function. They are any organized, systematic behaviour triggered by the appearance of a potential threat or stressor that predictably serves to achieve proximity to a selected caregiver [1]. Their general purpose is to achieve comfort and security – a purpose that can be achieved by all manner of behaviours, even if idiosyncratic to a particular child.

Attachment behaviours generally divide into three classes: signalling or distal communication (e.g. calling, crying); proximity-seeking (e.g. crawling, walking, reaching); and contact maintenance (e.g. clinging). Less frequently, monitoring the whereabouts and availability of an attachment figure is described as attachment behaviour. Attachment is characterized by *heterotypic continuity*, i.e. its basic functional organization shows continuity over time, while the child behaviours used to achieve comfort or security change radically in complexity and sophistication as children mature.

Attachment behaviour performs a kind of homeostatic function (see Figure 12.1). Its efficient operation requires environmental information – e.g. the nature and location of the threat, the caregiver's whereabouts, and contextual information regarding the potential efficiency of various forms of action, etc. Within attachment relationships, children develop internal working models of attachment that guide their thinking, feeling and behaviour in attachment situations. In the future, this will shape how they approach – and see themselves within – close relationships.

An attachment bond refers to the longer-term, stable tendency to seek out a selected parent figure when stressed. Processes leading to the establishment of long-term attachment bonds differ from those triggering attachment behaviour. Crucially, certain forms of attachment disturbance probably result from disruptions in the formation of attachment bonds (e.g. reactive attachment disorder or disinhibited social engagement disorder). Others result from experiences or influences altering how attachment behaviour is organized and triggered (e.g. disorganized attachment).

*Child Psychology and Psychiatry: Frameworks for Clinical Training and Practice,* Third Edition.
Edited by David Skuse, Helen Bruce and Linda Dowdney.
© 2017 John Wiley & Sons, Ltd. Published 2017 by John Wiley & Sons, Ltd.

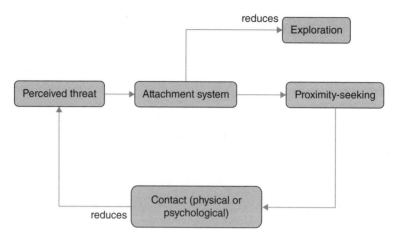

**Figure 12.1** Schematic diagram of the homeostatic function of attachment.

## Attachment Variations and Their Measurement

Mary Ainsworth's experimental *Strange Situation Procedure* is the most commonly used tool for studying attachment behaviour in infants aged 11–18 months [2]. It involves an encounter with a stranger and two, up to 3-minute, separations from a parent in an unfamiliar setting. Infant responses to these events are coded on four dimensions of behaviour, each of which are rated on a seven-point scale. Infant responses are divided into four broad categorical classifications – 'secure' (type B) and three types of 'insecure' attachment: type A (avoidant), type C (resistant) and type D (disorganized) (see Table 12.1). Research consistently indicates that the majority of infants in low-risk circumstances (approximately 65%) are described as 'secure'; approximately 15% are described as avoidant, 10% as resistant and 15% as disorganized. Clinically, the latter is of great interest as it appears most closely related to more severe forms of adverse parental care, and to a raised risk of psychopathology [3]. The prevalence of the different insecure subtypes varies considerably across cultures [4]. A host of similar measures have been developed for assessing attachment in older children [5].

## Causes of Variation in Attachment

An impressive database of longitudinal studies supports Ainsworth's original proposition that parental sensitivity and responsivity to the child's attachment signals (see Table 12.2) are critical determinants of attachment security [2,6]. Furthermore, randomized controlled trials of clinical interventions designed to improve sensitive parenting show an increase in the likelihood of secure attachment [7]. However, the effect sizes in correlational studies or clinical trials are not large and other factors – either different aspects of parenting or different causal influences – probably play a role. While sensitive care may be the most important proximal determinant of attachment security, many more distal or contextual factors are also consistently associated with

**Table 12.1** Attachment behaviour rating scales and classifications for the strange situation [2]

| Scale | Description |
|---|---|
| *Interactive behaviour scales* | |
| Proximity-seeking | The intensity and persistence to make contact on reunion with the caregiver. An infant scoring high on this scale makes a purposeful approach to the caregiver and takes initiative to make contact. |
| Contact-maintenance | The persistence in maintaining contact with the caregiver once it is achieved. A high score on this scale is given when an infant displays resistance to being put down (e.g. clinging), persistent efforts to remain close to the caregiver, or any sign the infant is not ready to terminate contact (e.g. a sinking embrace to mother). |
| Resistance | The intensity and duration of angry behaviour and resistance of contact directed towards the caregiver. Examples include pushing away, batting away, arching back, squirming to get down. |
| Avoidance | The intensity, duration and promptness of attempts to avoid contact/interaction with the caregiver. Examples of avoidance are averting gaze, moving away and ignoring the caregiver. |
| Disorganized/disoriented | Anomalous behaviour, e.g. sequential or simultaneous displays of contradictory behaviour; undirected, misdirected or incomplete behaviours; stereotypies, freezing, disorientation; fearful responses in presence of the caregiver. |
| *Infant attachment classification profiles* | |
| Secure | Secure infants use the caregiver as a secure base for exploration and as a source of comfort when needed. The infant is visibly aware of the caregiver's absence at separation. At reunion, the infant greets the caregiver with an approach, smile, gesture or vocalization and seeks contact with the caregiver if distressed. Contact is comforting and the infant is able to return to play. |
| Insecure-avoidant | An avoidant infant appears to be more interested in the environment than the caregiver throughout the procedure. During separation from the caregiver the infant is typically not upset. Upon reunion, the infant will ignore or actively avoid contact. |
| Insecure-ambivalent | An ambivalent infant prefers to maintain contact with the caregiver rather than explore the environment or exploration is limited. During separation the infant will be distressed. At reunion the infant displays angry behaviours towards the caregiver and/or is inconsolable. Contact with the mother is not effective in regulating the infant's state or supporting a return to play. |
| Insecure-disorganized | The infant's behaviour lacks an organized, coherent strategy in relation to the caregiver. See above for behavioural descriptions. |
| *Related disorders* | |
| Reactive attachment disorder | Consistently highly inhibited, emotionally withdrawn, rarely seeks or responds to comfort, minimal responsiveness to others, very little positive affect, occasional unexplained bouts of anger, fearfulness or distress even in seemingly unthreatening circumstances. Has experienced extremely insufficient care in early life. |
| Disinhibited social engagement disorder | Lack of fearfulness or appropriate reticence with strangers, overly familiar, especially physically, with strangers or unfamiliar adults, limited or no checking back with caregivers in unfamiliar situations, willingness of go off with strangers with little or no hesitation. Has experienced extremely insufficient care in early life. |

**Table 12.2** Scales of parenting sensitivity and frightened/frightening behaviour

| Scale | Description |
|---|---|
| *Maternal sensitivity scales* [2] | |
| Sensitivity vs insensitivity | The degree to which the infant cues are perceived, responded to promptly and appropriately. A sensitive parent is able to empathize with the infant's experience, promoting accurate interpretation of the infant's cues, resulting in appropriate and flexible responding. |
| Co-operation vs interference | The degree to which participation in the infant's ongoing experience is gentle, co-determined and supportive, rather than harsh, overwhelming, directive or controlling. |
| Availability vs neglecting | The degree to which the parent is physically and psychologically available to his/her infant. An available parent is perceptually alert and responsive to the infant even in the face of distraction or his/her own thoughts and feelings. |
| Acceptance vs rejection | The degree to which the parent is able to integrate the joys and stresses of being a parent, as expressed in her behaviour towards the child. An accepting parent will not direct or attribute negative feelings towards her child or become irritable, enabling her to maintain a positive and accepting stance towards her infant. |
| *Anomalous parenting behaviours* [14,15] | |
| Frightened or frightening parental behaviours | Behaviours towards the infant which are threatening, dissociative (e.g. 'spacing out'), frightened, timid/deferential, spousal/romantic or disorganized. |
| Disrupted affective communication | Behaviours which when displayed, particularly during times of stress, can result in unmodulated fear/arousal in the infant (e.g. contradictory signalling to the infant about the caregiver's availability, failure to respond to infant cues; displays that the caregiver is frightened by the infant; hostile/intrusive behaviours; dissociative and withdrawing behaviour) |

security and insecurity, including parental depression, social support, marital quality and poverty [8]. Importantly, genetic factors play a quite limited role in the development of infants' and preschoolers' attachments [e.g. 9], but may be more important in adolescence [10].

Unlike other insecure attachment categories, disorganized attachment does not appear to be linked to observed caregiver sensitivity. A different set of parenting features has been implicated, representing behaviour that has been described as frightened/frightening or extremely insensitive [11] (see Table 12.2). These clinically significant findings support Main and Hesse's intriguing theory about the causes of disorganized attachment behaviour [12]. They argue that the incoherent behaviour seen in disorganized attachment stems from the parent being experienced as the source of both comfort and threat. This creates an irreconcilable approach-avoidance conflict, causing disruptions in attachment behaviour (see Table 12.1). Data showing associations between disorganization and both frightening parenting behaviour and maltreatment support this hypothesis, although the precise mechanisms described by Main and Hesse [12] have never been directly verified.

**Attachment Disorders**

Although insecure attachment, and particularly disorganized attachment, is associated with a raised risk of later poor adjustment, the risk is relatively weak and probabilistic [13]. Insecure attachment patterns should therefore not be considered intrinsically problematic, and are not considered disorders. Disorders of attachment have been found when children have experienced the complete absence of a consistent carer, severe maltreatment (particularly neglect) or major disruption in the continuity of care – as in children raised in institutional or foster care. A significant number of children raised in such circumstances show quite pervasive patterns of disturbed social relatedness.

There are two types of relevant disorders in the *Diagnostic and Statistical Manual of Mental Disorders*, 5th edition (DSM-5). The first is reactive attachment disorder (RAD). This was previously known as RAD-inhibited subtype in DSM-IV. RAD is marked by a striking absence of attachment behaviour, extreme withdrawal, unexplained emotional volatility (e.g. fearfulness, anger) even during non-threatening interactions, a pervasive tendency not to seek comfort from carers when distressed, and a lack of social responsiveness or reciprocity.

The second disorder is known as disinhibited social engagement disorder (DSED) and was previously referred to as RAD-disinhibited subtype in DSM-IV. DSED is marked by indiscriminate social approach behaviour, lack of sensitivity to social/personal boundaries (e.g. non-normative physical contact or intimacy with strangers), over-friendliness and a lack of wariness of strangers (e.g. wandering off with strangers). However, DSED is no longer considered an attachment disorder within DSM-5, because evidence indicates that disinhibited behaviour can co-occur with otherwise seemingly normal attachment behaviour (even of the secure type) towards caregivers [14], although there is probably a close connection between attachment and the lack of selectivity of approach towards adults observed in DSED. The question of whether DSED should be considered a disorder involving attachment continues to be debated among scholars and clinicians [15]. There are a number of tools for assessing attachment disorders and related behaviours, including standardized questionnaires, interviews and observation schemes [16].

Critically, RAD and DSED are quite distinct from the normative patterns of attachment described earlier, in terms of both the behavioural definitions and the circumstances in which they arise. Variations in normative attachment patterns derive from differing styles or quality of parenting received by children who have formed one or more selective attachment bonds. In contrast, RAD and DSED most probably represent the consequences of severe disruption in the continuity of an attachment bond, or the failure to establish a selective attachment bond in the first place [3].

## Consequences of Variations in Attachment

Early attachment relationships appear to exert a significant and important influence on current and later relationships, well-being and psychological health. Longitudinal research suggests that securely attached children may have developmental advantages over their insecure counterparts in areas such as emotional regulation and understanding, social cognition and internalizing problems. While not all findings have been consistently replicated, recent meta-analyses report robust associations between insecure attachment and peer relationships and externalizing problems [13,17], and, to a lesser extent, internalizing problems [18]. With respect to the externalizing problems, the evidence indicates that Disorganized children are the most at-risk amongst the insecure subtypes [3,13].

The jury is still out on whether the effects of early attachment on later development represent the direct influence of early experience, or whether continuities over time in other individual and environmental intermediary processes are responsible. Considerable evidence suggests that some of the effects of insecure attachment result from these intermediary processes. For example, continuity in the quality of care is associated with longitudinal links between attachment and outcome [19]. On the other hand, some findings suggest that early experience can have specific and lasting effects – for example, particularly severe early deprivation is associated with DSED and its accompanying symptoms [3].

## Interventions

There are two broad types of attachment intervention, the majority of which focus on infants and toddlers. Preventive interventions are the most widely used. These aim to improve rates of secure attachment so as to promote resilience and reduce the risk for later emotional or behavioural problems. The second type focuses on children evidencing attachment problems – for instance, children who have experienced maltreatment and may be in foster care, or late-placed national or international adoptees.

### Preventive Interventions

An illustrative, highly successful preventive intervention is that undertaken with 100 highly irritable neonates randomly allocated to treatment or control groups. In the treatment group, home visits to mothers and infants focused on increasing maternal play behaviour and encouraging appropriate maternal responsiveness to infant cues and infant distress. Maternal sensitivity and infant attachment security improved and were maintained at the 3.5-year follow-up [20]. Another effective approach uses video-feedback to help parents and carers become attuned to their infants' or young children's attachment cues [21]. A meta-analysis of interventions aiming to increase maternal sensitivity and promote secure attachment in unselected or at-risk samples (e.g. maternal postnatal depression) identified variables associated with effective intervention [7]. These included the number of sessions (<16 was optimal); a behavioural orientation; a focus on sensitivity (rather than, for example, providing support); targeting a clinical population and interventions that started after infants were 6 months old. Critically, intervention effects on attachment were strongest when parental sensitivity increased and when the treated population included a large percentage of insecure infants – suggesting that appropriate targeting is associated with successful outcomes. Sensitivity-based interventions have also been shown to be partially effective at reducing rates of disorganization [22]. Promising treatments are available for preschoolers and older children.

### Interventions with Fostered and Adopted Children

A number of effective treatment packages address foster care and adoption. For instance, the Attachment and Biobehavioural Catch-Up programme uses video-feedback techniques and targets mutual parent–child processes thought to interfere with the child's self-regulation and attachment. These include parental attributions and interaction skills – as well as the effect of parental childhood history on current parenting attitudes and behaviour. Improvements in attachment behaviour and child stress (as measured by cortisol levels [23]) are reported. Similar programmes effectively reduced disorganized attachment among maltreated children (e.g. see Moss *et al.* [24]). A recent National Institute for Health and Clinical Excellence guideline [25] recommends video-feedback and caregiver sensitivity training programmes as evidence-based interventions for promoting attachment security for at-risk children – e.g. those children in care or on the edge of care due to very high risk of, or actual, maltreatment. This guideline is likely to have a substantial impact on future practice.

## Conclusions

The study of attachment highlights the potential importance of understanding the early relational roots of both adjustment and maladjustment. The field has also focused attention on the observation and measurement of child attachment and the sometimes subtle interactional processes taking place within parent-child relationships. Critically, this has led to the development of a range of quite effective treatment techniques designed to enhance the security of attachment relationships in early life. Important among these are video-feedback techniques and caregiver sensitivity training. However, the long-term effectiveness of such treatments for reducing risk for psychopathology and promoting resilience remains to be fully established, and is an important area for future clinical research.

## References

1 Cassidy J (2008) The nature of the child's ties. In: Cassidy J, Shaver PR (eds). The Handbook of Attachment: Theory, Research and Clincal Applications, 2nd edn. New York: The Guildford Press, pp. 3–22.

2 Ainsworth MS, Blehar MC, Waters E, Wall S (1978) Patterns of attachment: A psychological study of the strange situation. Hillsdale, NJ: Lawrence Erlbaum.

3 Rutter M, Kreppner J, Sonuga-Barke E (2009) Emanuel Miller Lecture: Attachment insecurity, disinhibited attachment, and attachment disorders: where do research findings leave the concepts? Journal of Child Psychology and Psychiatry, 50, 529–543.

4 Van IJzendoorn MH, Kroonenberg PM (1988) Cross-cultural patterns of attachment: A meta-analysis of the strange situation. Child Development, 59, 147–156.

5 Solomon J, George C (2008) The measurement of attachment security and related constructs in infancy and early childhood. In: Cassidy J, Shaver PR (eds) The Handbook of Attachment: Theory, Research and Clincal Applications, 2nd edn. New York: The Guildford Press, pp. 383–416.

6 De Wolff M, van Ijzendoorn MH (1997) Sensitivity and attachment: A meta-analysis on parental antecedents of infant attachment. Child Development, 68, 571–591.

7 Bakermans-Kranenburg MJ, van IJzendoorn MH, Juffer F (2003) Less is more: meta-analyses of sensitivity and attachment interventions in early childhood. Psychological Bulletin, 129, 195–215.

8 Belsky J, Fearon RP (2008) Precursors of attachment security. In: Cassidy J, Shaver PR (eds) The Handbook of Attachment: Theory, Research and Clincal Applications., 2nd edn. New York: The Guildford Press, pp. 295–316.

9 Bokhorst CL, Bakermans-Kranenburg MJ, Fearon RM et al. (2003) The importance of shared environment in mother-infant attachment security: a behavioral genetic study. Child Development, 74, 1769–1782.

10 Fearon P, Shmueli-Goetz Y, Viding E et al. (2014) Genetic and environmental influences on adolescent attachment. Journal of Child Psychology and Psychiatry, and Allied Disciplines, 55, 1033–1041.

11 Lyons-Ruth K, Bronfman E, Parsons E (1999) Atypical attachment in infancy and early childhood among children at developmental risk. IV. Maternal frightened, frightening, or atypical behavior and disorganized infant attachment patterns. Monographs of the Society for Research in Child Development, 64, 67–96; discussion 213–220.

12 Main M, Hesse E (1990) Parents' unresolved traumatic experiences are related to infant disorganized attachment status: Is frightened and/or frightening parental behavior the linking mechanism? In: Greenberg MT, Cicchetti D (eds) Attachment in the preschool years: Theory, research, and intervention The John D and Catherine T MacArthur Foundation Series on Mental Health and development. xix. Chicago, IL, USA: University of Chicago Press, pp. 161–182.

13 Fearon R, Bakermans-Kranenburg MJ, van IJzendoorn MH et al. (2010) The significance of insecure attachment and disorganization in the development of children's externalizing behavior: A meta-analytic study. Child Development, 81, 435–456.

14 Zeanah CH, Gleason MM (2015) Annual research review: Attachment disorders in early childhood – clinical presentation, causes, correlates, and treatment. Journal of Child Psychology and Psychiatry, and Allied Disciplines, 56, 207–222.

15 Lyons-Ruth K (2015) Commentary: Should we move away from an attachment framework for understanding disinhibited social engagement disorder (DSED)? A commentary on Zeanah and Gleason. Journal of Child Psychology and Psychiatry, and Allied Disciplines, 56, 223–227.

16 O' Connor T, Byrne G (2007) Attachment measures for research and practiice. Child and Adolescent Mental Health, 12, 187–192.

17 Groh AM, Fearon RP, Bakermans-Kranenburg MJ et al. (2014) The significance of attachment security for children's social competence with peers: a meta-analytic study. Attachment & Human Development, 16, 103–136.

18 Groh AM, Roisman GI, van IJzendoorn MH et al. (2012) The significance of insecure and disorganized attachment for children's internalizing symptoms: A meta-analytic study. Child Development, 83, 591–610.

19 Belsky J, Fearon RM (2002) Early attachment security, subsequent maternal sensitivity, and later child development: does continuity in development depend upon continuity of caregiving? Attachment & Human Development, 4, 361–387.

20 van den Boom D (1990) Preventive intervention and the quality of mother-infant interaction and infant exploration in irritable infants. In: Koops W, Soppe HJG, Linden JLvd, Molenaar PCM, Schroots JFF (eds) Developmental Psychology Behind the Dikes: An Outline of Developmental Psychological Research in the Netherlands. Amsterdam, the Netherlands: Eburon, pp. 249–270.

21 Juffer F, Bakermans-Kranenburg MJ, van IJzendoorn MH (2008) Promoting positive parenting: An attachment-based intervention. Promoting positive parenting: An

attachment-based intervention xix. New York, NY: Taylor & Francis Group/Lawrence Erlbaum Associates. Monographs in Parenting series.

22 Bakermans-Kranenburg MJ, van IJzendoorn MH, Juffer F (2005) Disorganized attachment and preventive interventions: a review and meta-analysis. Infant Mental Health Journal, 26, 191–216.

23 Dozier M, Peloso E, Lewis E et al. (2008) Effects of an attachment-based intervention on the cortisol production of infants and toddlers in foster care. Development and Psychopathology, 20, 845–859.

24 Moss E, Dubois-Comtois K, Cyr C et al. (2011) Efficacy of a home-visiting intervention aimed at improving maternal sensitivity, child attachment, and behavioral outcomes for maltreated children: A randomized control trial. Development and Psychopathology, 23, 195–210.

25 NICE (2015) Children's attachment: Attachment in children and young people who are adopted from care, in care or at high risk of going into care. London, UK: National Institute for Health and Care Excellence .

# 13

## Promoting Infant Mental Health

*Christine Puckering*

Developments in our understanding of the importance of infant mental health have resulted in it becoming a well-accepted priority in governmental, education and health strategies [1,2]. Widely endorsed papers such as *1001 Critical Days* [3,4] have become part of cross-party manifesto promises.

## Why the Early Years Matter

In the first 2 years of life, the foundations of later emotional and cognitive development are laid down. We have long been aware of the necessity of good early visual and auditory stimulation for children to develop normal vision and hearing. The cortex depends on such stimulation for the neural development needed to interpret light and sound. It has taken longer, however, to uncover the role of early experience across other domains of development, primarily because of the child's lack of narrative memory for this period. Nonetheless, these early experiences play a fundamental role in developing emotional control or habitual ways of responding to the world (Figure 13.1). Without emotional control, social interaction becomes fraught and learning disrupted by emotional reactivity. Underlying positive or negative cognitive schemata formed during childhood influence our habitual ways of responding to the world. For example, premises such as 'I am a worthwhile person' and 'the world is a benign place where help will be available if I need it' are likely to engender positive interactive responses to social stimuli, while the opposite is likely to hold for underlying negative schemata.

Research suggests that even very young children can show significant mental health problems affecting their early learning, social competence and, potentially, their lifelong physical health. They can, for example, show characteristics of anxiety disorders, conduct disorder and depression [5]. The signs may be more subtle than in older children and adults, who can articulate their experiences, but they are no less real.

The concept of 'toxic' stress has been invoked as an explanatory factor for the early development of some mental and physical health difficulties [6]. Part of normal development is that the child, with the aid of its caretaker, learns to tolerate normal levels of environmental stress. Overcoming such stressors may serve to build coping strategies and resilience. Stress becomes 'toxic' when it is chronic and uncontrollable and experienced in the absence of access to support from caring adults to help the baby modulate the stress. It is suggested that, during early development, toxic stress results

*Child Psychology and Psychiatry: Frameworks for Clinical Training and Practice,* Third Edition.
Edited by David Skuse, Helen Bruce and Linda Dowdney.
© 2017 John Wiley & Sons, Ltd. Published 2017 by John Wiley & Sons, Ltd.

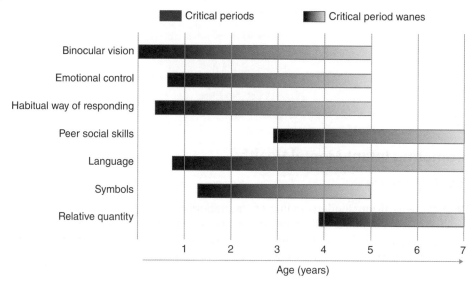

**Figure 13.1** Critical periods of brain development.

in the under-development of the executive functions of the prefrontal lobes, and the predominance of emotional processing in the amygdala, leaving the child constantly on 'high alert'. Toxic stress can lead to potentially permanent changes in all domains of learning and socio-emotional development, physiology and adaptive or maladaptive responses to future adversity [6].

A secure attachment can facilitate the baby's tolerance of stress and its capacity to use a caretaker to provide comfort and reduce stress, thus allowing the child freedom to explore, play and learn. Bowlby [7] first used the term attachment in this context. Although revised in the light of later understanding, his theory remains central in any understanding of infant mental health. Children develop close relationships in the first year of life with a small number of regular caregivers. The pattern of these relationships provides the base from which a child makes new relationships with peers and eventually romantic partners. The security of the parent–child relationship also predicts the capacity of the child to self-regulate, explore the environment and learn. Where children have a secure relationship with at least one regular caretaker, their future well-being is optimized (see Chapter 12). Attachment patterns (secure, avoidant, resistant and disorganized) tend to persist unless the child's circumstances change radically. In a 30-year follow-up, attachment history at 1 year was related to the growth of self-reliance, emotional regulation and social competence [8]. Any preventative measures or intervention to promote infant mental health must therefore look to promote secure child–carer attachment.

**Pregnancy and the Perinatal Period**

Early foetal development is a time of rapid neurodevelopment – new synapses are formed, pathways myelinated and synaptic pruning reduces the less used pathways and reinforces those found to be valuable [5]. Interest has grown, therefore, in exogenous factors that may affect foetal development and, potentially, longer-term outcome. For example, maternal antenatal stress is associated with infant outcome in a number of domains. The placental enzyme 11-β hydroxysteroid dehydrogenase type 2 (11-βHSD2) converts maternal cortisol to inactive cortisone. Increased maternal stress reduces its placental expression and increases foetal cortisol exposure [9]. The stressed baby is more likely to be born prematurely, at low birthweight, and carry an additional risk of psychological and physical problems [10]. High levels of maternal anxiety during pregnancy are associated with an increased risk of later child emotional and behavioural problems independent of other antenatal, obstetric and socio-demographic risks [11]. Both maternal stress and maternal amniotic cortisol levels predict infant cognitive and physical development at 17 months of age [12]. However, the infant's attachment status moderates outcome – the association between cognitive development and pre-natal amniotic fluid was nonsignificant in securely attached infants, suggesting that early environmental factors can moderate biological risk [12]. However, some caution is needed. In the Bergman *et al.* [12] study, for instance, there was a lack of association between amniotic fluid cortisol and prenatal maternal stress measures – i.e. there was 'no evidence that the prenatal stress effect on cognitive development was mediated by amniotic fluid cortisol' (p. 1029). Thus, while antenatal maternal stress consistently relates to infant developmental outcomes in a number of studies, exploration of the potential genetic, biological and environmental mediating and moderating factors continues.

## Intervention

### Antenatal and Postnatal Interventions

The recognition that social adversity and poor maternal mental health during pregnancy are associated with longer-term adverse outcomes in infant cognitive, social and emotional development has resulted in psychologically based intervention programmes focusing on mothers during the antenatal and post-birth period [13–15]. Participants report positively on these programmes and some improvements in mental health outcomes have been noted [15]. A recent systematic review of randomized control trials (RCTs) of *antenatal* interventions aiming to reduce maternal distress during pregnancy and post-birth showed mixed results. While treatment interventions significantly reduced maternal distress, preventive interventions failed to do so [16].

The Family Nurse Partnership programme (FNP) [17] provided a nurse home-visiting support programme for young, first-time, poorly educated and unemployed mothers beginning in early pregnancy and continuing for 2 years post-birth. RCT evaluation of the American FNP found a number of positive and long-lasting effects, including improved quality of parental care and improved infant and child developmental outcomes [17]. However, different findings emerged when this programme was rolled out in an RCT in the UK using trained health visitors. Early implementation sites reported good programme fidelity and positive views of the programme from parents and professionals. However, results from the RCT showed that the FNP had no impact on the primary outcomes of birthweight, maternal smoking, the need for emergency child medical care and hospital admissions, or further maternal pregnancies [18]. When set against the additional costs of the programme of around £2000 per family, the research team concluded that there was no basis for further implementation of the intervention. However, some secondary outcomes, including increased self-efficacy and confidence among the programme participants, and maternal reports of improved child language development, may have 'sleeper effects' over the longer term. A new RCT of Group Family Nurse Partnership (gFNP) is now under way. Based on the FNP curriculum and strengths-based approach, gFNP will be delivered in a group context, starting in pregnancy and lasting until infants are 12 months old [19].

**Intervention During Early Childhood**

Again, mixed findings are reported. The UK government Sure Start programme focused on high-risk families living in poverty, where no one was in employment, with targets that included improving children's developmental and educational outcomes, but also a strong emphasis on parents entering the workforce to improve the family's financial stability. The evaluation team was guarded in its appraisal of programme outcomes. No RCT was set up and the lack of a central curriculum or programme led to varying implementation and outcomes. There was some reduction in obesity and better child physical health in Sure Start areas, and mothers reported less chaotic family lives and less harsh discipline. However, by the time the children were aged 5 years, there were no demonstrable differences in child cognitive and social-emotional outcomes between those in the programme and comparison children who were not [20]. However, the evaluation team noted that the lack of differences in child outcome at age 5 years may, in part, have been influenced by comparison children's participation in free preschool education, although good preschool and school experiences still do not outweigh the strong effects of the home learning environment and the investment of parental time and energy in their child's cognitive development [21].

The relative value of universal and targeted services remains in the balance. In 2006, Glasgow City launched an ambitious programme of universal intervention based on the Triple P suite of programmes [22]. The programme was aimed at families with children aged 0–7 years. While those families who completed the interventions reported high levels of satisfaction and improvements in their parenting, emotional well-being and child behaviour, the final evaluation report concluded that the outcomes were disappointing. There were poor programme completion rates, particularly among the more deprived families and selective benefits for more affluent and better-educated families. Overall, there was a lack of improvement in the social and emotional adjustment of the majority of the children. The final recommendations were that there was little evidence to support further training and implementation in Triple P, but that a menu of alternative interventions more closely matched to the needs of each family be adopted and robustly monitored [22].

On the other hand, it has been suggested that early intervention is cost-effective over the longer term. The adult outcomes of those who participated as children in a compensatory preschool programme for low-income African American children aged 3–4 years has recently been evaluated [23]. The authors found that the programme substantially improved externalizing behaviours, which in turn improved employment outcomes and reduced criminal activities. Interestingly, socio-emotional abilities were noted to be as important as IQ and cognitive skills. The authors concluded that every

$1 spent in the early years saves $14 in later services. Late remediation is not as effective and is costly. Highly targeted and tailored interventions appear most effective and Heckman *et al.* [23] recommend supporting early childhood programmes meeting the following criteria:

- A focus on disadvantaged children aged 0–5 years.
- Professional staff who focus on developing children's cognitive and social skills.
- Offering parental support and education for parents that fosters their children's development.
- Collection and analysis of child development outcome and follow-up data.

## The Need for Supportive Services

### Primary Health Care Services

Health visiting services provide safe, accessible, non-stigmatizing primary care to all families and offer a safety net for the most troubled. A series of tragic deaths of small children at the hands of their carers led to a government recognition that child protection cannot be separated from policies to improve children's lives as a whole. Fortunately, recent depletions in the UK health visiting service are being reversed alongside government recognition that both universal services for every child and more targeted services for those with additional needs are essential [24].

### The Role of Child Mental Health Services

Infant mental health is a public health issue, where the role of psychiatry and psychology may be to offer skilled infant mental health consultation to trained nurses and health visitors. A sound understanding of attachment theory is essential. Child mental health services also have a role in liaison with antenatal services, which are understandably preoccupied by physical health and less likely to attend to a woman's state of mind, whether that is depression, anxiety or preoccupation with social and emotional stressors such as domestic violence and poverty. The bridge between adult and child services is often poor, and vulnerable children and perinatal mental health problems can remain unidentified until the damage has already been done, with the majority of the burden falling on the child and child services [25]. It behoves psychologists and psychiatrists, therefore, to have the skills and knowledge to act as supportive resources for public health, primary care and community services. Infant mental health matters.

## References

1 Scottish Government (2008) The Early Years Framework. Online: http://www.gov.scot /Resource/Doc/257007/0076309.pdf. Accessed: January 2017.
2 Department of Health (2013) Early Years Impact. Online: https://www.gov.uk /government/uploads/system/uploads/attachment_data/file/413129/2902452_Early _Years_Impact_2_V0_1W.pdf. Accessed: January 2017.

3  1001 Critical Days: The Importance of the Conception to age Two Period. (2013) Online: http://www.1001criticaldays.co.uk/sites/default/files/1001%20days_oct16_1st. pdf. Accessed: January 2017.

4  All Party Parliamentary Group for Conception to Age 2 – The First 1001 Days. Building Great Britons. February 2015. www.1001criticaldays.co.uk /buildinggreatbritonsreport.pdf.

5  Shonkoff J, Philips DA (eds) (2000) From Neurons to neighbourhoods: The science of Early Child Development. Washington DC: National Academy Press.

6  Shonkoff, JP, Garner, AS, Siegel BS et al. (2012) The lifelong effects of early childhood adversity and toxic stress. Pediatrics, 129, 232–246.

7  Bowlby J (1969) Attachment and loss. Volume 1.Attachment. New York: Basic Books.

8  Sroufe LA (2005) Attachment and development: A prospective, longitudinal study from birth to adulthood. Attachment & Human Development, 7, 349–367.

9  O'Donnell KJ, Bugge Jensen A, Freeman L et al. (2012) Maternal prenatal anxiety and downregulation of placental 11β-HSD2. Psychoneuroendocrinology, 37, 818–826.

10  Barker DJ (2002) Fetal programming of coronary heart disease. TRENDS in Endocrinology & Metabolism, 13, 364–368.

11  O'Connor TG, Heron J, Golding J et al. (2002) Maternal antenatal anxiety and children's behavioural/emotional problems at 4 years Report from the Avon Longitudinal Study of Parents and Children. The British Journal of Psychiatry, 180, 502–508.

12  Bergman K, Sarkar P, Glover V, O'Connor TG (2010) Maternal prenatal cortisol and infant cognitive development: moderation by infant–mother attachment. Biological Psychiatry, 67, 1026–1032.

13  Douglas H and Rheeston M (2009) The Solihull Approach. Keeping the baby in mind. Infant Mental Health in Practice, 29.

14  Sanders MR (2012) Development, evaluation and multinational dissemination of the Triple P-Positive Parenting Program. Annual Review of Clinical Psychology, 8, 345–379.

15  White J, Thompson LT, Puckering C et al. (2015) Antenatal parenting support for vulnerable women: an exploratory randomised controlled trial of mellow bumps versus chill-out in pregnancy or care as usual. British Journal of Midwifery, 195, 726–732.

16  Fontein-Kuipers YJ, Nieuwenhuijze MJ, Ausems M et al. (2014) Antenatal interventions to reduce maternal distress: a systematic review and meta-analysis of randomised trials. AN International Journal of Obstetrics and Gynaecology, 121, 389–397.

17  Barnes J (2010) From evidence-base to practice: implementation of the Nurse Family Partnership programme in England. Journal of Children's Services, 5, 4 – 17.

18  Robling M, Bekkers M, Bell K et al. (2015) Effectiveness of a nurse-led intensive home-visitation programme for first-time teenage mothers (Building Blocks): a pragmatic randomised controlled trial. The Lancet, 387, 146–155.

19  Barnes J, Aistrop D, Allen E et al. (2015) ISRCTN78814904: First steps: A trial of the effectiveness of the Group Family Nurse Partnership (gFNP) programme compared to routine care in improving outcomes for high-risk mothers and preventing abuse. Online: https://trialsjournal.biomedcentral.com/articles/10.1186/1745-6215-14-285. Accessed: January 2017.

20  The National Evaluation of Sure Start (NESS) Team (2010) The impact of Sure Start Local Programmes on five year olds and their families. Department for Education. http://www.ness.bbk.ac.uk/impact/documents/RR067.pdf. Accessed: January 2017.

21 Sylva K, Melhuish E, Sammons P et al. (2004) The Effective Provision of Pre-School Education (EPPE) Project:Findings from Pre-school to end of Key Stage1. Online: http://dera.ioe.ac.uk/18189/2/SSU-SF-2004--01.pdf. Accessed: January 2017.

22 Marryat L, Thompson L, and Wilson P (2017) No evidence of whole population mental health impact of the Triple P parenting programme: findings from a routine dataset. BMC pediatrics, 17(1), p.40.

23 Heckman J, Pinto R, and Savelyev P (2013) Understanding the mechanisms through which an influential early childhood program boosted adult outcomes. American Economic Review, 103, 2052–2086.

24 UK Government (2011) Health Visitor Implementation Plan 2011–2015. Online: https://www.gov.uk/government/uploads/system/uploads/attachment_data/file/213759/dh_124208.pdf. Accessed: January 2017.

25 Bauer A, Parsonage M, Knapp M et al. (2014) The Costs of Perinatal Mental Health Problems. Centre for Mental Health and London School of Economics.

# 14

# Promoting Children's Well-Being: The Prevention of Depression and Anxiety

*Paul Stallard*

Psychological problems of anxiety and depression in children are common, with cumulative rates suggesting that by early adulthood 15–18% will have experienced an impairing emotional disorder of anxiety or depression [1,2]. Emotional problems have a persistent and unremitting course, with longitudinal studies highlighting that child mental health disorders persist and increase the risk of other mental health problems in adulthood [3]. In the Victorian Adolescent Health Cohort Study, 1943 adolescents were assessed at eight time points from 15 to 29 years of age. Of those with a mental health problem in adolescence, 60% exhibited a further episode in young adulthood, with duration of adolescence episode being the strongest predictor of later problems [4].

Improving the mental health of children has been recognized as a national and global priority [5]. Although effective treatments are available for children with emotional disorders, the vast majority of those with problems remain unidentified and untreated [6] Given the limited availability and reach of traditional treatment services, alternative approaches are required in order to have a significant impact upon the mental health of children.

## Prevention

An alternative approach to intervention is through the widespread use of prevention programmes designed to reduce the prevalence of child and adolescent psychological problems whilst optimizing psychological well-being. Prevention programmes aim to reduce or mitigate the effects of known mental health risk factors whilst enhancing protective factors at the individual, family and community levels. In so doing, they help children to become more resilient and better able to cope with stress and adversity, thereby maintaining their healthy status.

Prevention programmes are typically conceptualized as universal, selective or indicated [7], with each having a different focus and aim (Table 14.1).

Universal programmes are provided to all of a target population irrespective of risk status, e.g. children of a certain age. Selective programmes target children at

*Child Psychology and Psychiatry: Frameworks for Clinical Training and Practice,* Third Edition.
Edited by David Skuse, Helen Bruce and Linda Dowdney.
© 2017 John Wiley & Sons, Ltd. Published 2017 by John Wiley & Sons, Ltd.

**Table 14.1** Universal, selective and indicated prevention

| Prevention | Provision | Advantages | Disadvantages |
|---|---|---|---|
| Universal prevention, e.g. anxiety prevention programmes for 9/10-year-old children | Universal – provided to all regardless of risk status | Far-reaching coverage<br><br>Opportunity for primary prevention, i.e. reduce prevalence of new disorders<br><br>Screening not required<br><br>Avoids need for labelling which could be stigmatizing<br><br>Low-cost, high volume | Limited resources used to provide interventions to many who are, and will remain, 'healthy'<br><br>Intervention effects are typically small<br><br>Face validity, relevance and engagement can be difficulties |
| Selective prevention, e.g. anxiety prevention programmes for children where parents are separating | Targeted – upon those at increased risk of developing problems through exposure to known risk factors | Resources focused upon 'at risk' groups<br><br>Opportunity for primary prevention | Potentially stigmatizing<br><br>Difficulties accurately identifying 'at risk' groups within the community |
| Indicated prevention, e.g. children with significant anxiety symptoms but not meeting full diagnostic criteria | Targeted – upon those displaying mild/moderate problems | Efficient use of limited resources<br><br>Provide early interventions for those with emergent problems<br><br>Demonstrate larger treatment effects | May require screening which can be costly and practically complicated<br><br>Potentially stigmatizing and unacceptable to some of the identified group. |

increased risk of developing problems through exposure to known risk factors, e.g. children of parents with a mental illness. Universal and selective programmes are primarily concerned with promoting well-being. They provide opportunities for prevention (e.g. maximizing potential), protection (e.g. developing competencies) and intervention (e.g. minimising impairment). Their widespread provision results in good reach and high acceptability, although their general focus may not be of sufficient depth or dosage to benefit those with more established disorders. Similarly, from an economic perspective, many of those who receive universal or selective interventions are healthy and are unlikely to require further intervention to maintain their well-being or maximize their potential. With limited public health funding, the justification for focusing limited finances in this way will be increasingly challenged.

Indicated prevention programmes provide early interventions on a targeted basis to those already displaying mild or moderate problems, e.g. children with symptoms of anxiety or depression. The aim of indicated approaches is to prevent these problems from worsening and developing into mental health disorders. Such programmes focus limited resources upon those with greater needs and their effects are often large, as initial levels of symptoms and the subsequent reductions are greater. However, they require accurate identification of the target group – a particular difficulty where children have emotional problems or disorders as these often go unrecognized [6].

## School-Based Prevention

School settings provide convenient and familiar locations to deliver prevention programmes to children [8]. School-based prevention programmes have good reach as the majority of young people attend school each day. The integration of emotional health programmes within the school setting and curriculum offers opportunities for the open discussion of mental health issues and also the promotion of psychological concepts and ideas as 'skills for life'. This open and more visible approach serves to normalize common psychological problems such as anxiety and depression, and can help to develop a supportive peer group culture where worries and problems can be more openly acknowledged and discussed.

In terms of effectiveness, systematic reviews of school-based emotional health prevention programmes suggest that universal and targeted/indicated approaches can have positive effects upon emotional well-being, although the results are variable [9,10]. The largest meta-analysis of universal school-based social and emotional learning prevention programmes to date assessed data from 270000 children [11]. Compared with controls, children who received prevention programmes demonstrated significantly improved social and emotional skills, attitudes, behaviour and academic performance [11]. In contrast, the results of programmes specifically addressing the mental health disorders of anxiety and depression were more variable. This chapter therefore focuses on such programmes, highlighting the issues and challenges that arise when they are delivered in school settings.

## Depression Prevention Programmes

A major review of school-based depression prevention trials found that the majority (76%) were based upon cognitive behavioural therapy (CBT) and 88% involved eight or more sessions. Two-thirds were led by graduate students, mental health practitioners or teachers. Indicated programmes were most effective in reducing symptoms of depression, with prevention programmes led by teachers tending to be the least effective. Variability in the effectiveness of programmes based upon the same theoretical model suggests that factors other than programme content or mode of delivery (universal vs targeted) *per se* may be important mediators of outcome [12].

A Cochrane review of depression prevention programmes analysed data from 53 studies involving 14 406 children and young people aged 5–19 years [13] and concluded that both universal and targeted interventions may prevent the onset of depression when compared with no intervention. However, many studies were of poor methodological quality, leading the authors to conclude that future evaluations should assess the effectiveness of these interventions when delivered under real-world conditions (pragmatic trials) and when utilizing placebo or attention control conditions.

When compared against other active control conditions, the results of depression prevention programmes are disappointing. For example, the Penn Resilience Programme (PRP) – a group-based CBT intervention – has been widely researched with a recent meta-analytic review failing to find any positive effect when compared with other active control interventions, a similar finding to a recent large trial in the Netherlands [14,15]. A recent pragmatic UK trial compared a universal CBT programme (Resourceful Adolescent Programme) with an attention control group and usual school provision. Young people ($n$ = 5030) aged 12–16 participated in the study and at 12 months there was no evidence that the CBT intervention was more effective than other conditions in reducing symptoms of depression [16]. This finding is consistent with those of other large pragmatic studies [17,18] and suggests that the widespread use of depression prevention programmes in school should not be pursued without further research.

## Anxiety Prevention Programmes

The results of school-based anxiety prevention programmes are more encouraging. A review of 27 randomized trials identified 20 different prevention programmes [19]. The majority (78%) were based upon CBT and were led by mental health practitioners (44%) or teachers (26%). Only four studies included children under the age of 9 years; 78% of interventions reported significant post-intervention reductions in symptoms of anxiety, with universal and targeted programmes being equally effective. Unlike depression prevention interventions, teacher-led interventions were found to be as effective as those led by mental health professionals. However, a direct comparison of programme leaders was only assessed in one small study. The review concluded that the widespread implementation of school-based anxiety prevention programmes, alongside rigorous evaluation of their longer-term outcomes, should be encouraged.

Of the anxiety prevention programmes that have been evaluated, 'FRIENDS for life' tends to have the largest evidence base [20]. The programme is manualized and can be delivered as a universal or indicated intervention. The 10-session programme is based upon CBT and has versions for young children (aged 4–6), children (aged 7–11) and youths (aged 12–16). The programme is very engaging and involves a mix of large and small group work, role plays, games, activities and quizzes and teaches children skills in three main areas. Cognitively, children are helped to become aware of their anxiety-increasing cognitions and to replace them with more helpful and balanced cognitions. Emotionally, they are helped to understand the anxiety response and their unique physiological reaction to stressful situations. This helps children to detect early signs of anxiety so that they can intervene to manage and reduce these unpleasant feelings. The final component addresses the behavioural domain and teaches children problem-solving skills and the use of graded exposure to systematically face and overcome their worries. FRIENDS can be led by trained teachers or mental health practitioners such as school nurses or psychology assistants.

The effectiveness of FRIENDS, particularly in Australia where it was developed, has been documented in a number of trials, with reductions in anxiety being maintained up to 3 years after the intervention [21]. However, other evaluations of FRIENDS have failed to find positive effects [22]. A recent pragmatic UK trial found that the effectiveness of FRIENDS depended upon who delivered the programme [23]. Trained health leaders, external to the school, achieved greater reductions in anxiety than trained school staff at 12 month follow-up.

## Future Developments and Challenges

Overall, the evidence is that anxiety and depression prevention programmes provided as universal or indicated interventions can be effective in the short term. Whilst this is encouraging the results are inconsistent and the evidence does not yet support the widespread implementation of these programmes in schools. Future research should address four key areas.

First, methodological weaknesses are common and include small sample sizes, a lack of medium-term follow-ups and few comparisons with other active interventions. Most studies have focused upon adolescents, failing to include younger children. CBT interventions, particularly for anxiety, show most promise, although there are considerable differences between programmes in length, core components and delivery. Variations in effectiveness within the same programme suggest the importance of mediating factors relating to programme leaders (e.g. professional experience, training, rapport and confidence) and moderating effects related to students (e.g. age, gender, ethnicity) and schools (e.g. class size, pedagogic orientation, emotional health awareness). Future work should identify the active ingredients and potential mediators and moderators of effective mental health prevention programmes.

Secondly, the majority of prevention programmes have assessed changes in psychological symptoms in the short term. There is little evidence to suggest that these programmes have a primary preventive effect in terms of maintaining psychological health and reducing the incidence of new disorders. Longer-term follow-ups are lacking. These are essential to demonstrate the primary preventive effect and also that short-term reductions in symptoms are maintained.

Thirdly, whilst schools are a convenient location to deliver anxiety and depression prevention programmes, integrating them within schools poses many practical issues. Schools are organizationally complex, with busy timetables and competing priorities that limit the time available to devote to these programmes. Whilst many schools are keen to develop the emotional health of their students, their ultimate aim, and upon which they are externally assessed, is the development of academic skills. Mental health prevention programmes will be more attractive to schools if they can be shown to benefit both mental health and academic performance.

Fourthly, robust trials are required to assess the benefits of mental health prevention programmes when provided in diverse everyday settings. To be sustainable, programmes need to be engaging, flexible, delivered within the available lesson time and contained within the school semester. However, intervention fidelity needs to be maintained, with current prevention trials evaluating the use of online CBT interventions [24,25]. In addition, future research should determine whether school staff can be trained to effectively deliver mental health prevention programmes or whether these should be delivered by trained professionals from outside of the school.

Finally, within the current context of financial constraints, perhaps the biggest barrier to the adoption of mental health prevention programmes will be funding. Pragmatic school-based mental health prevention programmes will result in additional costs which, within the current economic climate, may be beyond the finances available to many schools. Economic justification for prevention programmes more generally needs to rest upon demonstrations that their potential benefits in terms of reduced health and social care usage, and perhaps improved educational outcomes, will outweigh the cost of delivering them.

## References

1 Costello EJ, Mustillo S, ErkanI A et al. (2003) Prevalence and development of psychiatric disorders in childhood and adolescence. Archives of General Psychiatry, 60, 837–844.

2 Essau CA, Conradt J, Petermann, F (2000) Frequency, comorbidity, and psychological impairment of anxiety disorders in German adolescents. Journal of Anxiety Disorders, 14, 263–279.

3 Kim-Cohen J, Caspi A, Moffitt TE et al. (2003) Prior Juvenile Diagnoses in Adults with Mental Disorder Developmental Follow-Back of a Prospective-Longitudinal Cohort. Archives of General Psychiatry, 60, 709–717.

4 Patton GC, Coffey C, Romaniuk H et al. (2014) The prognosis of common mental disorders in adolescents: a 14-year prospective cohort study. Lancet, 383, 1404–1411.

5 Kieling C, Baker-Henningham H, Belfer M et al. (2011) Child and adolescent mental health worldwide: evidence for action. Lancet, 378, 1515–1525.

6 Ford T, Hamilton H, Meltzer H, Goodman R (2008) Predictors of service use for mental health problems among British schoolchildren. Child and Adolescent Mental Health, 13, 32–40.

7 Mrazek PJ, Haggerty RJ (1994) Reducing risks for mental disorders, frontiers for preventive intervention research. Washington DC: National Academy Press.

8 Fazel M, Harwood K, Stephan S, Ford T (2014) Mental health interventions in schools in high-income countries. The Lancet Psychiatry, 1, 377–387.

9 Adi Y, Killoran A, Janmohamed K, Stewart-Brown S (2007) Systematic review of the effectiveness of interventions to promote mental wellbeing in children in primary education. Report 1: universal approaches (non-violence related outcomes). London: National Institute for Health and Clinical Excellence.

10 Shucksmith J, Summerbell C, Jones S, Whittaker V (2007) Mental wellbeing of children in primary education (targeted/indicated activities). London: National Institute for Health and Clinical Excellence.

11 Durlak JA, Weissberg RP, Dymnicki AB et al. (2011) The impact of enhancing students' social and emotional learning: a meta-analysis of school based universal interventions. Child Development, 82, 405–432.

12 Calear AL, Christensen H (2010) Systematic review of school-based prevention and early intervention programs for depression. Journal of Adolescence, 33, 3, 429–438.

13 Merry SN, Hetrick SE, Cox GR et al. (2011) Psychological and educational interventions for preventing depression in children and adolescents (Review). The Cochrane Collaboration, Issue 12.

14 Brunwasser SM, Gillham JE, Kim E (2009) A meta-analytic review of the Penn Resilience Program's effect on depressive symptoms. Journal of Consulting and Clinical Psychology, 77, 1042–1054.

15 Tak YR, Kleinjan M, Lichtwarck-Aschoff A, Engels RC (2014) Secondary outcomes of a school-based universal resiliency training for adolescents: a cluster randomized controlled trial. BMC Public Health 14.1, 1171.

16 Stallard P, Sayal K, Phillips R et al. (2012) Classroom based Cognitive Behaviour Therapy in reducing symptoms of depression in high risk adolescents: a pragmatic randomised controlled trial. British Medical Journal, 345, e6058.

17 Sawyer MG, Pfeiffer S, Spence SH et al. (2010) School-based prevention of depression: a randomised controlled study of the beyondblue schools research initiative. Journal of Child Psychology and Psychiatry, 51, 199–209.

18 Araya R, Fritsch R, Spears M et al. (2013) School intervention to improve mental health of students in Santiago, Chile: a randomized clinical trial. JAMA Pediatrics, 167, 1004–1010.

19 Neil AL, Christensen H (2009) Efficacy and effectiveness of school based prevention and early intervention programmes for anxiety. Clinical Psychology Review, 29, 208–215.

20 Fisak BJ, Richard D, Mann A (2012) The prevention of child and adolescent anxiety: A meta-analytic review. Prevention Science, 12: 255–268.

21 Barrett PM, Farrell L, Ollendick TH, Dadds M (2006) Long-term outcomes of an Australian universal prevention trial of anxiety and depression symptoms in children and youth: an evaluation of the FRIENDS programme. Journal of Clinical Child and Adolescent Psychology, 35, 403–411.

22 Miller LD, Laye-Gindhu A, Liu Y et al. (2011) Evaluation of a preventive intervention for child anxiety in two randomised attention-control trials. Behaviour Research and Therapy, 49, 315–323.

23 Stallard P, Skryabina E, Taylor G, Phillips R, Daniels H, Anderson R, Simpson N (2014) Classroom-based cognitive behaviour therapy (FRIENDS): a cluster randomised controlled trial to Prevent Anxiety in Children through Education in Schools (PACES) Lancet Psychiatry, 1, 185–192.

24 Perry Y, Calear AL, Mackinnon A et al. (2015) Trial for the Prevention of Depression (TriPoD) in final-year secondary students: study protocol for a cluster randomised controlled trial. Trials 16.1, 451.

25 Teesson M, Newton NC, Slade T et al. (2014) The CLIMATE schools combined study: a cluster randomised controlled trial of a universal Internet-based prevention program for youth substance misuse, depression and anxiety. BMC Psychiatry 14.1: 32.

# 15

# Fostering Resilience in Adolescents

*Angela Veale*

## Introduction

Many adolescents who come to the attention of the mental health system have experienced multiple adversities in their lives, such as poverty, chaotic parenting, residential care, foster care or school expulsion. They live in systems that lack supportive capacity and are resource-impoverished. Significantly, these adolescents are also difficult to engage in therapeutic interventions, particularly because of a fear of stigmatization. There is a developmental challenge inherent in this situation – the health-seeking part of the psyche is outward-looking, and strives towards self-efficacy and autonomy, yet the prospect of engaging in therapy may reinforce unconscious fears of being 'mad' or a 'psycho'.

Environments that are chronically under-resourced have been implicitly assumed to produce poor developmental outcomes or impairments. New research highlights reciprocal dynamic transactions between biology, behaviour, environment, culture and resilience [1,2]. Fostering resilience involves a fundamental shift from a deficits perspective, focused on individualized negative functioning and vulnerability, to a dynamic, strengths-based, participative orientation. It involves a focus on building connections within developmental systems. This chapter outlines new theoretical resilience frameworks and links them to a participatory action research project with 'hard to reach' adolescents in an exploration of how resilience can be fostered in practice and community settings.

## What Do We Mean by Resilience?

Resilience can be defined as the 'capacity of a dynamic system to adapt successfully to disturbances that threaten the function, survival or development of the system'[1]. Systems operate at multiple levels ranging from the molecular neurobiological through to individual, social and economic levels [1]. For example, social world factors such as social support and social evaluation have effects on the structure, connectivity and function of the neural circuits involved in stress regulation, namely the amygdala and hippocampus and the prefrontal regions linked to these structures [2]. Tost *et al.* [2] show how a social-environmental risk factor such as exclusion and discrimination links to increased mental health risks for ethnic minority individuals. Negative social-evaluative experiences, if experienced repeatedly and consistently over time, can result in chronic

*Child Psychology and Psychiatry: Frameworks for Clinical Training and Practice,* Third Edition.
Edited by David Skuse, Helen Bruce and Linda Dowdney.
© 2017 John Wiley & Sons, Ltd. Published 2017 by John Wiley & Sons, Ltd.

stress which, in turn, can create lasting changes in neural stress-regulatory circuits. Social and cultural level factors can therefore act as negative forces shaping neural and stress responses, in a manner leading, for example, to undesirable physical and mental health consequences. Conversely, it appears from animal experimentation studies that these same factors can subsequently modify neural circuits in a positive direction. For example, the authors cite animal experiments showing that an enhanced environment of physical activity and social interaction with peers during juvenile development can alleviate the negative effects of early poor social experiences, creating effects at a neural level through richer dendritic branching and altered gene activity in multiple brain areas, resulting in enhanced behavioural and cognitive responses to stress [2].

A strengths-based, participative approach to fostering resilience is supported by new research on cognitive sensitivity to context. Ellis and Del Giudice [3] found that children who develop in harsh environments may specialize their abilities to match high-adversity contexts [3,4]. Adults who had experienced harsh childhoods had greater attentional flexibility (ability to switch attention quickly) than those not exposed to aversive childhood environments, so they demonstrated a skill in registering and responding to environmental cues quickly, which was *adaptive* in a high-risk environment. The authors argue that understanding such responses as coherent, functional responses to stress will enable us to work with, rather than against, differing adaptations to stress. This implies an altered focus on adaptation rather than maladaptation. Ellis argues that, instead of asking 'What is wrong'?, we need to ask 'What is right'? [4].

### Agency in Resilience

Cultural context, therefore, influences resilience, and there is increasing attention to cultural meanings, risk and protective processes [5,6]. Cultural models of resilience highlight the need to enhance agentive, mastery-oriented capacities. For Ungar, resilience involves both the capacity of individuals to harness health-sustaining resources and the capacity of the individual's family, community and culture to provide the needed resources and experiences in a way that is culturally meaningful [6,7].

### Mobilizing Social Networks to Foster Coping and Resilience

A further useful analysis of how social relationships foster resilience is provided in the Social Convoy model [8]. Social convoys are the multiple relationships in the lives of children and young people that facilitate the exchange of affective support, self-affirmation and direct aid. Importantly, the model extends the concept of attachment relationships to other close relationships and acknowledges that relationships between adults and children are characterized by mutuality of support and social exchange. That is, in adult–child relationships, children and young people have the capacity both to give and to receive nurturance and support, and furthermore this is a powerful motivational force in relationship formation and maintenance. The model is strengths-based as it posits an engaged young person who is active in reciprocal support relationships. This may be particularly relevant for adolescents engaged in the developmental task of negotiating a balance between autonomy and relatedness in relationships [9].

## Implications for Policy and Practice

The models outlined in the previous sections indicate the importance of supporting the agentive, help-seeking, mastery-oriented capacities of young people as they negotiate the support needed from those around them. Several challenges face practitioners if these models are to be successfully applied. Practitioners need to foster adolescents' capacities for mobilizing adaptive support systems; negotiating access to resources for healthy growth and development; and participating in social convoys characterized by reciprocal supportive relationships. They also need to foster resilience in situations when adolescent support systems may be damaged, unsupportive or unavailable as is often the case with the families of 'hard to reach' adolescents. Finally, they need to shift away from an emphasis on internal psychological processes, and clinician–patient-defined interventions, and become one part of the adolescent's total resilience system. In practice, this means initiating processes that facilitate young people in defining their own needs, priorities and best interests and in mobilizing their social networks and communities to support them as they address those needs.

## Mobilizing Resilience: An Illustrative Example

I outline here a participatory action research (PAR) social integration project with nine girls (aged 12–18 years), half of whom had received formal cautions from the police, and who had also been referred to an intensive support service for young people in crisis. A number were in foster or residential care, and some had actually been ejected from the latter. The remaining participants were community peers without formal contact with the police and who were not in crisis. Facilitator participants included a psychotherapist, a creative artist and two peer researchers from the same community. The author, a psychologist, was principal investigator.

### Summary of the Project

The intervention project unfolded in three phases over 24 weeks (see Table 15.1). It took the form of weekly creative arts workshops in which experiences of police, youth justice and social integration were explored. We anticipated that the girls would undertake a leading role in planning and decision-making: they would choose the art medium to work in; they would choose, design and implement a social action project that reflected their primary issues of concern; and they would control an allocated budget for their project. Throughout, the girls interacted with the outside world in ways determined by them – e.g. through visits to other social projects and meeting politicians, community leaders and other key actors to question them about matters of concern. Their final social project – a DVD outlining their issues with the justice and care systems, and social integration – was presented to Ireland's Ombudsman for Children, senior members of the Garda Juvenile Diversion service, local police, schools and community organizations.

**Table 15.1** Promoting resilience – a participatory action research project

| PAR project phases | Description | Fostering resilience |
| --- | --- | --- |
| **Phase 1** – Defining participation; question-posing; data-gathering; analyses | Twelve weeks of creative arts workshops facilitates:<br><br>• Exploration of participants' experiences with police, youth justice and social integration<br>• Identification of priority issues<br>• Opportunities to socialize<br>• Exploration of important themes<br>• Meeting key policy-makers to discuss priority issues<br>• Choice of social action project | Sharing of daily hassles and difficulties, and co-constructed art results in:<br><br>• Enhanced emotional regulation<br>• Communication skills<br>• Information-processing<br>• Behaviour respectful of group members and facilitators |
| **Phase 2** – Planning a social action | • Control of budget line<br>• Plan and implement social action project<br>• Choose method of action and dissemination (produce a DVD) | • Develop trust in their ownership of key project decisions<br>• Enhanced motivation<br>• Enhanced reflective capacity<br>• Responsible participation. |
| **Phase 3** – Implementing social action | Skills development culminating in girls' DVD production, *Girls Out Loud*. These include:<br><br>• Undertaking social action – visiting other relevant projects to learn about consultation with 'key' players, e.g. politicians and community leaders<br>• Make videos of project visits<br>• Interview other young people in social projects<br>• Use interviewing skills in visit to Irish parliament (Stormont)<br>• Identification of further research questions and themes<br>• Design and art skills – videoing and photography; drawing; storylines; animated puppet shows; video editing | The production of the story lines and DVD mobilized:<br><br>• Individual and collective mastery<br>• Confidence and self-esteem<br>• Persistence in the face of doubt and difficulty<br>• More powerful voice (making oneself heard)<br>• Effective communication |

| PAR project phases | Description | Fostering resilience |
|---|---|---|
| **Phase 4** – Analysis, reflection and dissemination of project findings | Present DVD and discuss issues with the justice and care systems with:<br>• Ombudsman for Children<br>• Garda Juvenile Diversion service<br>• Local police<br>• Local school<br>• Local communities<br><br>Subsequently, local youth organization starts participation initiative, consulting with parents. Our project participants:<br>• Train staff<br>• Develop consultation work with parents | Changes in:<br>• Perspective-taking and inter-subjectivity<br>• Ability to adopt the perspective of the 'other' in their communications |

### Implementing the Project

Some of the developmental stages of this project are outlined below.

**Getting the Girls to Engage with the Project**   was a key challenge – their experiences of feeling powerless and unheard within the social care and justice systems was evident in an early comment by one young participant: 'If you feel you're not being heard, there's no point, you feel there is no point in yourself making progress'

   Such experiences fed into a manifest reluctance to join in early workshop sessions. It was clear that the girls felt they had nothing to contribute and found it hard to imagine a project directed by them without adults structuring and controlling it. We tried engaging them in various ways. For instance, we included a drumming session to provide structure and focus while participants learned about the project and each other. It was difficult to get them to drum, making audible sounds. It often seemed as if the young people would disengage themselves from the project and that it was impossible for the group to find direction. This was evidenced in late arrivals, much leaving and returning to the room and a lot of mobile phone texting.

**The Need to Step Back**   and leave the control and ownership of the project in the girls' hands quickly became apparent, and gradually they became more engaged. For instance, they swiftly assumed control of choosing and ordering the end of session food; they developed their own rules for group meetings, including the fact that members needed to arrive ahead of time so they could chat together before the group meeting started; they chose the sessional art medium they would use. First, however, they 'interviewed' the group's creative artist, seeking information about his work, examining examples of it and asking questions. The group agreed that he was 'sound' and they could work with him.

**Emerging Group-Level Properties**   gradually become evident as the girls chose art activities, exchanged helpful ideas, and began to work alongside each other.

**Individual and Collective Mastery**   developed. Initially, participants were reluctant to use the arts materials – one was so inhibited at the start that the creative artist held her hand to scaffold her early drawing attempts. A 'transformational' came when the creative artist used the clay characters participants had made in a previous session to make an animated computer film. This provoked great enthusiasm and excitement. From then on, participants' assurance in their contribution to the group grew.

**A Sense of Ownership of the Group had Developed**   By session 6, members arrived on time, they reminded each other to turn off mobile phones and they more obviously helped each other, particularly if someone had missed a session. There was a sense of focus and flow. The group assumed significant responsibility for managing their session. One asked 'How many weeks have we left?' indicating how they valued the space. One requested that no new people should be allowed to join as 'this is the group now.' Over the next 6 weeks, their creative work and discussion about their lives opened up. They developed a puppet show and took charge of developing storylines. They began photographing their work.

**Participants Underwent Remarkable Changes**   as they gained in confidence, self-esteem, and optimism. Emotional control and regulation became apparent – in particular, inhibition of disruptive behaviour. They showed the capacity to plan and think ahead. Relationships between group members and with the facilitators came to be characterized by reciprocity and commitment to the achieving group aims.

Mobilizing supportive resilience systems flowed from the girls' progress and development. As they moved from being angry and antagonistic towards authority figures, such as the 'pigs' (police), they were able to engage constructively in discussions with them. Their new-found ability to tolerate multiple perspectives (theirs and those of the police) and increased maturity meant that when they showed their DVD to local police, their schools and local community projects, they were mobilizing supportive relationships that would enhance resilience within their immediate microsystems.

## Conclusion

Specific examples of the girls' enhanced resilient capacities are outlined in Table 15.1. In summary, our experience gained through this project has shown us that fostering resilience with 'hard to reach' adolescents means giving them a good or *positive* experience of power, control, ownership of decision-making and resource management in a way that stimulates their feelings of mastery (their mastery system). They gain a sense that they are able to impact on their world in ways that are chosen by them and meaningful to them, and that they can actively mobilize others to support them. These processes, so important in developing resilience when in difficult circumstances, may inadvertently be undermined by many of our more traditional clinical practices. As researchers and practitioners, our moment of enlightenment in this project came when the young people told the Irish Ombudsman for Children 'This was *our* project' and their sense of ownership was publicly celebrated and claimed.

# References

1 Masten AS (2015) Pathways to integrated resilience science. Psychological Inquiry 26, 187–196.
2 Tost H, Champagne FA, Meyer-Lindenberg A (2015) Environmental influence in the brain, human welfare and mental health. Nature Neuroscience 18, 1421–1431.
3 Ellis BJ, Del Giudice M (2014) Beyond allostatic load: rethinking the role of stress in regulating human development. Development and Psychopathology, 26, 1–20.
4 Ellis B (2015) Keynote presentation. Beyond Allostatic Load: Rethinking the Role of Stress in Regulating Child Development and Resilience. Pathways to Resilience III International Conference. Halifax, Canada. June, 2015.
5 Panter-Brick C, Leckman JF (2013) Editorial commentary: Resilience in child development-interconnected pathways to wellbeing. Journal of Child Psychology and Psychiatry, 54, 333–336.
6 Ungar M (2008) Resilience across cultures. British Journal of Social Work, 38, 218–235.
7 Ungar M (2015) Diagnosing childhood resilience- a systematic approach to the diagnosis of adaptation in adverse social and physical ecologies. Journal of Child Psychology and Psychiatry, 56, 4–17.
8 Levitt MJ (2005) Social relations in childhood and adolescence: The convoy model perspective. Human Development, 48, 28–47.
9 Mahler MS (1977) Separation-Individuation: Selected Papers of Margaret S. Mahler. New York: Aronson.

## 16

# Sexual Orientation, Sexual Health and Gender Dysphoria

*Justin Wakefield*

## Introduction

This chapter focuses on the relationships between the development of adolescent sexuality and gender identity with physical and mental health. Development of a positive and secure sense of identity, especially with regard to sexuality and gender, is a key task of childhood and adolescence. Clinicians require a framework for assessing sexuality and gender, due to the evidence of associations with adverse mental health outcomes.

## Sexual Orientation

The Royal College of Psychiatrists clearly states that homosexuality is not a psychiatric disorder, although historically it was labelled as such. It also remarks that there is no scientific evidence to support the notion that sexual orientation can be changed. In fact, attempts to do so can be harmful or distressing [1].

However, there are important associations with mental health presentations that have consequences for clinicians.

### Defining Sexual Orientation and Its Importance in Clinical Evaluation

Sexual orientation encompasses three different domains of an individual's identity and behaviour:

1) Romantic and sexual attraction – the gender to which individuals are romantically and physically attracted.
2) Sexual behaviour – the gender of person with which an individual has sexual relationships.
3) Sexual orientation identity – a term with which an individual chooses to define their overall sexual orientation.

Broadly speaking, the labels heterosexual, homosexual and bisexual can be applied to each of these three domains depending on whether they involve someone of the opposite gender, the same gender or both genders. One might expect consistency across the domains for adults. However, for a multitude of biological, developmental and psycho-social reasons, they may not be congruent during adolescence. For clinicians

*Child Psychology and Psychiatry: Frameworks for Clinical Training and Practice,* Third Edition.
Edited by David Skuse, Helen Bruce and Linda Dowdney.
© 2017 John Wiley & Sons, Ltd. Published 2017 by John Wiley & Sons, Ltd.

conducting assessments with adolescents, asking questions related to romantic attraction and sexual behaviour, rather than just identity, is important for a number of reasons:

1) It provides a more developmentally appropriate understanding of a young person's identity.
2) It demonstrates an understanding of the complex sense of self-identity that a young person might have.
3) It establishes important risk factors to inform treatment strategies.

### An Overview of the Literature Relating Sexual Orientation and Mental Health

Minority sexual orientation (homosexuality or bisexuality) is associated with an increased risk for adverse mental health outcomes in adults. An important meta-analysis that included 25 epidemiological studies identified relative risks in the region of 1.5–2 for suicide attempt, depression, anxiety and substance dependence [2].

Methodological problems, such as differing strategies to assign sexual orientation categories in adolescence, have made comparisons between studies challenging. However, epidemiological samples have now consistently replicated the majority of associations identified in adult samples. Many studies originate in the USA, which has routinely included questions related to sexual orientation and mental health in large youth risk behaviour surveys.

Data supports strong associations between sexual orientation and suicidality and suicide attempts [3], anorexia and features of disordered eating [4] and substance use [5]. There is growing concern regarding a complex syndemic of mental health difficulties, drug use and riskier sexual practices in gay men, which is of profound public health importance [6].

Associations with adverse mental health outcomes remain, no matter how sexual orientation is defined. Youths identified as bisexual seem to be at comparable or even higher risk for a range of adverse outcomes, including suicide attempts [7].

### Understanding the Associations Between Sexual Orientation and Mental Health

Most research has focused on the influence of adversity in psycho-social circumstances that mediates the association between sexual orientation and mental health outcomes.

Such experiences include victimization and bullying [8] and negative responses to disclosure of sexual orientation [9]. These experiences can inhibit development of emotional regulation skills, the very tools needed to manage such experiences [10]. Discriminatory experiences during development have a negative impact on the hypothalamic–pituitary axis, similar to those seen in depressive states [11].

### Intervening to Prevent Adverse Mental Health Outcomes

Evidence-based interventions exist to reduce the likelihood of such adverse mental health outcomes:

- Schools with systems in place to support sexual minority youths, such as gay–straight alliances, have lower rates of victimization and suicide attempts [12].
- Family connectedness and supportive caring adults are a protective factor [13], although there is far more research on unhelpful or negative parenting responses.

It is important that future research is longitudinal in nature, focuses on evaluating interventions and also develops understanding regarding models of resilience for sexual minority youth.

Box 16.1 provides practical implications of the available research for clinicians.

---

**Box 16.1  Practical clinical implications**

- An age-appropriate assessment of psychosexual development should be a standard component of any diagnostic assessment.
- Issues of confidentiality must be addressed.
- Clinicians should make an assessment of family dynamics and communication related to issues of sexual orientation or gender identity.
- Liaison with schools to advocate for the needs of young people is an important clinical intervention.
- Clinicians should be able to direct young people and families to community and professional resources for sexual minority youths.
- Clinicians should not offer treatment to alter or 'convert' sexual orientation.
- When communicating with adolescents:
  - Do not assume heterosexuality.
  - Use gender-neutral language in discussions regarding relationships.
  - Labelling sexual orientation identity is not necessary; enquire instead about the gender of partners or of people to whom he/she is attracted.
  - Ensure adolescents have the opportunity to speak without a parent or guardian present.
- Consider the use of language and representation of sexual minorities in literature and posters in waiting areas, promotional material and questionnaires.

*Source*: Adapted from Coker *et al.* [14] and Adelson [15].

---

## Sexual Health

The reciprocal relationships between mental health disorders and their treatment and sexual behaviour and health are important for clinicians. This remains the case whatever the sexual orientation.

### The Influence of Mental Health on Sexual Behaviour

Adolescents with psychiatric disorders are at higher risk of sexually transmitted infections. Symptoms [16] or a diagnosis of mania [17], depression [18] and attention deficit hyperactivity disorder [19] are known to be associated with increased sexual risk behaviour, although some risk is better predicted by the presence of broader behavioural or conduct problems.

Clinicians should feel confident in being able to identify individuals with an increased risk of sexual health problems. They can then work to promote sexual health and improve communication with families regarding sexual behaviours. Families with good communication in this domain had adolescents with lower sexual risk-taking [20].

**The Influence of Mental Health Treatment on Sexual Behaviour**

Side-effects of selective serotonin reuptake inhibitor antidepressants, such as reduced libido, erectile dysfunction and delayed ejaculation, are relatively common in adults (up to 30–40%). The available literature for adolescents suggests that antidepressant-induced sexual dysfunction does occur and can affect compliance, but it has not been sufficiently evaluated to comment on incidence or longer-term outcomes [21].

Antipsychotic medication is associated with high levels of sexual dysfunction in adults but this has not been sufficiently evaluated in adolescents. [22].

Clinical Implications

It is likely that sexual dysfunction occurs in adolescents as a result of psychotropic medication and that this can affect compliance as well as cause distress. Collaborative decision-making principles would suggest that sexual side effects should be discussed prior to starting psychoactive medication and be routinely enquired about during follow up consultations. The impact and acceptability of this for adolescents is a poorly understood area requiring further research.

# Gender Dysphoria

The clinical presentation of children and adolescents with extremes of gender variant behaviour or dissatisfaction with their birth gender is one that receives much popular interest, and is presenting with increased frequency at specialist treatment centres. However, local child and adolescent mental health services also have an important role to play in treatment.

### Diagnostic Issues

Gender variant behaviour describes behaving in a manner not ordinarily considered normal for someone's sex. Diagnostic and classification systems, which are themselves subject to review and change, define a spectrum of behaviours and subjective experiences which are considered abnormal.

*The Diagnostic and Statistical Manual of Mental Disorders*, 5th edition uses the term 'gender dysphoria' to describe individuals who:

- have incongruence between their assigned gender and their experience or expressed gender;
- insist that they in fact are, or want to be, the 'other' gender.

The *International Statistical Classification of Diseases and Related Health Problems*, 10th revision, currently classifies this presentation under the labels of gender identity disorder of childhood and transsexualism for adults.

### Epidemiology

The American Psychiatric Association estimates prevalence rates in adults of 0.005–0.014% for adult natal males and 0.002–0.003% for adult natal females. Referral data suggest that more males present for clinical evaluation with a sex ratio of between 2–4:1. There are no population-based studies to comment on prevalence in children or adolescents.

## Aetiology

Gender dysphoria represents an incredibly heterogeneous range of clinical presentations and presumed aetiologies. There has been considerable interest in identifying underlying biological mechanisms [23]. Possibilities include the role of genetics, although no consistent candidate genes have been found, and of prenatal sex hormones which are known to influence postnatal sex-dimorphic behaviour.

There is no clearly identifiable psycho-social factor contributing to the development of gender dysphoria. However, a thorough psycho-social and psychodynamic assessment has vital utility in developing a treatment plan, and may help to identify presentations with alternative explanations or diagnoses.

## Clinical Management in Childhood

The management of prepubertal children presenting with gender dysphoria is guided by the knowledge that the majority of these individuals will not persist with features of gender dysphoria after puberty. A more common outcome is of homosexuality or bisexuality [24].

Management therefore relies upon a thorough psycho-social assessment, psycho-education for parents and young people and consultation to the wider network. A common dilemma faced is how to respond to children wanting to dress in gender-variant clothing. It is important that parental reactions do not induce a sense of shame or guilt as this can lead to other emotional or behavioural psychopathology. A pragmatic approach, varied according to the strength of a child's conviction and degree of distress is normally suggested. Care should be taken to ensure a young person knows that it is always possible to reverse any transition they have made.

It is not yet possible to accurately predict which children will persist with gender dysphoria into adolescence and adulthood.

## Clinical Management in Adolescence

### Non-specialist care
Gender dysphoria should be assessed and diagnosed according to diagnostic criteria as early as possible. Over half of young people presenting with gender dysphoria have additional co-morbidities, such as mood, anxiety or behavioural disorders [25], which should be treated appropriately. There is additional interest in the increased prevalence of autistic spectrum disorders (ASDs) in this group of young people. A diagnosis of ASD does not preclude clinicians from making a diagnosis of, or treating a young person with, gender dysphoria [26].

Mental health services can provide important psycho-social support and liaison with other agencies such as education. They may additionally allow a young person to explore more thoroughly their desire for gender reassignment, and explore more conservative treatment options or lifestyle changes.

**Specialist Care**

Referral to a specialist gender dysphoria centre for adolescents allows more experienced clinicians to provide support and advice for families and the wider network in addition to therapeutic work. Specific medical treatment options [27] only available in specialist centres include:

- The use of gonadotrophin-releasing hormone analogues to suppress the development of secondary sexual characteristics – whether or not this treatment alters the natural history of gender identity development in gender dysphoria is currently under investigation.
- Cross-sex hormone treatment – the administration of sex hormones for the desired gender (normally reserved for those aged 16 or over).

Surgical management is not offered until after the age of 18 years. The hormonal treatment outlined above is associated with a reduction of symptoms of co-morbid disorder and an increase in measures of global functioning [28].

## Summary

All the presentations in this chapter prompt clinicians to understand and address issues of behaviour and identity that may, for some, seem challenging or uncomfortable.

Minority sexual orientation and gender dysphoria are associated with a wide range of psychiatric disorders, largely as a result of adverse psycho-social experiences, and it is therefore important to explore these associations and develop appropriate psychosocial interventions.

The reciprocal relationship between psychiatric disorders, their treatment and sexual risk and sexual behaviour demands that all clinicians incorporate a psychosexual assessment into routine clinical assessment.

## References

1 Croucher R (2014) Sexual Orientation: Royal College of Psychiatrists' Report.
2 King M, Semlyen J, Tai See S et al. (2008) A systematic review of mental disorder, suicide, and deliberate self harm in lesbian, gay and bisexual people. BMC Psychiatry, 8 SP-EP-(1), 70.
3 Stone DM, Luo F, Ouyang L et al. (2014) Sexual orientation and suicide ideation, plans, attempts, and medically serious attempts: evidence from local Youth Risk Behavior Surveys, 2001–2009. American Journal of Public Health, 104, 262–271.
4 Ackard DM, Fedio G, Neumark-Sztainer D, Britt HR (2008) Factors associated with disordered eating among sexually active adolescent males: gender and number of sexual partners. Psychosomatic Medicine, 70, 232–238.
5 Marshal MP, Friedman MS, Stall R et al. (2008) Sexual orientation and adolescent substance use: a meta-analysis and methodological review. Addiction, 103, 546–556.
6 Mustanski B, Andrews R, Herrick A et al. (2014) A syndemic of psychosocial health disparities and associations with risk for attempting suicide among young sexual minority men. American Journal of Public Health, 104, 287–294.

7   Saewyc EM, Skay CL, Hynds P et al. (2007) Suicidal ideation and attempts in North American school-based surveys: are bisexual youth at increasing risk? Journal of LGBT Health Research, 3, 25–36.

8   Rostosky SS, Owens GP, Zimmerman RS, Riggle EDB (2003) Associations among sexual attraction status, school belonging, and alcohol and marijuana use in rural high school students. Journal of Adolescence, 26, 741–751.

9   Rosario M, Schrimshaw EW, Hunter J (2009) Disclosure of sexual orientation and subsequent substance use and abuse among lesbian, gay, and bisexual youths: critical role of disclosure reactions. Psychology of Addictive Behaviors, 23, 175–184.

10  Hatzenbuehler ML (2009) How does sexual minority stigma 'get under the skin'? A psychological mediation framework. Psychological Bulletin, 135, 707–730.

11  Hatzenbuehler ML, McLaughlin KA (2014) Structural stigma and hypothalamic-pituitary-adrenocortical axis reactivity in lesbian, gay, and bisexual young adults. Annals of Behavioral Medicine, 47, 39–47.

12  Hatzenbuehler ML, Birkett M, Van Wagenen A, Meyer IH (2014) Protective school climates and reduced risk for suicide ideation in sexual minority youths. American Journal of Public Health, 104, 279–286.

13  Bouris A, Guilamo-Ramos V, Pickard A et al. (2010) A systematic review of parental influences on the health and well-being of lesbian, gay, and bisexual youth: time for a new public health research and practice agenda. Journal of Primary Prevention, 31, 273–309.

14  Coker TR, Austin SB, Schuster MA (2010) The health and health care of lesbian, gay, and bisexual adolescents. Annual Review of Public Health, 31, 457–477.

15  Adelson SL (2012) Practice parameter on gay, lesbian, or bisexual sexual orientation, gender nonconformity, and gender discordance in children and adolescents. Journal of the American Academy of Child and Adolescent Psychiatry, 51, 957–974.

16  Stewart AJ, Theodore-Oklota C, Hadley W et al. (2012) Mania Symptoms and HIV-Risk Behavior Among Adolescents in Mental Health Treatment. Journal of Clinical Child and Adolescent Psychology, 41, 803–810.

17  Brown LK, Hadley W, Stewart A et al. (2010) Psychiatric disorders and sexual risk among adolescents in mental health treatment. Journal of Consulting and Clinical Psychology, 78, 590–597.

18  Lehrer JA, Shrier LA, Gortmaker S, Buka S (2006) Depressive symptoms as a longitudinal predictor of sexual risk behaviors among US middle and high school students. Pediatrics. American Academy of Pediatrics, 118, 189–200.

19  Flory K, Molina BSG, Pelham WE Jr et al. (2006) Childhood ADHD Predicts Risky Sexual Behavior in Young Adulthood. Journal of Clinical Child & Adolescent Psychology, 35, 571–577.

20  Aspy CB, Vesely SK, Oman RF et al. (2006) Youth-parent communication and youth sexual behavior: implications for physicians. Family Medicine, 38, 500–504.

21  Levine A, McGlinchey E (2015) Assessing sexual symptoms and side effects in adolescents. Pediatrics. American Academy of Pediatrics, 135, e815–e817.

22  Correll CU, Carlson HE (2006) Endocrine and metabolic adverse effects of psychotropic medications in children and adolescents. Journal of the American Academy of Child and Adolescent Psychiatry, 45, 771–791.

23 Meyer-Bahlburg HFL (2010) From mental disorder to iatrogenic hypogonadism: dilemmas in conceptualizing gender identity variants as psychiatric conditions. Archives of Sexual Behavior, 39, 461–476.

24 Wallien MSC, Cohen-Kettenis PT. Psychosexual outcome of gender-dysphoric children. Journal of the American Academy of Child and Adolescent Psychiatry, 47, 1413–1423.

25 Wallien MSC, Swaab H, Cohen-Kettenis PT (2007) Psychiatric Comorbidity Among Children With Gender Identity Disorder. Journal of the American Academy of Child and Adolescent Psychiatry, 46, 1307–1314.

26 Vries ALC, Noens ILJ, Cohen-Kettenis PT, Berckelaer-Onnes IA, Doreleijers TA (2010) Autism Spectrum Disorders in Gender Dysphoric Children and Adolescents. Journal of Autism and Developmental Disorders, 40, 930–936.

27 Menvielle E, Gomez-Lobo V (2011) Management of children and adolescents with gender dysphoria. Journal of Pediatric and Adolescent Gynecology, 24, 183–188.

28 de Vries ALC, Steensma TD, Doreleijers TAH, Cohen-Kettenis PT (2011) Puberty suppression in adolescents with gender identity disorder: a prospective follow-up study. Journal of Sexual Medicine, 8, 2276–2283.

# 17

# Child Users of Online and Mobile Technologies – Risks, Harms and Intervention

*Peter K. Smith and Sonia Livingstone*

The relatively recent rapid growth in the development, accessibility and use of mobile phones and the internet has transformed the lives of young people, especially in developed countries. In the UK, Ofcom [1] found that ownership of a smartphone was 24% at 8–11 years, and 69% at 12–15 years by when 98% go online, and 74% have a social media profile (the most popular being Facebook). In the USA, 92% of teenagers aged 13–17 years report going online daily, 73% have access to a smartphone, and 71% use more than one social network site [2]. Across seven European countries, internet users aged 9–16 years are most likely to use the internet at home in their own bedroom (66%) and 68% have a social network profile [3].

Mobile, online and networked technologies bring enormous opportunities for pleasure and communication, knowledge-seeking and exchange. But they also bring risks, including cyberbullying, contact with strangers, sexual messaging (sexting) and pornography. These are the subject of public concern among parents, educators and clinicians, often amplified by the mass media. Concern about compulsive or excessive internet use ('addiction') has grown. Problematic internet use is characterized by a cognitive preoccupation with the internet, an inability to control its use, going online to relieve emotional distress, and continued use despite negative consequences [4]. It is associated with internet-related risks such as harassment, invasion of privacy and exposure to pornographic and violent content [4].

The EU Kids Online network [5] classified online risks to children on four dimensions: *aggressive, sexual, value-related* (e.g. visiting extremist sites) or *commercial*. Recognizing that children are themselves variously positioned in relation to such risks, they subdivided risks further into:

- *content risks* (which generally position the child as the recipient of mass produced content);
- *contact risks* (generally an adult-initiated online interaction which requires the child to participate, possibly unwittingly or unwillingly);
- *conduct risks* (where the child is an actor or interactor within a wider peer-to-peer network).

While interest is growing regarding value-oriented and commercial risks, most research to date has concentrated on aggressive and sexual risks, usually (and perhaps

*Child Psychology and Psychiatry: Frameworks for Clinical Training and Practice*, Third Edition.
Edited by David Skuse, Helen Bruce and Linda Dowdney.
© 2017 John Wiley & Sons, Ltd. Published 2017 by John Wiley & Sons, Ltd.

problematically) addressed separately. This review situates evidence on sexual and aggressive risks within the broader framework of risk, harm, and resilience. Online risks *afford* harm, this being a probabilistic negative outcome which depends on a host of contingencies. Similarly, online opportunities also afford but do not determine positive benefits for children. This helps in conceptualizing risk and protective factors, as well as suggesting beneficial interventions and enhancing resilience [6].

## Aggressive Risks: Cyber-Aggression and Cyberbullying

There are many types of electronic or cyber-aggression, including flaming, online harassment, cyberstalking, denigration (put-downs), masquerade, outing, exclusion, putting up false profiles and distributing personal material against someone's wishes. The victim may be known to the perpetrator offline (e.g. from school, or former girlfriends/boyfriends), may come from certain groups (e.g. ethnic, religious or sporting groups), but may also include celebrities, vulnerable people, school staff or victims known only from the internet [7].

Some researchers have used general terms such as cyber-victimization or online harassment [8], but much research has used the term cyberbullying, following criteria used for traditional bullying – intent to hurt, repetition and power imbalance. However, the repetition criterion is complicated in cyberbullying, as a single act by one perpetrator may be repeated by others and experienced many times by the victim. The power imbalance criterion is also contested, as neither physical strength nor strength in numbers is needed for cyberbullying, although other forms of power imbalance are possible, including anonymity [9,10].

Given differences in definition and measurement, estimates of cyberbullying prevalence vary widely [11]. The 25-country EU Kids Online survey of 9- to 16-year-olds in 2010 [5] found that 6% were bullied online, 3% by mobile phone or text, and 13% face-to-face. Figures for bullying others were 3%, 2% and 10% respectively. Other studies have reported substantially higher figures [9,11]. Overall, it seems that occasional or once-off occurrences may be reported by over 20% of young people, but serious or recent or repeated incidents are reported by only around 5% – less than for traditional bullying. There is some evidence of an age peak around 13–15 years. While boys are more engaged in traditional bullying than girls, girls can be equally as, or even more, engaged in cyberbullying, possibly because cyberbullying is more verbal or relational rather than physical, and is often located on social networking sites [9,11].

## Sexual Risks: Pornography, Sexting, Stranger Danger

Pornography can range from complete or partial nudity to depictions of sexual intercourse to violent or illegal images of abuse. Difficulties of investigation include the ethics of asking children what they have seen without introducing them to unfamiliar sexual ideas; social desirability effects when adolescents deliberately seek pornography but are unwilling to disclose this; and accidental exposure resulting from the internet 'pushing' pornography at those seeking informational, health or other content.

Sexting is generally defined as the sending, receiving and forwarding of sexually explicit messages, images or photos to others through electronic means. It is prevalent among young people, although again measures of incidence depend on the definitions and measures used [12,13]. EU Kids Online [5] found that 15% of 11- to 16-year-olds had seen or received a sexual message online, and this was more common among those characterized by more psychological difficulties, sensation-seeking or other risky online and offline behaviour. Predictors of risk of harm from receiving 'sexts' include being younger, female and showing greater psychological difficulties and less sensation-seeking. Qualitative research has identified young women as particularly at risk, as they often feel pressurized or coerced to send sexual images or 'sexts' [14].

Children make many contacts online with people they have not met face to face. EU Kids Online [5] found that 30% of 9- to 16-year-olds had made contact online in the previous year with someone they did not already know (from 13% at 9–10 years to 46% at 15–16 years), and 9% had gone to a meeting face-to-face with someone they first met on the internet. Harmful consequences remain rare although far from insignificant [15].

For sexual risks generally, the incidence of exposure to pornography, sexual messaging or stranger contact is generally found to increase over adolescence, but with higher risks for teenagers than adults.

## Trends Over Time

Although teenagers' internet use continues to rise, there is little evidence of a corresponding rise in exposure to online pornography, with incidence seemingly stabilizing at around one in six younger children, rising to a third of older teens [3,16], although it is possible that the extreme nature of what is viewed is changing.

Three waves of the nationally representative Youth Internet Safety Survey [16], conducted among US 10- to 17-year-olds in 2000, 2005 and 2010, found that unwanted sexual solicitations declined over the three time points, from 19% to 13% to 9%. Online harassment increased from 6% to 9% and then 11%, this being more marked for girls; unwanted exposure to pornography first increased from 25% to 34%, but then decreased to 23%. A survey by Net Children Go Mobile in 2013–2014 provided a follow-up of the EU Kids Online survey in 2010, in seven European countries [3,17]. They found an increase in online skills, but also an increase in most online risks – e.g. in being cyberbullied (from 7% to 12%), in meeting an online contact offline (from 8% to 12%), and in being bothered or upset by something on the internet (from 13% to 17%).

Over the period when access to online and mobile technologies increased dramatically, there was no equivalent evidence of a dramatic increase in either risk or harm to children. Nevertheless, there is evidence of an upward trend in many risks, and possibly of associated harm (see Box 17.1).

---

**Box 17.1  Child usage of online and mobile technologies – risks, harms and intervention**

- Increasing child and adolescent usage of online and mobile technologies is associated with a range of risks.
- Aggressive and sexual risks include cyberbullying/aggression; sexting, stranger danger.
- Evidence suggests that a range of adverse emotional and psychological harm can befall children and adolescents who use online and mobile technologies. This is particularly true for children with pre-existing vulnerabilities.
- Risk of harm is heightened by:
  - child psychological factors – such as propensity to risk-taking, low self-esteem, emotional or behavioural difficulties
  - social factors – such as lack of parental support and peer norms
  - digital factors – such as digital skills, online practices and specific online sites.
- Exposure to risk can also foster developmental resilience – particularly where children and adolescents receive support and are taught how to recognize and manage risk by parents, schools and colleges.
- Interventions are more likely to be successful when they are tailored to target groups and derive from evidence-based research identifying risk and resilience factors.

---

## The Harm Associated with Mobile and Online Risk

Not all online risks result in harm. It is not really known how many children have been harmed as a result of an online experience; researchers generally rely on subjective self-report measures, and few have conducted longitudinal studies that can track the later consequences of exposure to risk. Nonetheless, the evidence points to some evidence for harm.

### Aggressive Risks and Harm

Victims of cyberbullying express a variety of negative emotions. Cyber-victimization is associated in many cross-sectional studies with a range of psychosocial problems, including affective disorders, depression and behavioural problems, including substance use. This is not inevitable. A significant minority of young people report being not bothered, especially boys and those victimized less often. A few studies have assessed longitudinal relationships. Cyberbullying victimization has been found to predict later depressive symptoms, and also problematic internet use, with some evidence of a vicious cycle unfolding for victims over time [6].

A well-established finding is substantial overlap between victimization and perpetration online and offline [9,11]. Most studies find that those children who experience *both* types of bullying report worse symptoms and some also find the consequences worse if children are involved as both cyber-victims and cyber-perpetrators.

**Sexual Risks and Harm**

In the US, of 10- to 17-year-olds who had seen pornography, nearly half the 10- to 12-year-olds but only a fifth of the 16- to 17-year-olds said they were very or extremely upset [16]. With EU Kids Online [5], of the 9- to 16-year-olds who had seen online pornography, around one-third said that they had been bothered or upset. Among 11- to 16-year-olds who had seen or received a sexual message online, a quarter reported being bothered by it – a higher proportion of girls and younger children found this upsetting. The majority of sexual images and texts pass between consenting persons without harm. However, if sexually explicit images are disseminated without consent, if those involved are under-age, and if the images are used to cyberbully, there can be potentially serious outcomes.

# Factors that Increase Risk of Harm or Protect Against Them

Children who are already vulnerable offline are likely also to be vulnerable online, and, relatedly, those who take risks in one domain are also likely to take them in others [6]. The following factors appear important predictors of the risks of harm: personality factors (sensation-seeking, low self-esteem, moral disengagement, psychological difficulties), social factors (lack of parental support, peer norms) and digital factors (online practices, digital skills, the affordances of specific online sites and services).

# Interventions

Some kinds of aggressive and sexual risk-taking are illegal, depending on a plethora of national laws generally devised before the rise of the internet [18]. This complicates the context in which interventions are designed, implemented and evaluated so that best practice can be shared. For example, prevention of adolescent cyberbullying may involve general empathy training, modifying beliefs supportive of aggression, and more specific guidelines for internet behaviour, including actions young people can take themselves (such as not hitting back, reporting abuse, keeping evidence) [19–21].

A review of internet safety education programmes [22] pointed out the need for basing such programmes on research findings, tailoring them to developmental needs, and evaluating their effectiveness. A review of 13 intervention models for traditional and cyberbullying using information and communication technologies [23] found that only four programmes provided evidence of effectiveness. Independent evaluations of interventions are vital to learn from mistakes and share best practice.

**Challenges to Research**

The rapid changes in both technological advances and social practices of use mean that findings can date quickly and a focus on historical change is important. A related challenge comes from the shifting relations between online and offline risks. Often, risk is studied either online or offline, making it difficult to assess whether the advent of online and mobile technologies has extended the risk of harm to children or whether the proportion of children at risk is largely unchanged, with only the means by which it occurs changing.

### Policy Implications

Professionals need to be trained to recognize how the internet and mobile technologies may be implicated in mediating or exacerbating risk of harm to children. When clinicians and other professionals see a child showing signs of harm, they should inquire into the possible online as well as offline context. The more children use the internet, and the more digital skills and confidence they gain, the more deeply and broadly they use it, thus encountering more risks as well as opportunities. Finding the balance between treating online risk seriously and yet not overreacting is difficult. A world without risk is undesirable, and facing and coping with risk are important for developing resilience [24]. Paradoxically, therefore, a risk-averse society can exacerbate rather than reduce the very vulnerabilities it seeks to protect.

# References

1 Ofcom (2015) Children and parents: Media use and attitudes report. London: Office of Communications. Online: http://stakeholders.ofcom.org.uk/market-data-research/other/research-publications/childrens/children-parents-nov-15/. Accessed: January 2017.

2 Lenhart A (2015) Teens, social media, technology overview 2015. Pew Research Center. Online: http://www.pewinternet.org/2015/04/09/teens-social-media-technology-2015/. Accessed: January 2017.

3 Livingstone S, Mascheroni G, Ólafsson K, Haddon L (2014) Children's online risks and opportunities: Comparative findings from EU Kids Online and Net Children Go Mobile. LSE, London: EU Kids Online: http://eprints.lse.ac.uk/60513/. Accessed: January 2017.

4 Caplan SE (2010) Theory and measurement of generalized problematic Internet use: A two-step approach. Computers in Human Behavior, 26, 1089–1097.

5 Livingstone S, Haddon L, Görzig A, Ólafsson K (2011) Risks and safety on the internet: The perspective of European children. Full findings. LSE, London: EU Kids Online. Available at http://eprints.lse.ac.uk/33731/

6 Livingstone S, Smith PK (2014) Research Review: Harms experienced by child users of online and mobile technologies: The nature, prevalence and management of sexual and aggressive risks in the digital age. Journal of Child Psychology & Psychiatry, 55, 635–654.

7 Pyzalski J (2012) From cyberbullying to electronic aggression: typology of the phenomenon. Emotional and Behavioural Difficulties, 17, 305–317.

8 Finkelhor D, Turner HA, Shattuck A, Hamby SL (2015) Prevalence of childhood exposure to violence, crime, and abuse. JAMA Pediatrics, 169, 746–754.

9   Smith PK (2014) Understanding School Bullying: It's Nature and Prevention Strategies. Sage Publications.

10  Antoniadou N, Kokkinos M (2015) Cyber and school bullying: Same or different phenomena? Aggression and Violent Behavior, 25, 363–372.

11  Kowalski RM, Giumetti GW, Schroeder AN, Lattanner MR (2014) Bullying in the digital age: A critical review and meta-analysis of cyberbullying research among youth. Psychological Bulletin, 140, 1073–1137.

12  Klettke B, Hallford DJ, Mellor DJ (2014) Sexting prevalence and correlates: A systematic literature review. Clinical Psychology Review, 34, 44–53.

13  Mitchell KJ, Finkelhor D, Jones LM, Wolak J (2012) Prevalence and characteristics of youth sexting: A national study. Pediatrics, 129, 13–20.

14  Ringrose J, Harvey L, Gill R, and Livingstone S (2013) Teen girls, sexual double standards and 'sexting': Gendered value in digital image exchange, Feminist Theory, 14, 305–323. Online: http://eprints.lse.ac.uk/63960/. Accessed: January 2017

15  Whittle H, Hamilton-Giachritsis C, Beech A, Collings G (2013) A review of young people's vulnerabilities to online grooming. Aggression and Violent Behavior, 18, 135–146.

16  Jones LM, Mitchell KJ, Finkelhor D (2012) Trends in youth internet victimization: findings from three youth internet safety surveys 2000–2010. Journal of Adolescent Health, 50, 179–186.

17  Hasebrink U (2014) Children's changing online experiences in a longitudinal perspective. LSE, London: EU Kids Online: http://eprints.lse.ac.uk/60083/. Accessed: January 2017.

18  Lievens E (2014) Bullying and sexting in social networks: Protecting minors from criminal acts or empowering minors to cope with risky behaviour? International Journal of Law, Crime and Justice, 42, 251–270.

19  Ang RP (2015) Adolescent cyberbullying: A review of characteristics, prevention and intervention strategies. Aggression and Violent Behavior, 25, 35–42.

20  Schultze-Krumbholz A, Schultze M, Zagorscak P et al. (2016) Feeling cybervictims' pain – The effect of empathy training on cyberbullying. Aggressive Behavior, 42, 147–156.

21  Jacobs NCL, Vollink T, Dehue F, Lechner L (2014) Online Pestkoppenstoppen: systematic and theory-based development of a web-based tailored intervention for adolescent cyberbully victims to combat and prevent cyberbullying. BMC Public Health, 14, 396.

22  Jones LM, Mitchell KJ, Walsh WA (2013) Evaluation of internet child safety materials used by ICAC task forces in school and community settings. Final Report. US Department of Justice. https://www.ncjrs.gov/pdffiles1/nij/grants/242016.pdf. Accessed: January 2017.

23  Nocentini A, Zambuto V, Menesini E (2015) Anti-bullying programs and Information and Communication Technologies (ICTs): A systematic review. Aggression and Violent Behavior, 23, 52–60.

24  Coleman J, Hagell A (eds) (2007) Adolescence, risk and resilience: Against the odds. Chichester: Wiley.

## Internet Resources

Anti-bullying Alliance (UK): http://www.anti-bullyingalliance.org.uk/
Childnet International: http://www.childnet.com
ConnectSafely: http://www.connectsafely.org/
Cyberbullying Research Center (USA): http://cyberbullying.us/
EU Kids Online: www.eukidsonline.net
European Schoolnet: http://www.eun.org/
Insafe: http://www.saferinternet.org/
National Center for Missing and Exploited Children (USA):
http://www.missingkids.com/home
Safer Internet Centre (UK): http://www.saferinternet.org.uk/

Section 3

# The Impact of Trauma, Loss and Maltreatment

3a: Trauma and Loss

# 18

# Children Bereaved by Parent or Sibling Death

*Linda Dowdney*

Bereaved children grieve in similar ways to bereaved adults, reporting shock and disbelief, followed by sadness, anger, a longing for the dead person to return, and concentration, sleeping and eating difficulties [1].

## Children's Understanding of Death

There is developmental progression in children's biological concepts of death and also their ability to combine biological and supernatural explanatory frameworks [2,3]. Preschoolers believe that, and act as if, a dead person can return. Until the age of 7 years, children believe their thoughts and feelings can cause or reverse death. The biological concept of death is fully grasped by the age of 10–11 years, although it is acquired faster in verbally able children or those who have experienced bereavement. Eleven-year-olds are more likely than 7-year-olds to employ both biological and supernatural reasoning, e.g. accepting that the dead are insensate whilst imagining an afterlife where the dead enjoy favourite pastimes [2]. Adolescents can be troubled by the unfairness of death and by existential questions about life's meaning.

## How Children Express Grief

Children can distract themselves from grief through normative play or social activities, leading their carers to wonder whether they truly grieve. This uncertainty is compounded by young children's inability to verbalize their feelings. Children's curiosity about death takes new forms as they mature.

### Early Childhood

Young children search actively for the deceased. Their play and fantasies reflect their particular concerns and preoccupations. Their sense of loss, their carer's grief and changed daily routines can provoke bewilderment, developmental regression and unprovoked expressions of anger or aggression.

*Child Psychology and Psychiatry: Frameworks for Clinical Training and Practice,* Third Edition.
Edited by David Skuse, Helen Bruce and Linda Dowdney.
© 2017 John Wiley & Sons, Ltd. Published 2017 by John Wiley & Sons, Ltd.

**Middle Childhood**

Appropriate sadness exists alongside a resumption of normative activities. New sleeping difficulties vary by age: 5- to 7-year-olds experience difficulties settling to sleep, and older children report nightmares, although some derive comfort from dreaming about the deceased [1]. All children settle more easily when an attachment figure is nearby. From the age of 8 years, physical manifestations of distress such as headaches appear, as do temper outbursts, argumentativeness and concentration difficulties. Children's natural curiosity about death can sometimes reflect underlying anxieties about their 'responsibility' for what happened. Parental distress can silence children's questioning, allowing any misperceptions about death to persist. Separation anxiety focuses on the vulnerability of loved ones.

**Adolescence**

Grief takes various forms, including withdrawing from family activities, risk-taking behaviours such as alcohol or drug use, and/or seeking peer support. Adolescents' cognitive ability to review their relationship with the deceased may bring comfort or, for those troubled by guilt or regrets, increased distress. New family roles and responsibilities, and expectations of over-mature behaviour can occur. A sense of responsibility alongside a desire to protect grieving adults may result in disguised grief and giving mixed messages to others.

## Resilience and Positive Outcomes in Bereaved Children

The majority follow a normal developmental trajectory, with some children reporting positive changes in response to the experience. These include increasing independence, better school performance, heightened empathy to another's distress and a growth in spirituality [4]. Research suggests that 'resilient' bereaved children show greater coping efficacy and fewer negative appraisals than so-called 'non-resilient' children [5], but the lack of resilience may simply reflect the presence of vulnerability to mental health problems. Recent research suggests that parental bereavement can adversely influence adolescent functional competence [6], but a poor outcome is mediated in part by mental health issues in the parent or child prior to bereavement.

## Psychopathology in Bereaved Children

Differences in rates of child psychopathology stem from differences in study inclusion/exclusion criteria, recruitment practices and measures used. The best-controlled studies indicate that only one in five will show disturbance of clinical severity [7]. Some 10% experience impaired functioning up to 3 years post-bereavement [8].

**Commonly Agreed Bereavement Symptoms**  include dysphoria (a state of unease), headaches, stomach aches and separation anxieties. Grief symptoms normally attenuate within 4 months of the death [4,7]. A longing to be reunited with the deceased can lead to an expressed wish to be dead. Such statements need careful exploration, particularly if the child shows clinical disturbance or a family suicide has occurred.

**Children Bereaved by Family Murder or Suicide**   experience post-traumatic stress disorder (PTSD) and internalizing disorders. Rates and types of psychopathology are similar to those in other bereaved children [9], with a raised risk of depressive disorder up to 2 years after the event [10]. There is an increased risk of suicidal behaviour [11] and high levels of persistent anger, guilt, shame and social isolation [9]. Recent longitudinal cohort studies indicate that, up to early adulthood, parentally bereaved children have a significantly raised risk of all-cause mortality. The highest risk attaches to children bereaved by suicide [12]. Such associations may result from factors such as heritability of physical or mental health risk, or an interaction between psychosocial stressors and genetic susceptibility.

### Prolonged Complex Bereavement

Symptoms previously described as 'prolonged' or 'complicated' grief combine in the newly recognized prolonged complex bereavement disorder (PCBD) in the *Diagnostic and Statistical Manual of Mental Disorders*, 5th edition (DSM-5) [13,14]. The PCBD specifier 'traumatic bereavement' applies only to bereavement by homicide or suicide. Some claim that PCBD lacks validity with respect to children and risks pathologizing normal grief [15]. In contrast, others suggest PCBD is under-inclusive, and that applying DSM-5 criteria identifies approximately half of children with clinically impairing prolonged grief [13]. Further research clarifying developmental manifestations of adaptive and maladaptive grief, and developing appropriately validated child grief measures, are needed [16].

## Hypothalamic–Pituitary–Adrenal Axis (HPA) Dysregulation

The HPA axis mediates between stress and the pathophysiology of child psychiatric disorders [17]. Traumatic parental death has been linked to long-term dysregulation of the HPA axis in children [17]. Participation in a bereavement treatment programme may, through increasing effective parenting, for example, increase adolescent resilience as measured by their response to a cortisol stress test up to 6 years after the intervention [18]. Interpretation of these data is not straightforward, however, because of methodological shortcomings.

## What Influences Child Outcome?

Systematic examination of factors mediating or moderating bereaved children's outcomes is made difficult by the preponderance of unrepresentative samples. Recent national longitudinal cohort studies allow consideration of long-term health and mortality measures (see, e.g. Li *et al.* [12]).

Child morbidity is influenced by the age and sex of the child. Younger children develop behavioural or anxiety problems. Adolescents exhibit dysphoria or depression.

Generally, boys display higher rates of overall difficulties and acting out/aggressive behaviours than girls, who are more likely to show sleep disturbance, bedwetting and depressive symptoms.

Risk factors for persistent psychopathology include pre-existing psychiatric disorders in parents or children, marital conflict or separation and, post-bereavement, caregiver prolonged grief or depression [5,19]. Parental warmth, authoritative parenting and consistent discipline promote resilience [5].

## Interventions with Bereaved Children

### Theoretical and Cultural Influences

There are two main theoretical bases for interventions with bereaved children.

The first approach suggests that children need to complete a sequence of bereavement-related tasks in order to satisfactorily resolve their grief and so avoid maladaptive outcomes. Tasks include acceptance of the permanence of loss, constructing a positive internal image of the deceased and finding new and supportive relationships [20]. In children experiencing prolonged grief, therapy focuses on addressing psychological factors, such as PTSD, that prevent grief resolution [16]. The second approach views bereaved children's outcomes as the product of multiple, cumulative risk and protective factors [5]. Preventive intervention within this framework concentrates on increasing child protective factors, such as effective parenting, and reducing child emotional and behavioural symptomatology. However, the approach is least effective with more symptomatic children who may require a targeted mental health approach [5].

Beliefs about grief and mourning are socially constructed within cultural, social and familial contexts. These contexts, and each family's interpretation of them, vary between presenting children and require careful assessment. Therapists should be aware of how western conceptualizations of grief and mourning impact upon their own beliefs.

### What Do Bereaved Children Need?

Bereaved children benefit from receiving accurate information about the death and related events. Reassurance that they could not have changed or influenced either is helpful. Age-appropriate, clear and truthful explanations are needed. Euphemisms such as 'gone to sleep' will be interpreted literally by young children and can affect sleep. Little guidance is available where familial suicide or murder occurs. Open communication can be inhibited by protectiveness towards children or by adult survivors' guilt and shame. Guilt may also affect adolescent survivors of sibling suicide with unshared prior knowledge of their sibling's distress [11]. Adults worry that conveying understanding and empathy for the deceased might suggest to vulnerable children that violence or suicide are acceptable coping strategies [9,11]. Such families may be in particular need of supportive services.

Children benefit from the re-establishment of consistent daily routines, and the emotional availability of major caregivers. Children and adolescents benefit from having their developmental competencies fostered. Engagement in the wider social world, via activities and friendships, should be maintained. Adolescents find support in evolving friendship groups and in physical activities that help relieve depression or channel aggression [21]. Both adolescents and children report benefiting from talking with other bereaved children as this lessens their sense of isolation and difference.

Involvement in family expressions of grief, such as choosing flowers for the deceased, attending or speaking at the funeral service, is beneficial. Children report that physical comforting and sharing their thoughts and feelings within the family are helpful. Recognizing, normalizing and discussing their grief and concerns provides all children and adolescents with a sense that death can be managed and need not overwhelm them.

### What is Helpful for Parents?

Distressed parents can, understandably, be uncertain as to what and when to tell bereaved children. Often all that parents require is an opportunity to discuss their concerns and potential responses with an understanding and supportive adult, who can offer advice on management. Unexpected deaths require quick decisions from unprepared parents, who can be reassured that decisions they later regret can be addressed subsequently. For example, children who did not attend the funeral service can have it described to them and they can visit the burial site. Explanations that children's grief can take different forms and will attenuate over time reassure parents about the normality of their children's responses. Family reminiscing about the deceased is of particular help to children who appear not to be grieving [1]. Giving children mementos of their dead parent, or sibling, provides them with comfort and helps them to maintain a positive relationship with the deceased. Normal limit-setting increases children's sense of security. Schools can promote bereaved children's resilience by providing understanding and support and by incorporating preparation for trauma and loss into educational thinking and practice.

### Services for Bereaved Children

There has been a notable expansion in community-based services for bereaved children. Yet, quantitative evaluations of controlled bereavement interventions have highlighted few positive treatment effects [22,23]. Treatment effects may be limited by the fact that it is not necessarily the level of child distress that determines who receives services [5], and that outcome judged in terms of changes in psychopathology may be ill-matched to therapeutic inputs [22]. Interventions are neither neutral nor always helpful and infrequently measure potentially negative outcomes, such as an increase in child distress.

### The Role of Professionals

The majority of bereaved children need neither professional intervention nor therapy, although parents and children may benefit from talking with others in a similar position to themselves. Referral is appropriate where there is prolonged distress or disorder (Tables 18.1 and 18.2). It is essential to gain a detailed understanding of the circumstances of the death, what information and explanations the child has been given and how their knowledge was acquired. Relevant cultural or religious variables need to be understood.

**Table 18.1** Bereaved children – death and immediate aftermath

| Implications for management | Monitor if: |
| --- | --- |
| *Death occurs* | |
| Nature/circumstances of death | Traumatic, murder, suicide |
| *Children* | |
| Developmental level | |
| Information given to child | |
| Impact on routines/practical care | Trauma symptoms |
| Expression of grief tolerated | Prior child disturbance |
| Support available | |
| Involvement in rites/rituals | |
| Prior disturbance or disorder | |
| *Family* | |
| Patterns of communication | |
| Quality of relationships | Poor family relationships |
| Support available | Prior mental health problems |
| Prior parental mental health problems | |
| *Culture/religion/community* | |
| Beliefs | |
| Life, death, afterlife | |
| Roles of adults/children | Obstacles to culturally appropriate expression |
| Behaviour | |
| Rites and rituals | |
| Expression of grief | |

**Table 18.2** Bereaved children – short- and longer-term considerations

| Implications for management | Advise/consider referral if: |
| --- | --- |
| **Short-term (up to 4 months)** | |
| *Children* | |
| Whether routines/activities re-established | Absences from school |
| Ability to use support within family/from peers | Withdrawal/isolation |
| Whether/how grief is expressed and dealt with | Trauma symptoms persist |
| Withdrawal at home or school | Marked distress continues |
| Lack of stability, further losses | |
| *Family* | |
| Level of distress/mental health difficulties | If psycho-education required |
| Support available to adults | If support required |

| Implications for management | Advise/consider referral if: |
| --- | --- |
| **Longer term** | |
| *Children* | |
| Marked distress or trauma symptoms | Refer where symptoms impair daily functioning |
| Difficulties in peer relationships/bullying | |
| *Family* | |
| Mental health difficulties in adults | Refer where symptoms impair family functioning |
| Marked relationship difficulties | |

It is therapeutically useful to see children and parents separately and together. Individual meetings with children can highlight hidden worries, cognitive distortions, self-blame or symptoms of trauma. Individual meetings with parents can highlight concerns about what information to share with children. Seeing family members together can highlight which family processes to strengthen or modify. Widening family support networks is useful, e.g. via school consultations or reassuring parents that other trusted family members or friends can also help in managing children's grief.

## Conclusions

Children's understanding of death encompasses both biological and supernatural cognitive frameworks, and progresses developmentally. Children's expressions of grief are affected by their age, sex and developmental level. Grief-related distress does not indicate pathology. Parents appreciate information that normalizes children's grief and traumatic symptoms, and provides guidance on management. Bereaved children value opportunities to share their thoughts and feelings. The majority of families do not require psychological services. Consultation to other agencies in routine contact with children, such as schools, can enhance families' supportive community networks. It is essential to consider the impact of religious and cultural beliefs upon presentation.

Clinical disturbance affects approximately one in five children. Prolonged grief that impairs daily functioning indicates a need for professional help. Families bereaved by murder or suicide are particularly vulnerable and would benefit from extra support. The clinical validity of the new diagnosis of PCBD has been questioned. Research needs to focus on developmental manifestations of grief and appropriately validated child grief instruments.

## References

1  Worden JW (1996) Children and grief: When a parent dies. Guilford: New York.
2  Legare HL, Evans ME, Rosengren KS et al. (2012) The coexistence of natural and supernatural explanations across cultures and development. Child Development, 83, 779–793.

3 Monographs of the Society for Research in Child Development (2014) Children's Understanding of Death: Toward a Contextualised and Integrated Account. Monographs of the Society for Research in Child Development 79, 1–124.

4 Dowdney L (2000) Annotation: childhood bereavement following parental death. Journal Child Psychology and Psychiatry, 7, 819–830.

5 Sandler IN, Wolchik SA, Ayers TS et al. (2013) Family Bereavement Program (FBP) approach to promoting resilience following the death of a parent. Family Science, 4, doi: 10.1080/19424620.2013.821763.

6 Brent DA, Melhem N, Masten et al. (2012) Longitudinal effects of parental bereavement on adolescent developmental competence. Journal of Clinical Child & Adolescent Psychology, 41, 778–791.

7 Dowdney L, Wilson R, Maughan B et al. (1999) Bereaved children: psychological disturbance and service provision. British Medical Journal 319 354–335.

8 Melhem M, Porta G, Shamesedden W et al. (2011) Grief in children and adolescents bereaved by sudden parental death. Archives of General Psychiatry, 68, 911–919.

9 Cerel J, Jordan JR, Duberstein PR (2008) The impact of suicide on the family. Crisis, 29, 38–44.

10 Brent DA, Melhem N, Donohoe MB, Walker M (2009) The incidence and course of depression in bereaved youth, 21, months after the loss of a parent to suicide, accident, or sudden natural death. American Journal of Psychiatry, 166, 786–794.

11 Hung NC, Rabin LA (2009) Comprehending childhood bereavement by parental suicide: a critical review of research on outcomes, grief processes, and interventions. death studies, 33, 781–814.

12 Li J, Vestergaard M, Cnattingius S et al. (2014) Mortality after Parental Death in Childhood: A Nationwide Cohort Study from Three Nordic Countries. PLoS Med, 11, e1001679.

13 APA (2013) The Diagnostic and Statistical Manual of Mental Disorders, Fifth Edition (DSM-5). American Psychiatric Association.

14 Melhem, N, Porta G, Payne MW et al. (2013) Identifying Prolonged Grief Reactions in Children: Dimensional and Diagnostic Approaches. Journal of the American Academy Of Child And Adolescent Psychiatry, 52, 599–607.

15 Boelen PA, Prigerson HG (2012) Commentary on the inclusion of persistent complex bereavement-related disorder in DSM-5. Death Studies, 36, 771–794.

16 Kaplow M, Layne CM, Saltzman WR et al. (2013) Using multidimensional grief theory to explore the effects of deployment, reintegration, and death on military youth and families. Clinical Child and Family Psychology Review, 16, 322–340.

17 Kaplow J, Shapiro DN, Wardecker BM et al. (2013) Psychological and environmental correlates of HPA axis functioning in parentally bereaved children: preliminary findings. Journal of Traumatic Stress, 26, 233–240.

18 Luecken LJ, Hagan MJ, Sandler IN et al. (2014) Longitudinal mediators of a randomized prevention program effect on cortisol for youth from parentally-bereaved families. Prevention Science, 15, 224–232.

19 Stikkelbroek Y, Bodden DHM, Reitz E et al. (2015) Mental health of adolescents before and after the death of a parent or sibling. European Child & Adolescent Psychiatry 25, 49–59.

20  Baker JE, Sedney MA, Gross E (1992) Psychological tasks for bereaved children. American Journal of Orthopsychiatry, 62, 105–116.
21  Brewer JD, Sparks AC (2011) Young people living with parental bereavement: Insights from an ethnographic study of a UK childhood bereavement service. Social Science and Medicine, 72, 283–229.
22  Curtis K, Newman T (2001) Do community-based support services benefit bereaved children? A review of empirical evidence. Child: Care, Health and Development, 27, 487–495.
23  Currier JM, Holland JM (2007) The effectiveness of bereavement interventions with children: a meta-analytic review of controlled outcome research. Journal of Clinical Child and Adolescent Psychology, 36, 253–259.

## Internet Resources

Internet resources can help adults discuss death with bereaved children, recommend relevant children's books, and provide guidance for teachers and schools. Check appropriateness for individual families.

### For Families

http://www.griefencounter.org.uk/kids-zone/kids-resources/
http://support.childbereavement.org.uk/support_information/cbc_shop/free_downloadable_resources
http://www.partnershipforchildren.org.uk/resources/my-child-is-worried-about/bereavment/bereavement-links.html
http://www.youngminds.org.uk/for_parents/worried_about_your_child/bereavement/resources

### Resources for Schools and Teachers

http://www.childbereavementuk.org/support/schools/resources/
http://www.theguardian.com/education/teacher-blog/2013/jul/01/children-bereavement-help-at-school

### Advice on Different Faith and Belief Communities

http://amv.somerset.gov.uk/resources/religous-attitudes-to-death-and-grieving/
https://humanism.org.uk/education/parents/books-for-bereaved-children/

# 19

# Stress and Reactions to Stress in Children

*David Trickey*

## Reactions

Survival depends upon being able to adjust to various environmental stressors. In the face of a perceived stressor, humans react in a way that mobilizes biological and psychological resources to enable them to manage the stressor. This reaction to stress is much more than the simple 'fight–flight–freeze' response that is often referred to; it involves a number of biological and neuropsychological systems. These include the limbic system, the dopamine system, the adrenergic system, the hypothalamic–pituitary–adrenal (HPA) axis, the serotonin system, the endogenous opiate system and the immune system, interacting in an incredibly complicated and sophisticated response. A full overview is beyond the scope of this chapter, but a comprehensive overview is provided by Cohen *et al.* [1]. After the stressor has passed, the system can 'reset' itself and return to the non-stress mode. Carers can play a crucial role in this process for children by helping them to re-establish their sense of safety, to feel calm, to feel well supported and to feel as if they have some control over their worlds [2]. In this way, a good attachment can act as a buffer or an antidote to what would otherwise be overwhelming stress [3]. However, if individuals are exposed to too much stress, or are exposed to stress for too long, then they may become overwhelmed, which can lead to long-lasting difficulties.

In the United States, more than 9500 adults completed a short survey about childhood stressful events. The results demonstrated a strong link between experiencing more adverse childhood experiences and a number of adult outcomes, including alcoholism, depression, suicide attempts, smoking, obesity, ischaemic heart disease, cancer, chronic lung disease, skeletal fractures and liver disease, even when controlling for demographic factors [4]. The conceptual model underpinning the study suggests that such childhood experiences increase the risk of psychological impairment, which then leads to adopting more health-risk behaviours, which result in the physical health problems (e.g. Rose *et al.* [5]). Moreover, neuropsychological research indicates that early adversity is associated with atypical development of the HPA axis, structural differences in brain development (particularly the corpus callosum) and decreased activity in the prefrontal cortex [6]. Such neuropsychological changes may cause latent vulnerability to later psychological problems [7].

The most commonly studied persistent psychological reaction in children to overwhelming stress is post-traumatic stress disorder (PTSD). At the time of writing, the

*Child Psychology and Psychiatry: Frameworks for Clinical Training and Practice,* Third Edition.
Edited by David Skuse, Helen Bruce and Linda Dowdney.
© 2017 John Wiley & Sons, Ltd. Published 2017 by John Wiley & Sons, Ltd.

most recent incarnation of PTSD can be found in the *Diagnostic and Statistical Manual of Mental Disorders*, 5th edition, and, according to this set of diagnostic criteria, the person must have been exposed to an event or events that involved 'actual or threatened death, serious injury or sexual violence' [8]. However, a number of events that would not fulfil this criterion may also cause a child overwhelming stress and subsequent longer-term difficulties with a similar symptom profile to the DSM-5 description of PTSD. The World Health Organization (WHO) also publishes a system of diagnostic criteria for mental health problems, the *ICD-10 Classification of Mental and Behavioural Disorders*, 10th revision (ICD-10), in which the causal event is not so narrowly defined and must simply be 'of an exceptionally threatening or catastrophic nature' [9].

According to the DSM-5 criteria, which are used in most of the research studying PTSD, there are four distinct groups of symptoms that contribute to the diagnosis. Even if fulfilling criteria for a mental health diagnosis is not important, the groups of symptoms provide a useful framework for considering reactions to potentially traumatic events:

1) Intrusions (e.g. trauma-based play; memories of the event that intrude into consciousness of their own volition; flashbacks in which the person loses touch with the here and now because the re-experiencing of the event is so vivid; nightmares).
2) Avoidance of things related – even in tenuous ways – to the event or events (e.g. thoughts; memories; conversations; places; objects; people).
3) Adverse changes in cognitions and emotions (e.g. constant negative view of self, world, others; inaccurate and unhelpful thoughts about the cause or consequences of the event or events; unremitting negative feelings).
4) Physiological hyper-arousal (e.g. sudden and/or extreme temper; problems concentrating; hyper-vigilance; exaggerated startle response; sleep problems).

The DSM-5 criteria stipulate that the symptoms must continue for at least a month in order for them to be considered pathological and warrant a diagnosis of PTSD. This is consistent with the fact that the symptoms may be quite common in the initial days and weeks after a potentially traumatic event, but in many children the symptoms will diminish spontaneously (e.g. Le Brocque *et al.* [10]). Not all children exposed to potentially traumatic events develop PTSD – a meta-analysis found that, overall, 16% of children exposed develop PTSD [11]. According to a meta-analysis of risk factors, factors that existed before the potentially traumatic event (such as socio-economic status, gender, intelligence, previous adverse experiences, previous psychological problems) are only small risk factors. Those associated with the event itself (such as an objective measure of trauma severity, whether the child thought they would die, and whether the child was afraid at the time) are medium risk factors, and those that come after the event (such as whether the child feels unsupported, whether their family is not functioning well, whether their carers have a psychological problem) are medium to large risk factors [12]. Therefore, following potentially traumatic events, strengthening family functioning and enhancing support are likely to be effective ways of minimizing the risk of longer-term psychological impact. This is supported by the fact that the Child and Family Traumatic Stress Intervention (CFTSI), developed at the Childhood Violent Trauma Centre at Yale University, focuses on enhancing support from the caregiver and improving coping skills in the aftermath of potentially traumatic events, and has been shown in a randomized controlled trial to significantly reduce the likelihood of developing PTSD [13].

Post-traumatic stress disorder is not the only psychological problem that develops in children following events that elicit extreme or prolonged stress. Various psychological problems may occur as a result of such events, including depression, anxiety, developmental regression, behavioural problems and dissociation [14]. Furthermore, children may develop strategies to try to cope with their symptoms, which may ultimately prove unhelpful (e.g. using drugs to help them to sleep, staying at home to reduce anxiety about facing triggers).

Therefore, careful assessment is required to map out the full extent of the impact of the stress on the child and their family. Thorough assessment, which includes developmental history and specifically enquiring about potentially traumatic events, e.g. by using the Trauma History Profile included in the UCLA PTSD Reaction Index [15], will help to differentiate between PTSD and other difficulties that may share some symptoms, such as attention deficit hyperactivity disorder. The younger the child, the more the assessment will rely on the parental report of observable behaviour, such as changes in play and increased tempers [16]. However, many children may not be open about their symptoms in front of their carers in an attempt to 'protect' them, so it is important to interview children individually if possible [17]. Questionnaires such as the Child Post-traumatic Stress Scale may help clinicians to systematically enquire about symptoms in assessment and routinely monitor them over time.

## Cognitive Model of PTSD

The cognitive model of PTSD [19] provides a useful way to understand how overwhelming stress impacts children. The model helps clinicians to prepare for assessments, understand reactions to stress, develop a clinical formulation and plan interventions. Broadly speaking, the model proposes that problems following overwhelmingly stressful events are likely to be caused by the way that the *memories* for such events are stored [20] and/or by the *meaning* that is attributed to that event [21]. These two components often feed into each other and are usually *maintained* by a process of avoidance. Memories for overwhelmingly stressful events seem to be stored in an unprocessed 'raw' format and consist of vivid sensory information. Over time, memories for such events are usually processed (e.g. by talking it through with friends, family, colleagues or even pets). This develops a narrative memory associated with the sensory-bound memory, which provides the conceptual framework of words, meanings and stories. This in turn increases control over the memory, allowing it to be recalled as something from the past rather than it intruding and being re-experienced in the present [20]. However, if the event is too distressing to think or talk about, then this processing does not take place and the vivid memory persists and intrudes into consciousness. Most people can incorporate even difficult events into a helpful set of beliefs and expectations about the world, themselves and other people. If some events do not completely fit with expectations, it might be possible to distort or ignore such events as an alternative to changing beliefs. However, it is difficult to ignore traumatic events and, for some people, events of overwhelming stress shatter their assumptions, leaving them with beliefs and expectations that are coloured by the event. This can, in turn, drive behaviour which may perpetuate the beliefs. For example, if a child is physically assaulted, they may start to view the world as dangerous, other people as malevolent and themselves as vulnerable. So when a friend invites them out, they think that they will be at risk, which causes them anxiety. Therefore, in an attempt to avoid the feelings of anxiety, the child stays in. This means that they do not have new information that might challenge their view of the world, others and themselves, and so the avoidance ultimately strengthens their trauma-based belief system.

## Evidence-Based Interventions

There is an increasing body of research that supports the use of trauma-focused cognitive behavioural therapy (TF-CBT) in the treatment of children and young people with PTSD, and at the time of writing it is the only intervention recommended in the PTSD Clinical Guidelines produced by the National Institute for Health and Care Excellence [17]. Although there are different approaches to TF-CBT, they all contain similar basic elements depicted in Figure 19.1: working with the system around the child, enhancing safety, psycho-education, developing the therapeutic context and the therapeutic relationship, developing internal resources, reducing avoidant coping, processing the traumatic memory and cognitive restructuring [22].

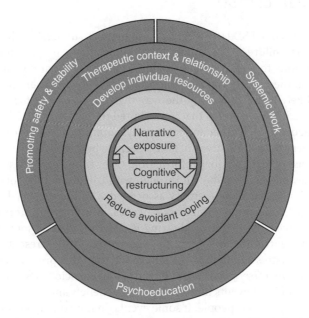

**Figure 19.1** Key contexts and key components of trauma-focused cognitive behavioural therapy.

There is also increasing evidence for the use of eye-movement desensitization and reprocessing (EMDR) [23]; this approach has many similar components to TF-CBT, but usually includes some form of bilateral stimulation (such as the client following the therapist's fingers from left to right) whilst focusing on the traumatic event.

## Conclusion

Children are more able to cope with stress and potentially traumatic events with the help and support of a carer to calm the child and help them make sense of events. Overwhelming stress can, however, have a longer-term impact on children, such as the development of PTSD. There are interventions that have been shown to help many children who develop such chronic problems.

## References

1 Cohen JA, Perel JM, DeBellis MD et al. (2002) Treating traumatized children clinical implications of the psychobiology of posttraumatic stress disorder. Trauma, Violence, & Abuse, 3, 91–108.

2 Hobfoll SE, Watson P, Bell CC et al. (2007) Five essential elements of immediate and mid–term mass trauma intervention: empirical evidence. Psychiatry, 70, 283–315.

3 Van der Kolk BA (2005) Developmental trauma disorder. Psychiatric Annals, 35, 401–408.

4 Felitti VJ, Anda RF, Nordenberg D et al. (1998) Relationship of childhood abuse and household dysfunction to many of the leading causes of death in adults: The Adverse Childhood Experiences (ACE) Study. American Journal of Preventive Medicine, 14, 245–258.

5 Rose SMS-F, Xie D, Stineman M (2014) Adverse childhood experiences and disability in US adults. PM&R, 6, 670–680.

6 McCrory E, De Brito SA, Viding E (2010) Research review: the neurobiology and genetics of maltreatment and adversity. Journal of Child Psychology and Psychiatry, 51, 1079–1095.

7 McCrory EJ, Viding E (2015) The theory of latent vulnerability: Reconceptualizing the link between childhood maltreatment and psychiatric disorder. Development and psychopathology, 27(Special Issue 02), 493–505.

8 American Psychiatric Association (2013)Diagnostic and statistical manual of mental disorders : DSM-5. APA.

9 World Health Organization (1992) The ICD-10 classification of mental and behavioural disorders: clinical descriptions and diagnostic guidelines: Geneva: World Health Organization.

10 Le Brocque RM, Hendrikz J, Kenardy JA (2010) The course of posttraumatic stress in children: Examination of recovery trajectories following traumatic injury. Journal of Pediatric Psychology, 35, 637–645.

11 Alisic E, Zalta AK, van Wesel F et al. (2014) Rates of post-traumatic stress disorder in trauma-exposed children and adolescents: meta-analysis. The British Journal of Psychiatry: the Journal of Mental Science, 204, 335–340.

12 Trickey D, Siddaway AP, Meiser-Stedman R et al. (2012) A meta-analysis of risk factors for post-traumatic stress disorder in children and adolescents. Clinical Psychology Review, 32, 122–138.

13 Berkowitz SJ, Stover CS, Marans SR (2011) The child and family traumatic stress intervention: Secondary prevention for youth at risk of developing PTSD. Journal of Child Psychology and Psychiatry, 52, 676–685.

14 Fletcher KE (1996) Childhood posttraumatic stress disorder. Child Psychopathology, 242–276.

15 Steinberg AM, Brymer MJ, Decker KB, Pynoos RS (2004) The University of California at Los Angeles post-traumatic stress disorder reaction index. Current Psychiatry Reports, 6, 96–100.

16 Meiser-Stedman R, Smith P, Glucksman E et al. (2008) The posttraumatic stress disorder diagnosis in preschool- and elementary school-age children exposed to motor vehicle accidents. American Journal of Psychiatry, 165, 1326–1337.

17 NICE (2005) The management of PTSD in adults and children in primary and secondary care. National Clinical practice Guideline.

18 Foa EB, Johnson KM, Feeny NC, Treadwell KR (2001) The Child PTSD Symptom Scale: A preliminary examination of its psychometric properties. Journal of Clinical Child Psychology, 30, 376–384.

19 Meiser-Stedman R (2002) Towards a cognitive-behavioral model of PTSD in children and adolescents. Clinical Child and Family Psychology Review , 5, 217–232.

20 Brewin CR, Gregory JD, Lipton M, Burgess N (2010) Intrusive images in psychological disorders: characteristics, neural mechanisms, and treatment implications. Psychological Review, 117, 210.

21 Ehlers A, Clark DM (2000) A cognitive model of posttraumatic stress disorder. Behaviour Research and Therapy, 38, 319–345.

22 Trickey D (2013) Post-traumatic stress disorders. In: Graham P, Reynolds S (eds) Cognitive Behaviour Therapy for Children and Families, 3rd edn. Cambridge University Press, pp. 235–254.

23 Rodenburg R, Benjamin A, de Roos C et al. (2009) Efficacy of EMDR in children: A meta-analysis. Clinical Psychology Review, 29, 599–606.

20

# Children's Developing Sense of Moral Agency, and the Disruptions Associated with War Exposure

*Cecilia Wainryb*

## The Development of Moral Agency

The study of moral development has traditionally focused on children's moral concepts and judgments, with contemporary research showing that even young children know that it is wrong to hurt others [1]. Still, in the course of their everyday lives, most children will occasionally engage in behaviours that cause harm to others, such as hitting a sibling, excluding a peer from a game, or betraying a friend's secret. These experiences challenge children's understandings of themselves as moral people, thus creating meaningful opportunities for moral growth. As children wrestle with, and attempt to explain to others, how and why they hurt someone despite knowing that causing harm is wrong, they tend to construct accounts that implicate not only what they did, but also what they wanted, thought and felt during that event. This means not merely that children possess a 'theory of mind' but that they habitually rely on their mentalization capacities to organize and make sense of their transgressive experiences. By relating their own actions to psychological aspects of their experiences, children come to understand their wrongdoing as being related to their own desires, beliefs and emotions, and thus construct a sense of their own *moral agency* [2,3]. Relating their actions to what they thought, felt or intended does not absolve children of responsibility or transform their hurtful actions into acceptable ones; rather, it helps children to recognize that harmdoing can arise from their imperfect attempts to balance their own and others' needs or from their limited understandings of others. This permits children to acknowledge the pain they caused and to recognize their potential for reparative action and their ability to behave differently in the future.

The ways in which children make sense of times when they hurt others vary with age [4,5]. By the early school years, children can already appreciate the negative effects of their actions and recognize their own, more or less, justifiable intentions, as well as mitigating circumstances that may serve to explain their actions, but often struggle to make sense of competing dimensions of their experiences. With age, children become increasingly able to coordinate the multiple psychological perspectives implicated in their transgression experiences, and by adolescence they begin exploring the implications of their actions for who they are and who they want to be. Parents play an important role in helping children grapple with the meanings of their own wrongdoing; parental strategies vary as a function of children's developing capacities [6,7]. Early on, parents help their children to recognize conflicts between their own and others' perspectives

*Child Psychology and Psychiatry: Frameworks for Clinical Training and Practice,* Third Edition.
Edited by David Skuse, Helen Bruce and Linda Dowdney.

by drawing attention to others' emotions as well as to children's own internally driven reasons for engaging in harmful behaviour. As children get older, parents help them to understand more complex and less transparent forms of psychological conflict, and by adolescence they help teens to situate their harmful actions in the context of their broader relationship histories and understandings of themselves and others.

In sum, although having a moral identity is often conceptualized as the subsuming of self to morality [8,9], the pervasive and inevitable complexity of moral life renders such a notion unfeasible; indubitably, the goal of moral development is not sainthood [2,10]. The living of a moral life necessarily involves interpersonal conflict and harm, and the process of moral agency creation helps children to construct a sense of themselves as flawed but fundamentally moral people.

## Challenges Posed by Exposure to War

Given that children construct a sense of themselves as moral beings in the context of their interactions with others, the harrowing backdrop of violence and injustice seen in war situations poses unique challenges [11,12]. The extreme forms of harm experienced and perpetrated by war-exposed youths probably challenge their basic faith in themselves and others as moral beings more deeply than do the mundane harms experienced by youths in non-violent contexts. Also, in war contexts, parents and other adults are often absent or overwhelmed and unavailable to listen to children and scaffold the process of agency construction; at the collective level, societies offer a polarized and dehumanizing public rhetoric. None of this helps children contain their anger, shame and guilt, and construct a complex sense of who they and others are. Rather, such environments undermine children's ability to believe that justice and welfare matter, as well as their motivation to consider these issues in making choices. Furthermore, extreme violence affects the development of basic regulatory processes and integrative functions and provokes the sort of hyperarousal that interferes with children's understandings of events; after the fact, numbing and avoidance arise to forestall pain and anger. Such processes hinder children's ability to think about their own and others' actions in psychological terms, thereby disrupting their construal of moral agency.

Therefore, although war-exposed youths develop moral concepts, these concepts are often divorced from what they expect themselves and others to actually do in real life [13]. War-exposed young people often find it difficult making sense of their experiences in ways that promote and preserve a sense of themselves and other people as moral agents; those difficulties are captured by disruptions in the ways they narrate their own experiences with harmdoing [11,12,14,15]. Three common disruptions are discussed in the following.

### Numb Agency

Numbing, a common psychological response following trauma [16], permeates war-exposed youths' accounts of their experiences. Numb accounts are devoid of references to goals, thoughts or emotions, and fail to articulate any sense in which the narrators' actions arise from their own psychological experience. Box 20.1 presents an account by a 14-year old Colombian former child-soldier of a time when he had harmed someone. The boy depicts a harrowing experience by providing the facts of who did what, without describing what he thought about what he was ordered to do, why he obeyed, or how he felt about doing so.

---

**Box 20.1  Numb Agency**

'So that, so that day, well, when they ordered me to kill someone and so – we went, we left like, like three and – we got there and, and, we killed a cop and, then we left, well, the guerrilla told me to kill someone, so then they ordered me, then we got there and, and we killed a cop and then we returned to – returned to our camp.'

*Source:* Wainryb and Recchia [15].

---

The numbing of agency in transgression accounts is consistent with findings indicating that, in the face of trauma, the capacities to think, organize and integrate experience collapse and dissociative mechanisms become activated [16]. Although numbing is protective in the short term, while traumatic events are taking place or shortly thereafter, in the longer term, numbing is linked to problematic developmental consequences that include the blunting of normative emotional responses, lack of empathy and remorse, and increased aggression and antisocial behaviour. It is unclear whether numbing reflects a passive dulling of psychological experience or an active attempt to avoid exploring the psychological implications of experiences. Nevertheless, given that numbing interferes with young people's ability to reconcile their own violent actions with their moral beliefs, this way of constructing a sense of their moral agency might result in young people developing a view of the world in which they cease to notice how their own actions, and perhaps also other people's actions, have moral relevance [12,14,15].

**Imbalanced Agency**

Young people often rely on group identities to make sense of some of their experiences; in war contexts, those collective identities may become increasingly salient and polarized and used to delegitimize the 'other' [17]. This delegitimization may be accomplished via an imbalanced representation of in-group and out-group members, as illustrated in Box 20.2 which contains an account of a 14-year-old boy from Papua New Guinea, a tribal society with a 350-year-long history of culturally sanctioned warfare. This boy describes engaging, together with his tribesmen, in harms against another group after learning that a girl from their own tribe had been raped by members of that group. The boy's actions and those of his tribesmen – both the engaging in and the ending of the violence – are represented as being related to what they knew or believed; their decisions and feelings are also described. In contrast, the 'others' in this conflict (the members of the other tribe) are not represented, individually or collectively, in ways that include any discernible psychological agency.

---

**Box 20.2 Imbalanced Agency**

'[Male name] saw the girl bleeding and shouted to all of us clansmen. Me and some of my clansmen heard that and we took our bushknives and ran to the Akupa. We entered the dancing ground and checked to see if any of the rapists' clansmen where there. There were lots and lots of people there but none of the rapists' clansmen were there. We were very frustrated and we burned all their mess houses, like tea-houses and flour-houses. . . . Then we went to another place in search of men to kill, but we couldn't find any. So we left their village and we went back to our village. Early the next morning my clansmen called out from every corner . . . they talked about the rape and said that we would go and attack the rapists' clan. After the discussion, we went to [village-name] and fought. We didn't bring any guns, we brought spears and arrows. We destroyed their gardens and we chopped down their big trees. . . . While we were destroying their places, they shot one of our clansmen with a spear. The war went on for about one week and we realized that we weren't winning so the elders stopped the war.'

*Source:* Wainryb and Pasupathi [11].

---

This kind of imbalanced construction of a restricted moral universe, wherein only the narrator and in-group members are represented as moral agents whose actions are guided by goals, beliefs and emotions, tends to confer on youths a measure of protection against war-related distress. Nevertheless, it also constitutes a significant risk, as it fosters the continuation and exacerbation of conflict and violence, laying the foundation for retribution and interfering with peacemaking efforts [11,18].

**Essentialized Agency**

Enduring negative self-views plague the accounts of war-exposed youths, especially those who, as combatants, engaged in killings or torture. These young people face unique challenges in their efforts to reconcile their brutal behaviours with their understandings of themselves as moral people, and many construct a sense of their own moral agency as essentialized – one for which change or redemption appear impossible or unlikely [12,14,15]. Box 20.3 presents an account by a 16-year-old former youth combatant in Colombia, who recounts an event where he was ordered to engage in devastating violence. Notably, he depicts his behaviour as arising not out of the orders he received but out of his own rage and desire for revenge. In this way, his account underscores his own sense of agency, but constructs it in an overly rigid manner.

In essentialized constructions of agency, the consequences and implications of certain actions for the sense of who youths are and who they can be appear inescapable, shackling them to their war experiences [14]. Often, these self-understandings are very negative and, whether they usher in antisocial pathways or pathways of redemption-seeking, they tend to perpetuate the grip of unresolved events and are linked to overwhelming distress and stunted growth [19,20]. For some young people, grappling with their actions as combatants produces an exalted view of themselves as brave, skilled or ferocious. Yet, inasmuch as their sense of themselves becomes organized around their war-related roles, these self-views, even when positive, may thwart their capacity to develop alternative self-conceptions, adapt to civil society and pursue more varied moral lives [12,15].

---

**Box 20.3 Essentialized Agency**

'So the day that I hurt a person was the day that they killed my cousins. We were fighting the Autodefensas Campesinas, and in the battle three of my cousins died. That day we captured – we killed 25 paracos [members of the paramilitary], we captured 10, and the comandante's order was to dismember them and to send the pieces to each of their families. And that day was when – from the rage of having seen my cousins killed by those same people we had caught – I was so enraged that I started out by removing the fingers off a person with a power-saw, I cut the fingers off both hands, then an arm, I cut off the arm all around until I got to the shoulders, then I started out with the feet, I removed everything until I cut off his head, I took off his tongue, and I cut off the eyes, and I sent it all to his mom. That day I will never forget and I always carry this burden. Being here I remember it and sometimes I feel like crying for having done this to a person. And a few days later I thought about it and said to myself – how will be my death, will it be like that or how?'

*Source:* Wainryb [14].

---

## Conclusions

Being a moral person involves not only knowing right from wrong and trying to do the right thing, but also recognizing one's capacity for hurting others and grappling with instances when one has done so. In normative contexts, children, in conversations with parents and other adults, wrestle with their own transgressions and reconcile their actions with positive self-views, building a sense of moral agency that acknowledges wrongdoing without becoming overly rigid and unsustainable.

War-exposed children, too, wrestle with the meanings of their actions, but as they do so they are often forced into pathogenic ways of thinking about themselves and others, and about justice in general. Although their transgression accounts offer insights into what has gone awry with them, their stories may also become an avenue for intervention, precisely because it is in the process of constructing and reconstructing accounts of one's experiences that a new or different sense of moral agency may emerge. This process is best accomplished via co-narration with others, as it is through such joint narration that children, especially, can garner new perspectives on actions and events and create different meanings.

The telling and re-telling of traumatic stories has long been used for therapeutic purposes, including with war victims [21]. But if used not solely for reducing post-traumatic stress disorder symptoms but for furthering the construction of moral agency, youths must be encouraged to recount their experiences in ways that help them reconstruct or reconstitute the details of the events and, especially, elaborate on their own and others' agency; such elaboration can help to mitigate numbing and imbalanced constructions [14]. In this respect, it is also important for adults assisting in the process not to deny the wrongness of these youths' actions or their responsibility for these actions, as doing so undermines their need to feel remorseful and their ability to construct a sense of their own complex agency [14]. Also important is recognizing the limits of redemptive storytelling [14,22]. Recounting experiences in growth-promoting ways does not entail transforming deeply hurtful actions into positive or redeeming ones. The goal is to help youths retell their stories in ways that allow them to integrate their past experiences with broader possibilities for future action; if righting past wrongs is impossible, new commitments can be made that include making amends and reparations to individuals and communities. Given the disrupted ecology of war-exposed youth, parents may be unavailable to offer such supports; the required assistance should be part of broader psychosocial interventions provided in the wars' aftermath.

## References

1  Smetana J, Jambon M, Ball C (2014) The social domain approach to children's moral and social judgments. In: Killen M, Smetana J (eds). Handbook of Moral Development, 2nd edn. New York: Psychology Press, pp. 23–45.
2  Wainryb C, Brehl B, Matwin S (2005) Being Hurt and Hurting Others: Children's Narrative Accounts and Moral Judgments of their Own Interpersonal Conflicts. Monographs of the Society for Research in Child Development, 70 (Serial No. 281).
3  Pasupathi M, Wainryb C (2010) Developing moral agency through narrative. Human Development, 53, 55–80.
4  Pasupathi M, Wainryb C (2010) On telling the whole story: facts and interpretations in autobiographical memory narratives from childhood through mid-adolescence. Developmental Psychology, 46, 735–746.
5  Recchia H, Wainryb C, Bourne S, Pasupathi M (2015) Children's and adolescents' accounts of helping and hurting: lessons about the development of moral agency. Child Development, 86, 864–876.
6  Wainryb C, Recchia H (eds) (2014) Talking about right and wrong: parent-child conversations as contexts for moral development. New York: Cambridge University Press.
7  Recchia H, Wainryb C, Bourne S, Pasupathi M (2014) The construction of moral agency in mother-child conversations about helping and hurting across childhood and adolescence. Developmental Psychology, 50, 34–44.
8  Frimer J, Walker L, Dunlop W, Lee B, Riches A (2011) The integration of agency and communion in moral personality: evidence of enlightened self-interest. Journal of Personality and Social Psychology, 101, 149–163.
9  Hardy S, Carlo G (2011) Moral identity: what is it, how does it develop, and is it linked to moral action? Child Development Perspectives, 5, 212–218.
10  Wainryb C, Pasupathi M (2015) Saints, and the rest of us: broadening the perspective on moral identity development. Human Development, 58, 154–163.
11  Wainryb C, Pasupathi M (2010) Political violence and disruptions in the development of moral agency. Child Development Perspectives, 4, 48–54.
12  Wainryb C, Bourne S. 'And I shot her': on war, and the creation of inequities in the development of youths' moral capacities. In: Horn S, Ruck M, Liben L (eds) Equity and Justice in Development Sciences: Implications For Diverse Young People, Families, And Communities (pp. 257–288). Academic Press.
13  Posada R, Wainryb C (2008) Moral development in a violent society: Colombian children's judgments in the context of survival and revenge. Child Development, 79, 882–898.

**14** Wainryb C (2011) 'And so they ordered me to kill a person': conceptualizing the impacts of child soldiering on the development of moral agency. Human Development, 54, 273–300.

**15** Wainryb C, Recchia H (2015) Youths' constructions of meanings about experiences with political conflict: implications for processes of identity development. In: McLean K, Syed M (eds) The Oxford Handbook of Identity Development. New York: Oxford University Press, pp. 369–386.

**16** Fonagy P (2003) The developmental roots of violence in the failure of mentalization. In: Pfäfflin F (ed.) A matter of security: the application of attachment theory to forensic psychiatry and psychotherapy. London: Kingsley, pp. 13–56.

**17** Bar-Tal D (2007) Sociopsychological foundations of intractable conflicts. American Behavioral Scientist, 50, 1430–1453.

**18** Hammack P (2011) Narrative and the Politics of Identity: the Cultural Psychology of Israeli and Palestinian Youth. New York: Oxford University Press.

**19** Bonanno G (2013) Meaning-making, adversity, and regulatory flexibility. Memory, 21, 150–156.

**20** Litz B, Stein N, Delaney E et al. (2009) Moral injury and moral repair in war veterans. Clinical Psychology Review, 29, 695–706.

**21** Schauer M, Neuner F, Elbert T (2005) Narrative exposure therapy: a short-term intervention for traumatic stress disorders after war, terror or torture. Gottingen: Hogrefe & Huber.

**22** Pals J, McAdams D (2004) The transformed self: a narrative understanding of posttraumatic growth. Psychological Inquiry, 15, 65–69.

# Section 3

# The Impact of Trauma, Loss and Maltreatment

3b: Maltreatment

# 21

# Child Maltreatment

*Danya Glaser*

## Introduction

Childhood maltreatment encompasses both abuse and neglect, with or without intention to harm. Child maltreatment is relatively common. At its worst, it is fatal. Non-fatal child maltreatment can cause physical injury. Although most of the harm is psychological and behavioural, in adulthood the harm extends to physical disease [1]. Different forms of maltreatment often co-occur (see Table 21.1)

Children who are maltreated are also more likely to be exposed to other forms of victimization, including conventional crime, exposure to violence and actual violence, i.e. polyvictimisation [2]. Adult retrospective studies suggest that different forms of abuse and neglect lead to different sequelae [3]. However, the co-occurrence of different forms of maltreatment make identifying the effects of each one difficult, although some robust associations are described later.

## The Nature of Maltreatment

Intention to harm children is not required for the definition of child maltreatment. Most maltreatment is intrafamilial, with harm being caused by either parents or primary carers [4]. The exception is sexual abuse, which is equally commonly perpetrated by siblings, an extended family member or someone else known to the child. Sexual exploitation of socially vulnerable older children – mostly girls – by gangs and organized male groups also occurs [5]. Child maltreatment is recognized in all cultures [4]. Some cultural practices, such as female genital mutilation, are harmful and constitute maltreatment.

Types of child maltreatment have different features (Table 21.2). Physical and sexual abuse may consist of single or repeated discreet events. Emotional abuse and neglect represent pervasive aspects of the primary carer–child relationship.

## Epidemiology

Rates of the various forms of maltreatment vary by study type. Self-reports by children and, retrospectively, of adults in community studies suggest that official child protection agencies' statistics underestimate their occurrence by as much as 10-fold [3].

*Child Psychology and Psychiatry: Frameworks for Clinical Training and Practice,* Third Edition.
Edited by David Skuse, Helen Bruce and Linda Dowdney.
© 2017 John Wiley & Sons, Ltd. Published 2017 by John Wiley & Sons, Ltd.

**Table 21.1** Forms of maltreatment and distribution within protection plans for England in 2014

| Type of maltreatment | Variants within type of maltreatment | Percentage of child protection plans (2014) |
|---|---|---|
| Neglect | Lack of provision | 43 |
| | Lack of supervision | |
| | Psychological neglect | |
| Physical abuse (inflicted injury) | Causing death, injury or visible marks such as bruises | 8 |
| | Fabricated or induced illness by: | |
| | • erroneous reporting of child's symptoms | |
| | • interfering with investigations, specimens and treatment | |
| | • direct interference with or harming the child so as to produce symptoms and signs | |
| Sexual abuse | Penetrative genital or oral contact | 4 |
| | Non-penetrative genital or genital–oral contact | |
| | Non-contact sexual exposure | |
| | Sexual exploitation | |
| Emotional abuse | Hostility and rejection | 36 |
| | Developmentally inappropriate interactions | |
| | Exposure to domestic violence | |
| | Using the child for the fulfilment of the adult's needs | |
| | Failing to promote the child's socialization | |
| More than one type | | 9 |

**Table 21.2** Differences between various forms of child abuse and neglect

| | Sexual abuse | Physical abuse | Emotional abuse and Neglect |
|---|---|---|---|
| Maltreating act or interaction | Hidden | Hidden or observed | Observable |
| Identity of the maltreating person | Usually in question | Sometimes known | Known |
| Abuser and primary carer | Usually different persons | Same or different persons | Same person |
| Immediate protection indicated | Yes | Usually, especially with young children | Rarely |
| Issue to be determined | Has it occurred and, if so, who is the abuser? | Is injury inflicted? | Is it harmful? |

For example, one UK retrospective random probability sample of parents or guardians, older children and young adults found that severe lifetime maltreatment was reported by 25.3% of the young adults [6]. The study found a general decline in reported experiences of harsh emotional and physical punishment by parents and caregivers, and also in experiences of physical violence, a finding replicating other studies. In contrast, in England in 2014, 48 300 children were subject to a local authority children protection plan based on a multidisciplinary consensus that the child *continues* to be at risk of harm, rather than on the substantiation of maltreatment (Table 21.1). These numbers are, therefore, a considerable underestimate of the actual prevalence of child maltreatment.

## Social and Family Factors

Families with abused or neglected children are more likely to live in adverse social circumstances where social disadvantage may compound the harm caused by maltreatment [7]. All those who maltreat children are troubled individuals, a proportion of whom have experienced abuse or neglect as children [8]. Emotional abuse, physical abuse and neglect are often found in families where one or both parents are suffering from mental illness, have a personality disorder or misuse drugs/alcohol. Violence between parents is also a risk factor. However, no single adult psychopathology is consistently associated with child maltreatment. Sexual abusers are mostly male.

Children of all ages may experience abuse and neglect. Physical neglect and emotional abuse often start early, continuing as enduring patterns of care and interaction throughout childhood and adolescence. Physical abuse in infancy may result from the parent's inability to cope with the baby's demands; this sometimes causes serious injury and even death. Later in childhood, physical abuse is more associated with inappropriate and harsh punishment. Sexual abuse occurs more commonly in adolescence and in girls, although young boys and girls are also sexually abused.

Fabricated or induced illness (previously known as Munchausen syndrome by proxy or factitious disorder by proxy) is included in physical abuse. It is nearly always perpetrated by mothers, and the child may also have a genuine illness.

Abuse and neglect may be self-limiting or single events but often continue over many years as a pattern of interaction within a particular parent–child relationship, as a form of child-rearing or, in child sexual abuse, as an addiction-like propensity that the same abuser extends towards more than one child.

## The Harm to the Child

Harm may be caused by a number of mechanisms (Table 21.3), which include physical effects, deprivation of experience, emotional neglect, stress and psychological trauma.

Children show differential susceptibility to maltreatment, depending on their genetic vulnerability [9] or resilience [10], their age [11] their gender, the nature and duration of the maltreatment, their relationship to the maltreater, the presence of *protective* relationships and a supportive social context.

Child adaptation to an abusive environment may lead to preferential attention to, and misperception of, threatening cues [12].

**Table 21.3** Mechanisms of harm associated with maltreatment

| Mechanism | Examples |
| --- | --- |
| Direct effects | Physical abuse causing injury or death |
| | Sexual abuse causing sexually transmitted diseases or unwanted pregnancy |
| | Effects of stress, deprivation and (mal)adaptive programming on the developing brain [16] |
| | Traumatogenic experiences (sexual abuse, exposure to violence, direct violence) leading to post-traumatic phenomena |
| | Exposure to antisocial and violent behaviour as a dysfunctional model for conflict resolution |
| | Hostility, denigration and rejection leading to low self-esteem |
| | Emotional neglect leading to emotional withdrawal or indiscriminate affection-seeking |
| | Deprivation of experience leading to developmental delay and poor cognitive functioning |
| Indirect effects | Effects on later health, including obesity, ischaemic heart disease, cancer |
| | Fabricated or induced illness leading to unnecessary investigations and treatments and reduced normal function |
| Effects of meaning of maltreatment | Sexual abuse leading to a sense of shame, depression, deliberate self-harm |
| Effects of associated emotional abuse | Most physical abuse and neglect are accompanied by emotional abuse |
| Effects of associated carer–child relationship | Sexual abuse may be associated with blame and non-belief of the child by the child's caregivers |
| Effects of associated social adversity | Poverty, social isolation, migration, natural disasters |
| Effects of intervention | Effects of removal of the child to inadequate alternative care |

**Psychosocial Development**

The greatest morbidity associated with child maltreatment is psychological, emotional and behavioural. Many maltreated children develop disorganized patterns of attachment [13], which are associated with maladaptive interpersonal relationships and poor educational progress. Physical abuse is associated with aggressive behaviour and low self-esteem. Emotional neglect leads to educational under-achievement and difficulties in peer relationships as well as to oppositional behaviour. Antisocial behaviour is significantly associated with prior child maltreatment. Sexual abuse is particularly associated with later depression, substance misuse and self-harm, post-traumatic phenomena and inappropriate sexual behaviour. The latter is particularly troublesome in young children [14].

**Educational Progress and Employment**

Comparisons of maltreated and non-maltreated children from similar socio-economic backgrounds indicate that neglect or physical and emotional abuse affects cognitive functioning and learning involving executive function, visuo-spatial processing, memory and language development. The considerable educational under-achievement of maltreated children is associated with later poor prospects for optimal employment, even when socio-economic effects are controlled for [15].

## Recognition of Maltreatment and Assessment of Harm and Need

Child maltreatment may be either suspected or recognized. Some forms of neglect and abuse are readily observable (Table 21.2).

The English National Institute for Health and Care Excellence (NICE) guideline on the features of suspected child maltreatment divides them into two categories: the *consider* category means that maltreatment is one possible explanation for the alerting feature; and the *Suspect* category means a serious level of concern about maltreatment, but is not proof of it. The guideline is appropriate for all professionals working with children [17]. The most common alerting features are as follows:

- *Physical abuse* is usually recognized by the physical marks it leaves (Table 21.4). The identification is usually made by hospital staff, such as paediatricians or radiologists, as is faltering growth and fabricated illness.
- *Physical neglect* is recognized by the discernible absence of normative provision of basic child care and supervision.
- *Sexual abuse* carries the hallmark of secrecy. As >80% of cases have no conclusive signs of abuse, recognition of such abuse relies strongly on children's verbal descriptions. Consequently, it is the child's words and credibility that are closely tested and challenged. Professionals receiving unexpected disclosures of abuse need to listen to the child, but not to probe or promise confidentiality. Rather, s/he needs to explain that social services will need to be told, and to explore any misgivings the child may have about this. It is vital that a written record is made of all such conversations.
- *Emotional abuse* is observable by the persistent harmful interactions with the child. It is the extent of harmfulness that is disputed. Emotional abuse cannot reliably be recognized by its effects on the child, as these are not specific to this form of maltreatment.

**Table 21.4** How child maltreatment comes to light

|  | Neglect | Physical abuse | Emotional abuse | Sexual abuse |
|---|---|---|---|---|
| Ill-treatment of the child observed | √ | May or may not | √ |  |
| Harmful effects to the child observed | √ | √ | May or may not | May or may not |
| Ill-treatment reported by the child |  | May or may not |  | √ |

When a child presents with difficulties suggestive of abuse or neglect, the process of identification and investigation is usually marked by caregiver or suspected abuser responses, signalling:

- absence of an acceptable explanation;
- some degree of denial of the possibility of abuse;
- a lack of, or only partial assumption of, responsibility for the child's difficulties.

Additionally, many professionals find it difficult to contemplate or accept the possibility that a parent (who may also be a patient) has harmed their own child [18]. They may also believe that the naming of child maltreatment will lead to the removal of the child from the family whose preservation, while clearly desirable, may conflict with the child's interests.

Almost invariably, therefore, there is some degree of dispute or doubt during the process of verifying child maltreatment. The fact that child maltreatment may also lead to criminal prosecution further complicates matters.

## Professional Response to Child Maltreatment

Following recognition of maltreatment, professional responses have several purposes. Some forms of maltreatment, such as sexual abuse and serious physical abuse, require *immediate protection of the child*. A minority of children in this category will require immediate medical or psychiatric treatment – including those who have been seriously injured or infected with a sexually transmitted disease, or those acutely traumatised. With neglect and emotional abuse, professionals usually work *towards child protection*. Both types of response aim to avoid recurrence of maltreatment. Child protection can be achieved by one of the following:

- A change in the maltreating parent or their circumstances through therapeutic or other work. The child will continue to be at risk during this period.
- Supervision of all contact between the child and the abuser. In practice, this is only sustainable for brief periods.
- Separation of the child from the maltreating person. This is the only way of ensuring the immediate safety of the child.

If the abuser is the child's primary caregiver, there is a significant emotional cost to achieving immediate protection. Even when the persons caring for the child are not the maltreating ones, it is nevertheless necessary to assess their capacity to protect the child from maltreatment by others. The most important determining factor here is the nature of the relationship between the non-abusing caregiver(s) and the abuser. The closer this is, the more precarious will be the child's position. 'Closeness' here includes love. It may also mean fear or dependency.

Immediate protection usually requires statutory measures either by a children's social care protection plan or through family (civil) court proceedings. The criminal law has little if any part to play in immediate child protection. Working towards protection by supportive and therapeutic work with the parents may be achieved without statutory measures.

## Treatment and Future Prevention

In planning intervention, it is helpful to organize information about the family in four tiers of concern (see **Table 21.5**). This allows the formulation of likely explanatory pathways to inform the focus and sequence of intervention (see **Figure 21.1**).

A comprehensive treatment plan includes:

- Help for the symptomatic child, following protection or accompanying work with the maltreating caregiver to prevent continuation of the maltreatment.
- Work with the maltreating parent(s).
- Support for the non-abusing caregiver(s).
- Work with the whole family, including siblings who may not be (or appear not to be) immediately involved.
- Attention to social/environmental disadvantage.

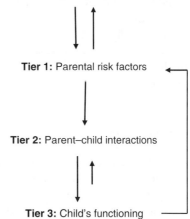

**Tier 0:** Family and social risk factors

**Tier 1:** Parental risk factors

**Tier 2:** Parent–child interactions

**Tier 3:** Child's functioning

**Figure 21.1** Explanatory relationships between tiers of concern.

When considering intervention, it should be borne in mind that there is no unitary post-abuse syndrome for any form of maltreatment. Also, evidence of effectiveness is variable [20]. Evidence-based therapeutic approaches are therefore indicated [21]. Children with post-traumatic stress disorder and inappropriate sexualized behaviour benefit from trauma-focused cognitive behavioural therapy [20]. Child developmental deficits and emotional difficulties following neglect may be addressed by supporting and improving parenting interactions. It may also require treatment of any adult mental health difficulties and substance misuse. However, experience shows that parents need to be willing to accept such help and that short, albeit intensive, interventions are less likely to lead to sustained change than is help that is maintained over time.

For children with disorganized attachments, the most efficacious intervention is increasing parental or caregiver sensitive responsiveness to their child's distress. Many children will also require educational remediation for associated educational under-achievement. Special attention is needed for any adolescent depression, substance misuse and self-harm following on from the experience of childhood or adolescent maltreatment.

**Table 21.5** Tiers of concern

| Tier | Description |
| --- | --- |
| Tier 0 | *Family and environmental factors* – including poverty, social isolation, poor housing, displacement |
| Tier 1 | *Parental risk factors* – including mental ill-health, substance misuse, history of significant own maltreatment, domestic violence [19] |
| Tier 2 | *Parent–child interactions* – forms of maltreatment, such as emotional abuse, neglect, physical abuse, sexual abuse |
| Tier 3 | *Child's functioning* – aspects that are attributable to maltreatment |

Additionally, child protection processes can lead to social disruptions for many maltreated children. They become preoccupied with separations and impermanence, and should be involved in age-appropriate decision-making. They require active support throughout.

Parents may initially oppose professional intervention. Acknowledging responsibility for the maltreatment, and sometimes for their inability to protect their child, is a difficult and painful process. They require support and specific therapy geared towards change.

## Conclusion

Child maltreatment carries a heavy burden of harm to the child, which may continue into adulthood and is a public health issue. Early recognition and intervention are necessary to aid prevention and ameliorate harm. Recognition and effective management involve a complex process requiring alertness to possible maltreatment alongside a coordinated, multidisciplinary and multi-agency approach. The family is of central importance to the child's well-being, although the child's own interests are paramount and sometimes these may not be achievable within the original family.

## References

1 Norman R, Byambaa D, De R et al. (2012) The long-term health consequences of child physical abuse, emotional abuse, and neglect: a systematic review and meta-analysis. PLOS Medicine, 9, e1001349.

2 Finkelhor D, Turner H, Hamby S et al. (2011). Polyvictimization: children's exposure to multiple types of violence, crime, and abuse. Juvenile Justice Bulletin. US Department of Justice, Office of Justice Programs.

3 Mullen P, Martin J, Anderson S et al. (1996) The long-term impact of the physical, emotional, and sexual abuse of children: a community study. Child Abuse and Neglect, 20, 7–21.

4 Pinheiro PS (2006) World Report on Violence Against Children. United Nations Secretary-General's study on violence against children. New York: United Nations.

5 Berelowitz S et al. (2013) 'If only someone had listened'. The Office of the Children's Commissioner's Inquiry into Child Sexual Exploitation in Gangs and Groups Final Report. London: Office of the Children's Commissioner.

6 Radford L, Corral S, Bradley C et al. (2011) Child Abuse and Neglect in the UK Today. London: NSPCC.

7 Sidebotham P, Heron J & Alspac Study Team (2006) Child maltreatment in the 'children of the nineties': a cohort study of risk factors. Child Abuse and Neglect, 30, 497–522.

8 Dixon L, Browne K, Hamilton-Giachritsis C (2005) Risk factors of parents abused as children: A meditational analysis of the intergenerational continuity of child maltreatment. Journal of Child Psychology and Psychiatry, 46, 47–57.

9 Ellis B, Boyce T (2009) Biological sensitivity to context. Current Directions in Psychological Science, 17, 183–187.

10 Cicchetti D, Rogosch F (2009) Adaptive coping under conditions of extreme stress: multilevel influences on the determinants of resilience in maltreated children. New Directions for Child and Adolescent Development, 124, 47–59.

11 Manly J, Kim J, Rogosch F et al. (2001) Dimensions of child maltreatment and children's adjustment: contributions of developmental timing and subtype. Development & Psychopathology, 13, 759–782.

12 Pollak S, Kistler D (2009) Early experience is associated with the development of categorical representations for facial expressions of emotion. Proceedings of the National Academy of Sciences, 99, 9072–9076.

13 Carlson V, Cicchetti D, Barnett D et al. (1989) Finding order in disorganization: Lessons from research on maltreated infants' attachments to their caregivers. In: Cicchetti D, Carlson V (eds) Child Maltreatment: Theory and Research on the Causes and Consequences of Child Abuse and Neglect. Cambridge: Cambridge University Press, pp. 494–528.

14 Glaser D (2015) Child sexual abuse. In: Thapar A, Pine D, Leckman J et al. (eds) Rutter's Child and Adolescent Psychiatry, 6th edn. Chichester: Wiley, pp. 376–388.

15 Mills R, Alati R, O'Callaghan M et al. (2011) Child abuse and neglect and cognitive function at 14 years of age: findings from a birth cohort. Pediatrics, 127, 4–10.

16 Teicher M, Samson J (2016) Enduring neurobiological effects of childhood abuse and neglect. Journal of Child Psychology and Psychiatry, 57, 241–266.

17 National Institute for Health and Care Excellence (NICE) (2009) When to Suspect Child Maltreatment: Clinical Guidelines CG89. NICE.

18 Gilbert R, Kemp A, Thoburn J et al. (2009) Recognising and responding to child maltreatment. Lancet, 373, 167–180.

19 Cleaver H, Unell I, Aldgate J (1999) Children's Needs – Parenting Capacity: The Impact of Parental Mental Illness, Problem Alcohol and Drug Use, and Domestic Violence on Children's Development. London: The Stationery Office.

20 MacMillan H, Wathen CN, Barlow J et al. (2009) What works? Interventions to prevent child maltreatment and associated impairment. Lancet, 373, 250–266.

21 Glaser D (2014) Child maltreatment. In: Fonagy P, Cottrell D, Phillips P et al. (eds) What Works for Whom? A Critical Review of Treatments for Children and Adolescents, 2nd edn. New York, NY: Guilford, pp. 411–451.

## 22

# The Neuroscience and Genetics of Childhood Maltreatment

*Eamon McCrory, Vanessa B. Puetz and Essi Viding*

## The Impact of Maltreatment on Brain Development

A growing body of research has investigated how stress, and specifically different forms of childhood maltreatment, can influence neural structure and function. These studies have employed both children who have experienced maltreatment and adults with documented childhood histories of early adversity. The main brain imaging modalities are summarized in Table 22.1. In this chapter we focus on studies of children, first considering those that have investigated differences in brain structure followed by a number of studies that have investigated the potential impact of maltreatment on brain function.

**Table 22.1** An overview of the characteristics, advantages and disadvantages of a number of brain imaging modalities used to investigate the impact of childhood maltreatment

ERP, event-related potential; fMRI, functional magnetic resonance imaging; DTI, diffusion tensor imaging.

| Imaging modality | How it works | Advantages | Disadvantages |
| --- | --- | --- | --- |
| ERP | Summarizes electrical activity at the scalp following stimulus presentation | • Relatively inexpensive<br>• High temporal resolution<br>• Easy to use with very young children | • Poorer spatial resolution<br>• Poorer spatial localization<br>• Limited to a predetermined set of waveforms |
| fMRI | Measures changes in blood oxygenation levels which is taken as a proxy of brain activity | • High spatial resolution<br>• Records from all regions of the brain simultaneously<br>• Can examine activity networks of brain regions<br>• Machine learning techniques can shed light on information-processing within a functional region | • Expensive<br>• Poorer temporal resolution<br>• Susceptible to motion artefacts |

*(continued)*

*Child Psychology and Psychiatry: Frameworks for Clinical Training and Practice,* Third Edition.
Edited by David Skuse, Helen Bruce and Linda Dowdney.
© 2017 John Wiley & Sons, Ltd. Published 2017 by John Wiley & Sons, Ltd.

**Table 22.1** (Continued)

| Imaging modality | How it works | Advantages | Disadvantages |
| --- | --- | --- | --- |
| DTI | Measures the direction of water diffusion to detect the integrity of white matter tracts | • High spatial resolution<br>• Technique that examines white matter tracts and measures connectivity | • Expensive<br>• Indirect measure of white matter integrity |

## Structural Differences

### Subcortical Structures: The Hippocampus and Amygdala

Animal research has shown that the hippocampus plays a central role in learning and various aspects of memory and that these functions are impaired when animals are exposed to chronic stress. Adults with post-traumatic stress disorder (PTSD) who have histories of childhood maltreatment, an early form of stress, consistently report that these individuals have smaller hippocampal volumes [1]. It is surprising then that structural magnetic resonance imaging (sMRI) studies of children and adolescents with maltreatment-related PTSD frequently fail to detect decreased hippocampal volume [2,3]. It is possible that the impact of stress is delayed and becomes manifest only later in development [4] or that heterogeneity in factors known to influence subcortical volumes, such as length or onset of maltreatment [5], obscure potential changes.

The amygdala, another key subcortical structure, plays a central role in evaluating potentially threatening information, fear conditioning, emotional processing and memory. Given that experiences of maltreatment typically occur in family environments characterized by unpredictability and threat, it might be expected that children growing up in such contexts would show increased amygdala volume, comparable to that found in stress-exposed animals who show increased dendritic arborization [6]. However, findings are inconclusive, with a meta-analysis of children with maltreatment-related PTSD reporting no significant differences in amygdala volume between maltreated and non-maltreated children [7] and others reporting smaller amygdala volumes [3]. By contrast, more recent studies have reported an increase in amygdala volume in maltreated children (e.g. Morey *et al.* [8]), suggesting that perhaps such effects are subtle and difficult to reliably detect or are associated with heightened forms of adversity experienced as a result of institutionalization.

A summary of structural and functional brain differences associated with maltreatment is given in Box 22.1.

### Cortical Structures: The Prefrontal Cortex and Cerebellum

The prefrontal cortex plays a major role in the control of many aspects of behaviour, regulating cognitive and emotional processes through extensive interconnections with other cortical and subcortical regions. In contrast to subcortical structures, several

---

**Box 22.1 Summary of structural and functional brain differences associated with maltreatment**

In summary, structural differences in several brain regions have been found to be associated with childhood adversity across studies even in the absence of concurrent psychiatric disorder, suggesting that maltreatment does indeed alter brain structure, even in those children who do not present with mental health problems. The emerging functional magnetic brain imaging research is largely consistent with findings from event-related potential studies indicating that maltreatment is associated with an increased amygdala response to threat-related cues. In addition, alterations in fronto-limbic networks have been demonstrated which are likely to compromise emotion regulation abilities as well as alter reward learning and cognitive control. These structural and functional changes may help to optimize the child's functioning in a hostile or unpredictable home environment in the short term, but over the longer term they point to mechanistic changes in emotional processing that may increase latent vulnerability to mental health problems.

---

studies have now reliably reported an association between the experience of maltreatment and volumetric reductions in grey [3,9–12] and white matter [13] in the orbitofrontal cortex (OFC), a brain region involved in emotion regulation and, in particular, fear extinction. Recently, we have shown that volumetric reductions in the OFC are associated with increased peer problems in both girls and boys exposed to maltreatment compared with typically developing peers [12].

In addition, decreased volume of the cerebellum in children and adolescents with a history of maltreatment has been a consistent finding in the literature [2], consistent with growing evidence that this structure plays an important role in emotion processing and fear conditioning via its connection with limbic structures and the hypothalamic–pituitary–adrenal axis. The cerebellum has also been shown to be involved in executive functioning, which has previously been shown to be impaired in children with a history of maltreatment [14].

**Corpus Callosum and Other White Matter Tracts**

The corpus callosum (CC) is the largest white matter structure in the brain and controls inter-hemispheric communication of a host of processes, including, but not limited to, arousal, emotion and higher cognitive abilities. With the exception of one study, decreases in CC volume have consistently been reported in maltreated children and adolescents compared with non-maltreated peers [2]. Recent studies that have employed diffusion tensor imaging have found differences in maltreated children in frontal and temporal white matter regions, including the uncinate fasciculus which connects the OFC to the anterior temporal lobe, including the amygdala (e.g. [15,16]). The extent of the white matter differences observed by Govindan *et al.* [15] was associated with longer periods within an orphanage and may underlie some of the socio-emotional and cognitive impairments exhibited by maltreated children.

## Functional Differences

In addition to the number of studies examining structural brain differences, a growing number are investigating the functional correlates associated with maltreatment using brain imaging techniques such as functional MRI (fMRI) or electrophysiological techniques. Such functional studies can capture more directly how the brain processes emotional information and are generally better able to shed light on potential underlying mechanisms of vulnerability in contrast to structural studies, which are often more difficult to interpret in terms of psychological processes.

### FMRI Studies

Building on the experimental evidence that maltreated children as young as 15 months show hypervigilance to threatening facial cues [17], several fMRI studies have examined the neural correlates of face-processing in this population. These studies have consistently reported that maltreated children are characterized by increased amygdala response to threatening cues in comparison to non-maltreated children [18,19], even if the facial cues are presented outside of conscious awareness (< 15 milliseconds; [20]). Other studies assessed response inhibition and observed increased activation in the anterior cingulate cortex in maltreated youths as compared with controls [11]. These results point to impaired cognitive control, which in turn could confer risk for psychopathology, notably anxiety-related disorders. Another study [21] used a monetary reward task and compared young adults who were maltreated as children with non-maltreated controls. Results suggested a weakened response in the reward circuit (i.e. globus pallidus) and less positive ratings of the reward cues in the maltreated group – a neural signature known from studies with patients with depression and PTSD. More research investigating how reward-processing is altered by maltreatment experience is warranted, given the accumulating evidence from clinical studies indicating that atypical reward-processing is associated with a number of psychiatric disorders.

### Event-Related Potential (ERP) Studies

Much of the existing ERP research has compared the pattern of brain response of adversely treated children and healthy children when processing facial expressions, an ability that is usually mastered by the preschool years. When compared with non-institutionalized peers, institutionalized children who have experienced severe social deprivation showed a pattern of cortical hypoactivation when viewing emotional facial expressions, and familiar and unfamiliar faces [22]. In contrast, a second set of important studies has provided convincing evidence that school-aged children who have been exposed to physical abuse show increases in brain activity specific to angry faces and require more attentional resources to disengage from such stimuli (e.g. [23]). These ERP findings are consistent with recent fMRI evidence and suggest that some maltreated children are allocating more resources and remain hypervigilant to potential social threat in their environment, probably at the cost of other developmental processes.

# The Role of Genetic Influences

It is a common but often striking clinical experience to find that two children who have experienced very similar patterns of early adversity have very different outcomes. While this may be partly due to specific environmental or psychological factors characterizing one child, but not the other, there is increasing evidence that such differential outcome may be due, at least in part, to genetic differences.

We now know that many of the psychiatric outcomes that are associated with maltreatment, such as PTSD, depression and antisocial behaviour, are partly heritable. However, it is incorrect to think that there are particular genes for these disorders. Rather, we are learning that there are a wide number of genetic variants that may subtly alter the structure and functioning of neural circuitry and hormonal systems that are crucial in calibrating our individual response to social affective cues and in regulating our stress response [24]. In recent years, researchers have focused, in particular, on the way in which such genetic variants and adverse environments may interact. Such gene X environment research has demonstrated that for a range of genetic variants (known as polymorphisms) childhood maltreatment can increase the risk of later psychopathology for some children more than others. For example, Caspi *et al.* [25] were the first to report on an interaction of a measured genotype (MAOA) and environment (maltreatment) for a psychiatric outcome and demonstrated that individuals who are carriers for the low-activity allele (MAOA-l) were at an increased risk for antisocial behaviour disorders following maltreatment. Imaging genetic studies suggest a neural mechanism by which MAOA genotype engenders vulnerability to reactive aggression following maltreatment [26].

In other words, gene X environment research suggests that a child's genotype may partly determine their level of risk and resilience for adult psychiatric outcomes, including depression and PTSD following childhood maltreatment (e.g. [27]). It is important to bear in mind, however, that positive environmental influences, such as social support, can promote resiliency, even in those children carrying 'risk' polymorphisms exposed to maltreatment [27]. This finding illustrates the important point that when considering a gene X environment interaction, positive environmental influences (such as contact with a supportive attachment figure) are as relevant to consider as negative environmental influences such as maltreatment.

## Clinical Implications

There is accumulating evidence pointing to a variety of neurobiological changes associated with childhood maltreatment. Such changes can, on the one hand, be viewed as a cascade of deleterious effects that are harmful for the child; however, a more evolutionary and developmentally informed view would suggest that such changes are, in fact, adaptive responses to an early environment characterized by threat. If a child is to respond optimally to the challenges posed by their surroundings then early stress-induced changes in neurobiological systems can be seen as 'programming' or calibrating those systems to match the demands of an early hostile environment. The theory of latent vulnerability has recently been proposed as a comprehensive model within which to think about how neurocognitive changes in children in response to maltreatment reflect patterns of adaptation that may carry longer-term costs, in particular increasing the likelihood of mental health problems in the future. [4]. An index of latent vulnerability can be thought of as capturing the degree to which an ostensibly healthy individual previously exposed to maltreatment is at future risk of developing a psychiatric disorder. For example, one candidate neurocognitive system relates to threat processing. Heightened responsiveness of this system (indexed by amygdala hyperactivation, as noted earlier) may be adaptive in an unpredictable home environment (increasing hypervigilance), but may be maladaptive when the individual is exposed to future stressors, increasing the risk of psychopathology [4].

Over the long term, the operationalization of latent vulnerability may enable the identification of a subgroup of children exposed to maltreatment who are at particularly high risk for psychopathology, thereby opening the possibility of targeted preventative interventions that would aim to reduce the risk of preventing disorders before they emerge. Future research should therefore investigate the influence of preventative clinical interventions as one positive environmental influence that may serve to moderate environmental and genetic risk. Such preventative strategies are most likely to include a systemic component. Indeed, emerging evidence from genetic and neurobiological research supports the importance of a reliable adult caregiver and the role they can play in helping to scaffold the child's ability to regulate stress [27]. Such work will begin to shed light on how professionals can intervene more effectively to promote better systemic structures around children that improve resilience and moderate the impact of maltreatment. Over the coming decade, we are likely to see an increasingly fruitful dialogue between developmental research, focused on a child's psychological representations of their social world, and neurobiological research, focused on putative neural mechanisms underlying adaptive responses to stress and effective emotional regulation.

## References

1 Jackowski AP, de Araújo CM, de Lacerda ALT et al. (2009) Neurostructural imaging findings in children with post-traumatic stress disorder: brief review. Psychiatry and Clinical Neurosciences, 63, 1–8.

2 McCrory E, De Brito S, Viding E (2011) The impact of childhood maltreatment: a review of neurobiological and genetic factors. Frontiers in Psychiatry, 2, 1–14.

3 Lim L, Radua J, Rubia K (2014) Gray matter abnormalities in childhood maltreatment: a voxel-wise meta-analysis. American Journal of Psychiatry, 171, 854–863.

4 McCrory EJ, Viding E (2015) The theory of latent vulnerability: Reconceptualizing the link between childhood maltreatment and psychiatric disorder. Developmental Psychopathology, 27, 493–505.

5 Hodel AS, Hunt RH, Cowell RA et al. (2015) Duration of early adversity and structural brain development in post-institutionalized adolescents. Neuroimage, 105, 112–119.

6 Lupien SJ, McEwen BS, Gunnar MR, Heim C (2009) Effects of stress throughout the lifespan on the brain, behaviour and cognition. Nature Reviews Neuroscience, 10, 434–445.

7  Woon FL, Hedges DW (2008) Hippocampal and amygdala volumes in children and adults with childhood maltreatment-related posttraumatic stress disorder: a meta-analysis. Hippocampus, 18, 729–736.

8  Morey RA, Haswell CC, Hooper SR, De Bellis MD (2015) Amygdala, hippocampus, and ventral medial prefrontal cortex volumes differ in maltreated youth with and without chronic posttraumatic stress disorder. Neuropsychopharmacology, 41, 791–801.

9  Andersen SL, Tomada A, Vincow ES et al. (2008) Preliminary evidence for sensitive periods in the effect of childhood sexual abuse on regional brain development. Journal of Neuropsychiatry and Clinical Neuroscience, 20, 292–301.

10  De Brito SA, Viding E, Sebastian CL et al. (2013) Reduced orbitofrontal and temporal grey matter in a community sample of maltreated children. Journal of Child Psychology and Psychiatry, 54, 105–112.

11  Kelly PA, Viding E, Wallace GL et al. (2013) Cortical thickness, surface area, and gyrification abnormalities in children exposed to maltreatment: neural markers of vulnerability? Biological Psychiatry, 74, 845–852.

12  Kelly PA, Viding E, Puetz V et al. (2015) Sex differences in socio-emotional functioning, attentional bias and gray matter volume in maltreated children: A multilevel investigation. Development and Psychopathology, 27, 1591–1609.

13  Hanson JL, Chung MK, Avants BB et al. (2010) Early stress is associated with alterations in the orbitofrontal cortex: a tensor-based morphometry investigation of brain structure and behavioral risk. Journal of Neuroscience, 30, 7466–7472.

14  Hostinar CE, Stellern SA, Schaefer C et al. (2012) Associations between early life adversity and executive function in children adopted internationally from orphanages. Proceedings of the National Academy of Sciences, 109(Supplement 2):17208–17212.

15  Govindan RM, Behen ME, Helder E et al. (2010) Altered water diffusivity in cortical association tracts in children with early deprivation identified with Tract-Based Spatial Statistics (TBSS). Cerebral Cortex, 20, 561–569.

16  Hanson JL, Adluru N, Chung MK et al. (2013) Early neglect is associated with alterations in white matter integrity and cognitive functioning. Child Development, 84, 1566–1578.

17  Curtis WJ, Cicchetti D (2013) Affective facial expression processing in 15-month-old infants who have experienced maltreatment: an event-related potential study. Child Maltreatment, 18, 140–154.

18  Tottenham N, Hare T, Millner A et al. (2011) Elevated amygdala response to faces following early deprivation. Developmental Science, 14, 190–204.

19  McCrory EJ, De Brito SA, Sebastian CL et al. (2011) Heightened neural reactivity to threat in child victims of family violence. Current Biology, 21, R947–948.

20  McCrory EJ, De Brito SA, Kelly PA et al. (2013) Amygdala activation in maltreated children during pre-attentive emotional processing. British Journal of Psychiatry, 202, 269–276.

21  Dillon D, Holmes A, Birk J et al. (2009) Childhood adversity is associated with left basal ganglia dysfunction during reward anticipation in adulthood. Biological Psychiatry, 66, 206–213.

22  Parker SW, Nelson CA (2005) An event-related potential study of the impact of institutional rearing on face recognition. Development and Psychopathology, 17, 621–639.

23 Pollak SD, Tolley-Schell SA (2003) Selective attention to facial emotion in physically abused children. Journal of abnormal psychology, 112, 323–338.

24 Viding E, Williamson DE, Hariri AR (2006) Developmental imaging genetics: challenges and promises for translational research. Development and Psychopathology, 18, 877–892.

25 Caspi A, McClay J, Moffitt TE et al. (2002) Role of genotype in the cycle of violence in maltreated children. Science, 297, 851–854.

26 Viding E, Frith U (2006) Genes for susceptibility to violence lurk in the brain. Proceedings of the National Academy of Sciences, 103(16), 6085–6086.

27 Kaufman J, Yang BZ, Douglas-Palumberi H et al. (2006) Brain-derived neurotrophic factor-5-HTTLPR gene interactions and environmental modifiers of depression in children. Biological Psychiatry, 59, 673–680.

# Section 4

## Atypical Development in Children and Adolescents

23

# Autism Spectrum Disorder – An Evolving Construct

*William Mandy*

Autism spectrum disorder (ASD) is a neurodevelopmental condition characterized by difficulties with social relationships and social communication; and inflexibility and atypical sensory processing [1]. Symptoms emerge in the second year of life (although in some cases they may not be obvious until later) and persist across the life span. In addition to these core features, people with ASD experience a range of neurodevelopmental, cognitive, emotional and behavioural atypicalities. As such, for children with ASD, co-morbidity is the rule rather than the exception, with the most common co-occurring difficulties being intellectual disability, attention deficit/hyperactivity disorder (ADHD), anxiety, speech and language problems, difficulties with emotional and behavioural regulation and executive dysfunction [2]. ASD is characterized by strengths as well as difficulties: whilst it has no consistent associated pattern of cognitive peaks and troughs, a non-specific unevenness of abilities across cognitive domains is a hallmark of the condition.

By current diagnostic criteria, ASD is a relatively common condition, affecting at least 1% of the population [3]. A person's chance of developing ASD is strongly influenced by their genes. Nevertheless, there is a growing awareness in the field that environmental exposures are also important in the aetiology of ASD and that previous heritability estimates of 90% or more were most likely inflated [4]. A recent influential synthesis of the literature concluded that, of the aetiological influences on ASD, 52% are attributable to additive genetic effects, 4% to non-additive genetic effects and 3% to *de novo* mutations [4]. This leaves 41% unaccounted for, which is likely to represent a range of environmentally mediated influences. Research to date has highlighted the potential importance of environmental exposures *in utero* (e.g. valproate) and during the first few months after birth (e.g. traffic-related pollution), suggesting that these exert their effects via interactions with genetic risk (for a review, see Mandy and Lai [5]).

In the last 10 years, understanding of the clinical characteristics of ASD has evolved rapidly and substantially. This is reflected both in recent changes to the definition of ASD in psychiatric nosology, marked by the move from the fourth to the fifth edition of the *Diagnostic and Statistical Manual of Mental Disorders*, and by broader shifts etc. Below I highlight these recent developments in how ASD is conceptualized, and outline some clinical implications.

*Child Psychology and Psychiatry: Frameworks for Clinical Training and Practice,* Third Edition.
Edited by David Skuse, Helen Bruce and Linda Dowdney.

## The Dimensionality of ASD

ASD is no longer considered to be categorically different from normal-range human variability in social competence and flexibility. Rather, ASD describes the difficulties of people who are at the extreme end of a trait distribution that extends throughout the general population. This is evidenced by the observation that when autistic traits are measured in general population samples, they are found to be continuously distributed with no natural cut-point between those with ASD and those without [6,7]. Further, twin studies and molecular genetic investigations suggest that aetiological influences on normal-range ASD trait variability overlap with influences on clinically severe autistic symptoms [8].

The emerging consensus that ASD is a dimensional disorder has engendered an interest in sub-threshold autistic traits (STATs), which we define as autistic symptoms that are not sufficiently severe to warrant clinical diagnosis. In the last decade, research has revealed that even mild childhood STATs confer risk for a range of maladaptive states [9]. These encompass conduct disorder, anxiety, depression, interpersonal difficulties, academic underperformance including school exclusion, and eating disorder [9–11]. Crucially there is evidence against the existence of a severity threshold at which STATs begin to impact upon well-being and functioning, such that even mildly elevated trait scores are associated with some increased risk of maladaptation [9]. On this basis, it is essential that when children are seen in mental health services and/or are struggling in education, even if they do not meet criteria for ASD, consideration should be given to the potential role of autistic traits in the development and maintenance of their difficulties. In particular, current evidence suggests that those seeking to understand and help boys with conduct problems [10] and adolescent girls with early-onset restricted eating difficulties [11] should routinely assess STATs in their clients.

## The Fractionation of the Autism Triad

The notion that ASD should be diagnosed when a person has a particular collection of social-communication and flexibility/sensory difficulties symptoms relies upon a fundamental assumption: that the diverse characteristics of autism cluster together because they share an underlying cause. It is surprising that, once autism had first been described in the scientific literature, it took 60 years before this assumption was tested. Happé *et al.* [12] used a twin sample to investigate the relationship between the social (i.e., social-communication and reciprocity) and non-social (i.e. flexibility/sensory) parts of the autism syndrome, and to model the degree of overlap between their genetic and environmental underpinnings. They discovered only modest overlap between different parts of the syndrome, with many people in their sample having social symptoms without non-social ones, and vice versa. Furthermore, it was estimated that the genetic influences on social autistic difficulties are substantially independent from genetic influences on flexibility/sensory traits.

This discovery that the autism syndrome is fractionable is corroborated in clinical samples by the observation that some children present with partial autism. Several reports exist of young people who have severe autistic social and communication difficulties, without marked inflexibility and sensory problems [13]. The converse profile also exists, namely inflexibility/sensory difficulties, in the presence of normal social communication abilities [14]. While such children do not fit neatly into current diagnostic systems, many experience serious difficulties and require clinical support. For example, autistic social-communication problems without inflexibility are a risk factor for diverse behavioural and emotional difficulties [13], while inflexibility/sensory problems without social impairment are associated with anorexia nervosa [15]. Thus, clinicians should expect to encounter children with some severe autistic difficulties who nevertheless do not meet criteria for ASD due to incomplete symptom profiles, and should be aware that despite not meeting full ASD criteria, they will require specific types of autism-relevant support.

## The End of Asperger's Disorder

During the era of DSM-IV there was a consensus that ASD comprised meaningfully distinct subtypes, named autistic disorder (AD), Asperger's disorder and pervasive developmental disorder – not otherwise specified (PDD-NOS). AD was defined as present when the full range of autistic impairments were observed, accompanied by a history of developmental delay, and was considered the prototypical ASD. Asperger's disorder was used to describe children with autistic difficulties who experienced no cognitive/linguistic developmental delay and PDD-NOS applied to those who had substantial autistic difficulties but who did not meet full criteria for AD or Asperger's. It emerged that clinicians could not reliably distinguish between these ASD subtypes, even when all used the same standardized measures [16]. Further, there is a lack of evidence that these subtypes are valid, as there is little to show that they differ from each other in terms of aetiology, prognosis and treatment needs (e.g. [17]). Therefore, the architects of DSM-5 decided to abolish the practice of distinguishing between autistic subtypes, choosing to subsume AD, Asperger's and PDD-NOS under the umbrella term ASD. In this system, heterogeneity within ASD is described by categorizing the severity of the disorder and by specifying whether intellectual disability, language impairment and a known genetic condition are present.

Whilst this decision to remove Asperger's disorder from psychiatric nosology is scientifically sound, it has attracted some criticism. The term 'Asperger's disorder/syndrome' is popular within the community of people with ASD and their parents, as it carries some positive connotations [18]. In this sense, while the diagnosis of Asperger's disorder lacks validity, it currently has some utility. It is likely that the term Asperger's disorder will survive its removal from official diagnostic systems, to be used informally to describe people with ASD who are verbally fluent and have average or above IQ.

## Gender Differences in ASD

Compared with boys, girls are at substantially elevated risk of their autistic symptoms being unrecognized: their difficulties are commonly mislabelled or missed entirely. In skilfully assessed, non-referred samples there are approximately three males for each female with ASD (e.g. [19]), whereas in clinically ascertained samples the male-to-female ratio is at least 4:1. This shows that many females with ASD never receive a clinical diagnosis and the help that comes with it. Even when females with ASD are identified, they receive their diagnosis (and associated support) later than equivalent males. Females require more severe autistic traits than males to come to clinical attention, and teachers under-report autistic traits in their female pupils [20].

One reason that females with autistic difficulties are at high risk of going unnoticed and unhelped is that there is a female autistic phenotype – a female-specific manifestation of autistic strengths and difficulties that does not fit the current, male-based consensus [1,20,21]. Research into the precise nature of ASD gender differences is at an early stage, but an empirically based account of the female autism phenotype is emerging, which has the following three key features.

### Higher Social Motivation

On average, females with ASD show greater interest in the social world than do equivalent males. This is reflected in a number of domains. For example, compared with males, females with ASD are more likely to have close friendships with peers, reflecting greater social motivation [22]. When social difficulties occur in girls with ASD, these can be less overt and therefore harder to identify than those of boys with ASD [23]. In terms of focused interests, females with ASD more often become fixated on topics with social relevance [21].

### Distinct Pattern of Risk for Co-Occurring Conditions

Reflecting gender differences in the general population, it has been observed that girls with ASD are at higher risk than males with ASD of developing internalizing problems and eating disorder, and at lower risk of having conduct problems [20,24].

### A Better Capacity to Camouflage and Compensate for Autistic Difficulties

Many people with ASD seek to mask their autistic characteristics in social situations ('camouflaging') and learn skills to compensate for ASD-related difficulties ('compensation'). This repertoire of behaviours has been memorably described by the author Lianne Holiday Willey, who herself has Asperger's syndrome, as 'pretending to be normal' and is considered to be especially characteristic of the female autism phenotype [25]. Examples include making a concerted effort to imitate a popular girl at school, including copying her clothes and learning how she uses gestures, and taking the decision to supress autistic self-stimulatory behaviours ('stimming') in public after realizing that these can attract negative attention [11].

Thus clinicians should be aware that girls with ASD are more likely to go unnoticed than boys with the condition. When assessing girls for ASD it is especially important to be aware that the presence of social motivation and the fact that a child may have established friendships should not automatically rule out an ASD diagnosis. Further, the possibility that some compensation and camouflaging may be present should be explored, both with the young person and with their parents. Finally, clinicians and educators must be aware that some girls with internalizing problems may have an underlying ASD. When standardized assessments are made that involve a detailed developmental history, sensitivity to the female autism phenotype can be high, even in young children [19].

# Conclusions

Autism spectrum disorder is a relatively common dimensional disorder that represents the extreme of a spectrum of behaviour that extends throughout the whole population. It is fractionable, and its presentation is partially gender-specific. Assessments should reflect this, in order to ensure that appropriate help is given to young people who are currently under-served by clinical services, namely children with sub-threshold traits, those with partial autistic presentations and girls with autistic difficulties.

# References

1 American Psychiatric Association (2013) Diagnostic and Statistical Manual of Mental Disorders, 5th edn (DSM-5). American Psychiatric Association.
2 Simonoff E, Pickles A, Charman T et al. (2008) Psychiatric disorders in children with autism spectrum disorders: prevalence, comorbidity, and associated factors in a population-derived sample. Journal of the American Academy of Child and Adolescent Psychiatry, 47, 921–929.
3 Baird G, Simonoff E, Pickles A et al. (2006) Prevalence of disorders of the autism spectrum in a population cohort of children in South Thames: the Special Needs and Autism Project (SNAP). Lancet, 368, 210–215.
4 Gaugler T, Klei L, Sanders SJ et al. (2014) Most genetic risk for autism resides with common variation. Nature Genetics, 46, 881–885.
5 Mandy W, Lai M-C (2016) Annual Research Review: The role of the environment in the developmental psychopathology of autism spectrum condition. Journal of Child Psychology and Psychiatry, Jan 19 [epub ahead of print]
6 Constantino JN, Todd RD (2003) Autistic traits in the general population: a twin study. Archives of Genener Psychiatry, 60, 524–530.
7 Posserud M-B, Lundervold AJ, Gillberg C (2006) Autistic features in a total population of 7–9-year-old children assessed by the ASSQ (Autism Spectrum Screening Questionnaire). Journal of Child Psychology and Psychiatry, 47, 167–175.
8 Robinson EB, Koenen KC, McCormick MC et al. (2011) Evidence that autistic traits show the same etiology in the general population and at the quantitative extremes (5%, 2.5%, and 1%). Archives of General Psychiatry, 68, 1113–1121.
9 Skuse DH, Mandy W, Steer C et al. (2009) Social communication competence and functional adaptation in a general population of children: preliminary evidence for sex-by-verbal IQ differential risk. Journal of the American Academy of Child and Adolescent Psychiatry, 48, 128–137.
10 Mandy W, Skuse D, Steer C et al. (2013) Oppositionality and socioemotional competence: interacting risk factors in the development of childhood conduct disorder symptoms. Journal of the American Academy of Child and Adolescent Psychiatry, 52, 718–727.
11 Mandy W, Tchanturia K (2015) Do women with eating disorders who have social and flexibility difficulties really have autism? A case series. Molecular Autism, 6, 6.1.
12 Happé F, Ronald A, Plomin R (2006) Time to give up on a single explanation for autism. Nature Neuroscience, 9, 1218–1220.

13 Mandy W, Charman T, Gilmour J, Skuse D (2011) Toward specifying pervasive developmental disorder-not otherwise specified. Autism Research, 4, 121–131.

14 Greaves-Lord K, Eussen MLJM, Verhulst FC et al. (2013) Empirically based phenotypic profiles of children with pervasive developmental disorders: interpretation in the light of the DSM-5. Journal of Autism and Developmental Disorders, 43, 1784–1797.

15 Pooni J, Ninteman A, Bryant-Waugh R et al. (2012) Investigating autism spectrum disorder and autistic traits in early onset eating disorder. International Journal of Eating Disorders, 45, 583–591.

16 Lord C, Petkova E, Hus V et al. (2012) A multisite study of the clinical diagnosis of different autism spectrum disorders. Archives of General Psychiatry, 69, 306–313.

17 Frith U (2004) Emanuel Miller lecture: confusions and controversies about Asperger syndrome. Journal of Child Psychology and Psychiatry, 45, 672–686.

18 Ruiz Calzada L, Pistrang N, Mandy WPL (2012) High-functioning autism and Asperger's disorder: utility and meaning for families. Journal of Autism and Developmental Disorders, 42, 230–243.

19 Zwaigenbaum L, Bryson SE, Szatmari P et al. (2012) Sex differences in children with autism spectrum disorder identified within a high-risk infant cohort. Journal of Autism and Developmental Disorders, 42, 2585–2596.

20 Lai M-C, Lombardo MV, Auyeung B et al. (2015) Sex/gender differences and autism: setting the scene for future research. Journal of the American Academy of Child and Adolescent Psychiatry, 54, 11–24.

21 Hiller RM, Young RL, Weber N (2015) Sex differences in pre-diagnosis concerns for children later diagnosed with autism spectrum disorder. Autism. Feb 25 [epub ahead of print].

22 Head AM, McGillivray JA, Stokes MA (2014) Gender differences in emotionality and sociability in children with autism spectrum disorders. Molecular Autism ;5, 19.

23 Dean M, Kasari C, Shih W et al. (2014) The peer relationships of girls with ASD at school: comparison to boys and girls with and without ASD. Journal of Child Psychology and Psychiatry, 55, 1218–1225.

24 Mandy W, Chilvers R, Chowdhury U et al. (2012) Sex differences in autism spectrum disorder: evidence from a large sample of children and adolescents. Journal of Autism and Developmental Disorders, 42, 1304–1313.

25 Willey LH (1999) Pretending to be Normal: Living with Asperger's Syndrome. Jessica Kingsley Publishers.

24

# Attention Deficit Hyperactivity Disorder

*Antonio Muñoz-Solomando and Anita Thapar*

## Definition

Attention deficit hyperactivity disorder (ADHD) is a childhood-onset, impairing, disorder [1] and a diagnostic category that is grouped as a neurodevelopmental disorder in the *Diagnostic and Statistical Manual of Mental Disorders*, 5th edition (DSM-5) [2]. Hyperkinetic disorder is the diagnostic term used in the *ICD-10 Classification of Mental and Behavioural Disorders*, 10th revision (ICD-10) [3] and captures a more severely affected group (specific criteria are listed in Box 24.1). Both diagnostic definitions require ADHD symptom presence in two or more settings and for symptoms to be impairing with an onset in childhood. ICD-10 also includes the category of hyperkinetic conduct disorder, which is helpful because children with both ADHD and conduct disorder have more severe symptoms of ADHD and a poorer clinical outcome than those with ADHD alone. DSM-5 differs from ICD-10 in several ways; notably it divides ADHD symptoms into two rather than three groups (hyperactive/impulsive and inattention). DSM-5 also differs from its predecessor, DSM-IV [4], in requiring an age of onset prior to 12 years rather than 7 years. It is helpful that DSM-5 now explicitly recognizes developmental stage, as the number of ADHD symptoms required has been adjusted for adolescents and adults. Also co-morbid diagnoses, which notably include autism spectrum disorder, are no longer an exclusion clause. For clinical purposes, ADHD is considered as a category. In the general population, as with blood pressure and blood glucose, it behaves as a trait.

Chronic irritability is a common, troublesome feature of ADHD [5]. It is typically but not always considered as a feature of co-morbid oppositional defiant disorder. DSM-5 will probably capture this group via a new diagnostic category called disruptive mood dysregulation disorder (DMDD) that is grouped with the depressive disorders. Although there is some evidence to link DMDD to later mood disorders, and this DSM-5 category circumvents the problem of inappropriate diagnosis of bipolar disorder in some countries, irritability is a clinical topic that requires further research. Box 24.2 shows a list of frequent ADHD co-morbid disorders.

*Child Psychology and Psychiatry: Frameworks for Clinical Training and Practice*, Third Edition.
Edited by David Skuse, Helen Bruce and Linda Dowdney.
© 2017 John Wiley & Sons, Ltd. Published 2017 by John Wiley & Sons, Ltd.

---

**Box 24.1 Symptoms of hyperkinetic disorder in *International Classification of Diseases*, 10th revision (ICD-10)**

---

**Hyperactivity**

- Often fidgets with hands or squirms in seat
- Difficulty remaining seated when required
- Runs about or climbs on things excessively in situations when it is inappropriate
- Exhibits a persistent pattern of motor activity (always on the go)
- Often noisy in playing or difficulty engaging quietly in leisure activities

**Inattention**

- Fails to sustain attention in tasks or play activities
- Often fails to follow through on instructions from others
- Often avoids tasks that require sustained mental effort
- Often easily distracted
- Often loses things that are necessary for tasks or activities
- Appears not to listen to what is being said to him/her
- Fails to pay attention to details, or makes careless mistakes
- Often forgetful in daily activities
- Often has difficulty organizing tasks and activities

**Impulsivity**

- Difficulty waiting turn in games or group situations
- Often blurts out answers before questions have been completed
- Often interrupts or intrudes on others
- Often talks excessively

**Other**

- Onset before the age of 7 years
- Impairment/interference
- Pervasiveness of symptoms

---

**Box 24.2 Frequent comorbidities of attention deficit hyperactivity disorder**

---

- Oppositional defiant disorder and conduct disorder
- Learning and developmental problems, including reading disability (dyslexia), developmental coordination disorder, speech and language problems
- Tic disorders, including Tourette syndrome
- Anxiety and depression
- Global learning/intellectual disability
- Pervasive developmental disorders/autism spectrum disorder

# Epidemiology

In the most recent UK epidemiological study [6], prevalence rates were 1.4% for DSM-IV ADHD combined type and 1% for ICD-10 hyperkinetic disorder. A more recent meta-analysis of published findings found the estimated prevalence of ADHD in children to be 3.4% [95% confidence interval (CI): 2.6–4.5] [7]. Like other neurodevelopmental disorders such as autism spectrum disorder and specific learning disorders, boys are more commonly affected than girls. The male:female sex ratio is higher in clinics (7–8:1) than in the community (3–4:1), suggesting that ADHD in females is under-recognized.

# Aetiology

Attention deficit hyperactivity disorder is a complex disorder influenced by the interplay of multiple risk factors (Box 24.3). No single risk factor is sufficient to result in disorder. Although there is a strong genetic contribution [8], non-inherited factors are also important. A number of environmental risk factors have been found to be associated with ADHD [8,9], but not all have been shown to be definitely causal

# Cognitive and Neurobiological Correlates

Routine cognitive testing is not necessary or diagnostically useful. Children with ADHD can underperform on IQ tests. They also show deficits on measures of executive function, response inhibition, prefrontal cortical function, delay aversion and

---

**Box 24.3  Risk factors in attention deficit hyperactivity disorder (ADHD)**

- **Genetic factors:** ADHD is highly heritable, like autism (heritability around 80%) and can run in families. Recent molecular genetic studies have revealed that multiple different types of genetic risks contribute to ADHD risk. The same risk contributes to different types of disorder.
- **Genetic syndromes:** syndromes such as fragile X, 22q11 microdeletion syndrome and tuberous sclerosis may lead to features of ADHD but are rare. Routine screening of genetic syndromes in non-learning-disabled children is currently unwarranted.
- **Maternal smoking and stress in pregnancy:** these are associated, but quasi-experimental evidence suggests that they might not be causal [10,11].
- **Alcohol use in pregnancy:** exposure to high doses of alcohol results in foetal alcohol syndrome. Evidence that mild alcohol use is important is sparse [10].
- **Low birthweight/prematurity** are associated [10].
- **Extreme early adversity** [12] involving early privation and institutional rearing can lead to features similar to ADHD. It is not known whether milder adversities are important.
- **Environmental toxins:** lead toxicity and early exposure to pesticides have been considered to be associated with ADHD, besides possibly dietary factors in some children.
- **Family adversity**, notably a negative mother–child relationship, appears to be a consequence of ADHD and seems to improve when ADHD symptoms are treated.

timing deficits. Structural imaging studies [13] show alterations, including reduced volume, in the basal ganglia and limbic regions of the brain, and delayed cortical maturation especially in the prefrontal regions; functional magnetic resonance imaging (MRI) studies implicate corticostriatal circuit involvement and alterations in networks considered relevant to attention and executive function. Diffusion MRI studies also find widespread white matter microstructure alterations. Early animal, genetic and pharmacological studies implicated involvement of dopaminergic pathways. More recent studies, including genetic ones highlight additional biological pathways (see Thapar & Cooper [9]).

## Diagnostic Assessment

Diagnosis is based on the presence of reported symptoms. The diagnostic process includes a detailed history from the family, observation of the child, and reports from school or other observers (Box 24.4).

### Information from Parents

This includes a developmental and psychiatric history. Asking for examples of the behaviour often illustrates the severity of problems and the level and types of impairment. The clinician should ask the parents to explain what they think could be causing the problems and their attitude to treatment. Finally, completion of rating scales such as the Strengths and Difficulties Questionnaire [14] Swanson, Nolan, and Pelham Rating Scale, fourth edition (SNAP-IV) [15] and Conners' Parental Rating Scale, third edition [16] provide baseline information on symptoms and can also be used for initial screening or to monitor treatment response. They are not substitutes for clinical questioning.

---

**Box 24.4  Key areas of assessment**

- Presence of ADHD symptoms as specified in ICD-10 or DSM-V
- Information from parents and child
- Neurodevelopmental assessment
- Establish degree of impairment and pervasiveness of symptoms
- Information from school or other informants
- Assess for co-morbidity and consider differential diagnoses
- Cognitive assessment of the child if learning difficulties suspected
- Physical examination, including height, weight and cardiovascular system checks
- Use of rating instruments such as the Strength and Difficulties Questionnaire and Conners' Rating Scale

ADHD, attention deficit hyperactivity disorder; DSM-V, *Diagnostic and Statistical Manual of Mental Disorders, 5th edition*; ICD-10, *International Classification of Diseases, 10th revision.*

---

### Child Information and Observation

These are important to assess ADHD symptoms and co-morbidity, and to consider differential diagnoses, such as anxiety and mood disorders. The clinician needs to consider the developmental age of the child. Observation while performing tasks that require a certain level of self-control and sustained attention can be helpful but the diagnosis should not be based purely on observed behaviours in clinic. When possible, a school visit can provide invaluable information to support the diagnosis. Teenagers can often describe their symptoms, for instance subjective feelings of restlessness, and provide information on their level of social functioning. However, self-reports of ADHD are not a substitute for reports from informants and should not be used alone to make the diagnosis [17].

### Report from School or Other Informants

After gathering consent, a report from the school or other informants is crucial. A school report from a teacher who knows the child well provides information on how the child's symptoms and behaviour manifest in a more structured environment, and on academic performance and social relationships. The use of instruments such as the Child ADHD Teacher Telephone Interview (CHATTI) [18] or teacher rating scales (e.g. the Conners Teacher Rating Scale) [19] can be valuable. Due to its frequent association with ADHD [20], autistic spectrum disorder symptomatology screening should be included in the assessment process. A cognitive assessment of the child may be necessary to identify intellectual disability, but is not routinely required. Some children require assessment by an occupational therapist or physiotherapist if motor coordination problems are noted. In young adults who have left school, informant reports still remain an important part of the diagnostic process.

### Physical Examination

This can be important in ruling out physical causes of the symptoms (e.g. hearing and vision problems). Physical examination needs to include checks on weight, height and the cardiovascular system, especially if medication is later prescribed as part of the treatment plan and the child has intellectual disability.

## Treatment

Current guidance supports the use of multimodal and multi-professional integrated packages of care for the treatment of ADHD; Box 24.5 shows the types of treatment used. Most families benefit from written information about the features and treatment of ADHD, and the addresses of reliable internet websites and voluntary organizations.

### Pharmacological Intervention

In preschool-aged children medication is rarely used. Instead, behaviourally oriented parent training programmes are the first treatment option. In school-aged children and young adults suffering with ADHD, stimulant medication such as methylphenidate and the non-stimulant atomoxetine have been shown to reduce hyperactivity and improve concentration. These drugs are endorsed by the National Institute for Health and Clinical Excellence [21]. Although there are short-term therapeutic effects of ADHD medication, there is uncertainty about long-term benefits [22]. Once medication has been started, the child's physical health, including weight and height, and ADHD symptoms need to be monitored regularly and the dosage titrated accordingly.

### Stimulants

Methylphenidate and dexamfetamine are central nervous system stimulants. The mode of action of methylphenidate is not entirely clear, although it appears to result in an increased dopamine concentration in the synaptic cleft by partially blocking the dopamine transporter (DAT). Methylphenidate is rapidly absorbed, reaching maximum plasma levels 2 hours after oral administration. Sustained-release formulations

---

**Box 24.5  Management of attention deficit hyperactivity disorder**

**Pharmacological interventions**

*First line*
- Methylphenidate*
- Dexamfetamine*

*Second line*
- Atomoxetine*
- Clonidine
- Modafanil
- Bupropion
- Tricyclic antidepressants

**Psychosocial interventions**

- Behaviour therapy, including parent training programmes*
- Cognitive behavioural therapy
- Social skills training
- Family support to reduce stress

**School interventions**

- Classroom interventions
- Management of general and specific learning difficulties

**Related areas**

- Elimination and supplementation diets

*Supported by evidence base.

with a therapeutic effect of 8–12 hours are also available, making single daily dose administration possible. Dexamfetamine also enhances dopaminergic neurotransmission in the central nervous system. The elimination half-life of dexamfetamine allows once- or twice-daily oral administration. A prodrug of dexamfetamine called Lisdexamfetamine has become available in many countries. Frequent short-term side-effects include:

- decreased appetite
- sleep disturbance
- headaches
- stomach aches
- drowsiness
- irritability
- tearfulness
- increased blood pressure and pulse.

The effect of methylphenidate on growth in the long term is unclear [23]. The use of drug holidays provides the opportunity to assess improvement of ADHD symptoms. Finally, the use of stimulant drugs in children with tics and seizures can be considered, but with caution. Stimulants have also been shown to be useful for treating ADHD in children with pervasive developmental disorders and intellectual disability [24].

### Non-Stimulants

Atomoxetine is a non-stimulant drug also used in the treatment of ADHD in children aged 6 years and over. The therapeutic effect of atomoxetine is currently considered to be related to the increase of noradrenaline in the cortex through inhibition of presynaptic reuptake. Atomoxetine can be administered as a once-daily dose, although some children benefit from divided daily doses. Common undesired effects of atomoxetine include:

- abdominal pain
- nausea and vomiting
- decreased appetite
- dizziness
- slight increases in heart rate and blood pressure.

Suicidal thoughts and liver damage have also been reported to be more frequent among children and adolescents treated with atomoxetine.

### Other Medications

There is limited evidence supporting the use of other drugs. However, drugs such as clonidine, bupropion and modafinil have been shown to produce some improvement in ADHD symptoms. Some uncontrolled studies have also suggested the use of tricyclic antidepressants such as imipramine and desipramine. These drugs should be used only as a second-line treatment and when other interventions have not been successful. The use of antipsychotic medication it is not recommended for the treatment of core ADHD symptoms.

### Psycho-Social Interventions

It is recommended that non-pharmacological interventions are also provided to children and adolescents suffering with ADHD. Clinicians must emphasize to parents the need to implement these interventions despite the use of pharmacological treatment. The largest trial to date, the Multimodal Treatment Study of ADHD [25], showed short-term benefits of medication, that adding behavioural treatment reduced the dosage of medication required, but that behavioural treatment alone was not helpful. Children with ADHD may benefit from scheduled activities and regular timetables. Reducing family stress by increasing support, either formally through social services or via voluntary organizations, can be helpful.

**Parent Training Programmes/Behaviour Therapy** are aimed at modifying symptoms and should be considered first for preschool children with ADHD [26]. Parenting packages, such as the Webster–Stratton programme [27], emphasize the use of behavioural interventions to improve the child's symptoms and behaviours. Parent training programmes have been shown to be effective in reducing behavioural problems [28], but not core ADHD symptoms [29].

**Cognitive Behavioural Therapy (CBT)** for older children and adolescents can help them to develop a better understanding of their feelings, thoughts and actions, and, theoretically, could improve core ADHD symptoms. There is some evidence to suggest that CBT techniques can be beneficial for adults who are already being treated with medication [30].

**Social and Organizational Skills Training** could be useful to help the child develop socially acceptable behaviours, and improve peer relationships and organizational skills. Social skills training includes the use of emotional regulation and problem-solving strategies. Although there is some evidence, more research is needed to support their use in this population.

### School Interventions

The management of ADHD in school-aged children needs to consider the school setting. Therefore, training of teachers about the condition and increased support in the classroom are important. Behavioural interventions include class placement, and the promotion of structure and routines in the classroom as well as during breaktimes and play activities.

### Other Interventions

There is some evidence that elimination of certain artificial colourings and preservatives from the individual child's diet can help a few selected individuals [31]. Some children could also benefit from the use of omega-3 and omega-6 polyunsaturated fatty acids to supplement their diet. However, the evidence base for these interventions is limited at present.

## Clinical Course

Symptoms of ADHD decline with age, but longitudinal studies show that ADHD and/or additional problems tend to persist into adolescence and adult life [32].
  Problems include:

- adult ADHD – continuing to meet diagnostic criteria;
- showing some ADHD symptoms with associated impairment;
- conduct disorder, antisocial behaviour, criminality;
- depression and anxiety;
- drug and alcohol misuse;
- educational and employment failure;
- relationship difficulties, driving offences;
- premature mortality [32].

Consideration must also be given to the possible effects of ADHD on safe driving among adolescents and young adults.

## References

1 Sonuga-Barke E and Taylor E (2015) ADHD and hyperkinetic disorders. In: Thapar A, Pine DS, Leckman JF, Scott S, Snowling MJ, Taylor E (eds) Rutter's Textbook of Child Psychiatry, 6th edn. Oxford: Blackwell

2 American Psychiatric Association (2013) Diagnostic and Statistical Manual of Mental Disorders, 5th edn, (DSM-V). Washington, DC: American Psychiatric Association.

3 World Health Organisation (1992) The ICD-10 Classification of Mental and Behavioural Disorders: Criteria for Research. Geneva: World Health Organization.

4 American Psychiatric Association (2000) Diagnostic and Statistical Manual of Mental Disorders, 4th edn, Text Revision (DSM-IV-TR). Washington, DC: American Psychiatric Association.

5 Shaw P, Stringaris A, Nigg J, Leibenluft E (2014) Emotion dysregulation in attention deficit hyperactivity disorder. American Journal of Psychiatry, 171, 276–293.

6 Ford T, Goodman R, Meltzer H (2003) The British Child and Adolescent Mental Health Survey 1999: the prevalence of DSM-IV disorders. Journal of the American Academy of Child and Adolescent Psychiatry, 42, 1203–1211.

7 Polanczyk GV, Salum GA, Sugaya LS et al. (2015) Annual research review: a meta-analysis of the worldwide prevalence of mental disorders in children and adolescents. Journal of Child Psychology and Psychiatry, 56, 345–365

8 Thapar A, Cooper M, Eyre O, Langley K (2013) What have we learnt about the causes of ADHD? Journal of Child Psychology and Psychiatry, 54, 3–16.

9 Thapar A, Cooper M (2015) Attention deficit hyperactivity disorder. Lancet, published online September 17, dx.doi.org/10.1016/S0140-6736(15)00238-X

10 Linnet KM, Dalsgaard S, Obel C et al. (2003) Maternal lifestyle factors in pregnancy risk of attention deficit hyperactivity disorder and associated behaviors: review of the current evidence. American Journal of Psychiatry, 160, 1028–1040

11 Thapar A, Rutter M (2009) Do prenatal risk factors cause psychiatric disorder? Be wary of causal claims. British Journal of Psychiatry, 195, 100–101

12 Stevens SE, Sonuga-Barke EJ, Kreppner JM et al. (2008) Inattention/overactivity following early severe institutional deprivation: presentation and associations in early adolescence. Journal of Abnormal Child Psychology, 36, 385–398.

13 Kelly AM, Margulies DS, Castellanos FX (2007) Recent advances in structural and functional brain imaging studies of attention-deficit/hyperactivity disorder. Current Psychiatry Reports, 9, 401–407.

14 Goodman R (1997) The strengths and difficulties questionnaire: a research note. Journal of Child Psychology and Psychiatry, 38, 581–586.

15 Swanson J et al. Categorical and Dimensional Definitions and Evaluations of Symptoms of ADHD: History of the SNAP and the SWAN Rating Scales. Online: http://www. adhd.net/SNAP SWAN.pdf.

16 Conners CK (2004) Continuous Performance Test II (CPT-II). New York: Multi-Health Systems Inc.

17 Barkley RA, Fischer M, Smallish L et al. (2002) The persistence of attention-deficit/ hyperactivity disorder into young adulthood as a function of reporting source and definition of disorder. Journal of Abnormal Psychology, 111, 279–289.

18 Holmes J, Lawson D, Langley K et al. (2004) The Child Attention-Deficit Hyperactivity Disorder Teacher Telephone Interview (CHATTI): reliability and validity. British Journal of Psychiatry, 184, 74–78.

19 Conners CK, Sitarenios G, Parker JD, Epstein JN (1998) Revision and restandardization of the Conners Teacher Rating Scale (CTRS-R): factor structure, reliability, and criterion validity. Journal of Abnormal Child Psychology, 26, 279–291.

20 Rommelse NNJ, Franke B, Geurts HM et al. (2010) Shared heritability of attention-deficit/hyperactivity disorder and autism spectrum disorder. European Child and Adolescent Psychiatry, 19, 281–295.

21 National Collaborating Centre for Mental Health (2009) Attention Deficit Hyperactivity Disorder: Diagnosis and Management of ADHD in Children, Young People and Adults. London: The British Psychological Society and The Royal College of Psychiatrists.

22 Jensen PS, Arnold LE, Swanson JM et al. (2007) 3-year follow up of the NIMH M TA study. Journal of the American Academy of Child and Adolescent Psychiatry, 46, 989–1002.

23 Poulton A (2006) Growth and sexual maturation in children and adolescents with attention deficit hyperactivity disorder. Current Opinion in Pediatrics, 18, 427–434.

24 Pearson DA, Santos CW, Roache JD et al. (2003) Treatment effects of methylphenidate on behavioural adjustment in children with mental retardation and ADHD. Journal of the American Academy of Child and Adolescent Psychiatry, 42, 209–216.

25 MTA Cooperative Group (1999) A 14-month randomized clinical trial of treatment strategies for attention-deficit/hyperactivity disorder. Multimodal Treatment Study of Children with ADHD. Archives of General Psychiatry, 56, 1073–1086.

26 Muñoz-Solomando A, Kendall T, Whittington CJ (2008) Cognitive behavioural therapy for children and adolescents. Current Opinion in Psychiatry, 21, 332–337.

27 Webster-Stratton CH (2011) Combining parent and child training for young children with ADHD. Journal of Clinical Child and Adolescent Psychology, 40, 191–203

28 Scott S, Gardner F (2015) Parenting programs. In: Thapar A, Pine D, Leckman JF et al. (eds) Rutter's Textbook of Child Psychiatry, 6th edn. Oxford: Blackwell.

29  Sonuga-Barke EJS, Brandeis D, Cortese S et al. and the European ADHD Guidelines Group (2013) Nonpharmacological interventions for ADHD: systematic review and meta-analyses of randomized controlled trials of dietary and psychological treatments. American Journal of Psychiatry, 170, 275–289.

30  Safren SA, Sprich S, Mimiaga MJ et al. (2010) Cognitive behavioral therapy vs relaxation with educational support for medication-treated adults with ADHD and persistent symptoms: a randomized controlled trial. Journal of the American Medical Association, 304, 875–80.

31  Dalsgaard S, Øtergaard SD, Leckman JF et al. (2015) Mortality in children, adolescents, and adults with attention deficit hyperactivity disorder: a nationwide cohort study. Lancet; published online Feb 26. DOI:10.1016/S0140-6736(14)61684-6.

32  Klein RG, Mannuzza S, Olazagasti MAR et al. (2012) Clinical and functional outcome of childhood attention-deficit/hyperactivity disorder 33 years later. Archives of General Psychiatry, 69, 1295–1303.

# 25

# Anxiety Disorders in Children and Adolescents

*Aaron Vallance and Elena Garralda*

Anxiety is an unpleasant feeling of apprehension accompanied by physiological (e.g. muscle tension), cognitive (e.g. worries, fears) and behavioural (e.g. avoidance) processes. Honed by millennia of natural selection to protect us from danger, the anxiety response is a normal human experience. However, the threshold between adaptive and maladaptive anxiety can be finely balanced; disorder ensues when anxiety arises disproportionately to the presenting threat, causing significant distress and/or impairment.

Anxiety occurs normally across different developmental stages (Table 25.1). Fears tend to occur at ages where they become evolutionarily adaptive: for a 2-year-old determined to explore, fear of animals is common and arguably protective. Cognitive skill meanwhile endows adolescents with the capacity to imagine and ruminate on increasingly complex and abstract threats. What is normal for a young child (e.g. separation anxiety) may be considered disordered in an older child.

## Diagnostic Features

The *International Statistical Classification of Diseases*, 10th revision (ICD-10) differentiates anxiety disorders according to the feared situation or the pattern of anxiety; all include physiological changes (Table 25.2). Subtypes probably evolved to optimize protection against particular dangers [1]. In contrast, the similarities of physiological effects (e.g. via the sympathetic nervous system) and behavioural responses (e.g. fight, flight, freeze and avoid) across subtypes may reflect an evolutionary need for flexibility

**Table 25.1** Fear and its typical developmental stages

| Age | Fears |
| --- | --- |
| 9 months to 3 years | Separation, strangers, sudden noises/movement |
| 3–6 years | Animals, darkness, 'monsters' |
| 6–12 years | Performance anxiety |
| 12–18 years | Social anxiety, fear of rejection |
| Adulthood | Illness, death |

*Child Psychology and Psychiatry: Frameworks for Clinical Training and Practice*, Third Edition.
Edited by David Skuse, Helen Bruce and Linda Dowdney.
© 2017 John Wiley & Sons, Ltd. Published 2017 by John Wiley & Sons, Ltd.

**Table 25.2** Epidemiological and diagnostic characteristics of paediatric anxiety disorder subtypes

| Anxiety Disorder | Diagnostic notes | Prevalence | Typical age of onset |
|---|---|---|---|
| Separation anxiety disorder | Excessive and/or developmentally inappropriate anxiety about separation from attachment figures or excessive worrying about the figure's welfare. | 2–4% | Pre-puberty; peaks at 7 years |
| | Impairment might include school refusal, particularly if there is concurrent school-related anxiety. | | |
| | ICD-10 requires onset < 6 years old and duration of 4 weeks. | | |
| Generalized anxiety disorder | Excessive worry, which is generalized and persistent, and not restricted to any particular situation. | 3% | Increased incidence in adolescence |
| | This 'free-floating' anxiety is hard to control and is usually accompanied by a more restricted set of somatic complaints as compared with adults, namely: restlessness, fatigue, muscle tension and sleep disturbance. | | |
| Social anxiety disorder | Marked persistent fear of embarrassment in social situations involving exposure to unfamiliar people or to scrutiny; these situations are then usually avoided, thereby reinforcing the anxiety associated with them and leading to social isolation. | 1–7% | 11–15 years |
| | ICD-10 differentiates 'social anxiety disorder in childhood' from 'social phobia'. The former occurs before 6 years old, during the developmental stage where such social anxiety reactions are age-appropriate, but where there is significant severity, persistence or impairment for at least 4 weeks. In contrast, social phobia reflects social anxiety later in life, and includes blushing, shaking or fear of vomiting, micturition or defecation. | | |
| | Social phobia that generalizes across various settings may carry greater chronicity, impairment and co-morbidity [2]. | | |
| Panic disorder | Recurrent and unexpected attacks of severe anxiety unrestricted to a particular situation. | 5% | Late teens |
| | The young person may show persistent apprehension about future attacks (anticipatory anxiety) or its feared implications. | | |
| | Consistent with ICD-10, DSM-5 now separates agoraphobia and panic disorder. | | |
| Specific or simple phobias | Excessive fears of discernible, circumscribed objects or situations that provoke an immediate anxiety response. | 2–4% | > 5 years |
| | Distinguished into animal, situational, nature/environment (e.g. water, heights) and blood injury subtypes, by virtue of varying symptoms, onset age, heritability and biological challenges [3]. | | |

| Anxiety Disorder | Diagnostic notes | Prevalence | Typical age of onset |
|---|---|---|---|
| Agoraphobia | An often-overlapping cluster of phobias relating to 2+ of: crowds, public places, leaving home or travelling alone. | 2.5% | Mid-teens |
| | Various specific worries may reinforce the anxiety, including fears of collapsing and being unable to escape. | | |
| | Persistent avoidance behaviour may act to restrict the anxiety, but isolate the individual and impair functioning. | | |

ICD-10, *International Statistical Classification of Diseases*, 10th revision; DSM-5, *Diagnostic and Statistical Manual of Mental Disorders*, 5th edition.

against uncertain or indefinable threats. Although anxiety can feature in obsessive compulsive disorder (OCD) and post-traumatic stress disorder (PTSD), the *Diagnostic and Statistical Manual of Mental Disorders*, 5th edition (DSM-5) does not classify these as anxiety disorders. DSM-5 does, however, include other subtypes, including: selective mutism, substance/medication-induced anxiety disorder, and anxiety disorder due to another medical condition.

## Epidemiology

Anxiety disorders are one of the most prevalent paediatric psychiatric conditions (Table 25.2). Over one-third of people with one anxiety disorder have at least an additional one. Co-morbidity with other psychiatric disorders is about 40%, while up to 84% of children with autistic spectrum disorder (ASD) have anxiety disorder.

## Aetiology

### Temperament

Longitudinal studies indicate that anxiety disorders can develop from pre-existing temperamental traits, including behavioural inhibition, passivity and shyness. The relationship is, however, complex and studies significantly vary [4].

### Genetic Factors

Family studies show a significant, but largely non-specific, association between parental anxiety and offspring depressive and anxiety disorders. Some twin studies indicate a shared genetic substrate across anxiety disorder subtypes (e.g. adult-onset panic episodes and childhood separation anxiety disorder [5]), while others indicate subtypes having distinct biological substrates [6]. Adult twin studies estimate genetic heritability of 40%, while estimates in children with specific phobia vary from 46% to 60%, and in separation anxiety disorder from 14% to 73%. These figures may, however, overestimate genetic contribution by incorporating gene–environment interaction [7]. Such inter-study variation could also occur if different genes come into play at different ages. One twin study found a specific genetic risk factor operating throughout childhood, while other genetic factors only appear in late adolescence and early adulthood [8].

Overall, genetic factors most likely endow a broad susceptibility towards anxiety in general as opposed to a specific disorder. This is consistent with anxiety disorder's largely non-specific familial transmission and heterotypic continuity.

### Environmental Factors and Parent–Child Interactions

Twin studies indicate significant contribution from shared and non-shared environmental factors. However their cross-sectional design limits what they tell us about *transmission* from parent to child [9]. In an innovative 'children-of-twins' paradigm, 876 adult twin pairs, their spouses and adolescent offspring were evaluated for anxious personality or symptoms [7]. By comparing correlations between child and parent, and contrasting this with correlations between the child and their parent's twin, as well as comparing monozygotic and dizygotic families, this design helps to disentangle the influence of living with one's parent from simply receiving half their genes. Although results indicate significant genetic influence on *adult* anxiety symptoms, parent-to-child transmission of anxiety was only mediated via environmental factors. One interpretation is that parental anxiety is genetically influenced, but with genes that only operate in adulthood.

In terms of potential environmental factors, retrospective and observational studies indicate that parents of anxious children have an excess of controlling and/or rejecting styles of child-rearing, high expressed emotion, and emotional over-involvement. It is unclear, however, whether parenting style contributes to the child's anxiety, or vice versa. However, in either case, such parental behaviour may impede the child's development of autonomy and coping ability and, through modelling, enhance threat perception.

Social adversity and adverse life events may also contribute [10]. Furthermore, maternal stress or anxiety in pregnancy correlates with later childhood anxiety [11] and neuroanatomical changes, e.g. reduced hippocampal volume and grey matter [12]. Such processes may have evolved to protect the offspring against the same potentially stress-inducing environment as experienced by its mother; however, maladaptation is a risk if anxiety is excessive.

### Neurobiology/Neuropsychology Factors

Neuroimaging studies have demonstrated amygdala–prefrontal circuitry abnormalities, areas associated with memory, learning and emotional regulation. Paediatric studies indicate reduced left hippocampal and left amygdala grey matter volume [13], with recovery following successful 8-week intervention with selective serotonin reuptake inhibitors (SSRIs) or psychotherapy. Such biological changes may be associated with information-processing biases, e.g. threat attention, threat appraisal and fear conditioning (Table 25.3) [14].

**Table 25.3** Information Processing Biases: Threat Attention and Threat Appraisal.

| Process | What is it? | Bias in anxiety disorder | Relative specificity to anxiety disorder sub-categories |
|---------|-------------|--------------------------|--------------------------------------------------------|
| Threat attention | Attention is rapidly directed towards environmental threats | Tendency to allocate attention automatically towards threats<br><br>As threat intensity increases, a tendency to avoid the threat develops | Low |
| Threat appraisal | Events are interpreted as meaningful and threatening to the individual | Children with anxiety disorders exhibit a reduced threshold for classifying stimuli as dangerous | High – for example, adolescents with social phobia exhibit a threat appraisal bias specifically for social stimuli |

### Respiratory Dysregulation

Recurrent dyspnoea, especially in asthma, increases risk particularly for separation anxiety and panic disorders [15].

## Assessment

Making an early diagnosis is important as anxiety disorders often remain unrecognized and untreated. Anxiety disorder also increases risk of suicidality and substance usage. Assessment involves evaluating aetiological factors and the ensuing distress and impairment, differentiating anxiety disorders from normal or developmentally appropriate anxiety. Appointments incorporating both individual time with the young person and collective family time can optimize information-gathering. School liaison is often helpful.

Differential and co-morbid diagnoses include ASD, conduct disorders, attention deficit hyperactivity disorder, depression, OCD and PTSD. Medical disorders (e.g. hyperthyroidism, arrhythmias, epilepsy, asthma, phaeochromocytoma) and drugs (e.g. steroids, sympathomimetics, caffeine, amphetamines and cocaine) can mimic or provoke anxiety states. Physical examination, targeted investigations and liaison with general practitioners and/or paediatricians may be indicated [16]. Various scales have been validated, including self-report (e.g. SCARED, Spence Children's Anxiety Scale) and clinician-operated (e.g. PARS).

## Prognosis

Although longitudinal studies indicate that childhood anxiety disorders generally remit, studies vary significantly and may depend on disorder subtype, co-morbidity and severity [17]. Furthermore, although evidence errs towards heterotypic continuity, so that a child with separation anxiety may develop generalized anxiety in adolescence and panic disorder in adulthood [17], other studies suggest more homotypic continuity. Overall, adolescent anxiety or depression predicts an approximate three-fold increase in risk for adult anxiety disorders, while over half of adults with anxiety disorder also had it in childhood.

## Treatment

The UK National Institute of Health and Clinical Excellence (NICE) guidance on generalized anxiety and panic disorders relates to adults, while guidance on social anxiety also includes children and adolescents. Both guidelines recommend psycho-education to help families' understanding and promote reassurance, while self-help may include written or electronic materials.

### Cognitive Behavioural Therapy (CBT)

The cognitive component encompasses reframing, challenging unhelpful thoughts, positive self-talk, and weighing up evidence for and against expected events, and requires a certain degree of cognitive maturity.

The behavioural component derives its principles from conditioning, social learning and information-processing paradigms. It includes relaxation training, modelling of and rewards for desirable behaviour, and role-play. Systematic desensitization and exposure and response prevention involve developing a 'fear hierarchy' of situations that would trigger increasing levels of anxiety. Carefully planned and performed in a stepwise manner over time, the child performs exposure 'experiments' to each situation, monitoring their anxiety in real time; repeated exposure eventually aims to desensitize at each level [18].

As Creswell *et al.* describe, CBT can be delivered through various media: books, therapist-guided, parent-delivered intervention, face-to-face manualized therapy (e.g. *Coping Cat*), and computerized CBT (e.g. *BRAVE, Camp-Cope-A-Lot, Cool Teens* and *Think, Feel, Do*) [19]. Studies show similar efficacy levels between computerized and clinic-based CBT [20]. Computerized CBT may be more accessible and help engage the young 'digitally native' generation, but motivation may be difficult to maintain, particularly with limited scope to tailor therapy [21].

Several meta-analyses have been published. A Cochrane review analysed 41 CBT face-to-face studies, rated generally as 'moderate' in quality [22]. CBT is significantly more effective than no therapy: remission rate was 58.9% for CBT compared with 16% for controls, with a number-needed-to-treat (NNT) of 6.0. Studies using CBT specifically adapted for children with ASD also showed efficacy. However, most studies used waiting-list controls, while the eight studies with active controls (e.g. psycho-education, bibliotherapy, therapist/peer support) showed *no* additional benefit of CBT. Efficacy did *not* vary significantly according to: group versus individual therapy, whether there was parental inclusion, and the number of sessions (although NICE recommends eight to 12 sessions). Age, severity, co-morbidity and gender were not found to predict clinical outcome.

In terms of subtype, one large multi-site study showed that generalized anxiety disorder was twice as likely to resolve following CBT compared with social anxiety disorder [23], perhaps reflecting the need for specifically tailored CBT for social anxiety. Recent studies have explored genetic predictors of CBT response; although results are inconsistent, variation in 5HTTLPR and NGF rs6330 genotypes may predict treatment outcome [24].

The evidence base for other psychological therapies is less robust. Parents may need additional support if they are also experiencing difficulties with anxiety or separation, while family therapy may help if family dysfunction is significant. Finally, CBT-based programmes in schools may have some preventive utility.

### Pharmacotherapy

The NICE guidance on generalized anxiety and panic disorders in adults advises that if symptoms remain after self-help or psycho-education, then CBT or medication is indicated. In contrast, NICE guidance on social anxiety advises not to routinely offer pharmacological interventions in children, even though several RCTs demonstrate that SSRIs can be effective and generally well-tolerated treatments (Table 25.4) [25]. In a Cochrane review and meta-analysis, 14 RCTs of SSRIs and serotonin–noradrenaline reuptake inhibitors (SNRIs) for paediatric anxiety disorders showed that the combined treatment response was significantly greater with medication (58.1%) than with placebo (31.5%), with an NNT of 4 [25]. It also showed that anxiety disorders were more treatment-responsive than OCD, with an overall effect size of 2.01. The evidence therefore suggests that SSRIs could be considered, particularly if CBT proves unsuccessful or if the child has difficulty engaging in CBT.

Potential side-effects of SSRIs include sedation, insomnia, agitation/hyperactivity, abdominal discomfort, headaches, nausea and vomiting. However, studies varied in statistical significance when comparing side-effects between treatment and placebo groups (Table 25.4). The Cochrane meta-analysis nevertheless showed that overall drug-related adverse events were significantly more frequent following medication than placebo, with a significant relative risk of 1.91. This, and the lack of evidence relating to efficacy by dosage, suggests that low doses should be tried first. Although adverse effects may limit SNRI usage, the Cochrane review found no difference in the tolerability of the SNRI venlafaxine versus SSRIs.

Two of the RCTs cited also had a psychological therapy arm. Beidel *et al.* [27] found that both fluoxetine and social effectiveness therapy (SET-C) were efficacious compared with pill placebo for paediatric social anxiety disorder, although SET-C was superior at specifically enhancing social skills. Walkup *et al.* [28] compared sertraline, CBT, combined sertraline with CBT, and placebo. Combined therapy was the most effective (80.7% response rate), while both sertraline (54.9%) and CBT (59.7%) were significantly more effective than placebo (23.7%).

The maximum duration of the RCTs cited was 16 weeks. However, two studies also conducted non-double-blinded extensions. Walkup *et al.*'s three active groups were followed up at week 36, with no significant differences (82.7%, 70.5%, and 71.5% response rates for the combined, sertraline and CBT groups respectively), although other measures showed durability of the additional benefit of combined treatment [29]. The Research Units on Pediatric Psychopharmacology (RUPP) study conducted a 6-month open-label extension to the initial RCT of fluvoxamine for social, generalized and separation anxiety disorders [30]. Out of the 35 fluvoxamine responders who were followed up, 33 showed maintenance or further improvement. The study also

**Table 25.4** Randomized control trials of selective serotonin reuptake inhibitors (SSRIs) and serotonin–noradrenaline reuptake inhibitors (SNRIs) for anxiety disorders

| Study[a] | Medication | Daily dose | Duration (weeks) | Disorder | Size | Cochrane quality score[b] | Adverse effects (significant difference towards drug group vs placebo group, $P < 0.05$) | Notes[c] |
|---|---|---|---|---|---|---|---|---|
| RUPP | Fluvoxamine | Flexible 50–300 mg | 8 | Social phobia, GAD, SAD | 128 | 28 | Abdominal discomfort. Increased motor activity | Weekly measurements. Statistical significance from week 3. Maximum effect by week 6. |
| Beidel et al. | Fluoxetine | Initially 10 mg, then increased by 10 mg every 2 weeks until 40 mg | 12 | Social phobia | 122 | 33 | Nausea | Four-weekly measurements. Fluoxetine's maximum effect by 8 weeks |
| Birmaher et al. | Fluoxetine | 10 mg for 1 week, 20 mg thereafter | 12 | Social phobia, GAD, SAD | 74 | 32 | Abdominal pain | Fortnightly measurements. Statistical significance by week 9 |
| Wagner et al. | Paroxetine | Flexible 10–50 mg | 16 | Social phobia | 322 | 30 | Insomnia | Nine measurements. Statistical significance by week 4 |
| Rynn et al. | Sertraline | 50 mg | 9 | GAD | 22 | 28 | Nil | Outcome only measured at week 9, statistically significant. |
| Walkup et al. | Sertraline | Flexible 25–200 mg | 12 | Social phobia, GAD, SAD | 488 | 40 | Nil | Outcomes measured at weeks 4, 8 and 12. Statistical significance by week 4 or 8, depending on measures used |

| Study | Drug | Dose | | Disorder | N | | Adverse effects | Comments |
|---|---|---|---|---|---|---|---|---|
| March et al. | Venlafaxine ER | Flexible 37.5–225 mg (partly weight-related) | 16 | Social phobia | 293 | 32 | Reduced appetite<br>Weight loss<br>Increased heart rate<br>Reduced mean PR interval on ECG<br>Increased diastolic BP | Eight measurements, but statistical analysis only report for week 16, showing significance |
| Rynn et al. | Venlafaxine ER | Flexible 37.5–225 mg (partly weight-related) | 8 | GAD | 313 | 30 | Weight loss<br>Reduced growth<br>Increased heart rate<br>Increased systolic and diastolic BP<br>Raised cholesterol[d] | Weekly measurements. Statistical significance from week 2 or 3, depending on measures used |
| Strawn et al. [26] | Duloxetine | Flexible 30–120 mg | 10 | GAD | 272 | Published subsequent to Cochrane review | Weight loss<br>Reduced appetite<br>Nausea<br>Vomiting<br>Oropharyngeal pain<br>Dizziness<br>Cough<br>Palpitations<br>Increased heart rate | Five measurements. Statistical significance from week 2 or 4, depending on measures used |

GAD, generalised anxiety disorder; SAD, separation anxiety disorder; RUPP, Research Units on Pediatric Psychopharmacology; BP, blood pressure.

[a] All references except Strawn et al. [26] are cited in Ipser et al. [25].

[b] Based on CCDAN Quality of Research Scale

[c] All statistical significance demonstrated in favour of the drug over placebo

[d] Only adverse effects which were analysed for comparisons between groups are cited in this table.

evaluated 14 non-responders; on switching them to fluoxetine, 10 participants' anxiety symptoms significantly improved. Limitations of these extension studies include the lack of double-blindness, the possibility of natural attenuation, and participants' use of additional treatment.

In paediatric studies analysed by the US Food and Drug Administration, antidepressants have been associated with suicidal ideation and non-fatal acts (in the order of 4%, vs ~ 2% in placebo groups) [31]. However in the Cochrane review of antidepressant use in anxiety disorders, the absolute rate of suicidal ideation was approximately 1%, mainly those taking paroxetine or venlafaxine. Furthermore, a re-evaluation by NICE of evidence related to depression has shown no increase in suicidal ideation in young people treated with antidepressants and psychological therapy compared with those treated with psychological therapy alone [32]. Ultimately, any risk of adverse effects needs balancing against the increased suicidality associated with anxiety disorders themselves.

The NICE recommendation is that fluoxetine's favourable risk–benefit profile makes it the first-line antidepressant for depression. The situation regarding anxiety disorders is less clear; the Cochrane review found little evidence for differences between SSRI agents in efficacy.

Benzodiazepines are generally not recommended in children: double-blind controlled trials have failed to demonstrate efficacy, while behavioural disinhibition and dependency are risks [25]. There is little paediatric data on β-blockers. Case reports and open trials indicate efficacy with buspirone.

## Conclusion

Anxiety disorders in children and adolescents are common, but can be disabling and relapse in later life. Detection is particularly important given the existence of effective and safe evidence-based interventions. Innovative research, such as using a children-of-twins design and longitudinal studies, may help to further elucidate the relative genetic and environmental mechanisms of transmission. Future research may help us better understand the individual- and treatment-related variables that influence intervention outcome.

## References

1 Marks I, Nesse R (1994) Fear and fitness: An evolutionary analysis of anxiety disorders. Ethology and Sociobiology, 15: 247–261.

2 Wittchen HU, Stein MB, Kessler RC (1999) Social fears and social phobia in a community sample of adolescents and young adults: Prevalence, risk factors and co-morbidity. Psychological Medicine, 29, 309–323.

3 Fyer AJ (1998) Current approaches to etiology and pathophysiology of specific phobia. Biological Psychiatry, 44, 1295–1304.

4 Degnan KA, Almas AN, Fox NA (2010) Temperament and the environment in the etiology of childhood anxiety. Journal of Child Psychology and Psychiatry, 51, 497–517.

5  Roberson-Nay R, Eaves LJ, Hettema JM et al. (2012) Childhood separation anxiety disorder and adult onset panic attacks share a common genetic diathesis. Depression and Anxiety, 29, 320–327.

6  Eley TC, Rijsdijk F, Perrin S et al. (2008) A multivariate genetic analysis of specific phobia, separation anxiety and social phobia in early childhood. Journal of Abnormal Child Psychology, 36, 839-848.

7  Eley TC (2015) The Intergenerational transmission of anxiety: A Children-of-Twins Study. American Journal of Psychiatry, 172, 630–637.

8  Kendler KS, Gardner CO, Lichtenstein P (2008) A developmental twin study of symptoms of anxiety and depression: evidence for genetic innovation and attenuation. Psychological Medicine, 38, 1567–1575.

9  Cresswell C, Waite P (2015) The dynamic influence of genes and environment in the intergenerational transmission of anxiety. American Journal of Psychiatry, 172, 597–598.

10  McLaughlin KA, Greif Green J, Gruber MJ et al. (2012) Childhood adversities and first onset of psychiatric disorders in a national sample of US adolescents. Archives of General Psychiatry, 69, 1151–1160.

11  Bergman K, Sarkar P, O'Connor TG et al. (2007) Maternal stress during pregnancy predicts cognitive ability and fearfulness in infancy. Journal of the American Academy of Child and Adolescent Psychiatry, 46, 1454–1463.

12  Glover V (2011) Annual Research Review: Prenatal stress and the origins of psychopathology: an evolutionary perspective. Journal of Child Psychology and Psychiatry, 52, 356–367.

13  Milham MP, Nugent AC, Drevets WC et al. (2005) Selective reduction in amygdala volume in pediatric generalized anxiety disorder: A voxel-based morphometry investigation. Biological Psychiatry, 57, 961–966.

14  Pine D (2007) Research review: a neuroscience framework for pediatric anxiety disorders. Journal of Child Psychology and Psychiatry, 48, 631–648.

15  Goodwin RD, Pine DS, Hoven CW (2003) Asthma and panic attacks among youth in the community. Journal of Asthma, 40, 139–145.

16  British Medical Journal Group - Best Practice (2012) Generalised Anxiety Disorder. http://bestpractice.bmj.com/best-practice/monograph/120/diagnosis/step-by-step.html.

17  Weems CF (2008) Developmental trajectories of childhood anxiety: identifying continuity and change in anxious emotion. Developmental Review, 28, 488–502.

18  Kendall PC, Robin JA, Hedtke KA et al. (2005) Considering CBT with anxious youth? Think exposures. Cognitive and Behavioral Practice, 12, 136–150.

19  Creswell C, Waite P, Cooper PJ (2014) Assessment and management of anxiety disorders in children and adolescents. Archives of Disease in Childhood, 99, 674–678.

20  Pennant ME, Loucas CE, Whittington C (2015) Computerised therapies for anxiety and depression in children and young people: A systematic review and meta-analysis. Behaviour Research and Therapy, 67, 1–18.

21  Richardson T, Stallard P, Velleman S (2010) Computerised cognitive behavioural therapy for the prevention and treatment of depression and anxiety in children and adolescents: A systematic review. Clinical Child and Family Psychology Review, 13, 275–290.

22  James AC, James G, Cowdrey FA et al. Cognitive behavioural therapy for anxiety disorders in children and adolescents. Cochrane Database of Systematic Reviews 2015, Issue 2. Art. No.: CD004690. DOI: 10.1002/14651858.CD004690.pub4.

23 Hudson JL, Keers R, Roberts S (2015) Clinical predictors of response to cognitive-behavioral therapy in pediatric anxiety disorders: The Genes for Treatment (GxT) Study. Journal of the American Academy of Child and Adolescent Psychiatry, 54, 454–463.

24 Hudson JL, Lester KJ, Lewis CM (2013) Predicting outcomes following cognitive behaviour therapy in child anxiety disorders: the influence of genetic, demographic and clinical information. Journal of Child Psychology and Psychiatry, 54, 1086–1094.

25 Ipser JC, Stein DJ, Hawkridge S et al. Pharmacotherapy for anxiety disorders in children and adolescents. Cochrane Database of Systematic Reviews 2009, Issue 3. Art. No.: CD005170. DOI: 10.1002/14651858.CD005170.pub2.

26 Strawn JR, Prakash A, Zhang Q et al. (2015) A randomized, placebo-controlled study of duloxetine for the treatment of children and adolescents with generalized anxiety disorder. Journal of the American Academy of Child and Adolescent Psychiatry, 54, 283–293.

27 Beidel DC, Turner SM, Sallee FR et al. (2007) SET-C versus fluoxetine in the treatment of childhood social phobia. Journal of the American Academy of Child and Adolescent Psychiatry, 46, 1622–1632.

28 Walkup JT, Albano AM, Piacentini J et al. (2008) Cognitive behavioral therapy, sertraline, or a combination in childhood anxiety. New England Journal of Medicine, 359, 2753–2766.

29 Piacentini J, Bennett S, Compton SN (2014) 24- and 36-week outcomes for the Child/Adolescent Anxiety Multimodal Study (CAMS). Journal of the American Academy of Child and Adolescent Psychiatry, 53, 297–310.

30 The Research Units on Pediatric Psychopharmacology Anxiety Study Group Treatment of Pediatric Anxiety Disorders (2002) An open-label extension of the research units on Pediatric Psychopharmacology Anxiety Study. Journal of Child and Adolescent Psychopharmacology, 12, 175–188.

31 Hammad TA, Laughren T, Racoosin J (2006) Suicidality in pediatric patients treated with antidepressant drugs. Archives of General Psychiatry, 63, 332–339.

32 Hopkins K, Crosland P, Elliott N (2015) Diagnosis and management of depression in children and young people: summary of updated NICE guidance. British Medical Journal, 350, h824.

# 26

# Childhood Behavioural Disorders

*Graeme Lamb and Ramya Srinivasan*

## Introduction

Childhood behavioural disorders (CBDs), including oppositional defiant disorder (ODD) and conduct disorder (CD) (see Box 26.1), continue to represent the most commonly presenting disorders at community child and adolescent mental health services [2,3]. Concern regarding childhood deviance is not a recent development. Since the time of Plato, societies have struggled with how to understand and manage the behaviour of out-of-control children, with ongoing debate as to the responsibility and culpability of children for their actions [4]. However, there is some evidence that antisocial behaviour has become more common over the last 25 years in high-income countries, particularly in adolescents [5], and this is reflected in the increasing media and public concern around such behaviours.

---

**Box 26.1  Definitions of ODD and CD**

**Oppositional defiant disorder (ODD)** – refers to a pattern of negative, hostile and defiant behaviour that is clearly outside the normal range of behaviour for a child of a given age and sociocultural context. These behaviours include a variety of features such as often losing one's temper, arguing with adults, refusing to comply with adults' requests, often being angry and spiteful, and deliberately annoying others; such children do not usually present with more severe dissocial or aggressive acts [1].

**Conduct disorder (CD)** – involves a repetitive and persistent pattern of behaviour in which the basic rights of others or major age-appropriate social norms are violated. Such behaviour includes aggression to people or animals, destruction of property, deceitfulness or theft, and serious violation of rules such as often staying out overnight or running away from home [1].

---

## Diagnostic Classifications and Subtyping

Childhood behavioural disorders (CBDs) are categorized in different ways in the two major diagnostic systems. In the *Diagnostic and Statistical Manual of Mental Disorders, 5th edition* (DSM-5) they fall within 'Disruptive, Impulse-Control and Conduct

*Child Psychology and Psychiatry: Frameworks for Clinical Training and Practice,* Third Edition.
Edited by David Skuse, Helen Bruce and Linda Dowdney.
© 2017 John Wiley & Sons, Ltd. Published 2017 by John Wiley & Sons, Ltd.

Disorders', whereas in the *International Classification of Mental and Behavioural Disorders in Children and Adolescents,* 10th revision (ICD-10), the behavioural disorders are described in 'Behavioural and emotional disorders with onset usually occurring in childhood and adolescence'. Also included in the DSM-5 section on 'Disruptive, Impulse-Control and Conduct Disorders' is intermittent explosive disorder (IED) [1] which is not explored in further detail in this chapter (see Box 26.2 for a description of intermittent explosive disorder).

---

**Box 26.2 Intermittent explosive disorder (IED)**

IED is a behavioural disorder characterized by impulsive or angry outbursts of aggression. These have a rapid onset, usually last for less than 30 minutes and occur in response to relatively minor provocation; the aggressive response is out of proportion to the provocation. These outbursts cause the individual distress or affect functioning, and are not explained by the presence of another mental health disorder [1]. IED was previously included in DSM-IV [6] and physical aggression was required for a diagnosis whereas significant verbal aggression is now included in DSM-5 [1]. DSM-5 also provides more specific criteria about the frequency and severity of the outbursts [1].

---

The DSM-5 has refined the criteria for ODD. Symptoms are now grouped into three types to reflect the presence of both emotional and behavioural symptomatologies as follows: angry/irritable mood, argumentative/defiant behaviour and vindictiveness [1].

In DSM-5, CD is divided into subtypes based on age of onset: childhood onset (with symptom onset prior to 10 years), and adolescent onset (with symptoms starting after 10 years) [1]. DSM-5 also utilizes the descriptive specifier of 'limited prosocial emotions', which relates to a callous or unemotional interpersonal style [1]. The presence of such traits, characterized by a lack of empathy for others, lack of guilt and inability to express emotions to others, does appear to signify a distinct subgroup of young people with a more severe form of disorder and different treatment response [7,8]. ICD-10 sub classifies CD as socialized, unsocialized and confined to the family context, reflecting the social context in which these behaviours occur [9].

There has been considerable debate regarding whether or not ODD and CD are distinct disorders or simply represent a continuum of increasingly challenging behaviour. Indeed, DSM-5 has removed CD as an exclusion criterion for ODD, reflecting the considerable symptom overlap between the two groups. Most research supports the distinction of oppositional behaviour and covert delinquent behaviour, but it is not yet clear whether aggression should represent a separate category of its own [10]. Whilst some children will grow out of ODD, in others it can be a precursor of CD, which in turn can lead to the later development of antisocial personality disorder (ASPD)[10].

One of the reasons for subtyping CBDs is to try to identify those who are likely to persist with such behaviours into adulthood. DSM-5 refers to the number and intensity of symptoms as clinical indicators of severity for both ODD and CD. Other factors to consider include the presence of overt (confrontational, such as fighting) versus covert (hidden, such as theft) symptoms, co-morbid mental health disorders, particularly attention deficit hyperactivityi disorder (ADHD), and early symptoms of ASPD [10].

## Epidemiology

As with many epidemiological studies of child mental health disorders, prevalence rates for childhood behavioural disorders are difficult to quantify due to changing diagnostic criteria and methodological variations in study design. In 1975, Rutter *et al.* [11] compared the rates of child mental health disorders in different settings within the UK, showing a prevalence rate for CBDs of 4% for rural populations, increasing to 9% in urban centres. Many studies have shown CD to be more common in boys than in girls. In more recent UK-based community surveys, CBDs occur in 6.9% of primary school-aged boys and 2.8% of girls, whilst in secondary school-aged children these prevalences rise to 8.1% and 5.1% respectively [12]. Despite the gender differences in prevalence, it is important to note that ODD and CD are relatively common diagnoses in girls, particularly in mental health settings. CD in girls is associated with significant outcomes, such as increased risk of ASPD, early pregnancy and a relationship with an antisocial partner [10].

There is also evidence of a clear increase in the prevalence of CD with age, with boys showing a linear rise from an early age throughout childhood, whilst girls show a different pattern, with rates increasing in adolescence [13]. However, different subsets of behaviours appear to have differing epidemiological trends. Whilst serious physical aggression and rule violations become more apparent in adolescence, lesser forms of aggression, such as fighting with peers, decline with age [13].

CBDs appear to show some longevity of symptoms, with 40% of 7 to 8-year-olds with CD becoming youth offenders in later life, whilst over 90% of such offenders have a history of CD as children [10,14]. Those children who develop CD at an earlier age will often have a worse prognosis than those who develop problems in adolescence [10,15].

Epidemiological studies also show a relationship between CBDs and other mental health disorders, including ADHD, depression and anxiety [10,15]. More than one-third of girls and almost half of boys with ODD or CD present with a co-morbid non-antisocial disorder [13].The presence of ADHD is particularly important; young people with CD and co-morbid ADHD have a much earlier age of onset of disruptive behaviour than those with CD alone [16].

## Aetiology

The development of CBDs incorporates a broad and complex range of biological and psychosocial risk factors.

Biological factors, including genetics, have long been implicated in the development of CBDs. Studies in the past decade show that the genetic effects appear to vary according to subtype. Children with callous-unemotional traits show much stronger heritability for antisocial behaviour than children without such traits (0.81 vs 0.30, respectively)[17].

In addition, more aggressive children who offend early have an increased heritability to do so [18].

Other biological risk factors include prenatal or perinatal exposure to toxins and early physical damage to the frontal lobe and other regions of the brain [18]. Research indicates a possible link between serotonin levels in the brain and aggressive behaviours, although the exact link has not been demonstrated [18].

Young people with aggressive behaviours have been shown to experience general autonomic under-arousal, as demonstrated by lower heart rates and skin conductance, indicating an associated lack of inhibitory anxiety, which may protect against antisocial behaviours [18].

Innate temperament has been shown to be predictive of future behavioural disorders [19]. Children with vulnerable temperamental characteristics are more likely to be subject to poor parenting styles. Adoption studies suggest that these children's behaviour may exacerbate a negative parenting response, leading to an additive effect [20]. Whilst attachment and CBDs display similar behavioural manifestations, supporting evidence for an aetiological connection between the two is weak [18].

Although cognitive and reading impairments are often thought to be related to behavioural disorders in children, research evidence is inconsistent due to confounding variables such as ADHD, poor school attainment and gender. Other factors, including impulsivity and social withdrawal, have been shown to be associated with antisocial behaviours, as have social skills deficits such as failing to notice relevant social cues, whilst misattributing hostile intent to others [18].

Children from socially disadvantaged areas have higher levels of CBDs [18,21]. However, much of this effect is thought to be mediated by intra-familial social processes associated with poor parenting and parental psychopathology [18], including mental illness, and alcohol and substance misuse.

Certain parenting styles have been consistently shown to link to behavioural disorders in children, including lack of parental involvement, harsh and inconsistent discipline and poor monitoring and conflict management. Children who have been exposed to sexual or physical abuse have a significantly increased risk of developing CBDs [18]. Peer relationships and community factors such as drug availability and crime rate may also influence the development of behavioural problems in children [18].

## Prevention and Treatment

There are many good reasons for trying to alleviate CBDs. As well as causing distress and damage to individual children and families, CBDs are known to have a considerable cost to the wider society. Scott *et al.* [22] showed that by the age of 28 years, costs for people with CD were 10 times higher than for those with no problems. These costs include crime, extra educational provision, foster and residential care and state benefits as well as smaller costs to the health service [22].

As parenting practices have been identified as important in the development and maintenance of CBDs there has been considerable interest in the use of parenting programmes as a form of prevention and treatment.

In 2006, the National Institute for Health and Clinical Excellence (NICE) and Social Care Institute for Excellence (SCIE) jointly commissioned a review of parenting programmes in the management of children aged 12 years or younger [23]. They concluded that group-based parenting/education programmes are to be recommended in the management of children with CBDs. For those parents with whom it is difficult to engage or for whom problems are more complex, similar individual-based programmes can be used instead.

The NICE clinical guideline on antisocial behaviour and conduct disorders in children and young people was published in 2013 and provide a number of recommendations on the recognition and management of these presentations. The guideline supports the use of group-based parenting/education programmes and particularly recommends these for the parents of younger children [3]. NICE also recommends selective prevention in the form of classroom-based emotional learning and problem-solving programmes for children aged 3–7 years old in schools with a high proportion of children identified to be at risk of developing ODD [3].

For older children, the guideline suggests group social and cognitive problem-solving programmes for those at high risk of, or with, ODD or CD, or those in contact with the criminal justice system due to antisocial behaviour. NICE also recommends multi-modal interventions, e.g. multi-systemic therapy for those aged between 11 and 17 years [3]. Multi-modal interventions are relatively expensive and, in practice, are usually reserved for those who cannot make use of other interventions.

In some circumstances, parenting programmes may not be feasible or as effective as hoped. Some families may be unwilling to take part in such programmes or there may be additional factors in the child which may reduce the potential effectiveness of this approach. In these cases, alternative approaches, such as individual cognitive problem-solving skills training such as those recommended for older children or multi-modal interventions, may need to be considered [3]. Other theoretical models such as attachment theory, systems theory or cognitive attribution theory may also be helpful [24].

Pharmacological interventions should not be used in the routine management of behavioural problems in children and young people [3]. However, children with CBDs often present with other co-morbid mental health disorders. These disorders may require treatment in their own right, which may in turn lead to a reduction in the behaviour problems. Studies have suggested that the treatment of ADHD may lead to an improvement in co-morbid oppositional behaviour and this is recommended by NICE [3]. Risperidone can be considered in the short-term management of severe aggression in young people with CD who have problems with explosive anger and emotional dysregulation and who have not responded to psychosocial interventions [3].

It is generally agreed within the scientific community that short-term interventions such as military-style boot camps, whilst often promoted within certain sections of the media, are not effective in the long term [25]. Frightening children, with the aim of reducing aggressive behaviour but without offering them any other behavioural alternatives, has the opposite effect of that intended, perhaps as a result of an increased fear-aggression reaction or due to modelling [25].

## Conclusion

CBDs have always been and still remain a common problem and, given current epidemiological trends, are likely to continue to be so for the foreseeable future. These disorders lead to considerable damage, in terms of both the quality of life for young people, their families and their victims, and the wider economic cost to society as a whole. Simple behavioural disorders can progress to much more serious personality disorders in adulthood. We know that there are effective treatments for CBDs and these are available across the country via parenting programmes. Our challenge remains to identify which factors within such programmes may be effective upon different symptom subtypes, to help identify those children who are not responsive to these approaches and consider which alternative methods may be best employed in these cases, and to spread effective treatments to those hard-to-reach families who perhaps need these most.

## References

1 APA (2013) Diagnostic and Statistical Manual of Mental Disorders, 5th edition (DSM-5). 2013, Washington DC: American Psychiatric Association.
2 Audit Commission for Local Authorities and the National Health Service in England and Wales (1999) Children in Mind. London: Audit Commission.
3 NICE (2013) Clinical Guideline 158: Antisocial behaviour and conduct disorders in children and young people: recognition, intervention and management, London: National Institute for Health and Care Excellence NICE.
4 Costello J, Angold A (2001) Bad behaviour: a historical perspective on disorders of conduct. In: Hill J, Maughan B (eds) Conduct Disorders of Childhood and Adolescence. Cambridge University Press, pp. 1–31.
5 Collishaw, S (2015) Annual research review: Secular trends in child and adolescent mental health. Journal of Clinical Child and Adolescent Psychology, 56, 370–393.
6 APA (2000) Diagnostic and Statistical Manual of Mental Disorders, 4th edition, text revision (DSM-IV-TR). Washington DC: American Psychiatric Association.
7 Rowe R, Maughan B, Moran P et al. (2010) The role of callous and unemotional traits in the diagnosis of conduct disorder. Journal of Child Psychology and Psychiatry, 51, 688–695.
8 Blair RJR, Leibenluft E, Pine DS (2014) Conduct disorder and callous–unemotional traits in youth. New England Journal of Medicine, 371, 2207–2216.
9 WHO (1992) The ICD-10 International Classification of Mental and Behavioural Disorders, 10th revision. World Health Organization: Geneva.
10 Loeber R, Burke JD, Lahey BB et al. (2000) Oppositional defiant and conduct disorder: a review of the past 10 years, Part I. Journal of the American Academy of Child & Adolescent Psychiatry, 39, 1468–1484.
11 Rutter M, Yule B, Quinton D et al. (1975) Attainment and adjustment in two geographical areas. The British Journal of Psychiatry, 126, 493–509.
12 Green H, McGinnity A, Meltzer H et al. (2004) Mental health of children and young people in Great Britain, 2005. Basingstoke: Palgrave Macmillan.

13 Maughan B, Rowe R, Messer J et al. (2004) Conduct disorder and oppositional defiant disorder in a national sample: developmental epidemiology. Journal of Child Psychology and Psychiatry, 45, 609–621.

14 Farrington DP (1995) The development of offending and antisocial behaviour from childhood: Key findings from the Cambridge Study in Delinquent Development. Journal of Child Psychology and Psychiatry, 6, 929–964.

15 Angold A, Costello J (1995) The epidemiology of disorders of conduct: nosological issues and comorbidity. In: Hill P, Maughan B (eds) Conduct Disorders of Childhood and Adolescence. Cambridge University Press, pp. 126–168.

16 Moffitt TE (1990) Juvenile delinquency and attention deficit disorder: Boys' developmental trajectories from age 3 to age 15. Child Development, 61, 893–910.

17 Viding E, Larsson H, Jones AP (2008) Quantitative genetic studies of antisocial behaviour. Philosophical Transactions of the Royal Society B: Biological Sciences, 363, 2519–2527.

18 Burke JD, Loeber R, Birmaher B (2002) Oppositional defiant disorder and conduct disorder: a review of the past 10 years, part II. Journal of the American Academy of Child & Adolescent Psychiatry, 41, 1275–1293.

19 Loeber R, Burke JD, Pardini DA (2009) Development and etiology of disruptive and delinquent behavior. Annual Review of Clinical Psychology, 5, 291–310.

20 Cadoret RJ, Yates WR, Troughton E et al. (1995) Genetic-environmental interaction in the genesis of aggressivity and conduct disorders. Archives of General Psychiatry, 52, 916–924.

21 Bywater T, Hutchings J, Daley D et al. (2009) Long-term effectiveness of a parenting intervention for children at risk of developing conduct disorder. British Journal of Psychiatry, 195, 318–324.

22 Scott S, Knapp M, Henderson J, Maughan B (2001) Financial cost of social exclusion: follow up study of antisocial children into adulthood. British Medical Journal, 323, 191.

23 NICE (2006) Parent-Training/Education Programmes in the Management of Children with Conduct Disorders NICE Technology Appraisal Guidance 102. London: National Institute for Health and Clinical Excellence, NICE.

24 Scott S, Dadds MR (2009) Practitioner review: when parent training doesn't work: theory-driven clinical strategies. Journal of Child Psychology and Psychiatry, 50, 1441–1450.

25 Steiner H, Remsing L (2007) Practice parameter for the assessment and treatment of children and adolescents with oppositional defiant disorder. Journal of the American Academy of Child & Adolescent Psychiatry, 46, 126–141.

27

# Depression and Suicidal Behaviour

*Julia Gledhill and Matthew Hodes*

## Introduction

This chapter focuses on depressive disorder [as defined by the *International Classification of Mental and Behavioural Disorders, 10th revision* (ICD-10), and *Diagnostic and Statistical Manual of Mental Disorders, 5th edition* (DSM-5) and suicidal behaviour. Whilst suicidal behaviour may be indicative of a range of difficulties, it may also be a symptom of depressive disorder. The epidemiology, aetiological factors, course, diagnostic assessment and management of depressive disorder and suicidal behaviour will be described.

## Depressive Disorder

Whilst there was little recognition of depressive disorders in children and adolescents before the 1970s, the use of symptom-oriented psychiatric interviews with children and adolescents led to an acknowledgement that depressive disorders resembling those seen in adults do occur in this age group; the current diagnostic criteria are the same as those used in adults – mood change (low mood/ irritability) or loss of enjoyment lasting at least 2 weeks, associated cognitive (e.g. guilt, pessimism about the future, suicidal ideation) and biological (e.g. change in appetite, sleep disturbance, fatigue) symptoms. DSM-5 requires functional impairment (at home, school or with regard to peer relationships), whereas ICD-10 describes functional impairment as a frequent accompaniment of depression.

### Epidemiology

The prevalence of depressive disorder increases from childhood to adolescence, with a reported prevalence in community samples of adolescents ranging from 1% to 8% [1–3]. It is equally common in girls and boys during childhood but during adolescence the female:male ratio increases to about 2:1 [4]. It has been suggested that pubertal status rather than age is associated with the increase in depressive disorders among adolescent girls [5]. Whilst the prevalence of depressive disorders in this age group has not changed greatly over the last 30 years, recognition and treatment have increased [6].

*Child Psychology and Psychiatry: Frameworks for Clinical Training and Practice,* Third Edition.
Edited by David Skuse, Helen Bruce and Linda Dowdney.
© 2017 John Wiley & Sons, Ltd. Published 2017 by John Wiley & Sons, Ltd.

Psychiatric co-morbidity, especially with anxiety disorders, conduct disorder and substance misuse, are common [7].

### Aetiological Factors

The aetiology of depressive disorder is multifactorial [4]; risk factors may be divided into those that predispose (increase vulnerability to) and those that precipitate (lead to development at a specific point in time) a depressive episode. These influences act through biochemical and psychological processes. Once established, depressive episodes may be prolonged by maintaining factors that treatment approaches aim to alleviate. These risks are described more fully in Table 27.1.

**Table 27.1** Aetiological factors for depressive disorders

| Risk factor | Evidence |
| --- | --- |
| *Predisposing factors* | |
| Genetic factors | • Greater genetic influence for adolescent than childhood depression<br>• Children of depressed parents at greater risk<br>• Twin studies – heritability 15–80% for depressive symptoms<br>• Indirect genetic influences, e.g. increased risk of experiencing more negative life events |
| Family environment | • Low levels of parental warmth, high levels of hostility and conflict are associated with increased depressive symptoms<br>• Parental mental health problems impact on parenting, make it more difficult to meet the child's emotional needs and provide a confiding relationship |
| Temperament/personality | • Children who are slow to adapt to new experiences, socially reticent, easily upset<br>• Elevated levels of anxiety, high self-criticism and negative attributional style – tendency to blame self rather than others |
| Early/chronic adversity | • Poverty/social disadvantage<br>• Physical, sexual or emotional abuse |
| Neurobiological factors | • Under-activity of cerebral amine systems<br>• Abnormalities in cortisol secretion<br>• Functional and anatomical brain differences in depressed and non-depressed young people |
| *Precipitating factors* | |
| Stressful life events | Examples include losses, e.g. parental separation or bereavement, disappointments and failures, e.g. peer problems, bullying, academic difficulties, failing exams |
| *Maintaining factors* | |
| Persistent depressive symptoms | Recognized as a risk factor for further depressive episodes |

| Risk factor | Evidence |
| --- | --- |
| Psycho-social scars | Individuals may experience residual effects from a depressive episode – 'psycho-social scarring', which increases the likelihood of further episodes |
| Persistent biological/ cognitive vulnerabilities | As above |
| Persistent adversity | Examples include family dysfunction, lack of a confiding relationship with mother, poor peer relationships |

## Diagnostic Assessment

This is facilitated by a mental state examination of the young person by interviewing him/her alone; adolescents themselves are the most accurate informants about internalizing symptoms which parents may not be aware of. Depressive disorder is often associated with psychiatric co-morbidity (40–70%) [4], particularly dysthymic disorder, anxiety disorders, eating psychopathology, conduct disorders and substance abuse. It is important to recognize co-morbidity, as this has implications for management and outcome.

## Outcome

The outcome of depressive disorder (assessed by episode duration or risk of recurrence) differs according to the population studied (mental health service referred or community); it is influenced by factors including age, symptom severity, past history of depressive episodes, co-morbid psychopathology and family factors, e.g. conflict and parental psychopathology. Recovery is the rule, with 88% recovering within a year in community samples [8], and 80–90% recovering by 12–18 months in clinic samples [9,10]. The median duration of depressive episodes is 9 months in clinic-referred samples [11] and 8–12 weeks in community samples [12], the former generally having more severe episodes. Recurrence is frequent: 12% relapse in 1 year among community samples [12] and 27% within 9 months among clinic samples [13]. Continuity into adulthood is high with an increased risk of self-harm, completed suicide and impaired psycho-social functioning [14].

## Management

The aims of management are:

1) to make an adequate assessment;
2) to treat the depressive disorder, and reduce associated psychosocial impairment;
3) to manage associated co-morbidity and risk factors;
4) to prevent relapse.

### Initial Assessment
This largely depends on the context in which the young person is seen and the expected level of severity of the problems. Thus, in primary care settings where youngsters with milder depression are seen, the brief assessment will focus on mood, including

self-harm risk, and current difficulties, including social function. Those seen in specialist child and adolescent mental health services are likely to have more severe depression with more co-morbidity and complex family situations. In this context, a more detailed assessment will cover developmental history and functioning at school, as well as family relationships and other problems.

### Treatment

Treatment of brief or minor depression will include exploration of difficulties, activity scheduling, and follow-up. Mild to moderate depression, where social function might be impaired, should be managed initially with psychological treatment [15]. That most frequently used is cognitive behavioural therapy (CBT), which starts with psycho-education and includes self-monitoring, e.g. diary keeping, increasing competence in emotion recognition, challenging cognitive distortions, and activity scheduling. An alternative appropriate psychological therapy is interpersonal psychotherapy for adolescents (IPT-A), which addresses problem relationship areas such as role conflict, transitions or losses. A recent meta-analysis supports CBT and IPT as the best available psychotherapies for children and adolescents, with IPT having fewer dropouts from therapy [15].

More persistent moderate or severe depression will require antidepressant medication. Recent studies, predominantly with adolescents, suggest that selective serotonin reuptake inhibitors (SSRIs), particularly fluoxetine, are helpful [16]. In recent years there has been a high level of concern regarding the possible increase of suicidal events with the use of SSRIs. Although the increased risk is slight, close monitoring is appropriate. Failure to respond to fluoxetine can be managed with a change to another SSRI, or another class of antidepressant such as venlafaxine, with the addition of CBT [17]. Poor progress or high risk of self-harm may require psychiatric admission.

### Managing Associated Co-Morbidity and Risk Factors

This means that additional interventions may be required. The associated anxiety or conduct problems might require specific interventions. For some youngsters, if the associated disorders are effectively treated, the depression might lift. Addressing problems in family relationships, school or with peers will require specific interventions.

### Preventing Relapse

If medication achieves remission it should be continued for 6–9 months. Psychological treatment sessions may also be required after the depression has improved. Relapse prevention includes recognition of stressors, promoting resilience and early identification of symptoms and timely commencement of booster psychological treatment sessions or use of antidepressants [4].

## Suicidal Behaviour

### Epidemiology

Suicide is very uncommon in childhood and early adolescence but the rate increases markedly in mid-adolescence [18]. The UK rate for suicide and undetermined deaths in

2011 was 6.6 for males aged 15–19 years and 3.1 per 100 000 for females. Males tend to use more violent methods, and rates vary by country and ethnicity.

Deliberate self-harm (DSH) is common in adolescents; studies report a 12-month prevalence rate of 7–9% [19,20], and it is approximately three times more common in females. However, only a minority (12.6%) of DSH episodes lead to hospital presentation [20,21]. The most common methods are self-poisoning and cutting. The term DSH is frequently used as it does not imply a specific level of suicidal intent.

Thoughts of suicide (in the absence of deliberate self-harm) are not uncommon, (approximately 15% in the previous year) and are more frequent in females [20].

## Aetiological Factors

These may be divided into predisposing factors (e.g. within the young person, their family and the wider environment) and precipitating factors.

## Predisposing Factors

### Individual
Psychiatric disorder, especially major depressive disorder, but also anxiety, substance misuse and conduct disorder, are key risk factors for DSH [20]. In the context of depression, feelings of hopelessness, despair, low self-esteem and a tendency to self-blame are particularly relevant. Psychological factors such as impulsivity and poor problem-solving skills reduce the ability to discuss and contemplate difficulties [22]. Young people who are socially or emotionally isolated, and particularly those who lack a family confidant with whom they can share problems, are at increased risk of self-harm [23]. Young people who have experienced abuse, particularly physical and sexual abuse, are at greater risk of DSH [20,21,24]. A history of DSH is predictive of future episodes; up to 30% report a previous episode (which may not have come to medical attention) [25].

### Family
Communication difficulties within the families of young people who self-harm are typical. This is also a risk factor for repeated compared with a single episode of self-harm [26]. A family history of mental health problems, particularly parental DSH is an additional vulnerability factor. Parental divorce is also more common in families of young people who self-harm [20].

### Wider Environment
School problems may be very relevant in this age group and include academic difficulties leading to under-achievement, pressure to achieve, as well as bullying. Difficulties with regard to relationships with peers, boy/girlfriends and teachers are also aetiologically important. Exposure to suicide or suicide attempts in family or friends also increases risk [25].

## Precipitating Factors

Deliberate self-harm is frequently precipitated by stressful life problems; often these are interpersonal conflicts or difficulties with parents or siblings, such as arguments, or rejection by boy/girlfriends or peers, and school problems such as academic difficulty and bullying. It is frequently an impulsive act, with many individuals thinking about it for just minutes before acting. Over 50% consult their GP in the month before DSH, but presentation is generally not with psychological symptoms [27].

### Risk Associated with Self-Harm

The factors associated with high risk from self-harm are given in Box 27.1. The physical severity of the self-harm is not a good indicator of intent as young people are often unaware of the objective degree of lethality of specific substances and quantities; it is their belief about potential lethality that is important.

---

**Box 27.1 Factors associated with high suicidal intent**

- Carried out in isolation
- Timed so that intervention is unlikely, e.g. after parents are at work
- Precautions taken to avoid discovery
- Preparations made in anticipation of death, e.g. leaving directions as to how possessions should be distributed
- Other people informed of individual's intention beforehand
- Advance planning of attempt
- Suicide note
- Failure to alert others following the attempt

---

### Course

At least 10% of adolescents who self-harm do so again in the following year; this is especially likely in the first 2 or 3 months. Factors that increase the likelihood of repetition include previous self-harm, personality disturbance, depression, substance misuse, extensive family psychopathology, poor social adjustment, social isolation and a poor school record [25]. Approximately 0.5% eventually kill themselves; risk factors include male gender, older age, high suicidal intent, mood disorder, substance abuse, violent method of self-harm and previous psychiatric admission.

### Management

The aims of management are:

1) to make an adequate assessment;
2) to treat the depressive disorder, and reduce associated psychosocial impairment;
3) to manage associated psychiatric disorder and risk factors;
4) to prevent further episodes of DSH.

### Type of Assessment

The type of assessment will depend on the context in which the young person is seen [28]. Thus, in primary care settings the main goal is to ascertain risk and consider whether self-harm has actually taken place, as this will often require referral to the appropriate local hospital accident and emergency service. In the hospital setting, paediatric management is required for physical effects of self-harm, coordinated with child and adolescent mental health assessment, and social work input. When referred to the hospital accident and emergency service out-of-hours, existing guidance is that admission is required overnight with the assessment taking place the following day [28]. The mental health assessment requires the identification of psychiatric disorder and range of risk factors. The assessment should include interviewing the young person alone as well as together with their parent(s). The purpose of this assessment is.

- to assess the current risk with regard to:
  - suicidality
  - further deliberate self-harm;
- to understand the young person and family's difficulties and how these have led to self-harm;
- to determine whether the young person is suffering with a psychiatric disorder, e.g. depression (and the level of hopelessness), drug or alcohol misuse;
- to assess the child's and family's resources.

It is important to establish whether the index episode of deliberate self-harm was associated with a high degree of suicidal intent (see Box 27.1); whilst a minority of patients may try to conceal their true intent, its assessment is best facilitated by obtaining a detailed understanding of the circumstances of the attempt and comparing this information with factors known to be associated with high intent. The outcome of this assessment will inform discharge and further management planning.

### Treatment

Treatment requires that the young person should be kept safe, which means restricting access to potentially harmful substances, such as drugs, used for self-harm as well as alcohol. Appropriate care and emotional support are needed [18]. These often require family intervention, such as family-based problem-solving therapy, which aims to improve communication and reduce conflict in the family, or attachment-based family therapy, which seeks to strengthen parent–adolescent attachment bonds. Individual psychological treatments include CBT [29] and newer interventions, dialectical behaviour therapy (DBT) and mentalization-based therapy. The evidence base suggests that DBT, CBT and mentalization-based therapies are the most effective treatments following DSH, and a strong family component was also associated with reduction in self-harm [30]. Unfortunately less than half of adolescents who self-harm, and their parents, will remain in therapy after the initial assessment. However, the assessment will reveal specific psychiatric disorders, such as depression, in a significant proportion of cases and treatment should then be targeted at the underlying disorder.

### Prevention

The main elements are identification of those at highest risk by the prompt recognition of depression or other problems associated with suicidal behaviour; establishing crisis intervention; reducing access to methods of self-harm, such as decreasing the availability of poisonous domestic gas; and restricting the pack size of analgesics in the UK [18].

# References

1 Cooper PJ, Goodyer IM (1993) A community study of depression in adolescent girls I: estimate of symptom and syndrome prevalence. British Journal of Psychiatry, 163, 369–374.

2 Ford T, Goodman R, Meltzer H (2003) The British Child and Adolescent Mental Health Survey 1999: The prevalence of DSM-IV Disorders. Journal of the American Academy of Child and Adolescent Psychiatry, 42, 1203–1211.

3 Lewinsohn PM, Rohde P, Seeley JR, Fischer SA (1993) Age-cohort changes in the lifetime occurrence of depression and other mental disorders. Journal of Abnormal Psychology, 102, 110–120.

4 Brent D, Maalouf F (2015) Depressive disorders in childhood and adolescence. In: Thapar A et al. (eds) Rutter's Child and Adolescent Psychiatry. Chichester, UK: John Wiley & Sons Ltd, pp. 874–892.

5 Angold A, Costello EJ, Wortham CM (1998) Puberty and depression: the roles of age, pubertal status and pubertal timing. Psychological Medicine, 28, 51–61.

6 Costello EJ, Erkanli A, Angold A (2006) Is there an epidemic of child and adolescent depression? Journal of Child Psychology and Psychiatry and Allied Disciplines, 47, 1263–1271.

7 Parker G, Roy K (2001) Adolescent depression: A review. The Australian and New Zealand Journal of Psychiatry, 35, 572–580.

8 Dunn V, Goodyer IM (2006) Longitudinal investigation into childhood and adolescence-onset depression: Psychiatric outcome in early adulthood. British Journal of Psychiatry, 188, 216–222.

9 Kovacs M, Feinberg TL, Crouse-Novak MA et al. (1984) Depressive disorders in childhood I. A longitudinal prospective study of characteristics and recovery. Archives of General Psychiatry, 41, 229–237.

10 McCauley E, Myers K, Mitchell J et al. (1993) Depression in young people: initial presentation and clinical course. Journal of the American Academy of Child and Adolescent Psychiatry, 32, 714–722.

11 Kovacs M, Obrosky DS, Gatsonis C, Richards C (1997) First-episode major depressive and dysthymic disorder in childhood: Clinical and sociodemographic factors in recovery. Journal of the American Academy of Child and Adolescent Psychiatry, 36, 777–784.

12 Lewinsohn PM, Clarke GN, Seeley JR, Rohde P (1994) Major depression in community adolescents: age at onset, episode duration and time to recurrence. Journal of the American Academy of Child and Adolescent Psychiatry, 33, 809–818.

13 Goodyer IM, Herbert J, Secher SM, Pearson J (1997) Short-term outcome of major depression: I Comorbidity and severity at presentation as predictors of persistent disorder. Journal of the American Academy of Child and Adolescent Psychiatry, 36, 179–187.

14 Weissman MM, Wolk S, Goldstein RB et al. (1999) Depressed adolescents grown up. Journal of the American Medical Association, 281, 1707–1713.

15 Zhou X, Hetrick SE, Cuijpers P et al. (2015) Comparative efficacy and acceptability of psychotherapies for depression in children and adolescents: a systemtic review and network meta-analysis. World Psychiatry, 14, 207–222.

16  Bridge JA, Iyengar S, Salary CB et al. (2007) Clinical response and risk for reported suicidal ideation and suicide attempts in pediatric antidepressant treatment: A meta-analysis of randomized controlled trials. Journal of the American Medical Association, 297, 1683–1696.

17  Brent DA, Emslie G, Clark GN et al. (2008) Switching to another SSRI or to venlafaxine with or without cognitive behavioural therapy for adolescents with SSR-resistant depression. Journal of the American Medical Association, 299, 901–913.

18  Hawton K, O'Connor R, Saunders K (2015) Suicidal behaviour and self-harm. In. Thapar A et al. (eds) Rutter's Child and Adolescent Psychiatry. Chichester, West Sussex: John Wiley & Sons Ltd, pp. 893–910.

19  Grunbaum JA, Kann L, Kinchen SA et al. (2002) Youth risk behaviour surveillance – United States 2001. Journal of School Health, 72, 313–328.

20  Hawton K, Rodham K, Evans E, Weatherall R (2002) Deliberate self-harm in adolescents: self report survey in schools in England. British Medical Journal, 325, 1207–1211.

21  Whitlock J J Eckenrode, D. Silverman (2006) Self-injurious behaviours in a college population. Pediatrics, 117, 1939–1946.

22  Kingsbury S, Hawton K, Steinhardt K, James A (1999) Do adolescents who take overdoses have specific psychological characteristics? A comparative study with psychiatric and community controls. Journal of the American Academy of Child and Adolescent Psychiatry, 38, 1125–1131.

23  Evans E, Hawton K, Rodham K, Deeks J (2005) The prevalence of suicidal phenomena in adolescents: A systematic review of population-based studies. Suicide and Life-Threatening Behaviour, 35, 239–250.

24  Dube SR, Anda RF, Felitti VJ et al. (2001) Childhood abuse, household dysfunction and the risk of attempted suicide throughout the lifespan. Journal of the American Medical Association, 286, 3089–3096.

25  Hawton K, James A (2005) Suicide and deliberate self-harm in young people. British Medical Journal, 16, 891–894.

26  Evans E, Hawton K, Rodham K (2004) In what ways are adolescents who engage in self-harm or experience thoughts of self-harm different in terms of help-seeking, communication and coping strategies? Journal of Adolescence, 28, 573–587.

27  Houston K, Haw C, Townsend E, Hawton K (2003) General practitioner contacts with patients before and after deliberate self harm. British Journal of General Practice, 53, 365–370.

28  National Collaborating Centre for Mental Health (2004) The short-term physical and psychological management and secondary prevention of self-harm in primary and secondary care. British Psychological Society & Royal College of Psychiatrists: London.

29  Harrington R et al. (2003) Cognitive behavioural therapy after deliberate self-harm in adolescence. In: King RA, Apter A (eds) Suicide in Children and Adolescents. Cambridge University Press: Cambridge.

30  Ougrin D, Tranah T, Stahl D et al. (2015) Therapeutic intervention for suicide attempts and self-harm in adolescents: systematic review and meta-analysis. Journal of the American Academy of Child and Adolescent Psychiatry, 54, 97–107.

# 28

# Eating Disorders in Adolescence

*Dasha Nicholls*

## Diagnosis and Classification

The term 'eating disorder' is restricted to disorders of eating behaviour driven by overvalued ideas about weight and shape. Within this narrow definition are three well-described disorders – anorexia nervosa (AN), bulimia nervosa (BN) and binge eating disorder (BED) – and some newer, less well validated presentations, including purging disorder and night eating syndrome. AN is characterized by determined food avoidance in pursuit of thinness, resulting in clinically significant weight loss, with or without so-called 'compensatory behaviours' to counteract the fattening effect of food. The *Diagnostic and Statistical Manual of Mental Disorders, 5th edition* (DSM-5) [1] recognizes a restrictive (AN-R; food restriction and exercise only) and a binge-purging (AN-BP) subtype and proposes a severity rating based on BMI at diagnosis, from evidence in adult patients. Two main features distinguish AN from BN. The first is the centrality of binge eating to BN, characterized by loss of control over eating. The second is that sufferers of BN are by definition not underweight. In BED, binge eating and associated impairment or distress are the core features; a lack of compensatory behaviours distinguishes BED from BN.

Despite features in common, each disorder has a distinct course, outcome and treatment response, with accumulating evidence for differential familial (including genetic), personality and neurodevelopmental risk.

Changes to the diagnostic criteria for the DSM-5 aimed to reduce the proportion of patients, previously around 60%, who did not meet the full diagnostic criteria. Studies estimate a 15–25% reduction in unspecified or atypical categories with the introduction of DSM-5 [2,3]. DSM-5 also introduced avoidant restrictive food intake disorder (ARFID), for which presence of weight and shape concern is an exclusion criterion. ARFID is as yet little researched, and includes patients previously diagnosed with Feeding Disorders of Infancy and Early Childhood, as well as those with food phobias and presentations for which terminology such as non-fat phobic AN, selective eating and orthorexia have been used [4]. There is no age limitation to the diagnosis of ARFID, which sits within the broad cluster of feeding and eating disorders, but is often excluded from workstreams around eating disorders such as service delivery, clinical guidelines, teaching curricula etc. (see Box 28.1)

*Child Psychology and Psychiatry: Frameworks for Clinical Training and Practice,* Third Edition.
Edited by David Skuse, Helen Bruce and Linda Dowdney.
© 2017 John Wiley & Sons, Ltd. Published 2017 by John Wiley & Sons, Ltd.

---

**Box 28.1  Making a diagnosis**

**The diagnostic process**

- Whole family interview
- Medical assessment
- Individual assessment with young person
- Semi-structured diagnostic interview, e.g. EDE [5,6], or questionnaire, e.g. EDE-Q

**Useful questions**

- How much would you like to weigh?
- How do you feel about your weight/shape?
- Are you or anyone else worried about your eating or exercising?
- Have you ever tried to make yourself sick?
- Consider using a screening tool such as the SCOFF [7] (not validated in younger patients)

EDE, Eating Disorder Examination; EDE-Q, Eating Disorder Examination Questionnaire.

---

## Epidemiology and Aetiology

Some form of eating disorder is experienced by around 13% of adolescents [8,9]; most would not meet full syndrome diagnostic criteria. For many young people this will be a transient period of eating pathology. In adolescent populations, around 0.8–1.7%% meet criteria for AN, 0.8–2.6% for BN, 2.3–3% for BED. The remainder have sub-threshold or atypical ED. Because of its chronicity, AN is often cited as the third commonest chronic illness of adolescence. The prevalence of BN is higher than that of AN, but only around 5% reach mental health services at present. The hidden nature of eating disorders means that when patients present, often because of parental concern, the problem is well established and should be taken seriously from the first consultation [10].

Eating disorders are biopsycho-social disorders of complex aetiology; no single factor accounts for the onset or maintenance of any given presentation. Table 28.1 outlines the best established risk factors as well as common behavioural indicators of a potential eating disorder, suggesting a full assessment is indicated. Familial factors are important; female relatives of someone with a clinical eating disorder are more than four times as likely to have BN and more than 11 times as likely to have AN than someone with no family history of eating disorders. This figure is probably higher for sub-clinical or partial syndromes. From twin studies, disordered eating behaviour has an estimated heritability of 55–60% [11] Emerging evidence suggests that specific cognitive profiles may be relevant to the aetiology of AN, including cognitive inflexibility, cognitive inhibition, visuo-spatial construction and memory [12,13]. The pattern for BN and BED is less clear. Similarities and differences in social cognition and emotional processing between patients with AN and those with autism spectrum disorders have also been

**Table 28.1** Risk factors for and behavioural indicators of eating disorders

| Risk factors for developing an eating disorder in adolescence | Psychological or behavioural markers of an eating disorder |
|---|---|
| Female sex | Reluctant attender |
| Repeated dieting | Seeks help for physical symptoms |
| Early puberty | Resists weighing and examination |
| Temperament – perfectionist personality | Covers or hides body with loose clothes |
| Teasing about weight and dieting | Secretive/evasive |
| Low self-esteem | Increased energy ± agitation |
| Losses and major life events | Gets angry when confronted |
| Family history of eating disorder | |

explored [14]. Neuroimaging studies show persistent processing deficits in relation to food and emotion regulation, reward sensitivity and body image perception [15].

A formulation of individual, systemic and cultural factors, framed as predisposing, precipitating, perpetuating and protective factors, is helpful for teasing out important elements for an individual, and can be a therapeutic tool to aid engagement. The aim is to not locate causation or blame with any one factor, event or individual. An example is given in Table 28.2. In eating disorders there is an interplay between dietary restraint, weight and eating, with issues such as negative affect, low self-esteem, adversity, shame, feelings of personal ineffectiveness or powerlessness, and, for young people, issues around growing up, identity formation, learning about risk taking and risk avoidance, other people's issues and cultural pressures. The formulation is a starting point for disentangling these themes; the emphasis in treatment is usually on maintaining factors rather than antecedents.

**Table 28.2** Hypothetical example of a formulation for an adolescent who has developed an eating disorder

| | Individual | Systemic | Cultural |
|---|---|---|---|
| Predisposing | Perfectionist nature<br>Picky eater from a young age | Grandmother hospitalized for weight loss as a teenager | |
| Precipitating | Onset of menses<br>Falling out with best friend | Older sister dieting | |
| Perpetuating | Social avoidance<br>Low mood | | Highly competitive group of friends |
| Protective | Enjoys school | Intact, motivated and supportive family | Supportive school<br>Maintained some links with peer group |

## Managing Eating Disorders

Assessment and management of a young person with an identified eating disorder must tackle medical, nutritional and psychological aspects of care, and be delivered by healthcare staff who are knowledgeable about normal adolescent development. Consideration should be given to the impact of the problem on siblings, who should be involved in treatment when possible. Admission to hospital is necessary if there is acute physical compromise, high psychiatric risk, or for intensive support with achieving specific aims. The purpose of hospitalization is not primarily weight gain, as this can be achieved in community settings, provided risks are manageable. The Junior MARSIPAN (Management of Really Sick Patients under 18 with AN) report contains a risk assessment framework to guide clinicians on risk assessment and decision-making [16].

### Medical Aspects

Medical complications of eating disorders can result from weight loss, poor nutrition or purging behaviours. They can be divided into acute and chronic complications, as summarized in Box 28.2. In adolescents, degree of underweight is best expressed as percentage BMI/median BMI for age and gender (also known as weight for height), as many patients are below the second centile for BMI (Figure 28.1). Using this terminology, less than 85% BMI would be considered underweight, and less than 70% BMI indicates severe malnutrition. Acute malnutrition is a medical emergency. Weight alone is not

---

**Box 28.2   Medical complications of eating disorders**

**Medical complications of calorie restriction**

- *Cardiovascular*: ECG abnormalities – bradycardia, T-wave inversion, ST-segment depression, prolonged Q–T interval, dysrhythmias (SVT, VT), pericardial infusions
- *Gastrointestinal system*: delayed gastric emptying, slowed GI motility, constipation, bloating, fullness, hypercholesterolaemia, abnormal liver function (carotenaemia)
- *Renal*: increased blood urea (from dehydration and reduced GFR) with increased risk of renal stones, polyuria (from abnormal ADH secretion), depletion of Na and K stores, peripheral oedema with refeeding due to increased renal sensitivity to aldosterone
- *Haematology*: leucopenia, anaemia, iron deficiency, thrombocytopenia
- *Endocrine*: sick thyroid syndrome (low $T_3$), amenorrhoea, growth failure, osteopenia
- *Neurological*: cortical atrophy, seizures
- *Death*

**Medical complications of purging**

- *Fluid and electrolyte imbalance*: low K, low Na, low Cl
- *Chronic vomiting*: oesophagitis, dental erosions, oesphageal tears, rarely rupture and pneumonia
- *Use of ipecac/laxatives*: myocardial damage, renal stones, low Ca, low Mg, low $KCO_3$
- *Amenorrhoea*

ECG, electrocardiogram; SVT, supraventricular tachycardia; VT, ventricular tachycardia; GI, gastrointestinal; GFR, glomerular filtration rate; ADH, antidiuretic hormone.

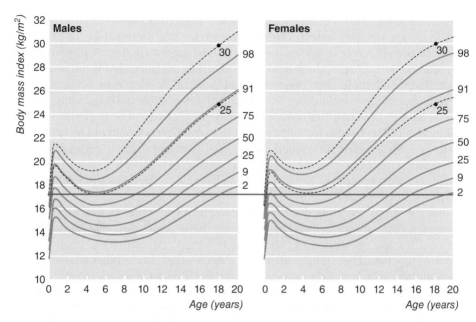

**Figure 28.1** Body Mass Index (BMI: weight in kg/square of height in m) varies with age and gender, so centile charts are needed to assess degree of underweight. The red line crosses through BMI of 17.5, defined as underweight in an adult, but which is in the normal range for an adolescent under 16.

adequate to assess medical risk, however. Table 28.3, based on the Junior MARSIPAN report, outlines the risk parameters that require assessment and when to be concerned.

**Table 28.3** Indicators of risk

BMI, body mass index; ECG, electrocardiogram

| Indicator | Comment |
| --- | --- |
| Very low weight or rapid weight loss | High concern at less than 70% of BMI for age and gender, or loss of over 1 kg for consecutive weeks in a low-weight child |
| Bradycardia | Symptomatic or with asymptomatic awake and resting heart rate < 45 beats/minute; prolonged QTc interval on ECG |
| Postural hypotension | Symptomatic or asymptomatic with a postural drop in systolic blood pressure of greater than 15 mmHg (note that some authorities recommend admission if the drop is greater than 10 mmHg) |
| Severe electrolyte imbalance | E.g. potassium < 3 mmol/L, hyponatraemia or hypernatraemia |
| | Hypoglycaemia |
| Severe-to-moderate dehydration | Difficult to assess clinically; will rely on history as well |
| Other severe medical complications | E.g. seizures or pancreatitis, hypothermia |
| Engagement with management plan | Violence from sufferer towards others, or towards the sufferer; risk of sexual abuse; parent/carer treatment non-attendance |
| Self-harm | E.g. suicidality, self-harm (e.g. head banging) or aggression |
| Activity levels | Uncontrolled exercise to the point of physical injury |
| Other | Muscular strength, acute confusion |

Refeeding in the context of severe malnutrition should be undertaken by a competent team in an appropriate context. Over-cautious refeeding carries risks, as does over-zealous refeeding. A recent randomized control trial suggests that most adolescents can start on a reasonably high-calorie intake provided they are being closely monitored [17].

In children and adolescents, assessment of pubertal development is important for determining risk for complications such as growth retardation and osteopenia, and also gives an indication of whether resumption of menses is likely to be the indicator that a 'healthy weight' has been achieved; a patient in early puberty would not be expected to menstruate. Serial pelvic ultrasound can be used to monitor pelvic organ maturation and predict onset of menses when this is in debate [18]. Puberty in boys runs about 2 years later than in girls, so boys are more vulnerable to the impact of low weight on growth and development.

Bones are at risk in eating disorders as a result of endocrine as well as nutritional inadequacy. Adolescence is the time of greatest bone acquisition. The most effective treatment for and prevention of osteopenia is weight restoration and resumption of endocrine function. There is no evidence for the role of calcium or other vitamin supplements, although some guidelines recommend them. Preliminary data suggest that oestrogen patches may be more effective than oral oestrogen, which is not recommended, in those patients in whom damage limitation needs consideration. Such treatments should only be undertaken in the context of a highly specialist multidisciplinary team.

Meal planning is a core component of treatment for all types of eating disorder, regardless of weight status, and should take into account pubertal stage and activity levels. Many underweight adolescent patients will need a higher calorie intake for adequate weight gain than that required by adult patients with eating disorders.

**Psychiatric Aspects of Management**

Eating disorders generate a lot of anxiety, often appropriately. Many seriously ill patients can be managed as outpatients provided an adequately skilled multidisciplinary team is involved and risks can be managed. Involving families in treatment and involving young people in decision-making increases cooperation, motivation and outcome.

Family interventions that directly address the eating disorder should be offered to adolescents with AN [19], usually in the form of family-based treatment [20], in a conjoint or separated family therapy format [21]. Individual therapy becomes the mainstay of treatment for AN when the young person is developmentally ready to take responsibility for managing their eating disorder [22], or when the eating disorder has become chronic. This may be in the form of cognitive–behaviour therapy, cognitive analytic therapy or other form of psychotherapy. Treatment should address the eating disorder, including weight and nutritional aspects. Adolescent-focused therapy (a specific manualized intervention) may also be offered as an alternative to family-based treatment when family support is not available for whatever reason [23], but as this treatment does not focus on managing disordered eating behaviours it should be supported by medical review and nutritional support/hospitalization as needed. Potentially useful psychotropic medications in AN include selective serotonin reuptake inhibitors (SSRIs) for co-morbid obsessive compulsive disorder or depression that has not improved with weight restoration. Occasionally, atypical antipsychotics such as olanzapine or risperidone are used to manage severe distress or emotional dysregulation, although there is no evidence to support this practice.

Adolescents with BN and BED can be treated with cognitive behavioural therapy (CBT) specific to the disorder [24], with the family included as appropriate, or with family-based treatment [25]. CBT can be delivered in a CD-ROM format with therapist support [26]. SSRIs are also potentially helpful as an adjunct to psychological treatment for BN, although there are no clinical trial data to support this.

Inpatient treatment has long been used as a therapeutic option when risks are high or when outpatient treatment response has been poor. Recent studies question the efficacy of inpatient treatment for treating AN, as well as its cost-effectiveness, and even suggest it may be counterproductive [27]. This has led to efforts to seek alternative treatments for the sickest patients, including increased use of paediatric wards for medical stabilization prior to outpatient treatment [28], or intensive family-based outpatient treatments such as multi-family therapy [29] or day-patient care [30]. Research is needed to understand who, in terms of illness stage, severity or motivation, benefits from inpatient care.

## Key Messages and Future Directions

Eating disorders are serious mental illnesses [31] with high morbidity and mortality [32]. The prognosis is good if appropriate treatment is started early [33], the majority of sufferers recovering within 5 years [34]. Models for early intervention are in development, focusing on parents/carers as the main source of support for the sufferer [35,36]. The trend is away from hospital-based treatment for adolescents, and towards treatment that allows relationships with peers and family members to be maintained, and for functional aspects of the sufferer's life, such as involvement in education, to be maintained.

## References

1 APA (2013) Diagnostic and Statistical Manual of Mental Disorders - DSM5. Vol. 5th edn. Washington DC: American Psychiatric Association.
2 Keel PK, Brown TA, Holm-Denoma J, Bodell LP (2011) Comparison of DSM-IV versus proposed DSM-5 diagnostic criteria for eating disorders: reduction of eating disorder not otherwise specified and validity. International Journal of Eating Disorders, 44, 553–560.
3 Caudle H, Pang C, Mancuso S et al. (2015) A retrospective study of the impact of DSM-5 on the diagnosis of eating disorders in Victoria, Australia. Journal of Eating Disorders, 3, 35.
4 Bryant-Waugh R, Markham L, Kreipe RE, Walsh BT (2010) Feeding and eating disorders in childhood. International Journal of Eating Disorders, 43, 98–111.
5 Bryant-Waugh R, Cooper PJ, Taylor CL, Lask BD (1996) The use of the Eating Disorder Examination with children: A pilot study. International Journal of Eating Disorders, 19, 391–397.
6 Cooper Z, Cooper PJ, Fairburn CG (1989) The validity of the eating disorder examination and its subscales. British Journal of Psychiatry, 154, 807–812.
7 Morgan JF, Reid F, Lacey JH (1999) The SCOFF questionnaire: assessment of a new screening tool for eating disorders. BMJ, 319,1467–1468.

**8** Stice E, Marti CN, Rohde P (2012) Prevalence, Incidence, Impairment, and Course of the Proposed DSM-5 Eating Disorder Diagnoses in an 8-Year Prospective Community Study of Young Women. Journal of Abnormal Psychology, 122, 445–457.

**9** Smink FR, van Hoeken D, Oldehinkel AJ, Hoek HW (2014) Prevalence and severity of DSM-5 eating disorders in a community cohort of adolescents. International Journal of Eating Disorders, 47, 610–619.

**10** Lask B, Bryant-Waugh R, Wright F et al. (2005) Family physician consultation patterns indicate high risk for early-onset anorexia nervosa. International Journal of Eating Disorders, 38, 269–272.

**11** Slane JD, Burt SA, Klump KL (2011) Genetic and environmental influences on disordered eating and depressive symptoms. International Journal of Eating Disorders, 44, 605–611.

**12** Lang K, Stahl D, Espie J et al. (2014) Set shifting in children and adolescents with anorexia nervosa: an exploratory systematic review and meta-analysis. International Journal of Eating Disorders, 47, 394–399.

**13** Lang K, Lopez C, Stahl D et al. (2014) Central coherence in eating disorders: an updated systematic review and meta-analysis. World Journal of Biological Psychiatry, 15, 586–598.

**14** Westwood H, Ivan E, William M et al. (2016) Using the autism-spectrum quotient to measure autistic traits in anorexia nervosa: a systematic review and meta-analysis. Journal of Autism and Developmental Disorders, 46, 964–77.

**15** Frank GK (2015) Recent advances in neuroimaging to model eating disorder neurobiology. Current Psychiatry Reports, 17, 559.

**16** Royal College of Psychiatrists (2010) Junior MARSIPAN: Management of Really Sick Patients under 18 with Anorexia Nervosa. Royal College of Psychiatrists.

**17** O'Connor G, Nicholls D, Hudson L, Singhal A (2016) Refeeding low weight hospitalized adolescents with anorexia nervosa: a Multicenter Randomized Controlled Trial. Nutr Clin Pract 31, 681–689.

**18** Mason HD, Key A, Allan R, Lask B (2007) Pelvic ultrasonography in anorexia nervosa: what the clinician should ask the radiologist and how to use the information provided. European Eating Disorders Review, 15, 35–41.

**19** National Institute for Health and Excellence (2004) Clinical, eating disorders: core interventions in the treatment and management of anorexia nervosa, bulimia nervosa and related eating disorders. UK: NICE.

**20** Lock J (2015) An update on evidence-based psychosocial treatments for eating disorders in children and adolescents. Journal of Clinical Child and Adolescent Psychology, 44, 707–721.

**21** Eisler I, Dare C, Hodes M et al. (2000) Family therapy for adolescent anorexia nervosa: the results of a controlled comparison of two family interventions. Journal of Child Psychology and Psychiatry, 41, 727–736.

**22** Dalle GR, Calugi S, Doll HA, Fairburn CG (2013) Enhanced cognitive behaviour therapy for adolescents with anorexia nervosa: An alternative to family therapy? Behaviour Research and Therapy, 51, R9–R12.

**23** Lock J, Le Grange D, Agras WS et al. (2010) Randomized clinical trial comparing family-based treatment with adolescent-focused individual therapy for adolescents with anorexia nervosa. Archives of General Psychiatry, 67,1025–1032.

24 Dalle Grave R, Calugi S, Sartirana M, Fairburn CG (2015) Transdiagnostic cognitive behaviour therapy for adolescents with an eating disorder who are not underweight. Behaviour Research and Therapy, 73, 79–82.

25 Le Grange D, Lock J, Agras WS et al. (2015) Randomized clinical trial of family-based treatment and cognitive-behavioral therapy for adolescent bulimia nervosa. Journal of the American Academy of Child and Adolescent Psychiatry, 54, 886–894.

26 Schmidt U, Lee S, Beecham J et al. (2007) A randomized controlled trial of family therapy and cognitive behavior therapy guided self-care for adolescents with bulimia nervosa and related disorders. American Journal of Psychiatry, 164, 591–598.

27 Gowers SG, Clark AF, Roberts C et al. (2010) A randomised controlled multicentre trial of treatments for adolescent anorexia nervosa including assessment of cost-effectiveness and patient acceptability – the TOuCAN trial. Health Technology Assessment, 14, 1–98.

28 Madden S, Miskovic-Wheatley J, Wallis A et al. (2014) A randomized controlled trial of in-patient treatment for anorexia nervosa in medically unstable adolescents. Psychological Medicine, 45, 415–427.

29 Knatz S, Murray SB, Matheson B et al. (2015) A brief, intensive application of multi-family-based treatment for eating disorders. Eating Disorders, 23, 315–24.

30 Herpertz-Dahlmann B, Schwarte R, Krei M et al. (2014) Day-patient treatment after short inpatient care versus continued inpatient treatment in adolescents with anorexia nervosa (ANDI): a multicentre, randomised, open-label, non-inferiority trial. Lancet, 383, 1222–1229.

31 Klump KL, Bulik CM, Kaye WH et al. (2009) Academy for eating disorders position paper: eating disorders are serious mental illnesses. International Journal of Eating Disorders, 42, 97–103.

32 Arcelus J, Mitchell AJ, Wales J, Nielsen S (2011) Mortality rates in patients with anorexia nervosa and other eating disorders. A meta-analysis of 36 studies. Archives of General Psychiatry, 68, 724–731.

33 Treasure J, Stein D, Maguire S (2014) Has the time come for a staging model to map the course of eating disorders from high risk to severe enduring illness? An examination of the evidence. Early Intervention in Psychiatry, 9, 173–184 .

34 Keel PK, Brown TA (2010) Update on course and outcome in eating disorders. International Journal of Eating Disorders, 43, 195–204.

35 Nicholls DE, Yi I (2012) Early intervention in eating disorders: a parent group approach. Early Intervention in Psychiatry, 6, 357–367.

36 Treasure J, Rhind C, Macdonald P, Todd G (2015) Collaborative Care: The New Maudsley Model. Eating Disorders, 23, 366–76.

# 29

# Emerging Personality Disorder

*Eileen Vizard*

## Definitions

### Temperament

Parents have long noted temperamental differences between infants early in life and still describe their babies and younger children as having 'sunny', 'restless' or 'placid' temperaments. Over half a century ago, researchers conducting the New York Longitudinal Study (NYLS) identified a nine-trait classification of infant temperament which clustered into three categories of infant temperament which are similar to parental perceptions, i.e. easy, difficult and slow to warm up [1].

Temperament is now thought to include individual differences in self-regulation, affect, attention and activity. These traits have a biological, partly genetic basis whilst at the same time their development is affected by maturation and life experience [2].

### Personality

Personality is a more complex, multi-dimensional construct than temperament and this may be partly why it is more likely to be applied to older children and adolescents. However, in a wide-ranging review of temperament and personality, the authors supported considering these two characteristics together because of their 'significant commonalities' [3, p. 183].

Many reviews and studies now confirm that children's temperament and personality traits can have lasting effects on both competence and resilience [2–4].

Continuities between childhood temperament and later personality traits have been described for certain clinical samples with presentations of antisocial behaviour, emerging severe personality disorder (ESPD) traits and borderline personality disorder (BPD) [5–7].

## Childhood Personality Traits and Adult Outcomes

Early research into childhood influences on later personality disorder tended to adopt a simple cause-and-effect model of investigation, rather than exploring interactions between possible risk factors. However, over 50 years ago, a study of youths and young adults aged between 15 to 26 years old ($N = 397$), in a range of settings including youth

*Child Psychology and Psychiatry: Frameworks for Clinical Training and Practice,* Third Edition.
Edited by David Skuse, Helen Bruce and Linda Dowdney.
© 2017 John Wiley & Sons, Ltd. Published 2017 by John Wiley & Sons, Ltd.

clubs, approved schools and special hospitals, found that 'there is strong evidence of a connection between severity of delinquency and some combination of parental deprivation, illegitimacy and brain damage' [8, p. 17].

An important recent research study, based on the Project Competence Longitudinal study of risk and resilience, investigated whether the childhood big five personality traits of extraversion, neuroticism, conscientiousness, agreeableness and openness predicted competence and resilience in adulthood [4,9,10].

A subsample of 176 children with complete data were selected from a group of 205 normative children for this study. They were assessed on various measures of personality at three stages – aged 10 years (childhood personality), 20 years (emerging adulthood) and 30 years old (young adulthood) – where the retention rates for the sample over the 20 year period were 88%, 98% and 90%, respectively [4].

The data were subject to both a variable-focused analysis and a person-focused analysis. A series of complex regression analyses used the variables of childhood personality traits and chronic adversity and their interaction to test whether or not this interaction predicted change and continuity in the children's competence over the three test periods. The person-focused analysis created within-sample groups of competent, resilient and maladaptive participants whose personality characteristics were then compared [4]. Correlations between the variables of big five personality traits, age and sex, chronic adversity in childhood and competence in academic achievement, rule-abiding conduct and social competence, were obtained.

The results showed that all of the competence outcomes were predicted by one or more personality traits, that females had higher levels of rule-abiding conduct and that the participant's exposure to chronic adversity had little impact on later competence outcomes [4]. It is claimed that these results support a 'main effects' model of childhood personality traits where those traits function as 'promotive effects' across adversity levels [4].

The study also shows that modest levels of positive personality traits are sufficient to allow those young people to attain resilient outcomes despite experiencing stress and adversity. In contrast, young people with more challenging personality traits (such as high levels of negative emotions, poor self-control, disagreeableness and disinterest in mastery development) are likely to continue to be at risk of a negative outcome, regardless of exposure to chronic adversity [4].

Perhaps unsurprisingly, the study also showed that children who achieve well on their developmental tasks, regardless of experiences of high or low adversity, will have the necessary abilities to self-regulate, to concentrate on schoolwork, to master new tasks and to show a capacity for empathy and connection. Finally, all of the big five childhood personality traits (except for extraversion) were found to be harbingers of adult competence and resilience [4].

Most research has focused on pathological outcomes, with the evidence linking certain childhood personality traits and behaviours to specific adult outcomes. For instance, children showing early neurocognitive problems (including early difficult temperament) and a 'life course persistent' trajectory of antisocial behaviour may develop conduct disorder and antisocial personality disorder (ASPD) in adult life [5,11]. A small number of high-risk children on this trajectory start offending earlier, commit more violent offences and have higher levels of recidivism [6,12]. This group has a substantial genetic risk of psychopathy and shows 'callous-unemotional' personality traits found in adult psychopaths [13,14].

The severity of childhood maltreatment may also be relevant in the development of personality pathology in adolescence. A study of 702 Indian adolescents showed that adolescents reporting higher severity of abuse and neglect also showed higher levels of personality pathology than those reporting less severe maltreatment [15].

A wide-ranging review of the evidence base for adolescent BPD supported a diathesis-stress approach to understanding the childhood origins of BPD, in which damage to the child's attachment relationships and mentalizing abilities 'may account for core features of BPD' [7, p. 1274].

## Relevant Neuroscience Findings

Recent neuroscientific evidence has increased understanding of some childhood personality traits. Brain studies suggest structural differences in the brains of children with callous-unemotional traits [16]. There are also suggested links between psychophysiological features, such as skin conductance measures, in early childhood and later psychopathy, as measured by self-report, at 28 years of age [17].

In fact, neuroscience research over the last 15 years or so has shown a strong consensus on certain aspects of adolescent brain development, attitudes and behaviours associated with stages of development and the implications of these findings for public policy [18]. It is now well established that the adolescent brain continues to grow, prune itself and establish new neural networks well into the early 20s and beyond [19]. It has been suggested that there are four specific structural changes that occur in the adolescent brain, as follows [18]:

- a decrease in grey matter in the prefrontal regions of the brain, reflective of synaptic pruning;
- significant changes in the density and distribution of dopamine receptors in pathways connecting with the limbic system;
- an increase in white matter in the prefrontal cortex, due to myelination of nerve fibres to improve the speed of transmission;
- an increase in the strength of connections between the prefrontal cortex and the limbic system which allows the executive functions of the prefrontal cortex to exert some control over the emotional responses of the limbic system.

## Personality Assessment and Personality Disorder in Clinical Practice

### Why Assess Childhood Personality?

Clinicians working with children do not routinely assess infant temperament or childhood personality. This may relate partly to a fear of stigmatizing children with what have historically been seen as adult diagnoses of 'personality disorder' as well as groundless fears that personality traits are unchangeable. In fact, it is accepted that they evolve and develop over time through transactions between individuals and their environments [3].

Recent research showed that all the big five childhood personality traits (except extraversion) were harbingers of later adult competence and resilience. This study also showed that whether or not they faced high or low adversity, children who did well developmentally had the important ability to self-regulate their emotions, to perform well at school and to develop a capacity for empathy and emotional connection to others [4].

This study and other clinical studies show the benefits of early identification of positive and negative temperamental and personality traits which are predictive of later good or bad outcomes, independent of experiences of adversity (see Table 29.1 [23]). Hence, the assessing clinician who has elicited this information about childhood personality traits and experiences of adversity, including maltreatment, is in a much better position to prognosticate about treatment needs and outcomes for that young person.

The usefulness of undertaking a careful clinical assessment of personality is also highlighted by research, which suggests that treatment interventions should be tailored to the personality of young participants [3].

## Diagnostic Issues

In DSM-5, the existing criterion-based diagnostic approach to personality disorders is presented along with a new, alternative, trait-specified (PD-TS), approach [20]. The existing system is categorical (diagnostic boxes are ticked or not), whereas the trait-specified (TS) approach is dimensional (some traits are present or not along a spectrum of the disorder).

In community-based clinical practice (child and adolescent mental health services, CAMHS), it may be unusual for a child or young person to present with the full criteria for any one personality disorder. However, the presence of sub-threshold (a few) traits of a personality disorder does not mean that there is no cause for concern. Rather, this situation should alert the clinician to the need for follow-up and reassessment of the child or young person to provide or modify treatment interventions. It has been noted that 'most children with one DSM diagnosis also have others. This mirrors reality: problems in young people's mental life are often multiple' [21, p. 225].

However, older adolescents with more complex needs seen in specialist services (Tier 4 NHS) may entirely fulfil criteria for more than one personality disorder, as well as having more than one psychiatric disorder. Co-morbidity for a range of other psychiatric and behavioural disorders is also the norm in samples of children (and also adults) referred to specialist services such as adolescent psychiatric units and forensic services [21,22].

In cases where there is concern about a child's personality traits or an emerging personality disorder, an assessment should be done, covering all aspects of the child's development including temperament, personality and family life (see Figure 29.1 [23, pages 22 & 23]). A family assessment of children at risk of ASPD or psychopathy is particularly important, given the role of family risk factors, including parental mental illness and criminality, in their development [5,6,11,23]. Parental ASPD may have major implications for the parenting, placement and care of high-risk children [24].

Some lessons for clinical practice are given in Box 29.1.

**Table 29.1** 'Big five' and possible positive and negative outcomes [23, pages 22 & 23]

| Trait | Positive outcome | Negative outcome |
| --- | --- | --- |
| Extraversion | Social competence, promotes good health, better romance/long-term relationships | Antisocial behaviour, callousness |
| Neuroticism | Conscience development, guilt when expected | Poor relationships, relation conflict, relation abuse, less competent parenting, risk for unemployment |
| Conscientiousness | School adjustment, educational and occupational achievement, job performance | Obsessive |
| Agreeableness | Social competence, positive parenting, responsible parenting | Exposure to risks |
| Openness | Exploring, friendliness, academic achievement | Exposure to risks |

*Source*: Adapted from Salekin [23].

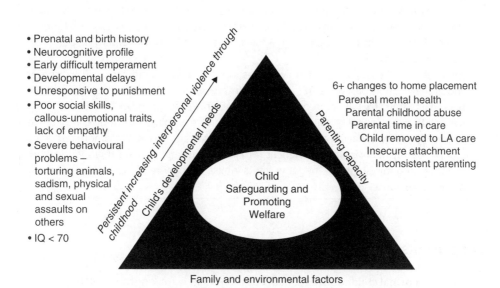

Cross-generational family history/genetics of ASPD/psychopathy and developmental disorders; cruelty / sexual abuse of animals; child exposed to domestic violence; schedule 1 offenders in family; inadequate sexual boundaries; adult sadistic and sexually perverted behaviour

**Figure 29.1** Emerging severe personality disorder. LA, local authority; ASPD, antisocial personality disorder. *Source*: Adapted from Vizard *et al.* [6] and Vizard [26].

---

**Box 29.1  Lessons for clinical practice**

- When taking a developmental history from parents or carers of referred children, clinicians should enquire about the child's temperament, general attitudes and behaviour from a very early age. Reference to the big five childhood personality traits may be useful here [23].
- Enquiries should also be made about co-morbidity for other psychiatric or developmental disorders, so that any interaction with pre-existing temperamental traits can be understood. A child with a diagnosis of ADHD may always have had an impulsive or careless approach to schoolwork and as a result may not have been conscientious about his/her schoolwork (big five trait 3). Or a child with school-based behaviour problems may not be agreeable or very much liked by other children, tending to be selfish and putting him/herself first (big five trait 4).
- The parents' early histories of temperament and personality traits should be noted along with any diagnoses of adult personality disorder. Of particular relevance may be the diagnosis of ASPD in one or both parents, which may bring risk factors for antisocial behaviour to the upbringing of the referred child [24]. Similarly, known callous-unemotional traits or a clinical diagnosis of psychopathy with associated convictions for violent offences, in parents or extended family members, may indicate a genetic risk for psychopathy [13].
- DSM-5 now provides a PD-TS model for assessing personality traits, based on five domains which are comparable (but not identical) to the big five childhood personality traits model mentioned previously [4,20]. Reference to the DSM-5, PD-TS model should be helpful for clinicians working with adolescents presenting with emerging personality disorder traits.
- An assessed child or young person who has signs of an emerging personality disorder should have a trait-based (PD-TS) treatment intervention which focuses on the specific personality traits that are currently causing concern. Research shows that all of the big five childhood personality traits except extraversion are harbingers of adult competence and resilience. Even having a few positive personality traits seems to promote resilience independently of adversity experiences [4]. Hence it makes sense for therapeutic work to focus on diminishing the negative traits whilst strongly reinforcing those likely to promote resilience.

## Conclusions

The study of normal childhood personality development is striking by its relative absence from the literature. However, earlier identification of a range of positive and negative personality traits in childhood would allow adaptive, positive traits to be encouraged, and negative, antisocial or interpersonal traits to be curtailed through specially adapted parenting interventions. Concerns about children acquiring personality trait 'labels' should be balanced against the benefits of building on their strengths.

Natural pathways exist which take the infant through a series of physical, emotional, cognitive and social developmental stages towards childhood, adolescence and adult life [25]. Links appear to exist between infant temperament, childhood personality traits and adolescent personality styles.

However, empirical research has not yet tracked these links across childhood and adolescence with detailed reference to a wide range of personality traits and outcomes, including diagnoses of adult personality disorders. Exceptions include research tracking adult outcomes for children with certain personality traits and behavioural profiles, such as conduct disorder, which are now reasonably well mapped and the onset, stability, course and adult outcomes for BPD [7,11].

Personality disorders carry a burden of psychopathology, relationship and parenting problems in adult life [24]. This is particularly the case with certain personality disorders such as BPD, where it has been noted that 'It is only through early active assessment and identification of youngsters with these problems that a lifetime of personal suffering and health system burden can be reduced or altogether avoided' [7]. Research on developmental trajectories in offending children has shown that the high-risk minority with callous-unemotional traits (a likely precursor to adult psychopathy) can be readily identified before 10 years of age with the clear implication that early identification and treatment can be offered to protect these children from adverse adult outcomes [6,26].

Overall, the positive message from research is that mental health practitioners' assessments of children and adolescents should routinely include reference to the child or adolescent's presenting temperamental style or personality and that attention should be given to any signs of emerging personality disorders so that intervention and treatment can be arranged, where needed.

# References

1 Thomas A, Chess S, Birch HG et al. (1963) Behavioral individuality in early childhood. New York: New York University Press.

2 Rothbart MK, Bates JE (2006) Temperament. In: Damon W, Lerner R (eds), N. Eisenberg (Volume Ed.),Handbook of Child Psychology, Vol. 3. Social, Emotional, and Personality Development (6th edn). New York: Wiley, pp. 99–166.

3 Caspi A, Shiner R (2008) Temperament and personality. In: Rutter M, Bishop D, Pine D et al. (eds) Rutter's Child & Adolescent Psychiatry, 5th edn. Blackwell Publishing, pp. 182–198.

4 Shiner RL, Masten AS (2012) Childhood personality as a harbinger of competence and resilience in adulthood. Development and Psychopathology. 24, 507–528.

5 Rutter M, Giller H, Hagell A (1998) Antisocial behaviour by young people. Cambridge: Cambridge University Press.

6 Vizard E, Hickey N, McCrory E (2007) Developmental trajectories towards sexually abusive behaviour and emerging severe personality disorder in childhood: the results of a three year UK study. British Journal of Psychiatry. 190, s27–s32.

7 Sharp C, Fonagy P (2015) Practitioner Review: Borderline personality disorder in adolescence – recent conceptualization, intervention, and implications for clinical practice. Journal of Child Psychology and Psychiatry, 56, 1266–1288.

8 Craft M, Stephenson G, Granger C (1964) The relationship between severity of personality disorder and certain adverse childhood influences. In: Adshead G, Jacob J (eds) Personality Disorder. The Definitive Reader.Forensic Focus 29. London: Jessical Kingsley Publishers, pp.13–21.

9 Garmezy N, Tellegen A (1984) Studies of stress resistant children: methods, variables and preliminary findings. In Morrison F, Keating D, Lord C (eds) Applied Developmental Psychology 1. New York: Academic Press, pp. 231–387.

10 Masten AS, Tellegen A (2012) Resilience in developmental psychopathology: Contributions of the Project Competence Longitudinal Study. Development and Psychopathology, 24, 345–361.

11 Moffitt TE (1993) Adolescence-limited and life-course-persistent antisocial behaviour: A developmental taxonomy. Psychological Review, 100, 674–701.

12 Hodgins S (2007) Persistent violent offending: what do we know? Assessment, risk and outcome in severe personality disorder. British Journal of Psychiatry, 190 (Supplement 49), s12–s14.

13 Viding E, Blair RJR, Moffitt TE, Plomin R (2005) Evidence for substantial genetic risk for psychopathy in 7 year olds. Journal of Child Psychology and Psychiatry, 46, 592–597.

14 Viding E, Frick PJ, Plomin R (2007) Aetiology of the relationship between callous-unemotional traits and conduct problems in childhood. British Journal of Psychiatry, 190, s33–s38.

15 Charak R, Koot HM (2015) Severity of maltreatment and personality pathology in adolescents of Jammu, India: A latent class approach. Child Abuse & Neglect, 50, 56–66.

16 De Brito SA, Mechelli A, Wilke M et al. (2009) Size matters: increased grey matter in boys with conduct problems and callous-unemotional traits. Brain, 132, 843–852.

17 Glenn AL, Raine A, Venables PH, Mednick SA ( 2007) Early Temperamental and Psychophysiological Precursors of Adult Psychopathic Personality. Journal of Abnormal Psychology, 116, 508–518.

18 Steinberg L (2012) Should the science of adolescent brain development inform public policy? Issues in Science and Technology, spring, 67–78.

19 Blakemore SJ, Choudhury S (2006) Development of the adolescent brain: implications for executive function and social cognition. Journal of Child Psychology and Psychiatry, 47, 296–312.

20 American Psychiatric Association (APA) (2013) Diagnostic and Statistical Manual of Mental Disorders, text revision. 5th edn (DSM-5)1000 Wilson Boulevard, Arlington, VA 22209–3901. www.psych.org.

21 Taylor E (2011) Diagnostic classification: current dilemmas and possible solutions. In: Skuse D, Bruce H, Dowdney L, Mrazek D (eds) Child Psychology and Psychiatry. Frameworks for Practice, 2nd edn. Chichester, UK: Wiley-Blackwell, pp. 224–228.

22 Bladon E Vizard E, French L, Tranah T (2005) Young sexual abusers: a descriptive study of a uk sample of children showing sexually harmful behaviours. Journal of Forensic Psychiatry & Psychology, 16, 109–126.

23 Salekin R (2009) Developmental pathways towards childhood psychopathy: The potential for effective early intervention. Presentation given at Department of Health Conference in London 2007: Vizard E, Jones A, Viding E et al. (eds) Early Intervention in Personality Disorder: MST and Other Treatments for Socially Excluded High Risk/High Harm Children and Families. http://www.personalitydisorder.org.uk/resources/emerging-pd/.

24 Adshead G (2003) Dangerous and severe parenting disorder? Personality disorder, parenting and new legal proposals. Child Abuse Review, 12, 227.

25 Shiner RL (2005) A developmental perspective on personality disorders: Lessons from research on normal personality development in childhood and adolescence. Journal of Personality Disorders, 19, 202–210.

26 Vizard E (2011) Emerging personality disorder. In: Skuse D, Bruce H, Dowdney L, Mrazek D (eds) Child Psychology and Psychiatry: Frameworks for Practice. John Wiley & Sons Ltd, pp. 217–222.

# 30

# Literacy Disorders

*Valerie Muter and Margaret J. Snowling*

## Definition, Incidence, Persistence and Co-occurrence

Disorders of literacy are arguably the most studied and best understood of all the cognitive disorders of childhood. In this chapter, we shall focus on both disorders of reading accuracy (dyslexia) and reading comprehension difficulties. Dyslexia is a common disorder affecting around 3–7% of children, with an over-representation of boys, especially in clinical samples [1]. A simple definition of dyslexia is a learning disorder that primarily affects reading and spelling development. The notion that in dyslexia 'reading achievement is substantially below expectation given the person's age and measured intelligence' has fallen from favour and this discrepancy definition is not used in the *Diagnostic and Statistical Manual of Mental Disorders*, 5th edition (DSM-5) [2]; rather, DSM-5 groups together reading disorders, mathematics disorders and disorders of written expression under a single over-riding diagnosis of specific learning disorders within the broader category of neurodevelopmental disorders. It is now recognized that dyslexia occurs across a wide range of abilities; dyslexia is not an 'all-or-none' category but rather a dimensional disorder with a number of behavioural outcomes. The importance of educational history is also critical in determining the clinical picture and it should be borne in mind that inadequate teaching may be a sufficient explanation for some children's poor reading skills. A debate considering whether 'dyslexia' is a meaningful construct and a useful label [3] has led to the proposal that the term should be reserved for those individuals who have not responded to robust and intensive intervention.

Dyslexia is a lifelong disorder and many affected individuals experience problems of reading fluency and spelling that persist into adulthood despite intervention. Dyslexia commonly co-occurs alongside other developmental difficulties, such as specific language impairment, mathematical problems, attention deficit hyperactivity disorder or motor difficulties [4].

The goal of reading is not only to access the printed word, but also to extract meaning from it. It is estimated that 7–10% of middle-school-age children can read words accurately but fail to understand what they read [5]. These 'poor comprehenders' are often not noticed because their fluent reading masks underlying difficulties.

*Child Psychology and Psychiatry: Frameworks for Clinical Training and Practice*, Third Edition.
Edited by David Skuse, Helen Bruce and Linda Dowdney.
© 2017 John Wiley & Sons, Ltd. Published 2017 by John Wiley & Sons, Ltd.

## Acquiring Literacy Skills

In order to understand why children fail to learn to read accurately and with understanding, it is important to have a clear picture of typical reading development. The Simple View of Reading proposes that variations in reading development can be understood in terms of two relatively separate underlying skills: word recognition and language comprehension.

Two critical foundation skills for acquiring *word recognition* skill during the first 2 years at school are phoneme awareness (the ability to analyse speech sounds within words) and letter-sound knowledge. Together these skills in preschool account for almost 90% of the variance in reading skill at age 6 years [6]. Performance on speeded naming tasks (naming pictures, colours, letters or digits as rapidly as possible) is also predictive of individual differences in reading, especially of reading fluency.

It has been argued that the ease of acquiring fluent and accurate reading depends on the writing system in which the child is learning [7]. The English orthography contains inconsistent letter-sound mappings and permits irregular forms; it is therefore classified as 'opaque'. In contrast, languages such as Italian, Greek and Finnish have a 'transparent' writing system in which sound-to-letter correspondences are regular and consistent. Although reading development proceeds faster in the more transparent than in the opaque orthographies [8], the predictors of individual differences in decoding (the skill that is impaired in dyslexia) are the same regardless of the transparency of the language [9]. It follows that the risks associated with dyslexia appear to be universal across languages and include problems of phonological awareness, naming and poor knowledge of the symbols of the writing system (e.g. letters) [10].

While learning to recognize printed words depends largely on creating 'mappings' between orthography and phonology, the development of *reading comprehension* depends on broader oral *language* skills, such as knowledge of word-meanings, the ability to understand sentences, to make inferences where appropriate and to remember what was read in order to create an integrated and cohesive sense of the text [11].

## The Nature of Impairment in Children with Literacy Disorders

Children with dyslexia fail to learn to read because of an underlying weakness in their phonological system. This weakness is indicated by poor performance on a wide range of phonological tasks, such as verbal short-term memory tests, deleting specified phonemes from words, speeded (rapid) naming and repeating non-words. Difficulties in processing, memorizing and analysing speech segments in words invariably result in problems of learning to decode in children with dyslexia. The most direct means of investigating this decoding deficit is to ask children to read non-words like '*kig*' and '*ploob*'. Children with dyslexia typically have great difficulty reading non-words, even when compared with younger children.

In contrast to children with dyslexia, poor comprehenders perform well on tests of phonological skills. They do, however, experience problems with a wide range of language-related tasks that assess oral language (vocabulary, grammar and oral expression), higher-level language skills (including narrative and use of figurative language), metacognitive processes (integration and inference making, knowledge of story conventions and structures) and executive processes (verbal working memory, suppression and inhibition). Nation *et al.* [12] carried out a longitudinal study of poor reading comprehenders from age 5 to 8 years; the children assessed as having reading comprehension difficulties at age 8 showed oral language problems that were present at school entry 3 years earlier. Such findings suggest that language problems are causally related to later reading comprehension difficulties.

Like most developmental disorders, dyslexia and reading comprehension difficulties occur along a continuum of severity. In dyslexia, the severity of the child's phonological deficit will influence the extent of their reading and spelling difficulties, and very likely also their response to remedial intervention. However, other cognitive risk factors also play a role, including lower non-verbal ability, weaknesses in auditory processing, slow language development and short-term verbal memory limitations. Indeed, there is growing evidence that a phonological deficit is one of a number of risk factors for dyslexia that accumulate towards a threshold which characterizes the disorder [13]. Children with dyslexia who also have language impairment will present with reading comprehension, as well as word recognition, problems. In considering the co-morbidity of dyslexia, language impairment and speech sound disorders, Pennington and Bishop [14] conclude that there are some risk factors that are general to all three disorders, especially difficulties in acquiring phoneme awareness (see Table 30.1). However, there are also risk factors that are specific to particular disorders; a deficit in rapid naming is specific to children with dyslexia, but is not always evident in children with language impairment.

## Patterns of Impairment from Preschool to Adolescence

It has been known for many years that dyslexia runs in families. A recent meta-analysis of family at-risk studies suggests that there is a 45% risk of a child developing dyslexia in families in which a first-degree relative is affected [15]. While dyslexia is most usually diagnosed in middle childhood, it is clear from prospective longitudinal studies that its effects are evident as early as 3 years of age and persist through adolescence into adulthood.

**Table 30.1** Risk factors for dyslexia in the preschool and early school years

| Stage of development | Risk factors for dyslexia |
| --- | --- |
| Birth | Affected family member |
| Preschool | Late talker |
| | Speech difficulties |
| | Slow to learn colours and letters |
| School entry | Poor knowledge of letters |
| | Poor rhyming or phoneme skills |
| | Expressive language difficulties |

Many children with delayed speech and language development later develop reading problems. In one prospective family-risk study, language-delayed preschoolers experienced persisting literacy difficulties through to adolescence when they also tended to present with low self-esteem in relation to their academic skills, avoidance of reading, and attentional and emotional difficulties [4]. Importantly, children from 'at risk' families who were reading within the normal range at the age of 8 years went on to experience difficulties in spelling and reading fluency at the age of 12; this finding elucidates potentially heritable weaknesses (endophenotypes) in dyslexia and protective factors that enable some family members to 'compensate' in order to circumvent poor reading, while others succumb to literacy problems. Finally, studies of children at family risk of dyslexia also remind us of the importance of gene–environment correlations, captured, for example, by differences, albeit subtle, in the home and literacy environment experienced by children of parents with dyslexia. For instance, teenagers with dyslexia avoid reading, and their parents read less frequently to them.

## Assessing Literacy Disorders

Most children with literacy disorders are referred for assessment in the middle-school years. However, there is increasing recognition of the importance of early identification before the child has fallen behind educationally and begins to experience declining levels of motivation and confidence. Since early screening batteries have tended to have low validity, a review for the UK government [16] recommended the identification of 'at risk' children via close monitoring of their response to reading instruction during the first 2 years at school. Children who fail to progress sufficiently in response to mainstream, differentiated and additional literacy support require further assessment for likely dyslexia or reading comprehension disorder (see Figure 30.1). More recent studies have suggested that being at family risk of dyslexia can provide an indication from a relatively early age (3 years) of whether a child is likely to experience later reading difficulties, especially if this is in combination with delayed speech and language development [17]. Early screening could lead to advice as to how parents could best support their child's emergent reading skills, bearing in mind that a home literacy environment rich in books and print-related interactions is associated with a good start in word decoding and comprehension.

A brief diagnostic assessment of dyslexia should include tests of single-word reading and spelling, a test of phonological awareness, a test of short-term verbal memory, a test of rapid naming and an (optional) test of arithmetic. If required, a short-form IQ test makes it possible to determine whether the child has a general learning difficulty or a more specific developmental disorder.

In order to determine why a child shows poor response to intervention, a more comprehensive evaluation is needed. Such an assessment needs to recognize that not all components of literacy skill will be equally impaired in a given child (see Table 30.2). For the child with suspected dyslexia, the nature of the child's underlying difficulty can be assessed using measures of phonological awareness, verbal short-term memory, rapid naming and decoding (non-word reading). For the child with reading comprehension difficulties, it is important to evaluate oral language skills and text comprehension strategies. Finally, in view of the common co-occurrence of developmental disorders,

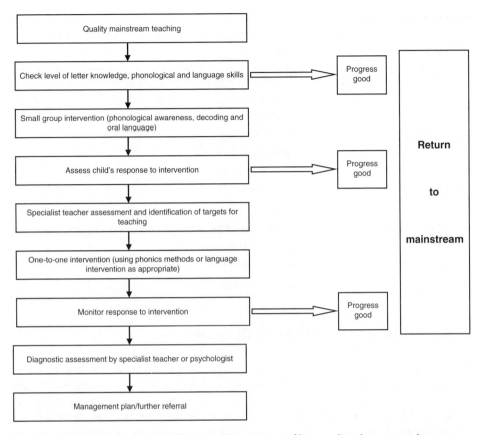

**Figure 30.1** Steps in the early identification and assessment of literacy disorders: a staged process.

the assessment needs to determine whether additional difficulties impact behaviour or school adjustment. Given time constraints, useful information can be sought from parents and teachers using standardized questionnaires which assess, for instance, attention or language difficulties.

**Table 30.2** Components of a comprehensive diagnostic assessment for reading disorders

| Construct | Test |
| --- | --- |
| Reading | Single-word reading |
| | Non-word reading (decoding) |
| | Reading fluency (single words and continuous text) |
| | Prose reading accuracy |
| | Reading comprehension (literal and inferential) |
| Spelling | Single-word spelling |
| | Spelling in free writing |

*(continued)*

**Table 30.2** (Continued)

| Construct | Test |
| --- | --- |
| Writing | Written narrative (structure and organization) |
| | Writing speed |
| | Quality analysis of handwriting |
| Mathematics | Mental arithmetic |
| | Mathematical reasoning |
| | Written arithmetic |
| Phonological skills | Phonological awareness |
| | Rapid naming |
| Verbal working memory | Verbal short-term memory span |
| | Non-word repetition |
| Language skills | Sentence repetition |
| | Grammar and morphology |

## Teaching Children with Literacy Disorders

There is considerable evidence showing that phonologically based reading interventions are effective in ameliorating children's word level reading/decoding difficulties, and a smaller evidence base showing that reading comprehension difficulties can be ameliorated by suitable interventions to boost vocabulary, broader oral language and text comprehension skills [18]. Preschool programmes aimed at strengthening the foundations of literacy (specifically oral language skills and phoneme awareness) can also have positive effects on reading comprehension [19].

Most interventions focus on remediating the child's difficulties. However, there is a place for encouraging children to draw on their cognitive strengths so that they can develop compensatory strategies. For example, the verbally able child with dyslexia encountering an unfamiliar word may be taught to supplement their (imperfect) attempt at decoding by using vocabulary knowledge.

As children get older, their needs extend beyond direct teaching of reading and spelling to include instruction in the use of information technology (computers, spellchecks and voice-activated software) and techniques for improving organizational skills and assessment arrangements (typically extra time in examinations but also possibly being supplied with a 'reader' or scribe).

Understandably, the teaching of children with dyslexia has focused largely on remediating reading and spelling problems. However, co-occurring difficulties need to be addressed in their own right. Management programmes should not be limited to literacy instruction, but should also consider the individual child's need for speech and language therapy, occupational/physiotherapy, medication or behavioural programmes for attention deficits and additional maths support.

# References

1  Snowling MJ (2009) Changing concepts of dyslexia: nature, treatment and co-morbidity. Journal Child Psychology & Psychiatry, 53, e1–3.
2  American Psychiatric Association (2013) Diagnostic and Statistical Manual, 5th edn. APA.
3  Elliott J, Grigorenko E (2014) The Dyslexia Debate. Cambridge: Cambridge University Press.
4  Snowling MJ, Muter V, Carroll JM (2007) Children at family risk of dyslexia: a follow-up in adolescence. Journal of Child Psychology and Child Psychiatry, 48, 609–618.
5  Clarke PJ, Snowling MJ, Truelove E et al. (2010) Ameliorating children's reading comprehension difficulties: A randomised controlled trial. Psychological Science, 21, 1106–1116.
6  Muter V, Hulme C, Snowling MJ et al. (2004) Phonemes, rimes, vocabulary and grammatical skills as foundations of early reading development: Evidence from a longitudinal study. Developmental Psychology, 40, 663–681.
7  Ziegler JC, Goswami UC (2005) Reading Acquisition, developmental dyslexia and skilled reading across languages: a psycholinguistic grain size theory. Psychological Bulletin, 131, 3–29.
8  Caravolas M, Lervag A, Defior S et al. (2013) Different patterns, but equivalent predictors, of growth in reading in consistent and inconsistent orthographies. Psychological Science, 24, 1398–1408.
9  Caravolas M, Lervag M, Mousikou P et al. (2012) Common patterns of prediction of literacy development in different alphabetic orthographies. Psychological Science, 23, 678–686.
10  Hulme C, Snowling MJ (2009) Developmental disorders of language, learning and cognition. Oxford: Wiley-Blackwell.
11  Cain K (2010) Reading development and difficulties. Oxford: Wiley-Blackwell.
12  Nation K, Cooksey J, Taylor J. et al (2010) A longitudinal investigation of the early language and reading skills in children with reading comprehension impairment. Journal of Child Psychology & Psychiatry, 51, 1031–1039.
13  Pennington BF, Santerre-Lemmon L, Rosenberg J et al. (2012) Individual prediction of dyslexia by single versus multiple deficit models. Journal of Abnormal Psychology, 121, 212–224.
14  Pennington BF, Bishop D (2009) Relations among speech, language, and reading disorders. Annual Review of Psychology, 60, 283–306.
15  Snowling M, Melby-Lervag M (2016) Oral language deficits in familial dyslexia: a meta-analysis and review. Psychological Bulletin, 142, 498–545.
16  Rose J (2009) Identifying and teaching children and young people with dyslexia and literacy difficulties. Online: http://www.interventionsforliteracy.org.uk/assets/Uploads/The-Rose-Report-June-2009.pdf. Accessed: January 2017.
17  Thompson PA, Hulme C, Nash HM et al (2015) Developmental dyslexia: predicting individual risk. Journal of Child Psychology & Psychiatry, 56, 976–987.
18  Snowling MJ, Hulme C (2011) Evidence-based interventions for reading and language difficulties: Creating a virtuous circle. British Journal of Educational Psychology, 81, 1–23.
19  Fricke S, Bowyer-Crane C, Haley AH et al (2013) Efficacy of language intervention in the early years. Journal of Child Psychology & Psychiatry, 54, 280–290.

# 31

# Challenges in Child and Adolescent Obsessive Compulsive Disorder

*Elaine Chung, Anup Kharod and Isobel Heyman*

## The 'Hidden Problem'

Young people and their families report that one of the most challenging aspects of dealing with obsessive compulsive disorder (OCD) is recognition of the problem. This includes realizing that the symptoms are part of OCD (Box 31.1).

Obsessive compulsive disorder generally responds to treatment, and the emotional, social and educational disabilities that children may acquire secondary to chronic OCD can be minimized by prompt intervention. Earlier detection will be promoted by greater public awareness, and early diagnosis and intervention improve long-term outcomes [1]. Around 50% of adults with OCD recall it started in childhood, but many failed to get help, with average delays in diagnosis of 12 years in adults and 3 years in children [2]. Although paediatric OCD was once considered rare, epidemiological studies have revealed a prevalence of 1–4%, with incidence rising exponentially with age [3].

A possible reason for delays in recognizing OCD is the nature of the illness itself. Individuals usually have good insight, realizing that their thoughts and behaviours are unnecessary. They often feel embarrassed by the symptoms and hide them for as long as possible, or fear that they will be asked to stop ritualizing and worry that this would be anxiety-provoking. Even in a brief primary care consultation, screening questions (e.g. the seven-item Short OCD Screener) can be used [4].

---

**Box 31.1  Symptoms of obsessive compulsive disorder**

**Obsessions**

- Intrusive, repetitive, distressing thoughts or images
- Most common themes – contamination, harm coming to others, sexual, aggressive, religious

**Compulsions**

- Repetitive, stereotyped, unnecessary behaviours
- Most common rituals – washing, checking, repeating, reassurance-seeking, ordering

---

*Child Psychology and Psychiatry: Frameworks for Clinical Training and Practice,* Third Edition.
Edited by David Skuse, Helen Bruce and Linda Dowdney.
© 2017 John Wiley & Sons, Ltd. Published 2017 by John Wiley & Sons, Ltd.

**When Do Ordinary Childhood Rituals Become OCD?**

Rituals are a part of normal childhood development (e.g. bedtime rituals), usually from the age of 2 to 7 years, and should not be confused with OCD [5]. Parents may not notice rituals are becoming more prolonged or distressing. A child's obsessions or rituals may be OCD if they:

- upset the child
- take up a lot of time (> an hour/day)
- interfere with the child's everyday life.

For a diagnosis of OCD, not only do compulsions and/or obsessions need to be present, but they also need to be causing functional impairment.

## Aetiology

The cause of OCD is not known, but there is increasing evidence for a biological basis [6], although it is highly responsive to psychological intervention.

Family and twin studies support a strong genetic role, with heritability in children ranging from 45% to 65% [7]; interestingly, this is higher than in adult cohorts, which is possibly suggestive of a developmental subtype [6]. The influence is polygenic. A promising approach for genetic, imaging and treatment studies is the consideration of OCD dimensions as quantitative phenotypes. OCD is a heterogeneous condition, and factor and cluster analytic studies in adults and children have identified four relatively independent symptom dimensions of contamination/cleaning, obsessions/checking, symmetry/ordering and hoarding [5].

Neuroimaging and neuropsychological studies support a frontal-striatal-thalamic model of OCD where hyperactivation of the orbitofrontal cortex may mediate persistent attention to perceived threat (obsessions), leading to compulsions to neutralize these [6]. Treatment with medication or cognitive behavioural therapy (CBT) is associated with a reversal of functional neuroimaging findings. The neurochemical basis is not known, but serotonergic, dopaminergic and glutamatergic systems, and their interactions, have been implicated [6].

A further finding implicating the basal ganglia in OCD, is that a subgroup of children may have the disorder triggered by infections. Streptococcal infections trigger an immune response, which in some individuals generate antibodies that cross-react with antigens in the basal ganglia. This subgroup have been given the acronym PANDAS (paediatric autoimmune neuropsychiatric disorder associated with *Streptococcus*), but recently the terms PANS (paediatric acute-onset neuropsychiatric symptoms) and CANS (childhood acute neuropsychiatric syndrome) have been used, given the sudden onset and uncertainty regarding aetiology [8].

## Assessment of the Young Person with Possible OCD

### Differential Diagnosis and Identifying OCD

Diagnosing OCD should involve asking the child direct questions about obsessions and compulsions, as these may not be revealed spontaneously. Clinicians need to consider alternative diagnoses, such as depression, anxiety disorders, developmental disorders, which include repetitive behaviours (e.g. autism spectrum disorders), and tic disorders. Psychological instruments can aid diagnosis and rating of severity. The best validated is the Children's Yale-Brown Obsessive Compulsive Scale (CY-BOCS) [9].

## Phenomenology of Obsessions and Compulsions

Children with OCD usually have both obsessions and compulsions, and an obvious link may be detected, e.g. contamination fears and excessive washing. The connection may be less obvious, e.g. fear of a parent's misfortune if the child doesn't touch something a certain number of times. Obsessions may not be present; a child may say that things are just 'not right' if they don't do their ritual. The distressing nature of obsessions can make it difficult for children to recognize them as their own thoughts. It is not unusual for younger children to call their obsessions 'voices', and careful examination of the psychopathology is needed to avoid confusing these experiences with psychotic phenomena. Children may have less insight into the irrational nature of obsessions and compulsions, and the *International Classification of Mental and Behavioural Disorders, 10th revision* (ICD-10) allows a diagnosis with reduced insight in young people. DSM-5 has removed the requirement for OCD symptoms to be perceived as excessive or unreasonable, adding an insight specifier (good, fair, absent.)

## Obsessions May Cause More Distress Than Compulsions

Particularly in teenagers, predominantly obsessional problems can be difficult to diagnose. The commonest obsessive themes – sexual, aggressive and religious – are often particularly embarrassing to disclose. It is helpful to enquire about these directly and explain that everyone has intrusive thoughts. It is important to explain that an obsessive thought should not be confused with an impulse to act, and in no way reflects the nature or behavioural leanings of the person experiencing it. This is especially important when someone has socially concerning obsessions, e.g. having sex with children. If these recurrent thoughts are not recognized as obsessions, an inappropriately high level of risk may be inferred, when there is none.

Secondary risks, the unintended consequences of compulsions or avoidance, should be considered, e.g. someone with contamination fears about food may restrict their dietary intake. Harm may also occur in individuals whose OCD is severe during critical phases of development; for example, withdrawal from school may mean they miss out on important social developmental experiences [10].

## Co-Morbidities

Consistent with adult studies, approximately 80% of young people with OCD have at least one co-morbid psychiatric disorder. The commonest co-morbidities in children are attention deficit hyperactivity disorder (ADHD, 34–51%), depression (33–39%), tics (26–59%), specific developmental disabilities (24%), oppositional defiant disorder (17–51%) and anxiety disorders (22%). Careful assessment is required both to distinguish symptoms of OCD from other disorders, and because some co-morbidities may influence response to treatment [11–13]. There appears to be a paediatric tic-related subtype of OCD, more common in boys, with earlier age of onset, and higher co-morbidity with ADHD and disruptive behaviours, and DSM-5 has included a specifier for the presence of tics in OCD. This subtype is less responsive to selective serotonin reuptake inhibitors (SSRIs) but CBT is equally effective [5,13].

## Treatment

Helping parents and young people to become informed about OCD is crucial, and there are several good publications available (see 'Further reading'). The UK charity OCD Action provides information and links to support groups. For many families, knowing they are not alone is the first step towards recovery.

There are two interventions of proven efficacy: CBT with exposure and response prevention (ERP), and medication, used independently or in combination. Direct comparison of CBT and SSRI medication in paediatric OCD showed that CBT and sertraline were associated with comparable levels of symptom reduction, but that combined CBT and SSRI treatment was associated with superior outcomes [15]. Meta-analyses of randomized control trials have found that whilst both CBT and medication are effective treatments for paediatric OCD, CBT is associated with greater efficacy than pharmacotherapy, with numbers needed to treat of 3 and 5, respectively [14] [15]. Combination treatment added little to concomitant CBT, but was superior to serotonin reuptake inhibitor (SRI) medication alone. In partial treatment responders, those who failed an SRI had better outcomes from adding CBT than continuing a SRI [16]. Those who failed CBT did as well continuing CBT as they did adding an SRI [16].

The UK's National Institute for Health and Care Excellence (NICE) recommends a 'stepped care' model, with increasing intensity of treatment according to clinical severity (Figure 31.1) [17]. CBT incorporating ERP is recommended as first-line treatment in children and adolescents, with the subsequent addition of an SSRI, then consideration of clomipramine and augmentation strategies with atypical antipsychotic medications as necessary. Admission to hospital is rarely indicated, but may be needed if there is risk to safety or physical health.

### Young People Becoming Experts

It is helpful for patients and families to have information about aetiology. Understanding that OCD is a neurobiological disorder helps them to realize it is not their fault. It is helpful to stress that treatments really work and that many successful people have coped with OCD.

### Cognitive Behavioural Therapy

Studies show that CBT is an effective treatment, with 40–88% of young people achieving remission. There is evidence that CBT for paediatric OCD can also be effectively delivered in groups, with promising early studies of treatment via telephone, webcam and internet [18] [19].

#### Anxiety

A key starting point in overcoming OCD and engaging in psychological treatment is understanding the role of anxiety (Figure 31.2).

| Who is responsible for care? | What is the focus? | Type of care |
|---|---|---|
| **Step 6**<br>CAMHS Tier 4 | OCD with risk to life, severe neglect, or severe distress or disability | Reassess, discuss options and care coordination<br><br>As per Step 4 and consider augmentation strategies, admission or special living arrangements |
| **Step 5**<br>CAMHS Tiers 3 and 4 | OCD with significant co-morbidity, or more severely impaired functioning and/or treatment resistance, partial response or relapse | Reassess, discuss options<br><br>As per Step 3 and consider referral to specialist services outside CAMHS if appropriate |
| **Step 4**<br>CAMHS Tier 2 and 3 | OCD with co-morbidity or poor response to initial treatment | Assess, review, discuss options<br><br>CBT (including ERP), then consider combined treatments of CBT (including ERP) with SSRI, alternative SSRI or clomipramine |
| **Step 3**<br>CAMHS Tiers 1 and 2 | Management and initial treatment | Guided self-help, CBT (including ERP), involve family/carers and consider involving school |
| **Step 2**<br>CAMHS Tier 1 | Recognition and assessment | Detect, educate, discuss treatment options, signpost voluntary support agencies, provide support to young people, families/carers/schools<br>Refer if necessary |
| **Step 1**<br>Individuals, public organisations, NHS | Awareness and recognition | Provide, seek and share information about OCD and its impact on individuals and families/carers |

**Figure 31.1** National Institute for Health and Care Excellence (NICE) stepped-care model for obsessive compulsive disorder (OCD) in children and adolescents [17]. CAMHS, Child and Adolescent Mental Health Service; CBT, cognitive behavioural therapy; ERP, exposure and response prevention; SSRI, selective serotonin reuptake inhibitor. *Source:* Adapted from NICE Guideline 31, The Stepped-Care Model, 2005.

### OCD as An 'Intruder'

An 'externalizing' approach to the disorder, giving it a name, and learning how to 'fight' it, is a useful technique in child and adolescent treatment [20]. The child is helped to see OCD as an 'intruder', who is spoiling their life by seeking to control their thoughts and actions. Treatment is aimed at giving the child and family effective means of controlling the intruder – saying 'no' to OCD.

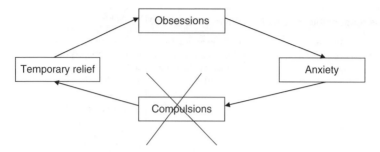

**Figure 31.2** The 'vicious cycle of obsessive compulsive disorder' (OCD). Obsessions generate anxiety, whilst compulsive rituals are performed to reduce the anxiety, but in fact this produces only temporary relief and reinforces the cycle. Exposure and response prevention (ERP) acts by exposing a young person to the feared situation whilst resisting compulsions, in a graded manner, to break this cycle.

CBT protocols are generally based on ERP: 'exposure' (facing up to the feared stimulus) and 'response-prevention' (resisting the urge to carry out a ritual in these circumstances) [20]. In adult and child studies, ERP appears to be a critical therapeutic component. Cognitive protocols, which tackle underlying beliefs about connections between thoughts and behaviours, are also being evaluated [21].

Cognitive behavioural therapy involves a detailed assessment of the problem, often starting with a symptom diary. Resisting compulsions makes OCD sufferers very anxious, and it is important for them to learn how to confront this anxiety. Step-by-step exposure to the anxiety-provoking situation, while resisting the urge to respond with compulsive behaviour, shows the patient that their anxiety levels steadily decrease under these conditions, and they come to realize that compulsive behaviour is not the only way to relieve their anxiety. The young person designs their treatment programme with the therapist, so that they can steadily overcome their fears. 'Accommodation', the participation by family members in OCD rituals, elicited by their child's distress and unwittingly reinforcing the OCD, is common, reported in up to 75% of parents [22]. Families need to learn about OCD and how to help their child fight back [22,23]. CBT is not usually a long treatment and most children respond in 8 to 12 sessions.

### Medication

There is extensive evidence demonstrating efficacy of SRIs in adults and young people. Clomipramine, an SRI, remains a useful drug for some, although its side-effect profile makes it generally less acceptable than SSRIs, which are now first-line medications. All SSRIs appear to be equally effective [15]. There has been concern about the use of SSRIs in depressed young people, with meta-analyses suggesting low levels of efficacy and increased behavioural activation including suicidal behaviours, although recent evidence is more positive. In contrast, SSRIs appear effective in paediatric OCD, with numbers needed to treat between 2 and 10, with no significant evidence of increased suicidality [24,25]. However, given concerns, there should be close monitoring for side-effects.

Only sertraline and fluvoxamine are licensed for OCD treatment in children in the UK, but other SSRIs could be used 'off-label' by a specialist in exceptional circumstances.

For example, in co-morbid depression, SSRIs should be used with caution, and only fluoxetine is licensed for depressed youths.

About 70% of individuals with OCD respond to medication, and if a first SSRI is ineffective or not tolerated, it is worth trying a second. Clomipramine and SSRIs have a delayed onset of action, with full therapeutic effects not apparent for 8–12 weeks. It is therefore worth awaiting a response at a moderate therapeutic dose, rather than moving rapidly to high doses that increase the chances of side-effects. The optimal dose is variable and should be determined by titrating from a low starting dose. Effective doses needed for adult OCD seem to be higher than for depression, which may also be the case in younger people.

## Prognosis and Ongoing Care

Early detection and treatment are likely to minimize secondary disabilities and continuation into adulthood, but few assertively treated early-onset cohorts have been followed up long term. These have found a persistence rate of 40%, and further studies into predictors of outcome and augmentation strategies are needed [26,27]. If a young person has responded to medication, treatment should continue for at least 6 months after remission [17]. CBT should give individuals strategies for dealing with transient symptom recurrence, and theoretically this obviates the need in some people for long-term medication. Many people with early-onset OCD respond to treatment and lead fully functioning lives. It is important that throughout the life span, people with OCD should have access to support as needed, and NICE recommends that if relapse occurs, they should be seen as soon as possible, rather than placed on routine waiting lists.

## References

1 Torp NC, Dahl K, Skarphedinsson G et al. (2015). Predictors associated with improved cognitive-behavioral therapy outcome in pediatric obsessive-compulsive disorder. Journal of the American Academy of Child & Adolescent Psychiatry, 54, 200–207.

2 Chowdhury U, Frampton I, Heyman I (2004) Clinical characteristics of young people referred to an obsessive compulsive disorder clinic in the United Kingdom. Clinical Child Psychology and Psychiatry, 9, 395–401.

3 Heyman I, Fombonne E, Simmons H et al. (2001) Prevalence of obsessive-compulsive disorder in the British nationwide survey of child mental health. British Journal of Psychiatry, 179, 324–329.

4 Uher R, Heyman I, Mortimore C et al. (2007) Screening young people for obsessive-compulsive disorder. British Journal of Psychiatry, 191, 353–354.

5 Leckman JF, Bloch MH, King RA (2009) Symptom dimensions and subtypes of obsessive-compulsive disorder: a developmental perspective. Dialogues in Clinical Neuroscience, 11, 21–33.

6 Pauls DL, Abramovitch A, Rauch SL et al. (2014) Obsessive-compulsive disorder: an integrative genetic and neurobiological perspective. Nature Reviews Neuroscience, 15, 410–424.

7  Van Grootheest DS, Cath DC, Beekan AT et al. (2005) Twin studies on obsessive-compulsive disorder: a review. Twin Research and Human Genetics, 8, 450–458.

8  Macerollo A, Martino D (2013) Pediatric autoimmune neuropsychiatric disorders associated with streptococcal infections (PANDAS): an evolving concept. Tremor Other Hyperkinet Mov, 3, tre-03-167-4158-7.

9  Scahill L, Riddle MA, McSwiggin-Hardin M et al. (1997) Children's Yale-Brown Obsessive Compulsive Scale: reliability and validity. Journal of the American Academy of Child and Adolescent Psychiatry, 36, 844–852.

10  Veale D, Freeston M, Krebs G et al. (2009) Risk assessment and management in obsessive-compulsive disorder. Advances in Psychiatric Treatment, 15, 332–343.

11  Storch EA, Merlo LJ, Larson MJ et al. (2008) Impact of comorbidity on cognitive-behavioural therapy response in pediatric obsessive-compulsive disorder. Journal of the American Academy of Child and Adolescent Psychiatry, 47, 583–592.

12  Sukhodolsky DG1, Gorman BS, Scahill L et al. (2013) Exposure and response prevention with or without parent management training for children with obsessive-compulsive disorder complicated by disruptive behavior: a multiple-baseline across-responses design study. Journal of Anxiety Disorders, 27, 298–305.

13  March JS, Franklin ME, Leonard H et al. (2007) Tics moderate treatment outcome with sertraline but not cognitive-behavior therapy in pediatric obsessive-compulsive disorder. Biological Psychiatry, 61, 344–347.

14  McGuire JF, Piacentini J, Lewin AB et al. (2015) A meta-analysis of cognitive behavior therapy and medication for child obsessive-compulsive disorder: moderators of treatment efficacy, response and remission. Depress Anxiety, 32, 580–593.

15  Ivarson I, Skarphedinsson G, Kornør H et al. (2015) The place of and evidence for serotonin reuptake inhibitors (SRIs) for obsessive compulsive disorder (OCD) in children and adolescents: Views based on a systematic review and meta-analysis. Psychiatry Research, 227, 93–103.

16  Skarphedinsson G, Weidle B, Thomsen PH (2014) Continued cognitive-behaviour therapy versus sertraline for children and adolescents with obsessive compulsive disorder that were non-responders to cognitive-behaviour therapy: a randomized controlled trial. European Child and Adolescent Psychiatry, 24, 591–602.

17  National Institute for Health and Care Excellence (2005) Obsessive-compulsive disorder: core interventions in the treatment of obsessive-compulsive disorder and body dysmorphic disorder. Clinical Guideline 31. London: NICE. http://www.nice.org.uk/nicemedia/pdf/cg031fullguideline.pdf.

18  Turner CM, Mataiz-Cols D, Lovell K et al. (2014) Telephone cognitive-behavioural therapy for adolescents with obsessive-compulsive disorder: a randomized controlled non-inferiority trial. Journal of the American Academy of Child and Adolescent Psychiatry, 53, 1298–1307.

19  Lenhard F, Vigerland S, Andersson E et al. (2014) Internet-delivered cognitive behaviour therapy for youth with obsessive compulsive disorder: an open trial. PLoS ONE 9, e100773.

20  Derisley J, Heyman I, Robinson S et al. (2008) Breaking Free from OCD. A CBT Guide for Young People and Their Families. London: Jessica Kingsley Publishers.

21  Williams TI, Shafran R (2015) Obsessive-compulsive disorder in young people. BJPsych Advances 21, 196–205.

22  Peris TS, Bergman L, Langely A et al. (2008) Correlates of accommodation of pediatric obsessive-compulsive disorder: parent, child and family characteristics. Journal of the American Academy of Child and Adolescent Psychiatry, 47, 1173–1181.

23  Freeman JB, Garcia AM, Coyne L et al. (2008) Early childhood OCD: preliminary findings from a family-based cognitive-behavioural approach. Journal of the American Academy of Child and Adolescent Psychiatry, 47, 593–602.

24  March JS, Klee, BJ, Kremer CM (2006) Treatment benefit and the risk of suicidality in multicenter, randomized, controlled trials of sertraline in children and adolescents. Journal of Child and Adolescent Psychopharmacology, 16, 91–102.

25  Bridge JA, Iyengar S, Salary CB, et al. (2007) Clinical response and risk for reported suicidal ideation and suicide attempts in pediatric antidepressant treatment: a meta-analysis of randomized controlled trials. Journal of the American Medical Association, 297, 1683–1696.

26  Pediatric OCD Treatment Study (POTS) Team (2004) Cognitive-behavior therapy, sertraline, and their combination for children and adolescents with obsessive-compulsive disorder: the Pediatric OCD Treatment Study (POTS) randomized controlled trial. Journal of the American Medical Association, 292, 1969–1976.

27  Micali N, Heyman I, Perez M et al. (2010) Long term outcomes of obsessive-compulsive disorder: follow-up of 143 children and adolescents. British Journal of Psychiatry, 197, 128–134.

## Further Reading

Derisley J, Heyman I, Robinson S et al. (2008) Breaking Free from OCD. A CBT Guide for Young People and Their Families. London: Jessica Kingsley Publishers.

March JS, Benton CM (2007) Talking Back to OCD: the Program that Helps Kids and Teens Say "No Way" – and Parents to Say "Way to Go." New York: Guildford Press. (both of these are CBT self-help books that young people could work through alone, or ideally with a parent or therapist).

Wagner A (2002) Up and Down the Worry Hill: A Children's Book about Obsessive-Compulsive Disorder and Its Treatment. New York: Lighthouse Press. (An illustrated book designed to help parents and professionals explain OCD to younger children through the story of "Casey", a young boy with OCD).

Waltz M (2000) Obsessive Compulsive Disorder: Help for Children and Adolescents. Patient Center Guides, USA. (Written by a woman with OCD who has two children with OCD, this book provides information about OCD, its diagnosis and treatment and advice for working with schools.)

Wells J (2006) Touch and Go Joe. An Adolescent's experience of OCD. Jessica London: Kingsley Publishers. (A revealing insight into the life of a teenager with OCD).

## Internet Resources

OCD youth: http://ocdyouth.iop.kcl.ac.uk/
OCD Action: www.ocdaction.org.uk
US OC Foundation: www.ocfoundation.org

32

# Medically Unexplained Symptoms/Functional Symptoms in Children and Adolescents

*Eve McAllister, Laura Markham, Anna Coughtrey and Isobel Heyman*

## Introduction

Medically unexplained symptoms (MUS) are somatic symptoms that are not explained by medical pathology. The most common MUS reported by children and young people are abdominal pain, headaches, musculoskeletal pain, fatigue, dizziness and loss of appetite [1]. These physical symptoms are usually transient but can be long-lasting and cause significant distress and impairment in children's functioning.

The term MUS has been widely criticized, as it implies that symptoms are all in the mind and reinforces dualistic conceptions of a separation between mind and body, which can lead to a failure to engage patients in appropriate treatments [2]. Current guidance in the United Kingdom recommends that when engaging or treating patients with MUS, patients are diagnosed with a specific syndrome which describes their key symptoms without inferring that the aetiology is psychological [3]. In paediatric settings, symptoms are classified depending on the system that they impact upon; for example, if the primary complaint is gastrointestinal, then a diagnosis of 'functional abdominal pain' (FAP) or 'irritable bowel syndrome' (IBS) may be given. Alternatively, in child mental health or psychiatric settings, symptoms are likely to be classified as 'somatic symptom and related disorders' including somatoform disorders and dissociative (conversion) disorders [*Diagnostic and Statistical Manual of Mental Disorders, 5th edition* (DSM-5) and *International Classification of Mental and Behavioural Disorders, 10th revision* (ICD-10)]. DSM-5 has also faced criticism due to the inclusion of patients with physical health problems, with some critics believing this may lead to misdiagnosis before full medical investigations have taken place [4]. Proponents conversely consider the inclusion of patients with physical health problems to be helpful, as many patients have physically understood symptoms in addition to functional symptoms and require access to psychological intervention to reduce their excessive functional disability.

The challenges in the classification of symptoms in this population are discussed widely elsewhere [1–3]. In this chapter, we will use specific diagnoses (e.g. IBS) throughout to describe children's central functional symptoms and will use the term FS to describe symptoms without a specific diagnostic label.

*Child Psychology and Psychiatry: Frameworks for Clinical Training and Practice,* Third Edition.
Edited by David Skuse, Helen Bruce and Linda Dowdney.
© 2017 John Wiley & Sons, Ltd. Published 2017 by John Wiley & Sons, Ltd.

## Epidemiology

To date, longitudinal prevalence studies have been limited by the use of retrospective reporting, not incorporating a medical examination and frequently failing to identify children who present with multiple symptoms. Nonetheless, several studies have consistently reported that FS are common, with approximately 24% of children and adolescents reporting weekly or bi-weekly FS [1], and 13% of children meeting DSM-IV diagnostic criteria for a somatoform disorder [5,6].

A recent meta-analysis of 58 studies found that FAP (including IBS) was the most common childhood FS, with a prevalence rate of 13.5% [7]. Estimates of the prevalence of chronic fatigue syndrome (CFS) were smaller, with rates ranging from zero in a telephone survey in Kansas, to approximately 2% in a community survey of 6- to 17-year-olds where diagnoses of CFS were confirmed by a paediatrician [8]. Conversion disorder, which includes children who experience functional motor and sensory symptoms such as abnormal movements and non-epileptic seizures, is less frequently identified (1.30 per 100 000 cases over a 12-month period in the UK) [8] and is normally treated in specialist settings. However, it is important to note that some children meet criteria for more than one disorder, that the presentation of FS can change over time, and that FS can co-occur with other psychiatric disorders (e.g. depression or an anxiety disorder) [5].

## Factors Relevant to the Development, Severity and Persistence of FS

There are multiple factors that are relevant to the development and maintenance of FS. These include co-morbidity with other psychiatric disorders, genetic and immune factors, sex (more common in females), family influences, traumatic life events and psychosocial factors. We have summarized some key findings in Box 32.1; however, these factors are covered in more detail in other papers [1,2,8–11].

A strong association between FS and anxiety and depressive symptoms in children is well established [7,9–11]. For example, FAP was found to be co-morbid with anxiety or depression in 82% of cases (42% anxiety, 26% depressive disorders), and headache was found to be co-morbid with a psychiatric disorder in 84% of cases, with anxiety disorders and depression being the most common (35% anxiety, 23% depressive disorders) [9]. As physical symptoms are central to the diagnosis of FS and to the diagnosis of anxiety disorders and depression, it may not be helpful for clinicians to make subjective judgments as to whether physical symptoms are explained by a mood disorder, or by FS. It has also been reasoned that FS may indicate an emotional disorder, even when cognitive symptoms of anxiety and depression are not recognized [11].

Several genetic, familial, infection-related, immune and endocrine factors have been implicated in the development of FS, although evidence for the specific role of these factors is unclear. Cross-sectional, retrospective-cohort and population-based studies have reported a viral illness preceding the onset of childhood CFS and/or evidence that the child has experienced the Epstein–Barr virus [8]. Several studies have also reported post-infectious IBS symptoms in children several years after an initial illness, although

---

**Box 32.1  Factors relevant to the development, severity and persistence of functional symptoms**

**Family factors**

Functional symptoms in children are associated with parental distress, depression in mothers, marital problems and mothers reporting of their own health difficulties. Children of mothers with chronic FS have higher numbers of GP consultations and reported health problems than children of mothers with explained chronic illness, or those without chronic illness [13]. An association between non-intact families, less parental education and family support and FS has also been demonstrated. Children who receive parental encouragement of illness behaviour, e.g. special privileges when reporting symptoms, have also been found to report more somatic symptoms [2].

**Traumatic life events**

A link has been demonstrated between childhood neglectful, abusive and traumatic experiences and FS in adults, although similar associations have not been strongly demonstrated in children. In a recent meta-analysis exploring FAP, it was found that significantly more children reported more frequent punishment by parents, parental job loss and hospitalization for another illness. In addition, any form of abuse was associated with an increase in the prevalence of FAP [7].

**Personality and psychosocial factors**

Lower socio-economic status and poverty, starting and changing school, poorer school attainment and difficulties in getting along with peers and teachers have predicted higher FS scores in children [2]. Anecdotal reports by experts have also reported both high achieving and compliant children falling ill with functional symptom disorders and equally young people with learning difficulties, although these links have been difficult to demonstrate. There is evidence however to suggest that parental expectations of IQ are significantly higher for young people with CFS than controls. Interestingly, children's own estimates of their IQ were not as high, and no actual differences were found on measured IQ between children with CFS and controls [8].

---

this pattern was not found in a prospective study in adults [12]. Genetic factors for FS have also been indicated, although no single disordered physiological process has been identified. Cross-sectional and twin studies have shown high rates of CFS and IBS reported within families. Additionally, abnormalities in immune function and endocrine factors have also been found in both children with CFS and those with IBS [8,12]. Stress reactivity, which is known to be a factor in internalizing disorders [2], is also likely to also play a role in FS, due to the high co-morbidity rates between these disorders.

**Course of Illness**

The majority of FS reported in children have been found to resolve after a few weeks, with only a minority of cases going on to result in greater impairment [1]. It has been shown, however, that when FS persist they are associated with distress, social difficulties, poor school attendance and performance. Single FS have also been shown to predict multiple FS later in life [1,2,11].

## Assessment

Children who have FS that result in clinically significant impairment should be referred to paediatricians or specialist child and adolescent mental health services. Children with minor symptoms should be managed by their general practitioner within primary care.

The partnership between the clinician and patient is very important and engagement is a key part of the assessment process. Clinicians should ensure they acknowledge the patients suffering and family concerns and have a non-judgmental approach to symptoms. It is important to determine what medical investigations have been carried out and is essential that clinicians convey that they believe the patient's experiences of FS to be genuine. In exploring FS, clinicians should consider developmental, cognitive, biological and psychosocial factors and gather information from the whole family, as poor concordance has been shown between parents and children's reporting of FS and functional impairment [2].

The goal of assessment is to develop a shared understanding of FS that emphasizes the link between the body and mind to avoid dualism. There should be an emphasis on treatment goals that focus on the restoration of function. The clinician should gradually assess mechanisms that may be contributing to the maintenance of symptoms. This may include assessing cognitive abilities through psychometric testing, if indicators are present that unidentified learning difficulties could be contributing to a child's presenting difficulties (e.g. poor attainment in school). It is also important to fully explore mental health difficulties due to their high rates of co-morbidity with FS and to offer evidence-based treatments for these difficulties when present.

A range of measures can be used to enable clinicians to discuss a child's somatic and mental health symptoms in a non-judgmental way (see Boxes 32.2 and 32.3).

---

**Box 32.2  Measures of somatization**

Measures include:

- the Child Somatization Inventory of the Child Behaviour Checklist
- the Child Somatization Inventory
- the Fatigue Scale
- the Functional Disability Inventory and objective measures of functional impairment such as school attendance rates and daily diaries of functional impairment, pain etc. [14].

Measures which explore mental health difficulties commonly co-morbid with FS, such as depression and anxiety, and those which consider illness attitudes (e.g. catastrophizing) will also provide useful information.

---

---

**Box 32.3 Referral to a child mental health team**

Referral to a child mental health team may be indicated when:

- function is significantly limited;
- the child presents with features of depression or anxiety, or another treatable mental health condition such as body dysmorphic disorder;
- reassurance, explanation, general advice and symptom specific standard treatment has not worked;
- patients may benefit from anti-depressant medication, cognitive behavioural therapy, or other behavioural interventions.

---

## Treatment

### Effectiveness of Psychological Treatment

Somatization in children is associated with marked impairment of daily functioning and high medical utilization [15]. Overall, the evidence concerning successful ways of managing and treating unexplained symptoms or disorders in children is surprisingly limited, considering the marked impact of these difficulties on daily functioning, high prevalence and significant medical utilization [2]. The literature also has important limitations, which in turn weaken the conclusions that can be drawn.

These limitations include the heterogeneity of conditions, inconsistent definitions of the disorder, variation in outcome measures and duration of follow-up. While there is a lack of methodologically rigorous clinical trials evaluating treatment for FS and there is no specific NICE guidance for treating MUS/FS, the Department of Health (2009) [16] clearly states that commissioning strategies need to address the psychological component of MUS.

Psychological therapies are increasingly emerging as effective interventions to treat children with FS, and recent reviews of the treatment of these are encouraging. Psychological interventions are specifically designed to alter psychological processes considered to underlie, contribute to or maintain pain, distress and disability. Psychological interventions that have been evaluated in randomized control trials include cognitive behavioural therapy (CBT) and relaxation and biofeedback. These aim to effectively control pain and alter situational, emotional, familial and behavioural factors that play a role in pain or related consequences [17]. The vast majority of these studies evaluate the effectiveness of these treatments for headaches and recurrent abdominal pain; however, there are also some studies exploring the effectiveness of psychological treatment for children with CFS and musculoskeletal or disease-related pain.

A recent Cochrane review [18] of psychological treatment for headache (including migraine), abdominal pain, chronic pain, fibromyalgia and IBS found that psychological treatments delivered face-to-face are effective in reducing pain intensity and disability for children and adolescents with headache, and therapeutic gains are maintained over follow-up (ranging from 3 to 12 months post-treatment). Psychological therapies were also beneficial at reducing anxiety post-treatment for headache. For non-headache conditions, psychological treatments were found to be beneficial for pain and disability post-treatment, but these effects were not maintained at follow-up. The review concludes that there is still limited evidence to suggest that psychological therapies for chronic pain have an effect on co-occurring anxiety and depression.

The most consistent evidence exists for CBT [17]. This model addresses biological, affective, behavioural and cognitive elements of the illness. The fundamental assumption of a CBT model is that the perpetuating domains interact to maintain symptoms, disability and distress, and that change in one domain will affect change in the others. There are an increasing number of controlled trials evaluating the effectiveness of CBT in treating FS. In FAP, Levy *et al.* [19] demonstrated the effectiveness of a three-session intervention of CBT treatment targeting parents' responses to their children's pain complaints and children's coping responses [19]. Compared with an educational control condition, children who completed the three-session CBT programme reported a reduction in pain and gastrointestinal symptom severity. Three randomized controlled trials have provided encouraging evidence for CBT treatment of CFS in young people. Following treatment there were improvements in levels of fatigue, school attendance and functionality [8].

Recent studies have highlighted the importance of exploring treatments targeting the co-occurring mental health disorders as part of the intervention [20]. Warner *et al.* [21] adapted an empirically supported anxiety intervention (Kendall's Coping Cat) to include a direct focus on chronic and impairing physical symptoms in children seeking medical care for FS (chest pain and headaches) and co-morbid anxiety. Adaptations included a focus on the link between physical sensations and emotions. Overall self- and parental ratings indicated reductions in children's somatic discomfort and anxiety. The results indicate that at a 3-month follow-up, the intervention group maintained clinical improvements with some indication of continued gains. This investigation suggests that a modified, empirically based intervention for anxiety disorders expanded to address pervasive FS may be effective for ameliorating children's differing types of somatic complaints.

### Psychopharmacological Treatment

Psychopharmacological treatments (e.g. selective serotonin reuptake inhibitors) have been found to be of limited efficacy in adults with FS [22]. There is inadequate published evidence for the efficacy of psychopharmacological interventions in childhood FAP and IBS [23]. Results are very preliminary, may include side-effects and often there is no long-term follow-up, with poor controls, or no control group.

Features of a treatment programme are given in Box 32.4.

## Current Challenges and Future Directions

The identification and treatment of children with FS is challenging because of the multiple settings in which they present and the lack of shared terminology and collaborative working between medical and mental health professionals. In future it will be important to increase consistency in the language used to describe FS and collaborative working between primary care, paediatric and child mental health systems. It will also be

---

**Box 32.4  Features of a treatment programme for functional symptoms**

There are few formally developed protocols for functional symptoms in children; however, cognitive behavioural therapy (CBT)-based treatment should include the following:

- Regular communication with all key professionals involved in a child's care to prevent unnecessary investigations, provide integrated care and enable professionals to work together to implement collaborative interventions and monitor progress.
- Working closely with the patient's network including school.
- Parent involvement.
- Determining the child's goals for recovery – set goals which aim to improve functioning.
- CBT techniques to reduce pain and anxiety (i.e. psycho-education, relaxation, cognitive restructuring, exposure to feared situations, etc.).
- Increased emphasis on the relationship between somatic symptoms and anxiety (e.g. daily monitoring of physical pain and anxiety).
- Expanded focus of cognitive restructuring to gain more detailed cognitions related to illness, such as, 'I will feel nauseous on the train, and I will not be able to find a bathroom'.
- Use of exposure tasks targeting physical pain (e.g. 'If I eat pizza my stomach will hurt').
- The programme should encourage a gradual return to previous activities, to reverse changes which are secondary to inactivity.
- Instruction in diaphragmatic breathing to reduce physical discomfort.
- It will also be important to address pain catastrophizing within treatment. Pain catastrophizing has been found to be associated with pain intensity. It has been found that pain catastrophizing may be a mediator of relationships between pain and disability, with greater pain catastrophizing resulting in greater functional impairment. Children's pain catastrophizing has also been found to be predictive of greater protective parenting responses [24].
- If a child experiences muscle pains following long period in bed or wheelchair-bound, it may be appropriate to recommend graded increases in physical activity with support from physiotherapy.

---

important to identify FS early and offer appropriate stepped-care treatment, with clear care pathways between the steps. Future directions include, identifying and treating common mental health conditions within children with FS, in addition to treating FS, due to the high co-morbidity rates with psychiatric disorders, particularly depression and anxiety disorders. Future research on the efficacy of psychological treatments for non-headache conditions such as musculoskeletal pain and complex regional pain will also be important in identifying appropriate psychological treatments, as will establishing the efficacy of online psychological interventions to increase accessibility to appropriate treatment.

Functional symptoms consume large amounts of healthcare time, represent substantial cost, and, if undetected or misunderstood, can result in prolonged, unnecessary and even harmful investigations and interventions. Identification in children can lead to early effective treatments and may prevent long-term disabilities.

# References

1 Schulte IE, Petermann F (2011) Somatoform disorders: 30 years of debate about criteria! What about children and adolescents? Journal of Psychosomatic Research, 70, 218–228.

2 Eminson DM (2007) Medically unexplained symptoms in children and adolescents. Clinical Psychology Review, 27, 855–871.

3 Improving Access to Psychological Therapies (2014) Medically Unexplained Symptoms/ FS: Positive Practice Guide. Online: https://www.uea.ac.uk/documents/246046/11991919/medically-unexplained-symptoms-positive-practice-guide-.pdf/ac806084-4058-4a2f-89f9-17d04eff6a3b. Accessed: January 2017.

4 Frances A (2013) The new somatic symptom disorder in DSM-5 risks mislabelling many people as mentally ill. British Medical Journal, 346, f1580.

5 Lieb R, Pfister H, Mastaler M, Witchen H-U (2000) Somatoform syndromes and disorders in a representative sample of adolescents and young adults: prevalence, comorbidity and impairment. Acta Psychiatrica Scandinavica, 101, 194–208.

6 Essau CA, Conradt J, Petermann F (2000) Haeufigkeit und Komorbiditaet Somatoformer Stoerungenbei Jugendlichen. Ergebnisse der Bremer Jugendstudie (Prevalence and comorbidity of somatoform disorders in adolescents). Results of the Bremen Youth Study). Z Klin Psychol Psychother, 29, 97–108.

7 Korterink JJ, Diederen K, Benninga MA, Tabbers MM (2015) Epidemiology of pediatric functional abdominal pain disorders: A meta-analysis. PLoS ONE, 10, 1371.

8 Lievesley K, Rimes KA, Chandler T (2014) A review of the predisposing, precipitating and perpetuating factors in chronic fatigue syndrome in children and adolescents. Clinical Psychology Review, 34, 233–248.

9 Liakopoulou-Kairis M, Alifieraki T, Protabora D et al. (2002) Recurrent abdominal pain and headache- psychopathology, life events and family functioning. European Child and Adolescent Psychiatry, 11, 115–122.

10 Egger HL, Costello EJ, Erkanli A, Angold A (1999) Somatic complaints and psychopathology in children and adolescents: Stomach aches, musculoskeletal pains, and headaches. Journal of the American Academy of Child and Adolescent Psychiatry, 38, 852–860.

11 Campo JV (2012) Annual Research Review: Functional somatic symptoms and associated anxiety and depression – developmental psychopathology in pediatric practice. Journal of Child Psychology and Psychiatry, 53, 575–592.

12 Sandhu BK, Paul SP (2014) Irritable bowel syndrome in children: Pathogenesis, diagnosis and evidence-based treatment. World Journal of Gastroenterology, 20, 6013–6023.

13 Craig TKJ, Cox AD, Klein K (2002) Intergenerational transmission of somatisation behaviour: a study of chronic somatizers and their children. Psychological Medicine, 3, 805–816.

14 Gledhill J, Garralda ME (2006) FS and somatoform disorders in children and adolescents: The role of standardised measures in assessment. Child and Adolescent Mental Health, 11, 208–214.

15 Hunfeld JAM, Perquin CW, Bertina W et al. (2002) Stability of pain parameters and pain related quality of life in adolescents with persistent pain: a three-year follow-up. Clinical Journal of Pain, 18, 99–106.

16 Department of Health (2009) Psychological assessment and treatment for medically unexplained symptoms and long-term conditions. Online: https://www.nice.org.uk/savingsandproductivityandlocalpracticeresource?ci=http%3a%2f%2farms.evidence.nhs.uk%2fresources%2fQIPP%2f29417%2fattachment%3fniceorg%3dtrue.

17 Deary V, Chalder T, Sharpe M (2007) The cognitive behavioural model of medically unexplained symptoms: a theoretical and empirical review. Clinical Psychology Review, 27, 781–797.

18 Eccleston C, Palermo TM, Williams AC et al. (2014) Psychological therapies for the management of chronic and recurrent pain in children and adolescents. Cochrane Database System Reviews, 5, CD003968.

19 Levy RL, Langer S, Walker LS et al. (2010) Cognitive Behavioural therapy for functional abdominal pain and their parents decreases pain and other symptoms. American Journal of Gastroenterology, 105, 946–956.

20 Campo JV, Bridge J, Ehmann M et al. (2004) Recurrent abdominal pain, anxiety and depression in primary care. Paediatrics, 113, 817–824.

21 Warner CM, Colognori D, Kim R et al. Cognitive behavioural treatment of persistent functional somatic complaints and paediatric anxiety: an initial controlled trial. Depression and Anxiety, 28, 551–559.

22 Kleinstäuber M1, Witthöft M, Steffanowski A et al. (2014) Pharmacological interventions for somatoform disorders in adults. Cochrane Database of Systematic Reviews, Nov 7, 11, CD010628. doi: 10.1002/14651858.CD010628.pub2.

23 Saps M, Youssef N, Miranda A et al. (2009) Multicenter, randomized, placebo-controlled trial of amitriptyline in children with functional gastrointestinal disorders. Gastroenterology, 137, 1261–1269.

24 Guite JW1, McCue RL, Sherker JL et al. (2011) Relationships among pain, protective parental responses, and disability for adolescents with chronic musculoskeletal pain: the mediating role of pain catastrophizing. Clinical Journal of Pain, 27, 775–781.

# 33

# Paediatric Bipolar Disorder

*Anthony James*

## Introduction

Paediatric bipolar disorder (PBD) (i.e. onset before 18 years) is a serious mood disorder defined by episodes of mania or hypomania and depression. It is often associated with considerable functional impairment and suicidality. There has been increased recognition of this disorder and, more recently, a clearer consensus upon definition.

### Diagnostic Criteria

The diagnosis of bipolar disorder in the *ICD-10 Classification of Mental and Behavioural Disorders, 10th revision* (ICD-10) [1] requires elation in a manic or hypomanic episode, as well as two or more episodes of hypomania, mania or depression. For mania this mood change must be prominent and sustained for at least a week, unless severe enough to require hospital admission [see Box 33.1 for the *Diagnostic and Statistical Manual of Mental Disorders, 5th edition* (DSM-5) [2] criteria].

According to DSM-5 there are three types of bipolar disorder:

- type I – least one manic episode (no major depressive episode required);
- type II – at least one hypomanic episode plus at least one major depressive episode;
- 'bipolar not otherwise specified" (BP-NOS) – symptoms not meeting criteria (duration) for a specific type of bipolar disorder.

The BP-NOS type is not endorsed by the National Institute for Health and Care Excellence (NICE) for use in younger children.

A major change in DSM-5 is the stipulation that irritable or euphoric mood in mania/hypomania should last 'most of the day nearly every day'. Previously, some US authorities had conceptualized bipolar disorder in children or adolescents as a chronic illness, with multiple fluctuations in mood states often occurring within a single day. Crucially, as for adults, bipolar disorder in children and adolescents is now regarded an *episodic* illness, with distinct periods (days to weeks) of mania, depression and euthymia.

*Child Psychology and Psychiatry: Frameworks for Clinical Training and Practice,* Third Edition.
Edited by David Skuse, Helen Bruce and Linda Dowdney.
© 2017 John Wiley & Sons, Ltd. Published 2017 by John Wiley & Sons, Ltd.

---

**Box 33.1 Diagnostic and Statistical Manual of Mental Disorders, 5th edition (DSM-5) criteria for bipolar disorder**

**Manic episode**

A manic episode includes a period of at least 1 week during which the person is in an abnormally and persistently elevated or irritable mood. This period of mania must be marked by three of the following symptoms to a significant degree. If the person is only irritable, they must experience four of the following symptoms:

1) Inflated self-esteem or grandiosity (ranges from uncritical self-confidence to a delusional sense of expertise).
2) Decreased need for sleep.
3) Intensified speech (possible characteristics: loud, rapid and difficult to interrupt, a focus on sounds, theatrics and self-amusement, non-stop talking regardless of other person's participation/interest, angry tirades).
4) Rapid jumping around of ideas or feels like thoughts are racing.
5) Distractibility (attention easily pulled away by irrelevant/unimportant things).
6) Increase in goal-directed activity (i.e. excessively plans and/or pursues a goal; either social, work/school or sexual) or psychomotor agitation (such as pacing, inability to sit still, pulling on skin or clothing).
7) Excessive involvement in pleasurable activities that have a high-risk consequence.

**Hypomanic episode**

A hypomanic episode is very similar to a manic one, but less intense. It is only required to persist for 4 days and it should be observable by others that the person is noticeably different from his or her regular self.

**Mixed episode**

A mixed episode would fulfil the symptom requirements for both a major depressive episode and a manic episode nearly every day, but the mixed symptoms only need to last for a 1-week period.

---

## Differential Diagnosis

Anxiety is a common co-morbid diagnosis. However, the symptom overlap between attention deficit hyperactivity disorder (ADHD) and PBD creates the greatest diagnostic problems. The symptoms of grandiosity, elated mood, flight of ideas and decreased need for sleep can reliably differentiate the two. Bipolar disorder can be associated with a sudden onset of severe behavioural disturbance. Such disturbance contrasts with the usually longer-standing conduct disorder. A family history of affective disorder rather than conduct or personality disorder may aid diagnosis. In children, mood instability and irritability associated with pervasive developmental disorders need to be noted, while in adolescence affective instability seen in cases of borderline personality disorder can cause diagnostic confusion. In the latter case there may well be considerable overlap, with reports of 15% of patients with bipolar disorder having borderline personality disorder. Psychosis in adolescence, particularly if florid with mood-incongruent hallucinations and thought disorder, has been misdiagnosed as schizophrenia. Factors in favour of a diagnosis of schizophrenia include premorbid personality abnormalities, schizotypal personality disorder, a family history of schizophrenia, and an insidious onset of psychosis. Mania needs to be distinguished from drug-induced states secondary to drug misuse or, rarely, from medical treatments such as steroids.

## Epidemiology

The peak onset of bipolar disorder is in the 15- to 19-year-old group, with males and females equally represented. Retrospective studies in adults with bipolar disorder report that over 50% of patients experience the onset of bipolar disorder before 20 years of age [3]. The initial presentation is mostly commonly depression; around 20–30% of depressed children, particularly those with psychosis, a family history of bipolar disorder and or pharmacologically induced mania, eventually develop bipolar disorder [4].

A meta-analysis of national epidemiological surveys found that the rate of narrowly defined PBD was 1.8% [5], with no significant difference between US and non-US studies, including prepubertal patients. However, when using broader diagnostic criteria, including BP-NOS, the rates of PBD rose to 6.7% in the US, which was significantly higher than the 2.4% reported in other countries.

In clinical settings, the prevalence of BD has increased markedly in the US in the past decade; similar trends are not as apparent in other countries. For example, a 40-fold increase in outpatient visits for PBD was reported in the US between 1994 and 1995 and between 2002 and 2003 [6]. However, recent work has shown that between 2000 and 2010 there was a 72-fold difference in discharge rates for PBD in children and adolescents between the US and England (US, 100.9/100 000 population vs England, 1.4/100 000 population), with no increase in rates during this period [7]. This disparity in discharge rates is specific for PBD, and points to likely differences in diagnostic practice in the US.

Partly as a result of the confusion and over-diagnosis of PBD in the US, 'disruptive mood dysregulation disorder' (DMDD) has been introduced into DSM-5. DMDD is characterized by severe persistent irritability with temper outbursts occurring at least three times weekly in young people aged at least 6 and with onset prior to age 10 [2]. Outcome research is needed show how this relates, if at all, to bipolar disorder.

## Assessment

The diagnosis of mania requires a distinct period of abnormally and persistently elevated or expansive mood. There has to be a change in the child's normal pattern of behaviour, which is not developmentally appropriate and which is associated with impairment. The stipulation that the behaviour is 'developmentally inappropriate' is crucial: open and excitable displays of high spirits, developmentally appropriate fantasy or oppositional behaviour, periods of feeling invulnerable and occasional boastfulness are all normal during childhood.

Paediatric bipolar disorder presents more often with depression than do adult-onset cases [8]. It is therefore important to recognize children and adolescents at risk of PBD, particularly those with recurrent depression, treatment-resistant depression, and family histories or a hypomanic response to antidepressant treatment. Specialist advice should be sought in these cases. Semi-structured instruments such as the Kiddie Schedule for Affective Disorders and Schizophrenia – Present and Lifetime (K-SADS-PL) [9], and, for children, the Washington University in St Louis-Kiddie Schedule for Affective Disorders and Schizophrenia (WASH-U-KSADS) [10] and the Young Mania Rating Scale (YMRS) [11] may aid diagnosis, but they do not replace the need for careful, multi-informant clinical appraisal. It is helpful to get a longitudinal perspective. Increasingly, mood monitoring using the internet or mobile phone is proving useful.

A family history of bipolar disorder in a first-degree relative raises concern about bipolar disorder in the child; however, children should be diagnosed and treated on the basis of the child's clinical presentation. For the assessment it is important to recognize that irritability is a non-specific symptom in childhood, associated with a wide range of childhood diagnoses. It is not predictive of later bipolar disorder [12], and it should not therefore be regarded as the core mood symptom of bipolar disorder in this age group

## Prodrome and Longitudinal Course

Bipolar disorder typically presents with depressive episodes after puberty [13]. In some high-risk children, sleep and anxiety disorders precede mood disorders by several years and reflect an increased vulnerability [13]. A staging model has been proposed whereby early exposure to adversity (e.g. exposure to parental illness, neglect from mother) and increased risk of psychopathology may be mediated through increased stress reactivity. Psychological processes including reward sensitivity, unstable self-esteem, rumination and positive self-appraisal appear to be risk factors for mood disorders.

With regard to outcome, the Course and Outcome of Bipolar Youth (COBY) study [14] of 413 children and adolescents (aged 7–17 years) with bipolar I disorder ($n$ = 244), bipolar II disorder ($n$ = 28) and BP-NOS ($n$ = 141) found that 25% of children and adolescents with bipolar II converted to bipolar I, and 38% of those with BP NOS converted to bipolar I or II. The outcome was not as chronic as was once thought: 24% were predominantly euthymic, 34.6% were moderately euthymic, 19.1% were ill with improving course, and 22.3% were predominantly ill. Each group were euthymic, on average, 84.4%, 47.3%, 42.8%, and 11.5% of the follow-up time, respectively. Better outcome was associated with higher age at onset of mood symptoms, less lifetime family history of bipolar disorder and substance abuse, and less history at baseline of severe depression, manic symptoms, suicidality, subsyndromal mood episodes and sexual abuse [15].

### Suicide

Bipolar disorder is a risk factor for suicide. Adolescents with bipolar disorder have higher rates of suicide and attempted suicide [16]. Suicide attempts are associated with female sex, older age, earlier illness onset, more severe/episodic PBD, mixed episodes, co-morbid disorders, past self-injurious behaviour, physical or sexual abuse, parental depression, family history of suicidality and poor family functioning. Co-morbid ADHD appears significantly associated with suicide attempts.

# Treatment

The treatment of PBD requires a multimodal approach. An assessment of co-morbid disorders such as substance abuse and conduct disorder needs to be undertaken, including an appraisal as to whether these are mood-dependent. Co-morbid disorders may need treatment in their own right. The treatment plan should take account of the developmental level of the child and adolescent. Treatment can be divided into two stages: acute treatment of mania or depression, and prophylaxis.

### Acute Phase

Pharmacotherapy is the mainstay of treatment for acute mania. The US Food and Drug Administration has given approval for risperidone, aripiprazole, quetiapine and olanzapine for the treatment of bipolar disorder. In children and adolescents, there is increasing use of second-generation antipsychotics (SGAs) as mood stabilizers, both in the acute manic phase and in the longer term. However, with perhaps the exception of aripiprazole, these agents are associated with adverse effects such as increased appetite, weight gain, lipid abnormalities and a risk of type 2 diabetes. Aripiprazole is recommended as a first-line treatment by NICE [17].

Expert guidance including that from NICE [17] recommends the initial use of SGAs and or an antiepileptic drug (Figure 33.1). However, sodium valproate is not recommended due to the risk of ovarian problems and teratogenic effects. A combination of medication is advocated if there is no response to a single medication (Figure 33.1). The choice of medication depends on the phase of the illness, presence of psychosis, presence of rapid cycling, risk of side-effects and, crucially, patient and family acceptance. SGAs are recommended for treating psychotic symptoms. Premature discontinuation of antipsychotic medication leads to a recurrence of psychotic symptoms in a large percentage of cases [28]. Lithium is an effective mood stabilizer [18]; however, although well tolerated, it requires regular blood level monitoring and it has a number of side effects – tremor, polyuria, hypothyroidism, hypercalcaemia etc. Treatment requires

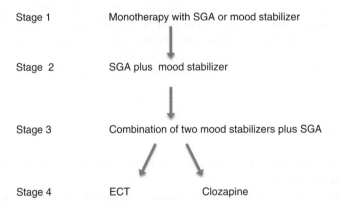

| | |
|---|---|
| Stage 1 | Monotherapy with SGA or mood stabilizer |
| Stage 2 | SGA plus mood stabilizer |
| Stage 3 | Combination of two mood stabilizers plus SGA |
| Stage 4 | ECT         Clozapine |

**Figure 33.1** Flow chart of pharmacotherapy for the treatment of paediatric bipolar disorder. SGAs, second-generation antipsychotics (aripiprazole, olanzapine, risperidone, quetiapine); mood stabilizers: lithium, sodium valproate, carbamazepine; ECT, electroconvulsive therapy.

good patient compliance. 'Classical' bipolar responds well to lithium, particularly those with a positive family history of bipolar disorder.

### Treatment of Depression in Bipolar Disorder

The first-line treatment for milder depression with PBD should be psychological [e.g. cognitive behavioural therapy (CBT) or interpersonal therapy (IPT)]. Selective serotonin reuptake inhibitor (SSRI) antidepressants can be used in conjunction with a mood stabilizer. There is limited evidence for the use of lamotrigine, but only in adolescents. For severe depression with or without psychotic symptoms, the combination of fluoxetine and olanzapine has been shown to be effective [19].

### Longer-Term Treatment

Lithium and SGAs can be used as longer-term treatment, although the evidence for efficacy in this age group is sparse; continued physical monitoring is required and weight gain remains a major problem with SGAs. Lithium is reasonably well tolerated and is not associated with weight gain. For sodium valproate and lithium use, counselling about teratogenic effects is necessary for those at risk of pregnancy.

Tapering or discontinuation of medication should be considered if the patient has achieved remission for a minimum of 12–24 consecutive months. However, for many patients, long-term or even lifelong pharmacotherapy might be indicated.

### Psychological Interventions

The treatment of bipolar disorder should involve psychological therapies. There are a limited number of psychological therapies for bipolar disorder in this age group, including Interpersonal and Social Rhythm Therapy for Adolescents (IPSRT-A) [20], Child- and Family-Focused Cognitive Behavioural Therapy (CFF-CBT) [21] and Dialectical Behaviour Therapy for Adolescents (DBT-A) [22]. Family psycho-educational approaches – a multi-family psycho-educational model psychotherapy (MF-PEP) [23,24] and family-focused treatment for adolescents (FFT-A) [25] – have the strongest evidence base. In addition to psycho-education, which includes information upon the appropriate use of medication, and appropriate adaption of lifestyle, particularly regulation of sleep, these approaches involve several components: mainly problem-solving and communication enhancement with family members. Family cohesion, adaptability and conflict appear to be predictors of the course of adolescent mood symptoms, while aggression is the strongest correlate of family functioning in PBD, and consequently needs to be a target for therapeutic work.

## References

1 WHO (1993) The ICD-10 Classification of Mental and Behavioural Disorders. Geneva: World Health Organisation.
2 APA (2013) Diagnostic and Statistical Manual of Mental Disorders, 5th edn. American Psychiatric Association.

3  Loranger AW, Levine PM (1978) Age at onset of bipolar affective illness. Archives of General Psychiatry, 35, 1345–1348.

4  Strober M, Carlson G (1982) Bipolar illness in adolescents with major depression: clinical, genetic, and psychopharmacologic predictors in a three- to four-year prospective follow-up investigation. Archives of General Psychiatry, 39, 549–555.

5  Van Meter AR, Moreira AL, Youngstrom EA (2011) Meta-analysis of epidemiologic studies of pediatric bipolar disorder. Journal of Clinical Psychiatry, 72, 1250–1256.

6  Moreno C, Laje G, Blanco C et al. (2007) National trends in the outpatient diagnosis and treatment of bipolar disorder in youth. Archives of General Psychiatry, 64, 1032–1039.

7  James A, Hoang U, Seagroatt V et al. (2014) A comparison of American and English hospital discharge rates for pediatric bipolar disorder, 2000 to 2010. Journal of the American Academy of Child and Adolescent Psychiatry, 53, 614–624.

8  Suominen K, Mantere O, Valtonen H et al. (2007) Early age at onset of bipolar disorder is associated with more severe clinical features but delayed treatment seeking. Bipolar Disorders, 9, 698–705.

9  Kaufman J, Birmaher B, Brent D et al. (1997) Schedule for Affective Disorders and Schizophrenia for School-Age Children-Present and Lifetime Version (K-SADS-PL): initial reliability and validity data. Journal of the American Academy of Child and Adolescent Psychiatry, 36, 980–988.

10 Geller B, Zimerman B, Williams M et al. (2001) Reliability of the Washington University in St. Louis Kiddie Schedule for Affective Disorders and Schizophrenia (WASH-U-KSADS) mania and rapid cycling sections. Journal of the American Academy of Child and Adolescent Psychiatry, 40, 450–455.

11 Youngstrom EA, Gracious BL, Danielson CK et al. (2003) Toward an integration of parent and clinician report on the Young Mania Rating Scale. Journal of Affective Disorders, 77, 179–190.

12 Stringaris A, Baroni A, Haimm C et al. (2010) Pediatric bipolar disorder versus severe mood dysregulation: risk for manic episodes on follow-up. Journal of the American Academy of Child and Adolescent Psychiatry, 49, 397–405.

13 Duffy A, Jones S, Goodday S, Bentall R (2015) Candidate risks indicators for bipolar disorder: early intervention opportunities in high-risk youth. International Journal of Neuropsychopharmacology. doi: 10.1093/ijnp/pyv071.

14 Birmaher B, Axelson D, Goldstein B et al. (2009) Four-year longitudinal course of children and adolescents with bipolar spectrum disorders: the Course and Outcome of Bipolar Youth (COBY) study. American Journal of Psychiatry, 166, 795–804.

15 Birmaher B, Gill MK, Axelson DA et al. (2014) Longitudinal trajectories and associated baseline predictors in youths with bipolar spectrum disorders. American Journal of Psychiatry, 171, 990–999.

16 Hauser M, Galling B, Correll CU (2013) Suicidal ideation and suicide attempts in children and adolescents with bipolar disorder: a systematic review of prevalence and incidence rates, correlates, and targeted interventions. Bipolar Disorders, 15, 507–523.

17 NICE (2014) Bipolar Disorder: the Assessment and Management of Bipolar Disorder in Adults, Children and Young People in Primary and Secondary Care. CG185. Online: http://www.nice.org.uk/CG185. Accessed: January 2017.

**18** Findling RL, Robb A, McNamara NK et al. (2015) Lithium in the acute treatment of bipolar I disorder: a double-blind, placebo-controlled study. Pediatrics, 136, 885–894.

**19** Detke HC, Del Bello MP, Landry J, Usher RW (2015) Olanzapine/fluoxetine combination in children and adolescents with bipolar I depression: a randomized, double-blind, placebo-controlled trial. Journal of the American Academy of Child and Adolescent Psychiatry, 54, 217–224.

**20** Hlastala SA, Kotler JS, McClellan JM, McCauley EA (2010) Interpersonal and social rhythm therapy for adolescents with bipolar disorder: treatment development and results from an open trial. Depression and Anxiety, 27, 457–464.

**21** Pavuluri MN, Graczyk PA, Henry DB et al. (2004) Child- and family-focused cognitive-behavioral therapy for pediatric bipolar disorder: development and preliminary results. Journal of the American Academy of Child and Adolescent Psychiatry, 43, 528–537.

**22** Fleischhaker C, Bohme R, Sixt B et al. (2011) Dialectical Behavioral Therapy for Adolescents (DBT-A): a clinical Trial for Patients with suicidal and self-injurious Behavior and Borderline Symptoms with a one-year Follow-up. Child and Adolescent Psychiatry and Mental Health, 5, 3.

**23** Cummings CM, Fristad MA (2007) Medications prescribed for children with mood disorders: effects of a family-based psychoeducation program. Experimental and Clinical Psychopharmacology, 15, 555–62.

**24** Fristad MA, Verducci JS, Walters K, Young ME (2009) Impact of multifamily psychoeducational psychotherapy in treating children aged 8 to 12 years with mood disorders. Archives of General Psychiatry, 66, 1013–1021.

**25** Miklowitz DJ, Axelson DA, Birmaher B et al. (2008) Family-focused treatment for adolescents with bipolar disorder: results of a 2-year randomized trial. Archives of General Psychiatry, 65, 1053–1061.

## 34

# Early Intervention in Psychosis

*Paolo Fusar-Poli and Giulia Spada*

## Introduction

Psychoses are a group of serious mental illnesses characterized by positive symptoms and negative symptoms. Positive symptoms include delusions, hallucinations, disorganized thinking, grossly disorganized or abnormal motor behaviour (including catatonia). Negative symptoms include social withdrawal and isolation [*Diagnostic and Statistical Manual of Mental Disorders*, 5th edition (DSM-5)] [1]. This chapter focuses on psychotic disorders such as schizophrenia. The prevalence of schizophrenia ranges from 2.6 to 6.7 per 1000 in the general population [2] (For bipolar disorder see Chapter 33.)

The onset of psychoses is usually preceded by a prodromal phase, characterized by initial changes in behaviour that last until the overt onset of psychosis, which can be either acute or insidious. There is then a pattern of chronic illness that can include periods of both remission and symptom relapse. Psychotic disorders are among the most disabling psychiatric disorders in young people, generally beginning in young adulthood, but 10–15% manifest prior to 18 years of age (early-onset psychosis, EOP), and 1–3% begin before the age of 13 years (very early onset, VEOP) [3].

## Early-Onset Psychosis

Compared with those with adult onset psychosis (AOP), young people with EOP frequently have more severe prodromal symptoms and poorer long-term symptomatic and social outcomes, characterized by chronicity of illness and severe impairments in social relationships and independent living [4]. At the time of onset, the prevalence of co-morbid disorders may delay the recognition of the syndrome. The onset of psychosis is also more likely to be less acute than in adulthood. In 75% of those with VEOP and 50% of those with EOP, the onset is insidious.

In DSM-5, the diagnostic criteria are the same for both EOP and AOP. However, symptomatology may be expressed differently at different ages. In EOP, elementary auditory hallucinations are the most frequent positive symptoms; delusions are less complex than AOP and are usually thematically related to childhood. Negative symptoms also show high prevalence rates in VEOP and EOP. School difficulties, cognitive deterioration and social withdrawal are frequent features of the prodromal phase.

*Child Psychology and Psychiatry: Frameworks for Clinical Training and Practice,* Third Edition.
Edited by David Skuse, Helen Bruce and Linda Dowdney.
© 2017 John Wiley & Sons, Ltd. Published 2017 by John Wiley & Sons, Ltd.

Whether the onset is in childhood, adolescence or adulthood, specialized treatment in early intervention centres leads to similar short-term outcomes. Over the longer term, those with EOP have similar or even better long-term outcomes than those with AOP, provided they are treated early [5]. The longer the period of *drug-untreated psychosis* and the *duration of untreated illness*, the worse the outcome [6,7]. Taken together, these factors underline that an early diagnosis and early intervention are positively associated with an improved prognosis.

## The Psychosis Prodrome

Birth cohort studies provide relatively consistent evidence that individuals who will later develop schizophrenic spectrum disorders exhibit a diversity of subtle premorbid developmental deficits during childhood [8]. These may include neurological 'soft signs' such as poor motor coordination, as well as language difficulties. Clinically significant psychiatric disorders, such as disruptive behaviour disorder, may also be present. Clinical symptoms that constitute a prodromal state, leading to clinical evaluation, may be progressive over childhood and adolescence. Non-specific developmental precursors are followed by clinically identifiable thought disorder. Development of the full clinical syndrome usually requires a degree of brain maturation that is not reached until later adolescence or early adulthood. Families with children who later become schizophrenic have often sought advice on their children's mental health prior to psychosis onset [5,9], which suggests that early identification and treatment should be possible. However, prodromal features cannot be used in clinical practice to alter the course of psychotic disorders, because they are only identified retrospectively in subjects who have already developed the illness. Therefore, early identification and intervention are of potential value but rest on the prospective early detection and treatment of young people who are beginning to develop overt symptoms of their acute illness [5]. The accurate prospective identification and recognition of symptoms that do differentiate children and adolescents at high risk for psychosis form the only viable approach to alter the course of these disorders in clinical practice [10].

## The Clinical High-Risk State

Research into first episodes of psychosis suggests that between 70% and 100% of cases are preceded by a lengthy period of attenuated symptoms [11]. Both positive and negative symptoms appear during the period preceding the onset of psychosis. The early at-risk psychosis state is characterized by attenuated negative symptoms, attenuated disorganized symptoms and cognitive impairments. The late at-risk psychosis state is characterized by attenuated positive symptoms and brief psychotic transient symptoms [12].

Together these prodromal phases represent the so-called 'clinical high-risk' state for psychosis (CHR). This is characterized by consistent and substantial impairments of functioning and a reduction in quality of life [13].

## Detecting the Clinical High-Risk State

Currently two main approaches are available to identify the CHR state in children and adolescents: the basic symptoms (BS) approach [14] and the ultra-high risk (UHR) approach [15], which apply to the early and late phases of the CHR respectively (see Figure 34.1).

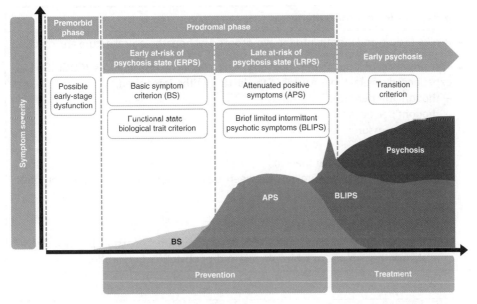

**Figure 34.1** Model of psychosis onset. The higher the line on the *y*-axis, the higher the symptom severity. BS, basic symptoms; APS, attenuated psychotic symptoms; BLIPS, brief limited intermittent psychotic symptoms. *Source*: Fusar-Poli *et al.* [9]. Reprinted with permission of American Medical Association.

### The BS Approach

The BS of psychosis are characterized by cognitive impairments in the form of subjectively experienced disturbances in different domains, including thought, speech and perception processes [9,11]. Unlike classic psychotic symptoms, BS are independent of abnormal thought content and are associated with intact reality testing. There is insight into the symptoms' psychopathological nature [9]. Appearing early in the development of the disorder, they possess a high specificity and a high positive predictive power [11]. BS criteria allow the clinician to assess the risk of the individual developing an overt psychosis before functional impairments appear. Requirements for meeting BS criteria are summarized in Box 34.1. Recent studies have assessed the value of BS using the Schizophrenia Proneness Instrument, an interview which has both an adult (SPI-A) and child and youth version (SPI-Y). The latter takes into account age-related developmental issues and symptom clusters [9]. Measure of BS focus on self-perceived cognitive and perceptual changes. These can be clustered into two partially overlapping subsets, one relating to 10 cognitive-perceptive basic symptoms (COPER) and the other to nine basic symptoms of cognitive disturbance (COGDIS), with the latter being the most specific and the more highly predictive of later psychosis [9,11].

### The UHR Approach

The UHR approach requires the presence of one or more of the following clusters of symptoms: attenuated psychotic symptoms (APS), brief limited intermittent psychotic symptoms and trait vulnerability plus a marked decline in psychosocial functioning (i.e. a combination of genetic risk and deterioration, GRD) [9] (see Box 34.2).These criteria

---

**Box 34.1  Basic symptom criteria**

- Reality testing and insight into the symptom's psychopathological nature are intact.

- The presence of one of the following nine cognitive disturbances (COGDIS [11]), experienced several times a week in the last 3 months, is required:
  - thought interference;
  - thought perseveration;
  - thought pressure;
  - thought blockages;
  - disturbance of receptive speech;
  - decreased ability to discriminate between ideas/perception, fantasy/true memories, unstable ideas of reference;
  - derealization;
  - visual perception disturbances;
  - acoustic perception disturbances and/or reduction of functional state plus first-degree relative with diagnosis of schizophrenia and/or obstetric complications.

---

**Box 34.2  Criteria for an ultra-high-risk state**

One or more of the following three symptom groups, coupled with a drop in social and/or occupational functioning (SOFAS), as defined in the following:

1) *Attenuated psychotic symptoms (APS)* include sub-threshold psychotic symptoms that are neither intense enough nor frequent enough to meet psychosis diagnostic criteria:
   - Unusual thought content (ideas of reference, delusional mood, thought disturbances)
   - Bizarre ideas (ideas of reference, delusional mood, thought disturbances)
   - Non-bizarre ideas (suspiciousness, persecutory ideas, grandiosity)
   - Perceptual abnormalities
   - DIsorganized speech

   PLUS

   - 30% drop in SOFAS score from premorbid level, sustained for a month, within past 12 months *or* SOFAS score < 50 for past 12 months or more

2) *Brief limited intermittent psychotic symptoms (BLIPS)* that include the presence of:
   - At least one psychotic symptom resolving spontaneously within 7 days with no antipsychotic interventions (hallucinations, delusions, formal thought disorders)

   PLUS

   - 30% drop in SOFAS score from premorbid level, sustained for a months, within past 12 months *or* SOFAS score < 50 for past 12 months or more

3) *Genetic risk and deterioration (GRD)* criteria require:
- First-degree relative with a diagnosis of schizophrenia or a schizophrenia spectrum disorder

PLUS

- 30% drop in SOFAS score from premorbid level, sustained for a month, within past 12 months *or* SOFAS score < 50 for past 12 months or more or a diagnosis of schizotypal personality.

SOFAS, Social and Occupational Functioning Assessment Scale.

reflect the later CHR phase ('late-at-risk' state) which carries a risk of developing a first psychotic episode within a year of their appearance. There are a number of adult interview measures for assessing UHR symptoms - for a fuller discussion of the measurement of both BS and UHR criteria, see (9,11).

### Using High-Risk Criteria with Children and Adolescents

Diagnosis in this age range is complicated by the fact that newly emerging BS and UHR symptoms appear in an evolving developmental context. Consequently, risk criteria may result from an undiagnosed medical condition (including metabolic and endocrinological disorders, and infections such as HIV). They may be associated with symptomatology that is unrelated directly to psychotic symptoms, including mood and behavioural disorders [such as anxiety, and attention deficit hyperactivity disorder (ADHD)], or with an early-emerging major psychosis associated with depression or bipolar illness [16].

While the evidence suggests that CHR criteria can be used successfully with older adolescents or adults [17], questions relate to their use in early adolescence and with children. Age-adapted tools for UHR symptoms are lacking. There has been insufficient validation of APS with respect to conversion to psychosis in this age group. There remains uncertainty about whether children themselves can reliably describe at-risk symptoms, and when and how parental information should be included [5]. Given their different developmental stages, children, adolescents and adults 'may need to be considered separately in terms of their presenting features, predictors and treatment needs' [9, p. 116].

### Transition to Psychosis

The utility of CHR criteria, in general, can be judged against how successful they are at predicting transition to a psychotic disorder. A recent meta-analysis of 27 studies, comprising 2502 patients (mean age 19.9 years, range 15–28) found follow-up transition risks of 18% at 6 months, 22% after 1 year, 29% after 2 years, and 36% after 3 years [14].

Meta-analyses find that the majority of UHR patients have APS [18] (see Box 34.2); in the absence of other symptom clusters, the conversion rate is 28.3% at the 3-year follow-up [19]. Symptom clusters comprising disorganized communication, suspiciousness, verbal memory deficits and decline in social functioning are also highly predictive of psychosis. In contrast, the GRD cluster alone (see Box 34.2) is not a good predictor of conversion [18].

Studies of adolescents report a wide range of different conversion rates. Some find a conversion risk that is similar to that of adults. Other studies have found a lower risk of conversion with the same symptom criteria, or longer prodromal periods with a more insidious onset. There are different conversion rates in the different UHR subgroups (see Box 34.2) [3,11,20].

## Intervention

On average, within highly developed healthcare systems, at least a year elapses from the first manifestation of psychotic positive symptoms to the initiation of adequate treatment [11]. There is emerging evidence that early intervention (EI) may be helpful. A recent meta-analysis of EI studies found significantly reduced conversion rates in adult UHR participants at short- to medium-term follow-up, with a risk ratio for active interventions versus placebo of about 0.54 [21]. Unfortunately, few outcome studies have reported equivalent data on children and adolescents, and there are no randomized controlled trials (RCTs) of early intervention in this age group. Early intervention during the CHR period might appear to be less effective with children than with adults, because the conversion to psychosis rate is lower in children and adolescents, and therefore it is hard to demonstrate benefit in a case–control comparison. Longer-term follow-ups are required [21].

A variety of early intervention treatments or management techniques are currently under investigation. These include clinical monitoring, pharmacological treatment, psychological treatment and psychosocial interventions, and nutritional supplements (such as omega-3 fatty acids) are being studied for their effectiveness in reducing the conversion risk and improving outcome [22]. At present, no clear and reliable effects have been found. For instance, RCTs have compared cognitive behavioural therapy (CBT) and olanzapine with CBT and a placebo condition, but found no additional benefit from the medication. Olanzapine alone was not effective, compared with placebo, but amisulpride plus a needs-based intervention may be moderately effective in reducing positive symptoms [23]. Overall, there is no high-quality evidence for or against the benefits of early pharmacological intervention [23]. Antipsychotics should not be used in this population. Some medications have highly prevalent and distressing side-effects, such as weight gain, that adolescents find particularly difficult to accept. They can also be stigmatizing. Interventions with antidepressants seem promising so far but require further replication [21]. Recent guidelines emphasize that the primary aim of pharmacological interventions should be to achieve symptomatic stabilization as a starting point for psychological interventions rather than to prevent conversion to psychosis [21].

Children and adolescents require an overall treatment plan that carefully monitors CHR symptoms and assesses their potential progression over an extended time period. Intervention should seek to improve psychosocial functioning and co-morbid mental health disorders. Treatment needs to be adapted, according to progress made by the patient.

## Future Directions

The CHR concept, which predicts the transition to psychosis with reasonable accuracy, has recently been debated [24]. There are limitations to this approach. For example, the epidemiological validity of purported CHR states is founded on research with unrepresentative opportunistic samples. Yet, alternative models of clinical applicability are lacking. In the future, treatment and management techniques based on the EI model discussed here may focus on a clinical staging model addressing a broader syndrome of early mental distress [24].

## References

1  American Psychiatric Association (2013) Diagnostic and Statistical Manual of Mental Disorders, 5th edn. Washington, DC.
2  Chong HY, Teoh SL, Wu DB et al. (2016) Global economic burden of schizophrenia: a systematic review. Neuropsychiatric Disease and Treatment, 12, 357–373.
3  Schultze-Lutter F, Michel C, Schmidt SJ et al. (2015) EPA guidance on the early detection of clinical high risk states of psychoses. European Psychiatry: the Journal of the Association of European Psychiatrists, 30, 405–416.
4  Hollis C (2000) Adult outcomes of child- and adolescent-onset schizophrenia: diagnostic stability and predictive validity. American Journal of Psychiatry, 157, 1652–1659.
5  Schimmelmann BG, Schultze-Lutter F (2012) Early detection and intervention of psychosis in children and adolescents: urgent need for studies. European Child & Adolescent Psychiatry, 21, 239–241.
6  Marshall M, Lewis S, Lockwood A et al. (2005) Association between duration of untreated psychosis and outcome in cohorts of first-episode patients: a systematic review. Archives of General Psychiatry, 62, 975–983.
7  Armando M, Pontillo M, De Crescenzo F et al. (2015) Twelve-month psychosis-predictive value of the ultra-high risk criteria in children and adolescents. Schizophrenia Research, 169, 186–192.
8  Welham J, Isohanni M, Jones P, McGrath J (2009) The antecedents of schizophrenia: a review of birth cohort studies. Schizophrenia Bulletin, 35, 603–623.
9  Fusar-Poli P, Borgwardt S, Bechdolf A et al. (2013) The psychosis high-risk state: a comprehensive state-of-the-art review. JAMA Psychiatry, 70, 107–120.
10  Millan MJ, Andrieux A, Bartzokis G (2016) Altering the course of schizophrenia: progress and perspectives. Nature Reviews Drug Discovery, 15, 485–515.
11  Klosterkotter J, Schultze-Lutter F, Bechdolf A, Ruhrmann S (2011) Prediction and prevention of schizophrenia: what has been achieved and where to go next? World Psychiatry: Official Journal of the World Psychiatric Association (WPA), 10, 165–174.
12  Cornblatt B, Lencz T, Obuchowski M (2002) The schizophrenia prodrome: treatment and high-risk perspectives. Schizophrenia Research, 54, 177–186.
13  Fusar-Poli P, Rocchetti M, Sardella A et al. (2015) Disorder, not just state of risk: meta-analysis of functioning and quality of life in people at high risk of psychosis. British Journal of Psychiatry : the Journal of Mental Science, 207, 198–206.

**14** Schultze-Lutter F, Ruhrmann S, Fusar-Poli P et al. (2012) Basic symptoms and the prediction of first-episode psychosis. Current Pharmaceutical Design, 18, 351–357.

**15** Yung AR, Phillips LJ, McGorry PD et al. (1998) Prediction of psychosis. A step towards indicated prevention of schizophrenia. British Journal of Psychiatry Supplement, 172, 14–20.

**16** Algon S, Yi J, Calkins ME, Kohler C et al. (2012) Evaluation and treatment of children and adolescents with psychotic symptoms. Current Psychiatry Reports, 14, 101–110.

**17** Spada G, Molteni S, Pistone C et al. (2015) Identifying children and adolescents at ultra high risk of psychosis in Italian neuropsychiatry services: a feasibility study. European Child & Adolescent Psychiatry, 25, 91–106.

**18** Fusar-Poli P, Cappucciati M, Borgwardt S et al. (2015) Heterogeneity of psychosis risk within individuals at clinical high risk: a meta-analytical stratification. JAMA Psychiatry, 73, 113–120.

**19** Cornblatt BA, Carrion RE, Auther A et al. (2015) Psychosis prevention: a modified clinical high risk perspective from the recognition and prevention (RAP) program. American Journal of Psychiatry, 172, 986–994.

**20** Schimmelmann BG, Walger P, Schultze-Lutter F (2013) The significance of at-risk symptoms for psychosis in children and adolescents. Canadian Journal of Psychiatry Revue Canadienne de Psychiatrie, 58, 32–40.

**21** Schmidt SJ, Schultze-Lutter F, Schimmelmann BG et al. (2015) EPA guidance on the early intervention in clinical high risk states of psychoses. European Psychiatry : the Journal of the Association of European Psychiatrists, 30, 388–404.

**22** Amminger GP, Schafer MR, Schlogelhofer M et al. (2015) Longer-term outcome in the prevention of psychotic disorders by the Vienna omega-3 study. Nature Communications, 6, 7934.

**23** Stafford MR, Jackson H, Mayo-Wilson E et al. (2013) Early interventions to prevent psychosis: systematic review and meta-analysis. BMJ (Clinical Research ed), 346, f185.

**24** Fusar-Poli P, Yung AR, McGorry P, van Os J (2014) Lessons learned from the psychosis high-risk state: towards a general staging model of prodromal intervention. Psychological Medicine, 44, 17–24.

# 35

# Developmental Language Disorder

*Gina Conti-Ramsden and Kevin Durkin*

## What is Developmental Language Disorder?

Children with language impairments have been labelled in various ways by both sci-
entists and practitioners. Until very recently, the most common label was 'Specific
Language Impairment' (SLI). Dissatisfaction with this term grew as research findings
indicated that language impairment, rather than being specific, is often associated with
other difficulties. Consequently, a new term has been recommended, namely 'Developmental Language Disorder'. DLD denotes language difficulties in the context of adequate
non-verbal skills, normal hearing, absence of frank neurological damage or autism (see
Box 35.1). For details of the debate on this issue see Refs. [4,5]. While we use the term
DLD here readers should be aware that – to describe the same disability – the term SLI
will still be encountered in much of the literature. Further, across the English-speaking

---

**Box 35.1  Definitions of Developmental Language Disorder (DLD)**

Debate centres on the level of language impairment required for diagnosis of DLD, and
whether there should be a mismatch of non-verbal abilities. For example:

- The *International Classification of Mental and Behavioural Disorders*, 10th revision [1]
  requires language difficulties greater than 2 standard deviations (SD) *below* the mean,
  with verbal skills at least 1 SD *below* measures of non-verbal cognitive functioning.
- The *Diagnostic and Statistical Manual of Mental Disorders* [2] requires language abilities
  to be substantially and quantifiably below those expected for age. What constitutes
  'substantial' is not defined operationally, though *functional impairment* is required, i.e.
  DLD interferes with academic or occupational achievement, or with social interaction.
  No criteria are specified in relation to non-verbal skills.
- The clinical research definition of DLD [3] works with threshold and discrepancy measures that enable consistent identification of DLD by speech and language therapists.
  It requires a combination of language difficulties, assessed on a composite standardized language measure, that fall 1.25 SDs *below* the mean (approximately, the 10th
  centile); plus adequate non-verbal cognitive functioning (i.e. a performance IQ > 1 SD
  below the mean, equating to a standard score of 85 or higher).

---

*Child Psychology and Psychiatry: Frameworks for Clinical Training and Practice,* Third Edition.
Edited by David Skuse, Helen Bruce and Linda Dowdney.
© 2017 John Wiley & Sons, Ltd. Published 2017 by John Wiley & Sons, Ltd.

world, there is variation both within and between countries as to how DLD is diagnosed. Diagnostic labelling is important as lack of agreement can affect which children have access to services. It can also impede research progress and makes it difficult to increase our understanding of the nature and causes of DLD. A multi-national, multi-disciplinary study undertaken to develop diagnostic and terminological consensus recommended the term developmental language disorder, which we use throughout this chapter [6].

Typically, DLD comes to the attention of clinicians as a result of concern from significant others about the child's progress with language learning. In practice, children with this condition rarely have difficulties with language alone. Furthermore, there is considerable variation not only in the severity but also in the nature of the language difficulties evident. These considerations raise challenges for the diagnosis, explanation and treatment of the disorder, in particular, as DLD presents substantial issues calling for the investment of clinical, educational and public health resources. DLD is a common disorder, estimated to affect approximately 7% of the population at school entry, with boys being more affected than girls at a ratio of 2:1. The new *Diagnostic and Statistical Manual of Mental Disorders*, 5th edition (DSM-5) term 'language disorders' provides is a useful generic label that is already in use in a variety of settings and is in line with the recommended term developmental language disorders [6]. Other labels used include 'speech, language and communication needs' (Royal College of Speech and Language Therapists); 'developmental language delay', 'language impairment', 'primary language difficulties' and other similar names (educational practice settings).

## What Causes DLD?

It has become clear that DLD is not a single-cause disorder. A number of theories have been put forward, all of which have received some empirical support. It seems likely that multiple risk factors are implicated. These include genetic, neurobiological, cognitive and environmental influences.

### Biological Bases of DLD: Genetic and Neurobiological Factors

There is strong evidence that DLD runs in families. The majority of children with DLD have a family history of language difficulties, with a first-degree relative usually affected. The contribution of genetic factors is most clearly indicated in twin studies, where identical twins have a much higher concordance for DLD than non-identical twins [7]. Patterns of inheritance appear to be complex, involving interactions among multiple genes. Technological advances have made it possible to examine brain development in children with DLD. However, few atypicalities have been identified. The most consistent neuroimaging findings suggest leftward asymmetry and atypical cerebral volume. Electrophysiological evidence indicates abnormal auditory processing [8]. However, these abnormalities have also been observed in other developmental disorders. Thus, further research is needed to identify distinctive features of brain development in individuals with DLD.

## Cognitive Bases of DLD: Non-Linguistic and Linguistic Factors

Different approaches emphasize different systems as influential in the aetiology of DLD. One prominent approach highlights memory impairments:

- Phonological short-term memory deficits have been extensively documented and there is evidence of heritability in this respect [9]. Such an impairment has a key impact on the child's ability to retain verbal information long enough to develop accurate speech and language representations.
- More general impairments in working memory have been identified in DLD and, more recently, difficulties with implicit, procedural memory [10]. Such deficits affect children's ability to extract the regularities of the language they are learning, such as suffixation, for example, the use of regular past tense '-ed' in English.

Other views focus on limitations in other areas of cognitive functioning, such as perceptual and information-processing capabilities, temporal auditory processing capacity, and executive functions. Some accounts assume that language structures are autonomous of other cognitive systems. These theories emphasize linguistic factors proposing deficits or immaturity in systems responsible for the representation of grammar, linguistic features or structural relationships.

### Environmental Influences

In general, samples of children with DLD contain disproportionately high numbers of individuals from socio-economically disadvantaged backgrounds. This could be interpreted as an outcome of disadvantage or as a consequence of intrafamilial transmission, or as due to some more complex interaction. Overall, present evidence supports the assumption of multicausality.

# What Types of Language Difficulties Do Children with DLD Have?

Developmental language disorders is heterogeneous. A number of different classification systems have been devised. The more enduring clinical types differentiate children with 'expressive' language problems only versus children with both 'expressive and receptive' difficulties:

- *Expressive DLD (E-DLD)* – children exhibit mainly language production difficulties in the context of adequate comprehension abilities. Subtle comprehension deficits, however, can be detected when using sufficiently sensitive instruments.
- *Mixed expressive-receptive DLD* (ER-DLD) – children have difficulties with both language comprehension and language production. Difficulties are usually evident at the word (vocabulary) and sentential levels, especially complex sentences.

It is not clear if these profiles of impairment are qualitatively different or represent different points on a continuum of severity, with ER-DLD representing the more severe cases. More recently, a third clinical type has received attention. These are children in whom the social use of language, i.e. pragmatic abilities, is the most prominent difficulty. Vocabulary and grammar can be relatively strong, i.e. sentences may appear well-formed, but comprehension of extended discourse is usually poor and social interactions can be odd (verbose or over-formal with poor turntaking skills). These children are currently referred to as having social communication difficulties (SCD, DSM-5). There is ongoing debate regarding the overlap between DLD, SCD and autism spectrum disorders (ASDs).

## Distinctive Features of Language in DLD

The language difficulties of children with DLD can be manifested in various areas of language functioning at varying levels. However, there are some noteworthy areas of difficulty.

The majority of children with DLD learning English have difficulties with grammar, in particular verb morphology. For example, they fail to mark tense accurately (they say 'play' for 'played, omitting '-ed') and do not always use auxiliaries ('I staying there' for 'I am staying there'). These difficulties are evident even when children with DLD are compared with younger typical children learning language. Grammar can be disproportionately affected in DLD and has been suggested as a hallmark of the disorder.

## Developmental Progression of Language Skills in DLD

It is a hallmark of DLD that most of these children are late talkers: they are late in acquiring their first words and in putting together their first word combinations. It is not the case that children with DLD start developing language normally and then stop and become delayed or lose what they have learned. Occurrence of 'language loss' in infancy is reported in some children with ASDs but not in children with DLD. This appears to be a distinguishing feature between the two disorders [11] which can be particularly useful for the differential diagnosis between DLD and ASD in the preschool period.

In childhood, difficulties with the sound system of the language, i.e. phonology, can co-occur with DLD. However, by middle childhood problems with sound production are usually resolved or less evident (unless there are oral-facial motor difficulties/apraxia) and most children with DLD are intelligible. It is also worth noting that a minority (5%) of children with DLD are not late talkers [12]. These children can develop problems late, after having acquired single words 'on schedule' (between 12 and 24 months). For these children, word combinations pose the biggest challenge in the trajectory of their language difficulties.

It used to be thought that DLD was a short-term difficulty in language learning which, with support, could be resolved by the early school years. Although this is true for a proportion of children (approximately 40%), developmental follow-up studies have shown that many children with DLD have persisting language difficulties well into adolescence and even adulthood. Research on the growth trajectories of individuals with DLD from childhood to adolescence and young adulthood is only just emerging. The evidence suggests that children with DLD show similar, parallel patterns of language growth in comparison to their typically developing peers. There is more variability in the rate of language growth of children with DLD in the preschool and early school years than later in develop-ment. Accelerated language growth and slowing down of growth are rare after the age of 7. Children with DLD develop language at a strikingly steady pace, with few exceptions [13].

## Associated Developmental Problems and Outcomes

Language is fundamental to human behaviour. Hence, it is not surprising to find that individuals with language disorders tend to have associated difficulties in other aspects of their lives. For example, recent research and theoretical multi-dimensional mod-els [14] indicate developmental interactions between oral language skills and areas of functioning such as literacy, memory skills and more general non-verbal abilities throughout middle childhood, adolescence and beyond [13,15].

Still more broadly, there is evidence that young people growing up with DLD expe-rience greater difficulties in social interaction than do typical children and adoles-cents [16]. These children are more vulnerable to social exclusion, behavioural and emotional difficulties, and to being bullied [17]. Their linguistic and literacy problems impact on their educational progress and attainment and on their uses of new tech-nologies [18]. As adolescents, they have greater difficulties in dealing with the myriad tasks of autonomous daily life [19]. A proportion of children with DLD develop broader phenotype autistic symptomatology in adolescence [20].

There is much debate with regard to the processes underpinning the above-mentioned developmental observations. Do they reflect the impact on language development of still more fundamental cognitive and perceptual capacities? Are they manifestations of co-morbid conditions that emerge during the developmental process? Are they devel-opmental manifestations of bidirectional interactions between language impairment and other areas of functioning? The answer to these questions requires further empiri-cal research and clinical data. However, what is clear is: (i) that oral language abilities matter throughout development; (ii) that children with DLD are likely to demonstrate a range of associated difficulties; and (iii) that these children are at risk of less successful developmental and educational outcomes.

## Implications

There is a need for the assessment of oral language abilities in children with DLD in middle childhood and beyond. Furthermore, because of the observed changing profiles of these individuals, when children and adolescents present with difficulties in learn-ing (mild-to-moderate learning disabilities), literacy (including dyslexia), behaviour or emotional and social functioning (including broader phenotype ASD), they should be assessed for their oral language skills. This is important not only because they may be in need of support for their development but because many of the foundations of intervention in clinical, educational and mental health practice involve the oral verbal medium. For example, language is the mode of educational instruction and a key ele-ment in interactions between clinician and client in cognitive behaviour therapy.

All practitioners who work with young people with developmental difficulties need to be sensitive to the possibility that these children may have, among other problems, language difficulties. The psychologist, clinical psychologist or other specialist dealing with children and young people in difficulties should consider the potential need to evaluate and, if required, obtain support for his or her oral language skills. Only in this way we will we be able to make it possible for individuals with DLD to have a good quality of life, find employment and establish long-term relationships.

## References

1 World Health Organization (1992) The ICD-10 Classification for Mental and Behavioural Disorders: Diagnostic Criteria for Research. Geneva: World Health Organization.

2 American Psychiatric Association (2013) Diagnostic and Statistical Manual of Mental Disorders, 5th edn. Arlington, VA: American Psychiatric Association.

3 Tomblin JB, Records NL, Zhang X (1996) A system for the diagnosis of specific language impairment in kindergarten children. Journal of Speech, Language and Hearing Research, 39, 1284–1294.

4 Reilly S, Tomblin B, Law J et al.(2014) SLI: a convenient label for whom? International Journal of Language and Communication Disorders 49, 416–451.

5 Bishop DVM (2014) Ten questions about terminology for children with unexplained language problems. International Journal of Language and Communication Disorders, 49, 381–415.

6 Bishop DVM, Snowling MJ, Thompson PA, Greenhalgh T, the CATALISE consortium. Identifying language impairment in children: a multinational and multidisciplinary Delphi consensus study. Manuscript under review.

7 Bishop DVM (2002) The role of genes in the etiology of specific language impairment. Journal of Communication Disorders 35, 311–328.

8 Webster RI, Shevell MI (2004) Neurobiology of specific language impairment. Journal of Child Neurology, 19, 471–481.

9 Falcaro M, Pickles A, Newbury DF et al. (2008) Genetic and phenotypic effects of phonological short-term memory and grammatical morphology in specific language impairment. Genes, Brain and Behavior, 7, 393–402.

10 Lum JAG, Conti-Ramsden G, Page, D, Ullman, M (2012) Working, declarative and procedural memory in specific language impairment. Cortex, 48, 1138–1154.

11 Pickles A, Simonoff E, Conti-Ramsden G et al. (2009) Loss of language in early development of autism and specific language impairment. Journal of Child Psychology and Psychiatry, 50, 843–852.

12 Ukoumunne OC, Wake M, Carlin J et al. (2012) Profiles of language development in pre-school children: a longitudinal latent class analysis of data from the Early Language in Victoria Study. Child: Care, Health and Development, 38, 341–349.

13 Conti-Ramsden G, St Clair MC, Pickles A, Durkin K (2012) Developmental trajectories of verbal and nonverbal skills in individuals with a history of specific language impairment: from childhood to adolescence. Journal of Speech, Language, and Hearing Research, 55, 1716–1735.

14 Ramus F, Marshall CR, Rosen S, van der Lely JKJ (2013) Phonological deficits in specific language impairment and developmental dyslexia: towards a multidimensional model. Brain, 136, 630–645.

15 St. Clair MC, Durkin K, Conti-Ramsden G et al. (2010) Growth of reading skills in children with a history of specific language impairment: The role of autistic symptomatology and language-related abilities. British Journal of Developmental Psychology, 28, 109–132.

16 Mok PL, Pickles A, Durkin K, Conti-Ramsden G (2014) Longitudinal trajectories of peer relations in children with specific language impairment. Journal of Child Psychology and Psychiatry, 55, 516–527.

17 St. Clair MC, Pickles A, Durkin K, Conti-Ramsden G (2011) A longitudinal study of behavioral, emotional and social difficulties in individuals with a history of specific language impairment (SLI). Journal of Communication Disorders, 44, 186–199.

18 Durkin K, Mok P L, Conti-Ramsden G (2015) Core subjects at the end of primary school: identifying and explaining relative strengths of children with specific language impairment (SLI). International Journal of Language & Communication Disorders, 50, 226–240.

19 Durkin K, Conti-Ramsden G (2010) Young people with specific language impairment: A review of social and emotional functioning in adolescence. Child Language Teaching and Therapy, 26, 105–121.

20 Conti-Ramsden G, Simkin Z, Botting N (2006) The prevalence of autistic spectrum disorders in adolescents with a history of specific language impairment (SLI). Journal of Child Psychology and Psychiatry, 47, 621–628.

## Internet Resources

RALLIcampaign, Raising Awareness of Language Learning Impairments: https://www .youtube.com/user/RALLIcampaign – *youtube channel with videoclips on SLI*

# 36

# Substance Misuse in Young People

*K. A. H. Mirza, Roshin M. Sudesh and Sudeshni Mirza*

## Introduction

Substance misuse is a major public health problem with substantial levels of morbidity and mortality, with the potential to alter the developmental trajectory of affected young people. Most children in their middle childhood are exposed to various substances, including alcohol and tobacco, and a substantial minority, as high as 10%, continue to use drugs into adolescence and adulthood [1, 2]. Many youngsters who misuse drugs have multiple antecedent and coexisting mental health problems, unrecognized learning difficulties, family difficulties, involvement with the justice system and deeply entrenched social problems. Substance misuse takes a high toll in terms of healthcare costs, violent crimes, accidents, suicides, social and interpersonal difficulties, and educational impairment [3].

## Epidemiology

In the UK, prevalence estimates for 2014 increased following a promising decline between 2003 and 2011. Not only are more young people using drugs than ever before, but this use is beginning at increasingly younger ages. The scale of the problem facing the UK is illustrated by annual data collected by the National Statistics Authority [4]. The level of any drug use in the last year was highest among 16- to 19-year-olds (19:3%) compared with all other age groups. The rates reported by younger children are also significant, with 5% of 11-year-olds reporting drug use on at least one occasion. Tobacco, alcohol and cannabis were the most commonly abused substances, with cocaine and heroin accounting for less than 10% [4,5]. Even though there is a declining trend in tobacco smoking in adults, over 200 000 young people took up smoking in 2013 and 43% of 11- to 15-year-olds admitted drinking alcohol at least once in the past year. In 2013, the average weekly alcohol intake for those aged 11–14 years was 10.4 units. Cannabis use is also widespread amongst 11- to 15-year-olds, with a prevalence of 7% in 2013. Approximately 1% of 11- to 15-year-olds and 3% of 16- to 24-year-olds surveyed also admitted to using Class A substances. A new class of drugs – the novel psychoactive substances (NPS; historically referred to as 'legal highs') – has been used by a significant number of young people, but we do not have systematic prevalence rates regarding these (see Table 36.1).

Most of the campaigns against substance misuse are directed at illegal drugs such as cannabis, heroin, cocaine and ecstasy. However, many more people die or develop problems,

*Child Psychology and Psychiatry: Frameworks for Clinical Training and Practice,* Third Edition.
Edited by David Skuse, Helen Bruce and Linda Dowdney.
© 2017 John Wiley & Sons, Ltd. Published 2017 by John Wiley & Sons, Ltd.

**Table 36.1** New psychoactive substances (NPS; historically called 'legal highs')[a] mimic psychoactive effects of drugs of abuse. There is little information on the pharmacology, toxicology and safety of NPS for humans; the potential health implications of these compounds are largely unknown

| Class of drug | Chemical structure/type of drugs | Popular brand names | Mechanism of action | Effects and dangers |
|---|---|---|---|---|
| *Stimulants* – drugs with actions similar to ecstasy or methamphetamine | Mephedrone – most common, piperazines, NRG drugs – naphyrone | Bubble, Miaow, MCAT, BZP pills, NRG-1, NRG -2 Rave, Energy, Fury, Jet | Action of many drugs not known, but seems to increase DA/ NA/5-HT | Acute effects due to symapthomimetic activity, including confusion, aggression, blurred vision, hallucinations, tachycardia, hyponatraemia, even death, acute myocarditis |
| *Synthetic cannabinoids; 'spice' and related products* – synthetic cannabinoids are dissolved in solvent and sprayed on to an organic herbal material | Naphthoyindoles, phenyl acetyl indoles, cyclohexyl phenols, benzoylindoles, classical cannabinoids | Black Mamba, Spice, Annihilation, Psyclone, Exodus, K2 | Acts similar to THC- and possess equal or higher affinity for cannabinoid receptors | Agitation, seizures, hypertension, vomiting and hypokalemia<br><br>Spice-like products are known to precipitate psychosis in vulnerable people and cause relapse in people with psychosis |
| *Hallucinogens* – plant-based products | *Salvia divinorum*, lysergic acid amide, psilocybin, *Amanita muscarita* | Diviner's sage, Hawaiian baby, Lion's ear | Hallucinogenic effects produced by plant based substances – effects on 5 HT/DA | The overall toxicity of *S. divinorum* products appears to be low. There is bad trip experience with dysphoria, anxiety, fear attacks and even suicidal thoughts, and three case reports of psychosis related to *Salvia* |

THC, tetrahydrocannabinol; DA, dopamine; NA, noradrenaline; 5-HT, serotonin.

[a] In 2016 the UK government banned all NPS as illegal, so there is no loophole to sell them legally online ('head shops').

either directly or indirectly, as a result of using tobacco and alcohol than all illegal drugs combined and the British classification of drugs has been a matter of controversy [6].

# Defining Substance Misuse in the Young: A Developmental Perspective

The notion of a drug-free society is almost certainly a chimera. Young people have always used substances to change the way they see the world and how they feel, and there is every reason to think they always will. The effects of a drug are not just dependent on the drug itself. The mindset of the individual who takes it and the setting in which it is used are crucial variables. Young people report that they take drugs for a variety of reasons: to gain pleasure, to conform to attitudes and values of the peer group, to block out traumatic and painful memories, and to relieve sadness and worries associated with their everyday lives. For some young people, use of drugs and alcohol may become a problem in itself, and a very small minority develop substance dependence. Early onset of substance use and a rapid progression through the stages of substance use are among the risk factors for the development of substance misuse [3]. Longitudinal studies have shown that the peak age for first use for both legal and illegal substances is between 15 and 18 years. This generally decreases by the age of 24 [7].

Given the natural history of substance use in young people and heterogeneity of the patterns of use, most researchers and clinicians struggle to define what constitutes substance misuse in young people.

## Definitions

International classificatory systems [*International Statistical Classification of Diseases* (ICD-10) and *Diagnostic and Statistical Manual of Mental Disorders*, 4th edition (DSM-IV)] suggest that adult categories like harmful use and dependence (ICD-10) and substance abuse and dependence (DSM-IV) could be reliably used to diagnose substance misuse in young people. Unfortunately, both systems lack developmental perspective in psychopathology, and the categories such as harmful use, dependence and substance abuse do not seem to capture all stages of substance use in young people [8,9]. For example, tolerance and withdrawal that typically develop in response to long periods of chronic substance use are rarely seen in young people.

## Alternative Classifications in Young People

Clinicians and researchers have proposed alternative criteria to classify substance misuse in young people [8,9]. Based on the seminal work by Joseph Novinsky and colleagues, Mirza and Mirza [6] proposed a developmentally sensitive and dimensional model to classify the stage of substance use in young people, starting with non-use at one end, moving through experimental stage, social stage, at-risk (prodromal) stage, and stage of harmful use to substance dependence on the other end. This model has the potential to ascertain stages of substance use across the dynamic continuum and choose the most appropriate intervention to suit the stage of substance misuse (see Table 36.2).

**Table 36.2** Stages of substance (alcohol and drugs) use and suggested interventions: a pragmatic classification

| Stage | Motive | Setting | Frequency | Emotional impact | Behaviour | Impact on functioning | Suggested interventions [32] |
|---|---|---|---|---|---|---|---|
| Experimental stage | Curiosity and risk-taking | Alone or with peer group | Rarely or very occasionally | Effect of drugs is usually very short-term | No active drug-seeking behaviour | Relatively little – may rarely result in dangerous consequences. | Universal prevention (drug education – formal or informal) |
| Social stage | Social acceptance/ need to fit in | Usually with peer group | Occasional | Mind-altering effects of drugs are clearly recognized | No active drug-seeking behaviour | Usually no significant problems – but some can go on to show features of the early at-risk stage | Universal prevention (drug education – formal or informal) |
| Early at-risk stage | Social acceptance/ peer pressure | Facilitated by peer group | Frequent, but variable, depending on peer group | Mind-altering effects of drugs are clearly recognized and sought | No active drug-seeking behaviour – but develops a regular pattern of drug/alcohol use | Associated with significant dangers including recurrent binge drinking or problems associated with intoxication | Targeted intervention Treatment by non-specialist services (e.g. GP, school health worker, young people's counselling services, healthcare staff working in CAMHS, paediatrics, etc.) |
| Later at-risk stage (substance use is not dominating mental state) | Cope with negative emotions or enhance pleasure | Alone or with a like-minded peer group | Frequent/ regular use | Uses drugs to alter mood or behaviour | Active drug-seeking behaviour is a key indicator of this stage | May be impairment in functioning in some areas (e.g. school and family) | Treatment by specialist services (e.g. CAMHS) – for both mental health issues and progression of substance use to further serious stages |

| Stage | | | | | | | |
|---|---|---|---|---|---|---|---|
| Stage of harmful use (similar to ICD-10) | Drug use is the primary means of recreation, coping with stress or both | Alone or with an altered (drug-using) peer group | Regular use, despite negative consequences | Negative effects on their emotions and ability to function | Active drug-seeking behaviour, despite negative consequences across many areas of life | Impairment in almost all areas of life and or distress within families or close relationships | Treatment[a] by specialist services (e.g. specialist substance misuse treatment services for young people and specialist substance misuse professionals within CAMHS) |
| Stage of dependence (similar to ICD-10) – only a rare minority of young people progress to this stage | To deal with withdrawal symptoms and stop craving | Alone or with like-minded peer group | Compulsive, regular or often daily use to manage withdrawal symptoms | Emotional impacts of drugs are very significant, withdrawal symptoms are prominent | Active drug-seeking behaviour, often loss of control over use, preoccupation with drug use, craving and behaviour may involve criminality | Physical and psychological complications, impairment in all areas of life | Treatment[a] by specialist services, including detoxification and some residential rehabilitation |

CAMHS, child and adolescent mental health services.

[a] For some the involvement of agencies and services, other than substance misuse services, may be required.

*Source:* Modified and reproduced with permission from Mirza and Mirza [6], Elsevier Publishers, London

## Aetiology: Risk and Protective Factors

Substance use does not occur in a vacuum. In vulnerable individuals, substance misuse is produced by the interaction of drugs with genetic, environmental, behavioural, psychosocial, and cultural factors (Table 36.3).

The complex mechanisms by which risk and protective factors (see Box 36.1) mediate and modulate development of substance misuse is beyond the scope of this chapter and interested readers may refer to excellent reviews or text books [10,11].

## Antecedent and Co-Morbid Mental Health Problems

Community-based longitudinal studies show that depression may predict alcohol dependence and cannabis use (see Box 36.2 for a list of high-risk groups) [12]. In addition, conduct problems in childhood predict substance abuse and dependence in early adulthood, after controlling for a range of social and other covariates [2]. Similarly, untreated attention deficit hyperactivity disorder (ADHD) has been shown to be a significant risk factor for development of substance misuse in adolescence and adulthood [13].

**Table 36.3** Risk factors for the development of adolescent substance misuse

| Domain | Risk factor |
| --- | --- |
| Neurobiological | Genetic susceptibility to substance misuse |
| | Psycho-physiological vulnerability (EEG, ERPs) |
| | Neurochemical abnormalities (DA, 5-HT, opioids, etc.) |
| Psychological | Depressive disorder Anxiety disorder |
| | Early/persistent conduct symptoms, ADHD |
| | Physical and sexual abuse |
| | Traumatic/stressful life events Early onset of drug use |
| | Sensation-seeking traits in personality |
| Family | Drug use by parents/other family members Family conflict and disruption |
| | Inconsistent or harsh discipline |
| | Lack of parental expectations about their child's future |
| Peer group/school | Peer rejection/alienation from peer group |
| | Association with drug-using peer group |
| | Poor commitment to school |
| | Academic failure/under-achievement |
| Social /cultural | Easy availability of drugs |
| | Social norms or laws favourable to drug use |
| | Extreme economic deprivation |
| | Disorganized, anomic neighbourhood |

EEG, electroencephalogram; ERP, event-related potential; 5-HT, serotonin; DA, dopamine; ADHD, attention deficit hyperactivity disorder.

---

**Box 36.1  Protective factors**

- Close, affectionate parent–child relationship
- Parental monitoring of young person
- Authoritative parenting style
- High educational aspiration/commitment
- Having a non-drug-using peer group
- Good social and interpersonal skills
- Sense of bonding to school or other social institutions (sports club, church, mosque)
- Acceptance of socially approved values and norms of behaviour

---

**Box 36.2  High-risk groups (based on longitudinal studies)**

- Young offenders
- Children of drug misusing parents
- Children excluded from school/truants
- Young people looked after by local authority
- Young people leaving care
- Young homeless people
- Teenage mothers
- Young people attending mental health services
- Regular attendees of accident and emergency services

---

The combination of conduct disorder and hyperactivity carries a particularly high risk. The risk of development of substance misuse is high in children exposed to neglect and maltreatment [14,15].

Significant rates of co-morbid psychiatric disorders were reported in the community and clinical samples of young people with substance misuse. [16,17], the most common being conduct disorder, major depression, ADHD (with or without co-morbid conduct disorder), anxiety disorders [post-traumatic stress disorder (PTSD) and phobias] and bulimia nervosa. Coexisting substance misuse has implications for the onset, clinical course, treatment compliance and prognosis for young people with psychiatric disorders [16,17]. Co-morbid substance misuse is the single most important factor that increases the risk of suicide in young people with psychosis or major depression [18].

## Consequences and Associated Features of Substance Misuse

A hallmark of substance misuse in adolescents is impairment in psychosocial and academic functioning. Impairment can include family conflict or dysfunction, interpersonal conflict and academic failure. Associated characteristics such as offending behaviour, other high-risk behaviours and co-morbid psychiatric disorders contribute further to risks and impairments. Injecting drug use is rare and only a small minority of young people develop physical dependence. Mortality is high due to accidents, suicides and physical complications of substance misuse.

## Clinical Assessment

For a detailed clinical assessment, please refer to Appendix 36.1.

## Treatment

The primary goal of treatment is to achieve and maintain abstinence from substance use. While abstinence should remain the explicit, long-term goal of treatment, harm reduction may be an interim, implicit goal, in view of both the chronicity of substance misuse in some young people and the self-limited nature of substance misuse in others. Treatment modalities used are largely psycho-social. Medication is used as an adjunct only, although it may offer a window of opportunity for young people to engage in psychosocial treatment [19,20]. Approximately 2% of young people treated for substance misuse in the UK in 2011 made use of coexistent pharmacological therapies [21].

### Evidence Base for Treatment

Reviews of the literature on adolescent treatment outcomes have concluded that treatment is better than no treatment [22]. Naturalistic follow-up of young people in a number of treatment settings in the USA showed decreased substance misuse and criminal involvement, as well as improved psychological adjustment and school performance, 1 year after treatment [22,23]. Family therapy approaches such as multisystemic therapy [24] and multidimensional family therapy [25] have the best evidence base for efficacy across a number of domains [26], although individual approaches such as cognitive behavioural therapy (CBT), both alone and in combination with motivational enhancement, have shown to be efficacious [27,28]. There is an emerging evidence base for brief motivational interviewing as well [29–31].

Most of the research on psychological treatment comes from the US, and is not necessarily directly applicable to the UK context, in terms of both the resources required and the cultural differences. However, there are significant overlaps between different forms of psychotherapies in both theoretical conceptualizations and therapeutic techniques, and building on existing skills of practitioners working across voluntary and statutory agencies in the UK could prove to be an effective and cost-effective way of delivering evidence-based interventions [32]. Essential elements of a successful treatment programme are given in Box 36.3.

---

**Box 36.3 Essential elements of a successful treatment programme**

- An empathic and non-judgmental therapist, who takes painstaking efforts to engage even the 'hard to reach' youngster in the treatment process and rekindles the ability to hope and dream.
- A therapeutic process that involves structured and personalized feedback on risk and harm to young people; emphasis on personal responsibility for change; and strategies to increase self-esteem, self-efficacy, practical problem-solving skills and social skills.
- Involvement of family and other 'systems of care' – such as school, judicial system, social services, to address the multiple complex needs of young people.
- A lengthy period of retention in service to ensure good aftercare.

---

Integrated, mental health and substance misuse treatment should be offered to young people with co-morbid psychiatric disorders [30,33]. Inpatient treatment is required for a very small minority: in those with severe and chaotic substance misuse, repeated failed community detoxification, intravenous drug use with complications, and those with severe mental illness and risk of self-harm. Variables consistently related to successful outcome are treatment completion, low pretreatment substance use, and peer and parent social support [22]. Other factors predictive of outcome are involvement of family, use of practical problem-solving, and provision of comprehensive services such as housing, academic assistance and recreation [27]·

Family/systemic interventions provide the best outcomes for young people with substance misuse, although even the most intensive forms of systemic therapies may fall short of producing enduring changes, especially for marginalized young people and communities. Appreciative inquiry is one of the most significant innovations in action research in the past decade and a method of producing long-lasting changes to the larger social system and there is anecdotal evidence for its efficacy in marginalized young people with drug and alcohol misuse, but large-scale studies are needed to substantiate these findings [34].

## Role of Child and Adolescent Substance Mental Health Services (CAMHS)

There are ongoing debates regarding the role of CAMHS in adolescent substance misuse. Professionals working in CAMHS have an unrivalled opportunity to play a significant role in the early identification and treatment of substance misuse, including children of substance-misusing parents and other high-risk groups [35]. Specific treatment of 'core' mental health problems such as depression, eating disorders, ADHD and PTSD is a primary role of the specialist CAMHS. CAMHS professionals could help to develop multi-agency treatment services and train other professionals in evidence-based interventions.

## Conclusions

The perception of substance misuse in young people has been marred by many myths held by both society and health professionals. Substance use is often seen as an acceptable and invariable part of adolescence, and treatment is commonly viewed as either unnecessary or futile. Research shows that early identification and comprehensive treatment of young people who show persistent difficulties could help to reduce the morbidity and mortality and prevent the derailment of their developmental trajectory. Everything that is done to help troubled and troublesome children should be informed by a sense of history, a reflective awareness of current value systems, economic and social factors, and a mature and balanced judgment of what is possible and what is not. Integrative, multi-agency treatments addressing a range of ecologically valid aetiological factors have the potential to engender a culture of therapeutic optimism.

## References

1 Newcomb MD (1997) Psychosocial predictors and consequences of drug use: a developmental perspective within a prospective study. Journal of Addictive Diseases, 16, 1–89.
2 Gilvarry E (2000) Substance abuse in young people. Journal of Child Psychology and Psychiatry, 41, 55–80.
3 The Home Office (2014) Drug Misuse: Findings from the 2013/14 Crime Survey for England and Wales. https://www.gov.uk/government/publications/drug-misuse-findings-from-the-2013-to- 2014-csew/drug-misuse-findings-from-the-201314-crime-survey-for-england-and-wales.
4 Health and Social Care Information Centre (2014) Statistics on Drug Misuse: England 2014. Online: http://www.hscic.gov.uk/catalogue/PUB15943/drug-misu-eng-2014-rep.pdf. Accessed: January 2017.
5 Hibbel B, Guttormsson U, Ahlström S et al. (2011) The 2011 ESPAD Report: Substance Use Among Students in 35 European Countries, The Swedish Council for Information on Alcohol and Other Drugs (CAN) Stockholm, 2009: Online: http://www.can.se/contentassets/8d8cb78bbd28493b9030c65c598e3301/the_2011_espad_report_full.pdf. Accessed: January 2017.
6 Mirza KAH, Mirza S (2008) Adolescent substance misuse. In: Psychiatry. London, UK: Medicine Publishing Group.
7 Kandel DB (ed.) (2002) Stages and Pathways of Drug Involvement: Examining the Gateway Hypothesis. Cambridge, UK: Cambridge University Press.
8 Halikas A, Lyttle M, Morse C (1990) Proposed criteria for the diagnosis of alcohol abuse in adolescence. Comprehensive Psychiatry, 25, 581–585.
9 Nutt D, King LA, Saulsbury W, Blakemore C (2007) Development of a rational scale to assess the harm of drugs of potential misuse. Lancet, 369, 1047–1053.
10 Hawkins JD, Catalano RF, Miller RF (1992) Risk and protective factors for alcohol and other drug problems in adolescence and early adulthood. Implications for substance abuse problems. Psychological Bulletin, 112, 64–105.
11 Swadi H (1999) Individual risk factors for adolescent substance use. Drug and Alcohol Dependence, 55, 209–24.
12 Pardini D, White Raskin H, Stouthamer-Loeber M (2007) Early adolescent psychopathology as a predictor of alcohol use disorders by early adulthood. Drug and Alcohol Dependence, 88, 38–49.
13 Wilens TE, Faroane S, Biederman J, Gunawardene S (2003) Does stimulant therapy of attention deficit-/hyperactivity disorder beget later substance misuse? A meta analytic review of the literature. Pediatrics, 111, 179–185.
14 Kendler KS, Bulik CM, Silberg J et al. (2000) Childhood sexual abuse and adult psychiatric and substance use disorders in women: an epidemiological and cotwin control analysis. Archives of General Psychiatry, 57, 953–959.
15 De Bellis MD (2005) The psychobiology of neglect: a review. Child Maltreatment, 10, 150–172.
16 Boys A, Farrell M, Taylor C et al. (2003) Psychiatric morbidity and substance use in young people aged 13–15 years: results from the Child and Adolescent Survey of Mental Health. British Journal of Psychiatry, 182, 509–517.

17 Roberts R, Roberts C, Yun X (2007) Comorbidity of substance use and other psychiatric disorders among adolescence. Evidence from an epidemiological survey. Drug and Alcohol Dependence, 88, 513–516.

18 Mirza KAH (2002) Adolescent substance use disorder: In Practical child and adolescent psychopharmacology, S. Kutcher, eds Cambridge Monograph Series. Cambridge University Press.

19 Marshall E, Mirza KAH (2000) Psychopharmacological treatment. In: Gilvarry E, McArdle P (eds) Clinics in Developmental Medicine, Alcohol, Drugs and Young people. Clinical Approaches. London: MacKeith Press.

20 Williams RJ, Chang SY. A comprehensive and comparative review of adolescent substance abuse treatment outcome. Clinical Psychological Science Practice, 7, 138–166.

21 Bateman J, Gilvarry E, Tziggili M et al. (2013) Psychopharmacological treatment of young people with substance dependence: a survey of prescribing practices in England. Child and Adolescent Mental Health. DOI: 10.1111/camh.12013.

22 Hser Y, Grella CE, Hubbard RL (2000) An evaluation of drug treatments for adolescents in four US cities. Archives of General Psychiatry, 58, 689–695.

23 Henggeler SW, Clingempeel WG, Brondino MJ, Pickrel SG (2002) Four year follow up of multisystemic therapy with substance abusing and substance- dependent juvenile offenders. Journal of American Academic Child Adolescent Psychiatry, 41, 868–874.

24 Liddle HA, Dakof GA, Parker K et al. (2001) Multidimensional family therapy for adolescent substance abuse: results of a randomised clinical trial. American Journal of Drug Alcohol Abuse, 27, 651–687.

25 Stanton MD, Shadish WR (1997) Outcome, attrition, and family-couple treatment for drug abuse: a meta-analysis and review of the controlled, comparative studies. Psychological Bulletin, 10, 35–44.

26 Williams RJ, and Chang SY (2000) A comprehensive and comparative review of adolescent substance abuse treatment outcome. Clinical Psychology Science Practice, 7, 138–166.

27 Waldron HB, Kaminer Y (2004) On the learning curve: the emerging evidence supporting cognitive-behavioural therapies for adolescent substance abuse Addiction, 99, 93–105.

28 Hulse GK, Robertson SI, Tait RJ (2001) Adolescent emergency department presentations with alcohol and other drug related problems in Perth, Western Australia, Addiction, 96, 1059–1067.

29 McCambridge J, Strang J (2004) The efficacy of single-session motivational interviewing in reducing drug consumption and perceptions of drug-related risk and harm among young people, results from a multi-site cluster randomised trial. Addiction 99, 39–52.

30 O'Leary TA, Monti PM (2004) Motivational enhancement and other brief interventions for adolescent substance abuse: foundations, applications and evaluations, Addiction, 99, 63–75.

31 Libby AM, Riggs PD (2005) Integrated substance use and mental health treatment for adolescents: aligning organizational and financial incentives. Journal of Child and Adolescent Psychopharmacology, 5, 826–834.

32 Gilvarry E, McArdle P, Mirza KAH et al. (2012) Practice standards for the assessment and treatment of children and young people with substance misuse. London, UK: The Royal College of Psychiatrists and Department of health. Online: http://www.rcpsych.ac.uk/pdf/Practice%20standards%20for%20young%20people%20with%20substance%20misuse%20problems.pdf. Accessed: January 2017.

33  Mirza KAH, Buckstein O (2010) Assessment and treatment of young people with ADHD, disruptive behaviour disorder and co morbid substance use disorder. In: Kaminer Y, Winters K (eds) Clinical Manual of Adolescent Substance Abuse Treatment. Washington DC: American Psychiatric Publishing.

34  McAdam E, Mirza KAH (2009) Drugs, hopes and dreams: appreciative inquiry with marginalized young people using drugs and alcohol. Journal of Family Therapy, 31, 175–193.

35  Mirza KAH, McArdle P, Gilvarry E, Crome I (eds) The Role of CAMHS and Addiction Psychiatry in Adolescent Substance Misuse. The National Treatment Agency. London, 2007. Online: http://www.nta.nhs.uk/uploads/yp_camhs280508.pdf. Accessed: January 2017.

## Appendix 36.1  Clinical Assessment

- Information should be obtained from a variety of sources, including the young person, parents/other caregivers, general practitioner, school, social services, youth justice system or any other social agencies involved. Clinical and research experience shows that young people are generally more reliable informants than might be assumed.
- The attitude of the clinician should be flexible, empathic and non-judgmental to engage the young person in the assessment process and to obtain a valid estimate of substance use.
- Explore the young person's leisure activities and gently guide them to talk about the nature and extent of substance use, context and its impact on various domains of their psycho-social functioning. This would enable the clinician to determine whether the current pattern of substance use constitutes normative stages of substance use or meets diagnostic criteria for harmful use or dependence.
- Detailed exploration of co-morbid psychiatric disorders and their relationship to substance misuse would help formulate a differential diagnosis and treatment plan.
- Substance misuse is almost always not the only problem and a comprehensive developmental, social and medical history should be undertaken to determine the multiple complex needs across different domains.
- Particular attention should be paid to the young person's vulnerability, resilience, hopes and aspirations.
- Evaluating the adolescent's readiness for treatment or stage of change may help determine the initial treatment goals or level of care.

### Mental State Examination and Physical Examination

- Physical examination including basic neurological examination should always be undertaken. Specific attention should be paid to signs of liver disease, tachycardia and high blood pressure, which may indicate excessive substance use or withdrawals states.
- Risk of harm to self and others should be systematically assessed, especially in young people with a history of offending behaviour and those with co-morbid psychopathology

- Young people may present with features of intoxication or withdrawal. Recent injecting sites, bloodshot eyes, nicotine stains on fingers, unsteady gait and tremulousness give indications of the extent of substance use. Inhaling solvents from the bag may lead to a rash around the mouth and nose.
- Perceptual abnormalities may suggest a primary psychotic illness or the use of drugs such as cannabis, alcohol, amphetamine or cocaine.

### Investigations

- Haematological and biochemical investigations like liver function tests are helpful to establish drug- and alcohol-related harm.
- Testing bodily fluids (urine, saliva, blood) for specific substances should be part of the initial evaluation, especially in inpatient settings and for court-mandated assessments. Most substances – except benzodiazepine, methadone and cannabis – are detectable in urine for a few days only. Considering this and the potential for adulteration of samples, a negative urine result does not necessarily mean that the young person is not using drugs.
- Hair test is more reliable as it gives a longer historical profile of drug use (up to 1 month).
- Some professionals argue that testing adds little to the verbal reports of substance use in young people, especially when clinicians have managed to nurture a trusting therapeutic relationship with them.
- There is little evidence at present to recommend repeated testing of bodily fluids to monitor routine clinical treatment.

# Section 5

# Assessment and Approaches to Intervention

# 37

# New Perspectives on the Classification of Child Psychiatric Disorders

*Elena Garralda[1]*

## Introduction

Classification is a tool for communication so that when clinicians or policy-makers or researchers refer to some feature they mean the same thing [1]. To classify is to arrange things in groups that have some characteristic in common, that are mutually exclusive and jointly exhaustive, and where definitions are supported by extensive and reliable data [2].

The classification of medical disorders remains crucial to communication between those involved with health services, and diagnoses are increasingly a requirement for service function and development. The two most widely used classification systems of mental health disorders are the World Health Organization's *International Classification of Diseases* (ICD) [3] and the American Psychiatric Association's *Diagnostic and Statistical Manual of Mental Disorders* (DSM) [4].

Their most recent revisions (DSM-5 and the forthcoming ICD-11) aim to reflect our current understanding of these disorders as well as clinical consensus and utility in practice. Overall psychiatric diagnoses, rather than immutable statements of objective phenomena, may be regarded as guide points or hypotheses for understanding, communicating and setting treatment.

## The Modern Area of Classification of Psychiatric Disorders

The modern area in psychiatric classification started with the development of a *Glossary of Mental Disorders and Guide to Classification* in 1974 (8th version of ICD), which brought order to the previous 'chaotic state of the classifications in use in psychiatry' [2], and in the USA with DSM-III's (1980) narrative description of the clinical features of disorders. There has been a concerted effort to harmonize DSM and ICD classifications, and recent versions are similar conceptually, in diagnostic terms and descriptions. Recent revisions have been guided by considerations that they are suitable for billing for service and the production of national statistics about mental disorders, and

---

1 The author has chaired WHO's ICD-11 Working Groups on Neurodevelopmental Disorders and Disruptive Dissocial Disorders. However, the views expressed here are the author's and they are not representative of the WHO or its Working Groups. Reference to ICD disorders reflects work still in progress.

*Child Psychology and Psychiatry: Frameworks for Clinical Training and Practice*, Third Edition.
Edited by David Skuse, Helen Bruce and Linda Dowdney.

that they serve as an internationally common language for researchers. They also aim to represent opinions of psychiatrists and other mental health personnel, and practice in different settings and cultures.

In medicine, there is often not a clear separating line between early clinical changes and treatable disorders, and this lies at the root of the debate about the advantages and disadvantages of the dimensional versus the dichotomous approach to health problems. When is elevated blood pressure a disease requiring treatment? When are adolescent mood changes a depressive disorder? Classificatory systems follow the taxonomical dichotomous tradition and aim to describe the crucial symptoms that cluster together into clinically recognizable entities that open the way to potentially efficacious treatments.

In contrast with general medicine, where the main job is to identify and treat physical diseases established by clinical syndromes that are supported by abnormal physical signs or laboratory findings, psychiatry puts emphasis on the concept of disorder supported by patient distress and suffering that cause impairment and interference with activities. Thus, both ICD and DSM define disorders by implying the existence of a clinically recognizable set of symptoms or behaviours associated in most cases with distress and interference with personal functions. The overall philosophy of their newer versions has been one of reducing the number of diagnozable disorders, leaving the best validated and most clinically helpful, and the general convention is one of allowing multiple diagnoses when present.

## Classification in Child and Adolescent Psychiatry

As in other fields, classification in child and adolescent psychiatry is a tool for communication amongst clinicians and researchers, for application of research to clinical problems, guidance on practice, explanations to patients and clinical reimbursement. For all these purposes, a good scientific classification should have the virtues of clarity, comprehensiveness acceptability to users and fidelity to nature. A scheme should also be flexible and change as understanding alters [1].

Earlier ICD classifications supported a multi-dimensional and multi-axial framework for child psychiatric diagnoses, as did DSM-IV for disorders across the age range. The multi-axial system allowed diagnoses in the following five areas:

- psychiatric syndromes
- developmental or personality disorders
- medical disorders
- psycho-social and environmental stressors
- overall clinical severity

It is particularly well suited to child psychiatric practice and avoids having to choose between two disorders in hierarchical classifications. Nevertheless, DSM-5 Working Parties concluded that the multi-axial system was no longer advisable and it no longer features in current revisions.

The previous hierarchical approach whereby one disorder would take precedence and encompass any accompanying symptoms from others is also now modified. Psychiatric co-morbidity is allowed, provided that the symptoms of each disorder are sufficiently extensive and impairing to justify more than one diagnosis and also that they are not better explained by a single psychiatric disorder.

# Child and Adolescent Psychiatric Disorders in DSM 5 and as Proposed for ICD 11

The ICD-10 classifies psychiatric disorders under three different umbrellas:

1) psychological development (affecting intellectual, learning and communication functions);
2) behavioural and emotional disorders occurring in childhood/adolescence and reflecting the immaturities of childhood (e.g. hyperkinetic, conduct, emotional disorders; social functioning disorders; tics, enuresis and encopresis, feeding and stereotyped movement disorders);
3) disorders applying across the age and developmental range, including mental retardation.

However, a decision was taken early on in DSM-5/ ICD-11 preparatory work to modify the placement of the more characteristic child psychiatric disorders and to spread and merge them across ICD-11 categories. It therefore became essential for all diagnoses to provide a lifetime perspective and an explicit set of instructions for the ways in which manifestations vary with age [5]. This decision is supported by the realization that most adult disorders can manifest in childhood, many young adults with psychiatric disorders have psychiatric diagnoses in childhood/adolescence, and there are strong continuities between child and adult disorders.

The DSM-5 begins with the neurodevelopmental disorders and in both systems the diagnostic categories most characteristic of childhood remain those that onset in the first few years of life, now grouped under the clusters of neuro-developmental and disruptive-dissocial disorders (Table 37.1).

## The Neurodevelopmental Disorders

In DSM-5 the neurodevelopment disorders are characterized by persistent behavioural and cognitive problems that affect brain-based functions, including intellectual function and learning, communication and social function, attention and motor control. Their onset is during the early childhood developmental period. They cause impairment in activities and performance and can persist into adulthood [6]. The neurodevelopmental cluster now includes intellectual disability and attention deficit disorders. ICD-11 neurodevelopmental disorders are generally congruent with this definition and classification, except for minor differences in terminology.

### Autistic Disorders

Both classificatory systems introduce important and largely comparable changes to the definition of autism, with a consolidation under this umbrella term of a number of related disorders (e.g. autism, asperger syndrome, disintegrative and pervasive developmental). The previously defining triad of impairment becomes a dyad with anomalies in two key dimensions: social communication and restricted repetitive behaviours [7]. In DSM-5 the diversity of the syndrome is represented by specifiers signalling the concurrent presence of intellectual disability or language disorder, of known medical conditions of co-morbid neurodevelopmental, mental or behaviour disorders or of catatonia,

**Table 37.1** Neurodevelopmental disorders and disruptive/dissocial/conduct disorders in the *Diagnostic and Statistical Manual of Mental Disorders* (DSM) and as proposed for the *ICD-11 Classification of Mental and Behavioural Disorders*

| DSM-5 | Proposed for ICD-11 |
|---|---|
| *Neurodevelopmental disorders* | *Neurodevelopmental disorders* |
| Intellectual disabilities | Disorders of intellectual development |
| Communication disorder | Developmental disorders of speech and language |
|   – includes language, speech sound, fluency, social/pragmatic | |
| Autistic spectrum disorder | Autism spectrum disorder |
| Attention deficit hyperactivity disorder | Attention deficit disorders |
| Specific learning disorder | Specific developmental learning disorders |
| Motor disorders | Specific coordination disorder |
|   – includes coordination, stereotypic, tics | Stereotyped movement disorder/tic disorder |
| *Disruptive, impulse-control and conduct disorders* | *Disruptive behaviour and dissocial disorders* |
| Oppositional defiant disorder | Oppositional defiant disorder |
| |   – with chronic irritability-anger |
| Conduct disorder | Conduct – dissocial disorder |
|   – with childhood/adolescent/unspecified onset |   – with childhood/adolescent onset |
|   – with limited prosocial emotions |   – with limited pro-social emotions |
| Intermittent explosive disorder | Intermittent explosive disorder |
| Pyromania and kleptomania | |

which often determine general management and the level of support required. It is also made explicit that autistic spectrum disorders are seen across the life span.

### Developmental Language or Communication Disorders

These continue to be characterized by persistent difficulties arising during early childhood in the acquisition, understanding, production or use of language, causing significant limitations in the ability to communicate. Problems that primarily involve expressive or pragmatic language (i.e. difficulties in the understanding and use of language in social contexts, such as making inferences, understanding verbal humour and resolving ambiguous meanings, *unaccompanied* by repetitive and restricted interests) can be separately identified.

## The Classification of Disruptive, Dissocial and Conduct Disorders

Comparable though not identical terminology defines disruptive disorders in both classificatory systems (Table 37.1). Noteworthy is the introduction of a limited prosocial emotions qualifier under conduct disorders, reflecting the growing literature on childhood 'callous and emotional traits' as being identifiable, relatively stable and linked to the more severe, aggressive and stable pattern of antisocial behaviour [8]. Both systems include, somewhat controversially, age of onset subtypes [9]. The childhood type involves earlier onset and more severe, complex and persistent problems. The two classificatory systems are, however, discrepant in the approach taken to the diagnosis of children presenting with both oppositional behaviour and marked irritability. In ICD-11 they would be regarded as having oppositional defiant disorders qualified by marked irritability, but DSM 5 classifies many of these children's problems under a new separate category, disruptive mood dysregulation disorder, as part of the depressive disorders group. This disorder has been criticized because of limited diagnostic reliability and high rates of overlap with other disorders [10].

## Future Approaches to Classification

A challenge to future versions of both DSM-5 and ICD-11 may come from research into brain functions underlying mental health problems. The USA's National Institute for Mental Health is advocating alternative research domain criteria [11]. These rest on a conceptualization of mental illnesses as dysfunction/disorders of brain circuits identified with the tools of clinical neuroscience, alongside expectations that genetics and clinical neuroscience will yield bio-signatures to complement clinical symptoms and signs. If this and similar initiatives lead to major breakthroughs in our understanding of the nature and management of mental health disorders, they may be expected to have a noticeable impact on future classifications.

## Classification and Child and Adolescent Mental Health Practice

In an increasingly globalized and better informed world, there is a strong drive to follow a common, empirically oriented terminology such as those of ICD and DSM. This is not always popular with clinicians and multidisciplinary child and adolescent mental health services (CAMHS), some of which advocate a broad diagnostic-*less* approach or local idiosyncratic classifications. Possible challenges to adopting the diagnostic approach include the following:

- Limited knowledge in the general population and amongst referring primary care workers about child and adolescent mental health problems, requiring ongoing educational efforts [12,13].
- The importance of psycho-social influences for child and adolescent mental health and the frequent use in CAMHS of *trans*-diagnostic treatment techniques, such as stress reduction, therapeutic empathy/understanding, work on parenting and family relationships. These may unwittingly obscure the centrality of diagnosis for the use of evidence-based, disorder-specific treatments [14].
- Insufficient appreciation that the diagnostic categorical/dimensional approaches are not opposites but complementary when summarizing children's problems and treatment progress [1,15]; also that diagnosis needs to be supplemented by a formulation

of the child's problems that details risk and protective predisposing, precipitant and maintaining factors [16].

- The misleading notion that complex childhood problems do not fit into diagnostic categories. Rather, problem complexity is often an expression of co-morbidity, as between neurodevelopmental and other psychiatric disorders, all of which need to be identified and inform management. It may also represent the early stages of severe mental or of emerging personality disorders [17].
- There is ongoing debate as to whether diagnosis stigmatizes children or whether it de-stigmatizes unusual behaviours and emotions by giving them a meaningful name that opens the way to effective treatments.

## Final Considerations

Psychiatric disorders are human constructs and works in progress. Diagnoses need to adapt and change in the light of new knowledge and expertise. Their ultimate goal is to integrate knowledge, aid communication between all those involved and open the way for a new and better understanding and management of mental health problems.

## References

1  Taylor E, Rutter M (2008) Classification. In: Rutter MJ, Bishop D, Pine D et al. (eds) Rutter's Child and Adolescent Psychiatry, 5th edn. Oxford: Blackwell.

2  Cooper JE, Sartorius N (2001) A companion to the classification of mental disorders. Oxford: Oxford University Press.

3  WHO (1992) The ICD-10 Classification of Mental and Behavioural Disorders: Clinical Descriptions and Diagnostic Guidelines, 10th edn. Geneva: World Health Organization.

4  American Psychiatric Association (2013) Diagnostic and Statistical Manual of Mental Disorders, 5th edn. Washington DC: American Psychiatric Association.

5  Rutter M (2011) Research review: child psychiatric diagnosis and classification: concepts, findings, challenges and potential. Journal of Child Psychology and Psychiatry, 52, 647–660.

6  Andrews G, Pine DS, Hobbs MJ et al. (2009) Neurodevelopmental disorders: Cluster 2 of the proposed meta-structure for DSMV and ICD11. Psychological Medicine, 39, 2013–2023.

7  Mandy PL, Chairman T, Skuse DH (2012) Testing the construct validity of proposed criteria for DSM-5 autism spectrum disorder. Journal of the American Academy of Child & Adolescent Psychiatry, 51, 41–50.

8  Frick JP, White SF (2008) Research review: the importance of callous unemotional traits for developmental models of aggressive and antisocial behaviour. Journal of Child Psychology and Psychiatry, 49, 359–375.

9  Fairchild G, van Goozen SHM, Calder AJ, Goodyer IM (2013) Review: evaluating and reformulating the developmental taxonomic theory of antisocial behaviour. Journal of Child Psychology and Psychiatry, 54, 924–940.

10 Lochman JE, Evans SC, Burke JD et al. (2015) An empirically based alternative to DSM-5's disruptive mood dysregulation disorder for ICD-11. World Psychiatry, 14, 30–33.

11 Insel T, Cuthbert B, Riegarvey M et al. (2010) Research domain criteria (RDoC) – toward a new classification framework for research on mental disorders. American Journal of Psychiatry, 167, 748–751.

12 MindEd. https://www.minded.org.uk. Accessed: November 2015.

13 Kramer T, Garralda ME. Assessment and treatment in non-specialist community health care settings. In Thapar et al (Eds), Rutter's Child and Adolescent Psychiatry 6th Edition. Oxford: Wiley-Blackwell; 2015.

14 National Institute for Health and Care Excellence. https://www.nice.org.uk. Accessed: November 2015.

15 Garralda ME (2009) Accountability of specialist child and adolescent mental health services. British Journal of Psychiatry, 194, 389–391.

16 Carrey N, Gregson J (2008) A context for classification in child psychiatry. Journal of the Canadian Academy of Child and Adolescent Psychiatry, 17, 50–57.

17 Tyrer P, Reed GM, Crawford MJ (2015) Personality disorder 1 – classification, assessment, prevalence, and effect of personality disorder. Lancet, 385, 727–734.

38

# Paediatric Neuropsychological Assessment: Domains for Assessment

*Jane Gilmour and Bettina Hohnen*

## Introduction

We provide here an introduction to the characteristics and parameters of specialist child neuropsychological assessments for clinical or research purposes. We discuss measurement issues, the main neuropsychological domains requiring specialized assessment, some relevant standardized assessments appropriate to these domains, alongside a consideration of their psychometric properties.

## Why Undertake a Specialized Neuropsychological Assessment?

For the purposes of this review, specialized tests are those that describe specific aspects of brain function, such as memory and language, as opposed to tests of general ability (IQ). Many specific areas of cognitive functioning contribute to IQ; therefore one would predict that an individual with an IQ < 70, for example (where the mean is 100 and the standard deviation is 15), would score in the low-performance bands of specialized tasks. On the other hand, some individuals, including those with average or high-range IQ scores, have a markedly low test performance in one or more areas of specific brain functioning relative to general ability. Such individuals are described as having a specific learning difficulty (SLD). Specialized neuropsychological assessment is therefore likely to be important in identifying the nature of an SLD for single clinical cases or groups in research.

## When is a Specialized Neuropsychological Assessment Justified?

Gaining an objective measure of IQ and attainment is usually the first stage of a clinical or research investigation into cognitive functioning and can be obtained by full administration of an age-appropriate standardized IQ assessment, such as the Wechsler Intelligence Scales for Children (WISC-V$^{UK}$) [1]. In many cases, no further testing is warranted, e.g. when an IQ test indicates that a child has general learning difficulties.

*Child Psychology and Psychiatry: Frameworks for Clinical Training and Practice,* Third Edition.
Edited by David Skuse, Helen Bruce and Linda Dowdney.
© 2017 John Wiley & Sons, Ltd. Published 2017 by John Wiley & Sons, Ltd.

However, there are two common scenarios where additional specialized neuropsychological assessment is justified:

- Groups or individuals with a markedly uneven IQ profile may require an assessment of specific cognitive functioning. Differences in general-ability domains that have statistical significance (i.e. the probability that the difference found between groups could have occurred by chance) are, by definition, relatively common, but discrepancies that have clinical significance (which considers how often this difference would be found in the population) are usually notably larger and may warrant further investigation. For example, individuals with a disproportionately low perceptual reasoning (PR) factor score relative to other factor scores (verbal comprehension, working memory and processing speed) on the WISC-V$^{UK}$ may have visual difficulties, dyspraxia (clumsiness), visual motor integration problems or – as a high PR score depends on a swift response – simply low motivation. Tests of specialized neuropsychological functioning can be used to exclude competing explanatory hypotheses.
- A child who has an attainment level significantly below the predicted level given their measured IQ may have an SLD such as primary literacy or numeracy dysfunction. It is important to note that low attainment relative to IQ is common in children of school age. Many factors could explain this profile, including emotional and behavioural difficulties or school-based variables. In other words, an SLD is a possible cause of poor school performance relative to general ability, but it is not the only feasible explanation.

## Measurement Considerations

A number of issues should be considered when assessing paediatric and clinical populations.

### Developmental Considerations

Broadly speaking there are relatively few specialized tests appropriate for preschool children. In part this is because very young children are a challenge to test reliably and their neuropsychological function is more difficult to capture. There are a few tests that are useful adjuncts to a general IQ assessment, such as tests of phonological processing [2], working memory [3] and declarative memory [4]. When interpreting data at this young age, bear in mind that some children may 'catch up' in their test performance over time because of neural plasticity or behavioural compensation strategies. For research studies in particular, it is often interesting to take a developmental approach in the assessment of specific areas of functioning.

### Be Sure of Why the Child Fails a Task – What is Their Route to Failure?

The non-specific abilities required to complete a given task should be considered, as there are many routes to failure. Many clinical populations have complex neuropsychological cognitive profiles. For example, there is a high degree of comorbidity between reading problems and attention deficit hyperactivity disorder (ADHD) [5]. Many, but not all, children with ADHD perform poorly on the Continuous Performance Task

(CPT) [6], a test of selective attention. McGee *et al.* [7] report that children with a reading disorder score significantly lower than non-reading-disordered groups on the CPT. For such reading-disordered children it would be wrong to conclude that a low score on the CPT necessarily indicates difficulty with the target skill, i.e. selective attention. Reading-disordered children have difficulty processing moving visual stimuli [8]. The CPT includes such stimuli, but the aim of the task is to capture the ability to attend to pertinent information and screen out irrelevant data, rather than to assess generic visual processing abilities. In other words, the CPT identifies children with target function difficulties (selective attention) and those who have problems with the non-specific demands of the test (processing dynamic visual stimuli).

Where possible, clinical populations should be assessed using a number of tests, presented in a variety of modalities that purport to assess the same target function so that core deficits can be identified.

### Psychometrics

#### Reliability and Validity

Some published tests have questionable psychometric properties. Reliability and validity are also important considerations when choosing a test and deciding how much weight to place on findings. There is no objective cut-off, but the general consensus is that, in relation to reliability, a correlation coefficient ($r$) of greater than 0.6 on test–retest is the accepted minimum for a test to be judged reliable. The validity of a test is measured in a number of ways, the most important of these being construct validity (the degree to which the test measures what it purports to measure). Even if reliability and validity are strong, it's also important to consider the size and character of the population on which the norms are based. In some cases $N$-values are surprisingly small which would affect the confidence that should be given to any interpretation.

#### Interpreting Scores

Be careful when considering test items not to overinterpret one or two outliers in the sample of tests as indicating real deficits. There is a risk of making a type 1 error (reporting a difference when there is none). Composite scores are created from individual subtest scores. These are more reliable than interpretations based on individual scores, as the standard error of measurement is reduced due to the larger number of items making up the score [9].

## Domains of Specialist Assessment

Tables 38.1–38.6 review a selection of published tasks assessing specific aspects of brain function. They include target functions and some of the non-specific skills required to complete the task.

### General Ability

Any specialized neuropsychological assessment relies on measured IQ to establish a general level of cognitive functioning as an indicator of general ability. A full IQ assessment

**Table 38.1** Memory assessment measures

| Assessment | Target function | Reference population (*n*) in each age band | Non-specific abilities[a] | Age range (years, to nearest whole year) | Comments |
|---|---|---|---|---|---|
| Automated Working Memory Assessment [11] | Memory – short-term and working memory<br><br>Visual-spatial and verbal | 59–67 | | 4–22 | Computer administration and scoring |
| Working Memory Test Battery for Children [3] | Memory – short-term and working memory<br><br>Visual-spatial and verbal | 59–100 | | 4.7–16 | |
| Children's Auditory Verbal Learning Test – 2 [12] | Memory – verbal, immediate and delayed recall and recognition | 30–81 | | 6–17 | |
| Wide Range Assessment of Memory and Learning [13] | Memory – verbal and visual, delayed and immediate, recall and recognition | 110–117 | | 5–15 | |
| Rey–Osterrieth Complex Figure [14,15] | Memory – visual, immediate, delayed and recognition | 18–48 | Planning, visuo–motor skills | 6–15 | |
| Children's Memory Scale [16] | Memory – visual, verbal, immediate, delayed recall, attention, recognition, learning | 100 | | 2–16 | It is possible to predict a General Memory Index Score from WISC FS IQ |

| Test | Memory domain | Other measures | n | Age range | Comments |
| --- | --- | --- | --- | --- | --- |
| Digit Span (WISC-V$^{UK}$) [1] | Memory – auditory working | | 74 | 6–16 | |
| Rivermead Behavioural Memory Test [17,18] | Memory – everyday tasks | | 100 | 5–14 | |
| The Visual Memory Battery [19] | Memory – working and stored, recognition and learning | Sustained attention (matching to sample subtest) | 40 | 4 to adult | Computer administration and scoring. Motor speed is controlled |
| NEPSY – memory subtests [20] | Memory – visual, verbal, immediate and delayed | | 100 | 3–16 | Appropriate subtests: names and faces; narrative; sentences; list learning |
| Color Object Assessment Test (COAT) [4] | Declarative memory | | 94–139 per 6-month age band | 18–36 months | Only preschool memory assessment |
| Child and Adolescent Memory Profile (CHAMP) [21] | Memory – visual, verbal, immediate and delayed | | 115–295 per year age band | 4–24 years | |

a   Intact senses and motivation are assumed in all cases.

**Table 38.2** Language assessment measures.

| Assessment | Target function | Reference population (n) in each age band | Non-specific abilities[a] | Age range (years, to nearest whole year) | Comments |
|---|---|---|---|---|---|
| Clinical Evaluation of Language Fundamentals-3 [24] | Language – spoken expressive and receptive | 151–267 | Auditory attention | 5 to adult | Test–retest reliability on some subtests is low |
| Clinical Evaluation of Language Fundamentals – preschool [25] | Language – spoken expressive and receptive | 100 | Auditory attention | 3–6 | Test–retest reliability on some subtests is low |
| Test for the Reception of Grammar (TROG) [26] | Language – spoken receptive grammar | 120–217 | | 4 to adult | TROG-E was published in 2005 and is a computerized version of same test |
| British Picture Vocabulary Scale [27] | Language – spoken receptive naming grammar | 183–423 | Visual discrimination | 3–16 | 1997 stimuli are less ambiguous than those in previous editions |
| Renfrew Language Scales [28] | Language – spoken comprehension, word finding, expression, narrative speech | 58–101 | | 3–8 | |
| Token Test [29] | Language – spoken receptive comprehension of language concepts | 29–53 | Short-term (working) auditory memory | 6–13 | |
| NEPSY – language subtests [20] | Language – expressive and receptive, cognitive processes related to language | 100 | | 3–16 | Appropriate subtests: phonological processing; speeded naming; repetition of non-words; comprehension of instructions |

a  Intact senses and motivation are assumed in all cases.

**Table 38.3** Attention assessment measures.

| Assessment | Target function | Reference population (*n*) in each age band | Non-specific abilities[a] | Age range (years, to nearest whole year) | Comments |
|---|---|---|---|---|---|
| Continuous Performance Test [6] | Attention – visual sustained attention and impulsivity (behavioural inhibition) | 40 | Age-appropriate reading | 6 to adult | Gender-differentiated norms |
| Test of Everyday Attention-2 [31] | Attention – auditory and visual sustained and selective attention, response inhibition | 29–58 | Basic numeracy is required for some subtests | 5–15 | |
| Cambridge Neuropsychological Test Automated Battery [19] | Attention – sustained, selective and divided | 40 | | 4 to adult | Computer administration and scoring. Motor speed is controlled |
| NEPSY – attention subtests [20] | Attention – auditory – selective and sustained (vigilance) | 100 | | 5–16 | Appropriate subtest: Auditory Attention and Response Set |

[a] Intact senses and motivation are assumed in all cases.

**Table 38.4** Spatial/visual assessment measures.

| Assessment | Target function | Reference population (n) in each age band | Non-specific abilities[a] | Age range (years, to nearest whole year) | Comments |
|---|---|---|---|---|---|
| Developmental Test of Visual Motor Integration [33] | Visual discrimination, motor skill and visuo-motor integration | 6–16 | Impulsivity may interfere with performance in the motor skill subtest | 2–14 | Some debate regarding the graduation of test item difficulty |
| Trail Making A and B [34–37] | Visual search and sequencing/motor output | 10–101 | Knowledge of number and alphabet sequence | 6–15 | Parts A and B measure different functions |
| NEPSY – geometric puzzles [20] | Visuo-spatial ability | 100 | | 5–16 | |
| Gestalt Closure – Kaufman Assessment Battery for Children [38] | Visual – meaningful stimuli naming | 200–300 | Knowledge of industrialized world objects | 2–13 | |
| Face Recognition Test [32] | Visual/spatial ability – face recognition | 19–59 | | 6–14 | |
| Judgement of Line Orientation [37] | Visual–spatial judgment | 23–50 | | 7–14 | |
| Rey–Osterrieth Complex Figure Test (copy condition) [14,15,39,40] | Visual/motor planning | 18–48 | | 6–15 | |
| Right-left orientation [41] | Spatial discrimination | 7–6 | | 6–16[b] | |
| NEPSY – visual spatial subtests [20] | Motor and visual perception; line discrimination | 100 | | 3–16 | Appropriate subtests: design copy; arrows; route finding |

a  Intact senses and motivation are assumed in all cases.
b  Some extrapolated norms.

is usually required, although for research purposes a short version of a test can often be used from which to calculate a pro rata full-scale IQ score. Crawford *et al.* [10] have published on the reliability of a short-form administration procedure for the WISC-IV though at the time of publishing this had not been updated for the WISC-V [1].

### Memory

Standardized tests in this domain (Table 38.1) assess explicit memory or conscious recollection (for facts or events) as opposed to implicit (for skills or procedures) traces. There are separate dimensions of memory – working (short-term), stored (long-term), verbal, spatial (visual) and learning capacity. Individuals may have impairment in one domain but not in another. In addition, it is important to test both delayed recall and recognition. Children who do poorly on a test of recall but accurately recognize previously presented items can often store information but have problems accessing it.

### Language

Tests of language assessment fall into two categories: receptive and expressive. Visual language channels are independent of spoken language channels, and so assessments that focus on spoken language (reviewed in Table 38.2) do not necessarily exclude

**Table 38.5** Motor assessment measures

| Assessment[a] | Target function | Reference population (n) in each age band | Age range (years, to nearest whole year) | Comments |
|---|---|---|---|---|
| Finger Tapping Test [42] | Motor speed | 20 | 6–14 | Gender-differentiated norms. Boys are significantly better at this task |
| Purdue Pegboard Test [43,44] | Motor dexterity (fine) | 23–40 | 5–15 | Practice effects are notable |
| Cambridge Neuropsychological Test Automated Battery [19] | Motor speed and reaction time | 40 | 4 to adult | Computer administration and scoring. Motor speed is controlled |
| Grip strength [42] | Motor strength | 20 | 6–14 (no norms for 9–11) | Sex and hand preference differentiated norms |
| NEPSY – sensorimotor subtests [20] | Motor dexterity and motor speed; imitation of sequences; graphomotor speed and accuracy | 100 | 3–16 | Appropriate subtests: fingertip tapping, imitating hand positions, manual motor sequences, visuo-motor precision |

[a]  Intact senses and motivation are assumed in all cases.

**Table 38.6** Executive function and social cognition assessment measures.

| Assessment | Target function | Reference population (*n*) in each age band | Non-specific abilities[a] | Age range (years, to nearest whole year) | Comments |
|---|---|---|---|---|---|
| Delis–Kaplan Executive Function System (D-KEFS) [52] | Executive function | Approx. 100 | | 8 to adult | Some parallel versions of tasks. Good variety of tasks |
| Behavioural Assessment of Dysexecutive Syndrome (BADS) [53] | Executive function – predicts everyday function | 22–32 | | 7–15 | Computer administration and scoring. Motor speed is controlled |
| Cambridge Neuropsychological Test Automated Battery [19] | Executive function – working memory and planning | 40 | Sustained attention (matching to sample subtest) | 4 to adult | Computer administration and scoring. Motor speed is controlled |
| Trail Making A and B [34–36] | Executive function – motor planning and disinhibition | 10–101 | Number and alphabet sequence ability | 6–15 (some extrapolated norms) | Parts A and B measure independent functions |
| Rey–Osterrieth Complex Figure Test (copy condition) [14,15,39,40] | Executive function–visual planning | 18–48 | Visuo-motor skills | 6–15 | |
| Wisconsin Card Sorting Test [54] | Executive function – cognitive flexibility; concept formation | 27–55 | Colour vision, basic numeracy | 6 to adult | There is a positive relationship between years in education and performance |
| Stroop Word and Colour Test [55,56] | Executive function – inhibition of a prepotent response | 14–29 | Colour vision, literacy | Collated norms for 7–16 | All three conditions must be administered to control for speed of processing |
| Diagnostic Analysis of Non-verbal Accuracy 2 [57] | Social cognition – receptive non-verbal ability; voice and face recognition | 25–305 | Sustained auditory attention | 3 to adult (collated norms)[b] | Body language subtest has been dropped for the most recent edition |
| NEPSY – attention and executive function subtests [20] | Executive function – inhibit automatic response, planning and organization, shift set | 100 | | 3–16 | Appropriate subtests: inhibition, clocks, animal sorting, design fluency, Statue |

a Intact senses and motivation are assumed in all cases.
b Child faces only.

written language problems. However, specific written language impairment and spoken language vulnerabilities often co-occur [22]. Assessments of written language are likely to be classed as assessments of attainment, such as subtests of the Wechsler Individual Attainment Test [23]. A significant finding on any test of language would warrant a consultation with speech and language therapy colleagues.

## Attention

Attention has two main components: sustained (effortful processing over a significant period of time) and selective (vigilance for target stimuli while ignoring distracter stimuli). Many children with ADHD do poorly on these tests but there is no diagnostic cognitive test for the condition. It is identified on the basis of a pervasive behavioural profile (assessed for example using the Conners Rating Scale) [30] rather than performance on a cognitive task. Until recently, many tests of attention for children were rather theoretical, attempting to define a core cognitive deficit in children who have the ADHD behavioural profile (the debate about the existence and nature of such a core deficit continues). The Test of Everyday Attention for Children - 2 (TEACh-2) [31] provides a battery of tests of attention and inhibition presented in a variety of visual and auditory modalities (see Table 38.3).

## Spatial Ability

Spatial skills include the ability to mentally rotate visual configurations in space and to recognize that same configuration, regardless of its orientation. The Benton Face Recognition Test [32] (see Table 38.4) is a good example of a visual orientation task that uses meaningful stimuli. The Geometric Puzzles subtest of the NEPSY-II [20] assesses orientation using abstract stimuli.

Spatial ability also includes the naming of objects – though it could be argued that naming makes such high demands on visual memory that it is better described as a visual memory skill rather than a spatial ability *per se*. The Gestalt Closure subtest of the Kaufman Assessment Battery for Children is a test of visual naming that is appropriate for children [38]

## Motor Skills

Motor tests (Table 38.5) assess a number of separate elements – strength, speed and dexterity. Many tests of motor dexterity include a visual component (e.g. the Rey–Osterrieth Complex Figure) [39,40]. A good example of this is the Visual Motor Integration Test [33]. It is important to refer to occupational therapy colleagues in the light of a significant finding on any test of motor skills.

## Executive Function

Executive function (EF) includes initiation, planning, inhibition, flexibility, self-regulation, concept generation and working memory (Table 38.6). It is argued that grouping these together into a unitary concept is flawed as they are so diverse [45]. There is also controversy over the construct validity of the tasks that profess to assess EF. There has been much debate and research into the importance of and ability to train working memory in recent years [46] There is strong clinical and theoretical justification to develop more refined classifications of the functions associated with EF, particularly as investigations of EF are often central to the assessment of many clinical conditions. Deficits in EF are implicated in many disorders (e.g. ADHD, autistic spectrum disorders and schizophrenia) [47–49]. In addition to the psychometric assessments of EF outlined in Table 38.6, the Behavioural Rating Index of Executive Function (BRIEF) [50,51], a parent, teacher and child rating questionnaire, provides information about behaviours that are associated with executive function difficulties (preschool and school age versions exist).

### Social Cognition

Social cognition (see Table 38.6) covers many high-order brain functions, such as the expression and understanding of emotion, facial expression and subtleties of language embedded in social interaction. 'Theory of mind' describes the ability to 'mentalize' and infer another person's state of mind. For the purposes of this review, theory of mind is not considered an aspect of social cognition, but is regarded as a theoretical concept. Describing theory of mind as a concept rather than a brain function is not an attempt to disregard the significant empirical data showing that children with autistic spectrum disorders, particularly low-functioning individuals, perform poorly in theory-of-mind tasks [58].

The measurement of social cognition relies on consensus opinion, in contrast to other brain functions, which can be quantified using objective right or wrong answers. The complex nature of social cognition may explain why there are few standardized tests assessing this aspect of functioning, but the paucity of standardized measurement is a challenge to those working in the specialist assessment of cognitive functions. The NEPSY-II (2007) has two subtests that measure 'theory of mind' (ability to understand mental functions such as belief, intention, deception, emotion, imagination and pretending, as well as how emotion relates to social context) and 'affect recognition' (ability to recognize affect) [20]. It should be noted that our current assessment of social cognition from a neuropsychological perspective has many limitations although it is an area ripe for development given the importance of the domain to functioning. As things stand currently social cognition is perhaps best assessed using a combination of a detailed standardized development interview (such as the 3Di) [59] and a semi-structured observation schedule (such as the Autism Diagnostic Observation Schedule-II) [60].

## Conclusions

This chapter outlines measurement and testing considerations in the field of paediatric neuropsychology, principles which apply equally to clinical cases and research populations. There are three key points to consider when interpreting test results in the context of neuropsychological theory – these are given in Box 38.1.

---

**Box 38.1  Key points to consider when interpreting test results in the context of neuropsychological theory**

- **Record** – there must be a clear record of the test profile, including highlights of strengths and vulnerabilities that are *clinically significant* relative to the general population.
- **Recommend** – the score profile must be considered in terms of recommendations. What can the child (or group) do to adapt in light of the results? This may include encouraging compensatory strategies such as using verbal commentary on non-verbal tasks to bolster performance. More commonly, recommendations include considerations of how the adults who support young people might change the environment to accommodate the child so that they can function more easily; for example, teachers may provide written instructions rather than dictate information to decease the load on working memory.
- **Reinforce** – perhaps the most important task of result interpretation is to reinforce the concept of a 'growth mindset' [61] in which the belief that persistence and application will develop skills. This approach has been linked to increased academic success and positive experiences in the face of learning challenges in the general population and those with learning difficulties [62].

---

# References

1 Wechsler D (2014) Wechsler Intelligence Scales for Children, 5th edn. Bloomington, MN: Pearson.

2 Torgesen JK (1999) Comprehensive Test of Phonological Processing. Pearson Education.

3 Pickering SJ, Gathercole SE (2001) The Working Memory Test Battery for Children. London: Harcourt.

4 Jordan CM, Johnson AL, Hughes SJ, Shapiro EG (2006) The Color Object Association Test (COAT): the development of a measure of declarative memory for 18-to-36 month-old toddlers. Child Neuropsychology, 14, 21–41.

5 Willcutt EG, Pennington BF (2000) Psychiatric comorbidity in children and adolescents with reading disability. Journal of Child Psychology and Psychiatry, 41, 1039–48.

6 Conners CK, n.d Multi-Health Systems Staff (2014) Conners' Continuous Performance Test Version 3.0. Toronto: Multi-Health Systems.

7 McGee RA, Clark SE, Symons DK (2000) Does the Conners' Continuous Performance Test aid in ADHD diagnosis? Journal of Abnormal Child Psychology, 28, 415–424.

8 Eden GF, VanMeter JW, Rumsey JM et al. (1996) Abnormal processing of visual motion in dyslexia revealed by functional brain imaging. Nature, 382, 66–69.

9 Lezak MD, Howieson DB, Loring DW et al. (2004) Neuropsychological Assessment. Oxford Unitversity Press.

10 Crawford JR, Anderson V, Rankin PM, MacDonald J (2010) An index-based short-form of the WISC-IV with accompanying analysis of the reliability and abnormality of difference. British Journal of Clinical Psychology, 49, 235–258.

11  Alloway TP (2007) Automated Working Memory Assessment (AWMA). Pearson Education.

12  Talley JL (1993) Children's Auditory Verbal Learning Test – 2. Professional Manual. Lutz, FL: Psychological Assessment Resources.

13  Sheslow D, Adams A (1990) Wide Range Assessment of Memory and Learning (WRAML). Wilmington, DE: Wide Range.

14  Kolb B and Wishaw I (1990) Fundamentals of Human Neuropsychology, 3rd edn. New York: Freeman.

15  Meyers JE, Meyers KR (1995) Rey Complex Figure Test and Recognition Trial: Professional Manual. Odessa, FL: Psychological Assessment Resources Inc.

16  Cohen M (1997) The Children's Memory Scale. San Antonio, TX: The Psychological Corporation.

17  Aldrich FK, Wilson B (1991) Rivermead Behavioural Memory Test for Children: a preliminary evaluation. British Journal of Clinical Psychology, 30, 161–8.

18  Wilson BA, Forester S, Bryant T et al. (1991) Performance of 11–14-year-olds on the Rivermead Behavioural Memory Test. Clinical Psychology Forum, 30, 8–10.

19  The Cambridge Neuropsychological Test Automated Battery (CANTAB) (2001) Cambridge, UK: CeNeS Pharmaceuticals.

20  Korkman M, Kirk U, Kemp S (2007) NEPSY-II: A Developmental Neuropsychological Assessment II. San Antonio, TX: Psychological Corporation.

21  Sherman EMS, Brooks, BL (2015) Child and Adolescent Memory Profile. Ann Arbour, MI: Western Psychological Services.

22  Snowling MJ, Adams JW, Bishop DV et al. (2001) Educational attainments of school leavers with a preschool history of speech-language impairments. International Journal of Language and Communication Disorders, 36, 173–183.

23  Wechsler D (2005) Wechsler Individual Attainment Test. London: The Psychological Corporation.

24  Semel E, Wiig EH, Secord WA (2006) Clinical Evaluation of Language Fundamentals, 3rd edn. London: The Psychological Corporation.

25  Wiig EH, Secord W, Semel E (2006) The Clinical Evaluation of Language Fundamentals – Pre-school Version. San Antonio, TX: The Psychological Corporation.

26  Bishop DVM (2003) Test for the Reception of Grammar. Manchester, UK: Chapel Press.

27  Dunn L, Dunn D (2009) The British Picture Vocabulary Scale, 3rd edn. Windsor, UK: NFER-Nelson.

28  Renfrew C (1995) The Renfrew Language Scales. Oxford: Winslow.

29  De Renzi E, Faglioni P (1978) Development of a shortened version of the token test. Cortex, 14, 41–49.

30  Conners CK, Multi-Health Systems Staff (2008) Conners Rating Scale Third Edition. Toronto: Multi-Health Systems.

31  Manly T, Crawford J, George M, Underbjerg M and Robertson IH (2016) Test of Everyday Attention for Children - 2 (TEACh-2). Bury St Edmunds: Thames Valley Test Co.

32  Benton AL (1994) Neuropsychological assessment. Annual Review of Psychology, 45, 1–23.

33  Beery KE (1997) The Visual Motor Integration Test: Administration, Scoring and Teaching Manual, 4th edn. Cleveland, OH: Modern Curriculum Press.

34  Reitan RM (1971) Trail making test results for normal and brain-damaged children. Perceptual and Motor Skills, 33, 575–581.

35  Spreen O and Gaddes WH (1969) Developmental norms for 15 neuropsychological tests age 6 to 15. Cortex, 5, 170–191.

36  Army Individual Test Battery (1994) Trail Making B Manual of Directions and Scoring. Washington, DC: War Department, Adjutant General's Office.

37  Lindgren SD and Benton AL (1980) Developmental patterns of visuospatial judgement. Journal of Pediatric Psychology, 5, 217–225.

38  Kaufman AS and Kaufman NL (2004) Kaufman Assessment Battery for Children. Circle Pines, MN: American Guidance Service.

39  Rey A (1941) L'examen psychologique dans un cas d'encephalopathie traumatique. Archives of Psychology, 28, 286–340.

40  Osterrieth PA (1944) Le test de copie d'une figure complexe: contribution à l'étude de la perception mémoire. Archives of Psychology, 30, 286–356.

41  Benton AL (1959) Right-Left Discrimination and Finger Localization. New York: Hoeber.

42  Finlayson MAJ and Reitan RM (1976) Handedness in relation to measures of motor and tactile function in normal children. Perceptual and Motor Skills, 43, 475–481.

43  Tiffin J (1968) Purdue Pegboard: Examiner Manual. Chicago, IL: Science Research Associates.

44  Gardner RA, Broman M (1979) The Purdue Pegboard: normative data on 1334 school children. Journal of Clinical and Child Psychology, 8, 156–162.

45  Halperin JM (2016) Executive functioning – a key construct for understanding developmental psychopathology or a 'catch-all' term in need of some rethinking? Journal of Child Psychology and Psychiatry, 57, 443–445.

46  Cortese S, Ferrin M, Brandeis D et al. (2015) Cognitive training for attention-deficit/hyperactivity disorder: Meta-analysis of clinical and neuropsychological outcomes from randomized controlled trials. Journal of the American Academy of Child and Adolescent Psychiatry, 54, 164–174.

47  Kempton S, Vance A, Maruff P et al. (1999) Executive function and attention deficit hyperactivity disorder: stimulant medication and better executive function performance in children. Psychology and Medicine, 29, 527–538.

48  Ozonoff S, Strayer DL, McMahon WM, Filloux F (1994) Executive function abilities in autism and Tourette syndrome: an information processing approach. Journal of Child Psychology Psychiatry, 35, 1015–1032.

49  Bryson G, Whelahan HA, Bell M (2001) Memory and executive function impairments in deficit syndrome schizophrenia. Psychiatry Research, 102, 29–37.

50  Gioia GA, Isquith PK, Guy SC, Kenworthy L (2000) Behaviour Rating Inventory of Executive Function. Odessa, FL: Psychological Assessment Resources.

51  Sherman EM, Brooks BL (2001) Behaviour Rating Inventory of Executive Function – Preschool Version (BRIEF-P): test review and clinical guidelines for use. Child Neuropsychology, 16, 503–519.

52  Delis DC, Kaplan E, Kramer JH (2001) The Delis–Kaplan Executive Function System (D-KEFS). San Antonio, TX: Psychological Corporation.

53  Emslie H, Wilson F, Burden V et al. (2003) Behavioural Assessment of Dysexecutive Syndrome. Thames Valley Test Company.

54  Heaton RK, Chelune GJ, Talley JL et al. (1993) Wisconsin Card Sorting Test Manual – Revised and Expanded. Lutz, FL: Psychological Assessment Resources.

55  Golden JC (1992) Stroop Word and Colour Test: A Manual for Clinical and Experimental Uses. Chicago: Stoelting.

56 Comalli PE, Wapner S, Werner H (1962) Interference effects of the Stroop Colour Word Test in childhood, adult and aging. Journal of Genetic Psychology, 100, 63–65.

57 Nowicki S, Duke MP (1994) Individual differences in the non-verbal communication of affect. The diagnostic analysis of a non-verbal accuracy scale. Journal of Non-Verbal Behaviour, 18, 9–35.

58 Brunsdon VEA, Colvert E, Ames C et al. (2015) Exploring the cognitive features in children with autism spectrum disorders, their co-twins, and typically-developing children within a population-based sample. Journal of Child Psychology and Psychiatry, 56, 893–902.

59 Skuse D, Warrington R, Bishop D et al. (2004) The developmental, dimensional and diagnostic interview (3di): a novel computerized assessment for autism spectrum disorders. Journal of American Academy of Child and Adolescent Psychiatry, 43, 548–558.

60 Lord C, Rutter M, DiLavore PC et al. (2012) Autism Diagnostic Observation Schedule, 2nd edn. Torrance, CA: Western Psychological Services.

61 Dweck CS (1986) Motivational processes affecting learning. American Psychologist, 41, 1040–1048.

62 Mangels JA, Butterfield B, Lamb J et al. (2006) Why do beliefs about intelligence influence learning success? A social cognitive neuroscience model. Social Cognitive and Affective Neuroscience, 1, 75–86.

39

# Cognitive Behavioural Therapy for Children and Adolescents

*Cathy Creswell and Thomas G. O'Connor*

Cognitive behavioural therapy (CBT) is a treatment approach based on the general notion that a psychological disorder is caused or maintained by 'dysfunctional' thought patterns and lack of positively reinforced adaptive behavioural coping strategies. CBT is a class of treatment; all cognitive behavioural treatments aim to identify and reduce cognitive biases or distortions (such as those in Box 39.1) and build effective coping and problem-solving skills.

---

**Box 39.1  Examples of key cognitions associated with common emotional and behavioural disorders in childhood and adolescence**

**Characteristics of clinically anxious children**

- Vigilant to threat
- Interpret ambiguity as more threatening
- Come to faster conclusions about threat
- Underestimate personal coping ability
- Anticipate distress (often exaggerated) in the face of threat

**Characteristics of clinically aggressive children**

- Attend to less social cues
- Direct attention towards hostile social cues
- Interpret stimuli in a hostile manner
- Generate fewer solutions to social problems
- Positively appraise aggressive responses
- Positively appraise own ability to perform aggressive response

**Characteristics of clinically depressive children**

- Selectively attend to negative features of events
- Report negative attributions (i.e. internal, stable explanations for positive events and external, unstable explanations for negative events)

---

*Child Psychology and Psychiatry: Frameworks for Clinical Training and Practice,* Third Edition.
Edited by David Skuse, Helen Bruce and Linda Dowdney.
© 2017 John Wiley & Sons, Ltd. Published 2017 by John Wiley & Sons, Ltd.

After decades of extensive research on CBT in adult populations [1], CBT is now well established as an effective treatment for psychological disorders in child and adolescent populations.

## Basic Premises of the CBT Approach and its Administration

Several clinical and developmental models have informed and been informed by research into the processes by which distorted cognitions are developed and influence behavioural/emotional problems. One example, the social information processing model [2], was developed in the context of conduct disorder but has proved useful for other childhood disorders, including depression and anxiety. The model focuses on the following:

- the child's attending to, encoding and interpreting social cues (e.g. Why did that child step on my foot?);
- developing goals for one's own behaviour (e.g. What do I want to do now?);
- generating potential solutions and evaluating their effects (e.g. What would happen if I hit back at him?).

Cognitive behavioural therapy is often tailored for a particular disorder (see the studies cited below), but it is possible to make several basic statements about how CBT is administered. In general, CBT interventions seek to break the cascade of maladaptive thoughts and feelings that lie between the cognitive distortion and the destructive behaviour. This occurs in a logical, stepped manner usually lasting eight to 16 sessions, typically on a one session/week schedule (Box 39.2). A first step is often to collate detailed information about the settings that lead the child to feel, for example, anxious and unable to cope with a particular situation. A second step is typically to help the child/adolescent to identify and differentiate thoughts, feelings, behavioural responses and somatic reactions linked with these situations. Often there is a focus on self-talk, or helping the child to recognize how certain kinds of self-talk can maintain the problem ('I'll look silly') and promoting positive self-talk ('I have done this OK before'). Using these skills, children are then supported to develop a hierarchy of anxiety-producing situations which they gradually face, with a clear reward structure in place. Throughout treatment children are helped to evaluate their newly developed coping skills in 'real life' settings, and these are rewarded where appropriate. This can continue for several sessions, as the child learns to test new strategies and, through trial and error, to find strategies that work and diagnose why other strategies do not. Homework throughout the treatment process fosters understanding of why negative feelings develop and how they might be managed effectively.

---

**Box 39.2 Typical steps in cognitive behavioural therapy for childhood anxiety**

- Recognize feelings and physical reactions
- Identify associated thoughts (e.g. interpretations, attributions and expectations)
- Cognitive restructuring/coping self-talk/ putting thoughts to the test
- Imaginary/*in vivo* (graded) exposure
- Self-evaluation and reward

---

CBT programmes value rapport but do not construct the treatment as working through the relationship with the therapist. Instead, the CBT therapist guides the child/adolescent to reshape attributions, expectations and behaviour. Treatments including a family component are increasingly common and typically this means an ancillary focus on the parents' behaviour. Overall, good outcomes can be achieved following CBT regardless of whether there are additional parental sessions. However, active parental involvement that emphasizes contingency management or transfer of control may support long-term maintenance of treatment gain (e.g. [3]).

## Developmental Considerations

It is somewhat surprising that little is known or hypothesized about the developmental constraints around CBT-based treatments and their effectiveness. This may be because the predictors so far considered (e.g. age) are weak indicators of the cognitive and social processes that are required for successful CBT. So, for example, the traditional CBT model is not explicit about why the approach might work with a 12-year-old but not with a 3-year-old. Nonetheless, it is clear that CBT can be effective even with comparatively young children. For example, in their meta-analysis of CBT for anxiety disorders in children aged 4–19 years, James *et al.* [4] reported a response rate for remission of any anxiety diagnosis of 59.4% for CBT versus 17.5% for wait-list controls. Although the available evidence suggests that CBT appears to be equally effective across a wide age range, it may be that further research assessing moderators (see later) identifies cognitive or affective processes (which may show developmental change) that predict treatment outcomes.

More recent research is beginning to identify how the cognitive behavioural model and its clinical application may differ for children and adolescents. One example concerns the role of threat interpretation (Box 39.3). The tendency to interpret ambiguity in an overly threatening way – a hallmark of anxious adolescents and adults – may not distinguish anxious from non-anxious pre-adolescent children [6]. Rather, both anxious and non-anxious pre-adolescents show a tendency to interpret ambiguity as threatening, but what distinguishes them appears to be their response to threat, particularly avoidance. These findings are consistent with suggestions from a recent multi-centre trial comparing CBT, sertraline and sertraline with CBT [7]. This research found that particular gains were made during the exposure phase (compared with the 'cognitive' phase) of CBT for pre-adolescent children and that treatment gains were mediated by changes in perceived coping and not by changes in negative automatic thoughts [8]. The focus in treatment on exposure and coping in younger children, rather than on addressing distorted cognitions through verbal methods (such as thought records), may be especially noteworthy, particularly given that what may be presumed to be 'distorted' cognitions can be demonstrated in young children. Murray *et al.* [9] reported spontaneous expressions of hopelessness in 5-year-old children of depressed mothers. Other studies using different methodologies also suggest that cognitive biases or distorted 'filters' exist in young children: 2- to 6.5-year-olds with an insecure attachment showed poorer understanding of negative emotions compared with securely attached children. In other words, these children had more difficulty explaining or making sense of negative emotions [10]. Findings from these and related studies may yield practical lessons

---

**Box 39.3 Sample responses to ambiguous scenarios**

**You have arranged to have a party at 4pm and by 4.30pm no one has arrived**

*Cognitive bias – What do you think is most likely to have happened?*

- Anxious: 'Nobody wants to come to the party'
- Aggressive: 'Nobody wants to come to the party'
- Non-clinical controls: 'They might be late because there is bad traffic'

*Behaviour – What will you do about it?*

- Anxious: 'Nothing. Feel upset.'
- Aggressive: 'Get cross and when I see them at school I will tell them I don't want to be friends with them'
- Non-clinical controls: 'Phone around and see where they are and when they will arrive'

**You are playing inside and your dog starts barking and growling outside**

*Cognitive bias – What do you think is most likely to have happened?*

- Anxious: 'There is someone I don't know trying to get into my house'
- Aggressive: 'Someone is stealing my bike from outside'
- Non-clinical controls: 'Another dog is walking past outside'

*Behaviour – What will you do about it?*

- Anxious: 'Hide'
- Aggressive: 'Find the thief and hit them'
- Non-clinical controls: 'Look out of the window and tell my dog to be quiet'

*Source:* Adapted from Barrett *et al.* [5].

---

for assessing young children, but the presence of cognitive distortions does not mean that these cognitive processes are causally linked with disorder or that altering these cognitions will necessarily produce positive behavioural change in young children.

## Recent Advances and Future Directions for CBT for Children and Adolescents

Recent clinical research findings on CBT in children and adolescents are noteworthy in several respects. One is the expanded range of conditions for which CBT has produced large, reliable and clinically meaningful findings as established by meta-analytic methods. These include depression [11], anxiety (for children with and without autistic spectrum conditions) [4], post-traumatic stress disorder [12] and obsessive compulsive disorder [13]. Furthermore, good outcomes have been found not just in specialist research clinics but also in conventional clinical settings (e.g. [14]).

Another advance in work on CBT in children and adolescents is the focus on comparative effectiveness, particularly in relation to medication. Probably the best-known studies are the Treatment for Adolescents with Depression Study (TADS) [15] and the Child Anxiety Multisite Study (CAMS) [16].

In the TADS study, follow-up at 36 weeks post-randomization showed that treatment-group differences apparent in the earlier phases of treatment diminished over time, with the result that there was convergence among the CBT-only, medication-only (fluoxctinc) and CBT plus mcdication conditions [15]. The rate of adolescents with suicidal ideation (none committed suicide in the trial) was considerably higher in the medication-only group (15%) than in the combined (8%) or CBT-only (6%) conditions. This is naturally a major consideration when making treatment decisions.

The CAM study, in contrast, compared outcomes of children aged 7–14 years with a diagnosed anxiety disorder randomized to either 14 sessions of CBT, sertraline, a combination of sertraline and CBT, or a placebo drug [16]. Based on clinicians' global impressions of improvement, 60% of children were reported as 'much' or 'very much' improved following the CBT condition. The same was true for 55% of children in the sertraline condition and 81% of children in the combination treatment. All intervention outcomes were superior to placebo outcomes (24%). Importantly acute selected serotonin reuptake inhibitor (SSRI) use was found to generally be tolerable, although it was associated with more adverse effects than the no-SSRI conditions, particularly for pre-adolescent children. The researchers conclude that it 'may be prudent, especially for children less than 12 years of age, to consider treatment with CBT first' [17, p. 186]. These findings show that assumptions about CBT being appropriate only for milder cases is no longer supported. Indeed, although its impact is even greater when coupled with medication, CBT is an important stand-alone treatment and, in terms of its effectiveness and side-effect profile, can be considered as a first-choice treatment rather than an add-on to other approaches.

Based on these findings, a question now for mental health professionals is not whether CBT is a reasonable treatment option, but rather how to increase the availability of CBT to children and families – and how to do that in an efficient, cost-effective manner. That is, the question here is: in what way can CBT be used so as to have a public health impact on children's mental health? Attempts in several countries to increase access to CBT are underway (e.g. [18]). Recent developments in this area consider low-intensity interventions delivered online [19] or via books for parents. The use of internet-based approaches for public health promotion have been widely discussed and are seen as a viable, and cost-efficient option (e.g. [20]). Translating CBT for child mental health to this format is clearly a valuable future direction. Application of CBT within school-based programmes to promote mental well-being is another avenue with potentially large-sale benefit. School-based programmes that focus on reducing anxiety appear to be effective in the short term [21]. These developments are significant because they demonstrate that CBT can be used as a general tool, and across a variety of settings, without requiring highly specialized clinical settings or therapists. There is, however, a need for caution before seeing CBT as a panacea for all types of emotional and behavioural problems.

Future research is also needed on the mediators of treatment effects (why does treatment work?) and the moderators of treatment effects (what predicts who will respond to treatment and who will not?). Findings from this type of research are important for improving our understanding of the treatment process (e.g. by identifying the most 'active' elements of the treatment regimen) and also for better targeting of those who are most likely to benefit from treatment. To date, there is little consistency across studies in what mediates or moderates treatment outcome. This may reflect the fact that most CBT studies explore these questions retrospectively (e.g. they were not designed or powered to identify robust treatment predictors). The increased focus on precision medicine – the proposal that treatment will be optimized to the extent that it accounts for individual variability in genetic background, lifestyle and psychosocial context – may spur further research on moderators of CBT outcomes in children.

## Conclusion

Children's cognitions about their social world reflect developmental histories that shape behaviour. CBT is concerned with how these cognitive processes may be altered and, when altered, if there are consequential reductions in psychiatric symptoms and improvements in social functioning. Results from many clinical trials have shown that CBT reliably improves mental health outcomes in children. Recent studies show that CBT should no longer be considered only for milder cases, and that the list of targeted disorders appropriate for CBT is increasing to include, e.g. depression, anxiety, post-traumatic stress disorder and obsessive compulsive disorder. CBT can be regarded as an important stand-alone treatment for many conditions. Additionally, CBT has been shown to be as effective as, perhaps better than, and possibly a useful adjunct to, medication. These findings are important for instilling confidence in recommending treatment for ill and distressed children and their families. A next step is to develop increasingly efficient and varying modes of delivery to provide wider access to this effective form of treatment and so increase its public health impact.

## References

1 Elkin I, Gibbons RD, Shea MT et al. (1995) Initial severity and differential treatment outcome in the National Institute of Mental Health Treatment of Depression Collaborative Research Program. Journal of Consulting and Clinical Psychology, 63, 841.

2 Crick NR, Dodge KA (1994) A review and reformulation of social information-processing mechanisms in children's social adjustment. Psychological Bulletin, 115, 74.

3 Manassis K, Lee TC, Bennett K et al. (2014) Types of parental involvement in CBT with anxious youth: A preliminary meta-analysis. Journal of Consulting and Clinical Psychology, 82, 1163.

4 James AC, James G, Cowdrey FA et al. (2013) Cognitive behavioural therapy for anxiety disorders in children and adolescents. Cochrane Database Syst Rev, 6.

5 Barrett PM, Rapee PM, Dadds MR, Ryan SM (1996) Family enhancement of cognitive style in anxious and aggressive children. Journal of Abnormal Child Psychology, 24, 187–203.

6 Waite P, Codd J, Creswell C (2015) Interpretation of ambiguity: Differences between children and adolescents with and without an anxiety disorder. Journal of Affective Disorders, 188, 194–201.

7  Peris TS, Compton SN, Kendall PC et al. (2015) Trajectories of change in youth anxiety during cognitive—behavior therapy. Journal of Consulting and Clinical Psychology, 83, 239.

8  Kendall P, Cummings C, Villabø M et al. (2016) Mediators of change in the Child/ Adolescent Anxiety Multimodal Treatment Study. Journal of Consulting and Clinical Psychology, 84, 1–14.

9  Murray L, Woolgar M, Cooper P, Hipwell A (2001) Cognitive vulnerability to depression in 5 year old children of depressed mothers. Journal of Child Psychology and Psychiatry, 42, 891–899.

10  Laible DJ, Thompson RA (1998) Attachment and emotional understanding in preschool children. Developmental Psychology, 34, 1038.

11  Zhou X, Hetrick SE, Cuijpers P et al. (2015) Comparative efficacy and acceptability of psychotherapies for depression in children and adolescents: A systematic review and network meta-analysis. World Psychiatry, 14, 207–222.

12  Gillies D, Taylor F, Gray C et al. (2013) Psychological therapies for the treatment of post-traumatic stress disorder in children and adolescents (Review). Evidence-Based Child Health: A Cochrane Review Journal, 8, 1004–1116.

13  McGuire JF, Piacentini J, Lewin AB et al. (2015) A meta analysis of cognitive behavior therapy and medication for child obsessive-compulsive disorder: moderators of treatment efficacy, response and remission Depression and Anxiety, 32, 580–593.

14  Creswell C, Murray L, Cooper P (2014) Interpretation and expectation in childhood anxiety disorders: age effects and social specificity. Journal of Abnormal Child Psychology, 42, 453–465.

15  March JS, Silva S, Petrycki S, Curry J, Wells K, Fairbank J, ... & Severe J (2007) The Treatment for Adolescents With Depression Study (TADS): long-term effectiveness and safety outcomes. Archives of General Psychiatry, 64(10), 1132–1143.

16  Walkup JT, Albano AM, Piacentini J et al. (2008) Cognitive behavioral therapy, sertraline, or a combination in childhood anxiety. New England Journal of Medicine, 359, 2753–2766.

17  Rynn MA, Walkup JT, Compton SN et al. (2015) Child/Adolescent Anxiety Multimodal Study: Evaluating Safety. Journal of the American Academy of Child & Adolescent Psychiatry, 54, 180–190.

18  Payne KA, Myhr G (2010) Increasing access to cognitive-behavioural therapy (CBT) for the treatment of mental illness in Canada: A research framework and call for action. Healthcare Policy, 5, e173.

19  Pennant ME, Loucas CE, Whittington C et al. (2015) Computerised therapies for anxiety and depression in children and young people: A systematic review and meta-analysis. Behaviour Research and Therapy, 67, 1–18.

20  Bennett GG, Glasgow RE (2009) The delivery of public health interventions via the Internet: actualizing their potential. Annual Review of Public Health, 30, 273–292.

21  Neil AL, Christensen H (2009) Efficacy and effectiveness of school-based prevention and early intervention programs for anxiety. Clinical Psychology Review, 29, 208–215.

## Further Reading

Graham P, Reynolds S. Cognitive behaviour therapy for children and families: Cambridge University Press; 2013.

40

# Psychodynamic Psychotherapy
# for Children and Adolescents

*Eilis Kennedy*

## Introduction

An interest in applying psychoanalytic ideas to therapeutic work with children and adolescents arose out of the thinking of Anna Freud and Melanie Klein, and received further impetus from work showing the impact upon children of their experiences of separation and loss during the Second World War [1]. Over time, psychoanalytically informed therapeutic approaches have expanded beyond individual work with the child to include work with families, groups, parent–infant psychotherapy and parent–couple work. This chapter focuses on psychodynamic psychotherapy for children and adolescents presenting with a range of clinical problems.

## Basic Premises of a Psychodynamic Approach

Key concepts guiding the therapeutic process include an interest in unconscious processes and the 'internal' world of the child. Children's play is thought to provide a window onto the child's unconscious thoughts and feelings. The child's play and behaviour are therefore used by the therapist to understand the child's inner world [2]. Attunement to the child in order to be receptive to the minutiae of what is being emotionally exchanged is one of the primary tasks [3]. The ability to gather fine details regarding how the child responds to the setting and relates to the therapist is essential. Where possible, the work is undertaken in a regular consistent setting. When working individually with young children, the psychotherapist prepares a box for each child with suitable toys and drawing materials to facilitate the child's creative play, exploration and non-verbal communication. It is usual practice for the child's parents/carers to attend parallel psychotherapeutic sessions. The psychotherapeutic model is deeply embedded in a developmental approach to children's difficulties, and an excellent account of a psychoanalytic perspective on personality development from infancy to adolescence can be found in Waddell [4]. Increasingly, research from neuroscience and developmental psychology is used to complement this model and enhance understanding of work with children with neurodevelopmental disorders or those who have experienced severe maltreatment [5]. An American Academy of Child and Adolescent Psychiatry Practice Parameter [6] presents guidelines for the practice of psychodynamic

*Child Psychology and Psychiatry: Frameworks for Clinical Training and Practice,* Third Edition.
Edited by David Skuse, Helen Bruce and Linda Dowdney.
© 2017 John Wiley & Sons, Ltd. Published 2017 by John Wiley & Sons, Ltd.

psychotherapy with children and is available to download at https://www.aacap.org/aacap/Resources_for_Primary_Care/Practice_Parameters_and_Resource_Centers/Practice_Parameters.aspx.

## The Evidence Base for Psychodynamic Child Psychotherapy

The evidence base for psychodynamic child psychotherapy is somewhat limited as randomized controlled trials (RCTs) have been few in number. A 2004 systematic review identified 32 studies, noting that many had limitations in study design and sample size. Only five were RCTs and four were quasi-RCTs [7]. A more recent systematic review has identified three additional RCTs [8]. A meta-analysis in 2013 of short-term psychodynamic models concluded that there were preliminary data that short-term psychodynamic psychotherapy (STPP) may be effective for a range of conditions in children [9]. As in the adult literature there is evidence of a 'sleeper effect', i.e. that the effects of treatment continue following the end of treatment. A National Institute for Health Research (NIHR) multi-centre RCT, comparing cognitive behavioural therapy, short-term psychodynamic psychotherapy and specialist clinical care, in the treatment of adolescents with major depression, is due to report shortly (see the NIHR website: http://www.nets.nihr.ac.uk/projects/hta/060501). This will be the largest randomized trial to date to include psychodynamic child psychotherapy as a treatment arm [10].

## Examples of Research with Children and Young People Presenting with Various Clinical Problems

### Children Who Have Experienced Abuse

An RCT by Trowell *et al.* [11] compared individual psychodynamic psychotherapy with a psycho-educational group-based intervention for girls who had been sexually abused. While both types of intervention were found to be effective at substantially reducing psychopathological symptoms, and participants in both groups evidenced improved functioning, individual therapy led to a greater improvement in symptoms of post-traumatic stress disorder. The authors note that the small sample size, and the lack of a control group limit conclusions about changes attributable to treatment.

### Internalizing and Externalizing Disorders

#### Disruptive Behaviour Disorders

There is limited intervention research in this area, although a retrospective study of the case notes of 763 children attending the Anna Freud Centre found poorer outcomes for those diagnosed with conduct or oppositional defiant disorders [12]. Outcomes were, however, better for younger children and those with mixed emotional and behavioural disorders.

#### Internalizing Disorders

Research evidence here suggests that children with depressive and/or anxiety disorders respond positively to a psychodynamic therapeutic approach.

In a quasi-randomized 2-year follow-up of children aged 6–11 years with depressive or anxiety disorders, Muratori *et al.* [13] compared those assigned to either a time-limited psychodynamic psychotherapy (PP) intervention condition or to community services. The results of the study indicated that PP was effective in treating internalizing disorders at the time of intervention and at the 6-month follow-up. A 'sleeper' effect for PP was also found at the 2-year follow-up, in so far as only children in the PP group moved into the non-clinical range on standardized assessments, while those in the control group remained at the same level of clinical severity.

A multi-centre randomized trial compared focused individual psychodynamic therapy and parallel therapeutic work with parents (FIPP) with a systemic integrative family therapy approach (SIFT), in a sample of children aged 10–14 years who met criteria for major depressive disorder and/or dysthymia [14]. Significant reductions in disorder rates for both groups were found such that clinical depression had remitted in more than 70% of participants in both types of intervention, and reductions in co-morbid conditions were evident. Improvements were persistent, with a 6-month follow-up indicating that none of the FIPP participants remained depressed, compared with 81% of SIFT participants, although the loss of four cases to follow-up in the SIFT group limited assessment of effectiveness rates. While the final outcome of these interventions appears similar, a different pattern of responses was found. Family work appeared to have highly effective initial impact, whereas the response to individual work was slower but possibly more sustained.

### Mixed Diagnoses

A number of studies have focused on children presenting in middle childhood with a range of difficulties rather than belonging to a particular diagnostic category. One randomized trial of such children, aged 5–9 years, compared time-unlimited or time-limited (12 sessions), psychodynamically oriented treatment with a minimal-contact control group (four sessions) [15]. All groups showed significant improvements from pre-test to post-test, although changes in family functioning in the control group were significantly greater than those in the time-unlimited group. At the 4-year follow-up, all three groups did well on a variety of outcome measures, although the control group did rather better, being the only group to report significant improvements on severity of target problems and measures of family functioning. The researchers speculate that the four-session 'minimal contact control' group may have proved most effective because the families' own capacities for coping and resilience had been harnessed.

A further RCT compared the effectiveness of structural family therapy with individual psychodynamic child psychotherapy and a 'recreational' control in boys aged 6–12 years presenting with mixed diagnoses [16]. Attrition was greatest in the control group (43%) and greater in the family therapy group compared with the individual therapy (16% vs 4%). Both family therapy and individual psychodynamic therapy were equally effective in reducing behavioural and emotional problems on a variety of outcome measures that included family systems and individual psychodynamic rating scales. Findings on measures of family functioning were mixed: the control group showed no significant change; the family therapy group improved; those receiving individual psychodynamic psychotherapy showed deterioration at 1-year follow-up. This finding may possibly be biased as an intention-to-treat analysis was not carried out despite variable drop-outs in the three groups, but it may also be attributable to the fact that the individual psychodynamic child therapy was undertaken in the absence of any parallel parent work, contrary to usual practice. The study underlines the importance of working with the wider family system in conjunction with individual work with the child.

## Young People with Poorly Controlled Diabetes

Moran and colleagues undertook a series of studies assessing the effectiveness of psychoanalytic psychotherapy for children with poorly controlled diabetes [17,18]. A quasi-randomized study compared two groups, each containing 11 diabetic children with unstable insulin-dependent diabetes. Those in the treatment group received intensive psychoanalytic psychotherapy (up to three to four times a week) for an average of 15 weeks; those in the control group received only routine psychological input without individual psychotherapy. A significant improvement in diabetic control was noted in the experimental group compared with the controls, with 91% of participants in the treatment group showing a reduction in glycosylated haemoglobin, in contrast to only 36% of controls. This improvement was maintained at 1-year follow-up.

As part of this study, three children with diabetes and growth retardation were studied, using a single-case experimental design methodology; in all three cases there were gains in height over the predicted height following psychotherapeutic treatment [18].

## Long-Term Outcomes

### The Anna Freud Centre Long-Term Follow-up Study

#### Adult Outcome
In this study [19], the adult outcome of 34 children who had received psychotherapeutic treatment at the Anna Freud Centre was compared with the outcome of 11 of their untreated siblings. In general, those who had received treatment in childhood were found to be functioning well, reporting low levels of adversity, relatively few severe life events and good health. They displayed adequate personality functioning across a range of domains and a low rate of personality disorders.

Interestingly, while adversity in childhood was greater in the treated children, the untreated siblings were found to experience more negative life events in adulthood. In relation to personality functioning, the entire sample appeared to be doing well in the work domain. In the area of intimate relationships, those children successfully treated in childhood appeared to be doing better than their untreated siblings.

Possible adverse effects of treatment were highlighted in relation to attachment security. While a secure adult attachment status was common in those who had moved from poor functioning in childhood to high functioning in adulthood, the attachment style of those who had been *unsuccessfully* treated in their childhood was predominantly preoccupied/entangled. Those children in the sample who did not receive psychoanalytic treatment were found to be predominantly dismissing in their adult attachment style. Treated participants demonstrated a balanced and accurate memory of their childhood experiences, although in contrast to their siblings, their memories tended to be more painful.

*Patients' Perspectives*

Another aspect of this study assessed the perspective of the patient by exploring the memories of adults who were in therapy as children and examining the meaning participants gave to the experience of therapy in the context of their later lives [20].

Two-thirds of participants were able to describe some aspect of the experience of child psychotherapy that had felt helpful at the time of treatment. Some were more confident about the positive impact than others. Several described how being able to talk and 'unburden' themselves was helpful. One described how the treatment provided a 'sort of canvas' to 'express myself in a way that I wouldn't necessarily have been able to talk to anyone else about these problems.' Some noted how the therapist's attention made them feel more confident and how therapy enabled them to cope better.

Others questioned the potentially negative impact of the therapy. Some of their comments included feelings that the therapy was 'pointless' and had made no difference, or that it had set them apart from others. As one observed, 'the last thing I wanted was to feel different.' In some participants, this sense of being different created or exacerbated a sense that they were somehow 'damaged' and that there was 'something wrong' with them.

## Potential Adverse Effects of Treatment

In contrast to research on pharmacological treatments, there has been a tendency not to look systematically for adverse effects of psychotherapeutic treatments. However, existing research suggests some potentially adverse consequences of treatment that would benefit from scrutiny in future research. For example, there are indications that individual psychotherapy undertaken in the absence of concurrent parent/family work may have a negative impact on family functioning. There is a suggestion also that unsuccessful treatment during childhood may result in a preoccupied/entangled attachment style in adulthood. In addition, some adults who received treatment in childhood describe how the treatment itself compounded a sense they had that there was 'something wrong with them' and for some there was an anxiety that it may have resulted in a tendency to be overly introspective.

## Conclusion

The application of psychoanalytic understanding to psychotherapeutic work with children has a long tradition. Hopefully this work will continue to evolve and develop with the contribution of new insights from large-scale treatment trials, developmental psychology and neuroscience.

## References

1 Likerman M, Urban E (2009) The roots of child and adolescent psychotherapy in psychoanalysis. In: Lanyado M and Horne A (eds) The Handbook of Child and Adolescent Psychotherapy: Psychoanalytic Approaches, 2nd edn. London: Routledge, pp. 15–26.

2 Lanyado M and Horne A (2009) The therapeutic setting and process. In: Lanyado M and Horne A (eds), The Handbook of Child and Adolescent Psychotherapy: Psychoanalytic Approaches, 2nd edn. London: Routledge, pp. 157–174.

3 Hunter M (2002) Psychotherapy with Young People in Care: Lost and Found. Sussex: Brunner-Routledge.

4 Waddell M. (2002) Inside Lives: Psychoanalysis and the Development of the Personality, revised edn. London: Karnac.

5 Music G (2010) Nurturing Natures: Attachment and Children's Emotional, Sociocultural and Brain Development. London: Psychology Press.

6 Kernberg PF, Ritvo R, Keable H; AACAP, CQI (2012) Practice parameter for psychodynamic psychotherapy with children. Journal of the American Academy of Child and Adolescent Psychiatry, 51(5), 541–557.

7 Kennedy E (2004) Child and Adolescent Psychotherapy: A Systematic Review of Psychoanalytic Approaches. London: North Central London Strategic Health Authority.

8 Midgley, N., Kennedy, E (2011) Psychodynamic Psychotherapy for Children and Adolescents: A Critical Review of the Evidence Base. Journal of Child Psychotherapy, 37, 1–2.

9 Abbass AA, Rabung S, Leichsenring F, Refseth JS, Midgley N (2013) Psychodynamic psychotherapy for children and adolescents: a meta-analysis of short-term psychodynamic models. Journal of the American Academy of Child and Adolescent Psychiatry, 52, 863–875.

10 Goodyer IM, Tsancheva S, Byford S et al. (2011) Improving mood with psychoanalytic and cognitive therapies: a pragmatic effectiveness superiority trial to investigate whether specialised psychological treatment reduces the risk for relapse in adolescents with moderate to severe unipolar depression. Trials, 12, 175.

11 Trowell J, Kolvin I, Weeramanthri T et al. (2002) Psychotherapy for sexually abused girls: psychopathological outcome findings and patterns of change. British Journal of Psychiatry, 180, 234–247.

12 Fonagy P, Target M (1994) The efficacy of psychoanalysis for children with disruptive disorders. Journal of the American Academy of Child and Adolescent Psychiatry, 33, 45–55.

13 Muratori F, Picchi L, Bruni G et al. (2003) A two-year follow-up of psychodynamic psychotherapy for internalizing disorders in children. Journal of the American Academy of Child and Adolescent Psychiatry, 42, 331–339.

14 Trowell J, Joffe I, Campbell J et al. (2007) Childhood depression: a place for psychotherapy. An outcome study comparing individual psychodynamic psychotherapy and family therapy. European Child and Adolescent Psychiatry, 16, 157–167.

15 Smyrnios K, Kirby R (1993) Long term comparison of brief versus unlimited psychodynamic treatments with children and their parents. Journal of Consulting and Clinical Psychology, 61, 1020–1027.

16 Szapocznik J, Murray E, Scopetta M et al. (1989) Structural family versus psychodynamic child therapy for problematic Hispanic boys. Journal of Consulting and Clinical Psychology, 57, 571–578.

17 Moran G, Fonagy P, Kurtz A et al. (1991) A controlled study of the psychoanalytic treatment of brittle diabetes. Journal of the American Academy of Child and Adolescent Psychiatry, 30, 926–935.

18 Fonagy P, Moran C (1990) Studies of the efficacy of child psychoanalysis. Journal of Consulting and Clinical Psychology, 58, 684–695.

19 Schachter A, Target M (2009) The adult outcome of child psychoanalysis: The Anna Freud Centre long-term follow-up study. In: Midgley N, Anderson J, Grainger E et al. (eds), Child Psychotherapy and Research: New Approaches, Emerging Findings. London: Routledge, pp. 144–156.

20 Midgley N, Target M, Smith J (2006) The outcome of child psychoanalysis from the patient's point of view: a qualitative analysis of a long-term follow-up study. Psychology and Psychotherapy – Theory, Research and Practice, 79, 257–269.

# 41

# Systemic and Family Approaches to Intervention

*Philip Messent*

## Introduction

The word 'systemic' has many meanings that have changed and evolved over time according to historical and political contexts [1]. With practice ever-changing and evolving, approaches that have been researched are unlikely to be at the cutting edge of practice. Most of the approaches researched thus far belong to modernist early systemic approaches rather than to later postmodern approaches that are less amenable to manualizing and randomized control trials (RCTs). Modernism here refers to the rationalist, materialist and reductionist view that an objective understanding of a shared, universal and measurable reality is achievable. In contrast postmodernist approaches see our understanding of the world as tentative and provisional, elaborated by individuals within particular communities. Such approaches are inherently sceptical about the universal applicability of any treatment approach.

Research trials assessing the effectiveness of family-based approaches to common problems exhibited by children and young people have recently been reviewed [2]. Here I focus on the most promising approaches, following Carr [2] in using a broad definition of systemic interventions, before noting evidence of treatment effectiveness of more recent postmodernist practices drawn from a different research tradition.

## Externalizing Disorders

### Attention Deficit Hyperactivity Disorder (ADHD)

Systemic interventions for ADHD comprising sessions with families, school staff and young people are best offered as elements of multi-modal programmes involving stimulant medication [3], with systemic interventions playing an increasingly important role in the longer term [4]. Family therapy for ADHD focuses on helping families to develop patterns of organization conducive to effective child management: a high level of parental cooperation, clear intergenerational boundaries, warm, supportive family relationships, clear communication and clear, moderately flexible rules, roles and routines [5]. The finding in a large multi-modal treatment study [6] that stimulant medication ceased to have a therapeutic effect after 3 years (and had negative side-effects) underlines the importance of the use of systemic interventions alongside the briefer use of such medication, to help children and parents develop skills in managing symptoms.

*Child Psychology and Psychiatry: Frameworks for Clinical Training and Practice,* Third Edition.
Edited by David Skuse, Helen Bruce and Linda Dowdney.
© 2017 John Wiley & Sons, Ltd. Published 2017 by John Wiley & Sons, Ltd.

### Conduct Problems in Adolescence

Baldwin *et al.* [7] in a meta-analysis of 24 studies evaluating the effects of Brief Strategic Family Therapy [8], Functional Family Therapy (FFT) [9], Multisystemic Therapy (MST) [10] and Multidimensional Family Therapy (MDTF) [11] found that all four forms of family therapy were effective compared with non-treatment control groups (with an effect size of 0.7) and somewhat more effective than alternative treatments (with an effect size of 0.2). These results are consistent with a previous meta-analysis of eight family-based treatment studies of adolescent conduct disorder [12], which found that family-based treatments including FFT, MST and Multi-Dimensional Treatment Foster Care (MDTFC) [13] were more effective than routine treatment in reducing time spent in institutions, the risk of rearrest and recidivism 1–3 years following treatment. MST and FFT are discussed in Chapter 43.

The transferability of these multi-dimensional systemic treatment approaches developed in the USA to a UK setting has yet to be established. All of these treatment approaches are resource-intensive and during a time of a reduction of public services, evidence will need to provide compelling evidence of effectiveness to justify such costly investment. In the UK many pilot projects have dissolved after initial central government funding has come to an end.

### Substance Misuse in Adolescence

In a systematic narrative review of 45 trials of treatments for adolescent drug users, Tanner-Smith *et al.* [14] found that family therapy approaches were more effective than other types of outpatient treatment, including cognitive behavioural therapy (CBT), motivational interviewing, psycho-educational and individual and group counselling.

Effective programmes include those mentioned earlier as effective for conduct problems. MDTF is a multi-dimensional approach which Rowe and Liddle [15] found was effective in reducing alcohol and drug misuse, behavioural problems, emotional symptoms, negative peer associations, school failure and family difficulties associated with drug misuse. Family therapy with young people who misuse substances was more effective than routine individual or group psychotherapies in engaging and retaining them in therapy, and in improving psychological, educational and family adjustment. Brief Strategic Family Therapy as developed by Robbins *et al.* [8] for use with ethnic minority and particularly Hispanic families, focuses on resolving adolescent drug misuse by improving family interactions directly related to substance misuse, and Santisteban *et al.* [16], in their review of research on this approach, concluded that it was effective in engaging adolescents and their families in treatment, reducing drug abuse and recidivism and improving family relationships.

## Emotional Problems

### Anxiety

Systematic reviews such as Reynolds *et al.* [17] show that a family-based treatment for anxiety disorders is at least as effective in alleviating symptoms of anxiety as individual CBT, and more effective where parents also have anxiety disorders, and in improving the quality of family functioning. Barret's FRIENDS programme [18] involving 10 weekly group sessions of 90 minutes for children with parents joining each group for the last 20 minutes is a well validated example of such an approach.

### Depression

Effective family-based interventions for children and adolescents with depression aim to decrease family stress and enhance social support within the family context through the facilitation of clear parent–child communication, the promotion of family-based problem-solving, the disruption of negative critical parent–child interaction and the promotion of secure parent–child attachment. Stark *et al.* [19] reviewed 25 trials of family-based treatment programmes and concluded that these were as effective as individual CBT or interpersonal therapy, leading to remission in 66–75% of cases at the 6-month follow-up, and were more effective than individual treatment in maintaining post-treatment improvements.

### Self-Harm and Attempted Suicide

Family interventions have been found to improve the adjustment of adolescents who have attempted suicide [20], while a version of MST adapted for such young people was more effective than emergency hospitalization and treatment by a multidisciplinary psychiatric team [21]. Effective approaches begin with engaging young people and families in an initial risk assessment process, then developing a clear plan for risk reduction involving individual therapy for adolescents alongside systemic therapy for members of the family and social support networks. King *et al.* [22] describe a manualized Youth-Nominated Support Team approach that involves the young person naming four people to be part of their 'support team'. This team, which might include individuals in schools, extended family or religious community, is encouraged to maintain weekly contact with the adolescent, and themselves receive input aimed at facilitating their understanding of the young person and their provision of appropriate support. Compared with psychotherapy and antidepressant medication, this approach led to improvements in the level of suicidal ideation for girls, although not significantly for boys.

Self-Harm Intervention Family Therapy (SHIFT) is a UK national study [23] which is currently examining the best methods of helping young people [11–17] overcome self-harm, assessing the effectiveness of a specialist family therapy programme compared with treatment as usual for this group.

## Eating Disorders

### Adolescent Anorexia Nervosa

Family therapy approaches here as described by Eisler [24] involve:

1) an 'engagement' phase, making contact with each adolescent's family member and emphasizing a primary task of overcoming anorexia, rather than understanding its causes;
2) helping the family to 'challenge the symptoms';
3) as concerns around eating recede, exploring issues of individual and family development more broadly;
4) ending with a discussion of future plans.

He notes also the usefulness of a multiple family day programme whereby different families can meet and establish group cohesion in a supportive atmosphere in which new solutions can be tried.

Eisler's [24] systematic review of 11 family therapy trials for adolescent anorexia nervosa found that by the end of treatment between a half and two-thirds of participants had achieved a healthy weight. At follow-up, 60–90% had fully recovered. This contrasts with the rates of relapse of 25–30% for first inpatient admission and 55–75% for further admissions. This evidence is reflected in the National Institute for Health and Care Excellence (NICE) guidelines [25] that 'family interventions directly addressing the eating disorder should be offered to children and adolescents with anorexia nervosa'. Some caveats are noted by Eisler, however, including the small number of studies, their methodological limitations, and that there is little research comparing family therapy with other treatments. He notes, too, that systematic evaluations have been largely confined to family therapy with a strong 'structural' flavour [24].

### Obesity

Meta-analyses such as Kitzmann *et al.* [26] have found that family-based behavioural weight reduction programmes are more effective than dietary education and other routine interventions. Nowicka and Flodmark [27] have, for example, described Standardized Obesity Family Therapy (SOFT), which is based on systemic and solution-focused theories and has shown positive effects on children and adolescents with respect to degree of obesity, physical fitness, self-esteem and family functioning. The distinguishing features of SOFT are the focus on family interactions as an important source for implementing and maintaining lifestyle changes, the multidisciplinary team approach, and a limited number of sessions (three to four per year).

## First Episode Psychosis

While antipsychotic medication is considered to be the primary treatment for first episode psychosis, reviews of controlled trials such as Kuipers *et al.* [28] show that combining this with psycho-educational family therapy reduces relapse rates, and that multi-family psycho-educational therapy is particularly effective [29].

## A Different Sort of Evidence

Narrative/postmodernist family therapists would argue that an exclusive reliance on knowledge drawn from RCTs of manualized approaches to treatment overestimates the degree of knowledge that has been achieved to date and ignores the more 'local' knowledge and expertise in managing difficulties developed by clinicians, clients, families, services and communities. As Wren [30] writes:

> in most areas, we have very limited certainty about the value of the research evidence and little agreement about how best to proceed. As clinicians, we operate in the zone of complexity where we must go forward on a trial and error basis, conscious of our fallibility, where creativity and innovation are required to develop new understandings of how to act.

Alongside such creativity and innovation, therapists from this tradition emphasize the need above all to pay careful attention to how questions and interventions are being received and understood by client families. Timimi *et al.* [31] describe one way of placing the client's experience of the heart of what was offered within one British child and adolescent mental health service, by using routine outcome monitoring, with the whole service primed to adapt practice according to the feedback thus received.

Such an approach generates a 'practice-based evidence' [32], building a framework to guide practice 'from the ground up'. Young and Cooper [33] describe a study exemplifying such an approach in which families who had received therapy reviewed tapes of their own clinical sessions. Families were asked to stop the tape at 'meaningful moments' and then interviewed. The following themes were generated:

- Family members commented upon the importance of their **therapists' stance** – for example, a 14-year-old commented, 'I liked hearing that she was accepting that if I didn't want to answer a question then she would be fine with that . . .'
- **Giving people back their words** – an 11-year-old commented that, 'with her reviewing the stuff I said, it just really helped me 'cause it was in my brain more . . .'
- **Externalizing conversations** – a mother of an 8-year-old said: 'What she was doing in terms of how she was phrasing things, because she said "the worry puts thoughts in your head" and my son was immediately saying, like echoing back what she was saying, "the worry does this . . ." so I was starting to feel that this was looking good.' [laughs]

Such action-based research can help to ensure that clinicians are attentive to the experience of service users and that their practice is responsive and effective. It also acts as a counterweight to knowledge derived from the research on trials of manualized treatment approaches that have formed the bulk of this chapter. This emphasis on what clinicians bring to their work and how they learn and develop is an important complement to lessons about effectiveness drawn from larger-scale quantitative studies. It has long been found that the specific technique or approach used by therapists is not as important in accounting for effectiveness as non-specific factors linked to the quality of the relationship that is developed between client (family) and therapist (as evidenced, for example, by Chatoor and Kupnick's [34] review of the literature). The responsible and ethical systemic practitioner will be able to draw from the research knowledge base developed for the particular problem areas described earlier, and continue to learn from their practice with individual clients in their specific working context what it is that contributes to the development of relationships that client families will find helpful.

## References

1 Fredman G (2006) Working systemically with intellectual disability: why not? In: Baum S, Lynggaard H (eds) Intellectual Disabilities: A Systemic Approach. London: Karnac, pp. 1–20.
2 Carr A (2014) The evidence base for family therapy and systemic interventions for child-focused problems. Journal of Family Therapy, 36, 107–157.
3 Hinshaw S, Klein R, Abikoff H (2007) Childhood attention-deficit hyperactivity disorder: nonpharmalogical treatments and their combination with medication. In P Nathan P & J Gorman (eds) A Guide to Treatments that Work, 3rd edn. New York: Oxford University Press, pp. 3–28.

4 Jensen P, Arnold L, Swanson J et al. (2007) 3-year follow-up of the NIMH MTA Study. Journal of the American Academy of Child and Adolescent Psychiatry, 46, 989–1002.

5 Anastopoulos A, Shelton TL, Barkley R (2005) Family-based psychosocial treatments for children and adolescents with attention-deficit/hyperactivity disorder. In: Hibbs E & Jensen P (eds) Psychosocial Treatments for Child and Adolescent Disorders: Empirically Based Strategies for Clinical Practice, 2nd edn. Washington DC: American Psychological Association, pp. 327–350.

6 Swanson J, Volkow N (2009) Psychopharmacology: concepts and opinions about the use of stimulant medications. Journal of Child Psychology and Psychiatry, 50, 180–193.

7 Baldwin S, Christian S, Berkeljon A et al. (2012) The effects of family therapies for adolescent delinquency and substance misuse: a meta-analysis. Journal of Marital and Family Therapy, 38, 281–304.

8 Robbins M, Horigian V, Szapocznik J, Ucha J (2010) Treating Hispanic youths using brief strategic family therapy. In: Weisz J, Kazdin A (eds) Evidence-based Psychotherapies for Children and Adolescents, 2nd edn. New York: Guilford, pp 375–390.

9 Alexander J, Waldron H, Robbins M, Neeb A (2013) Functional Family Therapy for Adolescent Behaviour Problems. Washington: American Psychological Association.

10 Henggeler S, Schaeffer C (2010) Treating serious antisocial behaviour using multisystemic therapy. In: Weisz J, Kazdin A (eds) Evidence-based Psychotherapies for Children and Adolescents, 2nd edn. New York: Guilford, pp 259–276.

11 Liddle H (2010) Treating adolescent substance misuse using multidimensional family therapy. In: Weisz J, Kazdin A (eds) Evidence-based Psychotherapies for Children and Adolescents, 2nd edn. New York: Guilford, pp. 416–432.

12 Woolfenden S, Williams K, Peat J (2002) Family and parenting interventions for conduct disorder and delinquency: a meta-analysis of randomised controlled trials. Archives of Diseases in Childhood, 86, 251–256.

13 Holmes L, Ward H, McDermid S (2012) Calculating and comparing the costs of multidimensional treatment foster care in English local authorities. Children and Youth Services Review, 34, 2141–2146.

14 Tanner-Smith E, Wilson SJ, Lipsey M (2013) The comparative effectiveness of outpatient treatment for adolescent substance abuse: a meta-analysis. Journal of Substance Abuse Treatment, 44, 145–158.

15 Rowe C, Liddle H (2008) Multidimensional family therapy for adolescent alcohol abusers. Alcoholism Treatment Quarterly, 26, 105–123.

16 Santisteban S, Suarez-Morales L, Robbins M, Sxapocznik J (2006) Brief Strategic Family Therapy: lessons learned in efficacy research and challenges to blending research and practice. Family Process, 45, 259–271.

17 Reynolds S, Wilson C, Austin J, Hooper L (2012) Effects of psychotherapy for anxiety in children and adolescents: a meta-analytic review. Clinical Psychology Review, 32, 251–262.

18 Pahl K, Barrett P (2010) Interventions for anxiety disorders in children using group cognitive-behavioural therapy with family involvement. In: Weisz J, Kazdin A (eds) Evidence-based Psychotherapies for Children and Adolescents, 2nd edn. New York: Guilford, pp. 61–79.

19 Stark K, Banneyer K, Wang L, Arora P (2012) Child and adolescent depression in the family. Couple and Family Psychology: Research and Practice, 1, 161–184.

20 Harrington R, Kerfoot M, Dyer E et al. (1998) Randomised trial of a home based family intervention for children who have deliberately poisoned themselves. Journal of the American Academy of Child and Adolescent Psychiatry, 37, 512–518.

21 Huey S, Henggeler S, Rowland M et al. (2004) Multisystemic therapy reduces attempted suicide in a high-risk sample. Journal of the American Academy of Child and Adolescent Psychiatry, 43, 183–190.

22 King C, Kramer A, Preuss L et al. (2006) Youth-nominated support team for Suicidal Adolescents (Version 1): A randomised control trial. Journal of Consulting and Clinical Psychology 74, 199–206.

23 Wright-Hughes A, Graham E, Farrin A et al. (2015) Self-Harm Intervention: Family Therapy (SHIFT), a study protocol for a randomised controlled trial of family therapy versus treatment as usual for young people seen after a second or subsequent episode of self-harm. Online: www.ncbi.nlm.nih.gov/pubmed/26537599. Accessed: January 2017.

24 Eisler I (2005) The empirical and theoretical base of family therapy and multiple family day therapy for adolescent anorexia nervosa. Journal of Family Therapy, 27, 104–113.

25 NICE (2004) Eating Disorders: Core Interventions in the Treatment and management of Anorexia Nervosa, Bulimia Nervosa and Related Eating Disorders. London: The British Psychological Society and Gaskell.

26 Kitzmann K, Dalton W, Stanley C et al. (2010) Lifestyle interventions for youth who are overweight: a meta-analytic review. Health Psychology, 29, 91–101.

27 Nowicka P, Flodmark C (2011) Family therapy as a model for treating childhood obesity: useful tools for clinicians. Clinical Child Psychology and Psychiatry, 16, 129–145.

28 Kuipers L, Leff J, Lam D (2002) Family Work for Schizophrenia, 2nd edn. London: Gaskell.

29 McFarlane W (2002) Multifamily Groups in the Treatment of Severe Psychiatric Disorders. New York: Guilford.

30 Wren B (2015) 'There is no room in CAMHS for providing intervention without an evidence base': The case against. Context 139, 27–31.

31 Timimi S, Tetley D, Burgoine W, Walker G (2013) Outcome Oriented child and Adolescent Mental health services (OO-CAMHS). A whole service model. Clinical Child Psychology and Psychiatry, 18, 169–184.

32 Madsen W, Gillespie K (2014) Collaborative Helping: A Strengths Framework for Home-based Services. New York: Wiley.

33 Young K, Cooper S (2008) Towards composing an evidence base: the narrative therapy revisiting project. Journal of Systemic Therapies 27, 67–83.

34 Chatoor I, Kurpnick J (2001) The role of non-specific factors in treatment outcome of psychotherapy studies. European Child and Adolescent Psychiatry 10, S19–S25.

# 42

# Mentalization

*Dickon Bevington*

## Introduction

Two decades ago the term 'mentalizing' was rarely heard, but this has changed dramati-cally, particularly since the publication of a randomized study [1–3] showing how this concept, linked to a manualized therapeutic approach, mentalization-based treatment (MBT), offers effective treatment for the adult borderline personality disorder. What accounts for this proliferation in interest and applications, and how have theory and practice changed since then? This chapter explains mentalization and its relevance in a field not lacking in existing frameworks and interventions. After describing its devel-opmental origins, there is a brief overview of the clinical applications for children and adolescents to which this understanding has been applied.

## Definition

The standard definition [4] of mentalizing is deceptively simple; it refers to an *imagina-tive activity of mind required to make sense of behaviour*. When mentalizing is active, it reveals itself in an inquisitive, tentative, not-knowing stance; the ability to attempt a broadly coherent narrative as to how and why a state of affairs might have arisen; acceptance of the limits of one's knowing, with minds seen as at least partly opaque rather than openly knowable; a capacity to trust and forgive; and gently self-deprecating humour (an ability to enjoy the 'comedy of errors' that human interaction so often entails.) To have one's actions made sense of in this way is generally to experience a degree of compassion [5] as one's own perspective and state of mind are taken seriously.

There are several important qualifiers to this definition.

First, implicitly, the theory accommodates both pre-conscious as well as conscious determinants of behaviour. It is the reflection ('metacognition') upon contextual factors that might have been at play (beliefs, hopes, fears and intentions) that help to make sense of why a particular course of action might have unfolded at a particular point in time. Here we emphasize the adjective 'imaginative' in the core definition above – this is an 'imperfect science' that human brains (this mind-mindedness is almost exclu-sively human) engage in, and does not end in certainty. Even if on later reflection those beliefs are seen as mistaken, or the logic as clouded by emotion, mentalizing refers to the effort to grasp the 'gestalt' of mental contents at that time to explain the behaviour.

*Child Psychology and Psychiatry: Frameworks for Clinical Training and Practice,* Third Edition.
Edited by David Skuse, Helen Bruce and Linda Dowdney.
© 2017 John Wiley & Sons, Ltd. Published 2017 by John Wiley & Sons, Ltd.

Understanding this definition helps to explain the name; in *'mentalizing'* a behaviour, there is implicitly the attribution of a *mentality* (an intentional mind) behind it. In addition, there is the implicit attribution of an *agentive* self, operating upon the world in purposive ways. In many ways, this is a non-original folk psychology (people behave as they do because of what goes on in their minds) offering an integrative stance that is respectful of (and draws upon) social-cognitive, systemic and psychoanalytic frameworks, led by experimental evidence and neuroscience.

Second, crucially, 'mentalizing' refers to this particular form and focus of thinking, regardless of whether it is directed towards behaviour conducted by oneself or by another person. There is evidence from functional magnetic resonance imaging studies [6,7] to support the aggregation of these 'acts of making sense of behaviour on the basis of mental states' regardless of whether by self or other.

Third, mentalizing is a fragile mental capacity, prone to momentary lapses and recovery in the normal ebb and flow of social interaction. With the exception of people on the more severe end of the autistic spectrum who lack theory of mind, it is a fairly universal capacity mostly occurring implicitly and automatically (quietly in the background), occasionally more explicitly (summoned into controlled conscious attention by puzzlement or concern); however, it is easily subject to being overturned by relatively small alterations in affect. In situations of stress or arousal, limbic circuits overwhelm this delicate prefrontal 'playing with reality' and drive different, more primitive, forms of thought, more suited to addressing survival needs. For instance, *psychic equivalence* (characterized by certainty that one's thoughts about other people's minds and intentions are directly equivalent to objective reality), *teleological* thinking (considering the resolution of distress solely in terms of physical, observable outcomes – such as violence, self-injury, substance use, etc.) or *pretend mode* thinking (denying affective realities, retreating into coherent, even clever wordiness which avoids the 'elephant in the room' – long-winded justifications for past offences, mere theorizing in the face of immediate danger, etc.)

## Development

Fonagy *et al.* [4] describe mentalizing and attachment as 'loosely coupled' systems. An expectant mother's capacity to mentalize is more predictive of her child's secure attachment than is her own attachment style [8], and mentalizing develops in the context of attachment relationships, even though the activation of the attachment system may overwhelm mentalizing.

Mentalizing is explicitly and exclusively *relational*. It develops from early infancy through repeated experiences of *being mentalized*, especially in the context of secure attachment relationships. Attachment figures (principally mothers) use 'marked mirroring' to reciprocate and signal mentalized understanding of the child, whose imagined state of mind is represented back to them through facial expression and tone of voice (a mother playfully frowning as she soothes her screaming baby.) 'Marking' distinguishes this from straightforward mirroring; she does not scream back at the baby, but instead 'frames' her imitation of what she imagines the baby's state of mind to be – with a sing-song tone of voice, etc., offering contingent care that fits (her perception of) what might help. Through iterative experiences of accurate mirroring, the child comes to recognize its own mind in different states as these are 'benignly caricatured' by the parent, developing an awareness of self and agency. Securely attached mothers only offer fully contingent matching in about 30% of interactions; but this is enough [9]. Times when her attention is elsewhere, or she misinterprets (a grimace as a grin, for instance) stimulate the child in turn to mentalize her mind, finding 'mind-minded' explanations for her failures.

## Relevance

Mentalizing offers the huge evolutionary advantage of allowing for complex predictions about behaviour, facilitating complex kinship relationships and navigation through complicated and variable cultures without recourse to violence.

Mentalizing is intimately connected to learning, especially of the 'cognitively opaque' social knowledge required to manage life in sophisticated culturally diverse societies; for instance customs not explicitly signposted but signalling belonging and respect. Gergely, Csibra and colleagues suggest that humans are evolutionarily primed to establish a particular form of ('epistemic') trust in the value of the social knowledge that another person holds *when they experience that person as mentalizing them accurately*. This has been demonstrated in elegant experiments with toddlers [10]. When epistemic trust is established, the subject not only learns that the 'teacher' likes (or does not like) something, but also generalizes this learning, applying it to the social world beyond. It is argued [11] that establishing epistemic trust is a key common factor in successful therapies - more important than the (often widely divergent) specific techniques or explanatory theories that underpin them.

Caspi *et al.* [12], repeated in Patalay *et al.* [13] for adolescents, describe analyses of psychiatric diagnoses, symptoms, and their stability through time. Both analyses suggest that a (thus far imaginary) 'general psychopathology' *p*-factor (analogous to *g* in IQ measurements) offers the best fit for predicting the long-term stability of psychopathological symptoms rather than existing diagnoses or clusters (internalizing and externalizing). Fonagy *et al.* [14] suggest that a low level of epistemic trust ('epistemic hypervigilance' – which may be genetically predisposed or represent an adaptive response to a hostile early environment) may be a useful proxy for high *p*-factors, implying as it does the relative impermeability to therapeutic alliance, and the capacity to make use of treatment. The aetiology of this lies in the interplay between genetic and environmental influences, but the implication is that while patients with relatively low *p*-factor scores will probably respond well to straightforward manualized, evidence-based practices, those with high scores (lacking epistemic trust) require more specific attention and adaptation in order to help them.

## Applications

### The Mentalizing Stance

Workers are encouraged to adopt a therapeutic 'stance' of inquisitive not-knowing, sharing thoughts and impressions openly ('thinking aloud') and tentatively, broadcasting the expectation that through improved understanding of the patient's mind, both parties will be enriched in mutually beneficial ways. The mentalizing stance is active; when non-mentalizing is identified, deliberate steps are taken to punctuate or terminate this and to rekindle reflection ('I notice you've become very certain in the way you are talking just now, which seems different from how you appeared a few minutes ago when you were wondering about the different ways people may have experienced you. Do you notice this shift, too? I wonder if I've got us into this by bringing up these difficult matters too quickly?')

In keeping with simple behaviourist techniques, the worker attends to any evidence of positive mentalizing by the patient, marking and positively reinforcing these ('I really like the way you've got hold of that "calm-puzzling-out" style of thinking that we've discussed again – it's hard to hold onto it when we're talking about strong feelings') There is an element of straightforward psycho-education in this process, using plain language, humour and real-time interactions to elucidate mentalizing as a valuable capacity of mind.

Finally, the worker tries to hold a series of elements in approximate balance across sessions: mentalizing the patient as well as oneself and others in the patient's wider social world, attending to cognitions as well as to associated affect, to here-and-now interactions as well as to relevant episodes from outside the sessions.

Coupled with this general stance promoting a lively, even at times playful, learning environment in which affect is explicitly moderated, there is also a basic structure to sessions. Focus is applied to noticing and naming one or more particularly salient scenarios (and ways) in which the patient's mentalizing capacity is liable to collapse. Improving mentalizing of these ultimately supports the development of strategies for generalization, mitigating their impact in other areas of life.

### Specific Interventions

The strong emphasis on the developmental origins of mentalizing means that it is unsurprising that applications for use in children, young people and families have been quick to develop. What follows is a brief and by no means exhaustive sketch of a selection of these applications.

#### Mentalization-Based Treatment

Mentalization-based treatment is directed particularly at adults with borderline personality disorder (BPD), but has been adapted (MBT-adolescents, MBT-A) for use with self-injurious adolescents with emergent traits of BPD as well as depressive and anxiety-related symptoms. A randomized trial showed favourable outcomes in terms of reduction of self-injury, as well as reduction of emergent borderline traits and improved mentalizing, compared with treatment as usual in a UK child and adolescent mental health services setting [15]. In adult MBT, weekly individual sessions are supplemented by regular mentalizing group therapy sessions; poor evidence for group therapy with self-injurious adolescents means MBT-A replaces these with regular MBT-family sessions.

#### MBT-Families

MBT-families [16] has shown encouraging outcomes and high service user acceptability in a small pilot study, and an adaptation for Looked After Children and foster carers is currently under trial. MBT-F (see www.tiddlymanuals.com) views systemic practice through a mentalizing lens, offering a flexible 12 session format. Where appropriate it introduces a rich variety of games and activities, providing a structured context in which family interactions can be observed and worked with. Activities mitigate the unhelpful effects of high affect, common in highly conflicted families, which paradoxically reduces the mentalizing capacity that therapy aims to foster.

### Adaptive Mentalization-Based Integrative Treatment (AMBIT)

Adaptive Mentalization-Based Integrative Treatment applies mentalizing theory and techniques in teams working with complex, risky, co-morbid youths with low help-seeking behaviour [17,18]. Not a single specific intervention, it instead directs workers to apply mentalizing techniques across four broad areas, creating contexts in which evidence-based approaches (including, but not limited to, mentalization-based methods) have the greatest likelihood of supporting sustainable positive change (see Table 42.1)

AMBIT is an 'open source' approach to developing effective interventions, emulating the 'deployment-focused' method of treatment development espoused by Weisz and Simpson Gray [21], building effective methods through repeated field-based iterations, outcome evaluations and local adaptation to different cultural and organizational contexts.

**Table 42.1** Scope of Adaptive Mentalization-Based Integrative Treatment (AMBIT) mentalizing practice

| Area of work | Intent behind mentalization-based practices |
| --- | --- |
| Clients | Increase engagement, effectiveness and sustainability of a wide range of evidence-based interventions, and improve 'relationship to help'. |
| Team | Enable workers to support and develop trustworthy mentalizing individual relationships by ensuring these key workers (vulnerable to the 'entropic' impact of such work) are themselves proactively supported by, and model healthy dependency upon, a mentalizing 'team around the worker' using disciplined methods of communication. |
| Networks | Reduce unintended but inevitable 'dis-integration' (different, sometimes contradictory, explanatory models, operational criteria, agency priorities, etc.) through systematic application of mentalizing across multi-agency/multi-professional networks. Avoiding the destructive impact of (non-mentalizing) explanations of dis-integration by negative attributions (incompetence, laziness, etc.) that all networks are at risk of. |
| Learning | Service improvement [19] by establishing learning organizations that consistently interrogate their outcomes and co-produce innovative online 'wiki' manuals of local practice, blending centrally curated evidence-based practice with local practice-based evidence (see www.tiddlymanuals.com) Teams become part of a wider 'community of practice' [20] sharing emerging best practice via this local *manualization*, which is seen as analogous to mentalization by a team ('*Why do we do what we do?*') |

# References

1 Bateman A, Fonagy P (1999) Effectiveness of partial hospitalization in the treatment of borderline personality disorder: a randomized controlled trial. American Journal of Psychiatry, 156, 1563–1569.

2 Bateman A, Fonagy P (2001) Treatment of borderline personality disorder with psychoanalytically oriented partial hospitalization: an 18-month follow-up. American Journal of Psychiatry, 158, 36–42.

3 Bateman A, Fonagy P (2008) 8-year follow-up of patients treated for borderline personality disorder: mentalization-based treatment versus treatment as usual. American Journal of Psychiatry, 165, 631–638.

4 Fonagy P, Gergely G, Jurist EL, Target, M (2004) Affect Regulation, Mentalization, and the Development of the Self. New York: Other Press.

5 Gilbert P (2009) Introducing compassion-focused therapy. Advances in Psychiatric Treatment, 15, 199–208.

6 Lieberman, MD (2007) Social cognitive neuroscience: a review of core processes. Annual Review of Psychology, 58, 259–289.

7 Dimaggio G, Lysaker PH, Carcione A, Nicolò G, Semerari A (2008) Know yourself and you shall know the other.. to a certain extent: multiple paths of influence of self-reflection on mindreading. Consciousness and Cognition, 17, 778–789.

8 Fonagy P, Steele M, Steele H et al. (1991), The capacity for understanding mental states: The reflective self in parent and child and its significance for security of attachment. Infant Mental Health Journal, 12, 201–218.

9 Beebe B Jaffe J, Markese S et al. (2010) The origins of 12-month attachment: a microanalysis of 4-month mother-infant interaction. Attachment & Human Development Journal, 12, 3–141.

10 Egyed K, Király I, Gergely G (2013) Communicating Shared Knowledge in Infancy. Psychological Science, 24, 1348–1353.

11 Fonagy P, Allison E (2014) The role of mentalizing and epistemic trust in the therapeutic relationship. Psychotherapy (Chicago), 51, 372–380.

12 Caspi A, Houts RM, Belsky DW et al. (2014) The p factor: One general psychopathology factor in the structure of psychiatric disorders? Clinical Psychological Science, 2, 119–137.

13 Patalay P, Fonagy P, Deighton J et al. (2015) A general psychopathology factor in early adolescence. British Journal of Psychiatry, 207, 15–22.

14 Fonagy P, Luyten P, Campbell C, Allison L (2014, December) Epistemic trust, psychopathology and the great psychotherapy debate. Online: http://www.societyforpsychotherapy.org/epistemic-trust-psychopathology-and-the-great-psychotherapy-debate. Accessed: January 2017.

15 Rossouw TI, Fonagy P (2012) Mentalization-based treatment for self-harm in adolescents: a randomized controlled trial. Journal of the American Academy of Child and Adolescent Psychiatry, 51, 1304–1313.

16 Asen E and Fonagy P (2012) Mentalization-based therapeutic interventions for families. Journal of Family Therapy 34, 347–370.

17 Bevington D, Fuggle P, Fonagy P et al. (2012) Adolescent Mentalization-Based Integrative Therapy (AMBIT): A new integrated approach to working with the most hard to reach adolescents with severe complex mental health needs. Child and Adolescent Mental Health, 18, 46–51.

18 Bevington D, Fuggle P, Fonagy P (2015) Applying attachment theory to effective practice with hard-to-reach youth: the AMBIT approach. Attachment & Human Development, 17, 157–174.

19 Fuggle P, Bevington D, Cracknell E et al. (2014) The Adolescent Mentalization-based Integrative Treatment (AMBIT) approach to outcome evaluation and manualization: adopting a learning organization approach. Clinical Child Psychology and Psychiatry, 20, 419–435.

20 Lave J, Wenger E (1991) Situated Learning: Legitimate Peripheral Participation. Cambridge: Cambridge University Press.

21 Weisz JR, Simpson Gray J (2008) Evidence-based psychotherapy for children and adolescents: data from the present and a model for the future. Child and Adolescent Mental Health, 13, 54–65.

# 43

# Parenting Programmes for Conduct Problems

*Stephen Scott and Sajid Humayun*

## Evidence Linking Parenting to Child Psychopathology

The finding that parent–child relationship quality is associated with aggressive behaviour, conduct disorder and delinquency is one of the most widely reported in the literature, repeatedly found in large-scale epidemiological investigations, intensive clinical investigations and naturalistic studies of diverse samples using a mixture of methods [1]. The sort of parenting behaviours associated with these outcomes are high criticism and hostility, harsh punishment, inconsistent discipline, low warmth, low involvement, low encouragement and poor supervision.

The link with depression, anxiety and other emotional problems (e.g. somatic complaints, social withdrawal) is clear, although smaller than that found for disruptive outcomes [2]. There is also a connection between parenting and quality of a child's peer relationships, mediated by social cognitions and behavioural strategies learned from interacting with parents.

## Programmes for Children Based on Social Learning Theory

Programmes based on social learning theory have evolved for more than 40 years and there is a large evidence base. Most are aimed at antisocial behaviour as their proximal target outcome. The content and delivery of a typical programme are shown in Box 43.1. Most basic programmes take eight to 12 sessions, lasting 1.5–2 hours each. Full accounts of programmes are given by the developers [3,4] (Box 43.1).

---

**Box 43.1  Features of effective parenting programmes based on social learning theory**

**Content**

- Structured sequence of topics, introduced in set order during 10–12 weeks
- Curriculum includes play, praise, rewards, setting limits and discipline

---

*(continued)*

*Child Psychology and Psychiatry: Frameworks for Clinical Training and Practice*, Third Edition.
Edited by David Skuse, Helen Bruce and Linda Dowdney.
© 2017 John Wiley & Sons, Ltd. Published 2017 by John Wiley & Sons, Ltd.

> **Box 43.1 (Continued)**
>
> - Parenting seen as a set of skills to be deployed in the relationship
> - Emphasis on promoting sociable, self-reliant child behaviour and calm parenting
> - Constant reference to parent's own experience and predicament
> - Theoretical basis informed by extensive empirical research and made explicit
> - Plentiful practice, either live or role-played during sessions
> - Homework set to promote generalization
> - Accurate but encouraging feedback given to parent at each stage
> - Self-reliance prompted (e.g. through giving parents tip sheets or book)
> - Emphasis on parents' own thoughts and feelings varies from little to considerable
> - Detailed manual available to enable replicability
>
> **Delivery**
>
> - Strong efforts made to engage parents (e.g. home visits if necessary)
> - Collaborative approach, typically acknowledging parents' feelings and beliefs
> - Difficulties normalized, humour and fun encouraged
> - Parents supported to practise new approaches during session and through homework
> - Parent and child can be seen together, or parents only seen in some group programmes
> - Crèche, good-quality refreshments, and transport provided if necessary
> - Therapists supervised regularly to ensure adherence and to develop skills

## Format of a Typical Social Learning Programme

### Teaching a Child-Centred Approach

The first session covers play. Parents are asked to follow the child's lead rather than impose their own ideas. Instead of giving directions, teaching and asking questions during play, parents are instructed simply to give a running commentary on their child's actions. As soon as the parent complies, the practitioner gives feedback. After 10–15 minutes, this directly supervised play ends and the parent is 'debriefed' for half an hour or more alone with the clinician.

The second session involves elaboration of play skills. The previous week's 'homework' of playing at home is discussed with the parent in considerable detail. Often there are practical reasons for not doing it ('I have to look after the other children, I've got no help') and parents are then encouraged to solve the problem and find ways around the difficulty. For some parents there may be emotional blocks ('It feels wrong – no one ever played with me as a child'), which need to be overcome before they feel able to practise the homework.

After this discussion, live practice with the child is carried out. This time the parent is encouraged to go beyond describing the child's behaviour and to make comments describing the child's likely mood state (e.g. 'You're really trying hard making that tower', or 'That puzzle is making you really fed up'). This process has benefits for both the parent and the child. The parent gets better at observing the fine details of the child's behaviour, which makes them more sensitive to the child's mood. The child gradually gets better at understanding and labelling his/her own emotional states.

### Increasing Desirable Child Behaviour

Praise and rewards are covered here. The parent is required to praise their child for lots of simple everyday behaviours such as playing quietly on their own, eating nicely, and so on. In this way the frequency of desired behaviour increases. However, many parents find this difficult. Usually, with directly coached practice, praise becomes easier. Later sessions go through the use of reward charts.

### Imposing Clear Commands

A hallmark of ineffective parenting is a continuing stream of ineffectual, nagging demands for the child to do something. Parents need to be taught to reduce the number of demands, but make them much more authoritative. This is done through altering both the manner in which they are given, and what is said. The manner should be forceful (standing over the child, fixing him/her in the eye, and in a clear firm voice giving the instruction). The emotional tone should be calm, without shouting and criticism. The content should be phrased directly ('I want you to . . . '). It should be specific ('Keep the sand in the box') rather than vague ('Do be tidy'). It should be simple (one action at a time, not a chain of orders), and performable immediately. Commands should be phrased in terms of what the parent wants the child to do, rather than what the child should stop doing ('Please speak quietly' rather than 'Stop shouting'). Instead of threatening the child with vague, dire consequences ('You're going to be sorry you did that'), 'when–then' commands should be given ('When you've laid the table, then you can watch television').

### Reducing Undesirable Child Behaviour

Consequences for disobedience should be applied as soon as possible. They must always be followed through: children quickly learn to calculate the probability that consequences will be applied, and if a sanction is given only every third occasion, a child is being taught he/she can misbehave the rest of the time. Simple logical consequences should be devised and enforced for everyday situations (e.g. if a child refuses to eat dinner, there will be no pudding). The consequences should 'fit the crime', should not be punitive, and should not be long-term (e.g. no bike riding for a month), as this will lead to a sense of hopelessness in the child, who may see no point in behaving well if it seems there is nothing to gain. Consistency of enforcement is central.

Time out from positive reinforcement remains the final 'big one' as a sanction for unacceptable behaviour. The point here is to put the child in a place away from a reasonably pleasant context. Parents must resist responding to taunts and cries from the child during time out, as this will reinforce the child by giving attention. Time out provides a break for the adult to calm down also.

## Interventions with Youth

In adolescence somewhat different approaches are necessary, with more emphasis on negotiation and close supervision when the young person is out of the home. Also, whilst many components of programmes based on social learning theory are incorporated, additional elements may be required. In particular, there may need to be more of a focus on the wider systems around the youth, be they the wider family, school or peer networks. Thus interventions tend to be one of two types: family-based interventions or multi-component interventions.

### Family-Based Interventions

Being based on systemic family therapy theories, family-based interventions typically attempt to alter the structure and functioning of the family unit. The best known in the context of delinquency is Functional Family Therapy (FFT) [5]. It is designed to be practicable and relatively inexpensive: eight to twelve 1-hour sessions are given in the family home, to overcome attendance problems common in this client group; for more intractable cases, 26–30 hours are offered, usually over 3 months.

There are three phases to treatment; the first is the *engagement and motivation* phase. Here the therapist works hard to enhance the perception that change is possible. The aim is to keep the family in treatment and then to move on to find what precisely the family wants. Techniques include reframing, whereby positive attributes are enhanced (e.g. a mother who continually nags may be labelled as caring, upset and hurt). The next phase is not commenced until motivation is enhanced, negativity decreased and a positive alliance established.

The second phase targets *behaviour change*. There are two main elements to this: communication training and parent training. This stage is applied flexibly according to family needs. Thus, if there are two parents who continually argue and this is impinging on the adolescent, the 'marital subsystem' will be addressed, using standard techniques. Parent training techniques are similar to those found in standard approaches.

The third and final phase is *generalization*. Here the goal is to get the improvements made in a few specific situations to generalize to other similar family situations and to the wider community; for example, to help the youth and family negotiate positively with community agencies such as school and to help them get the resources they need. Sometimes this phase may require the therapist to be a case manager for the family.

### Multi-Component Interventions

These attempt to target multiple risk factors in multiple domains, with the best known being Multisytemic Therapy (MST) [6]. The initial focus of MST is an assessment that will identify the youth's difficulties in relation to the wider environment. Difficulties are understood as a reaction to a specific context, not seen as necessarily intrinsic deficits. At the same time, strengths will be identified that can be used as levers for positive change. These may be in the young person, the parents, the wider family, peers, the school or the community.

Interventions are designed to promote responsible behaviour and decrease irresponsible behaviour with the aim of helping the youth become independent and develop prosocial life skills. They will be focused in the present and be action-oriented with well-defined specific goals. This requires daily or weekly efforts by family members, which enables frequent practice of new skills, positive feedback for efforts made and rapid identification of non-adherence to treatment.

Intervention effectiveness is evaluated continually, with the intervention team assuming responsibility for overcoming barriers to successful outcomes. Whilst the way the therapy is delivered is closely controlled, the precise nature of moment-to-moment interaction is not tightly prescribed. In a sense, MST is a set of operating principles that draw on the evidence for whatever works – e.g. cognitive behavioural therapy, close monitoring and supervision – rather than one specific therapy.

## Effectiveness

### Social Learning Approaches

Systematic reviews and meta-analyses of studies, usually with 'no treatment controls', confirm that these approaches work well for antisocial children aged 3–10 years [7]. Mean effect sizes across studies vary from around 0.4 to 1.0 according to outcome, thus showing good effectiveness.

### Youth Interventions

Adolescents are generally found to do less well in parenting programmes for antisocial behaviour. However, studies on adolescents generally have the most severe, persistent cases. When cases of similar severity are compared directly there is no age effect [8]. The results for FFT and MST are reasonably impressive, at least in the USA [9,10]. Whilst evaluations outside the USA are either lacking or mixed, there has been one UK trial of MST showing effectiveness, at least for non-violent offences [11]. A recent UK trial of FFT, however, found that it did not improve outcomes more than usual youth offending services [12].

## Mediators and Moderators of Change

In recent years, researchers have begun to investigate the factors that mediate outcome. This research helps to identify the 'active ingredient' of therapy. Both reductions in negative parenting (critical, harsh and ineffective practices) [13] and increases in positive parenting [14] have been shown to mediate a reduction in child symptoms. At the same time, some individual factors have been shown reduce the effectiveness of therapy. Most notably, children and youth with callous-unemotional traits have been regarded as more difficult to treat [15]. However, that prevailing view is increasingly being challenged [16,17].

## Dissemination: The Role of Therapist Skill

Therapist performance can be divided into three parts: the alliance, which could be defined as how well, both personally and collaboratively, the client and therapist get on together; fidelity or adherence to specific components of a model, which concerns the extent to which the therapist follows the actions prescribed in the manual; and the skill or competence with which the therapist carries out the tasks (i.e. how well the therapist performs the actions). A meta-analysis of youth studies found that the alliance contributed, on average, an effect size of 0.21 standard deviations to outcome; this finding held across treatment types, and across youth, parent and family approaches [18]. In a trial under regular clinical conditions [19], therapist skill had a large effect on child outcomes – the worst therapist made outcomes slightly worse. These findings have major implications for service delivery, as they suggest that, at least for multi-problem, clinical cases, a high level of therapist skill is required, and staff training will need to reflect this.

## Conclusion

The best parenting programmes incorporate empirical findings from developmental studies and are effective in using these to alter dimensions of parenting, which in turn improve child outcomes. In future, better assessments of parenting are needed so that programmes can be tailored to specific needs rather than 'one size fits all'.

## References

1 Hoeve M, Dubas JS, Eichelsheim VI et al. (2009) The relationship between parenting and delinquency: A meta-analysis. Journal of Abnormal Child Psychology, 37, 749–775.
2 Wood J, McLeod B, Sigman M et al. (2003) Parenting and childhood anxiety: theory, empirical findings, and future directions. Journal of Child Psychology and Psychiatry, 44, 134–151.
3 Markie-Dadds C, Sanders M (2006) Self-directed triple P (positive parenting programme) for mothers with children at-risk of developing conduct problems. Behavioural and Cognitive Psychotherapy, 34, 259–275.
4 Webster-Stratton C, Reid J (2003) The incredible years parenting program. In: Kazdin A, Weisz J (eds) Evidence-based Psychotherapies for Children and Adolescents. New York: Guilford Press, pp. 224–240.
5 Sexton TL, Alexander JF (2000) Functional Family Therapy. Washington, DC: U.S. Department of Justice.
6 Henggeler SW, Rowland MD, Randall J et al. (1999) Home-based multisystemic therapy as an alternative to the hospitalization of youths in psychiatric crisis: clinical outcomes. Journal of the American Academy of Child and Adolescent Psychiatry 38, 1331–1339.
7 Maughan B, Denita R, Christiansen E et al. (2005) Behavioural parent training as a treatment for externalizing behaviours and disruptive behaviour disorders: a meta-analysis. School Psychology Review, 34, 267–286.
8 Ruma PR, Burke R, Thompson RW (1996) Group parent training: is it effective for children of all ages? Behaviour Therapy, 27, 159–169.
9 Woolfenden SR, Williams K, Peat J (2001) Family and parenting interventions in children and adolescents with conduct disorder and delinquency aged 10–17. Cochrane Database of Systematic Reviews, 2, CD003015.
10 Littell JH (2005) Lessons from a systematic review of effects of multisystemic therapy. Children and Youth Services Review, 27, 445–463.
11 Butler S, Baruch G, Hickey N et al. (2011) A randomized controlled trial of multisystemic therapy and a statutory therapeutic intervention for young offenders. Journal of the American Academy of Child & Adolescent Psychiatry, 50, 1220–1235.

12 Humayun S, Herlitz L, Chesnokov et al. (in press) Randomized Controlled Trial of Functional Family Therapy for offending and antisocial behavior in UK youth. Journal of Child Psychology and Psychiatry.

13 Beauchaine T, Webster-Stratton C, Reid J (2005) Mediators, moderators and predictors of 1-year outcomes among children treated for early-onset problems: a latent growth curve analysis. Journal of Consulting and Clinical Psychology, 75, 371–378.

14 Gardner F, Burton J, Klimes I (2006) Randomised controlled trial of a parenting intervention in the voluntary sector for reducing child conduct problems. outcomes and mechanisms of change. Journal of Child Psychology and Psychiatry, 47, 1123–1132.

15 Hawes DJ, Dadds MR (2007) Stability and malleability of callous-unemotional traits during treatment for childhood conduct problems. Journal of Clinical Child Adolescent Psychology, 36, 347–355.

16 Waller R, Gardner F and Hyde LW (2013) What are the associations between parenting, callous–unemotional traits, and antisocial behavior in youth? A systematic review of evidence. Clinical Psychology Review, 33, 593–608.

17 O'Connor TG, Humayun S, Briskman J et al. Sensitivity to parenting in adolescents with Callous/Unemotional Traits: observational and experimental findings. Journal of Abnormal Psychology, 125, 502–513.

18 Shirk S and Karver M (2003) Prediction of treatment outcome from relationship variables in child and adolescent therapy: a meta-analytic review. Journal of Consulting and Clinical Psychology, 71, 452–464.

19 Scott S, Spender Q, Doolan M et al. (2001) Multicentre controlled trial of parenting groups for childhood antisocial behaviour in clinical practice. British Medical Journal 323, 1–7.

## 44

# Paediatric Psychopharmacology – Special Considerations

*Paramala Santosh and Rakendu Suren*

## Introduction

Problems of mental health and behaviour in children are multidisciplinary, and optimal treatment is multi-modal. The number of children in the USA taking prescription drugs for emotional and behavioural disturbances is growing dramatically and has given rise to multiple controversies, ranging from concerns over off-label use and long-term safety to debates about the societal value and cultural meaning of pharmacology and treatment of childhood behavioural and emotional disorders. More than 80% of the worldwide use of stimulant medications takes place in the USA, and the use of antidepressants and antipsychotics is many times greater in the USA than in other countries [1]. Variability in use reflects differences in diagnostic systems, clinical practice guidelines, drug regulation, health services organization, availability and allocation of financial resources, and cultural attitudes towards childhood behavioural and emotional disturbances [1]. This chapter focuses on aspects of psycho-pharmacology that have special relevance in children and adolescents; it provides relevant information about classes of medication, rather than disorder-specific treatment recommendations.

## Information to Assist Judicious Prescribing

Apart from a thorough diagnostic assessment, the following information is important:

- full medical history – current and past;
- detailed medication history, including over-the-counter medications;
- history of substance misuse to ascertain potential misuse liability and interactions with prescribed medication;
- detailed family history, including history of mental illness, suicide, substance abuse, neurological/medical conditions (especially early-onset coronary artery disease), and the response of the family members to psychotropic medication.

*Child Psychology and Psychiatry: Frameworks for Clinical Training and Practice*, Third Edition.
Edited by David Skuse, Helen Bruce and Linda Dowdney.
© 2017 John Wiley & Sons, Ltd. Published 2017 by John Wiley & Sons, Ltd.

## Medication as a Part of Multi-Modal Treatment Package

Treatment plans should be individualized according to the pattern of target symptoms and strengths identified in the evaluation. Treatment should target situations in which symptoms cause most impairment, and treatment progress should be monitored by custom-designed target symptom scales or daily behavioural report cards. The designation of a case manager is essential for chronically disabled individuals to coordinate the wide range of services necessary for their care and to ensure periodic diagnostic reassessments. As pharmacological treatment is symptom-based in most psychiatric conditions, it is useful to conceptualize it, as described below [2].

### Symptom-Based Pharmacotherapeutic Strategy

- *Symptoms that require and are likely to respond to medication alone* – inattention, impulsivity, hyperactivity, tics, obsessions, psychotic symptoms, labile mood.
- *Symptoms that are less likely to respond to medication alone, requiring both medication and psychosocial interventions* – aggression, rituals, self-injury, depression.
- *Symptoms that are unlikely to respond to medication and need specific remediation* – skill deficits in academic, social, or sports domain.

## The Art of Prescribing Medication

Besides neurochemical effect of any given agent, the response to medication also depends on an inherent 'placebo response', as well as the therapeutic concordance achieved by obtaining agreement and acceptance of why the medication is prescribed and what is the expected response. Rewards experienced from medication treatment include improvement in symptoms, school performance and family relationships, and reduced level of parenting stress. Identified costs include the impact of adverse side-effects, social stigma, lack of response, fears of addiction, and changes in the child's personality [3]. Acceptance of the diagnosis influences adherence, while medication education has varying effects. Families' attitudes, beliefs and perceptions about psychiatric illness and treatment play a large role in medication treatment decisions. A trusting relationship with the clinician has a positive effect on adherence, but psycho-social treatment alternatives are usually preferred. With maturation, adolescents have more influence on decisions related to adherence [3].

These characteristics are enhanced when: parents and patients feel understood; parents, patients and clinicians agree on the need and type of treatment; the patient and parents are involved in medication decision-making; and medication is started in small doses using the principles of effective dosing with minimum side-effects (EDMS) [4,5]. The EDMS is the minimum dose with which 'acceptable' improvement with minimal side-effects is achieved. Medication should be initiated in small doses (usually in doses that are one-eighth to one-sixth of the final anticipated dose), increasing the dosage after about every five half-lives of the drug, which in practice is usually every 3–7 days, over a period of 4–6 weeks, to identify the EDMS [5].

## Use of Non-Licensed Psychotropic Medication

Most psychotropics – other than stimulants, atomoxetine for attention deficit hyperactivity disorder (ADHD), and imipramine for enuresis – are not licensed for use in children. Unlicensed psychotropics are not contraindicated in children, and doctors can prescribe any medication approved by the appropriate agency (e.g. the Food and Drug Administration or European Medicines Agency), to any age group, if they believe that there is a reasonable clinical indication. Thus, licensing of medication constrains drug companies but leave doctors free to prescribe unlicensed drugs or to use licensed drugs for unlicensed indications. The drug companies are not legally liable if any untoward reaction occurs in children treated without their knowledge, using such non-licensed medication. It is therefore important that the parents and patients (as appropriate) are given this information as part of the informed consent. The Royal College of Psychiatrists has published a consensus statement on the use of licensed medicines for unlicensed use [6]. Before prescribing a drug off-label, exclude licensed alternatives and ensure familiarity with the evidence base for the intended unlicensed use, document discussions and patient's consent.

## Factors Affecting Pharmacotherapy in Children

Understanding the pharmacokinetics and pharmacodynamics of drugs used in psychopharmacology across the paediatric age spectrum from infants to adolescents represents a major challenge for clinicians. In paediatrics, treatment protocols use either standard dose reductions for these drugs for children below a certain age or less conventional parameters such as weight for allometric dosing; the rationale behind this, however, is often lacking. Key factors for consideration are in Box 44.1.

---

**Box 44.1 Pharmacotherapy in children – key factors**

- **Absorption and hepatic metabolism.** The rate of absorption is faster in children and peak levels are reached sooner. Hepatic metabolism is highest during infancy and childhood (1–6 years), is about twice the adult rate in prepubertal children (6–10 years) and is equivalent to that in adults by the age of 15 years [7]. This is important clinically because younger children may require higher doses (mg/kg) of hepatically metabolized medication, compared with older children and adults.
- **Fat distribution.** Substantial fat stores slow the elimination of highly lipid-soluble drugs (e.g. fluoxetine) from the body. Fat distribution varies in children, increasing during the first year and gradually falling until puberty.
- **Protein binding and volume of distribution.** These differ in children, affecting pharmacokinetics by modifying the fraction of drug that is active (unbound) [8].
- **Incomplete maturation of neurotransmitter system.** The noradrenergic system does not fully develop anatomically and functionally until early childhood [9]. This may be one of the reasons for poor antidepressant response in childhood depression.
- **Cardiotoxicity.** The rates of maturation of the sympathetic and parasympathetic systems vary, although vagal and sympathetic modulations follow a similar pattern. This may lead to accentuation of the related of loss of vagal modulation associated with tricyclic antidepressants [10].

---

## Medications

The dose ranges of the majority of psychotropics used in children and adolescents along with their main indications are shown in Table 44.1.

**Table 44.1** Dose range of psychotropic medication used in children and adolescents

| | | |
|---|---|---|
| **Stimulant medication** | | |
| Methylphenidate IR | 5–60 mg/day | Inattention, hyperactivity, impulsivity and behavioural problems related to ADHD |
| Concerta XL | 18–72 mg/day | |
| Equasym XL | 10–60 mg/day | |
| Medikinet XL | 10–60 mg/day | |
| Dexamfetamine | 2.5–40 mg/day | |
| Lisdexamfetamine (Elvanse) | 30–70 mg/day | |
| **Non-stimulant medication** | | |
| Atomoxetine | 1–1.2 mg/kg body weight/day | |
| Clonidine | 0.05–0.4 mg/day | Hyperactivity, impulsivity, inattention, insomnia, tics, oppositionality, aggression |
| Guanfacine | 0.05–0.12 mg/kg/day | |
| **Tricyclic antidepressants** | | |
| Imipramine, desipramine | <6 years: 10–20 mg/day | Bedwetting, hyperactivity, impulsivity, inattention |
| | >6 years: 10–75 mg/day | |
| Clomipramine | 10–200 mg/day | Obsessions, compulsions |
| **SSRI** | | |
| Fluoxetine | 10–60 mg/day | Depression (only fluoxetine approved), obsessions and compulsions (high doses may be needed), self-injurious behaviour and anxiety-related aggression in ASD (low doses) |
| Fluvoxamine | 50–300 mg/day | |
| Sertraline | 25–150 mg/day | |
| Paroxetine | 10–60 mg/day | |
| Citalopram | 10–60 mg/day | |
| **SNRI** | | |
| Venlafaxine | 37.5–150 mg/day | Symptoms of ADHD and depression in adults |
| **Antipsychotic medication** | | |
| Haloperidol | Pre-pubertal: 0.5–8 mg/day | Low doses (< one-third of dose for psychosis) |
| | Post-pubertal: 1–16 mg/day | |
| Clozapine[a] | 50–600 mg/day | tics, severe aggression, and self-injury; |
| Risperidone | 0.25–6 mg/day | |
| Olanzapine | 2.5–20 mg/day | Low dose Aripiprazole and Risperidone in ASD with ADHD |
| Quetiapine | 25–300 mg/day | |
| Aripiprazole | 1–15 mg/day | |

**Antiepileptic medication**

| | | |
|---|---|---|
| Carbamazepine | 5–10 mg/L (serum level | Epilepsy, symptoms and |
| Sodium valproate | 50–100 mg/L (serum level) | prophylaxis of bipolar illness. Sodium valproate should not be used in post-pubertal girls. |
| Clonazepam | 0.5–4 mg/day | Epilepsy, akathisia, sleep disorders |

**Other medications**

| | | |
|---|---|---|
| Lithium carbonate | 0.4–1.0 mEq/L (serum level) | Bipolar disorder, aggression in the learning disabled, augmentation in depression |
| Buspirone | 10–45 mg/day | ?Anxiety, hyperactivity, aggression |
| Melatonin | 0.5–9 mg/day | Sleep problems |
| Naltrexone | 12.5–50 mg/day | Severe resistant self-injurious behaviour in ASD |

ADHD, attention deficit hyperactivity disorder; ASD, autistic spectrum disorder; SNRI, serotonin norepinephrine reuptake inhibitor; SSRI, selective serotonin reuptake inhibitor.
a Only for psychosis and tardive dyskinesia.

### Stimulants

Stimulants have been used for decades and there is good research evidence supporting their short-term use in ADHD. More recently, various stimulant delivery systems have been developed [the osmotic controlled-release system (OROS), Concerta XL; the wax matrix-based beaded system, Metadate CD or Equasym XL; the patch release system, Daytrana, etc.], resulting in long-acting preparations that make it possible to avoid the administration of medication in school, reducing stigmatization and embarrassment. The release systems and preparation of stimulants (pro-portion of immediate release versus slow release) allow the tailoring of the long-acting preparations to suit individual children [11]. Lisdexamfetamine is a prodrug, where dexamphetamine is complexed with the amino acid lysine, and in this form is inactive. Once ingested and absorbed, it is gradually broken down by enzymes to dexamphetamine.

Stimulants are contraindicated in schizophrenia, hyperthyroidism, cardiac arrhythmias, angina pectoris and glaucoma, and in patients with a history of hypersensitivity. Stimulants can be used with caution in hypertension, depression, tics (or family history of Tourette syndrome), autism spectrum disorders (ASDs) and severe mental retardation (Table 44.2).

### Antipsychotics

#### Second-Generation Antipsychotics (SGAs)

These are prescribed most frequently – aripiprazole, risperidone, quetiapine, olanzapine, ziprazidone and amisulpride. They are dopamine receptor blockers (hence they reduce positive symptoms but can produce extrapyramidal symptoms and many produce hyperprolactinaemia) and 5HT-2A receptor blockers.

**Aripiprazole** is a dopamine partial agonist or dopamine stabilizer and also has actions at 5HT-2A and D3 receptors, and partial agonists of 5HT-1A receptors. Symptoms may improve in the first week, but it is recommended to wait 4–6 weeks to determine efficacy, owing to pharmacokinetics of the drug. The mean elimination half-life of aripiprazole is

**Table 44.2** Specific side-effects of stimulants

| Side-effect | Precautions | Comment |
| --- | --- | --- |
| Seizure | No evidence of decreasing seizure threshold; can be used in well-controlled epilepsy | If seizures appear or worsen, change to dexamfetamine; avoid atomoxetine |
| Growth retardation | Reduced height and weight centiles possible over time | Advisable not to start stimulants in children who are short or biologically predisposed to short stature |
| Cardiovascular problems | Increases heart rate and blood pressure – monitor regularly | High risk in those with structural cardiac defects; monitor with ECG. Avoid Adderall in cardiac high-risk groups |
| Abuse potential | Possible abuse of stimulants by others with access | Self-initiated increase in dose by emotionally unstable patients with substance-use disorders is possible and should be monitored; atomoxetine, bupropion, or Concerta XL (drug delivery system makes it difficult to abuse) can be used |
| Psychotic symptoms | Can induce or worsen psychotic experience | Avoid in those who have first-degree relatives with a psychotic disorder or in children who have psychotic or quasi-psychotic experiences; atomoxetine, tricyclic antidepressants, clonidine, bupropion, or risperidone can be used |

ECG, electrocardiography.

75 hours, and that of the major metabolite, dihydro-aripiprazole, is 94 hours. There is little published evidence on its use in managing non-psychotic disruptive behaviours in developmental disorders, although clinical experience suggests that very small doses (2–5 mg daily) are sufficient (Table 44.3). This is known to produce hypoprolactinaemia.

**Table 44.3** Specific side-effects of selected psychotropic medication

| Drug | Precautions | Side-effects |
| --- | --- | --- |
| **Non-stimulants** | | |
| Atomoxetine (noradrenaline reuptake inhibitor) | Contraindicated in hepatic impairment, glaucoma, uncontrolled seizures or a history of hypersensitivity to drug; use with caution in hypertension, tachycardia, cardiovascular problems and patients with long QT interval or family history of QT prolongation or cerebrovascular disease | *Growth retardation*: reduction of two to three percentiles in mean height, and some weight loss<br><br>*Seizure liability*: not to be used in patients with uncontrolled seizures, and should be discontinued in those who develop or have an increased frequency of seizures<br><br>*Cardiovascular*: increases heart rate (by increasing noradrenergic tone) and small increase in blood pressure; QT-interval prolongation |

| Drug | Precautions | Side-effects |
|---|---|---|
| **Non-stimulants** | | |
| | | *Suicide risk*: monitor for signs of depression, suicidal thoughts and behaviour |
| | | *Liver dysfunction*: severe liver injury – rare. Abnormal liver enzymes are more common. Discontinue on first symptom or sign of liver dysfunction, e.g. pruritus, dark urine, jaundice, right upper quadrant tenderness or unexplained flu-like symptoms |
| Guanfacine | Can cause syncope, hypotension and bradycardia<br><br>Caution in patients with hypotension, heart block, bradycardia or cardiovascular disease or history of QT prolongation<br><br>*Contraindications*: hypersensitivity to the active substance, patients with galactose intolerance, glucose or galactose malabsorption | Somnolence, headache, abdominal pain and fatigue are very common. Decreased appetite, depression, anxiety, affect lability, insomnia, bradycardia, hypotension, vomiting, diarrhoea, nausea and constipation are common |
| Tricyclic antidepressants – imipramine, amitriptyline, nortriptyline, desipramine and clomipramine | Use has declined due to concerns of cardiac arrhythmias and case reports of sudden death | Cardiotoxicity, danger of accidental or intentional overdose, troublesome sedation, anticholinergic side-effects, lowered seizure threshold |
| **Newer antidepressants** | | |
| SSRIs – fluoxetine, fluvoxamine, sertraline, paroxetine, citalopram, escitalopram<br><br>SNRI – venlafaxine<br><br>NRI – reboxetine, mirtazapine | It is currently advised that children or adolescents being started on, or dose being increased of, antidepressants should be monitored closely for emergence or worsening of suicidal ideation or behaviour | *Antidepressant-related suicidal ideation and behaviour*: consistently there has been increased suicidal ideation with use of antidepressants in childhood depression. This has to be balanced with genuine suicidal risk in untreated severe depression.<br><br>*SNRI*: venlafaxine should be avoided<br><br>*Antidepressant-induced behavioural activation*: increased motor activity, restlessness, excitability, and impulsivity that occurs usually early in treatment and may be reduced by using the EDEM principle; managed by reducing the dose, and with a benzodiazepine for a few days |

(*continued*)

**Table 44.3** (Continued)

| Drug | Precautions | Side-effects |
| --- | --- | --- |
| **Non-stimulants** | | |
| **Antipsychotic medications** | | |
| *FGAs* – haloperidol, chlorpromazine *SGAs* – risperidone, olanzapine, quetiapine, aripiprazole, ziprazidone, clozapine | Monitor movement disorders at baseline and regularly during antipsychotic treatment – extrapyramidal side-effects such as tardive dyskinesia are more common in FGAs. Aripiprazole and clozapine are useful in those who require antipsychotics but have developed tardive dyskinesia *Metabolic syndrome*: monitor weight, waist circumference, and body mass index at baseline and every 6 weeks; serum prolactin, fasting lipids, fasting cholesterol, fasting glucose and liver function tests at baseline and every 6 months. Be cautious if there is a family history of obesity, dyslipidaemia, early-onset hypertension, cardiovascular disease, cerebrovascular accident or diabetes | *Extrapyramidal side-effects* such as tardive dyskinesia are more common in FGAs. Aripiprazole and clozapine are useful in those who require antipsychotics but have developed tardive dyskinesia *Hyperprolactinaemia*: common with risperidone and FGAs *Risk of weight gain and metabolic dysfunction*: high – clozapine, olanzapine; moderate – risperidone, quetiapine, sertindole; low – amisulpride, aripiprazole, ziprazidone *Treatment of SGA-induced metabolic dysfunction*: preventive healthy lifestyle counselling; regular monitoring of body weight and metabolic variables; cognitive behavioural therapy and motivational interviewing to address unhealthy diet, physical inactivity and smoking; metformin therapy may become necessary in severe cases |

FGA, first-generation antipsychotic; MED, minimum effective dose; NRI, noradrenaline reuptake inhibitor; SGA, second-generation antipsychotic; SNRI, serotonin noradrenaline reuptake inhibitor; SSRI, selective serotonin reuptake inhibitor.

A black box warning exists as a result of analyses showing more frequent suicidal ideation in clinical trials of children treated with atomoxetine [12]

In December 2003, the Committee on Safety of Medicines concluded that the evidence was adequate to establish effectiveness only for fluoxetine in the treatment of depressive illness in children and adolescents, and advised against the use of the other SSRIs [13].

The US Food and Drug Administration has insisted on black box warnings for all SSRIs regarding the possibility of suicide-related behaviour as a side-effect in children [6].

**Risperidone** is the most used SGA; it is a potent dopamine D2 receptor blocker (and hence produces hyperprolactinaemia) and can lead to extrapyramidal symptoms.

**Quetiapine** is an effective SGA with a moderate effect on weight; it usually needs to be taken at least twice daily because of relatively weak receptor binding.

**Ziprazidone** is the only SGA that is weight-neutral; however, it has a greater impact on cardiac rhythm and the QTc interval.

**Clozapine** is used in those with resistant psychoses or tardive dyskinesia, but can lead to neutropenia, sialorrhoea and significant weight gain.

**Olanzapine** is used less in children and adolescents because of the propensity to weight gain and metabolic syndrome. Evidence from adults suggests that clozapine, olanzapine, and low-potency conventional antipsychotics such as chlorpromazine are associated with an increased risk of insulin resistance, hyperglycaemia and type 2 diabetes mellitus.

Risperidone and aripiprazole are now licensed to use in children and adolescents with ASD and irritability.

Autism spectrum disorder is frequently associated with co-morbid disorders such as intellectual disability, anxiety disorder, ADHD, depression, obsessive compulsive disorder and tic disorder. Evidence suggests that the deficits in social communication and co-morbid symptoms can be managed by focused behavioural interventions, medication, and medication coupled with behavioural interventions [6].

### Mood Stabilizers

Carbamazepine, sodium valproate, lamotrigine, lithium carbonate, and SGAs are mood stabilizers.

**Sodium valproate or valproic acid** is the most frequently used mood stabilizer and is best avoided in girls of child-bearing age due to its teratogenicity effects, as well as the possible side-effect of polycystic ovarian disease.

**Lithium** use warrants regular blood level monitoring, which is often problematic in children.

**Lamotrigine** is especially useful when significant depressive symptoms exist in bipolar disorder. Valproic acid markedly increases the half-life of lamotrigine and the likelihood of developing severe drug rashes, including Stevens–Johnson syndrome. Lamotrigine is to be started at very low doses (as low as 5 mg/day) and increased slowly over a couple of months.

As antipsychotics, antidepressants and anti-manic agents are more closely associated with the development of obesity and sexual/reproductive adverse events in African-American patients, practitioners need to carefully weigh the risks/benefits of prescribing psychotropic agents to African-American children, taking into consideration pre-existing/co-morbid conditions or individual risk factors for adverse reactions, especially when multiple medications are prescribed [14].

### Disruptive Mood Dysregulation Disorder (DMDD)

Disruptive mood dysregulation disorder is a newcomer to the psychiatric nosology. Treatment is often based on what has been helpful for other disorders that share the symptoms of irritability and temper tantrums. These disorders include ADHD, anxiety disorders, oppositional defiant disorder, and major depressive disorder [15] Psychological treatments (psychotherapy, parent training and computer-based training) should be tried before considering any medical treatments. There is evidence that, in children with irritability and ADHD, stimulant medications also decrease irritability. Antidepressant medication is sometimes used to treat the irritability and mood problems associated with DMDD. Risperidone and aripiprazole are approved by the US Food and Drug Administration for the treatment of irritability associated with autism and are sometimes used to treat DMDD [15].

## Drug Interactions

Detailed reviews of the cytochrome P450 enzyme system in children and guidelines to the prediction of drug–drug interactions are available [16,17]. It is advisable to look through this list before prescribing concomitant medication. Terfenedrine, ketoconazole, azetamazole and erythromycin, if co-administered with selective serotonin reuptake inhibitors, can in theory lead to cardiac arrhythmias. Fluvoxamine can significantly increase clozapine levels; sodium valproate significantly increases lamotrigine levels, and imipramine, when added to erythromycin, can lead to toxic delirium.

## Ethical Issues in Paediatric Psychopharmacology

Research on psychopharmacological treatment in children and adolescents is the object of ongoing ethical discussion, as minors with mental disorders constitute a vulnerable patient group. Incentives for the conduct of clinical trials with children comparable to those contained in US legislation are now provided in the EU. Research to develop 'me too' preparations or drugs that are just similar to already existing drugs may have less benefit for children, but can cause research burden and detract from clinically more important projects by utilizing limited investigator time and patient resources [18]. The issues of avoiding undue influence from funders and conflicts of interests remain a prominent concern that can be solved by declaring conflicts and publishing all results of studies extensively.

## Conclusion

Pharmacokinetics studies may bring more individualized treatment approaches into child psychiatry but they remain at present a promise for the future. A holistic biopsychosocial formulation and management of the child's problem is essential, as psychopharmacotherapy is only part of a package of care. Use of the EDMS principle assists in titrating initial dose increments to the expected target dose based on treatment response and emergent adverse effects. Paediatric pharmacovigilance for psychotropic agents and true long-term studies on efficacy and side-effects are essential. Evidence regarding treatment impact on co-morbid disorders, cost and impact on quality of life is sparse and urgently needs to be addressed. Until such detailed data become available, it is safe to assume that paediatric populations are at least as (or more) vulnerable to adverse effects as adults.

## References

1 Vitellio B (2008) An international perspective on pediatric psychopharmacology. International Review of Psychiatry, 20, 121–126.
2 Santosh PJ, Baird G (1999) Psychopharmacotherapy in children and adults with intellectual disability. Lancet, 354, 233–242.

3  Hamrin V, McCarthy EM,Tyson V (2010) Pediatric psychotropic medication initiation and adherence: a literature review based on social exchange theory. Journal of Child and Adolescent Psychiatric Nursing, 23, 151–172.

4  Santosh PJ (2009) Medication for children and adolescents – current issues. In: Gelder M, Andreason N, Lopez-Ibor J, Geddes J (eds) New Oxford Textbook of Psychiatry. Oxford: Oxford University Press, pp. 1793–1799.

5  Santosh PJ, Singh J (2016) Drug treatment of autism spectrum disorders and their comorbidities in children. BJPsych Advances, 22, 151–161.

6  Food and Drug Administration (2007) Antidepressantuse in Children, Adolescents and Adults. US FDA. Online: http://www.fda.gov/Cder/drug/antidepressants/default.htm. Accessed: January 2017.

7  Bourin M, Couetoux du Tertre A (1992) Pharmacokinetics of psychotropic drugs in children. Clinical Neuropharmacology, 15(Suppl 1), 224A–225A.

8  Paxton J, Dragunow M (1993) Pharmacology. In: Werry J, Aman M (eds) Practitioner's Guide to Psychoactive Drugs for Children and Adolescents. New York: Plenum.

9  Goldman-Rakic PS, Brown RM (1982) Postnatal development of monoamine content and synthesis in the cerebral cortex of rhesus monkeys. Brain Research, 256, 339–349.

10  Mezzacappa E, Steingard R, Kindlon D et al. (1998) Tricyclic antidepressants and cardiac autonomic control in children and adolescents. Journal of the American Academy of Child and Adolescent Psychiatry, 37, 52–59.

11  Banaschewski T, Coghill D, Santosh P et al. (2006) Long-acting medications for the hyperkinetic disorders. A systematic review and European treatment guideline. European Child and Adolescent Psychiatry, 15, 476–495.

12  Strattera Medication Guide. n.d  Online: http://www.fda.gov/downloads/drugs/ drugsafety/ucm089138.pdf. Accessed: January 2017.

13  Committee on Safety of Medicines (2004) Report of the CSM Expert Working Group on the Safety of Selective Serotonin Reuptake Inhibitor Antidepressants. Online: http:// www.mhra.gov.uk/home/groups/pl-p/documents/drugsafetymessage/con019472.pdf. Accessed: January 2017.

14  Jerrell JM (2010) Adverse events associated with psychotropic treatment in African American children and adolescents. Journal of the National Medical Association, 102, 375–383.

15  National Institute of Mental Health (NIMH) Disruptive Mood Dysregulation Disorder. Online: http://www.nimh.nih.gov/health/topics/disruptive-mood-dysregulation- disorder-dmdd/disruptive-mood-dysregulation-disorder.shtml. Accessed: January 2017.

16  Nemeroff CB, DeVane CL, Pollock BG (1996) Newer antidepressants and the cytochrome P450 system. American Journal of Psychiatry, 153, 311–320.

17  Oesterheld JR, Shader RI (1998) Cytochromes: a primer for child and adolescent psychiatrists. Journal of the American Academy of Child and Adolescent Psychiatry, 37, 447–450.

18  Kolch M, Ludolph AG, Plener PL et al. (2010) Safeguarding children's rights in psychopharmacological research:ethical and legal issues. Current Pharmaceutical Design, 16, 2398–2406.

# 45

# Paediatric Liaison

*Peter Hindley*

## Overview

Paediatric liaison psychiatry lies at the interface between physical and mental health. Historically, paediatric liaison services in the UK have tended not to concern themselves with psychiatric emergencies in the acute hospital setting. However, services in larger teaching hospital settings provide both daytime emergency and ward outpatient services. This chapter follows this model.

In contrast to adult liaison mental health services, paediatric services are relatively under-developed in the UK. The most recent national survey of liaison mental health services [1] found that only 20% of hospitals with paediatric services had on-site dedicated paediatric liaison services. It is unclear why this is so but difficulties in encouraging physical and mental health commissioners to work together may partly account for the difference. Moves to more integrated models of commissioning may help to overcome some of these problems.

## Paediatric Liaison and Child and Adolescent Mental Health Emergencies

Self-harm represents the commonest emergency presentation in the acute setting. The estimated number of children and young people who self-harm in any one year ranges from 10% to 20% [2]. Not all of these young people present to hospital but those who have taken overdoses or used more violent methods to harm themselves are far more likely to present. Self-harm is an important symptom of social and/or psychological distress, but not all children and young people who self-harm intend to kill themselves. However, the risk of completion of suicide rises significantly in the 3 months following an episode of self-harm. The risk of completion of suicide rises with a concurrent history of mental illness, especially depression, recent discharge from inpatient care and a family history of suicide. Important dynamic risk factors fall into two groups: those young people who plan a suicide attempt for whom intensifying suicidal thoughts is a key risk indicator; and those who act impulsively where a combination of impulsivity, brief but intense periods of low mood and disinhibition via drugs or alcohol interact to increase risk. National Institute for Health and Care Excellence (NICE) guidance recommends

*Child Psychology and Psychiatry: Frameworks for Clinical Training and Practice,* Third Edition. Edited by David Skuse, Helen Bruce and Linda Dowdney.
© 2017 John Wiley & Sons, Ltd. Published 2017 by John Wiley & Sons, Ltd.

inpatient paediatric admission for young people under 16 and a comprehensive psycho-social assessment [3]. Children and young people who have been admitted to hospital are referred to community services for 7-day follow-up but many do not attend (up to 60% in some areas). Follow-up offered by the assessing clinician tends to improve follow-up rates. A promising intervention is the Therapeutic Assessment [4], which allows assessing clinicians to include a therapeutic intervention, improves young people's understanding of why they self-harm and offers alternative strategies to self-harm.

First presentation of psychosis, acute behavioural disturbance in children and young people with neurodevelopmental disorders and delirium are the next most commons emergency presentations. All three presentations require careful assessment of the young person's physical and mental health. Although most young people presenting with first episode psychosis will not have an underlying physical illness, a small proportion will. Disorders such as autoimmune encephalitis, especially N-acetyl D-aspartate receptor (NMDAR) [5], can present as primarily psychiatric in nature and careful screening for disturbances of consciousness should be an integral part of emergency assessments in accident and emergency. Instruments such as the Paediatric Anaesthesia Emergency Delirium (PAED) scale [6] can help in screening for delirium. Children and young people with disorders such as autism spectrum disorder (ASD), especially those with limited communication skills, may present with behaviour disturbance secondary to physical health problems, especially occult pain such as from a dental abscess. Young people presenting with a first episode of intoxication, due to either alcohol or street drugs, are not always referred to paediatric liaison or community child and adolescent mental health services. However, where there is a recurrent pattern of attendance, indicating a possible substance misuse disorder, this would be indicated.

## Paediatric Liaison and the Mind–Body Interface

Western medicine, in training, in service provision and in lay thinking, perpetuates a division between the mind and the body. And yet it is increasingly clear that non-western models of the indivisible nature of mind and body more accurately reflect reality. Physical pain and mental pain are mutually entwined, all symptoms are experienced in the mind and all symptoms exert a function in our biopsycho-social world [7]. Understanding the function and meaning of symptoms, physical and mental, is central to paediatric liaison psychiatry. Mayou *et al.* [8] developed a powerful tool for making sense of symptoms (see Figure 45.1). As the clinician develops a better understanding of each patient's condition and circumstance, information can be mapped onto the chart. The chart allows the clinician to understand the interaction between different factors in various different domains of a patient's life. It can be used to share this understanding with colleagues and patients and their families.The addition of the medical domain helps us understand how the patient's interaction with the medical world (beliefs, expectations, relationships, communications, tests and treatments) act as a powerful factor in determining the function and meaning of symptoms in the lives of children and young people, their families and their wider worlds (especially school).

The function of parents' response to physical symptoms is most starkly seen in pain. Children are more likely to display recurrent abdominal pain if their parents display a highly emotionally concerned response pain [7] and see pain as allowing the child to be relieved of key responsibilities (attending school, undertaking household chores, etc.).

| Domain | Predisposing | Precipitating | Perpetuating | Protective/positive |
|---|---|---|---|---|
| Biological | | | | |
| Psychological | | | | |
| Social | | | | |
| Medical | | | | |

**Figure 45.1** Mayou et al.'s [45] tool for making sense of symptoms.

And yet at the same time we know that many long-term conditions (e.g. sickle cell disease, inflammatory bowel disease) are associated with powerful experiences of pain.

How children, parents, carers and siblings respond to physical symptoms and illness will depend on a range of factors: personal and family beliefs about illness; the child's age and developmental status; the extent of personal and social resources that are available to them; and the range of other stressors (social, psychological, practical) that the child and the family members are currently experiencing. It is important to bear in mind that frequent hospital attendance brings with it a range of financial and practical stressors (fares, food in hospital, missing work, care of other children at home, etc.). Finally, cultural factors are always important to bear in mind. In many communities (e.g. those of West African origin) beliefs about spirit possession as a cause of illness are common and important to consider when understanding how the family is responding to the child's symptoms and or illness.

Somatization, or the tendency to express psychological distress as physical symptoms, is a common process [7]. Sympathetic activation when under stress is a contributory factor, often reinforced by excessive attention to physical symptoms and underlying cultural beliefs (see earlier). However, it is important to remember that not all physical illnesses are easily or immediately recognized. Psychological explanations are often the first resort in circumstances where we do not understand the significance of physical symptoms. It is very important to distinguish between not knowing and positing a psychological explanation and having an explanation in which the role of psychological and social factors can be clearly demonstrated.

This becomes particularly important when considering the role of somatization in children with long-term conditions. Many of the symptoms that children with long-term conditions experience (e.g. pain in sickle cell disease, non-epileptic seizures in children with epilepsy) cannot be understood purely as a manifestation of the physical disease process. All of the factors outlined above influence symptom emergence and perpetuation in children with long-term conditions. In fact, with very regular experience of investigation and medical interventions, one could argue that they are even more important. Using Mayou *et al.*'s formulation approach with children and their parents and carers can be useful in understanding these complex processes. However, at heart is the willingness to listen to a child and a parent's story and to give it due respect and weight in making sense of their experience.

Children with long-term conditions are also at greater risk of mental health problems. This arises from a combination of factors: the physical impact of the illness, when you feel unwell you are less resilient; the impact of treatments (drug side-effects, regular injections); the impact on a child's lifestyle (dietary restrictions, restrictions to activities, school absences etc); and the impact of stigma, which arises in relation to physical illness almost as much as mental illness. Conditions which put children and young people particularly at risk include: diabetes; chronic renal failure; all forms of cancer; and painful conditions such as sickle cell disease. For a comprehensive review see Shaw & DeMaso [9].

However, the risk of mental health problems increases exponentially with conditions that involve the central nervous system (CNS). Epilepsy is the exemplar condition. Children with epilepsy are at greater risk of all forms of developmental disorders, emotional disorders and psychotic disorders [10]. This increased vulnerability reflects all of the processes outlined earlier. For example, all anticonvulsants have psychotropic effects, and epilepsy is universally one of the most stigmatized conditions. The key difference with CNS disorders is that damage to the CNS itself can cause psychiatric symptoms and disorders.

A good example of this is the group of autoimmune encephalitides which have been recognized over the past 20 years. Anti-NMDAR encephalitis has been extensively studied and a wide range of psychiatric disorders (delirium, psychosis, catatonia, depression, anxiety) are commonly seen. However, their management is complicated by the co-occurrence of severe neurological disturbance (see Barry *et al.* [5])

Delirium, a disturbance of the sensorium, with confusion, disorientation, abnormal experiences such as visual and auditory hallucinations and hypo- or hyperactivity, occurs in the context of severe physical illness of all kinds [11]. However, it is often missed in children. It requires active management, based on the treatment of the underlying cause, with environmental and psychopharmacological interventions.

## Paediatric Liaison: Management, Commissioning and Value for Money

Paediatric liaison has historically suffered from 'falling between two stools' – neither physical nor mental health commissioners have seen it a priority. However, with the growing awareness of the importance of the interaction between physical and mental health [12,13] and a move towards more integrated commissioning this may start to change. There is some evidence that paediatric liaison services can help to significant cost savings by the more effective management of somatization and long-term conditions [14]. Allied to this is a growing awareness of the uneven spread of urgent and emergency care for children and young people in mental crisis. Increasing resourcing to paediatric liaison services may be one way of improving patient experience.

## Conclusions

Paediatric liaison psychiatry is a rich and varied speciality. Its position at the interface between mental and physical health and its focus in understanding and valuing the experience of children and families make it crucial in a world where the two systems are increasingly coming together.

# References

1 Barrett J, Aitken P, Lee W (2016) Report of the 2nd Annual Survey of Liaison Psychiatry in England. Online: http://www.crisiscareconcordat.org.uk/wp-content/uploads/2015/10/2a-Report-of-the-2nd-Annual-Survey-of-Liaison-Psychiatry-in-England-20-.pdf. Accessed: January 2017.

2 Wasserman D, Hoven C, Wasserman C et al. (2015) School-based suicide prevention programmes: the SEYLE cluster-randomised, controlled trial. The Lancet, 385, 1536–1544.

3 Nice (2004) Self-harm in over 8s: short-term management and prevention of recurrence. Online: https://www.nice.org.uk/guidance/cg16. Accessed: January 2017.

4 Ougrin D (2016) Therapeutic Assessment. Online: http://www.therapeuticassessment.co.uk/TAteam.html. Accessed: January 2017.

5 Barry H, Byrne S, Barrett E et al. (2014) Anti-n-methyl-d-aspartate encephalitis: review of clinical presentation, diagnosis and treatment. Psychiatric Bulletin, 39, 19–23.

6 Janssen N, Tan E, Staal M et al. (2015) On the utility of diagnostic instruments for pediatric delirium in critical illness: an evaluation of the Pediatric Anesthesia Emergence Delirium Scale, the Delirium Rating Scale 88, and the Delirium Rating Scale-Revised R-98. Intensive Care Medicine, 37, 1331–1337.

7 Garralda M (2010) Unexplained physical complaints. Child and Adolescent Psychiatric Clinics of North America, 19, 199–209.

8 Mayou R, Sharpe M, Carson A (2003) ABC of Psychological Medicine. London: BMJ Books.

9 Shaw R, Demaso D (2010) Pediatric Psychosomatic Medicine. Washington DC: American Psychiatric Association.

10 Wallace S, Farrell K (2004) Epilepsy in Children. London: Arnold.

11 Smith HD, Fuchs C, Pandharipande P et al. (2009) Delirium: an emerging frontier in the management of critically ill children. Critical Care Clinics, 25, 593–614.

12 Independent Mental Health Taskforce to the NHS in England (2016) The Five Year Forward View For Mental Health. Online: https://www.england.nhs.uk/wp-content/uploads/2016/02/Mental-Health-Taskforce-FYFV-final.pdf. Accessed: January 2017.

13 Department of Health (2015) Future in Mind: Promoting, Protecting And Improving Our Children and Young People's Mental Health and Wellbeing. Online: https://www.gov.uk/government/uploads/system/uploads/attachment_data/file/414024/Childrens_Mental_Health.pdf. Accessed: January 2017.

14 North C, Eminson M (1998) A review of a psychiatry-nephrology liaison service. European Child & Adolescent Psychiatry, 7, 235–245.

# 46

# Promoting Educational Success: How Findings from Neuroscience can Guide Educators to Work Optimally with the Brain

*Bettina Hohnen*

## Education and Neuroscience: The Debate

There is a movement across the world to use knowledge from neuroscience to inform formal education, evidenced by the significant increase in the number of papers linking the two [1]. With the advent of improved technology such as functional magnetic resonance imaging (fMRI), we can see the brain at work and track changes throughout childhood, teaching us much about brain function and the processes underlying brain development. However, some are sceptical of the productivity of this relationship [2], arguing that it is a 'bridge too far'. Bishop [3] concurs, saying that pure measures of brain function offer little additional explanatory power or practical implications over an explanation at the cognitive or behavioural level. For example, if training A improves reading via changing functioning in brain region X, it is only of relevance that the reading changed, not which region was involved. Moreover, we are a long way from being able to use individual brain scans to inform practice. Yet, neuroscientists can say which brain regions and circuits are involved in many cognitive activities and how this changes with age [3]. This paper shows that valid neuroscientific facts and concepts can be a useful resource for guiding educators, helping them to understand basic brain functioning and the course of brain development to ensure they work optimally with the brain while teaching and learning at different ages. A disregard for such factors may, in fact, delay or prohibit educators from accurately diagnosing the source of student difficulty and identifying factors impeding each child to attain optimal educational success.

## Neuro-Myths

One of the barriers to neuroscience's application to education has been the rise of the so-called 'neuro-myths'. These are ideas and theories about how the brain works which are not factually correct but carry with them recommendations for how to work with individuals [4]. These myths can do more harm than good, leading to wasted time, money and effort [5,6]. The most strongly believed myths among professionals are outlined in Table 46.1 [7].

These myths persist, Pasquinelli [5] argues, because of cultural conditions such as 'neurophilia', which is the growing presence of brain images into newspaper reports and because explanations at the brain level are alluring and fulfil a 'soothing' function when

*Child Psychology and Psychiatry: Frameworks for Clinical Training and Practice,* Third Edition.
Edited by David Skuse, Helen Bruce and Linda Dowdney.
© 2017 John Wiley & Sons, Ltd. Published 2017 by John Wiley & Sons, Ltd.

**Table 46.1** Most prevalent 'neuro-myths' [7]

| Neuro-myth | Description |
| --- | --- |
| Learning styles | Individuals learn better when they receive information in their preferred learning styles such as auditory, visual, kinaesthetic |
| Left brain, right brain | Individuals are either left or right brain dominant, which explains how they learn best |
| Brain gym exercises | Short bouts of coordinated exercise can improve integration of left and right hemispheric brain function |
| We use 10% of our brains | We only use 10% of our brains |

anxiety about children's education is high. In the face of poor scientific knowledge, most of the population are not able to be truly discerning about findings – and hence the tendency for brain facts that lack any evidence to persist [8].

It is clear from research that teachers are curious about the brain and keen to take on and apply knowledge about brain development [9]. Yet this backdrop of scepticism about how neuroscience can inform education means a missed opportunity for educators, professionals, teachers and even students themselves to understand some of the solid findings about brain functioning and developmental changes. Hohnen and Murphy [10] try to address this gap by proposing the model 'The Optimum Context for Learning', which draws together key findings from neuroscience to guide teachers' behaviour in the classroom to enable optimal performance from students.

## Optimum Context for Learning: A Neuroscientific Model [10]

The Optimum Context for Learning is a neurologically informed model that incorporates findings from neuroscience and takes into account the hierarchy of information-processing in the brain to consider what might get in the way of a child's learning. Rather than trying to reduce learning to a neurological level for the individual, this approach takes a whole view of brain processing based on well-established neuroscientific data. In a similar vein to Maslow's hierarchy of needs [11], the model proposes that if stronger foundation levels are achieved, there is a greater chance of a child reaching the top of the model and succeeding. To reach the top, where learners are passionate and engaged, lower levels need to be firmly established.

## Background to Brain Development

Genes and the environment both play a part in developing the brain. While genes clearly play a role, development will not take place without environmental stimulation, which is required for neurones and their synapses to connect and stabilize through processes of myelination and pruning of brain connections.

While brain plasticity remains throughout life, 'developmental plasticity', where the brain is chemically predisposed to be modified by experience, and where synaptic changes occur with ease, is thought to end sometime during the third decade of life [12,13]. Moreover, research is beginning to unveil a pre-programmed order of development within the cortical and subcortical brain where different regions become predisposed to receive certain experiences at certain times [14]. It seems a brain has sensitive periods or windows for growth during which time regions become highly sensitive to specific experiences [15].

### Level 1

As shown in Figure 46.1, the first level of need is to provide safety for the child which comes from being in a positive relationship with the teacher and where the environment is stress-optimal (too much stress and too little stress are avoided). Heightened stress, a lack of feeling safe and a poor student–teacher relationship will set off the brain's fight-or-flight alarm system, which results in midbrain activation. This acts in conflict with higher brain functioning which is required for thinking and learning as the brain prioritizes emotional processing to ensure safety and survival [16,17].

### Level 2

The second level of need is to ensure the child is functioning at their achievable challenge level, a similar concept to Vygotsky's 'zone of proximal development' [18]. No two children are the same in terms of either current knowledge or capacity to take on new learning due to genetic factors and experience. Yet in order to enter the positive cycle of learning, where dopamine is released and circuits are built and strengthened

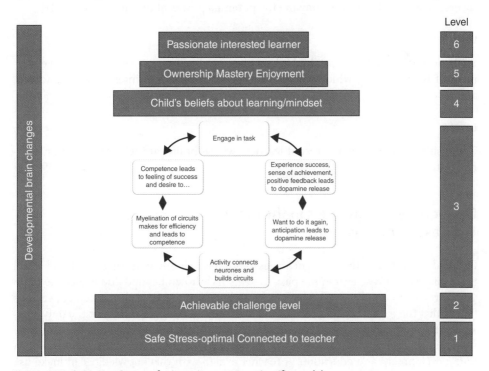

**Figure 46.1** Optimum Context for Learning: a neuroscientific model.

(myelinated), the challenge level needs to be right for each child or they risk midbrain activation due to stress or boredom. Knowledge about general and specific learning difficulties is essential here.

### Level 3

The child can then engage in the positive cycle of learning, which will begin with an action potential in neurones and result in growth of myelinated circuits. Myelinated circuits correlate with skill and competence, which in turn bring success and so the cycle continues.

### Level 4

Children's beliefs about their ability and potential to learn, or their 'mindset' has been shown to have an impact on behaviour and learning. Dweck [19] provided robust evidence that children who have a *fixed* mindset about their intelligence, believing intelligence to be an inherent trait, inhibit their learning. Believing themselves to be 'intelligent' results in them holding onto their status, thereby reducing opportunities for risk-taking, critical feedback and learning. If they believe themselves to be 'unintelligent', applying themselves persistently to their studies is pointless. On the other hand, the child who holds a *growth* mindset, believing intelligence and abilities are learnt through effort and persistence, seeks critique and takes on risks and challenges with determination and effort. This mirrors the message from brain plasticity beautifully, showing children that greater synaptic connection and speed come from repetition which is the result of determination and hard work. Dweck and her colleagues have linked academic success to a growth mindset showing the potential power of this approach [20,21].

### Level 5

With lower levels in place the child is best placed to begin to have ownership and enjoyment of their learning which will lead to mastery through uninterrupted application and repetition.

### Level 6

The result is passionate, interested learners whose brains are functioning in an optimal state.

## Developmental Changes in the Brain: The Case of Adolescence

Our understanding of the different stages of brain development during childhood is still in its infancy, but research in the past 15 years has shown beyond doubt that the brain goes through a complex set of changes kicked off by puberty [22], correcting previous beliefs that the earliest years of children's lives offered the greatest, if not the only, possibility for brain development. The finding of significant brain reorganization and sensitivity during the adolescent years has implications for education at this crucial time in both development and education. A teacher armed with this knowledge can make use of developmental drives and avoid conflicts that work against brain functioning.

The key areas of growth in the teenage brain impacting on functioning can be summarized as changes in relation to reward, regulation and relationships [23], along with opportunities for the development of creativity and higher-order thinking.

## 1. Reward

Reward sensitivity is a well established finding in the area of adolescent brain development [24]. Studies using fMRI measures have repeatedly shown exaggerated neural activation in reward centres in the brain at this time, particularly the ventral striatum [25-27]. This means adolescents are driven to experience reward more intensely and experience pleasure more astutely than either younger children or adults.

## 2. Regulation

At the same time, the prefrontal cortex (PFC), which subserves systems of behavioural and emotional regulation as well as impulse control, is undergoing significant reorganization during which time its functioning is suboptimal. The dual systems model [28] uses this temporal gap between the early maturing reward systems in the brain and the slower maturing cognitive control system, the PFC, to explain adolescent behaviours of risk-taking. The neural imbalance leads to greater sensitivity and motivation for pleasure, with less regulation capacity explaining the increase in pleasure-seeking behaviour in the classroom. A better understanding of this by educators may alter expectations as well as encourage them to make use of adolescents' intense interests and passions as a driver for motivation and success.

## 3. Relationships

Adolescence is a time of heightened social importance where peer relationship and acceptance become fundamental to experience and self-worth. This is thought to be related to the significant development that goes on in the social brain during adolescence [29]. Rather than telling adolescents to leave their social brain outside the classroom, Lieberman [30,31] advocates leveraging on this social bias in the brain to change how we educate adolescents to include a social element in the classroom. For example, this might involve taking care not to strip away the rich social cognitive drama in history and instead using this to engage social thinking. In English, rather than focusing on spelling and grammar he advocates using the motivation of mind to mind transfer of ideas to persuade and inform, which would create a social motivation [31]. For maths and sciences, using the social motivation of peer-to-peer learning is recommended, particularly given preliminary evidence that moving the focus from *learning* content to *teaching peers* content engages the mentalizing network of the brain in adults [32].

## 4. Creativity and Higher-Order Thinking

Just as the sensory and motor cortices are sensitive to development during the early years as brain reorganization takes place [33], so the skills subserved and interconnected with the PFC may also be particularly sensitive to development during adolescence while reorganization in this brain region takes place [34]. If this is the case, then the teenage years and secondary school education offer an exciting opportunity for learning higher-order cognitive skills such as goal-directed persistence, sustained effort, organization, prioritizing and activating workloads, decision-making, critical analysis and creativity. Such skills are considered highly valued in the 20th-century labour force [35] and should be a focus of secondary school education.

## References

1  Howard-Jones P (2014) Neuroscience and Education: A Review of Educational Interventions and Approaches Informed by Neuroscience. Education Endowment Foundation.

2  Bruer J (1997) Education and the brain: a bridge too far. Educational Researcher, 26, 4–16.

3  Bishop, DVM (2014) What is Educational Neuroscience? Online: 10.6084/ m9.figshare.1030405. Accessed: January 2017.

4  Geake J (2008) Neuromythologies. Education Educational Research, 50,123–133..

5  Pasquinelli E (2012) Neuromyths: why do they exist and persist? Mind Brain and Education, 6, 89–96.

6  Sylvan LJ, Christodoulou JA (2010) Understanding the role of neuroscience in brain based products: a guide for educators and consumers. Mind Brain and Education, 4, 1–7.

7  Dekker S, Lee NC, Howard-Jones P, Jolles J (2012) Neuroscience myths in education; prevalence and predictors of misconceptions among teachers. Frontiers in Psychology, 3, 429.

8  Lindell AK, Kidd E (2013) Consumers favour 'right brain' training: the dangerous lure of neuromarketing. Mind, Brain, and Education, 7, 35–39.

9  Hook CJ, Farah MJ (2013) Neuroscience for educators: what are they seeking, and what are they finding? Neuroethics, 6, 331–341.

10  Hohnen B, Murphy T (2016) The optimum context for learning; drawing on neuroscience to inform best practice in the classroom. Educational & Child Psychology, 33, 75–90.

11  Maslow AH (1943) A theory of human motivation. Psychological Review, 50, 370–396.

12  Sowell ER, Peterson BS, Thompson PM et al. (2003) Mapping cortical change across the human life span. Nature Neuroscience, 6, 309–315.

13  Spear LP (2013) Adolescent Neurodevelopment. Journal of Adolescent Health, 52, s7–s13.

14  Gogtay N, Giedd JN, Lusk L et al. (2004) Dynamic mapping of human cortical development during childhood through early adulthood. Proceedings of the National Academy of Science, 101, 8174–8179.

15  Greenough WT, Black JE, Wallace CS (1987) Experience and brain development. Child Development, 58, 539–559.

16  Le Doux J (1996) The Emotional Brain. New York: Simon Schuster.

17  Pawlak R, Magarinos AM, Melchor J et al. (2003) Tissue plasminogen activator in the amygdala is critical for stress-induced anxiety-like behaviour. Nature Neuroscience, 6, 168–174.

18  Vygotsky LS (1978) Mind in Society: The Development of Higher Psychological Processes. Cambridge, MA: Harvard University Press.

**19** Dweck CS (1986) Motivational processes affecting learning. American Psychologist, 41, 1040–1048.

**20** Blackwell LS1, Trzesniewski KH, Dweck CS (2007) Implicit theories of intelligence predict achievement across an adolescent transition: a longitudinal study and an intervention. Child Development , 78, 246–263.

**21** Mangels JA, Butterfield B, Lamb J et al. (2006) Why do beliefs about intelligence influence learning success? A social cognitive neuroscience model. Social Cognitive and Affective Neuroscience, 1, 75–86.

**22** Casey BJ (2013) The teenage brain: an overview. Current Directions in Psychological Science, 22, 80–81.

**23** Steinberg L (2014) Age of Opportunity: Lessons from the New Science of Adolescence, Mariner Books.

**24** Galvan A (2013) The teenage brain: sensitivity to rewards. Current Directions in Psychological Science, 22, 89–93.

**25** Ernst M., Nelson E, Jazbec S et al. (2005) Amygdala and nucleus accumben in response to recept and omission of gains in adults and adolescents. NeuroImage, 25, 1279–1291.

**26** Galvan A, Hare T, Parra C et al. (2006) Earlier development of the accumbent relative to orbitofrontal cortex might underlie risk-taking behaviour in adolescents. Journal of Neuroscience, 26, 6885–6892.

**27** van Leijenhorst L, Zanolie K, van Meel C et al. (2010) What motivates the adolescent? Brain regions mediating reward sensitivity across adolescents. Cerebral Cortex, 20, 61–69.

**28** Steinberg L (2010) A dual systems model of adolescent risk-taking. Developmental Psychobiology , 52, 216–224.

**29** Somerville LH (2013) The teenage brain: sensitivity to social evaluation. Current Directions in Psychological Science, 22, 121–127.

**30** Lieberman MD (2012) Social: Why Our Brains Are Wired To Connect. Oxford University Press.

**31** Lieberman MD (2012) Education and the social brain. Trends in Neuroscience and Education, 1, 3–9.

**32** Mitchell JP, Macrae CN, and Banaji MR (2004) Encoding-specific effects of social cognition on the neural correlates of subsequent memory. Journal of Cognitive Neuroscience, 24, 4912–4917.

**33** Hebb DO (1949) The Organisation of Behaviour. New York: Wiley.

**34** Blakemore S (2006) Brain Development during Adolescence and Beyond. The Institute for Cultural Research Monograph Series No 51.

**35** Robinson K (2013) Finding Your Element: How to Discover your Talents and Passions and Transform your Life. Penguin.

# 47

# Continuities and Discontinuities in Youth Mental Healthcare

*Helen Bruce and Linda Dowdney*

## Introduction

Prospective longitudinal studies provide consistent evidence that psychopathology in children and adolescents predicts adult psychopathology [1,2]. While some psychiatric disorders such as anxiety onset during childhood, others such as mood and substance disorders are more likely to have an onset during adolescence [3]. Mood disorders show a nearly two-fold increase between 13 and 17/18 years of age [3], and suicide increases markedly between mid-adolescence and early adulthood. Child and adolescent psychopathology is also associated with other adverse outcomes in early adulthood, such as educational drop-out, involvement in the criminal justice system, unemployment, relational instability and early parenthood [4].

Taken together, these findings suggest the importance of both the availability of mental health services for adolescents as they progress into young adulthood, and the need for a smooth transition between child and adolescent mental health services (CAMHS) and adult mental health services (AMHS). However, this transition process has become a focus of concern for clinicians, researchers and successive UK governments [5,6]. One major UK study of adolescent transition between CAMHS and AMHS found that only 58% of those leaving CAMHS transferred into AMHS and that the majority of transitions were poorly planned and executed, with less than 5% being classed as optimal [5]. Such difficulties are not confined to the UK, with a forthcoming research trial planning to investigate the issue in the European-wide collaborative Milestone project (see the 'Internet resources' section at the end of this chapter). The focus of this chapter, however, is on the CAMHS in the UK that provide a multi-disciplinary service for children with the most serious mental health needs. While there are differences in the way these services are organized in the constituent parts of the UK, similar transitional difficulties are described in each country setting [6]. These can arise from a variety of service and client characteristics that poorly match existing service provision.

## Service Characteristics

**Service entry criteria** differ between CAMHS and AMHS. Children and families are eligible for CAMHS services when a child or adolescent has a mental health difficulty that impairs their own and/or their family's daily functioning. Entry into AMHS is likely

*Child Psychology and Psychiatry: Frameworks for Clinical Training and Practice,* Third Edition.
Edited by David Skuse, Helen Bruce and Linda Dowdney.
© 2017 John Wiley & Sons, Ltd. Published 2017 by John Wiley & Sons, Ltd.

to require the presence of a 'severe and enduring mental illness'. Successful transition between the two services is most likely when adolescents exiting CAMHS meet the diagnostic criteria for such a severe disorder or have had specialist inpatient treatment [5]. The majority of young people attending CAMHS are unlikely to meet these criteria, even though demonstrating a wide range of serious mental health difficulties that can be compounded by risk-taking behaviour, accommodation needs and early parenthood. A further complexity arises from the difficulty in distinguishing between normal adolescent turmoil and the non-specific prodrome of serious mental illness. The inflexibility of AMHS diagnostic entry requirements results in a serious service gap for those eligible by age, but not in terms of diagnoses, to enter AMHS services – unless their condition deteriorates into a mental health crisis, rendering them eligible for AMHS support.

**Differences in Service Ethos** between CAMHS and AMHS also have an impact upon transition. For instance, the focus within CAMHS on the developmental needs of children and adolescents results in both child and family involvement in treatment, either together or in parallel. This is associated with a variety of psychologically based treatment models, such as systemic therapy and psychotherapy. The focus on biological disorders in AMHS results in an emphasis on medication, individual treatment and client autonomy that largely excludes family involvement [7]. While some adolescents welcome this approach, for others it is less helpful. For example, in CAMHS eating disorder (ED) services, adolescents and their families work together to 'fight the ED'. The exclusion of the family from treatment upon entry into AMHS in a client group likely to have major maturational issues can be 'bewildering and dangerous for patients and their families' [8, p. 399]. Another example relates to confidentiality. Within CAMHS, negotiated limits to client confidentiality allow the sharing of information with parents where child/adolescent safety issues arise. Within AMHS, client information deemed confidential is not shared with parents even where they are providing support for a seriously unwell adolescent. A lack of adequate preparation for such practice changes can result in parental distress and confusion and mar the transition process.

**Policies, Guidelines and Protocols on Service Transition** have been produced by successive governments, the voluntary sector and professional bodies for service users, professionals and commissioners of services (e.g. [9–13]). Clinicians and commissioners now have easy access to supportive internet resources illustrating model protocols and good practice models. Nonetheless, research indicates that only a minority of CAMHS services have developed protocols based on these practice guidelines – and not all have implemented them [5]. Transition protocols between CAMHS and AMHS services differ, as does the assessment and recording of care needs and electronic record-keeping systems [5]. AMHS can be reluctant to plan around the needs of those ineligible for their service, and transition planning within mental health is not always integrated into the transition pathways produced by education and social care [14].

## Client Characteristics

These can be poorly matched with existing service provision. First, because youth mental health difficulties may not meet the strict diagnostic entry criteria for AMHS. Second, because there is a lack of AMHS that are appropriate for youth with particular diagnoses, especially neurodevelopmental disorders such as autism spectrum disorders (ASDs) [5] and attention deficit hyperactivity disorder (ADHD) [15]. Such groups are likely to have particular difficulties coping with the changes in education, living accommodation and employment that can occur concurrently with the need for service transition [14].

Adolescents with high-functioning ASD (HFASD) are likely to be ineligible for entry into adult learning disabilities services as they do not meet impairment entry criteria. While some 70% of those with HFASD meet the criteria for an additional psychiatric disorder [16], they are unlikely to meet diagnostic criteria for entry into AMHS, or indeed for adult social care. Their difficulties in coping with all transitions will be exacerbated where AMHS staff lack specific training in ASD [16].

Adolescents with ADHD are also likely to encounter diagnostic specific difficulties, and AMHS staff with a poor understanding of their disorder [15]. For example, the amelioration of some key ADHD symptoms as part of the adolescent maturational process can lead to diagnostic uncertainty. Consequently, some adult psychiatrists challenge the validity of the disorder in early adulthood and fail to recognize the need for AMHS provision [17]. Developmental transitions, increasing adolescent autonomy and a lack of appropriate transition services combine to result in a drop in pharmacological prescriptions for ADHD at this stage [18]. The complex profile of many neurodevelopmental disorders may well indicate the need for continuing pharmacological and mental health intervention. There are likely to be co-morbid diagnoses, with a high risk of, for example, substance misuse and involvement in the criminal justice system. Given the complex needs of this group, their often chaotic lifestyles, attentional difficulties and impulsivity, inter-service transitions need to be managed carefully.

## Ways Forward

As noted previously, there is an abundance of policy documentation, with model commissioner and service transition protocols. Recent examples envisage a transition process that incorporates a developmental perspective and research findings on both professional and service user views [19]. These suggest a number of ways forward. To counteract negative service user experiences, there should be youth involvement in the development, planning and evaluation of transition services; access to peer and multimedia resource support; adequate preparation for service transfer and an identified transition worker coordinating the transition process. Professionals involved should have training or experience in working with young people and understand the impact of contemporaneous youth transitions in social, educational and workforce spheres. Recommendations reflecting professional concerns include IT systems aligned between adult and child services; clarity over who bears clinical responsibility during the transition period; and joint training of AMHS and CAMHS staff to reduce the risk of misunderstandings and service misperceptions. While proper implementation of, and improvement in, transition protocols at the local level can smooth the transfer process, good practice alone will not address differences in eligibility criteria between services, the absence of services for specific groups of youth or the need for a shift towards a socially inclusive, preventive intervention focus [20].

A number of local service initiatives have sought to address the gaps between services. Some, such as youth services for those with ADHD or ASD [16,21] offer a short-term solution but fail to address the lack of appropriate adult services further down the line.

More recently, joint health and social care initiatives providing specialist adult ASD teams, or outreach specialist workers for youths with ASD, have been reported [14].

Adult mental health services or CAMHS have also extended their age boundaries to address the needs of young people with severe mental health impairments, e.g. by extending aspects of an early intervention psychosis service to 14- to 18-year-olds [22]. Others have suggested a broadening of entry criteria and a reduction of the referral threshold within AMHS [23].

A more radical approach is advocated by those who argue that the child–adult split at 16–18 years is no longer 'fit for current purpose' and that major service reorganization is required [23]. Examples include the establishment of services for the 16- to 25-year age group, e.g. the national 'headspace' service in Australia, the Headstrong service in Ireland and Youthspace in Birmingham [24]. While there are organizational differences between these services, they share a number of common features, including a focus on enhanced primary care services, flexible service provision and easy accessibility in a low-stigma youth-friendly environment. These models reflect a move away from symptom reduction and containment to prevention and wider social inclusion [24]. Youth input into service design and delivery alongside internet-based mental health support enhance accessibility and relevance. Developments in progress are establishing links between such services and more specialist providers of psychiatric care.

Current commissioning and funding arrangements, and financial constraints, are likely to impinge upon a national roll-out of such services in the NHS. It is noticeable that both the Irish Headstrong and Birmingham Youthspace initiatives represent a public–private funding arrangement. There are, of course, boundaries to overcome between existing mental health services and the new transitional provision. Concerns have been raised, too, about whether the development of youth services will result in financial constraints in child mental health services [23].

### Evaluation of Transition Outcomes

Such evaluation is limited, localized, variable in quality and fails to meet standard research criteria such as case–control trials. It is unclear what would constitute the best 'outcome' measures – e.g. youth drop-out rates, or user satisfaction – and how valid and reliable measures of these would be developed. The proposed Milestone randomized clinical trial of transition services offers the possibility of addressing these problems (see Internet resources).

## Conclusions

Transitions between CAMHS and AMHS have proved problematic. Only a small minority of those moving between these services report an optimal experience. Many youths exiting CAMHS are ineligible for entry into AMHS due to the latter's rigid diagnostic entry criteria. Local initiatives have developed transition services for those most affected (e.g. those with neurodevelopmental disorders) but fail to address the lack of subsequent adult service provision. Policy and protocol transitions guidelines abound, but their implementation often falters due to differences in CAMHS and

AMHS working practices, service ethos and professional misunderstandings. Ways forward within current service frameworks include adequate implementation of existing guidelines alongside widening of AMHS entry criteria and more integrated commissioning arrangements. New developments include youth mental health services from 16 to 25 years, deriving from public–private funding initiatives. Their innovative focus on prevention and social inclusion is allied to the provision of 'stigma-free' service environments with easier access to support from social care, health, education and employment. Good transition practices will still be needed at the boundaries of such services. Standardized and valid measurement of service transition outcomes in methodologically adequate research trials have yet to be undertaken.

# References

1 Reef J, van Meurs I, Verhulst FC et al. (2010) Children's problems predict adults' DSM-IV disorders across 24 years. Journal of the American Academy of Child and Adolescent Psychiatry, 49, 1117–1124.
2 Patton GC, Coffrey C, Romaniuk H et al. (2014) The prognosis of common mental disorders in adolescence: a 14 year prospective cohort study. Lancet, 383, 1404–11.
3 Merikangas KR, He J-P, Burstein M et al (2010) Lifetime prevalence of mental disorders in US Adolescents: Results from the National Comorbidity Study-Adolescent Supplement (MCS-A). Journal of the American Academy of Child and Adolescent Psychiatry, 49, 980–989.
4 Copeland W, Wolke D, Shanahan L et al. (2015) Adult functional outcomes of common childhood psychiatric problems – a prospective, longitudinal study. JAMA Psychiatry, 9, 892–899.
5 Singh SP, Paul M, Ford T et al. (2010) Process, outcome and experience of transition from child to adult mental healthcare: a multiperspective study British Journal of Psychiatry, 197, 305–312.
6 Dowdney L, Bruce H (2014) Transiting out of child and adolescent mental health services – influences on continuities and discontinuities. In: Byrne P, Rosen A (eds) Mental Health Care in Early Intervention in Psychiatry: EI of Nearly Everything for Better Mental Health. Wiley-Blackwell, pp. 79–91.
7 McLaren S, Belling R, Paul M et al. (2013) 'Talking a different language': an exploration of the influence of organizational cultures and working practices on transition from child to adult mental health services. BMC Health Services Research, 13, 254.
8 Treasure J, Schmidt U, Hugo P (2005) Mind the gap: service transition and interface problems for patients with eating disorders. British Journal Psychiatry, 187, 398–400.
9 Department of Health & Department for Children, Schools and Families (2007) A transition guide for all services. Department of Health.
10 Department for Children, Schools and Families and Department of Health (2008) Transition: Moving on Well. A Good Practice Guide for Health Professionals and their Partners on Transition Planning for Young People with Complex Health Needs or a Disability. Department of Health.
11 Department of Health (2010) 'Fulfilling and Rewarding Lives' – The Strategy for Adults with Autism in England. Department of Health.

**12** Lamb C, Hill D, Kelvin R, Van Beinum M (2008) Working at the CAMHS/Adult Interface: Good Practice Guidance for the Provision of Psychiatric Services to Adolescents/Young Adults. A Joint Paper from the Interfaculty Working Group of the Child and Adolescent Faculty and the General and Community Faculty of the Royal College of Psychiatrists, May 2008. Royal College of Psychiatrists.

**13** Young Minds (2011) CAMHS Transition Guides. Online: http://www.youngminds.org .uk/about/our_campaigns/transition. Accessed: January 2017.

**14** Beresford B, Moran N, Sloper P et al. (2013) Transition to Adult Services and Adulthood for Young People with Autistic Spectrum Conditions. Research Works, Social Policy Research Unit, University of York, York. Online: http://www.york.ac.uk /inst/spru/research/summs/transitionsASC.html. Accessed: January 2017.

**15** Hall CL, Newell K, Taylor J et al. (2013) 'Mind the gap' – mapping services for young people with ADHD transitioning from child to adult mental health services. BMC Psychiatry 13, 186.

**16** McConachie H, Hoole S, Le Couteur AS (2011) Improving mental health transitions for young people with autism spectrum disorder. Child: Care, Health and Development, 37, 764–766.

**17** Moncrieff J, Timimi S (2010) Is ADHD a valid diagnosis in adults? No. British Medical Journal, 340, c547.

**18** McCarthy S, Asherson P, Coghill D et al (2009) Attention-deficit hyperactivity disorder: treatment discontinuation in adolescents and young adults British Journal of Psychiatry, 194, 273–277.

**19** Department of Health (2015) Model Specification for Transitions from Child and Adolescent Mental Health Services. Online: https://www.england.nhs.uk/wp-content /uploads/2015/01/mod-transt-camhs-spec.pdf. Accessed: January 2017.

**20** Thomas N, Pilgrim D, Street C et al. (2012) Supporting young people with mental health problems: lessons from a voluntary sector pilot. Mental Health Review Journal, 17 14–25.

**21** Verity R, Coates J (2007) Service Innovation: transitional attention-deficit hyperactivity disorder clinic. Psychiatric Bulletin, 31, 99–100.

**22** Sainsbury M, Goldman R (2011) Mental Health Service Transitions for Young People. Social Care Institute for Excellence. Available at http://www.scie.org.uk/publications /guides/guide44/files/guide44.pdf. Accessed: January 2017.

**23** Lamb C, Murphy M (2013) The divide between child and adult mental health services: points for debate. British Journal of Psychiatry, 202, s41–s44.

**24** McGorry P (2015) Arguments for transformational reform of mental health care for young people. Irish Journal of Psychological Medicine, 32, 9–11.

## Internet Resources

### Youth mental health support

Headspace, Australia: http://headspace.org.au
Headstrong, Ireland: https://www.headstrong.ie
Youthspace, Birmingham: http://www.youthspace.me
Young Minds: http://www.youngminds.org.uk/for_children_young_people/guide_to _mental_health_services

## For Professionals and Commissioners of Services

The Milestone Project: http://www.milestone-transitionstudy.eu/about-milestone
/project-summary
Young Minds: http://www.youngminds.org.uk/search?q=transitions – *offers a series of
guides and examples of good transition practice*
The CHIMAT website: http://www.chimat.org.uk/camhs/transitions – *has a range of
supportive materials for professionals and commissioners of services*
The Social Care Institute for Excellence (SCIE) website: www.scie.org.uk/ – *includes
guidance, research, case studies and examples of practice (see, e.g., Guide 44, SCIE
'Mental Health Service Transitions for Young People')*

# 48

# The Children and Young People's Improving Access to Psychological Therapies (CYP IAPT) Programme in England

*Peter Fonagy, Kathryn Pugh and Anne O'Herlihy*

## Introduction

The Children and Young People's Improving Access to Psychological Therapies (CYP IAPT) programme was initiated in 2011 by the Department of Health [1]. It aimed to improve the access of children, young people and their families to evidence-based psychological therapies (EBPTs) and to seek their participation in all aspects of care, service delivery and design.

The CYP IAPT programme benefited from lessons learned from the earlier implementation of the adult IAPT programme – a programme described as the most extensive and centralized attempt to implement EBPTs [2]. This had focused on widening the availability of EBPTs to adults with depression and anxiety (see Layard & Clark [3]). CYP IAPT had a more extensive focus, aiming to address the broad range of mental health difficulties commonly presenting to community-based child and adolescent mental health services (CAMHS). The formalized framework for implementation of CYP IAPT was published in 2012 [4]. Government funding of £52 million covered the initial 4-year implementation period. The aim was to transform CAMHS into an evidence-based, outcome-focused, collaborative service. However, successful implementation of CYP IAPT required an understanding of the challenges then facing CAMHS, alongside an implementation strategy designed to address them.

## Challenges Facing CAMHS

Numerous inquiries into CAMHS (e.g. [5]) had identified problems with service structure and treatment delivery. In brief, service user and referrer accounts pictured an inaccessible service, with lengthy waiting lists, inflexible diagnostic entry requirements, and limited involvement of carers and young people in decision-making. Services were seen as stigmatizing, especially for minority groups. Interventions were lengthy. Preventive and resilience-building treatments were largely absent, as were national data to enable monitoring of service effectiveness and to support planning. For fuller discussions, see Chapter 47 and McGorry *et al.* [6].

Staff of CAMHS attributed service shortcomings to a significant shortage of adequately trained professionals, alongside vacant posts and redundancies. Consequently, few services could offer self-referral routes, and support was often lacking for clients

*Child Psychology and Psychiatry: Frameworks for Clinical Training and Practice*, Third Edition.
Edited by David Skuse, Helen Bruce and Linda Dowdney.

transitioning between child and adult services, or needing referral across other NHS or agency boundaries. There were also insufficient resources for monitoring and evaluation of individual and service performance (see Chapter 47). These difficulties were set against a background of rising rates in community mental health problems alongside increasing referrals [7,8]. Nonetheless, only between one-quarter and one-third of those with mental health problems found their way to mental health services, while in adolescent males the proportion was thought to be below 15% [9].

## Implementation

Addressing the above challenges and delivering this ambitious programme involved the support of service and commissioner partnerships, educational collaboratives and a series of implementation initiatives. There was a deliberate decision to not set up a standalone CYP IAPT service, and to actively discourage areas from doing so. As the aim was whole-system change there was a phased dissemination of a set of clinical principles (an outcome focus, increased patient and parent participation and the use of EBPTs) implemented through local partnerships and collaborations across a range of services [10].

The programme took advantage of pre-existing CAMHS partnerships between public commissioners of mental health services and the NHS, local authorities and the charity and voluntary sector service providers (in this chapter to be known as commissioner and provider service partnerships – CPSs). These partnerships had built up, in some form, over the previous 6 years. Together these bodies would be responsible for the delivery of CYP IAPT. For full details of the implementation process, see Fonagy *et al.* [11].

### Partnerships and Collaboratives

The initial implementation stage required CPSs to work with training providers based in higher education institutions (HEIs) to establish CYP IAPT learning collaboratives. Thirteen potential collaboratives applied to deliver the programme, and three were chosen in the first year through a competitive process. The selection was made on the basis that they were ready to make the necessary service culture change; to initiate training of managers and supervisors; to ensure services were ready to support the delivery of EBPTs; and to gather routine outcome monitoring (ROM) data. These partnerships were to implement a coherent set of principles governing service organization and delivery and, over time, to become country-wide.

Partnerships worked closely and iteratively with the HEIs to implement a national curriculum developed by expert consensus, using a modular approach [12,13]. This approach recognizes that children present with multiple problems and disorders, that treatment needs to evolve within episodes of care, and that practitioners require expertise in many EBPT protocols.

### Implementation Initiatives

Five systematic and interdependent initiatives were implemented. These covered the delivery of training to clinical staff, clinical service leaders and service managers. Other initiatives focused on developing and implementing a model of genuine user participation and collaborative relationships with service staff.

## Training Initiatives

Two initiatives focused on training. The first concentrated on training CAMHS staff in two NICE-approved EBPTs – cognitive-behavioural therapy (CBT) for anxiety and depression, and parent training for conduct problems. Two years later, training extended to systemic family practice for depression, self-harm, conduct disorder and eating disorders, as well as interpersonal psychotherapy for young people with anxiety or depression. In its third year, the programme included providing training in the basic principles of EBPT to less well-qualified practitioners using a curriculum that incorporated e-learning via an internet-based resource (MindEd e-learning – see 'Internet resources'). The second initiative focused on managers and service leaders within participating CPSs who were concurrently trained in service change, demand and capacity management, and leadership. Training was also provided to senior clinicians providing supervision in EBPT, and to newly trained therapists in monitoring outcomes.

## User Participation Initiatives

User participation was the focus of the remaining initiatives that aimed at delivering genuine, and empowering, user participation at different service levels. First, children/ young people and their families became involved in service design and delivery at both national and local levels. They also participated in service staff training events organized by the learning collaboratives. Secondly, CPSs were required to set up easily accessible and convenient mechanisms to enable children/young people and their carers to self-refer. Thirdly, on entering the service, users were empowered by becoming involved in the choice of treatment, in formulating their individual therapeutic goals, and by participating in routine session-by-session feedback on symptoms, treatment progression and satisfaction. User participation, alongside ROM data of this kind, has been shown to have therapeutic and service effectiveness benefits (see, e.g., [14,15]).

Such user empowerment was seen as an essential part of CYP IAPT. Developing services based on a spirit of collaborative care and trust was particularly important for the largely socially disadvantaged children and young people who attend CAMHS, whose previous experiences of healthcare are likely to have made them suspicious of both the motives of others and the information they impart. The transformed services sought to offer a different set of experiences based on the belief that experiencing their therapists think about them and respond to their preferences, thoughts and feelings would enhance young people's capacity to absorb and respond to information both in therapy and in their wider social world [16].

## Monitoring User Participation and Training Initiatives

In CYP IAPT, mandatory ROM measures of user participation typically take the form of standardized questionnaires used before each treatment session to gauge the severity of the patient's problems, their sense of progress towards their goals, and the extent to which their expectations of treatment were met. The effectiveness of staff training is monitored via staff supervision, ROM feedback data and videotaping of trainees' performance in the workplace. This combination facilitates treatment fidelity, immediate feedback and opportunities for trainee practice repetition. It assists in avoiding biases that can affect trainees' learning, such as confirmatory and hindsight basis [17]. It also aids trainees and supervisors to develop detailed plans for improvement. During implementation, the close collaboration of trainers at the HEIs, clinical supervisors, service leaders and the central CYP IAPT implementation team is critical in ensuring that high standards of competence are reached.

## Service Development Outcomes

At the beginning of 2016, year 5 of CYP IAPT, there were 94 CPSs covering 82% of 0- to 19-year-olds nationally. Within these, by 2015, 372 therapists, 86 supervisors and 51 service leaders had been trained. National coverage is expected to be 100% by 2018.

Successful user participation has been a major achievement. It led to initiatives such as the development of a Mental Health Services Passport held by young people and carers (see, Internet resources'). These are written jointly by young people and practitioners. They contain a summary of service users' issues, history and preferences. A further initiative commissioned a young people's mental health charity (YoungMinds) to facilitate user contributions to service design and delivery, to establish a network for parents and carers, and to develop a resource toolkit for service users, commissioners and providers ('Parents Say' toolkit – see 'Internet resources').

Quality frameworks for the accreditation of CYP IAPT training courses and services have been developed by the newly formed National Accreditation Council [18]. From 2016, the outcome measures developed to support CYP IAPT will be incorporated into the mandatory Mental Health Services Data Set.

## Evaluation

A full audit of service and user outcomes has not been possible due to difficulties beyond the scope of the programme in developing an accessible computerized system for recording a full national minimum data set. Nonetheless, based on the measures available, an internal audit revealed a number of achievements. The audit derives from interviews with 92 staff, 45 children/young people and 42 parents. Informants came from 12 CSPs covering 6803 children/young people, 11 services and 43 clinical teams [19].

### Improved Access and Efficiency

Between 2010 and 2014, the time between referral and first appointment decreased by 75% (from 239 to 64 days) and the average time between referral and assessment decreased by 21% to 235 days. Staff attributed these improvements to the use of ROM. Service accessibility improved via new self-referral routes, single points of access, outreach services and evening and weekend appointments. The average number of self-referrals increased by 195%.

### Evidence-Based Interventions

Around 83% of clinicians trained in NICE-recommended therapies were continuing to provide them and receive related supervision. They expressed increased confidence in choosing and delivering an EBPT. Nonetheless, a substantial proportion of young service users were still not receiving the recommended evidence-based treatment.

### ROM and User Engagement

Use of ROM increased and facilitated shared decision-making. Users saw it as help-ing to 'keep things focused'. There was increased service user participation in service organization and management, including staff appraisal and selection. Improved user engagement was reflected in an increase of 22% in the proportion of cases closed by mutual agreement.

### Challenges to Implementation

Concurrent cost efficiency initiatives, competing organizational changes and contract tendering processes substantially disrupted the implementation of CYP IAPT at some sites. Staff morale was negatively affected as increased referrals occurred alongside staffing reductions and time lost to training. Insufficient time was provided to embed new practices and to learn new systems and processes. ROM generated some anxiety among practitioners, particularly when service users did not report positive change. As noted above, there were programme failures in information governance and technology.

Both adult IAPT services and the CYP IAPT transformation programme have their critics, who share, for example, concerns over what they regard as an over-medicalized diagnostic focus and a therapeutic reliance on a traditional CBT approach [20,21]. How-ever, CYP IAPT training curricula developments have resulted in many more systemic family practitioners, interpersonal psychotherapists and parenting therapists than CBT therapists [10]. It has also been suggested that IAPT therapeutic interventions are constrained by unrealistic time limits and an over-focus on the targets and measures needed for contract tendering purposes [20,21]. Against this needs to be set the CYP IAPT audit data outlined earlier, and also other qualitative feedback from the same dataset. This indicates that 61% of clinicians thought that service access had improved for their local population; well over half reported often or always using outcome data to review or inform therapy; and more than three-quarters reported frequent engagement in shared decision-making activities with all service users [10].

## Future Directions

CYP IAPT is the foundation for a wider continuous transformation process in CAMHS [22]. New funding will create a nationwide programme based on CYP IAPT principles, with training extended to include community-based eating disorder services, perinatal care, service users with learning disabilities and those with an ASD. The number of EBPTs will continue to widen and will include counselling and psychopharmacological treatments, with supportive curriculum initiatives to educate clinicians in these approaches and pro-vide the developmental understanding needed for the 0–18 years' age range.

## References

1 Department of Health (2011) Talking Therapies: A Four-Year Plan of Action. London, UK: Department of Health. Online: https://www.gov.uk/government/uploads/system/uploads/attachment_data/file/213765/dh_123985.pdf. Accessed: January 2017.

2 McHugh RK, Barlow DH (2010) The dissemination and implementation of evidence-based psychological treatments. A review of current efforts. American Psychologist, 65, 73–84.

3 Layard R, Clark D (2014) Thrive: The power of evidence-based psychological therapies. London, UK: Allen Lane.

4 Centre for Mental Health, Department of Health, Mind, NHS Confederation Mental Health Network, Rethink Mental Illness, Turning Point (2012) No Health Without Mental Health: Implementation Framework. Crown copyright; Online: https://www.gov.uk/government/uploads/system/uploads/attachment_data/file/216870/No-Health-Without-Mental-Health-Implementation-Framework-Report-accessible-version.pdf. Accessed: January 2017.

5 Kennedy I (2010) Getting it Right for Children and Young People. Overcoming Cultural Barriers in the NHS so as to Meet their Needs. Independent Review. Crown Copyright. Available from: http://www.dh.gov.uk/prod_consum_dh/groups/dh_digitalassets/@dh/@en/@ps/documents/digitalasset/dh_119446.pdf. Accessed: January 2017.

6 McGorry P, Bates T, Birchwood M (2013) Designing youth mental health services for the 21st century: Examples from Australia, Ireland and the UK. British Journal of Psychiatry Supplement, 54, s30–35.

7 Bor W, Dean AJ, Najman J, Hayatbakhsh R (2014) Are child and adolescent mental health problems increasing in the 21st century? A systematic review. Australian and New Zealand Journal of Psychiatry, 48, 606–616.

8 NHS Benchmarking Network (2015) CAMHS Benchmarking Report. Manchester: NHS Benchmarking Network.

9 Green H, McGinnity A, Meltzer H et al. (2005) Mental Health of Children and Young People in Great Britain, 2004. A survey carried out by the Office for National Statistics on behalf of the Department of Health and the Scottish Executive. Basingstoke, UK: Palgrave Macmillan. Online: http://www.esds.ac.uk/doc/5269/mrdoc/pdf/5269 technicalreport.pdf. Accessed: January 2017.

10 Fonagy P, Clark DM (2015) Update on the Improving Access to Psychological Therapies programme in England: Commentary on . . . Children and Young People's Improving Access to Psychological Therapies. BJPsych Bulletin, 39, 248–251.

11 Fonagy P, Myles P, Pugh K, Shafran R (2014) Transformation of mental health services for children and young people in the UK. In: Beidas RS, Kendall PC (eds) Child and Adolescent Therapy: Dissemination and Implementation of Empirically Supported Treatments. New York, NY: Oxford University Press, pp. 158–178.

12 Chorpita BF, Bernstein A, Daleiden EL (2011) Empirically guided coordination of multiple evidence-based treatments: An illustration of relevance mapping in children's mental health services. Journal of Consulting and Clinical Psychology, 79, 470–480.

13 Weisz JR, Chorpita BF, Palinkas LA et al. (2012) Testing standard and modular designs for psychotherapy treating depression, anxiety, and conduct problems in youth: a randomized effectiveness trial. Archives of General Psychiatry, 69, 274–282.

14 Miller SD, Hubble MA, Chow D, Seidel J (2015) Beyond measures and monitoring: Realizing the potential of feedback-informed treatment. Psychotherapy (Chic), 52, 449–457.

15 Bickman L, Kelley SD, Breda C et al. (2011) Effects of routine feedback to clinicians on mental health outcomes of youths: Results of a randomized trial. Psychiatric Services, 62, 1423–1429.

16 Fonagy P, Allison E (2014) The role of mentalizing and epistemic trust in the therapeutic relationship. Psychotherapy (Chic), 51, 372–380.

17 Tracey TJ, Wampold BE, Lichtenberg JW, Goodyear RK (2014) Expertise in psychotherapy: An elusive goal? American Psychologist, 69, 218–229.

18 York A, Kingsbury S, Rayment B et al. (2013) 'Delivering With and Delivering Well'. CYP IAPT Principles in Child & Adolescent Mental Health Services. Values and Standards. London, UK: CAMHS Press; 2013. Online: https://www.england.nhs.uk /wp-content/uploads/2014/12/delvr-with-delvrng-well.pdf. Accessed: January 2017.

19 Edbrooke-Childs J, O'Herlihy A, Wolpert M et al. (2015) Children and Young People's Improving Access to Psychological Therapies: Rapid internal audit national report. London: Evidence-based Practice Unit, the Anna Freud Centre and UCL;.

20 Binnie J (2015) Do you want therapy with that? A critical account of working within IAPT. Mental Health Review Journal, 20, 79–83.

21 Timimi S (2015) Children and Young People's Improving Access to Psychological Therapies: Inspiring innovation or more of the same? BJPsych Bulletin, 39, 57–60.

22 Department of Health (2015) Future in Mind: Promoting, Protecting and Improving our Children and Young People's Mental Health and Wellbeing. London: NHS England. Online: https://www.gov.uk/government/uploads/system/uploads/attachment_data /file/414024/Childrens_Mental_Health.pdf. Accessed: January 2017.

## Internet Resources

MindEd e-learning: https://www.minded.org.uk/mod/page/view.php?id=1259 – *a resource for the MindEd curricula in children's/young people's mental health*

NHS England: https://www.england.nhs.uk/mental-health/cyp/iapt/ – *information about the CYP IAPT programme, with links to useful resources including the Mental Health Services Passport*

Parents Say: http://www.youngminds.org.uk/psaytoolkit – *information about YoungMinds' 'toolkit' to support CAMHS to implement and encourage parent participation in all aspects of their work*

# Index

Page numbers in **bold** refer to Tables; those in *italics* refer to Figures.

*Child Psychology and Psychiatry: Frameworks for Clinical Training and Practice,* Third Edition.
Edited by David Skuse, Helen Bruce and linda Dowdrey.
© 2017 John Wiley & Sons, Ltd. Published 2017 by John Wiley & Sons, Ltd.